Microsoft®
Visual Basic®
Game Programming
with DirectX®

Jonathan S. Harbour

PREMIER PRESS

GAME DEVELOPMENT

D1708937

Premier

p

Press ™

Premier Press is a registered trademark of Premier Press, Inc.

Publisher: Stacy L. Hiquet

Associate Marketing Manager: Heather Buzzingham

Managing Editor: Sandy Doell

Acquisitions Editors: Mitzi Foster, Emi Smith

Project Editor: Cathleen D. Snyder

Editorial Assistant: Margaret Bauer

Technical Reviewer: Joshua Smith

Copy Editor: Elizabeth Agostinelli

Interior Layout: Bill Hartman

Cover Design: Phil Velikan

Indexer: Sharon Shock

Proofreader: Jenny Davidson

ISBN: 1-931841-25-X

Library of Congress Catalog Card Number: 2001096481

Printed in the United States of America

02 03 04 05 RI 10 9 8 7 6 5 4 3 2

For Kayleigh Rebecca

Acknowledgments

I would like to thank everyone who helped to make *Visual Basic Game Programming with DirectX* a reality. First, I thank God for giving me the skill to take it on and the resolve to complete the manuscript. Thanks to my family and friends for their support. Thank you, Jennifer, for putting up with my mood swings during the past six months, with mounting deadlines and source code that often just did not work like it was supposed to. Thank you, Jeremiah and Kayleigh, for being a pleasant distraction and the joy of my life.

I owe a big thank you to everyone at Premier Press who helped to create this book. Jody Kennen (who is now with New Riders) originally brought up the idea for this book and asked me to think about writing it. Emi Smith has been simply wonderful at coordinating everything, followed by Mitzi Foster, who helped acquire the screenshots and a lot of other last-minute things. Cathleen Snyder was a terrific project editor; she did a great job editing the final manuscript, which was *very* marked up, and is an extremely friendly person. Thank you, Cathleen, for your patience and perseverance. Thanks go to Joshua Smith, the technical editor, for doing a fine job at pointing out errors in the source code; Elizabeth Agnostinelli, the copy editor, for correcting my spelling and grammatical errors; and Arlie Hartman, the CD-ROM producer. Thanks to Bill Hartman and Mike Tanamachi, who prepared the final layout and artwork.

I would like to thank two buddies of mine, Raul Aguilar and Chris Henson, who were in the thick of it early on, providing suggestions and feedback. Thanks for meeting with me once a week just to go over the early chapters and talk about how to develop the book. Many of your comments helped to direct the content later on. Thanks to John Striker for helpful feedback and for play-testing the sample games.

Thanks to Edgar Ibarra for contributing the 3-D artwork used in the book and for doing all the graphics for Stellar War. The asteroids, ships, and black holes look great!

Thanks to Steve Fowler at Microsoft for providing some high-quality screenshots of *HALO*. Speaking of which, you guys at Bungie are so awesome, it's kind of freaky.

Thanks also go out to William White and the "Circuit Scramblers" at Vera C. O'Leary Junior High in Twin Falls, Idaho, for reviewing chapters of the book and providing helpful input.

I owe a debt of gratitude to André LaMothe for his encouragement and suggestions for this book, and for all of his previous books that helped to set the standard for others to follow.

ABOUT THE AUTHOR

Jonathan S. Harbour is the author of *Pocket PC Game Programming,* also by Premier Press. He has been writing games for 14 years, having created his first game on a Tandy 1000 in 1988. He has worked on commercial games and has developed information systems for cellular, aerospace, pharmeceutical, education, and medical research companies. Jonathan is currently living in Phoenix, Arizona, working as a software consultant. In his spare time, Jonathan enjoys writing Pocket PC games, reading science fiction, and spending time with his wife and two children.

CONTENTS AT A GLANCE

Part IV
Complete Game Projects 777

Part V
Appendixes.................................993

CONTENTS

CHAPTER 3
VISUAL BASIC PROGRAMMING IN
A NUTSHELL..53

CHAPTER 4

GETTING TO KNOW THE WINDOWS API 89

CHAPTER 5

OPTIMIZING VISUAL BASIC WITH OBJECTS 131

CHAPTER 6
SUPERCHARGING VISUAL BASIC WITH DIRECTX

PART II
THE NUTS AND BOLTS OF GAME
DEVELOPMENT 195

CHAPTER 7
BREAK OUT THE BITMAPS 197

CHAPTER 8
SUPERSONIC SPRITES 251

CHAPTER 9

LET THE ANIMATION BEGIN 315

CHAPTER 10

DIVING INTO DIRECTDRAW 373

CHAPTER 11

PLAYING SOUND AND MUSIC WITH
DIRECTX AUDIO 423

CHAPTER 12

GETTING A HANDLE ON USER INPUT 463

CHAPTER 13

BUILDING THE DIRECTX GAME LIBRARY....529

CHAPTER 17

NETWORK PROGRAMMING WITH

DIRECTPLAY 721

CHAPTER 18

EFFECTIVE GAME DESIGN TECHNIQUES 755

Part IV
Complete Game Projects 777

Chapter 19
Block Attack! Classic Arcade Game . . . 779

CHAPTER 20
WARBIRDS 1944: SCROLLING
SHOOTER GAME 811

PART V
APPENDIXES 993

APPENDIX A
VISUAL BASIC GAME LIBRARY
REFERENCE 995

APPENDIX B
DIRECTX FOR VISUAL BASIC
REFERENCE 1009

FOREWORD

In this book, Jonathan Harbour presents a comprehensive overview of game development using Visual Basic. One very important point he covers concerns Visual Basic versus C++. After almost 20 years of software development, one of the things I can attest to is that it's not the language that makes or breaks the program, but the knowledge, skill, creativity, and dedication of the programmers. While it may be next to impossible to program a game like *Quake Arena* in COBOL, you will find that you usually have more than one language to choose from when deciding how to program your game.

In 1983, I started working on a major project named *Starquest*. C was the programming language of choice for many, and C++ was maybe two years old, but we chose a language called FORTH. We believed that the raw programming power and flexibility of that language would ultimately make it the best choice for programming then and in the future. Sadly for FORTH, C and C++ continued to gain appeal, and FORTH all but disappeared; some younger programmers these days haven't even heard of it. But that project, on which I worked with the four other people who comprised Binary Systems, was a game we eventually renamed *Starflight*. It was published by Electronic Arts in 1986 and has sold several hundred thousand copies on six different computer platforms.

I don't want to tell you that back in my day we had to walk five miles to school in snow up to our knees, but in terms of programming *Starflight* in the early '80s, that's what it may sound like. We undertook this venture in what you could call the early days of computer game publishing. To put some perspective on this, think for a moment about how many games Electronic Arts has produced—we were something like contract number five or six!

Our BIG compiler machine was an IBM AT that had a whopping 10MB hard disk and a CPU that we overclocked to get a blistering 12MHz processor speed. We used CGA artifact mode to get 16 brilliant colors, and came up with laser blasts and explosion sounds that could be played through the PC speaker because there were no sound cards yet. The game was so huge when it was completed that it shipped on not one, but *two* 360K floppy disks. I mention all this because *Starflight*, with its primitive graphics and sound, still engenders fan mail from people who tell us how much they loved the game and ask us where can they find a copy that will run on their Pentium IV.

Starflight came together perhaps more "organically" than you would see for games of its magnitude that are produced today. I was in my last quarter of my Linguistics major in San Diego when I started the project, and Greg Johnson was my roommate at the time. He was intrigued by the project and started using an early computer graphics program on an Atari 800 to draw the major characters of the game, just for fun. He joined the company a couple of months after I did to help out with design work, and as his ideas blossomed into major portions of the game, he took on the lead designer role. Bob Gonsalves came on board to develop an interleaved disk I/O methodology that ended up being scrapped because we changed platforms; he stayed on to develop all the planet-side activity in the terrain vehicle and the combat sequences in space. Tim Lee joined and brought with him a high-powered graphics idea he was working on that we used for our planetary orbit animation and landing sequence; he also developed the graphics primitives and the database that supported all the objects and events in the game. I wrote the code for all the starport interaction, space travel and ship operations, and all encounters which used a linguistically based expert system for alien communications. Rod McConnell was the guy who kept the whole thing together; he even took on a second job to help pay the meager salaries we drew so we could pay our rent.

What *Starflight* was when I started was not what it became by the time we launched the product. It was always going to be "the ultimate space adventure," but it changed from an open-ended game of exploration to a complex story with interwoven plots and twists. As we joined the project, we each injected our own unique personalities into the game. Many of the messages and artifacts a player finds on planet surfaces were put there because of something significant in our lives. Everyone on the team created at least one artifact with some special name. My own was the "Red Herring," an artifact that was 0.1 cubic meters too large to fit inside the terrain vehicle, so a player could never pick it up! There was no master plan detailing each and every task to be done. We had an idea of what the major modules had to be and we added a lot of final design as we got into programming each of the modules. Somehow when it was done, they all fit and worked together.

What I think is particularly important is that *Starflight*'s success transcends technology. We certainly did things that no one had done before. There were 270 star systems and 811 planets in the game—all unique and based upon fractal math. The filled-polygon landing sequence was a great special effect. We compressed data every way we could think of to make the whole thing fit onto those two diskettes. And of course, Electronic Arts had a great marketing division that built anticipation and demand for the game. But all those factors wouldn't mean anything if the game didn't have the rich personality we gave it. What really made *Starflight* such a long-term success was the people who worked at Binary Systems.

When you start programming your own games, remember that technology is only a part of what you need. I don't want to sound trite, but it's true that no matter what cool special effect you put into a game, someone will come up with something cooler. What makes a game special, what makes it unique, is that you put part of yourself into it. So what are you waiting for? Read this book and go write that game!

Alec Kercsó

LETTER FROM THE SERIES EDITOR

I never thought I would say this, but the time has finally come that Visual Basic is a valid language to create high-speed 2-D and 3-D games!

For all you VBers who have for years stood by Visual Basic and hoped and prayed that one day you would be able to make high quality games with the language, the time is finally here. Visual Basic has matured into a robust language and set of tools to create object-oriented applications that rival the speed and complexity of C++. But it's been a long hard road. I think that the software engineering elite have always looked down upon the words "Visual Basic," since BASIC is for beginners and hence Visual Basic must be a toy. Well, as we both know, it's not. VB is actually Microsoft's flagship language, and a huge amount of resources goes into the development of the language. Although I personally think that if they had simply named it something else from Day One, history would be different. But that's electrons through the gate....

Now is the time that you, Visual Basic, and *Visual Basic Game Programming with DirectX* alone are enough to create just about any game you can think of on the PC. This book is without a doubt one of my favorites. The reason why is because it is simply so well done. Jonathan Harbour has really written a perfect book here. It's like a movie where everything happens just the way you want it; that's how this book feels. I have read it and read it again, and it's just about as good as it can possibly get. You, the reader, are really going to love this book; it has so much that it's really amazing. Typically, books about Visual Basic and Visual Basic game programming show you how to use the Windows GDI and media services to make a Blackjack game or something. This book does no such thing. *Visual Basic Game Programming with DirectX* is a serious book about creating serious games for the PC using DirectX technology.

This book starts off showing you the basics of Visual Basic programming and how to integrate graphics and sound using the standard VB components. Once you have that under your belt, the book covers DirectX 7.0 and 8.0 and illustrates how to use every single major DirectX component—from DirectDraw, DirectSound, and DirectInput to Direct3D. Along with the discussions are beautiful annotations and tons of demos. Furthermore, the code in the book is some of the best I have seen; it's clear, well commented, and efficient. Jonathan really is a master of VB; he knows all the pitfalls of game programming under this platform and hence guides you smoothly from topic to topic without leaving out details or making assumptions.

After the initial coverage of DirectX, the game programming material ensues, and boy does it! Artificial intelligence, basic physics, game theory, and more. The book even covers multiplayer networked games with VB! That's a first! The book concludes by showing you how to create complete games, rounding out the theory with concrete examples.

In conclusion, I can't recommend this book highly enough. Even if you're a C/C++ game programmer, you should really read this book. It will open your eyes and might give you some options to try things with VB. If you're a VB programmer already, then this is the book for which you have waited 10 years. *Visual Basic Game Programming with DirectX* will without a doubt become a classic and a wonderful treasure for any game programmer's library. Heck, why not buy two!

Sincerely,

André LaMothe
Series Editor

INTRODUCTION

Welcome to *Visual Basic Game Programming with DirectX*. Like so many titles in the Premier Press Game Development Series, this book tackles a subject that has never before been covered in so much detail, providing you with tips, tricks, and techniques for doing things that most would have disregarded. This is the first comprehensive book that teaches you how to write complete games with Visual Basic and DirectX.

WELCOME TO THE ADVENTURE!

Make no mistake—Visual Basic is an awesome language! Nearly half of the three- to four-million programmers in the world are using Visual Basic on a daily basis. Most programmers entered the field due to the influence of a game at one time or another. Not everyone, of course. But of the millions of Visual Basic programmers in the world, a large number of them do enjoy playing games, myself included.

The problem, as I see it, is that few game developers have considered Visual Basic a serious game development language. For one reason or another, most Visual Basic programmers themselves do not even believe that Visual Basic is suitable for game programming. It's a common belief that Visual Basic is just too slow to write a decent game.

I believe the reason why Visual Basic is not taken seriously is because C++ is the dominant language today in this field. Most of the printed books and online resources are geared toward C++, leaving little room for other languages to get into the gaming action. Visual Basic programmers just do not have the required information needed to get started writing games with their favorite language.

It is my primary goal with this book to show you every trick and technique that I have learned over the years for getting the absolute most out of Visual Basic. I will teach you how to harness the tools necessary to write cutting-edge games with Visual Basic, using the Windows API, DirectDraw, and the entire DirectX 8.0 API.

This book is most definitely *not* a comprehensive guide to DirectX. On the contrary, this is a book dedicated to game programming with Visual Basic. DirectX is an integral part of this book, without a doubt. But DirectX is not dissected in this book with the same amount of tenacity that other books use to tackle the subject. I will teach you Visual Basic first and foremost, followed by the Windows API, and then I will dig into the components of DirectX. I cover the Windows API in the early chapters and even include two complete games based on this functionality, as a means to properly demonstrate the code. Using functions like BitBlt and LoadImage, I show you how to use double buffers and dirty rectangles to achieve extremely high frame rates—without DirectX. After I've shown you how to create a complete game with the Windows API, I jump into DirectDraw and build a complete sprite engine using DirectDraw surfaces. Finally, I make use of Direct3D to build a more powerful sprite engine using D3DXSprite.

The coverage of DirectX includes the following components:

- DirectX Graphics (DirectDraw and Direct3D)
- DirectX Audio (DirectSound, DirectSound3D, and DirectMusic)
- DirectInput
- DirectPlay

In addition, I have dedicated three entire chapters to multiplayer programming. One chapter covers the Windows Sockets API, another covers DirectPlay, and a third chapter builds a complete client/server game called *Stellar War*.

LEARNING BY EXAMPLE

I wholeheartedly believe that the best way to learn is by example. Mastery of a subject comes from practice, practice, practice! For that reason, this book is about 50 percent theory and 50 percent exercise. There is a lot of source code presented in this book (the projects on the CD-ROM include over 33,000 lines of code!), but I explain every function in detail before it is used. I usually include code snippets throughout a chapter to explain how something works.

After all, what is more exciting—talking about a 1968 Shelby Cobra or actually driving one?

Here is how I cover most subjects:

1. Explain the subject in detail.
2. Demonstrate the subject with source code.
3. Develop a reusable class for the subject.

In particular, Part IV of the book is dedicated to the development of complete games that demonstrate the topics covered in the book. The first three parts of the book do not include any games, but rather include sample programs that demonstrate each subject (such as DirectSound, artificial intelligence, multiplayer game programming, and game design).

TARGET AUDIENCE

This book is *not* a beginner's guide to programming games with Visual Basic. Ironically, this book started out life as an absolute beginner's book for game programming, but ended up being much, much more. I wanted to help newcomers who love games learn how to write their own games, and that is the emphasis throughout the book. I don't jump into any subjects that are too difficult to understand.

However, that is only the beginning. The first half of the book teaches the basic mechanics of building a double buffered sprite engine, while the second half of the book delves into numerous subjects that are more advanced (such as positional sound effects). Overall, I believe that I have achieved the goal of making this book accessible to all—from beginner to experienced developer. Because there were no other books on which to base this work, I had to approach this project as a C++ programmer. As you will see throughout the pages found herein, there are very few lines of pure Visual Basic code. Most of the subjects and samples are based on modern game development techniques, not on modern Visual Basic code for building applications.

The end result is a book that any beginner can use to learn how to write games with Visual Basic. Advanced games! Cutting-edge games! I'm not talking about Tic-Tac-Toe and Solitaire, but rather scrolling arcade games, space shooters, 3-D arcade games, and strategy games. But be prepared for a roller-coaster ride in later chapters, because there's no turning back when it comes to the more advanced subjects.

This book teaches the *right* way to create games from the start. You will not find comfortable point-and-click walk-throughs in these pages. I do not provide you with drag-and-drop ActiveX controls. If you were hoping to register an ArcadeGame.ocx control, drop it onto a form, and then call it a game, you will be in for a disappointment. Most of the sample games just use the standard form that comes with a new project: Form1. Any necessary controls are added to the program at run-time. That's right: Most of the time, you won't even touch the form, not even to add a PictureBox!

Hopefully, this is not too much of a disappointment. After all, if you want to create the best games possible, why not learn how to do it right? What I do give you—rather than an ubiquitous ActiveX "game control"—is hardcore treatment of the subject of game programming, along with a no-holds-barred approach to the sample code listings found herein.

I recommend that you read this book if you meet any of the following criteria:

- You have never written a computer game in your life, but you want to learn how to do it.
- You are just starting out as a programmer, you know maybe one or two programming languages, and you want to pick up Visual Basic.
- You are a capable Visual Basic programmer who has already written many applications, but you want to expand your skills to include multimedia (games, graphics, sound, input, 3-D, and so on).
- You are an accomplished game developer who is intrigued by Visual Basic and you want to learn more about it.

YOUR EXPECTATIONS

Since I have no way to tell exactly what topics you would like to learn about ahead of time, my goal is to cover as much material as possible within a finite amount of space. Every page is important, and every topic is crucial to the subject at hand. While I can't please everyone, it is my hope that every person who reads this book will learn something valuable. Even if you know almost everything that I have covered, it is my hope that you will find something new to enhance your game development efforts. There are enough pages in this book that you are likely to learn something new even if you have been writing games for many years.

MY EXPECTATIONS

My expectations while writing this book have been simple. I want to present you with everything you need to develop games with Visual Basic—games that rival those developed with other languages. I have set my sights on providing a complete solution for writing extremely high-quality, professional games with Visual Basic. When you are finished with this book, I expect you will need no other reference on the subject (until such time as the technologies presented herein become obsolete, which is inevitable in the game and computer industries).

My only expectation is that you keep an open mind, filled with creativity, and that you are willing to learn. There is no black box or black art to game programming. It all just amounts to a lot of hard work, self-learning, and good information. The cutting edge becomes dull quickly in the gaming world, and the latest and greatest game engine soon fades into obscurity. By keeping up with programming trends (such as the latest version of DirectX), you ensure that the games you create are fun, even on the latest computer hardware!

Just keep this in mind: Technology is not nearly as important as playability.

SYSTEM REQUIREMENTS

Most of the source code in this book will run on a mid-range computer, with the exception of some of the Direct3D code. Low-end PCs have had some problems running the sample games, such as Warbirds 1944 (a vertical-scrolling arcade game) and Pong 3D (a game that runs entirely in 3-D). DirectX 8.0 requires that you have a 3-D accelerator card to make use of most of the features provided by Direct3D, even when working on 2-D games (using Direct3D sprites).

In general you will want the most powerful computer system you can get your hands on for game development. But the code in this book is pretty forgiving of computer hardware and will run on most systems without any trouble. However, just to be thorough, here are my recommendations for the minimum system requirements:

- Pentium II 500MHz
- 128MB memory
- 6GB hard drive
- 16MB 3-D accelerator card (which supports DX8)
- 19" monitor

BOOK SUMMARY

This book is divided into five parts, as described in the following paragraphs.

Part I: Introducing Visual Basic and DirectX. Part I will teach you how to get started programming Visual Basic, with an introduction to the language, an in-depth study of the variable types, and how to get the most performance out of the language. I have included benchmarks with several sample programs to demonstrate how one method is superior to another, along with comparable Windows API routines that provide even more speed. This Part is wrapped up with an introduction to DirectX, with two sample programs showing how to harness DirectX in the Visual Basic environment.

Part II: The Nuts and Bolts of Game Development. Part II is where the most important subjects are covered for programming games with Visual Basic. This Part begins with coverage of bitmaps and sprites, and then delves into sound effects, music, and user input using various DirectX libraries. By the end of Part II, the game library will be a foundation for quickly building prototype games, with support for double buffering, dirty rectangle animation, transparency, and numerous other topics that form the basis of most games.

Part III: Hardcore Game Programming. Part III covers advanced game programming topics that extend your code base and the game library with higher-level functionality that is not focused so much on the actual code. This Part includes coverage of multiplayer game programming with sockets, as well as DirectPlay. Artificial intelligence is also explained, with coverage of game state, adaptive programming, and genetic algorithms, as well as practical solutions for controlling sprites. DirectX Graphics is also discussed in Part III, with detailed explanations and source code for handling 2-D sprites and 3-D objects with Direct3D.

Part IV: Complete Game Projects. Part IV includes four complete games that are created from scratch using all of the source code and techniques covered in the book, including support for the feature-rich game library. The sample games are varied and show off what can be done with Visual Basic, given the right tools. There are single-player, multiplayer, 2-D, and 3-D sample games included, with detailed analyses of how they are built, as well as the full source code for each game.

Part V Appendixes. Part V includes the appendixes, with a game library reference, a DirectX reference, a list of DirectInput scan codes, interesting Web sites, and recommended reading.

SUMMARY

Visual Basic is a fascinating language, and DirectX is a fascinating game development library. By combining the two you can create wonderful games that no one has thought of before! This book will help you get the most out of each by combining them into a seamless game programming paradigm that will give you and others great enjoyment for years to come.

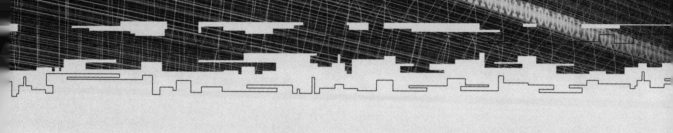

PART I

INTRODUCING VISUAL BASIC AND DIRECTX

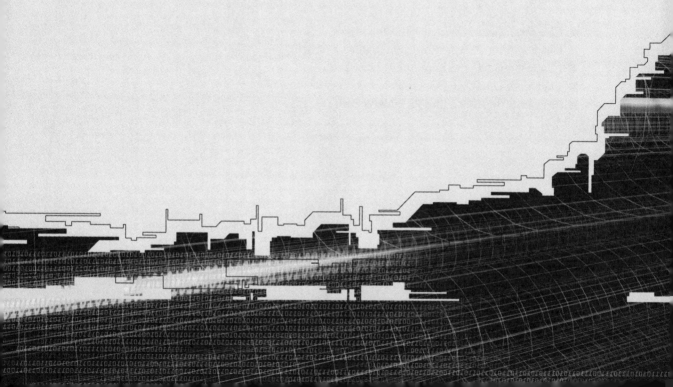

Welcome to Part I of *Visual Basic Game Programming with DirectX*. Part I includes six chapters that introduce you to Visual Basic and DirectX programming. It begins with an overview of the basic capabilities of Visual Basic for game programming, and then proceeds to explain how to get up to speed in a short amount of time with the use of sample code and illustrations.

In this part, you will learn some of the advanced features available by tapping into the core functionality of the Windows API, as well as how to optimize Visual Basic to get the most performance out of the language—an essential requirement for game programming. Part I includes an introduction to DirectX, explaining each of the DirectX components and how they can be used by Visual Basic to create more advanced games, and includes a sample DirectX program.

By the time you are finished with Part I, you will have a solid understanding of the Visual Basic language, how to optimize Visual Basic for speed, how to tap into advanced Windows API functions, and how to initialize DirectX to gain full-screen exclusive access using DirectDraw.

Part I includes the following chapters:

- Chapter 1: Game Programming Basics
- Chapter 2: Getting Started with Visual Basic
- Chapter 3: Visual Basic Programming in a Nutshell
- Chapter 4: Getting to Know the Windows API
- Chapter 5: Optimizing Visual Basic with Objects
- Chapter 6: Supercharging Visual Basic with DirectX

CHAPTER I

GAME
PROGRAMMING
BASICS

This chapter introduces the basics of game programming by exploring the subject from several viewpoints and taking you on a short jaunt through the history of the game industry. Then, I will explain the relationship between Visual Basic and DirectX, and how you can use them to write your own high-performance games. Finally, the chapter explains how the Visual Basic Game Library (which is developed in later chapters) will make game programming simple and fun.

This chapter covers the following topics:

- Welcome!
- What is a Video Game?
- Rewriting Your Favorite Game
- Video Games Versus Computer Games
- Gaming Hardware
- The Impact of DirectX
- Visual Basic is a Cool Language!
- Visual Basic Game Library
- Promotions

WELCOME!

Welcome to the fascinating world of *Visual Basic Game Programming with DirectX*! Game programming is a rewarding career, an enjoyable hobby, and an entertaining pastime for many people. The primary goal of this chapter is to introduce the subject of game programming and provide you with a little insight into what this book is about. As your host, I will take you through the first chapter of the adventure that will challenge your assumptions about Visual Basic and teach you how to write exciting, high-quality games.

Visual Basic Games

Visual Basic is a truly *awesome* programming language that is fully capable of supporting game development. Visual Basic has proven itself as a multi-purpose language that millions of programmers worldwide use on a daily basis. What many people overlook, however, is that Visual Basic is also a capable language for writing cutting-edge games.

Visual Basic is far too often dismissed as a serious language for game programming, but this assumption comes from lack of experience and lack of in-depth knowledge of the language. In my experience, poor performance in Visual Basic programs comes primarily from poorly written code! For this reason, I have dedicated two chapters to the subject of optimization: Chapter 4, "Getting to Know the Windows API" and Chapter 5, "Optimizing Visual Basic with Objects." I want to convince you that Visual Basic is an awesome language that is great for writing games! I will prove this to you using sound arguments, as well as actual benchmarks that compare different methods of drawing figures and bitmap images.

A Glimpse at DirectX

This book is heavily involved with DirectX programming from the start. In fact, as the title suggests, DirectX will be the core of most of the code in the book. I will touch upon the subject in this chapter and the next few chapters, and you will have an opportunity to write your first DirectX program in Chapter 6, "Supercharging Visual Basic with DirectX."

Since DirectX is the backbone of this book, I will show you how to get the most out of it using Visual Basic. But first things first! Before jumping into full-blown DirectX programming, I will start at the beginning and teach you some graphics programming with Visual Basic, followed by more advanced features in the Windows API. There are a few things you need to learn before you jump into DirectX.

I will start with intrinsic Visual Basic graphics code, and then add some punch with some really awesome Windows API functions that allow you to get under the hood, so to speak. After you have learned everything you need to know to write a complete game *without* DirectX, I will then show you how to do the same thing *with* DirectX.

I like to compare it to taking a walk to the park. There is so much to see, so many sounds, faces, nature, and landmarks to enjoy. When you jump into a car and drive to the park, it is fast and comfortable, but you miss something along the way. Likewise, there is a certain amount of enjoyment to be had from manipulating pixels on the screen without any help from a library like DirectX. Besides, software evolves quickly, so it is a good idea to understand how things work behind the scenes.

Game Programming Topics

If you are reading this as a complete novice who has never written a game before, you will not have any problem with DirectX programming. This book starts at the very beginning!

Visual Basic Game Programming with DirectX is *the* book on game programming with Visual Basic, covering not only the basics (such as drawing sprites with Windows API functions), but also the advanced subjects (like DirectDraw and Direct3D). DirectX is used almost exclusively by professional game developers today, because it has the complete support of the hardware industry (the companies that make sound cards and video cards, for instance). DirectX is fully supported in Visual Basic. This book makes the most of it, and you should have no problem developing full-blown DirectX games in a short time.

WHAT IS A VIDEO GAME?

Okay, here's a simple question: What is a computer game?

A computer game or video game is a program written in a programming language, such as C++ or Visual Basic, that allows a player to interact with and respond to events in an imaginary world. The goal of a video game is usually to compete with other players in a cooperative or adversarial competition (or to play solo), with an emphasis on setting the high score or completing the game.

Why Do We Play Video Games?

Video games are fun because they are very good at simulating another world and drawing the player into that world. Video games are excellent for developing keen hand-eye coordination and problem-solving skills through the achievement of goals with specific rewards. Often the completion of the game alone is reward enough, but many games do not have a specific solution. Rather, some games are suited for pitting two or more friends against each other, either at the same time or in turn. Other games are pointless and endless and continue playing in a never-ending loop, while continually increasing the difficulty until the player can no longer play.

Competition is not a bad thing. On the contrary, competition helps people to develop the skills they need to work with others and strive to better themselves.

Video games are fascinating works of art (yes, art!) that reflect the wild imaginings of a game designer. As such, game designers are like painters with a virtual canvas, capable of transporting someone to another world. The most exciting games are those with endless replay value, since consumers have made it clear that no

> **TIP**
>
> **Video games are excellent for developing keen hand-eye coordination and problem-solving skills through the achievement of goals with specific rewards.**

amount of graphical wizardry can make up for mediocre gameplay. Once a game has achieved a minimum acceptable standard on the visual and audio level, players expect the game to entertain through a gripping story or fantastic goal. Once in a while, a rare game comes along that achieves both visual wizardry and fantastic gameplay. *HALO: Combat Evolved* is one such game, developed by Bungie for the Microsoft Xbox. The physics and environment are so realistic that it makes the game seem to come alive.

The Game Engine

Every game, from the simplest card game to the most complicated 3-D first-person shooter game, has what is called a game engine. The *game engine*, shown in Figure 1.1, is the core set of routines that are executed repeatedly in a main animation loop. Such routines include displaying images on the screen, playing sound effects, and handling user input.

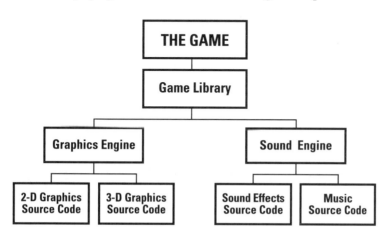

Figure 1.1

Games are made up of source code that is best organized in a game library (or game engine).

Of course, this is a simplified definition, as a large percentage of games (and the engines that power them) are written completely from scratch.

The best-developed games showcase the game engine, which is of more interest than the game itself. Games such as *Quake III Arena* and *Unreal Tournament* feature an engine that is licensed to other game developers who may not have the time, willingness, or ability to develop a comparable game engine on their own. Licensing a game engine is an excellent way to allow a game designer to focus on the aspects of gameplay and story, rather than spending that valuable time developing the technology for the game. Figure 1.2 illustrates the concept of licensing the game engine from one game to another.

> **BUZZWORD**
>
> The *game engine* is the core set of routines that are executed repeatedly in the main loop, including displaying images on the screen, playing sound effects, and handling user input.

Another reason why a development team might license software technology rather than develop it is the amount of time involved in creating an advanced 3-D engine. Most games are developed quickly, compared to the time involved in creating the engine itself. For this reason, a development company is usually able to recoup some of the costs for development by licensing the technology to others. It is a win-win situation for many.

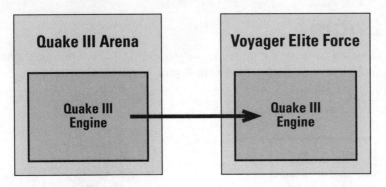

Figure 1.2

The Quake III *engine powers numerous games, including* Voyager Elite Force.

Game Graphics

In the old days, all games used two-dimensional images called sprites. The source image for a sprite usually has a background color that is defined as the *transparent* color—a pixel color that is not displayed when the sprite is drawn on the screen, allowing anything in the background to show through.

Most games developed today run entirely in 3-D and feature three-dimensional objects throughout the game world, rather than simple sprites. Both PC and console games have made the transition to 3-D, although consoles seem to be a step behind PC graphics technology. This was not the case in past generations of console video games. In the past, most consoles set the standards for graphics and immersion. Now it seems that console manufacturers are building video game machines that are more like PCs, with multiplayer options.

> **BUZZWORD**
> A *sprite* is a small image that may or may not be animated, with properties that define how it will move around on the screen.

The Microsoft Xbox console is a prime example of this manufacturing. Featuring a high-end Pentium III CPU (*Central Processing Unit*), a custom Nvidia GPU (*Graphics Processing Unit*) that is based on the GeForce 3 chip, and a 256-channel DSP (*Digital Signal Processor*), this console is bristling with PC technology. Xbox will forever change the console industry by combining the best of both worlds into a single $299 unit. Figure 1.3 illustrates the three primary processors in a computer system and the functions they perform in a game.

This book uses several techniques to display graphics on the screen. Starting with intrinsic Visual Basic graphics functions, you will be introduced to Windows API functions that display graphics objects. You will dig into DirectDraw through the DirectX 7.0 library, followed by DirectX Graphics with the DirectX 8.0 library. However, as I have mentioned before, I will show you how to write graphics code the hard way before you jump into DirectX full speed.

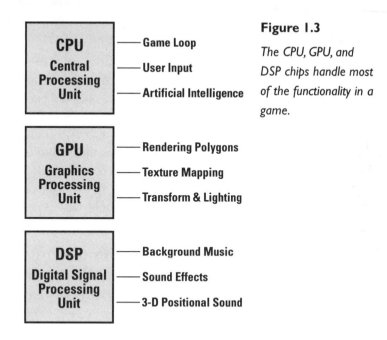

Figure 1.3

The CPU, GPU, and DSP chips handle most of the functionality in a game.

Sound Effects and Music

Sound is quite often more important than the graphics in a game. It is clear that we humans interact primarily through speech and sound. It should, therefore, be no surprise that sound is a vital part of every game. A game without sound might be acceptable on a fancy cell phone or wristwatch, but on any serious game hardware, sound is a major factor.

The development of a good sound effects library will be helpful when you select the sound effects for a new game. However, equally important is the source code that will play the sound files.

Getting Input

User input is always needed, no matter what type of game you are writing. After all, a game without user input is nothing more than a technology demo!

Visual Basic is capable of handling just about any type of input device that you can plug into your PC, including the newer USB (*Universal Serial Bus*) force-feedback joysticks and driving wheels. These topics will be explored in depth with coverage of DirectInput, the component of DirectX that handles input devices.

BUZZWORD

USB is a new type of high-speed communications port that is gradually replacing aging interfaces like serial ports, parallel ports, and joystick ports. IEEE 1394, or FireWire, is another high-speed port that is competing with **USB** and is capable of higher data transmission rates.

Artificial Intelligence

Computer-controlled players are needed for most types of games, and are absolutely essential for single-player games. Some multiplayer games, such as FPS (*First-Person Shooter*) games, do not always have computer-controlled players, and thus do not need AI (*Artificial Intelligence*) code. But the vast majority of games do—especially strategy games—so it is important to learn the tricks and techniques for simulating intelligence and challenging the player with competitive computer players. Some games use self-running mini programs called *bots* for the computer players. These bots are often programmable plug-ins for the game, which allows fans to develop their own AI players. Chapter 21, "Stellar War: Multiplayer Space Combat Game," includes a bot program that you can modify and run on the Stellar War server while playing the game.

Supporting Multiple Players

Nearly every game written today has multiplayer features that allow two or more players to compete or work cooperatively in the game. Most games also allow you to run your own game server on your PC and invite your friends to join your game over the Net. Since this is such a basic aspect of games today, it is important that you learn how to write multiplayer code and support networking in your own games. There is still a strong market for single-player games (such as the phenomenal game, *Civilization III*), but that market is dwindling as players flock to massively-multiplayer games like *Operation Flashpoint*.

One sub-genre is called MMORPG, which is short for "massively-multiplayer online role-playing game." These types of games were once only theoretical, until *Ultima Online, EverQuest*, and other large-scale games built an industry for themselves. These games usually require a monthly fee for access, because the developers are constantly improving and expanding the game and adding new worlds for the players to explore.

The online network created for Blizzard's games is called Battle.net, and is one of the most successful online game services in the industry—while remaining free for anyone who buys one of the supported games. Battle.net was created for the original *Diablo* and has been expanded to support all of Blizzard's games since, including *StarCraft, Diablo II*, and *WarCraft III*.

REWRITING YOUR FAVORITE GAME

Since technology is such a large focus of game development today, with numerous game libraries and game engines available, it can be a bit overwhelming for someone who is trying to get his foot in the door. You probably have a favorite game and would like to recreate it with your own embellishments. That is exactly how I got started writing games! I was an avid fan of sci-fi games like space shoot-em-ups and space exploration games (before *Master of Orion* re-defined the genre), and I wanted to create my own Star Trek game that incorporated all of the best features of the best games.

Perfecting an Already-Perfect Game

Two of my all-time favorite games are *Starflight* and *Star Control*. These two games fascinated me more than any other. I loved the open-ended nature of *Starflight*, and I also loved the intense gaming action of *Star Control*. The sequels to these games were even better! *Starflight II* and *Star Control II* were filled with plenty of creativity and replay value. Today, the galactic conquest genre has dominated sci-fi games, due to modern gaming advancements like multiplayer Internet support and the popularity of RTS (*Real-Time Strategy*) games. Now there are massive games like *Master of Orion II* and *Imperium Galactica II* that have yet to be bested in the genre. But those two originals were more like adventure games, rather than galactic conquest games, with a personal element that drew players into the game.

> **NOTE**
> *Starflight III* is in the works, with support from the authors of the original game. Take a look at http://www.starflight3.net for more information.

Building Your Ultimate Game

Whatever your interest, it is a good idea to have a major game idea in the back of your mind as you read through this book. If you already have a favorite type of game that you would like to write, that's great! If you are starting out without a prototype game of your own design, you should try to come up with one soon. Having a game idea in your mind as you read this book will make the subjects and source code covered look like bright spots in your mind's eye, as you learn how to implement each part of your game. Numerous sample games in later chapters will give you the examples you need to write your own game.

None of that will be of much use unless you have a side project, a hobby of sorts, a vision of that game you have always dreamed of writing. The important thing will not be whether the game lives up to your stratospheric expectations; the only thing that matters is that you finish writing the game.

The games in this book come from my own imagination, which is largely influenced by factors in my life, such as the books I read and the movies I watch. The sample games were inspired by my experience as a gamer, so I'm pretty sure that these games are fun. However, you might disagree, since everyone has different opinions and assumptions. For this reason, having your own game project in mind will be very helpful.

Making Your Game Ideas into Reality

You must apply the technology in this book to make your ideas a reality. The technology alone—such as the game library developed in this book—is not sufficient to create a game. Anyone, even RPG II and Cobol database programmers, can write a game. (I should know, since I have worked on large corporate databases.)

The difference between a run-of-the-mill card game and a new genre buster is an ephemeral quality which comes from the magical part of your mind that is capable of leaping beyond facts and working intuitively. Grasp that part of your inner being and you will build something masterful.

What Makes a Game Tick?

You might be wondering, what exactly makes a game tick? What is inside a game that makes it run, display the graphics, play the sounds, and interact with the player? It is difficult to answer those questions without a basic understanding of game architecture.

While you may or may not understand these steps at this point, I would like to show you how a game runs. Here are the basic steps that are processed during the run of a typical game:

1. Display the title screen.
2. Load the sprites and sounds.
3. Create a double buffer.
4. Display a static or rendered background image.
5. Save the image under each sprite.
6. Erase all sprites from the double buffer.
7. Check for user input and update the player's position.
8. Process enemy positions using A.I.
9. Move each sprite to the new location.
10. Check for collisions between the sprites.
11. Increment the animation frame for each sprite.
12. Draw all sprites to the double buffer.
13. Quickly transfer the double buffer to the screen.
14. Loop back to Step 5.
15. Delete all game objects and free memory.
16. End the game.

Although the details of each step are not displayed, this is a pretty good list of activities that occur while a game is running. Since I don't want to get into the habit of listing pseudo-code (which I have always felt was redundant), I will just explain what each step does.

Steps 1 through 4 are handled when the game first starts running. They initialize the game by loading all of the graphics, sounds, and setup of the game screen.

Steps 5 through 14 make up the game loop and are executed repeatedly while the game is running. These steps must run in order to display each frame in the game. Therefore, when you hear that some games run at 60 FPS (*Frames Per Second*), you must realize that a lot of work is being done during each frame. Too often, gamers will compare two or more games based solely on the frame rate. This is unfortunate, because some games do a lot more behind the scenes than others! Some games have far more intelligent computer players, while other games might run at twice the frame rate but have poor computer players.

Steps 15 and 16 are executed at the end of the game.

There are many more steps in an actual game, but this simplified list should give you a good idea how a game runs internally. The goal of a game library is to make these steps as simple as possible by handling the complicated details behind the scenes.

Video Games Versus Computer Games

The IBM PC was never meant to be a game machine, so I'm sure no one would disagree with the irony that today, most computer games run on descendants of the original IBM PC. In comparison to computer technology today, the original IBM PC and its clones were ridiculously primitive. It was only through sheer ingenious wizardry (with a dash of highly-optimized assembly language) that games were ever created for the PC at all.

While my friends were blasting aliens (with multi-channel digital sound and loads of color) on their Atari ST and Amiga 500 computers, I was pecking away at my PC, trying to make sense of the four colors available with my CGA video card and finding new ways to squeak something out of the PC speaker. So it is a wonder that the PC made it at all! Look at computers today—they are mind-boggling in complexity and power. It is absolutely amazing to think that a modern PC with a GeForce 3 card can crank out graphics in real-time that rival the digital artistry of feature films like *Jurassic Park* and *The Phantom Menace*.

How It All Started

The current generation of gamers, those who got into it in more recent times and have computers that come standard with 3-D graphics acceleration and 3-D positional sound, do not appreciate the old days with the same nostalgia that older gamers feel for games such as *Starflight*, *Battlehawks 1942*, *Star Control*, *Archon*, *King's Quest*, *Power Monger*, and *Lode Runner*. It is easy to take computer hardware for granted today, when it is so powerful and inexpensive!

For example, the original IBM PC came with 64k of RAM and one 360k floppy drive. The next version, the IBM PC/XT, had the option for a 5MB Winchester hard drive for several hundred dollars. Now, let's put this into perspective. The Intel Pentium III processor has a built-in instruction cache of 256k that keeps the processor from waiting for data to be loaded from memory (which is much slower than the processor). This cache is made up of more transistors than the entire 8086 processor at the core of the original IBM PC.

In the early days, before the Adlib or Sound Blaster cards, the IBM PC had only a simple internal speaker for making sounds. Early PC games had dreadful sound support, to put it mildly. Gamers were lucky to find a game with even rudimentary sound effects, and most commercial games (which were presumably cutting-edge) were even lacking.

> **NOTE**
> The Nvidia GeForce 3 chip, which accelerates 3-D games and features advanced transform and lighting (T&L) instructions, has over 40 million transistors, exceeding even the Pentium 4 processor in complexity.

In 1988, Access Software released an amazing game called *Mean Streets*. This futuristic action/adventure game featured standard VGA graphics (common in all PC games at the time). But what really made *Mean Streets* shine was the full-blown digital music and sound that permeated the game! Right from the start, the musical score for *Mean Streets* gave the player a taste of what to expect throughout the game. Each character in the game featured a real voice actor and limited video-capture sequences.

Access Software followed suit with *Crime Wave* and several follow-up games in the series. A few years after the release of *Mean Streets* and *Crime Wave*, sound cards like the Sound Blaster and Pro Audio Spectrum appeared on the market, and high-quality sound was finally possible on the PC.

Home Consoles

Home video game machines, also called consoles, have been around since the original Atari 2600. In the early 1980s, a Japanese coin-operated arcade game manufacturer called Nintendo came out with the Nintendo Entertainment System (NES) for homes. Nintendo had been building arcade machines (like *Donkey Kong*) for years. Nintendo's new console helped to invigorate the struggling video game industry at the time.

Arcade games and video games have led the pace in graphics and gameplay for many years. However, in recent years, PCs have actually surpassed arcade and video game machines. The line dividing computer games and video games is not as distinct as it was in the past. Now, games are ported from arcade to console, from PC to console, and vice versa. Development tools are also becoming more standardized as industry leaders strive for content. Software is more important than hardware, and the video game industry has finally figured out that gamers just want to play fun games, regardless of the platform. Dynamic, creative, and exciting new games that cross the barriers of game genres are the ones that sell.

Sega should also be credited for many advances in video game design, with three excellent home consoles: the Genesis, Saturn, and Dreamcast. These consoles greatly helped to keep the industry competitive with giants like Nintendo and Sony. Even in the midst of highly advanced consoles like the PlayStation 2, Microsoft Xbox, and Nintendo GameCube, the Sega Dreamcast is still very popular and an affordable alternative to comparable games. Sega might be out of the hardware business, but it is hardly out of the games business!

GAMING HARDWARE

There should be little difference in the hardware requirements for playing games and developing them. Game developers arc often solely responsible for the massive hardware upgrades that take place with the release of awesome new games that push existing PCs into obsolescence. However, the games covered in this book will run on a modest PC without all of the latest and greatest hardware.

You can get away with much less, but here are the hardware specifications of the PC that I used while writing the sample programs in upcoming chapters. This is a baseline for the frame rates mentioned in the book:

- Mobile Pentium-850 Processor
- 512MB PC100 RAM
- 30GB 5400 RPM Hard Drive
- 32MB ATI Mobility M4 Graphics Chip

NOTE

Thanks to the marketing wizards at Intel, we now have about a dozen versions of the Pentium brand to keep track of. There are three different versions of the Pentium III alone! To make things easier from this point on, I am going to use the word *Pentium* to refer to the Pentium III, Celeron, and Pentium 4 processors. Similarly, I will use the word *Athlon* to refer to the various AMD Athlon and Duron processors.

Notebooks: The New Gaming Rigs

Game development has now entered a new era in which notebook computers (also called laptops) are capable of running games that once required top-of-the-line desktop gaming machines.

Notebook computers once lagged behind desktop computers by several years, which is a lifetime in computing terms. However, miniaturization technology has developed some remarkable new devices at a scale that is simply staggering. The computer industry's continual price war has resulted in incredibly powerful desktop and notebook computers at the price range once reserved for the low-end budget market.

Quite honestly, a modest sum will not only buy the absolute latest and greatest computer today, it will buy all of the accessories too! What is even more startling is that the same amount may be used to buy a notebook computer of comparable power. Even year-old computing technology was once considered grossly obsolete by high-end users (most notably, gamers). But today, the low-end budget PCs are capable of running some of the most advanced games. This state of affairs should keep game programmers employed for at least the next few years.

Instant LAN Party

LANs (*Local Area Networks*) were once only found in large businesses. As the technology improved and prices dropped, small- to medium-sized businesses were able to network their office computers together, as were savvy hobbyists at home. Today, a significant number of households have two or more computers with a high-speed Internet connection, and a home network just makes sense. The ability to share drive space, Internet connectivity, and printers is appealing to most people, and especially to gamers.

LAN parties are now common forms of entertainment around the world, as friends get together (usually at a site with a high-speed Internet line and a network router), toting their massive tower cases jammed full of every conceivable type of drive and accessory and gigantic 19" or 21" monitors (the only way to play, in the opinion of many). Now picture a newcomer with a lightweight notebook computer, featuring most of the same high-end features and accessories, in a leather case strapped to his shoulder, and you get an idea about how far the computer industry has come in recent years.

Wireless LAN Cards

Wireless networking is now a viable technology and may soon change the way networks are planned and configured. While past home and office networks required endless streams of CAT-5 cable, modern networks built with wireless network cards and hubs are definitely the wave of the future. There's nothing quite as much fun as playing games and browsing the Web with a laptop, while sitting on the back porch or on the living room couch—without a network cable. Leading technologies include the original 802.11, the faster 802.11b, HomeRF, and OpenAir. Proxim has an excellent wireless system that supports both HomeRF and OpenAir at a reasonable price, and they even have a new CompactFlash card available for portable devices like Pocket PCs.

This bodes well for gamers and makes the concept of the instant LAN party even more of a reality. In the near future, most systems will likely be wireless, including notebook and handheld computers. The only problem with wireless technology is a lack of security. Just about anyone can tap into a wireless network unimpeded. As with any new technology, this will have to be addressed in time, by adding more robust encryption to the myriad of signals traveling through the air.

3-D Acceleration to Go

Most new games today require 3-D acceleration in order to run, due to the intense graphics featured in these games. 3-D acceleration has only been available since about 1996, with the advent of the 3Dfx Voodoo card. However, 3-D acceleration is now available for the first time on notebook computers featuring the ATI Mobility and Nvidia GeForce2Go chips. These high-end graphics processors are capable of supporting nearly all of the latest games that normally would run only on high-end desktop systems.

THE IMPACT OF DIRECTX

DirectX is a significant development in the PC gaming world, and has been a successful library on consoles like the Dreamcast and Xbox as well (get it, "X" box?). The standardization that comes with DirectX has done much to further the computer game and video card industries.

When a company develops a new game that supports the latest version of DirectX, they are guaranteed that nearly every Windows PC will be able to run the game. Similarly, when a graphics card company invents a new graphics chip with new features, it is also guaranteed sales by providing DirectX drivers with the new graphics chip.

DirectX has helped the software and hardware sides of gaming come to terms, whereas in the past hardware and software have always been somewhat at odds. Today, with the latest version of DirectX, both hardware and software seem to be more consistent, with neither far ahead of the other. Years ago it was common for an awesome new game to compel gamers to upgrade their computers. Today, game developers are lucky if they are able to push the latest PC hardware to its limits. How things have changed!

VISUAL BASIC IS A COOL LANGUAGE!

The premise behind the use of Visual Basic for game development is the language's versatility. Visual Basic is capable of handling large database programs as well as advanced 3-D games. Not many programming languages can claim such a feat. Often, a language will be well-suited for a particular task. But now it is possible to use Visual Basic to do many things that once might have been spread across two or more languages. Many Web servers that once used Perl or C++ scripts now use VBScript, and many ASP (*Active Server Pages*) Web sites also use VBScript, because it is so easy to use and supports many different types of databases for Web development.

Power, Flexibility, Saturation, and Speed

Put simply, Visual Basic has the power to handle the most challenging computing tasks, including advanced 3-D games. It has the flexibility to handle a multitude of different tasks. Visual Basic now compiles native executable program files that run under Windows without an interpreter (as in previous versions, such as 4.0). Finally, Visual Basic is used by millions of programmers on a daily basis, which means that the language has saturated business and home users alike.

Visual Basic and DirectX in the Same Sentence?

It might seem odd for a C or C++ programmer to consider using Visual Basic to create DirectX games. After all, DirectX is a COM (*Component Object Model*) library that was built with C++, and would be best utilized with the native language of Windows.

However, starting with DirectX 7.0, Microsoft has provided a type library for writing DirectX programs with Visual Basic. This type library contains the link between the DirectX library and Visual Basic that allows you to take full advantage of every feature in DirectX without limitation. Yes, you can even write Direct3D programs in Visual Basic, with performance close to what can be done in C or C++. For an example, check out the game in Chapter 22, "Pong 3D: Modern Arcade Game."

THE VISUAL BASIC GAME LIBRARY

The goal of this book is to teach game programming with Visual Basic and DirectX first and foremost, and the best way to do that (in my opinion) is through practice. Therefore, you will write numerous sample programs throughout the course of this book. In the process, I will show you how to build an advanced game library that uses all the features and functionality of the Windows API and DirectX.

The Visual Basic Game Library, which is assembled in Chapter 13, "Building the DirectX Game Library," will start off with all of the code you need to write games with Visual Basic (in other words, without DirectX). I'll show you how to enhance the library with Windows API functions that will drastically increase the speed of graphics functions that are essential for writing high-speed games. Later, I will show you how to add DirectX support to the library. In the end, you will have a full-featured game library suitable for building any type of game, from the simplest card game to the most advanced real-time strategy game. It will be a simple matter to add the necessary game library files to your project or simply reference the compiled game library as a DLL.

PROMOTIONS

At this early stage, you might consider yourself a white-belt *Newbie Gamer*. I assume that you know how to *play* games (that is, your brain is sufficiently developed to make the connection between your eyes and your hands), but that is about all that I will assume. As you learn and demonstrate skill in increasingly advanced subjects, you will be promoted!

The ranks look like this:

1. Newbie Gamer
2. Apprentice Hacker
3. Skilled Programmer
4. Veteran Coder
5. Master Developer
6. Adept Game Designer

Each new level in the ranking is an order of magnitude higher than the one before, in relation to the amount of information you will learn. If you are already an experienced programmer, you might progress through the ranks quickly, but later ranks will be extremely challenging and you must demonstrate your prowess with the subjects to advance. The final rank of Adept Game Designer requires a great deal of study and skill that can only be honed by developing complete games. To quote Master Yoda, "My own counsel will I keep on when you are ready!"

Basically, you will have to write lines of code as easily as you breathe air, and be able to call up algorithms and function libraries from memory. You must be able to control every aspect of game creation so that it is second nature to you. You will no longer work with mere functions and structures, but with whole libraries of code that do your bidding. You must build your own game engine and learn how to master it.

Remember at the end of *The Matrix*, when Neo began to see the *real* world? That is how you must see games and code to reach the final rank of Adept Game Designer, by pondering a higher plane of gaming design that transcends mere source code. Most of our peers are Skilled Programmers. A smaller number are Veteran Coders, while a select few are Master Developers. Needless to say, Adept Game Designers are rare, at the top of their genre. Study the material herein, practice by writing code, leave no idea unexplored, and one day you might find yourself sharing stories with John Carmack, Sid Meier, and Peter Molyneux.

SUMMARY

The most important factor in game development is this: Be creative! Visual Basic is a fun language to use for writing games, and it handles all of the complexities of Windows programming for you. So use this opportunity to focus on creativity and gameplay! Go the extra mile and put the extra bells and whistles into a game. Put all of your energy into it.

This chapter has presented the subject of game development with Visual Basic and DirectX as an achievable concept—something that you can easily do with a little bit of know-how. If you find yourself intimidated by new games that come out full of awesome features, then all you need is a little experience creating games of your own. This book will teach you how to do that! Visual Basic and DirectX work well together, and you are going to have a lot of fun learning how to write games in later chapters.

This is only the beginning and I haven't even scratched the surface of what is possible. In Chapter 2, "Getting Started with Visual Basic," I'll give you a formal introduction to Visual Basic, explain all the features of the language, and show you the various versions available. So put on your seatbelt and get ready, because it's full speed ahead.

CHAPTER 2

GETTING STARTED WITH VISUAL BASIC

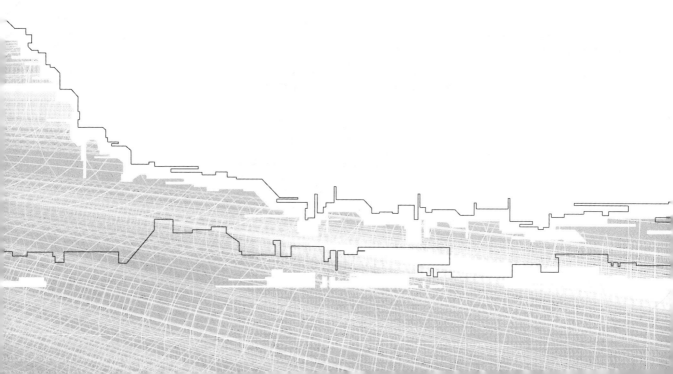

This chapter is an introduction to Visual Basic with a history of the language and a discussion of the various versions available. The primary features of the language are explored, including a tour of the IDE (*Integrated Development Environment*) and a tour of the help system for Visual Basic, which is called MSDN (*Microsoft Developer Network*). There are numerous versions and editions of Visual Basic, which are covered in this chapter along with a tutorial on installing Visual Basic 6.0.

This chapter covers the following topics:

- Breaking the Rules
- History of Visual Basic
- Compiler Version Support
- Choosing the Best Version
- Innovations in Visual Basic.NET
- Installing Visual Basic
- Exploring the Visual Basic IDE
- Using Microsoft Developer Network

Breaking the Rules

Let me fill you in on a little-known secret: Visual Basic is a rogue language. That's right, VB does not follow the rules! VB started out by committing simple misdemeanors, but has developed many felony crimes over the years and now shows complete disregard for authority! Visual Basic is so simple that many programmers disregard it after spending only a few minutes with the compiler. That is the crime of VB—fooling unsuspecting programmers into a false belief that the language is for beginners, causing them to make the mistake of underestimating the language.

What do I mean by this? Visual Basic is more of a product than a language in the strictest sense. The VB language is a descendant of the original BASIC language, but has so departed from the roots of BASIC that it might now be considered a new language. VB breaks the laws set forth in computer science academia by providing simple solutions to complex problems.

Need quick access to a database table? Throw a few controls on a form, set a few properties, and go. Need to write a game with DirectX? Reference the DirectX library, throw a PictureBox on top of a form, and go!

You see, VB does not assume that you have a complex problem that requires an algorithm. (Yikes, that word makes my spine tingle!) VB assumes that you can solve a problem by assembling simple objects into complex solutions. Figure 2.1 illustrates this concept by showing the primary components that can be used by a VB program.

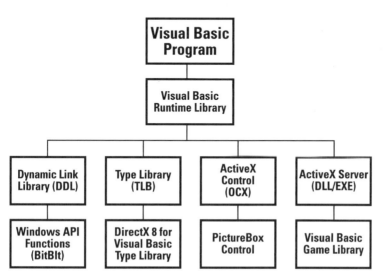

Figure 2.1

Visual Basic provides numerous system components to enhance programs.

Language Barriers

What does it mean when someone claims to know C++? That person's skill is usually limited to his preferred platform, such as Linux. Try compiling a Visual C++ program using GNU C++, or vice versa. It just doesn't work. In fact, C++ programmers take pride in their conversions (also called *ports*) from one platform to another, because the task is often monumental. Another problem is that a large percentage of C++ programmers really do not know or use any parts of the "++" in the language—they are still programming in straight C.

How can you tell the difference? It's pretty easy. A typical game written in C will have mostly function prototypes, structs, and variables at the top of source code files, rather than objects.

Visual Basic does have a limited form of OOP (*Object-Oriented Programming*) built in. You can dramatically enhance your games by using these simple OOP features, mainly through classes and properties. Some C diehards claim that C++ is inefficient and will bog down a game. This is true only if you abuse the C++ features by overloading and inheriting everything. (Those subjects will be covered in Chapter 5, "Optimizing Visual Basic with Objects.") The power of VB lies in its extensibility. Any time you need to extend a program or reuse existing code, you can reference a type library with the Project References dialog or use a Declare statement to call an external function. I will explain the subject of extensibility more in Chapter 13, "Building the DirectX Game Library."

So how does VB accomplish so much when it is supposedly light-years behind other modern languages? VB is modest, subtle in exposing its features. At first glance, VB is plain, unsophisticated, and feature-poor for beginners. But what happens once you get to know VB? You discover that underneath the shroud of the drag-and-drop GUI "front" is a sleek, smooth, and powerful language.

Standards, Schmandards

What is a standard in the programming language market? It is a document prepared by a governing body (such as ANSI, the *American National Standards Institute*) that defines the semantics of a language in an attempt to promote cross-product and cross-platform compatibility. The problem is, standards are always a few years behind the leading edge. By the time the ANSI C++ standard came along, the vendors (such as Microsoft, Borland, Lattice, and Watcom) had all created their own hybrid versions of the language, with hordes of followers ready to give their all in defense of this or that version of what is supposed to be a standardized language.

Nothing supersedes the drive in a free-market economy to produce the best and dominate all others. Despite the standards' intentions to keep languages within a tightly-held pattern, market forces shape and mold compilers—like many software products—to perfection.

Since VB is a singular product as well as a language, it does not suffer from cross-platform incompatibilities. Unfortunately, VB is only available for Windows.

Visual Basic Makes Its Own Rules!

Visual Basic is a highly standardized programming language because it is the product of Microsoft. No other company can create another form of Visual Basic because Microsoft owns it. This status differs from most traditional programming languages, which are public domain or licensed in theory, and then implemented by competing companies. Over time, the most prolific or feature-rich compiler will dominate the market for that particular language.

Visual Basic is one language, one country, one king. It has no standard because it defines itself. You can count on the fact that this bad boy is stable and here to stay. If you are planning to pour all of your energy into a single technology, VB will not leave you high and dry. Sure, drastic things are happening with VB.NET, but I'm sure you won't mind trading a bumpy, pothole-riddled asphalt highway for a shiny, new, concrete super-freeway. VB.NET isn't leaving us behind, it is taking us to new heights and perfecting a language that was already good enough for most of us. Feature glut? No way! These features help programmers be more productive. The whole Windows API is available to VB.NET through a class hierarchy, so there is no longer a need to declare any of the Windows functions.

Visual Basic is unattractive to many people precisely because it has no open standard and it is maintained by a single company, which affords the language no opportunity for improvement (at least not through competition). But let's face it: No one can do VB better than Microsoft. So if it came down to licensing the product for Mac or Linux, Microsoft would have to do it. Since those platforms are direct competition for Windows, it will not likely happen. In the end, I would speculate that VB is largely the reason for each new release of Microsoft Visual Studio. It is a significant product for the company—a flagship product, not just another development tool.

HISTORY OF VISUAL BASIC

The original BASIC (*Beginner's All-Purpose Symbolic Instruction Code*) language was developed in 1964 and ran on mainframe computers. The idea behind BASIC was to teach students how to program with an easy language before getting into more advanced languages that are difficult to learn, such as Cobol and Assembly.

Visual Basic was based on the original BASIC language. Therefore, one might argue that VB goes back to 1974 when Bill Gates and Paul Allen developed their first product together, Altair BASIC. Following this version, Gates and Allen wrote versions of BASIC for Apple, Commodore, and Amiga computers, and founded Microsoft on sales of BASIC. So it should be no surprise that the latest incarnation of BASIC is still Microsoft's leading development tool.

A few years later, Microsoft developed DOS (*Disk Operating System*) for IBM's new Personal Computer. This came to be known as PC-DOS (along with a separately-licensed version called MS-DOS for IBM-compatible PCs). IBM released a version of BASIC with PC-DOS called BASIC-A. This version would only run on actual IBM computers (not clones), but Microsoft released an identical version with MS-DOS called GW-BASIC.

Since GW-BASIC was only an interpreter, incapable of compiling executable programs, Microsoft provided another product for use in compiling BASIC programs, called QuickBasic. QuickBasic was a revolutionary update to the language, featuring true structured programming with callable procedures instead of line numbers. The free version of QuickBasic, released with later versions of MS-DOS, was called Q-Basic.

Alan Cooper is regarded as the father of Visual Basic because he developed the first working prototype of a drag-and-drop programming environment with a toolbox of widgets (controls). Cooper's width toolbox was the key to his recognition in this respect. Cooper's program was called Tripod, and he had the opportunity to show the program to Bill Gates (who, in case you only recently landed on Earth, is the chairman of Microsoft) back in 1988. Gates apparently loved the program and offered to buy it from Cooper. The new Microsoft product was code-named Ruby, and the rest is history. Oddly enough, Microsoft stripped the widget toolbox out of Ruby and shelved Tripod. Only later did the development team resurrect the concept of plug-in widgets, per Gates' insistence. Had the team not done this, Visual Basic would have likely failed as a development tool. But since developers had an opportunity to add their own widgets to the drag-and-drop toolbox, VB had an edge over other visual languages.

Version History

Each new version of Visual Basic has been significantly more powerful than the last, and has been released to great fanfare and acclaim. Later versions generated almost as much fervor as Microsoft's Windows operating system and Office products. Following is a short description of each version of Visual Basic.

Visual Basic 1.0. The first official version of Visual Basic (code-named Thunder) debuted in 1991. It was actually a combination of QuickBasic and Ruby, and could be used to create Windows programs with a simple drag-and-drop interface and instant interpreted runtime. This was Microsoft's first visual language, and its drag-and-drop control toolbox and event-driven programming model allowed programmers to create Windows 3.0 programs without using the clumsy Microsoft C compiler that ran under MS-DOS.

Visual Basic 2.0. This version was released in 1992 and greatly helped the language grow in popularity. VB 2.0 featured ODBC (*Object Database Connectivity*—a database driver standard) support, MDI (*Multiple-Document Interface*) forms, object variables, and a new Professional Edition.

Visual Basic 3.0. This version came out in 1993 and had several new advancements, including integration of the Access JET database engine, OLE (*Object Linking and Embedding*) automation, and rudimentary reporting.

Visual Basic 4.0. This version, which debuted in 1995, added support for COM (*Component Object Model*) components, including support for ActiveX DLL and OCX files. VB 4.0 was a hybrid version, supporting both 16-bit Windows 3.1 and 32-bit Windows 95. The most significant new feature of VB 4.0 was the addition of classes, which gave VB programmers a taste of the object-oriented programming world.

Visual Basic 5.0. This version was released in 1997 and added additional support for COM with the ability to create custom ActiveX controls (whereas VB 4.0 only allowed you to use them, not create them). It was directly aligned with Microsoft's new focus on Internet development. VB 5.0 also included a native code compiler, resulting in much faster programs, and added the `WithEvents` statement.

Visual Basic 6.0. This version came out in 1998 with great success and achieved widespread acceptance, pushing Visual Basic to the top position in development tool popularity. VB 6.0 offered some spectacular new features (particularly involving databases), including the Data

Environment for creating database connection classes, WebClasses for Internet development, windowless controls, and a scaled-down version of Crystal Reports.

Visual Basic.NET. This version was released in 2002 and might be thought of as VB 7.0. This version is a grand departure from previous versions of Visual Basic and is comprised of more than just new features. VB.NET revolutionizes the language and is a complete rewrite of the compiler (which is shared by other Visual Studio languages). In fact, it might be argued that VB.NET is not even really Visual Basic any more, and that VB 6.0 was the last true version. These new features are discussed in more detail later, in the section titled "Innovations in Visual Basic.NET."

COMPILER VERSION SUPPORT

The source code presented in this book is comprised of source code for various classes, sample demonstration programs, and several complete games. Early on, I wanted to fully support VB.NET in the book since most people enjoy learning about the latest and greatest products. In the end, I decided to focus on the most popular (and stable) version, Visual Basic 6.0, rather than using untested and unproven technology in the form of VB.NET, despite the compelling new features. As of this time, some of the minor features in VB.NET are not even grounded, and there are some problems porting DirectX code to VB.NET. It would have been a major undertaking to support both VB 6.0 and VB.NET, because this would have required two separate versions of the game library.

As an alternative, I have included versions of the code in this book for VB 5.0 and VB 6.0. You will find the projects for each version on the CD-ROM. The VB 5.0 projects are unsupported and provided as a bonus.

Visual Basic 5.0

Visual Basic 5.0 is very similar to 6.0, so the source code from the book is easy to port back to this version. You should have no trouble loading the projects and running the code. DirectX is also referenced in the same manner as 6.0, and DirectX 8.0 is fully supported. The source code from the book has been converted to VB 5.0 format and is located on the CD-ROM in the \Sources\VB5 directory. This version of the source code is not supported but is provided simply as bonus material for your convenience. The splash screen for the Visual Basic 5.0 Professional Edition setup program is shown in Figure 2.2.

Figure 2.2

The Visual Basic 5.0
Professional Edition
splash screen

Visual Basic 6.0

Visual Basic 6.0 is the version fully supported in the book, and all of the source code listings should ideally be compiled under VB 6.0. The source code for all the sample programs in the book is located on the CD-ROM in the \Sources\VB6 directory.

Visual Basic.NET

Visual Basic.NET, like all of the development tools in Visual Studio.NET, has been radically changed from 6.0 and rebuilt from the ground up as a product. I'll cover VB.NET in more detail later in this chapter. This version provides some awesome new features that should definitely be exploited for game programming. However, take care when developing game programming classes because too much structure can actually slow down a game.

I had originally planned the game library for this book as an ActiveX custom control, containing all of the source code wrapped around a single sub-classed PictureBox control. This would have provided a means to easily and quickly handle the core functionality of a game within the library. Unfortunately, the overhead involved in using ActiveX controls made the code significantly slower than if I just used procedures and classes. Therefore, the game library will be a simple ActiveX DLL instead. (I'll cover this in more detail in Chapter 13, "Building the DirectX Game Library.")

CHOOSING THE BEST VERSION

There are several versions of Visual Basic from which to choose, and each step up in price offers additional features. You probably did not know there were actually six versions of Visual Basic, did you? I was surprised when I discovered this for myself. Based on this, it is pretty clear that Microsoft takes Visual Basic very seriously and considers it the company's flagship development product. As for game programming and running the code in this book, I recommend Visual

Basic 6.0, either the Professional Edition or the Enterprise Edition. Both editions are functionally similar, and differ only in the included tools. However, the free version of Visual Basic 5.0, called the Custom Control Edition, can compile the code. So if you just want to learn without buying an expensive compiler, you have that option.

Minor Editions

Following is a list of the minor editions of Visual Basic.

Control Creation Edition. One of the best ways to learn Visual Basic is by downloading the free Visual Basic 5.0 Control Creation Edition from Microsoft.com. (Alternatively, you can search for it on the Internet.) This version has most of the features of the full-blown commercial version of Visual Basic 5.0, and you can write and run complete VB programs with it.

There are two downsides to this edition. First, you cannot compile executable versions of your programs, but can only run them inside the Visual Basic IDE. Second, this free edition was only made available for Visual Basic 5.0. But don't worry! Most source code written with VB 6.0 will still run under VB 5.0. This is a great way to learn how to program Visual Basic without the costly expense of a full-blown compiler. Personally, I suspect that Microsoft had intended to ship VB5CCE with Windows at some point, but that idea never worked out.

Applications Edition. The Visual Basic Applications Edition used to be called Visual Basic for Applications, but the acronym VBA is still the same. This edition, which is more of a sub-edition than a full-blown product, is a licensed form of the language that third-party software companies can incorporate into their own products, thus adding the capability to customize those products with VB code.

Microsoft Office 97 and later versions include VBA so that programmers can customize Excel spreadsheets, Word documents, and—most importantly—Access databases. The strength of VBA revolutionized the capabilities of Access 97, which previously featured a limited macro language. Now, it is possible to port database applications to and from Access and VB with little effort. In fact, a common practice in database circles is to develop a prototype database with Access and then move the code over to full-blown VB using an ODBC (*Object Database Connectivity*) connection. Once the stand-alone VB application is working with the Access data, the data can be moved to Microsoft SQL Server, MSDE (*Microsoft Data Engine*), Oracle, SQL Anywhere, or any other ODBC-compliant database server.

Despite the strengths of this edition for creating applications and enhancing products, VBA is not suitable for game programming.

Scripting Edition. The Visual Basic Scripting Edition, also called VBScript, was created to enhance Internet Explorer with functionality to rival Netscape's JavaScript browser language during the great browser war of the late 1990s.

VBScript is the language of choice for creating Web sites with ASP, using Microsoft InterDev or (more commonly) through manually-coded pages. ASP is an awesome Web development component of IIS5 (*Internet Information Server 5.0*—Microsoft's Web server product). ASP support has also been added to Web servers like Apache (a popular Linux program) using a product called Instant ASP from Halcyon Software (http://www.halcyonsoft.com).

VBScript is also the engine behind Embedded Visual Basic—the Windows CE compiler. You might consider this a shameless plug, but if you are interested in developing games for Windows CE, check out my other book: *Pocket PC Game Programming: Using The Windows CE Game API* (Premier Press, Inc., 2001).

VBScript can be used to create Web-based games for the Microsoft Internet Explorer browser or any other Web browser that supports VBScript. However, it is not suitable for general game programming.

Major Editions

Following is a list of the major editions of Visual Basic.

Learning Edition. The Visual Basic 6.0 Learning Edition is an affordable alternative to the expensive Professional and Enterprise editions of the language. The Learning Edition costs about $100 and is similar to the VB 5.0 CCE, but supports all of the features and project files of VB 6.0. If you are considering buying Visual Basic 6.0 and would like to evaluate it first, this is a good low-cost alternative.

The Learning Edition comes with a tutorial on CD, is fully capable of running the sample programs in this book, and supports DirectX. Additionally, if you purchase the Learning Edition first, you will be able to upgrade it to the Professional Edition at a significant discount. (As it turns out, this costs less than buying the Professional Edition at the retail price.)

Professional Edition. The Visual Basic 6.0 Professional Edition is the most common edition used for developing both applications and games. This version includes the optimizing native code compiler that allows you to compile your programs into executable files. If you are considering purchasing Visual Basic, this is the best option for game programming, and is the edition that I use on a daily basis. However, you might want to consider buying the Learning Edition first, because you can then upgrade it to the Professional Edition for less than the full retail price.

Enterprise Edition. The Visual Basic 6.0 Enterprise Edition is the ultimate edition of Visual Basic, which includes absolutely everything that Microsoft has developed for applications programming. Numerous database tools and ActiveX controls come with this edition. Since

these extras aren't needed for game programming, the Enterprise Edition is certainly imprac-
tical, considering that it is four times as expensive as the Professional Edition. In fact, even if
you have the Enterprise Edition, you will likely not install the extras. This is a case where if
you already own it, that's great, but there is no compelling reason for an individual developer
to purchase the Enterprise Edition.

Visual Studio Packs a Punch

In addition to the stand-alone versions of Visual Basic, Microsoft has packed several development
tools into a package called Visual Studio. In previous versions, this was called Developer's Studio.
There are two versions of Visual Studio:

- Visual Studio 6.0 Professional Edition
- Visual Studio 6.0 Enterprise Edition

Both editions include the same selection of software, but the Enterprise edition includes additional server components, utilities, source code control, and custom controls.

Regardless of the edition, Visual Studio 6.0 includes the following development tools:

- Visual C++ 6.0
- Visual Basic 6.0
- Visual InterDev 6.0
- Visual FoxPro 6.0
- Visual J++ 6.0

Following is a short description of each version.

Visual C++ 6.0. This is the premier Windows C++ compiler on the market, and the one used
by nearly every studio today for DirectX game development. Even those developers who write
cross-platform code find it difficult to avoid supporting Visual C++ and DirectX due to the
established user base.

Visual Basic 6.0. This is, of course, the language of choice for writing games based on the
source code and information in this book.

Visual InterDev 6.0. This is a lesser-known development tool for creating Web sites. InterDev
treats a complete Web site as a programming project and each Web page as an ASP (*Active
Server Pages*) program. Like the other Visual Studio tools, InterDev provides the resources for
connecting to databases and is helpful when creating large data-driven Web sites. While it is
possible to write games using VBScript—the scripting language of choice for ASP pages—it is
something of a specialty and is not suitable for serious game development.

Visual FoxPro 6.0. This database development environment and language is on the decline and not as popular as it once was, due to the success of SQL Server and Access, as well as the database features in Visual Basic.

Visual J++ 6.0. This is Microsoft's version of the Java language, developed and maintained by Sun Microsystems (through a spin-off called JavaSoft). J++ received a lot of flak early on from Java developers since Microsoft apparently did not follow Java coding standards when trying to incorporate ActiveX and other features into J++ that are popular in the other Visual Studio languages (which is acceptable). Java is an excellent language for game development, with many features that were borrowed from C++. Visual J++ became somewhat obsolete with the release of Microsoft C# (pronounced "see sharp"), a more versatile language.

If you have the full-blown Visual Studio, then you have the option of what languages you would like to install. Naturally, for the code presented in this book, you will need only Visual Basic. The other languages are optional and probably do not need to be installed.

INNOVATIONS IN VISUAL BASIC.NET

Visual Basic.NET, or VB.NET, is the first version of Visual Basic to support full-blown OOP techniques. In fact, the entire spectrum of Visual Studio development tools includes new .NET versions, which may be thought of as version 7.0. This book focuses primarily on Visual Basic 6.0, but due to the radical changes present in VB.NET, I thought it would be a good idea to at least introduce you to the new features that will revolutionize the language. Some of this information is for advanced programmers, so feel free to skim over it if this does not interest you.

Object-Oriented Programming Features

The new version of Visual Basic supports implementation inheritance, overloading (also called *polymorphism,* a term meaning "many forms"), and parameterized constructors (which allow you to initialize a class when it is created). Please note that this information is only of use as a reference for VB.NET development, and might not be applicable to the source code presented in this book (which was written with VB 6.0).

Implementation Inheritance. Visual Basic 6.0 currently supports a limited form of implementation inheritance through the keyword Implements. In order to share a base class, you must create a skeleton class with function definitions (but no actual source code). Sub-classes will then implement those skeleton functions, allowing the main program to handle different classes with a standard calling mechanism. (The DirectPlay chat program developed in Chapter 17, "Network Programming with DirectPlay," demonstrates how to use Implements to handle incoming messages from DirectPlay.)

VB.NET takes that rudimentary inheritance to the next level with full-blown implementation inheritance of a base class, including support for `Private` and `Public` variable and accessory methods (that is, functions which allow you to change private variables from outside the class). VB Forms also support inheritance. You have the ability to actually modify the source code that drives a Form. VB.NET inheritance is accomplished with the `Inherits` keyword, and also supports function overriding with the `Overrides` keyword. Here is a simplified example:

```
BitmapClass
    Overridable Function Draw()
    ...
    End Function
SpriteClass
    Inherits BitmapClass
    Overrides Function Draw()
    ...
    End Function
```

Overloading. Function overloading allows you to declare several functions with the same name but with different parameters, usually employed to handle different data types. For example:

```
Overloads Sub FireMissile( MissileNumber as Long )
...
End Sub
Overloads Sub FireMissile( MissileName as String )
...
End Sub
```

Parameterized Constructors. Constructors have been present in VB 6.0 through the `Class_Initialize` and `Class_Terminate` events, but never to the extent that VB.NET supports them. Full-blown support for constructors takes Visual Basic up to the level of C++, and is necessary for effective class inheritance. For example:

```
Class WaveSound
    Private SoundFile as String
    Constructor WaveSound( Filename as String)
    ...
    End Constructor
End Class
Public Sub Form_Load()
    Dim wave = New WaveSound("explosion.wav")
    ...
End Sub
```

Modern Language Features

In addition, VB.NET also includes modern language features like free threading, structured exception handling, strict type checking, shared members, and initializers. Following are brief explanations for these features.

Free Threading. Threads are separate processes that run parallel with the main program (asynchronously) and make it possible to scale a program by running multiple threads across several processors or even several computers in a cluster. This means that VB programs are able to support multiple processors (such as the dual-CPU systems that some power gamers own).

Structured Exception Handling. Exceptions are errors that occur in a program that could potentially stop the program from running if they are not handled properly. In VB 6.0 and previous versions, errors were handled with the On Error Goto statement. The problem with this method of error handling is that it is difficult to test each line of a program to determine exactly where an error occurred (unless you are good at breaking down programs into small functions, in which case the error messages are more obvious). VB.NET adds the Try...Catch...Finally statement for error handling, which allows you to group sections of code for error checking.

Strict Type Checking. VB 6.0 and earlier allowed programmers to declare variables without any data type. Such variables are automatically set to Variant unless you wisely use the Option Explicit statement in every source code listing. In VB.NET, there is no Variant data type because everything is an object. The new Option Strict statement (which is a step above Option Explicit) requires that all variables be given specific data types when declared. With strict type checking enabled, VB will generate an error when a type conversion fails.

Shared Members. This feature is also necessary for inheritance in VB.NET. Shared members are variables and functions that are global to the class, retaining state across all instances of the class. For instance, you can declare a shared variable that keeps track of the number of times that class is used by incrementing a counter variable each time the class is created, and then decrementing the variable when the class is terminated.

Initializers. Initializing variables when they are declared saves a lot of time and reduces the length of the code that is normally required to set variables to their starting values. For example, in VB 6.0 you can declare and initialize a variable like this:

```
Dim SpriteWidth as Long
SpriteWidth = 32
```

Using VB.NET, these two lines can be combined into a single initializer. This feature alone is compelling, making Visual Basic look more like the modern C++ language.

```
Dim SpriteWidth as Long = 32
```

INSTALLING VISUAL BASIC

The process of installing a compiler like Visual Basic 6.0 is similar to installing any other Windows application. Normally, you select a destination folder, decide on a few options, and then let the installer do its thing. However, there are several editions of Visual Basic to choose from, and the whole Visual Studio package as well, so things can get a bit complicated if you've never installed VB before. In this section, I'm going to quickly run through the installation process for Visual Studio 6.0 (by far the most complicated), followed by Visual Basic 6.0. Along the way, I'll show you what features you will or will not need to run the code in this book. This might seem like overkill, but I know how frustrating it can be when you are presented with a plethora of setup options for a new program. My intent is to help you identify what options you will need specifically for the code in this book. Ensuring that the compiler is set up properly from the start should give you a warm, fuzzy feeling (or not).

Installing Visual Studio 6.0

Visual Studio 6.0 is the complete development suite that includes several compilers and numerous tools, as explained earlier in the chapter. Since this is the most comprehensive set of installation options, I will explain the installation of VS 6.0 in detail first, and then breeze through the installation of just the Visual Basic compilers. The specific version I am covering here is Visual Studio 6.0 Enterprise Edition.

1. To start the installation, use Windows Explorer to locate the setup.exe file on the first Visual Studio 6.0 CD-ROM. Run it by double-clicking the file. The Installation Wizard screen will appear (as shown in Figure 2.3). Click Next to continue.

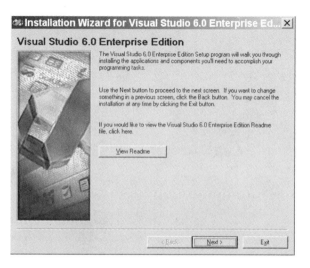

Figure 2.3

The Visual Studio 6.0 Installation Wizard

2. The End User License Agreement is then displayed, as shown in Figure 2.4. Select the I Accept the Agreement option and then click Next.

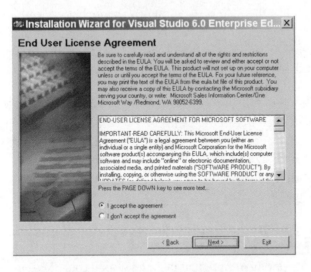

Figure 2.4

The End User License Agreement for Visual Studio 6.0

3. The Product Number and User ID dialog box appears next, as shown in Figure 2.5. The Product ID is located on the back of the VS 6.0 CD-ROM jewel case.

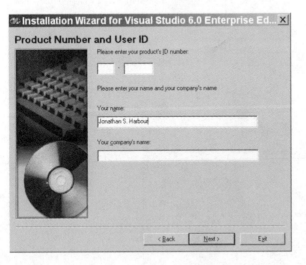

Figure 2.5

The Product Number and User ID dialog box

4. Next, the Enterprise Setup Options dialog box is displayed (see Figure 2.6), allowing you to select what category group to install. Select the Products group and click Next.

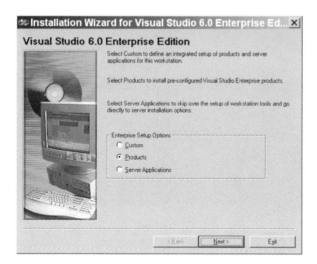

Figure 2.6

The Enterprise Setup
Options dialog box

5. The next dialog asks you to choose the Common Install Folder (see Figure 2.7). Normally, you will just accept the default.

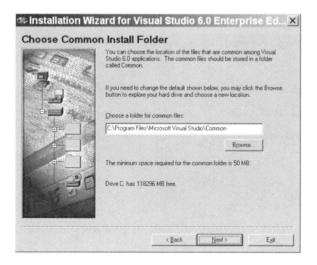

Figure 2.7

Selecting the Common
Install Folder

6. The final step for the Installation Wizard (before the Visual Studio setup program actually takes over) is the Visual Studio Individual Tools Setup dialog box (see Figure 2.8). Select the Visual Basic 6.0 Enterprise Edition option.

Unless you will be specifically using one of the other compilers, you do not need to install them at this time. If you find that you need additional compilers or tools later, you can always run the Installation Wizard again later and add components.

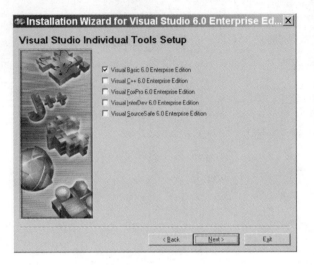

Figure 2.8

The Visual Studio Individual Tools Setup dialog box is where you select the compilers to install.

7. Now that the Installation Wizard has gathered all of the preliminary information from you, the Visual Studio 6.0 Enterprise Setup program will kick in and actually start installing the programs and tools to your hard drive. Figure 2.9 shows the title screen for the installer.

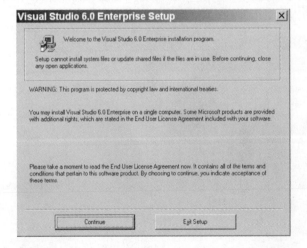

Figure 2.9

The Visual Studio 6.0 Enterprise Setup title screen

8. The next dialog box allows you to select the individual compiler components you would like to install (as shown in Figure 2.10). This is where things can start to get messy.

    You can keep the defaults, but for solo game development you probably don't need Visual SourceSafe or the Enterprise Tools. Just make sure Visual Basic 6.0 is selected. You can also

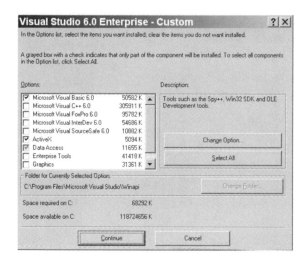

Figure 2.10

The Component Options dialog box allows you to select exactly what you want to install.

check the Graphics option, since it installs several hundred graphics files (such as icons) to your hard drive. These graphics are useful when you want to add a flashy mouse cursor or icon to your game.

9. Click Continue and the setup program will finish installing Visual Studio 6.0 to your hard drive.

Installing Visual Basic 6.0

If you have either Visual Basic 6.0 Enterprise Edition or Visual Basic 6.0 Professional Edition, then the following tutorial on installing the compiler will apply to you. The setup options are similar to the Visual Studio 6.0 Setup program after the Installation Wizard has finished gathering information and started the actual install process.

It is important to note that the stand-alone Visual Basic 6.0 compiler is exactly the same as the one included with Visual Studio 6.0, regardless of the edition (although the Learning Edition is not capable of compiling an executable). While the two editions are similar, I am covering the Enterprise Edition here since it has the most options and, therefore, may be the most confusing. The Professional Edition installer looks similar.

1. Start the installation process by running the setup.exe program on the Visual Basic 6.0 CD-ROM. The Installation Wizard startup dialog box will appear, as shown in Figure 2.11.

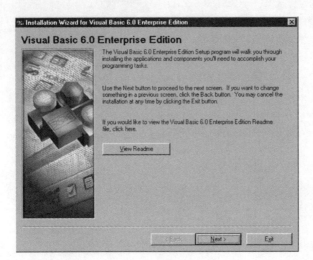

Figure 2.11

The Visual Basic 6.0 Enterprise Edition Installation Wizard

2. The next dialog box that appears is the End User License Agreement (see Figure 2.12).

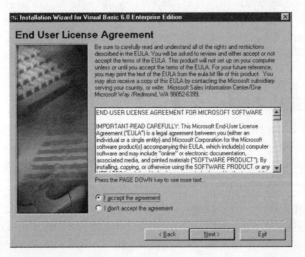

Figure 2.12

The Visual Basic 6.0 End User License Agreement

3. Next, the Product Number and User ID dialog box appears, as shown in Figure 2.13. This dialog box asks for the Product ID (located on the back of the VB 6.0 CD-ROM jewel case) and your name.

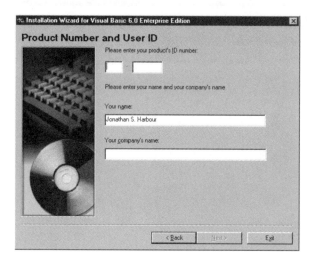

Figure 2.13

The Product Number and User ID dialog box

4. The next screen is the Server Options dialog box, shown in Figure 2.14. It allows you to selectively install VB 6.0 or enterprise server applications. Normally, you will not need any server applications, so keep the default Install Visual Basic 6.0 Enterprise Edition option.

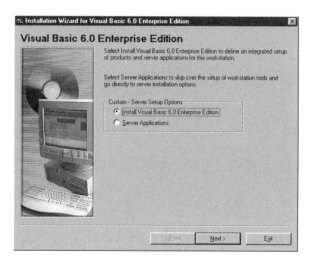

Figure 2.14

The Server Options dialog box

5. At this point, the Visual Basic 6.0 Setup program will kick in and start the Visual Basic 6.0 Installation program. Figure 2.15 shows the title screen for the actual installer.

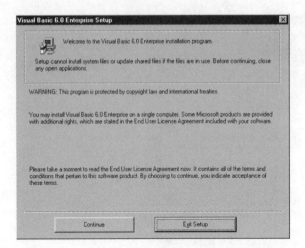

Figure 2.15

The Visual Basic 6.0 Enterprise Installation title screen

6. The Installation Type dialog box, shown in Figure 2.16, allows you to select a Typical install or a Custom install. Since the Typical install includes a bunch of database stuff you won't need, click the Custom button to bring up the Custom Installation dialog box.

Figure 2.16

The Installation Type dialog box lets you select a Typical or Custom install.

7. The default Installation Options dialog box (shown in Figure 2.17) lists the components that you can select. I recommend that you disable the Microsoft Visual SourceSafe 6.0 option; disable the Enterprise Features and Tools option; and enable the Graphics option, which includes several hundred bitmaps, icons, and cursors. After you make these selections, click Continue to start the installation with the options you have selected.

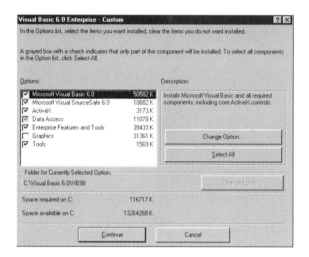

Figure 2.17

*The Installation
Options dialog box
allows you to select
custom components.*

Installing the MSDN Library

MSDN is the comprehensive help system that comes with Visual Studio (and also with the individual compilers, if you purchased them separately). The MSDN Library comes on three CD-ROMs unless you have the DVD version, in which case the MSDN Library comes on a single disc. Figure 2.18 shows the MSDN help system running. To bring up MSDN, simply highlight an object or keyword in Visual Basic and press the F1 key.

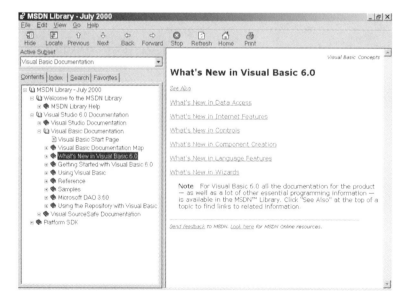

Figure 2.18

*MSDN is the help
system for Visual
Basic 6.0.*

1. When you start the MSDN Library Setup program, you are presented with the title screen, shown in Figure 2.19.

Figure 2.19

The MSDN setup title screen, showing the edition in use (July 2000)

2. The next dialog that appears is the Installation Options dialog box. There are three installation options for the MSDN Library, as shown in Figure 2.20. These include Typical, Custom, and Full. If disk space is not an issue and you can spare about two gigabytes, then select Full. The entire library will be installed, end of subject. However, if disk space is important—and it usually is—then click the Custom button.

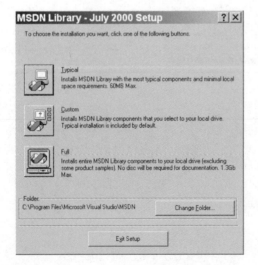

Figure 2.20

The Installation Options dialog box for the MSDN Library setup

3. The next dialog box is Custom Options, shown in Figure 2.21. It allows you to select the individual components of the MSDN Library to be installed. This is a rather complicated list and you might be tempted to just select everything, especially if disk space is plentiful. However, I will show you what options you don't need as an alternative.

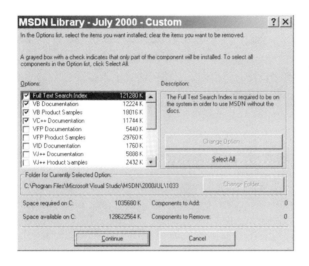

Figure 2.21

The Custom Options dialog box for the MSDN Library setup

Normally, you could get away with just installing the Visual Basic documentation and related files. But this is game programming! You're going to be doing things far beyond the default capabilities of VB, so you will need some extra help files. Namely, you need the Windows API documentation, which includes several Visual C++ help files, too.

I have installed MSDN many times, and it can be very frustrating when you are in the middle of a fast and furious coding session and you suddenly need to know the calling parameters for a Windows API function that is not included in the API Text Viewer (such as the GetBitmapBits function, for instance). So you don't want to leave out any essential MSDN topics; but at the same time, you might not want to install topics that are never needed.

Once again, if you don't care about disk space, then you can just click the Select All button and install everything. But if disk space is important, then I recommend you install just the following topics.

- Full Text Search Index (121MB)
- VB Documentation (12MB)
- VB Product Samples (18MB)
- VC++ Documentation (11MB)
- Platform SDK Documentation (216MB)
- VS Shared Documentation (3MB)
- Knowledge Base (92MB)
- All Other Files (560MB)

The last two topics in the list of MSDN options—Knowledge Base and All Other Files—are not essential, so if you can't spare the hard drive space, you can safely remove them. I do recommend you install these topics, however. Quite often in MSDN, you will be searching for a keyword and find that it was not installed. In such cases, MSDN will ask you to insert one of the CDs to retrieve the information. By installing these last two topics, you avoid running into that problem.

> **TIP**
>
> The most important MSDN help topic is the Platform SDK documentation. This topic is essential for game programming because it includes the function calls for all of the Windows GDI graphics functions, such as `BitBlt`.

Downloading the Latest Service Pack

It is an unfortunate fact that most software companies release buggy programs. Despite the earnest efforts of the most comprehensive quality assurance (QA) teams, bugs are inevitable. Given the complexity of the Visual Basic compiler and IDE, it is a given that bugs will be fixed and features added over time.

Microsoft's solution to bug fixes and feature requests is to release periodic Service Packs. At the time of this writing, the latest service pack for Visual Studio 6.0 is Service Pack 5 (SP5). You can download the service pack from the Microsoft Web site at http://msdn.microsoft.com/vstudio/sp/vs6sp5/default.asp. Since Web pages change so frequently, you can also go to http://msdn.microsoft.com and perform a search for "visual basic service pack" to help you locate the latest version.

EXPLORING THE VISUAL BASIC IDE

The Visual Basic IDE (*Integrated Development Environment*) includes everything you'll need to write and compile VB programs. The VB 6.0 IDE is loaded with features, so I am going to explain the most important features to you in this section, and then show you how to get around in VB. For reference, the VB 6.0 IDE is shown in Figure 2.22.

The Program Menu and Toolbar

The program menu includes the following menus: File, Edit, View, Project, Format, Debug, Run, Query, Diagram, Tools, Add-Ins, Window, and Help. Whew, that's a lot of functionality (and you thought VB was for beginners?). After a while, you probably won't use the menus very often, because there are keyboard shortcuts for all of the frequently used commands in VB. The usual Ctrl+C, Ctrl+X, and Ctrl+V will copy, cut, and paste selections of text.

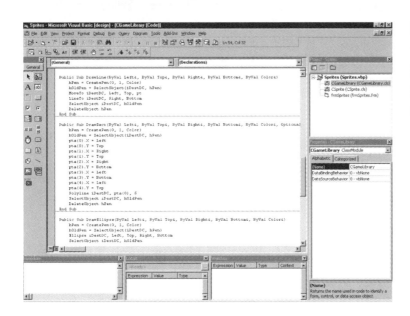

Figure 2.22

*The Visual Basic 6.0
Integrated
Development
Environment*

The toolbars are even more complicated because they show only little icons that you must learn. To see what an icon does, hover the mouse cursor over the icon for a few seconds and a tool tip will appear with the icon's description. The neatest thing about the toolbars is that you can move them around the edges of the IDE to any location you want.

To add or remove toolbars, simply right-click one of the toolbars and you will see a short list. The available toolbars are: Debug, Edit, Form Editor, and Standard. I regularly keep the Debug toolbar visible because it has two icons for automatically adding and removing comments from selections of text—very handy indeed when you need to comment or uncomment large portions of code during development.

Table 2.1 shows some of the most common (and useful) keyboard shortcuts.

The Project Explorer

The Project Explorer, located at the upper-right portion of the screen, displays all of the files in your project and the files in other projects that are part of a project group. You can add new projects to an existing project (thus creating a new project group) by selecting Add Project in the File menu. This is a convenient way to build a game library, for instance, since you can have the game library and test program projects in a shared project group.

Table 2.1 Visual Basic 6.0 IDE Keyboard Shortcuts

Shortcut	Description
F1	Invoke MSDN help on highlighted word
F2	Invoke object browser
Shift+F2	Go to definition of highlighted object
Ctrl+F	Search for text in project
F3	Find next occurrence of search text
F4	Open properties window
F5	Run program
Ctrl+F5	Run program with full compile
F8	Debug program line-by-line and jump to called procedures
Shift+F8	Debug program line-by-line and skip over procedure calls
F9	Set or remove breakpoint at current line
Ctrl+F9	Set next statement to be executed (debug mode)
Ctrl+O	Open project
Ctrl+N	New project
Ctrl+S	Save current file in edit window

To add new files to a project, right-click anywhere within the Project Explorer and move the mouse cursor over the Add menu item. A list of files is displayed, with the following options:

- Form
- MDI Form
- Module
- Class Module
- User Control
- Property Page

- User Document
- DHTML Page
- Data Report
- WebClass
- Data Environment
- Add File

Of these options, only the first few will be used in this book. I will explain these items in Chapter 3, "Visual Basic Programming in a Nutshell."

The Properties Window

The Properties window, located at the lower-right portion of the screen, is probably the most important part of the Visual Basic IDE, at least in terms of GUI (*Graphical User Interface*) development. Every type of form, designer, property page, class, and ActiveX control in VB has properties. Even the main project has a single property: the project name. When you create an ActiveX control, you have an opportunity to include your own properties for the control, which are then displayed in the Properties window (although I don't cover ActiveX controls in this book).

The Toolbox Window

The Toolbox window contains all of the ActiveX controls available to a program and is extremely dependent on the references and components you have installed in the project. You can see the references by selecting the References item in the Project menu. Likewise, you can see the components by selecting the Components item in the Project menu.

References are usually type libraries (refer back to Figure 2.1) that allow VB to get into custom DLLs used by Windows. For example, in order to write DirectX code in VB, you need to reference DirectX 8 for Visual Basic Type Library from the References dialog. If the type library is not visible, most likely the library is not installed. (You can search by pressing the key that corresponds to the first letter in the type library, such as "D.") VB does a good job of identifying all of the libraries in the system, but might occasionally miss one. (This usually happens when you are creating your own ActiveX library and you compile it several times while developing it.) When this happens, you can click the Browse button and manually select the file to be referenced (usually a DLL or TLB file).

Components are ActiveX controls that are registered in the system. They are selected in the same manner in which you select references.

The Editor Window

The Editor window is where you will spend most of your time entering the code listings found in this book. The Editor window is used for browsing and editing code, and for editing GUI components when a form or ActiveX control is opened for editing.

Editing in the Visual Basic Editor window is one of the most rewarding experiences I've had as a programmer, because VB was a pioneer language in developing a technology called *IntelliSense*. This is such a phenomenal time-saving feature that I find it nearly impossible to write code without it (in other languages). IntelliSense displays a pop-up list of objects that are in scope with whatever object you have just typed, followed by a period. If the object is a UDT (*User-Defined Type*) or enumeration, the IntelliSense pop-up will display all of the items in whatever list is relevant at that position in the code. If nothing is relevant, then pressing the period key does nothing.

IntelliSense saves hundreds of hours over the development life cycle, by saving programmers from having to look up the members of UDTs and objects. IntelliSense is also wonderful when you are exploring a new object that you have referenced. It is even possible to write code with an object without a reference manual simply by browsing the function listing of an object with IntelliSense.

Writing code in the VB Editor window is something of a shock for programmers of C++ and other languages where the syntax is up to the programmer. In Visual Basic, the syntax is rigidly controlled by the compiler. You simply can't enter a line of code that is meaningless unless you prefix it with the comment character (a single quote). When you move the cursor off a line of code, Visual Basic immediately validates that line of code to verify that it is legal. If the line has a syntax error, an error message is displayed right away and the line is highlighted in red. Of course, once you have mastered the language, this feature can be a nuisance. In that case, you can turn the feature off from the Options menu. But until you have mastered the language, this is a welcome feature that will keep you on your toes.

The Immediate Window

The Immediate window is primarily a debugging tool, but it is also a live platform for entering commands while a program is running. It supports some of the old-school BASIC statements like `Print` and `?`. Usually you will use the Immediate window when stepping through the code or when the compiler hits a breakpoint that you have set up (sort of a roadblock in the program). Once a program is paused, Visual Basic will highlight the current line of code with the default color of yellow, which makes the line look alive. You can then enter commands in the Immediate window. For instance, you can enter a Print command to display a status variable in your program or from an object.

The Immediate window is also a fantastic debugging tool. Visual Basic has an object called Debug which, in turn, has a function called `Print`. `Print` sends lines of text to the Immediate Window (as `Debug.Print` statements). Feel free to litter `Debug.Print` statements throughout your code, because they are stripped out by the compiler when you create an executable.

The Locals Window

The Locals window is another powerful debugging feature in VB. I highly recommend that you keep the Locals window open when debugging a program line-by-line. The Locals window displays all of the variables that are within scope as the program runs. When execution enters a function or procedure, the Locals window displays all of the variables that are within scope. When execution leaves that function, the variables are removed and new ones are added in scope. You can open the Locals window from the View menu.

The Watches Window

The Watches window is a powerful debugging tool that is similar to the Locals window, but is not affected by scope. If you would like to track the value of a global variable, simply highlight that variable name in the Editor window, then release the mouse and drag the highlighted text over the Watches window to add that variable to the watch list. The variable will remain in the watch list until you specifically remove it. This is handy when you want to keep track of a variable when it goes out of scope and comes back into scope again, or if there is a global variable that you need to watch.

USING MICROSOFT DEVELOPER NETWORK

Starting with Visual Basic 6.0 (and all of the tools in Visual Studio 6.0), Microsoft introduced a completely new help system called MSDN, a comprehensive collection of everything in the Windows API and all other libraries in Windows, including DirectX. The MSDN help system (refer back to Figure 2.18) is a stand-alone program that Visual Basic calls whenever you need help on a keyword or GUI object (such as an ActiveX control).

Getting Help

You can invoke MSDN by hitting F1 on a keyword or GUI object, or you can start MSDN from the Program menu (look for a submenu called Microsoft Developer Network). Once inside MSDN, if the result of your initial help invocation does not return a helpful result, you can click the Index tab and type in a keyword, which usually works for finding help on a topic.

Depending on the options you selected when you installed MSDN, you might have access to all of the Windows API from here. If you elected to leave out most of the MSDN options, then you can simply insert the correct MSDN CD-ROM when you search for help on a topic that was not installed but is listed in the index. The primary strength of MSDN is that it effectively replaces an entire library of Windows API reference books and includes countless tutorials that are invaluable when researching a topic. Nothing beats sample code!

Online Resources

Quite often, you will need information about an obscure function (like `GetBitmapBits`) and won't be able to find the information you are looking for with your installed copy of MSDN. Microsoft actually has the entire up-to-date MSDN Library available online at http://msdn.microsoft.com. The online interface includes the table of contents with all of the same information that is installed with a local MSDN copy, but has the additional benefit of providing the latest and greatest topics.

If you have a high-speed Internet connection, I highly recommend you use the online version of MSDN for all of your referencing needs.

SUMMARY

Since there are so many versions and editions of Visual Basic, it can be quite confusing at times. Selecting the right compiler is not exactly an easy choice. This chapter explained all of the different forms that Visual Basic has taken in recent years, including the most recent version, Visual Basic.NET.

Visual Studio is the largest development suite that Microsoft offers, and the list of installation options is quite long. For that reason, this chapter included a section on installing the components of Visual Studio that are necessary for running the Visual Basic code in this book. A short tutorial on installing the stand-alone Visual Basic 6.0 was also provided, along with help on installing and using MSDN.

Now that you have a better understanding of what Visual Basic is all about, it's time to start learning how to write games with Visual Basic. Chapter 3, "Visual Basic Programming in a Nutshell," is an introduction to Visual Basic programming where you will have an opportunity to write a simple graphics program. Following that, Chapter 4, "Getting to Know the Windows API," covers the Windows API and shows you how to tap into a wealth of features not available to native VB.

CHAPTER 3

VISUAL BASIC PROGRAMMING IN A NUTSHELL

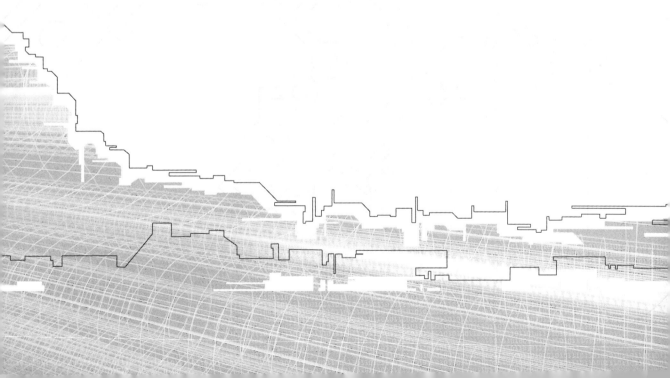

This chapter is a hands-on tutorial on Visual Basic programming from the ground up. Even if you have never written a Visual Basic program before, you will be able to quickly get up to speed with the help of this chapter. Visual Basic is an amazing language that allows even a complete beginner to write programs with very little effort. As soon as you have grasped the language, I will show you how to set up a game window and do some graphics. Much of Visual Basic falls outside the realm of this book (specifically, setting up forms and programming custom controls), so I'll only get into subjects that specifically help with game programming. For additional resources on specific subjects of the language, see Appendix E, "Recommended Reading," for a list of books.

This chapter covers the following topics:

- Programming Language Basics
- Elements of a Visual Basic Program
- Writing Your First Visual Basic Program
- Running the ChunkyPixels Program
- Understanding the VB Object

Programming Language Basics

Programming languages can be categorized into a hierarchy or abstraction that defines what those languages are capable of doing, as related to the computer hardware. Trying to differentiate between *languages* and *products* might be confusing, so I will use those two words interchangeably. By my own estimation, there are six primary programming language categories, as shown in Table 3.1. Notice that Visual Basic falls into the category of BASIC languages.

Machine Language

At the lowest-level of hardware, there is a CPU (*Central Processing Unit*). The CPU runs instructions fed into it through a program, which must be a binary executable file (machine language). The operating system (for example, MS-DOS or Windows) handles all the details of actually loading the program into memory and feeding it to the CPU. This happens when you run a program on the hard drive. Programs may be represented by icons on your Windows desktop (which point to EXE files on the hard drive).

Table 3.1 Programming Language Categories

Category	Languages
Machine Language	Binary Executable
Assembly Language	Macro Assembler
Low-Level Language	C
Mid-Level Language	C++
High-Level Language	BASIC, Java, Pascal, C#
Scripting Language	HTML, VBScript, JavaScript, XML, Perl

Machine language contains the raw binary instructions that tell the CPU what to do. Even something as simple as displaying a dialog box in VB translates to thousands of binary machine language instructions. The architecture behind Windows that handles most of the work numbers in the hundreds of millions of binary instructions. In the early days of vacuum tube and transistor computers, machine language was the *only* language, and programs were written by manually setting binary switches.

Assembly Language

Assembly is a language and a category unto itself that dates back to the early days of computing (akin to the Stone Age). There is a distinction between an *assembler* and a *compiler*. Most compilers actually convert program source code into assembly. In the old days, this was how all compilers worked. First, you compiled the program into an ASM file, assembled it into a BIN file, and then linked it into an EXE. Assembly was once a great way to squeeze performance out of MS-DOS games, but it is not used much anymore, since libraries like DirectX and OpenGL handle the low-level stuff now.

MASM—the Microsoft macro assembler—is one example. Modern compilers are extremely advanced and have so many features that most of us completely take these features for granted. It wasn't so easy in the good old days. Then again, I wouldn't exactly call Windows programming easy. But that's where Visual Basic comes in.

Low-Level Language

Low-level languages are one step above assembly. These languages make it easier to write programs while, at the same time, keeping a very close eye on the actual hardware. C is a low-level language that was was actually invented for building the UNIX operating system. Statements in C translate closely to several assembly instructions each, so that the resulting assembly source code is similar to the C code. Obviously, things have changed since C was invented, as developers wrote new and competitive versions of their own compilers with support for graphics and so forth. These features are added to a low-level language using libraries. A LIB file containing one or more compiled BIN files of common routines can be reused by several programs.

Mid-Level Language

Typically, you will only hear of low-level and high-level languages, but I have added mid-level because I believe the distinction between low and high is too great. Like the low-level languages, mid-level languages compile to a native executable. For example, C is a low-level language, while VB is a high-level language. Where, then, does Visual C++ fit in? It might be argued that C++ is a low-level language, but I disagree. C++ was originally developed as an extension of C. It used a pre-processor that created C code, which was then compiled to ASM, and on to a binary. While most C++ compilers include support for straight C, the actual C++ language does not include some of the C constructs (like pointers, which were replaced by references). But for competitive reasons (and for convenience), every C++ compiler that I know of is capable of compiling straight C programs.

Other mid-level languages include products like Borland C++ Builder and Kylix (the Linux version of Delphi, which is a modern Pascal), and a public domain compiler called DJGPP, which is available for multiple platforms. I should also mention CodeWarrior, because it is a common cross-platform C++ compiler that is used by both PC and console game developers.

High-Level Language

Visual Basic is a high-level language. This means that VB does not run close to the hardware, but is abstracted, with something else helping the VB code run after it has been compiled. Even though Visual Basic is available only for Windows, it could have been ported to other platforms. I would have enjoyed running VB under Linux, but doing so would undercut the sale of Windows. (There was actually a slick Linux version of Visual Basic called Instant Basic that, oddly enough, could read VB project files and forms and could compile VB programs into Java programs. Talk about strange!)

The same is true of other high-level languages, such as Java, C#, and the Microsoft .NET development tools, all of which use a new Common Language Runtime and forms engine. These languages interface through a virtual machine that abstracts the actual hardware beneath.

VB 6.0 uses the Visual Basic runtime engine, which lives in a file called MSVBVM60.DLL. This stands for "Microsoft Visual Basic Virtual Machine 6.0 Dynamic Link Library." While it is true that VB 6.0 compiles native executable programs, there is no getting around the fact that the runtime library is still needed. You cannot simply compile a VB program into an EXE and expect it to run without the runtime being installed.

The same applies to Java, which is an implementation-independent language. It is not tied to specific computer hardware. The Java Virtual Machine (JVM) is an open architecture that has been implemented on every platform, including IBM RS/6000, Solaris, Linux, Mac, and PC. There is even a mobile version of JVM for cell phones and PDAs, leaving no doubt that Java is versatile. Most virtual machines now include a Just-In-Time (JIT) compiler that translates Java byte codes into native instructions that run much faster.

Other high-level languages include Borland, Delphi, and JBuilder. One distinction can be made for all of these high-level languages: They are all RAD (*Rapid Application Development*) tools. You can quickly prototype and run a program written with a RAD tool, and then fully develop it later, usually without the need to compile. These languages often feature both interpreted and compiled execution.

Scripting Language

At the highest level is the scripting language, which is usually a programmable interface to a larger system. For instance, Microsoft's Internet Explorer browser supports a scripting language called Visual Basic Script (VBScript), a subset of VB that was covered in Chapter 2, "Getting Started with Visual Basic." VBScript allows you to customize a Web page and is interpreted by Internet Explorer when you open the page. The primary use of VBScript is for developing Web databases, but it is also a versatile scripting language.

An even more common scripting language is HTML (*Hypertext Markup Language*), the format that launched the World Wide Web into a global phenomenon. HTML uses markers to define blocks of text that should be formatted in a specific way. It also supports image files, embedded sounds, and even videos. Extensions to HTML have provided for advanced Web development without the need for VBScript or another supplemental language. Unlike the other language categories, a scripting language will always be 100 percent platform independent because the platform is irrelevant to the interpreted script. (In other words, scripting languages are not compiled into binary programs.)

ELEMENTS OF A VISUAL BASIC PROGRAM

Visual Basic, like most development tools, provides several ways to accomplish a task. This applies to database programming as well as game programming. For instance, to modify a database table, you could use a data control on a form with fields tied to that control. Or you could write the ADO (*ActiveX Data Objects*) code to do it, which is the better solution. How about writing a game? You could do it entirely with the features built into Visual Basic—with a Form, a PictureBox control (for graphics), and the Multimedia control (for sound). You could also use the Windows API along with a sound library like WaveMix to write a game. Alternatively, you could use DirectX, which is the best solution overall. Why? Because DirectX provides everything you need to write a cutting-edge game, including all of the latest features available in computer hardware, with an easy-to-use interface.

GUI Versus Code

Visual Basic programs tend to be centered around the user interface. In fact, most of the events and functions in a VB program are related to user input. The alternative to a GUI-centered program is a code-centered program.

The problem with a GUI-centered program is that it tends to keep a programmer in the application-programming mindset, rather than in a game-programming mindset. The GUI is neat and fun to use. But what use does a game have for a horizontal scrollbar or a button? The problem with that very question is that many VB programmers will try to mold a game into that GUI framework. This limits the potential greatness for a game. To write a truly killer game, you must stop thinking like a VB programmer—an application programmer—and start thinking like a game developer. What do you want to see in the main menu, a form with some gray buttons or a cool background scene with glowing, pulsating buttons, along with an evil finger for a mouse cursor?

Games do not need the clunky, slow GUI controls that are built into Windows. What a game needs is a blank screen—a canvas—upon which to do some magic. DirectX provides a means for choosing a video mode and going full screen, but we haven't reached that point yet! (After all, you're still a Newbie Gamer, and I wouldn't want to frighten you.) The alternative is a form with a PictureBox on top. Surprisingly, this is the basis for all of the sample programs developed in this book—even the DirectX samples!

> **TIP**
> **Stop thinking like an application programmer and start thinking like a game developer.**

I'll show you how to get started soon, but first you need a little background information. After all, if you don't know the inner details of the source code on which you are working, your game will be called a knock-off. It would be like ripping the graphics and sounds out of *Doom* and inserting your own, and then calling it your own creation. Don't do that! You want to create a game from scratch and understand it at every level. Don't take shortcuts and use someone else's so-called game engine until you understand how to create your own! Cloned games are seldom taken seriously, no matter how much creativity you pour into them.

> **NOTE**
>
> *Half-Life* was based on the original *Quake* engine, but was modified extensively with real-world weapons physics and other features so that in the end, it only peripherally resembled Quake.

Forms

There are two types of forms that can be used in Visual Basic programs, the standard dialog-style SDI form and the MDI form.

- **Dialog (SDI) Form.** The standard form is a dialog-style application, which might be familiar to Visual C++ programmers. The program does not really feature a document at all, but simply a slate upon which controls might be placed. Forms are the most common objects in Visual Basic. Without forms, Visual Basic would not be very useful, since the language revolves around them. A Visual Basic program might have dozens of forms, although professional games will usually feature only a single form (or, more likely, will run full-screen). In fact, as you will see in later chapters, even a full-screen DirectX program requires a window handle; in VB, this is provided by a form. The sample programs in this book will all use a single standard form. See Figure 3.1 to see what a dialog-style program looks like.

- **MDI Form.** *Multiple-Document Interface* is the standard way of handling multiple open files in a program. For instance, Microsoft Word has an MDI interface which can handle dozens of open Word documents at the same time. Most MDI interfaces include the standard Window menu that displays all of the open windows in the application. The presence of the Window menu is a sure sign that a program features an MDI. MDI programs are commonplace in applications, but are not really suitable for a game. Figure 3.2 shows a sample MDI application.

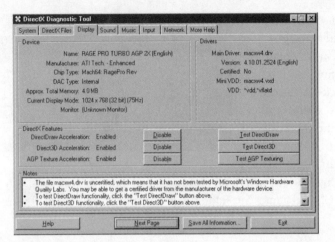

Figure 3.1

The DirectX Diagnostic Tool features a dialog-style interface.

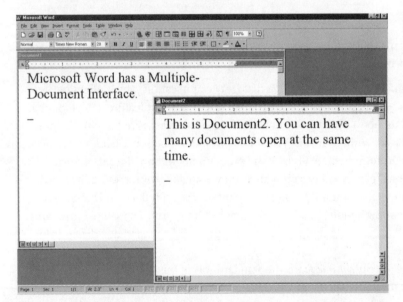

Figure 3.2

Microsoft Word 97 features a Multiple-Document Interface (MDI).

ActiveX Controls

Visual Basic 5.0 and 6.0 both have the capability to create compiled ActiveX COM (*Component Object Model*) objects. These include controls, in-process servers, and out-of-process servers. Whoa, what does that mean? It's simple. (You knew I was going to say that, didn't you?) The three types of ActiveX objects are OCX, DLL, and EXE files. Controls are contained within an OCX. In-process servers are stored within a DLL, which is loaded into the memory space of your program. Out-of-process servers are stored within an EXE, which is loaded into its own memory space.

Now for the confusing part—as if that wasn't confusing enough. All three of these ActiveX objects can contain controls, classes, forms, code modules, property pages—just about anything that you can put into a regular program can be put into one of these ActiveX objects. Do you see why some people laugh when "VB" and "game" are both used in the same sentence? This is a misnomer that I intend to correct! Yes, VB does support all kinds of obnoxious application-development features, the likes of which will make your head spin. But you do not need any of that stuff to write a game—a serious game, that is.

But now, back to the subject of controls. There are several hundred ActiveX controls available for VB from Microsoft and third-party vendors. Ignore all of those controls! The only thing you need to write a game in VB is a PictureBox. In fact, when using DirectDraw and full-screen mode, all you need is the form. Anything more is uncivilized!

The PictureBox control is an advanced ActiveX OCX and is very easy to spot in the VB IDE. The Toolbox (see Figure 3.3) shows all of the ActiveX controls that are available to your program by default.

Figure 3.3

The Control Toolbox shows all of the available ActiveX controls.

The list is dependent upon the objects or components you have referenced in the program (via the Project menu). By default, VB includes the following ActiveX controls (in order of appearance):

- PictureBox
- Label
- TextBox
- Frame
- CommandButton
- CheckBox
- OptionButton
- ComboBox
- ListBox
- HScrollBar
- VScrollBar
- Timer
- DriveListBox
- DirListBox
- FileListBox
- Shape
- Line
- Image
- Data
- OLE

At first glance, you might conclude that VB has a lot of support for games already. After all, it offers the PictureBox, Timer, Shape, Line, and Image controls by default! It's true; VB does include some graphics controls that can be used to write simple games. You might even squeeze a really neat game out of them, but not likely. These controls are much too slow for any serious game development. Card games? Yes. Arcade games? No.

I will use the PictureBox control extensively in the sample programs in this book to show you how to get the most out of a PictureBox control before jumping into DirectX. While the features built into VB are sluggish, the Win32 API is not. The Windows API has some terrific features you can tap into to enhance a game in VB. All you need to know is the Declare statement for an API function and you're in business. Since this is such an important step in Visual Basic game development, I have dedicated an entire chapter to the subject—Chapter 4, "Getting to Know the Windows API."

Code Modules

Visual Basic code resides primarily in source code modules as stand-alone BAS files and as the source code underlying a form (closely tied to the user interface). While it is possible to write an entire VB program using nothing but controls, you will not be able to do much with a program like that, other than perhaps build a prototype.

VB forms and controls are programmable through code modules. The VB IDE makes it easy for you to identify and use the GUI objects from the code editor. To open the code editor, double-click a form or control, or click the code icon at the top-left corner of the Project Explorer. Alternatively, you can open the View menu and select the Code menu item. Or, from the code editor, select Object to return to the form editor.

There are four basic types of procedures you can use in a VB program:

- Sub
- Function
- Property
- Event

Events are not strictly procedures, but are similar enough to warrant inclusion in this list.

Subs

A *sub* is a procedure that can accept parameters, but does not return a value. Basically, any time you need to perform a specific task in a page or less of code, you should put that code into a reusable sub that can be called from other locations in the program.

```
Public Sub Test_Sub()
    Debug.Print "Hello from Test_Sub"
End Sub
```

Functions

A *function* is a procedure that does return a value and can accept parameters. The return value can be any intrinsic data type, an array, a user-defined type, an enumeration, or an object.

```
Public Function Test_Function() As Long
    Debug.Print "Hello from Test_Function"
    Test_Function = 0
End Function
```

Properties

A *property* is a special-case procedure that can have up to three forms, any of which can be used for your own custom properties:

- **Property Get.** This form of the property returns a value and is similar in functionality to a function. This should normally be a private variable, declared in the code module or class module, which keeps track of the value of the property. In the following example, it is sLocalVariable. A Property Get procedure looks like this:

  ```
  Public Property Get Test_Property() As String
      Test_Property = sLocalVariable
  End Property
  ```

  The property is read by using the property name directly in code, and works the same whether it is a built-in property or a property of your own design. For example:

  ```
  Debug.Print "Property value = " & Test_Property
  ```

- **Property Let.** This form of the property sets a value and is similar in functionality to a sub. A single parameter is passed to Property Let, along with the value to which the property should be changed. A Property Let procedure looks like this:

  ```
  Public Property Let Test_Property(ByVal sNewValue As String)
      sLocalVariable = sNewValue
  End Property
  ```

  A private variable should be used to store the value of the property. In this case, it is sLocalVariable. For example:

  ```
  Test_Property = "Super Shooter Arcade Game"
  ```

- **Property Set.** This form of the property is used to set an object when the property variable is an actual object, such as a form or a control, but more often when a custom object is implemented as a class. A Property Set procedure looks like this:

```
Public Property Set Property4(ByRef objNewObject As StdPicture)
    Set objLocalObject = objNewObject
End Property
```

Note how the Property Set procedure uses the Set keyword when assigning the local object to the passed object. This is a limited form of polymorphism, where the property acts differently depending on the including parameter. When the Set keyword is left out in the main program that uses the property, it invokes the Property Let. But when the Set keyword is used in the main program, it invokes Property Set. The difference is that Set always refers to an object, while Let always refers to a variable.

Assuming that you have created a custom property (Test_Property) that includes a Property Set procedure, and you have declared a private variable of type Object for use by the property, the following example could be used:

```
Set Test_Property = Form1.Picture
```

Properties allow you to create highly readable code by providing the object-oriented feature of *encapsulation*. This hides the actual data from a calling routine, promotes code reuse, and helps prevent bugs. Code written with properties is also easy to maintain. New features can be added without difficulty, since the logic behind assignments is hidden away in the property's procedures.

Events

An *event* is a callback procedure that is triggered inside your program in a pre-defined event routine, telling your program that something noteworthy has happened. This could be something as simple as a key-press or mouse click, or something as complicated as a sprite collision. Events are everywhere in VB, and the user interface is handled entirely with events in your program. But the real power of events in VB is the ability to create new, custom events that you can raise yourself!

In order to use a form or class that has events, you must declare it using the WithEvents keyword, like this:

```
Dim WithEvents splash As frmSplash
```

The form or class that defines events must declare the events at the top of the code listing. For example, suppose that frmSplash has an event that is triggered when the user clicks the OK button. The event might look like this:

```
Public Event Finished()
```

> **TIP**
>
> When you declare an object using WithEvents, you cannot use the New keyword in the same declaration. Instead, you first declare the object using WithEvents and then set the object with the New keyword in Form_Load (or another appropriate startup procedure).

Then, elsewhere in the code, you can actually trigger that event by calling it with the following syntax:

```
RaiseEvent Finished
```

Of course, you can also pass variables through an event. Declaring parameters in an event is the same as any other type of procedure. For example, it might be convenient to notify the user when a sprite on the screen is clicked. (Sprites are covered in Chapter 8, "Supersonic Sprites.") You could then raise an event called Clicked with the X and Y location of the mouse pointer, or perhaps with the name of the sprite. Events can be even more complex. You can have a sprite handler trigger an event when two sprites collide on the screen!

The cool thing about an event is that as soon as you declare the object using WithEvents, VB adds it to the object drop-down list located at the top-left of the code window. You can then select the object (in this case, splash). The procedure listing in the drop-down list located to the right of the object list will show the events in that object. When you select the event, it is added to your code window automatically, and might look something like this:

```
Private Sub splash_Finished()
    Debug.Print "User is finished with the splash screen"
End Sub
```

Events are tremendously powerful in VB. I will show you how to use them to their fullest extent in later chapters. You will be amazed by how much can be accomplished with events alone. Events can significantly affect how you write a game; for example, information can be passed *to* your program, rather than your program having to poll information from a game loop. Events are also critical when you're working with sockets and DirectPlay in a multiplayer game (which will be covered in Chapter 16, "Multiplayer Programming with Windows Sockets," and Chapter 17, "Network Programming with DirectPlay").

Data Types and Parameters

Because you will be using the Windows API extensively in later chapters, it is vitally important to understand data types and how parameters are passed from one procedure to another in VB. The API functions are very strict in the types of parameters they can accept.

Data Types

A *data type* is the attribute of a variable that determines what kind of data it represents. There are 12 intrinsic data types in VB, as shown in Table 3.2 (with String and Variant each having two versions). I have rounded off the values in order to make them easier to comprehend. In my experience, the extreme range of a data type should not be an issue. However, pushing your variables to

Table 3.2 Intrinsic Data Types

Data Type	Bytes	Range
Byte	1	0 to 255
Boolean	2	True or False
Integer	2	+/- 32,767
Long	4	+/- 2.147 Billion
Single	4	+/- 3.402823E38
Object	4	Object Reference
Double	8	+/- 1.79769E308
Currency	8	+/- 922.337 Trillion
Date	8	Jan 1, 100 to Dec 31, 9999
Decimal	14	+/- 7.9228E24
String (Fixed)	Length	1 to 65,400
String (Variable)	10 + Length	0 to 2 Billion
Variant (Numeric)	16	+/- 1.79769E308
Variant (String)	22 + Length	0 to 2 Billion

the limit is dangerous. You might want to consider using larger data types, because overflowing a variable will crash your game.

When deciding what data types to use in a game, consider the number of bytes for each variable and select the most efficient data types. However, you must take care not to limit the variables too much, even if you think they will never exceed the data type range. In Chapter 5, "Optimizing Visual Basic with Objects," I will show you how to set the compiler options so that VB doesn't check for out-of-range errors, which greatly speeds up execution time.

This is not a license to write buggy code, but simply a reminder that you can always make a game stable later. Remember, it is difficult to optimize a program after you have written most of the code. Selecting the data types ahead of time is vitally important from the beginning.

Most of the time, I use the Long, Double, and Variable String data types. This keeps the code simple and gives the program room to breathe without sacrificing speed. When working with arrays of bitmap or wave data, I use the Byte data type, which also handles characters well. Surprisingly, you can even use a Variable String for reading waves and other binary files, because Variable Strings have a large capacity and are actually treated as Byte arrays. Notice also that VB supports a fixed-length string, but it is far more efficient to just declare text variables as String, without the length. Fixed-length strings are terribly slow, as demonstrated by the benchmarks in Chapter 5, "Optimizing Visual Basic with Objects."

Data Type Shortcuts

VB allows you to declare variables using shortcut characters to reduce the amount of typing when entering code. There is a shortcut character for most of the intrinsic data types. Table 3.3 lists the shortcut characters for the most common data types.

For example, if you would like to declare a string variable, but you are tired of typing in As String every time, you can simply declare variables like this:

```
Dim sPlayerName$
Dim lArmorClass&
Dim dShieldRechargeRate#
```

Of course, if you are declaring an array or a fixed-length string, you will not be able to use the shortcut character in the definition. Keep a bookmark on this page, because you might want to refer back to this table.

Table 3.3 Data Type Shortcut Characters

Data Type	Shortcut
Integer	%
Long	&
Single	!
Double	#
Currency	@
String	$

Parameter Types

There are three types of parameters that you can pass to procedures in VB:

- **ByVal**. This parameter type means "by value" and indicates that a copy of the value is passed to the procedure. ByVal parameters can accept a variable or a literal. A literal is a real value, such as 1, 2, 3, 4, or "hello," while a variable is a data type or object that is assigned a value, such as lNumber or sFirstName. A procedure with a parameter passed by value might look like this:

```
Public Sub Debug_Print(ByVal strMessage As String)
    Debug.Print strMessage
End Sub
```

- **ByRef**. This parameter type means "by reference" and indicates that the address of a value is passed to the procedure, rather than the value itself. This allows you to make changes to the variable without needing to return a value. This is as close to a pointer as you will get in VB (excluding the AddressOf operator). A procedure with a parameter passed by reference might look like this:

```
Public Sub Swap_Strings(ByRef sText1 As String, _
    ByRef sText2 As String)
    Dim sTemp As String
    sTemp = sText1
    sText1 = sText2
    sText2 = sTemp
End Sub
```

- **Optional**. This parameter type is actually a prefix for ByVal and ByRef. It indicates that the parameter is optional, and can also have a default value assigned to it for cases where the parameter is not supplied. The IsMissing function can be used to determine whether an optional parameter is present, but is not needed when a default value is supplied. For example:

```
Public Sub Increment(ByRef lValue As Long, Optional ByVal lAmount = 1)
    lValue = lValue + lAmount
End Function
```

Optional parameters allow you to give procedures great versatility. You could call the Increment procedure by either of the following methods:

```
Increment lngIndex
Increment lngIndex, 10
```

Variable and Procedure Scope

When you declare a variable or a new procedure, you have the option of declaring it with the following keywords (exceptions noted below):

- **Dim.** The Dim keyword is the most common shortcut keyword for declaring variables, and is equivalent to declaring variables as Private. Dim cannot be used to declare the scope of a procedure, only a variable.
- **Public.** The Public keyword allows you to declare variables and procedures that are visible outside that code module, form, or class.
- **Private.** The Private keyword allows you to declare variables and procedures that are not visible outside that code module, form, or class, but are visible only within the current scope.
- **Static.** The Static keyword allows you to declare variables (but not procedures) that retain their value even after the scope has been lost. This is equivalent to declaring global variables, but is limited to the current scope (which is usually inside a procedure).
- **Global.** The Global keyword allows you to declare a global variable in a code module that is visible throughout the entire scope of the program, regardless of whether the code is located in a code module, form, or class.
- **Friend.** The Friend keyword allows you to declare a procedure (but not a variable) that is visible throughout the project, but not to the calling routine that has an instance of the object. Friend can appear only in forms and classes (not code modules).

Coordinate Systems, Sizing, and Scaling

Visual Basic is versatile in that it allows multiple scaling modes to exist in a program, usually centered around the resolution of a printed page. The scaling modes available in VB include the following:

- 0 - User
- 1 - Twip
- 2 - Point
- 3 - Pixel
- 4 - Character
- 5 - Inch
- 6 - Millimeter
- 7 - Centimeter

When you set the ScaleMode property for a form to 3 - Pixel, for instance, the ScaleWidth and ScaleHeight values will reflect the actual pixel resolution of the form. However, if you change the

ScaleMode to 5 - Inch, you will have to work with inches and fractions of an inch. This can be helpful in certain types of applications that need measurements in inches, but I can't think of any game that would benefit from it.

The default ScaleMode is 1 - Twip, which is comparable to a printed page and varies depending on the capabilities of your video card. Since games use pixel sizes for bitmaps and sprites, it is best to use pixels as a scale mode in a VB program.

One of the more interesting features of scaling is that you can actually set the pixel scale to a stratospheric number and VB will automatically scale objects within that resolution. For instance, you can place a PictureBox on a form, set the ScaleMode to pixels, and then set the width and height values both to 10,000. This gives that PictureBox an effective resolution of 10,000 pixels. You could literally load a bitmap file with a resolution of 10,000 by 10,000 pixels, and it would be fully displayed in the PictureBox (albeit with a poorly-rendered scale). Of course, the PictureBox is way too slow for doing this in a real-time game environment, but it is an interesting feature to keep in mind for other uses.

WRITING YOUR FIRST VISUAL BASIC PROGRAM

Visual Basic is very much a hands-on development tool, and the user interface is intuitive to this fact. Just move the mouse over a toolbar icon in the VB IDE for a couple seconds and a tool tip will appear, describing what the icon does.

> **BUZZWORD**
>
> A *tool tip* is a small pop-up message that describes an object under the mouse pointer. Tool tips make an application more intuitive, allowing you to become familiar with the user interface more quickly, often eliminating the need for a user manual.

In this section, I am going to walk you through the process of writing a complete program in VB. However, you're in for a treat, because this is not just a typical "Hello, World!" program, but actually a graphics demo called ChunkyPixels. What better way to get the hang of VB than by starting with graphics, right?

Visual Basic Project Types

Let's get started! Fire up VB, and you should be presented with the New Project dialog box, as shown in Figure 3.4.

Visual Basic is a multi-purpose language with the functionality to handle many programming problems that would be very difficult to handle using another language, such as Visual C++. The

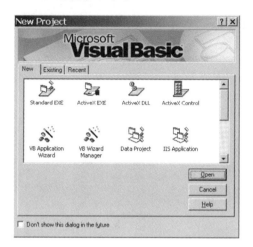

Figure 3.4

The New Project dialog box allows you to select a project type.

heart of a Visual Basic project is a project file with an extension of VBP. This file actually describes all the source code files and components that comprise a project.

Depending on the version of Visual Basic that you are using, the following list of project types might vary. (This list comes from the Professional Edition.)

- Standard EXE
- ActiveX EXE
- ActiveX DLL
- ActiveX Control
- VB Application Wizard
- VB Wizard Manager
- Data Project
- IIS Application
- Addin
- ActiveX Document DLL
- ActiveX Document EXE
- DHTML Application
- VB Pro Edition Controls

The four most common project types are listed at the top of the New Project dialog box. Most of the time, you will select the first icon, labeled Standard EXE. Select it now and click the Open button. The project will be created and the default form, called Form1, will be added to the project, as shown in Figure 3.5.

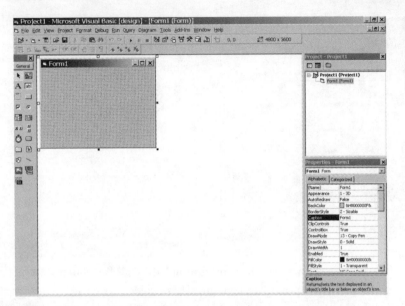

Figure 3.5

The new project includes only a blank form.

Building the User Interface

Now I would like to make an important point, because this is the part where most experienced VB developers jump in and start building the user interface for an application. Whether you are new to VB or experienced with it, you must not let the application development mindset kick in.

This is game programming!

If you even *start* along the app design path, you are already off track. I am passionate about this, because I have gone down that path myself and it takes an incredible amount of willpower to keep from manipulating the GUI at the start of a new game project. This dominant factor is evident in the game library that I will help you create in later chapters. Just think of it this way: As far as game programming goes, there is *no user interface*.

Don't Take Shortcuts

Now, I do make exceptions during development and testing. However, those exceptions usually involve only a few Label controls here and there for diagnosing the state of a game while it is running. The Debug.Print statement is also very useful, since it sends output to the Immediate window instead of the program form. Most of the time, I just print status information right on the game screen.

I will be using code most of the time to set up the user interface. First, it is far easier to print a dozen lines of code than to walk you through every step of setting values in the Properties window. Second, it is important to start thinking like a game developer rather than an application programmer. Game developers don't mess with user interfaces; they write code. The fact that, with VB, you have a rich assortment of tools to aid in game development does not mean that you should take shortcuts.

The last thing you want to see is a hundred hidden PictureBox controls on a giant form, housing all of the graphics in a game. *Gasp!* So many have suggested this route in the past, it's no wonder VB has been given a bad rap as a game programming language. I have even seen app developers suggest using a PictureClip to store sprite animations. (Select Project, Components and then scroll down to Microsoft PictureClip Control 6.0 or the equivalent.) What a terrible suggestion! This same mindset expects to do DirectX programming by dropping a DirectX-enabled PictureBox (written by someone else) on a form. That's just not the way things are done! Any time you come across this sort of thinking, feel free to label that person a Newbie Gamer.

Unconventional Bitmap Magic

You might be wondering, without PictureBox controls, how do you load graphics into a game? Even if bitmaps are stored on disk, there must be a PictureBox to load them into, right? Historically, this is how it has been done. However, that comes from thinking like an app developer. Remember, this is *game programming*! You do things differently in game-land. I will show you how to load bitmaps into memory using the LoadPicture procedure and then use a bitmap handle and device context to manipulate the image, as it is done in Visual C++. Surprised? I'll show you how to do it in Chapter 7, "Break Out the Bitmaps."

Unfortunately, there are some properties that are read-only at runtime, meaning they cannot be set after the program has started running, and can be set only during design time. But not to worry, I will show you how to size the form and primary display surface (a simple PictureBox) before the program starts running, along with the initial properties you need to get started.

Setting Up the Form

Now that you have a default project with a single form, it's time to start programming the core functionality of the drawing surface. Visual Basic forms are limited to running in the screen resolution that you have configured within Windows. In the early days of Windows game development, it was common for games to require you to set a specific video mode (like 640 × 480 and 8-bit color) in order to run the game, which was a terrible solution. You can grab the whole screen by maximizing a form, but this still leaves the Taskbar and Start Menu at the bottom to run at the current Windows resolution. Only when you have progressed to DirectX (see Chapter 6, "Supercharging Visual Basic with DirectX" and Chapter 10, "Diving into DirectDraw") will you be able to enter full-screen mode with whatever resolution you want. Until then, you will have to work with a drawing surface (PictureBox) on a window (Form) of fixed size.

Initial Property Values

Your new project should have a form called Form1, and it should be already visible in the edit window. If you click the form once, the form will be highlighted (if it is not already). You can recognize the highlighted form by the drag-ingots at the corners and sides of the form. Highlighting an object sets the Property window with the values for that object, which is what you want to do with Form1. Drag the ingot at the bottom-right to enlarge the form so it will be easier to use. Don't worry about the pixel resolution of the form because that will be set later with code.

Once the form is selected and resized, notice the properties for the form. If the Properties Window (shown in Figure 3.6) is not visible, simply press F4 or select it from the View menu.

Figure 3.6

The Properties window, showing the properties for Form1

The first property on the list is (Name), with a value of Form1. Most of these properties will be set in the startup source code for the program. The only properties that are important to this program and can't be changed with code are MaxButton and StartUpPosition. Scroll down the list of properties until you find MaxButton, and then double-click it to set it to False. You can also highlight MaxButton and press the F key to change it to False. Alternatively, you can select False from the drop-down list. By setting the MaxButton property to False, you prevent the user from maximizing the game form (which does not look good with a fixed-size PictureBox in the middle).

Now scroll down the property list to the bottom, where you will find the StartUpPosition property. Once again, change the property using one of the aforementioned methods until it is set to 2 - Center Screen.

That's it, only two properties need to be set from the GUI—all of the other properties will be set manually with code. Trust me; you save a lot of work in the end by doing it this way. I find it most convenient to double-click or press the appropriate key to change a property. Since all of the enumerations (or lists of values) for properties start with a number, it is also easy to press that number after highlighting a property name (once you become familiar with all of the values).

Don't worry about the caption, width, height, or scale mode, since these values will all be set later with code.

Adding the Primary PictureBox Control

Look at the first icon in the Control Toolbox. It should be the PictureBox. (If you aren't sure, hover the mouse cursor over the icon for a tool tip.) Select the PictureBox icon and then drag a small rectangular region right on top of the form to create the new PictureBox. When you release the mouse button, the new PictureBox is added to the form (see Figure 3.7).

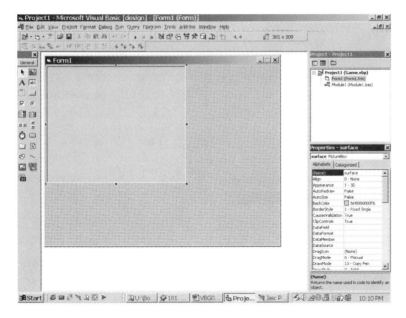

Figure 3.7

A new PictureBox control has been added to the form.

Look at the properties for the PictureBox. VB has given it the default name of PictureBox1. Change the name of the PictureBox. Highlight the (Name) property and change the name to "surface." I know this is a strange name to give a PictureBox, but it is in line with the sample programs set up in later chapters, leading up to DirectX. For now, just trust me that surface is a good name for a display canvas (and it also helps to get out of the icky VB application mindset too). We aren't actually working with an ActiveX control; it's really a magical drawing surface.

The size and placement of the PictureBox doesn't matter. Again, this will all be handled by the source code; so don't worry about it right now. All that matters is that you have a PictureBox named surface, to which the code will refer.

Creating the Code Module

This project is code-based rather than form-based. This means that Sub Main will start rather than Form1. Whenever you need to add a new file in VB, you do so by right-clicking the Project Explorer at the top-right, as shown in Figure 3.8.

Figure 3.8

The Project Explorer shows the files in your project.

A pop-up menu will appear with a list of options. Move the mouse cursor over the menu item labeled Add and you will see a list of file types that can be added to your project, as shown in Figure 3.9.

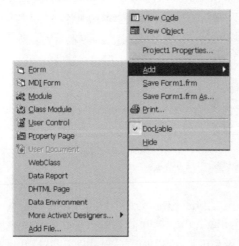

Figure 3.9

Adding a new file to the project

In order to base the program on code rather than on a form, you need to add a module to the project, so select that option from the list.

The Add Module dialog will appear (as shown in Figure 3.10), allowing you to select the default Module file or load an existing module into the project (by clicking the Existing tab).

TIP

The file extension of a module is **BAS**, which goes back to the original Microsoft QuickBasic and **GW-BASIC days.**

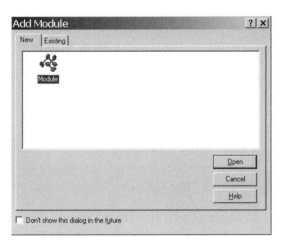

Figure 3.10

The new module will contain the source code for the program.

Since this is a new project that does not need any pre-existing files, just click the Open button. (This condition will change once you start working on the game library.) A new module will be added to the project, called Module1. If you double-click Module1 in the Project Explorer, you will see that the new file is empty. This is where you will start entering the code for the program.

Since procedures are what make up a program, it is helpful to be able to crank out procedure names quickly. The easiest way to create a new procedure is by selecting Add Procedure from the Tools menu. The Add Procedure dialog box is shown in Figure 3.11.

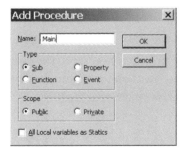

Figure 3.11

The Add Procedure dialog will stub the code for a new procedure for you.

The Add Procedure dialog lets you create a new sub, function, property, or event, and you can select Private or Public scope. The dialog box comes in handy, especially when you need to create a new property but you can't remember the exact format for properties.

Setting the Startup Object

Now you should set the project so that Sub Main starts running instead of Form1. Click the Project menu and select Project1 Properties, or right-click the project name in the Project Explorer window. The Project Properties dialog box will appear, as shown in Figure 3.12.

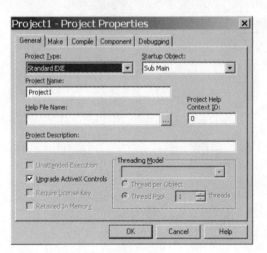

Figure 3.12

The Project Properties dialog box shows the property values for your project.

I will explore the Project Properties dialog box in more detail in Chapter 5, "Optimizing Visual Basic with Objects." Until then, you only need to be concerned with the General tab on the dialog box, which is open by default. The Project Type list allows you to change the project to an ActiveX control, DLL, EXE, or Standard EXE, which is what it should show now.

But it is the Startup Object field that is of interest right now. It currently shows Form1, which invokes the Form_Load routine when the project starts. Now, if you click the drop-down list, you should see two items:

- Sub Main
- Form1

Select Sub Main and click the OK button. The project is now set to start running at Sub Main rather than Form1. This affords you the most control over a VB program, since you have the option of displaying any form you want and can even create a form object.

Sample Program Source Code

At this point, you have only typed two lines of code for this program in the code module, and no code at all in the form module. In fact, the form won't have any code at all in this program. Everything will be handled by the code module.

If you haven't already done so, save the project now. VB will ask you for the filename of the form and module. You can make up some creative names if you'd like, or just leave it at Form1 and Module1. For the project, name it ChunkyPixels, since that describes what this program is all about.

Now open Module1 and enter the following lines of code into the code editor. After you have finished entering this code, save the project and run it by pressing F5.

```
'================================================================
' Visual Basic Game Programming
' Chapter 3: Visual Basic Programming in a Nutshell
' ChunkyPixels Program Source Code File
' Demonstrates the game window and display surface.
'================================================================


'create reference to game window
Dim window As Form

'create reference to display surface
Dim surface As PictureBox

'define the standard screen resolutions
Public Enum RESOLUTIONS
    Res320x240 = 1
    Res640x480 = 2
    Res800x600 = 3
    Res1024x768 = 4
End Enum


'================================================================
' Function CreateWindow
' Creates a reference to an existing Form and initializes
' the form to one of the standard screen resolutions.
'================================================================
Public Function CreateWindow(ByRef frm As Form, _
    ByVal res As RESOLUTIONS) As Form
    'create the reference
    Set CreateWindow = frm

    'set up the form
    frm.AutoRedraw = False
    frm.BorderStyle = 1
    frm.ClipControls = False
    frm.KeyPreview = True
    frm.ScaleMode = 3
```

```vb
        'resize the form to a standard resolution
        Select Case res
            Case Res320x240
                frm.Width = 320 * Screen.TwipsPerPixelX
                frm.Height = 240 * Screen.TwipsPerPixelY

            Case Res640x480
                frm.Width = 640 * Screen.TwipsPerPixelX
                frm.Height = 480 * Screen.TwipsPerPixelY

            Case Res800x600
                frm.Width = 800 * Screen.TwipsPerPixelX
                frm.Height = 600 * Screen.TwipsPerPixelY

            Case Res1024x768
                frm.Width = 1024 * Screen.TwipsPerPixelX
                frm.Height = 768 * Screen.TwipsPerPixelY


        End Select
End Function


'=======================================================
' Function CreateSurface
' Creates a reference to an existing PictureBox and
' resizes the control to the parent form.
'=======================================================
Public Function CreateSurface(ByRef window As Object) As PictureBox
    'create the reference
    Set CreateSurface = window.surface

    'set up the surface
    CreateSurface.AutoRedraw = False
    CreateSurface.BorderStyle = 0
    CreateSurface.ClipControls = False
    CreateSurface.ScaleMode = 3
    CreateSurface.BackColor = RGB(0, 0, 0)

    'resize the surface to the parent window
    CreateSurface.Left = 2
    CreateSurface.Top = 2
```

```
        CreateSurface.Width = window.ScaleWidth - 4
        CreateSurface.Height = window.ScaleHeight - 4
    End Function


    '================================================================
    ' Sub Main
    ' Starting point for the program.
    '================================================================
    Public Sub Main()
        Dim X As Long
        Dim Y As Long
        Dim Count As Long
        Dim Color As Long

        'initialize the game window
        Set window = CreateWindow(Form1, Res800x600)
        window.Caption = "Chunky Pixels"

        'initialize the display surface
        Set surface = CreateSurface(window)

        'display the game window
        window.Show
        DoEvents

        'draw 100,000 chunky pixels
        Randomize
        surface.DrawWidth = 5
        For Count = 1 To 100000
            X = surface.ScaleWidth * Rnd
            Y = surface.ScaleHeight * Rnd
            Color = RGB(Rnd * 256, Rnd * 256, Rnd * 256)
            surface.PSet (X, Y), Color
        Next Count

        'delete the object references
        Set surface = Nothing
        Set window = Nothing
    End Sub
```

RUNNING THE CHUNKYPIXELS PROGRAM

The ChunkyPixels program demonstrates how to reference and use a form and PictureBox without going through the typical event-driven user interface, and without any code in the form module. The program was written like this to expose you to a code-based program that does not rely on any events or properties until the program starts running. Referencing the PictureBox as a drawing surface, rather than using it directly, allows you to abstract the display and separate it from the program logic. This method also prepares you for the DirectX chapters to come. I won't keep writing the programs like this one, now that you understand the functionality; I just wanted to demonstrate a point. The output from the ChunkyPixels program is shown in Figure 3.13.

Figure 3.13

Running the ChunkyPixels sample program

Does it seem strange that you might run a VB program before compiling it? Remember, VB is a RAD tool because it allows you to quickly put together complete programs with very little code. You can actually drag controls onto a form, customize the properties of those controls, and run the program, all without writing a single line of code. For this reason, VB is an excellent language for prototyping large applications. VB also allows you to write games more rapidly than you can in other languages.

There is an option in VB that will cause a program to compile every time instead of just running the interpreter inside the IDE. The option is called Compile On Demand. You will want to turn off this feature so that VB will completely compile your programs before running them in the interpreter. I will explain how to do this in the "Background Compilation" section.

This is actually a good idea, because a full compile will catch any errors in the program. However, it is true that most often you will run your VB game before actually compiling it! In the VB world, you only really compile the program when you are ready to distribute it or send it off to be tested by others. Most of your development time will take place in the VB IDE, which is where you will run the program most often. After getting used to the instantaneous startup of VB programs, it is actually frustrating to use another language that requires a full compile before the program will run (like Visual C++). In fact, when you run a Visual C++ program inside the IDE, it is actually running the EXE file on disk. Sure, the EXE might be full of debugging information and proprietary to the Visual C++ IDE, but that differs greatly from the way VB runs programs inside its own IDE. That's because Visual C++ is not a RAD tool.

Background Compilation

Most programmers who discover Visual Basic for the first time—particularly Windows programmers with a C or C++ background—are astonished by the speed at which Visual Basic seems to compile and run programs. The fact is, Visual Basic does not always compile the program before running it! Rather, Visual Basic compiles the code as you type it in and checks the syntax of the statement. Have you noticed that Visual Basic automatically formats each line of code? The formatting takes place as the line is compiled. If that seems strange, consider that Visual Basic is rooted in the original BASIC language, which was capable of executing statements in the editor. For example, in the original GW-BASIC that came with MS-DOS, any statement that you type in without a line number is executed immediately after you press the Enter key.

> **TIP**
>
> Once you have mastered Visual Basic, the syntax-checking feature will get in the way. Nothing is more annoying than having a message pop up while you're trying to type in code. That's helpful during the learning process, but you will soon tire of it. To disable syntax-checking, go to the Tools menu, select Options, and disable the Auto Syntax Check option.

To disable the Compile On Demand feature, select Options from the Tools menu. When the Options dialog box appears, as shown in Figure 3.14, select the General tab. There is an option called Compile On Demand with a sub-option called Background Compile. Just uncheck the Compile On Demand option and that will take care of the problem. As soon as you do, the program will run differently. If you have any typos with variable names in obscure corners of the program, this new setting will pick up those problems immediately, rather than when the program comes to that point. Compile On Demand works well in conjunction with the Option Explicit statement to reduce bugs.

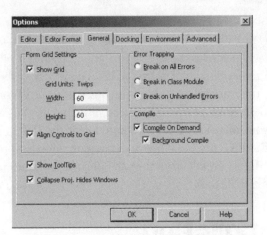

Figure 3.14

The Options dialog box is where you change settings in the VB IDE.

Early and Late Binding

Now, keep in mind, Visual Basic only checks the syntax of a statement during design time. It does not always check the validity of a statement containing objects, regardless of whether those objects are created with early-binding or late-binding. An early-bound object is identifiable during design time with IntelliSense. The following descriptions should help to clarify the matter.

- **Early-Binding**. This occurs when Visual Basic recognizes the object during compilation and has an opportunity to verify that the object is being used correctly.
- **Late-Binding**. This occurs when Visual Basic does not recognize the object during compilation and must assume that the object will function correctly during runtime.
- **IntelliSense**. This feature allows you to view the contents of an object by typing the name of the object followed by a period, which displays a pop-up list of items contained in that object. This feature saves hours of time that you might have spent looking up object definitions, and immediately shows if an object is early-bound or late-bound.

The Debug Object

A somewhat contradictory situation comes up when you're using the Debug object. The Debug object includes two functions: `Print` and `Assert`. The `Print` function displays messages in the Immediate window when you run the program in the Visual Basic IDE. Visual Basic will immediately complain if the Debug statement is used improperly.

TIP

Debug statements are stripped out when you compile the program into an executable, so use them liberally! It never hurts to include too many Debug statements, since they do not affect runtime speed and they usually save a lot of time tracking down bugs.

To see how syntax-checking works, create an empty project or just open the code window for an existing program. Find a blank line inside a function or sub—`Form_Load` will work fine. Type `Debug.Print "Hello"` and press Enter. Note that as soon as you type `Debug` followed by the period, IntelliSense kicks in and shows you the two functions that Debug owns. If you type `Debug.Print` alone, it will send a blank line to the Immediate window. Including text in quotes will print that text.

> **NOTE**
>
> The Immediate window is only functional when the program is running. If you try to type in a `Print` command during design time, an error message will be displayed.

You can also display object properties and variables. For example, you can start a program line-by-line by pressing F8. As soon as the first line of the program is highlighted with a yellow background, open the Immediate window (Ctrl+G) and type `Print Me.Caption`. The caption of the main program form should be displayed in the Immediate window. Since you are already in the Immediate window, the Debug object is not needed, so you are simply using the intrinsic `Print` function.

UNDERSTANDING THE VB OBJECT

Visual Basic has numerous built-in procedures that you can use, all contained within an object called VB. (Surprised?) To see the list of properties and procedures in the VB object, simply open a code window and type **VB** followed by a period. You should see a list of things contained within the VB object, including other objects. Following is the list of items in the root VB object:

- App (object)
- Clipboard (object)
- Forms (object)
- Global
- Licenses (collection)
- Load (procedure)
- LoadPicture (procedure)
- LoadResData (procedure)
- LoadResPicture (procedure)
- LoadResString (procedure)
- Printer (object)
- Printers
- SavePicture (procedure)
- Screen (object)
- Unload (procedure)

I will cover the VB object procedures (such as LoadPicture) in due time. But for now, I would like to explain the sub-objects that are contained within VB.

The App Object

The App object includes information about the program and basically summarizes all of the fields that you can modify in the Project Properties, such as Major and Minor (the version), Title, CompanyName, and other useful pieces of information.

The most useful App property, and one that will be used extensively, is the App.Path property. This gives you the directory where the program executable is located and is invaluable for loading data files, bitmaps, waves, and the like.

The Clipboard Object

The Clipboard object gives you access to the Windows Clipboard for copy, cut, and paste operations. Basically, you check the type of data currently stored in the clipboard with the GetFormat function and then call either GetData or GetText to retrieve a binary object (such as an image) or a text string.

You can also send information to the clipboard using the SetData and SetText procedures, which can be useful for providing data to other programs (such as a screenshot of the game in progress).

The Forms Object

The Forms object can be useful when you have numerous forms in a program and would like to iterate through them all. This is usually a common feature in an MDI application, and is not very useful in a game. However, if you would like to get a list of all the forms in the program (which must be running), you can try the following code:

```
Dim frm As Form
For Each frm In VB.Forms
    Debug.Print frm.Name
Next
```

The Screen Object

The Screen object is useful if you would like to know the resolution of the Windows desktop. It also provides the functions `TwipsPerPixelX` and `TwipsPerPixelY`, which are essential when you're resizing a form (as you did in the ChunkyPixels program). The Screen object also provides information about ActiveX controls and fonts, and allows you to change the mouse cursor.

SUMMARY

This chapter was a crash course in VB programming, and it showed you that it is possible to take VB seriously as a game programming language when you get into the proper mindset. Trying to mold a game into the VB user interface is the wrong approach. Rather, this chapter focused on developing coding habits and the use of code modules, with minimal focus on the main form (which usually gets all of the attention). The sample program, ChunkyPixels, showed that forms and controls do not need to be the focus in a VB program. Properly handled, these objects will serve your game programming needs.

The next chapter shows you how to enhance Visual Basic for speed by calling upon functions built into Windows. These functions are integral parts of the operating system and are collectively called the Windows API. These functions will greatly enhance your game programming skills and will eventually form the core of the game library that is developed in later chapters.

CHAPTER 4

GETTING TO
KNOW THE
WINDOWS API

This chapter covers the gritty details of the Windows 32-bit Application Programming Interface, also known as the Windows API. This is a huge collection of procedures available to all Windows programs. You can tap into this treasure trove of routines in Visual Basic with a little effort. The Windows API provides functionality that can duplicate all of the routines built into VB, and these routines often run faster. I will show you, through hands-on examples, how to make use of these routines to speed up graphics processing in VB, which in turn will translate into faster game code.

This chapter covers the following topics:

- Introducing the Windows API
- Giving Visual Basic a Boost
- Using the Windows API
- Speeding Up Drawing Routines
- Identifying the Host System

INTRODUCING THE WINDOWS API

The Windows API is the heart and soul of Microsoft Windows, regardless of which version of Windows you are using. In a way, the Windows API actually *is* Windows, because without it, Windows would be nothing but a small core.

Figure 4.1 is an illustration showing where the Windows API fits in with the other parts of the Windows operating system, and the level at which a Visual Basic game must run.

> **NOTE**
> The Windows 2000 core, without the Windows API or virtual memory management or any other desktop features, actually powers the Microsoft Xbox video game console.

Origins of the Windows API

The Windows API goes back to the mid-1980s, when Microsoft started developing Windows. While the early versions of Windows were used to power specialized applications like desktop publishing programs, it was not actually a real operating system. In fact, even Windows 3.0, which is considered by many to have been the first *real* version of Windows, was not an operating system because it was riding on top of MS-DOS.

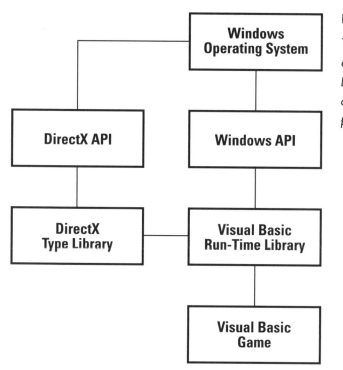

Figure 4.1

The Windows API sits at the midpoint between the Windows core and a Visual Basic program.

But for all practical purposes, Windows 3.0 might as well have been an operating system because it extended MS-DOS by leaps and bounds. By the time Windows 3.1 and Windows for Workgroups 3.11 were released, Windows had started to gain serious attention and was grudgingly accepted by some game developers. At the time, Windows was just a 16-bit operating system because MS-DOS was *still* only a 16-bit operating system. Since Windows 3.11 could only see 16 bits, the Windows API was also limited to 16 bits.

When Windows 95 came along, it was a full 32-bit operating system, no longer riding on MS-DOS. Windows 95 included support for a new 32-bit Windows API, so the differences were noted as Win16 and Win32. Visual Basic 4.0, which was released soon after Windows 95, supported both 16-bit and 32-bit programs, and supported both Windows 3.11 and Windows 95.

BUZZWORD

Bit depth defines the amount of information that a computer system can crunch at a time, and can be thought of as the highway upon which data travels (also called the *bus*). The result is that a larger data path can handle either more pieces of data or larger pieces of data, but not necessarily both at the same time. A 128-bit bus can handle 200 percent more data than a 64-bit bus, which is why the Sega Dreamcast blows away the Nintendo 64 and Sony PlayStation.

As you can imagine, things were pretty messy at the time. With two versions of the Windows API cohabiting the operating system, it was difficult to upgrade existing programs to the new 32-bit way of things. Variable data types changed, which meant that new Windows API procedures had to be referenced, often with new parameters.

32-Bit Windows

Now we are safely beyond the confusing years and Windows 3.1 is long gone. There is a standard 32-bit Windows API and DirectX, both of which are fully supported by Visual Basic. VB itself is also a full 32-bit programming language, having left behind its 16-bit roots with version 4.0. A single compiler with VB 6.0 is now capable of compiling code that will run on all of Microsoft's operating systems, including Windows 95, 98, 2000, Me, XP, and NT. The bottom line is that these are all 32-bit operating systems, all with the same basic core API, so VB programs should have no problem running on any of them. There are some incompatibilities between 9x and NT (such as function names), but these issues don't often cause a problem.

Visual Basic Runtime Library

The key lies in the Visual Basic Runtime Library. Despite VB's ability to compile native executable programs, most of the functionality of a VB program (such as the forms engine) is located in the runtime file, not in the executable that is created by VB when you compile a program.

> **TIP**
>
> The runtime file for VB 6.0 is called **MSVBVM60.DLL** and must be installed before a VB program will run on a target system.

VB Holds Its Own

VB does include much of the Windows API as intrinsic procedures, but VB was designed for ease of use. There is a large portion of the Windows API that VB does not support internally. In fact, despite the fact that the Windows API provides a general-purpose, bitmap-drawing function called BitBlt (which is short for *bit-block transfer*), VB actually implements its own bitmap-drawing procedure called PaintPicture, which is part of the PictureBox control. This is unfortunate, because the BitBlt function is a device driver function that is usually implemented by the video card's hardware chip, and is therefore very fast.

> **BUZZWORD**
>
> A *device driver* is an interface to a hardware device using a standardized API. Different vendors of the device—such as a video card—can provide operating system support by simply writing a device driver that the operating system can use.

Why would the VB development team choose to duplicate features that are built into Windows? I have pondered that question myself, as have others. I think it basically comes down to portability—not relying upon the operating system for key features. Ironically, VB is available only for Windows.

GIVING VISUAL BASIC A BOOST

Let's be honest—Visual Basic was not intended as a tool for creating high-performance commercial games. The language absolutely excels for application development and particularly database development. I have worked on some large database systems using VB, and I can tell you from personal experience that VB absolutely rocks in this arena.

This is exactly why many have not taken VB seriously as a game development language. But isn't that to be expected? Most programmers would argue that you should select the right tool for the job. As far as game programming goes, that tool should be Visual C++ and DirectX. But what about Java, Delphi, and other fascinating languages, including Visual Basic? It is largely a matter of preference. But VB does have an edge since it is widespread, mainstream, and used all over the world on countless software projects. And when VB isn't the main development tool, it is the de facto support tool for building prototypes and quick utilities.

Now that I've gotten that off my chest, I hope you understand what I mean when I say that VB is not perfectly suited for writing games. The library that is built into VB is not really optimized for creating high-performance games. But the very same thing applies to Visual C++. What does Visual C++ have intrinsically that makes it so great for game development? Nothing really, other than native access to the Windows API.

There's the key! VB also has access to the Windows API, and those API functions run just as fast in VB as they do in Visual C++. There, now you know the truth, so the language might not really matter after all!

Now, back to the subject at hand. How do you tap into the Windows API from VB?

Filling In Missing Functionality

VB has an inherent trait in that it does the things it can do natively very well, and it is very easy to make use of all of the features of the language. There is no need to declare prototype functions before using them, like you would do in C or C++. You just create a procedure anywhere you like in the VB project. In fact, you can create procedures in multiple source code modules, and as long as they are all part of the same project and the procedures are declared as Public, you can call them from anywhere.

VB also has built-in graphics routines that you can use to draw points, lines, rectangles, circles, and bitmaps (the primary components of a game). The only problem is, VB doesn't do these things particularly fast. Quite often, a programming language must sacrifice speed for ease-of-use, and VB is no exception.

C and C++ share a similar circumstance. It is well known that C code runs very fast at a lower level than C++. The extensions to the language that differentiate C++ from C also add overhead to the code, just like the VB runtime library or the Java virtual machine add overhead—sort of like bureaucracy or paperwork within the parts of a language that make things run.

However, most compilers are capable of overcoming this overhead through advanced optimization of the compiled code at the assembler level. So it is not always true that C code will run faster than C++, Java, or VB, for that matter.

Enhancing Existing Functionality

How do you identify VB features that need to be optimized with the Windows API? The best way is to benchmark some code running in native VB, and then compare that to similar code also running in VB, but using Windows API routines.

Later in this chapter, I will show you several benchmark programs that will show the differences between native VB and *enhanced* VB—so to speak.

Using the Windows API

The Windows API consists of hundreds of functions contained in dozens of DLLs (*Dynamic Link Libraries*). The most commonly used libraries are GDI32 and USER32. These DLLs provide the core routines needed to optimize VB for graphics handling, and include the well-known and over-worked BitBlt function for displaying bitmaps.

The Declare Statement

Declaring and using Windows API functions is surprisingly straightforward when you consider that these functions were created with Visual C++ and comprise the core functionality of Windows itself. The basic syntax of the Declare statement looks something like this:

```
[Public | Private] Declare [Function | Sub] ProcedureName _
    Lib "libname" [Alias "aliasname"] _
    (Parameter1, Parameter2, […]) _
    [As ReturnType]
```

When you declare a function as Public, it is visible to all other code modules, while functions declared as Private are visible only within the current code module.

The procedure must be declared as either Function or Sub. If the procedure returns a value, you must declare it as a Function; procedures that do not return a value are declared as Sub, just like a regular VB procedure.

The Lib and Alias values define the actual name of the procedure and the local name that you would like to give the procedure. There are many API functions with obscure names, so it is convenient to use the Alias to point to the actual API name, while defining the Lib to any name you want.

The parameter list should look like the list for any VB procedure, and the data types must match those of the API function. Generally, any time an API function requires a pointer or a Window handle, you declare the data type As Long (the most common data type used in Declare statements).

Common API Structures

There are three structures that come up more often than all others when you're working with graphics in Windows, regardless of the language you use: POINT, RECT, and RGBQUAD. In the declarations that follow, notice that they are all declared as Private, which is a requirement for adding structures or functions to class modules. If you add these declarations to code modules, then you are free to declare them as Public.

> **NOTE**
> Notice that DirectX defines its own version of these structures, so you will run into problems if you declare and pass them to DirectX functions. To get around this, you will want to use the DirectX-specific structs when possible. For example, if you are using DirectDraw, you will want to declare the RECT as DxVbLib.RECT.

- **POINT.** The POINT structure is used throughout the Windows API as a means to send a single point from one routine to another without requiring two parameters for the X and Y component (which represents the position of a pixel on the screen). This structure is also very useful when you want a function to return a point value without resorting to the use of reference parameters.

```
Private Type POINT
    X As Long
    Y As Long
End Type
```

■ **RECT.** The RECT structure is also used throughout the Windows API for the same reason as POINT—it drastically saves time when sending parameters from one function to another. The RECT structure consists of four variables that keep track of the four sides of a rectangular region on the screen. Windows itself uses RECT structures to update the display any time you resize or move a program window on the screen, so it is very common.

```
Public Type RECT
    Left As Long
    Top As Long
    Right As Long
    Bottom As Long
End Type
```

■ **RGBQUAD.** The RGBQUAD structure is not as common as POINT and RECT, but it is helpful any time you need to work with color on a 32-bit display (the default used in this book). The four components of this structure (Blue, Green, Red, and Alpha) keep track of all the information needed to store a color for a 32-bit pixel. As the structure shows, this equates evenly into four bytes, and can be used to directly modify video memory.

```
Private Type RGBQUAD
    Blue As Byte
    Green As Byte
    Red As Byte
    Alpha As Byte
End Type
```

Common API Functions

Among the hundreds of Windows API functions, only a few are needed to enhance VB for game development. They are primarily focused on graphics functions such as BitBlt. But there are other equally important functions that fill the gaps in the VB library. The most notable lack is the ability to load a bitmap into memory without the use of a PictureBox or Image control. I will cover this topic in Chapter 7, "Break Out the Bitmaps," so it is only important that you understand what the Windows API provides, and not necessarily how to use each function at this point.

■ **GetTickCount.** This function taps into the low-resolution system timer and is useful for keeping a program running at a stable speed regardless of the frame rate. A high frequency timer exists with much finer time increments, but GetTickCount is usually sufficient for timing game loops. There might be a time when you will need more resolution than is provided by this function. For example, if you want to get a precise benchmark on the execution time of a routine, you might want to look into the high-resolution timer using `QueryPerformanceCounter` and `QueryPerformanceFrequency` (which are not covered in this book).

```
Private Declare Function GetTickCount Lib "kernel32" () As Long
```

- **SetPixel**. This function allows you to draw a single pixel on a drawing surface such as a PictureBox. The four parameters provide the destination, the location, and the color of the pixel. See the Pixels program later in this chapter for a demonstration.

```
Private Declare Function SetPixel Lib "gdi32" ) _
    ByVal hDC As Long, _
    ByVal X As Long, _
    ByVal Y As Long, _
    ByVal crColor As Long _
) As Long
```

- **GetPixel**. This function is the complement of `SetPixel` in that it returns the color of a pixel at a specific location on the drawing surface. The three parameters provide the destination and the location of the pixel. The return value is a Long, which is compatible with the RGB function.

```
Private Declare Function GetPixel Lib "gdi32" ( _
    ByVal hDC As Long, _
    ByVal X As Long, _
    ByVal Y As Long _
) As Long
```

- **Ellipse**. This function draws an ellipse to the destination drawing surface. The five parameters include the destination and the four sides of a rectangular region that bounds the desired shape. Setting the rectangle is an easy way to see how the ellipse will be drawn. The color and line style must be set in advance using a custom drawing pen. See the Circles program later in this chapter for a demonstration.

```
Private Declare Function Ellipse Lib "gdi32" ( _
    ByVal hDC As Long, _
    ByVal X1 As Long, _
    ByVal Y1 As Long, _
    ByVal X2 As Long, _
    ByVal Y2 As Long _
) As Long
```

- **MoveTo**. This function moves the current drawing pointer to a new location on the destination drawing surface. The four parameters include the drawing surface, the location, and a POINT that is returned as ByRef with the old location of the pointer.

```
Private Declare Function MoveTo Lib "gdi32" Alias "MoveToEx" ( _
    ByVal hDC As Long, _
    ByVal X As Long, _
    ByVal Y As Long, _
    lpPoint As POINT _
) As Long
```

- **LineTo.** This function draws a line from the current pointer position to a new location on the drawing surface. The color and line style must be set in advance using a custom drawing pen. See the Lines program later in this chapter for a demonstration of MoveTo and LineTo.

```
Private Declare Function LineTo Lib "gdi32" ( _
    ByVal hDC As Long, _
    ByVal X As Long, _
    ByVal Y As Long _
) As Long
```

- **PolyLine.** This function draws a series of lines stored inside an array of points that mark the endpoints of each line segment. The color and line style must be set in advance using a custom drawing pen. See the Rectangles program later in this chapter for a demonstration.

```
Private Declare Function Polyline Lib "gdi32" ( _
    ByVal hDC As Long, _
    lpPoint As POINT, _
    ByVal nCount As Long _
) As Long
```

- **CreatePen.** This function is used to create a custom drawing pen for use with the drawing functions like LineTo and PolyLine. The pen is identified with a returned Windows handle, much like a hWND, and is stored as a system resource in Windows. It is therefore very important that you delete a pen when you are finished using it. The three parameters include the pen style, the drawing width, and the RGB color. The Lines program demonstrates the use of this function.

```
Private Declare Function CreatePen Lib "gdi32" ( _
    ByVal nPenStyle As Long, _
    ByVal nWidth As Long, _
    ByVal crColor As Long _
) As Long
```

- **SelectObject**. This function is used to select an object into a device context (Windows terminology for a drawing surface). Selecting an object in this manner has the effect of associating the object with a specific device context, for instance, a pen created with the CreatePen function. When using a public object such as the primary Windows desktop, for example, it is very important that you select OUT the object when you are finished. For this reason, the SelectObject function returns the old object handle. After you are done with the device, you can then select the old object handle back into it. The Lines program demonstrates the use of this function.

```
Private Declare Function SelectObject Lib "gdi32" ( _
    ByVal hDC As Long, _
    ByVal hObject As Long _
) As Long
```

- **DeleteObject**. This function deletes a system resource that was created with a function such as CreatePen (or any of the other numerous functions related to Windows handles). Deleting the   object not only frees up the memory used by that object; it also frees up valuable finite system resources. The Lines program demonstrates the use of this function.

```
Private Declare Function DeleteObject Lib "gdi32" ( _
    ByVal hObject As Long _
) As Long
```

- **GetObject**. This function retrieves information about an object with a Windows handle, and is useful for reading the header information for a bitmap image. The three parameters provide the handle, the size of the header, and the destination buffer for the data (such as a BITMAP structure). The Bitmaps program demonstrates the use of this function.

```
Private Declare Function GetObject Lib "gdi32" _
    Alias "GetObjectA" ( _
    ByVal hObject As Long, _
    ByVal nCount As Long, _
    lpObject As Any _
) As Long
```

- **CopyMemory**. This extremely valuable function copies bytes of memory from one memory buffer to another and is able to work with just about any type of buffer you can throw at it, including byte arrays, strings, even portions of system memory. The actual API function name is RtlMoveMemory, but it was renamed to CopyMemory using an alias so that it is easier to use. Three parameters provide the destination buffer, the source buffer, and the number of bytes to copy. This function is demonstrated in later chapters, and is provided here only for reference.

```
Private Declare Sub CopyMemory Lib "kernel32" _
    Alias "RtlMoveMemory" ( _
    lpvDest As Any, _
    lpvSource As Any, _
    ByVal cbCopy As Long _
    )
```

SPEEDING UP DRAWING ROUTINES

To fully understand and appreciate the power of the Windows API, I am going to show you several demonstration programs that actually benchmark the performance of VB functionality and equivalent API functionality using the functions listed earlier (such as SetPixel and PolyLine). The benchmark programs include a test for drawing points, lines, rectangles, circles, and bitmaps.

These programs are a little more dependent upon forms and controls, because they are not actual games—they're just benchmarks. The only problem with dependency on forms and controls is that it is easy to mess up a program by simply setting a property to the wrong value. For this reason, I prefer to use code as much as possible, but will make an exception now and then to illustrate a point (no pun intended).

Drawing Fast Points

Figure 4.2 shows a program called Points. This program demonstrates the difference between drawing points using the intrinsic PSet procedure (on the left side of the figure) and the Windows API SetPixel function (on the right side of the figure). As you can see from the figure, PSet has drawn 94,380 points per second, while the SetPixel function has drawn 108,470 points per second. The difference may vary on your PC, but in this case the API function is capable of drawing points at least 15 percent faster than the equivalent VB function.

However, if you refer to Figure 4.3, you will notice that the same program reports a much slower score for the PSet function. In fact, at 31,213 points per second, this version is only running at one-third the speed of the previous one. What's the difference? No, it wasn't running on a slower computer. The program in Figure 4.2 was compiled to an executable, while the program shown in Figure 4.3 was run from within the VB IDE! At the same time, note that the difference between each version of SetPixel is not very great.

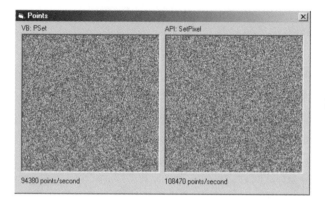

Figure 4.2

The SetPixel *API function is much faster than the intrinsic* PSet *procedure.*

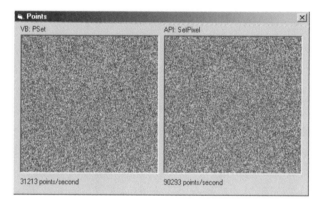

Figure 4.3

The Points program reports different results inside the VB IDE.

This demonstrates an important point. Before judging a procedure or algorithm as inadequate, always be sure to compile the program and run it stand-alone, because VB's optimizing native code compiler usually compiles code that runs much faster than the interpreted code that runs inside the IDE.

TIP

Windows API routines will often (though not always) make a program run at nearly the same speed in the IDE as it runs as a compiled executable.

Creating the Points Program

To create this program yourself, start a new project and resize the form so that Width = 7600 and Height = 4600. Set ScaleMode = 3 – Pixel and KeyPreview = True. Now add two PictureBox controls to the form, Picture1

TIP

Make sure you always set KeyPreview = True in the main form for a program, in order to handle keyboard events. Otherwise, the keyboard events will all be captured by the controls on the form.

and Picture2. For each PictureBox, set ScaleMode = 3, Width = 230, and Height = 230. Add a label above each PictureBox called Label1 and Label2. Add another label below each PictureBox called Label3 and Label4. For each Label control, set AutoSize = True.

Source Code for the Points Program

Following is the source code for the Points program. Simply type this code into the code module for Form1. To quickly jump to the code module, double-click the form.

```
'=================================================================
' Visual Basic Game Programming With DirectX
' Chapter 4 : Getting To Know The Windows API
' Points Program Source Code
'=================================================================


Option Explicit
Option Base 0


'this function returns the current system timer tick count
Private Declare Function GetTickCount Lib "kernel32" () As Long


'this function draws a pixel to a destination hHD
Private Declare Function SetPixel Lib "gdi32" _
    (ByVal hDC As Long, ByVal X As Long, ByVal Y As Long, _
     ByVal crColor As Long) As Long


'global variables
Dim done As Boolean


'=================================================================
' Random
' Generate a random number from 0 to num using Rnd
'=================================================================
Public Function Random(ByVal num As Long) As Long
    Random = CLng(num * Rnd)
End Function


'=================================================================
' Form_KeyDown
' This event is triggered when you press a key.
' Hitting the ESC key will end the program.
```

```
'=================================================================
Private Sub Form_KeyDown(KeyCode As Integer, Shift As Integer)
    If KeyCode = 27 Then
        done = True
    End If
End Sub


'=================================================================
' Form_Load
' This event occurs when the form is first loaded, and is
' actually the startup form for this program.
'=================================================================
Private Sub Form_Load()
    Dim iStart As Long
    Dim iLeft As Long
    Dim iTop As Long
    Dim iColor As Long
    Dim iCount As Long

    'display the form before doing anything else
    Me.Show
    DoEvents
    done = False

    'keep drawing points until user presses ESC
    Do Until done
        'Draw points using PSet VB function
        iCount = 0
        iStart = GetTickCount

        'draw points for 1 second
        Do While GetTickCount < iStart + 1000
            iLeft = Random(Picture1.ScaleWidth)
            iTop = Random(Picture1.ScaleHeight)
            iColor = RGB(Random(256), Random(256), Random(256))
            Picture1.PSet (iLeft, iTop), iColor
            iCount = iCount + 1
        Loop

        'display results of test
        Label3.Caption = iCount & " points/second"
```

```
            iCount = 0
            DoEvents

            'Draw points using SetPixel API function
            iCount = 0
            iStart = GetTickCount

            'draw points for 1 second
            Do While GetTickCount < iStart + 1000
                iLeft = Random(Picture2.ScaleWidth)
                iTop = Random(Picture2.ScaleHeight)
                iColor = RGB(Random(256), Random(256), Random(256))
                SetPixel Picture2.hDC, iLeft, iTop, iColor
                iCount = iCount + 1
            Loop

            'display results of test
            Label4.Caption = iCount & " points/second"
            iCount = 0
            DoEvents
        Loop

        'when user presses ESC, the loop is broken
        End
End Sub
```

Drawing Fast Lines

A program called Lines shows the difference between the intrinsic Line procedure and the
Windows API MoveTo/LineTo functions (see Figure 4.4). The VB routine can draw 27,421 lines per
second, while the API routines can draw 28,255 lines per second.

The difference isn't that great in this case—only three percent! Usually such an insignificant
improvement would not be worth the effort, but there is actually a case to be made here for the
API functions. In the source code listing that follows, you will notice that the MoveTo/LineTo
functions are actually wrapped by lines of code that create and destroy a drawing pen for every
single line that is drawn. This is not exactly the fastest way to handle it, which means there is
room for improvement in the code. The API functions are, at any rate, still faster than the VB
Line function.

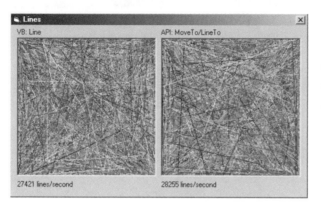

Figure 4.4

The Lines program shows the difference between VB and API line-drawing functions.

Creating the Lines Program

To create this program yourself, start a new project and resize the form so that Width = 7600 and Height = 4600. Set ScaleMode = 3 – Pixel and KeyPreview = True. Now add two PictureBox controls to the form, Picture1 and Picture2. For each PictureBox, set ScaleMode = 3, Width = 230, and Height = 230. Add a label above each PictureBox called Label1 and Label2. Add another label below each PictureBox called Label3 and Label4. For each Label, set AutoSize = True.

Source Code for the Lines Program

Following is the source code for the Lines program. Simply type this code into the code module for Form1. To quickly jump to the code module, double-click the form.

```
'===============================================================
' Visual Basic Game Programming With DirectX
' Chapter 4 : Getting To Know The Windows API
' Lines Program Source Code
'===============================================================

Option Explicit
Option Base 0

'structure to store points
Private Type POINT
    X As Long
    Y As Long
End Type

'Windows API function declarations
Private Declare Function GetTickCount Lib "kernel32" () As Long
```

```
Private Declare Function MoveTo Lib "gdi32" Alias "MoveToEx" ( _
    ByVal hDC As Long, ByVal X As Long, ByVal Y As Long, _
    lpPoint As POINT) As Long

Private Declare Function LineTo Lib "gdi32" ( _
    ByVal hDC As Long, ByVal X As Long, ByVal Y As Long) As Long

Private Declare Function CreatePen Lib "gdi32" ( _
    ByVal nPenStyle As Long, ByVal nWidth As Long, _
    ByVal crColor As Long) As Long

Private Declare Function SelectObject Lib "gdi32" ( _
    ByVal hDC As Long, ByVal hObject As Long) As Long

Private Declare Function DeleteObject Lib "gdi32" ( _
    ByVal hObject As Long) As Long

'global variables
Dim done As Boolean


'===================================================================
' Random
' Generate a random number from 0 to num using Rnd
'===================================================================
Public Function Random(ByVal num As Long) As Long
    Random = CLng(num * Rnd)
End Function


'===================================================================
' DrawLine
' Draws a line defined by the four corners of a rectangular region
' using the MoveTo/LineTo API functions.
'===================================================================
Public Sub DrawLine(ByVal Left As Long, ByVal Top As Long, _
    ByVal Right As Long, ByVal Bottom As Long, ByVal Color As Long)

    Dim pt As POINT
    Dim hPen As Long
    Dim hOldPen As Long
```

```
    'create custom drawing pen and select it
    hPen = CreatePen(0, 1, Color)
    hOldPen = SelectObject(Picture2.hDC, hPen)

    'set starting point of line
    MoveTo Picture2.hDC, Left, Top, pt

    'draw line to destination point
    LineTo Picture2.hDC, Right, Bottom

    'delete the custom pen
    SelectObject Picture2.hDC, hOldPen
    DeleteObject hPen
End Sub


'==================================================================
' Form_KeyDown
' This event is triggered when you press a key.
' Hitting the ESC key will end the program.
'==================================================================
Private Sub Form_KeyDown(KeyCode As Integer, Shift As Integer)
    If KeyCode = 27 Then done = True
End Sub


'==================================================================
' Form_Load
' This event occurs when the form is first loaded, and is
' actually the startup Sub for new programs by default.
'==================================================================
Private Sub Form_Load()
    Dim lLeft As Long
    Dim lTop As Long
    Dim lRight As Long
    Dim lBottom As Long
    Dim lColor As Long
    Dim lStart As Long
    Dim lCount As Long

    'display the form
    Me.Show
    DoEvents
```

```
'keep drawing lines until users hits ESC
Do Until done
    'Draw lines using VB Line function
    lStart = GetTickCount
    lCount = 0

    'draw lines for 1 second
    Do While GetTickCount < lStart + 1000
        lLeft = Random(Picture1.ScaleWidth)
        lTop = Random(Picture1.ScaleHeight)
        lRight = Random(Picture1.ScaleWidth)
        lBottom = Random(Picture1.ScaleHeight)
        lColor = RGB(Random(255), Random(255), Random(255))
        Picture1.DrawWidth = 1
        Picture1.Line (lLeft, lTop)-(lRight, lBottom), lColor
        lCount = lCount + 1
    Loop

    'display results of the test
    Label3.Caption = lCount & " lines/second"
    lCount = 0
    DoEvents

    'Draw lines using API MoveTo/LineTo functions
    lStart = GetTickCount
    lCount = 0

    'draw lines for 1 second
    Do While GetTickCount < lStart + 1000
        lLeft = Random(Picture2.ScaleWidth)
        lTop = Random(Picture2.ScaleHeight)
        lRight = Random(Picture2.ScaleWidth)
        lBottom = Random(Picture2.ScaleHeight)
        lColor = RGB(Random(255), Random(255), Random(255))
        Picture2.DrawWidth = 1
        DrawLine lLeft, lTop, lRight, lBottom, lColor
        lCount = lCount + 1
    Loop
```

```
        'display results of the test
        Label4.Caption = lCount & " lines/second"
        lCount = 0
        DoEvents
    Loop

    'when loop exits, the program ends
    End
End Sub
```

Drawing Fast Rectangles

Figure 4.5 shows the Rectangles program, which compares the VB Line function (using the B option for Box) and the PolyLine API function. In this instance, the VB version is drawing 30,769 rectangles per second, while the API version is drawing 33,200 rectangles per second, resulting in a speed increase of eight percent. This amount is significant when you consider that the intrinsic Line procedure is a single-line instruction, while the PolyLine API function requires several lines of support code to set up the drawing pen and the line array.

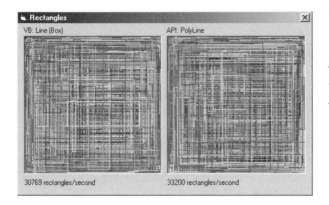

Figure 4.5

The Rectangles program demonstrates the speed of the PolyLine API function.

The MoveTo and LineTo API functions that you saw earlier in the Lines program would have resulted in a similar score because, despite the lack of a line array, there would be four function calls to draw all four sides of the rectangle, while PolyLine draws them all at once. Experimentation is the best policy, at any rate.

In most cases you would probably want to use the simpler MoveTo/LineTo functions, but it is nice to at least know how PolyLine works. Once again, it is a given that this code will run faster if you create and destroy the custom drawing pen outside of DrawRect. I have written it this way for clarity. Even with this slower method, the API code runs faster than the VB code.

Creating the Rectangles Program

To create this program yourself, start a new project and resize the form so that Width = 7600 and Height = 4600. Set ScaleMode = 3 – Pixel and KeyPreview = True. Now add two PictureBox controls to the form, Picture1 and Picture2. For each PictureBox, set ScaleMode = 3, Width = 230, and Height = 230. Add a label above each PictureBox called Label1 and Label2. Add another label below each PictureBox called Label3 and Label4. For each of the Label controls, set AutoSize = True.

Source Code for the Rectangles Program

Following is the source code for the Rectangles program. Simply type this code into the code module for Form1. To quickly jump to the code module, double-click the form.

```
'=================================================================
' Visual Basic Game Programming With DirectX
' Chapter 4 : Getting To Know The Windows API
' Rectangles Program Source Code
'=================================================================


Option Explicit
Option Base 0

'define structure to store points
Private Type POINT
    X As Long
    Y As Long
End Type

'Windows API function declarations
Private Declare Function GetTickCount Lib "kernel32" () As Long

Private Declare Function Polyline Lib "gdi32" _
    (ByVal hDC As Long, _
    lpPoint As POINT, ByVal nCount As Long) As Long

Private Declare Function CreatePen Lib "gdi32" _
    (ByVal nPenStyle As Long, ByVal nWidth As Long, _
    ByVal crColor As Long) As Long
```

```vb
Private Declare Function SelectObject Lib "gdi32" _
    (ByVal hDC As Long, ByVal hObject As Long) As Long

Private Declare Function DeleteObject Lib "gdi32" _
    (ByVal hObject As Long) As Long

'global variables
Dim done As Boolean

'declare the DrawRect variables global for speed
Dim hPen As Long
Dim hOldPen As Long
Dim pta(4) As POINT
Dim pt As POINT


'======================================================================
' Random
' Generate a random number from 0 to num using Rnd
'======================================================================
Public Function Random(ByVal num As Long) As Long
    Random = CLng(num * Rnd)
End Function


'======================================================================
' DrawRect
' Draw a rectangle using a line array and the PolyLine API function
'======================================================================
Public Sub DrawRect(ByVal Left As Long, ByVal Top As Long, _
    ByVal Right As Long, ByVal Bottom As Long, ByVal Color As Long, _
    Optional ByVal Filled As Boolean = False)

    'create a custom drawing pen
    hPen = CreatePen(0, 1, Color)
    hOldPen = SelectObject(Picture2.hDC, hPen)

    'set up the line array
    pta(0).X = Left
    pta(0).Y = Top
    pta(1).X = Right
    pta(1).Y = Top
```

```
        pta(2).X = Right
        pta(2).Y = Bottom
        pta(3).X = Left
        pta(3).Y = Bottom
        pta(4).X = Left
        pta(4).Y = Top

        'draw the lines in the array
        Polyline Picture2.hDC, pta(0), 5

        'delete the custom drawing pen
        SelectObject Picture2.hDC, hOldPen
        DeleteObject hPen
End Sub


'=================================================================
' Form_KeyDown
' This event is triggered when you press a key.
' Hitting the ESC key will end the program.
'=================================================================
Private Sub Form_KeyDown(KeyCode As Integer, Shift As Integer)
    If KeyCode = 27 Then
        done = True
    End If
End Sub


'=================================================================
' Form_Load
' This event occurs when the form is first loaded, and is
' actually the startup form for this program.
'=================================================================
Private Sub Form_Load()
    Dim lStart As Long
    Dim lLeft As Long
    Dim lTop As Long
    Dim lRight As Long
    Dim lBottom As Long
    Dim lColor As Long
    Dim lCount As Long
```

```
'display the form before doing anything else
Me.Show
DoEvents

'keep drawing rectangles until user presses ESC
Do Until done
    'Draw rectangles using VB Line function
    lStart = GetTickCount
    lCount = 0

    'draw rectangles for 1 second
    Do While GetTickCount < lStart + 1000
        lLeft = Random(Picture1.ScaleWidth)
        lTop = Random(Picture1.ScaleHeight)
        lRight = Random(100) + 10
        lBottom = Random(100) + 10
        lColor = RGB(Random(255), Random(255), Random(255))
        Picture1.DrawWidth = 1
        Picture1.Line (lLeft, lTop)-(lRight, lBottom), lColor, B
        lCount = lCount + 1
    Loop

    'display results of test
    Label3.Caption = lCount & " rectangles/second"
    lCount = 0
    DoEvents

    'Draw rectangles using PolyLine API function
    lStart = GetTickCount
    lCount = 0

    'draw rectangles for 1 second
    Do While GetTickCount < lStart + 1000
        lLeft = Random(Picture2.ScaleWidth)
        lTop = Random(Picture2.ScaleHeight)
        lRight = Random(100) + 10
        lBottom = Random(100) + 10
        lColor = RGB(Random(255), Random(255), Random(255))
        Picture2.DrawWidth = 1
        DrawRect lLeft, lTop, lRight, lBottom, lColor
        lCount = lCount + 1
    Loop
```

```
        'display results of test
        Label4.Caption = lCount & " rectangles/second"
        lCount = 0
        DoEvents
    Loop

    'when user presses ESC, the loop is broken
    End
End Sub
```

Drawing Fast Circles

Figure 4.6 shows the Circles program, which compares the VB `Circle` procedure with the `Ellipse` API function. As you can see from the figure, the VB function is drawing 18,864 circles per second and the API function is drawing 19,758, demonstrating that the API function is about five percent faster than the VB function.

Again, note that this is an unoptimized use of the API function, since the `CreatePen` and `DeleteObject` functions increase the overhead of the API code when called repeatedly. A more effective use would be to move the custom pen code into a class or possibly into the `Form_Load` and `Form_Unload` events, so that the pen isn't created and destroyed thousands of times per second.

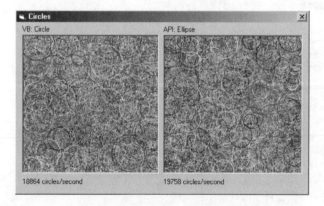

Figure 4.6

The Circles program benchmarks the VB Circle *and* Ellipse *API functions.*

Creating the Circles Program

To create this program yourself, start a new project and resize the form so that Width = 7600 and Height = 4600. Set ScaleMode = 3 – Pixel and KeyPreview = True. Now add two PictureBox controls to the form, Picture1 and Picture2. For each PictureBox, set ScaleMode = 3, Width = 230, and

Height = 230. Add a label above each PictureBox called Label1 and Label2. Add another label below each PictureBox called Label3 and Label4. For each Label control, set AutoSize = True.

Source Code for the Circles Program

Following is the source code for the Circles program. Simply type this code into the code module for Form1. To quickly jump to the code module, double-click the form.

```
'=================================================================
' Visual Basic Game Programming With DirectX
' Chapter 4 : Getting To Know The Windows API
' Circles Program Source Code
'=================================================================


Option Explicit
Option Base 0

'Windows API function declarations
Private Declare Function GetTickCount Lib "kernel32" () As Long

Private Declare Function CreatePen Lib "gdi32" _
    (ByVal nPenStyle As Long, ByVal nWidth As Long, _
    ByVal crColor As Long) As Long

Private Declare Function SelectObject Lib "gdi32" _
    (ByVal hDC As Long, ByVal hObject As Long) As Long

Private Declare Function DeleteObject Lib "gdi32" _
    (ByVal hObject As Long) As Long

Private Declare Function Ellipse Lib "gdi32" ( _
    ByVal hDC As Long, ByVal X1 As Long, ByVal Y1 As Long, _
    ByVal X2 As Long, ByVal Y2 As Long) As Long

'global variables
Dim done As Boolean
Dim hPen As Long
Dim hOldPen As Long


'=================================================================
' Random
```

```vb
' Generate a random number from 0 to num using Rnd
'====================================================================
Public Function Random(ByVal num As Long) As Long
    Random = CLng(num * Rnd)
End Function

Public Sub DrawEllipse(ByVal lLeft As Long, ByVal lTop As Long, _
    ByVal lRight As Long, ByVal lBottom As Long, ByVal lColor As Long)

    hPen = CreatePen(0, 1, lColor)
    hOldPen = SelectObject(Picture2.hDC, hPen)
    Ellipse Picture2.hDC, lLeft, lTop, lRight, lBottom
    SelectObject Picture2.hDC, hOldPen
    DeleteObject hPen
End Sub


'====================================================================
' Form_KeyDown
' This event is triggered when you press a key.
' Hitting the ESC key will end the program.
'====================================================================
Private Sub Form_KeyDown(KeyCode As Integer, Shift As Integer)
    If KeyCode = 27 Then done = True
End Sub


'====================================================================
' Form_Load
' This event occurs when the form is first loaded, and is
' actually the startup form for this program.
'====================================================================
Private Sub Form_Load()
    Dim lStart As Long
    Dim lLeft As Long
    Dim lTop As Long
    Dim lColor As Long
    Dim lRadius As Long
    Dim lCount As Long

    'display the form
    Me.Show
    done = False
```

```
    'keep drawing lines until users hits ESC
    Do Until done
        'Draw circles using VB Circle function
        lStart = GetTickCount
        lCount = 0

        'draw circles for 1 second
        Do While GetTickCount < lStart + 1000
            lLeft = Random(Picture1.ScaleWidth)
            lTop = Random(Picture1.ScaleHeight)
            lColor = RGB(Random(255), Random(255), Random(255))
            lRadius = Random(20) + 10
            Picture1.DrawWidth = 1
            Picture1.Circle (lLeft, lTop), lRadius, lColor
            lCount = lCount + 1
        Loop

        'display results of the test
        Label3.Caption = lCount & " circles/second"
        lCount = 0
        DoEvents

        'Draw circles using the Ellipse API function
        lStart = GetTickCount
        lCount = 0

        'draw circles for 1 second
        Do While GetTickCount < lStart + 1000
            lLeft = Random(Picture2.ScaleWidth)
            lTop = Random(Picture2.ScaleHeight)
            lColor = RGB(Random(255), Random(255), Random(255))
            lRadius = Random(20) + 10
            Picture2.DrawWidth = 1
            DrawEllipse lLeft - lRadius, lTop - lRadius, lLeft + lRadius, lTop +
lRadius, lColor
            lCount = lCount + 1
        Loop

        'display results of the test
        Label4.Caption = lCount & " circles/second"
```

```
        lCount = 0
        DoEvents
    Loop

    'when loop exits, the program ends
    End
End Sub
```

Drawing Fast Bitmaps

The key to game programming on any platform is the ability to load and display bitmap images in the game, whether it runs in 2-D or 3-D. The source bitmaps can be stored in any graphics file format, and VB even supports several of them, including BMP, GIF, and JPG.

Figure 4.7 shows the Bitmaps program, which compares the intrinsic PaintPicture procedure with the Windows API BitBlt function. As you can see from the figure, the VB function is drawing 6,662 bitmaps per second, while the API function is drawing 36,055 bitmaps per second, demonstrating that the API function is about 550 percent faster! This is by far the most significant example for the speed of the API functions, and is even more significant when you consider that bitmaps are far more important to game programming than points, lines, or circles.

TIP

Keep in mind that GIF and JPG files are compressed, which is not a good format for game graphics that were edited on a pixel-by-pixel basis. For game graphics, it is a good idea to stick with an uncompressed format, such as BMP.

NOTE

I'll cover bitmaps and sprites in more detail in later chapters. For now, I will stick to showing you *what* is happening, and I'll explain *how* at a later time.

Creating the Bitmaps Program

To create this program yourself, start a new project and resize the form so that Width = 7600 and Height = 4600. Set ScaleMode = 3 – Pixel and KeyPreview = True. Now add two PictureBox controls to the form, Picture1 and Picture2. For each PictureBox, set ScaleMode = 3, Width = 230, and Height = 230. Add a label above each PictureBox called Label1 and Label2. Add another label below each PictureBox called Label3 and Label4. For each Label control, set AutoSize = True.

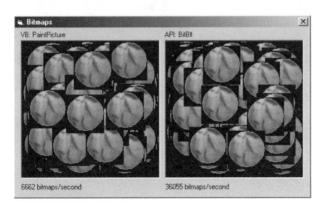

Figure 4.7

The Bitmaps program compares `PaintPicture` *to* `BitBlt`.

Add a third PictureBox called picSource and place it below Label3 so that it is not visible on the form. For picSource, set ScaleMode = 3, AutoRedraw = True, and AutoSize = True. The colorball.bmp image will be loaded into picSource when the program starts running, as long as the file is located in the same directory as Bitmaps.exe (or the project file, if you are running it from within the IDE).

I did notice an anomaly with this program when I was running it on extremely fast computers (particularly one with a good video card). The 1,000-millisecond delay is actually missed because the `BitBlt` function is running so fast. If you get erratic results from this program, simply change the 1,000-millisecond delay to 5,000, and then divide lCount by 5 when displaying the results—this should provide a cleaner result.

> **NOTE**
>
> In Chapter 7, "Break Out the Bitmaps," I will show you how to load a bitmap directly into memory so that there is no need for a PictureBox at all! Until then, the PictureBox helps you keep the source code listing much shorter.

Source Code for the Bitmaps Program

Following is the source code for the Bitmaps program. Simply type this code into the code module for Form1. To quickly jump to the code module, double-click the form.

```
'===========================================================================
' Visual Basic Game Programming With DirectX
' Chapter 4 : Getting To Know The Windows API
' Bitmaps Program Source Code
'===========================================================================
```

```vb
Option Explicit
Option Base 0

'Windows API constants
Private Const SRCCOPY = &HCC0020

'Windows API functions
Private Declare Function GetTickCount Lib "kernel32" () As Long

'fast bit-block transfer function
Private Declare Function BitBlt Lib "gdi32" ( _
    ByVal hDestDC As Long, _
    ByVal X As Long, _
    ByVal Y As Long, _
    ByVal nWidth As Long, _
    ByVal nHeight As Long, _
    ByVal hSrcDC As Long, _
    ByVal xSrc As Long, _
    ByVal ySrc As Long, _
    ByVal dwRop As Long) As Long

'program variables
Dim done As Boolean

'================================================================
' Random
' Generate a random number from 0 to num using Rnd
'================================================================
Public Function Random(ByVal num As Long) As Long
    Random = CLng(num * Rnd)
End Function

'================================================================
' Form_KeyDown
' This event is triggered when you press a key.
'================================================================
Private Sub Form_KeyDown(KeyCode As Integer, Shift As Integer)
    ' Hitting the ESC key will end the program
    If KeyCode = 27 Then done = True
End Sub
```

```vb
'===============================================================
' Form_Load
' This event occurs when the program starts running.
'===============================================================
Private Sub Form_Load()
    Dim lStart As Long
    Dim lLeft As Long
    Dim lTop As Long
    Dim lColor As Long
    Dim lCount As Long

    'display the form
    Me.Show
    DoEvents
    done = False

    'load the source picture
    picSource.Picture = LoadPicture(App.Path & "\colorball.bmp")

    'keep drawing until user presses ESC
    Do Until done
        'draw bitmaps using PaintPicture
        lCount = 0
        lStart = GetTickCount

        'draw bitmaps for 1 second
        Do While GetTickCount < lStart + 5000
            lLeft = Random(Picture1.ScaleWidth - picSource.ScaleWidth)
            lTop = Random(Picture1.ScaleHeight - picSource.ScaleHeight)
            lColor = RGB(Random(256), Random(256), Random(256))
            Picture1.PaintPicture picSource.Picture, _
                lLeft, lTop, _
                picSource.ScaleWidth, picSource.ScaleHeight, _
                0, 0, _
                picSource.ScaleWidth, picSource.ScaleHeight, _
                SRCCOPY
            lCount = lCount + 1
        Loop

        'display results of test
        Label3.Caption = lCount \ 5 & " bitmaps/second"
```

```
            lCount = 0
            DoEvents

            'draw bitmaps using BitBlt
            lCount = 0
            lStart = GetTickCount

            'draw bitmaps for 1 second
            Do While GetTickCount < lStart + 5000
                lLeft = Random(Picture2.ScaleWidth - picSource.ScaleWidth)
                lTop = Random(Picture2.ScaleHeight - picSource.ScaleHeight)
                lColor = RGB(Random(256), Random(256), Random(256))
                BitBlt Picture2.hDC, lLeft, lTop, _
                    picSource.ScaleWidth, picSource.ScaleHeight, _
                    picSource.hDC, 0, 0, SRCCOPY
                lCount = lCount + 1
            Loop

            'display results of test
            Label4.Caption = lCount \ 5 & " bitmaps/second"
            lCount = 0
            DoEvents
        Loop

        'when loop exits, end program
        End
End Sub
```

IDENTIFYING THE HOST SYSTEM

There are many different versions of the Windows operating system, not all of which are 100 percent compatible with the rest. To ensure that your code will run on as many systems as possible, it is a good idea to identify any incompatibilities that might exist and work around them.

For instance, Windows 98 and later versions include an API function called `TransparentBlt` that can be used to draw a bitmap transparently. Unfortunately, this function does not exist on Windows 95 or Windows NT 4.0. While you can always state the system requirements for a game, you should also try to support older operating systems if possible, and try not to let a single missing function prevent the game from running. Usually you will want to resort to the lowest common denominator when working on a game. This means using only functions that you know for sure will work on every system.

So, how might you detect the version of Windows running? There are hundreds of functions in the Windows API, as you have learned, and some of them are reserved for identifying the system. I'll show you some of these API functions and how to use them, since this code might be useful for working around issues with older versions of Windows. The sample program called SystemInfo (also included on the CD-ROM) demonstrates all of these system-identification API functions, and is shown in Figure 4.8.

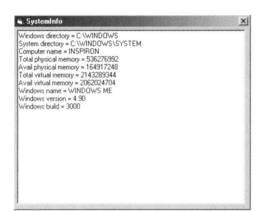

Figure 4.8

The SystemInfo program displays information about the host computer system.

Windows and System Directories

There might be times when you'll need to know exactly where Windows was installed. The C:\Windows default might not always be used on every system, so if you hard-code that directory into a game to save settings or for any other reason, the program might not work. You should first find out where the Windows directory is located. Two API functions help in this case: GetWindowsDirectory and GetSystemDirectory. The function declaration for GetWindowsDirectory looks like this:

```
Private Declare Function GetWindowsDirectory Lib "kernel32" _
    Alias "GetWindowsDirectoryA" ( _
    ByVal lpBuffer As String, _
    ByVal nSize As Long _
) As Long
```

And here is the function declaration for GetSystemDirectory:

```
Private Declare Function GetSystemDirectory Lib "kernel32" _
    Alias "GetSystemDirectoryA" ( _
    ByVal lpBuffer As String, _
    ByVal nSize As Long _
) As Long
```

Like many system functions, these require that you pass a fixed-length string; therefore, a standard variable-length string in VB will not work. You must first fill the string with spaces using the Space$ function, so that it has a fixed length, like this:

```
Dim temp$
temp$ = Space$(255)
```

Putting this code into a simple function that returns the directory is straightforward, as the following listing shows:

```
'return the Windows directory
Public Function GetWindowsDir() As String
    Dim temp$
    temp$ = Space$(255)
    GetWindowsDirectory temp, 255
    GetWindowsDir = temp
End Function
```

```
'return the System directory
Public Function GetSystemDir() As String
    Dim temp$
    temp$ = Space$(255)
    GetSystemDirectory temp, 255
    GetSystemDir = temp
End Function
```

Computer Name

The computer name is used to identify your PC on a network, and is found using the GetComputerName function. Don't worry about the "A" at the end of the function name; this is common in the Windows API, and it signifies that it is an ANSI function rather than a Unicode function. Unicode is the character format used by Windows NT and Windows CE, but not on Windows 95, 98, or Me (all of which use ANSI). If this sounds confusing, don't worry about it; just take my word for it that the function declarations will work.

```
Private Declare Function GetComputerNameA Lib "kernel32" ( _
    ByVal lpBuffer As String, _
    nSize As Long _
) As Long
```

Putting this function to use is a little more complicated than the `GetWindowsDir` function, because `GetComputerName` needs a string filled with zeros (the null character). First, a string is created with the `String$` function, and then it is passed to the API function. Then the last null character is stripped out before it is returned to the caller.

```
Public Function GetComputerName() As String
    Dim temp$
    Dim res&
    temp = String$(80, 0)
    res = GetComputerNameA(temp, 80)
    GetComputerName = Mid$(temp, 1, InStr(1, temp, Chr$(0)) - 1)
End Function
```

Memory Status

It is a good idea to keep track of the available memory in the system before you load large amounts of data, or before the game loop even starts if the game requires a minimum amount of memory in order to run. A single API function called `GlobalMemoryStatus` provides information about physical memory, virtual memory, and the page file.

To use `GlobalMemoryStatus`, you must declare a structure called MEMORYSTATUS and pass this as a variable to the function. Here is what the structure looks like:

```
Private Type MEMORYSTATUS
    dwLength As Long
    dwMemoryLoad As Long
    dwTotalPhys As Long
    dwAvailPhys As Long
    dwTotalPageFile As Long
    dwAvailPageFile As Long
    dwTotalVirtual As Long
    dwAvailVirtual As Long
End Type
```

The `GlobalMemoryStatus` function itself is a simple function declaration that requires a single parameter—a variable declared as MEMORYSTATUS. The function then fills the structure with information about system memory.

```
Private Declare Sub GlobalMemoryStatus Lib "kernel32" ( _
    lpBuffer As MEMORYSTATUS _
)
```

Before calling the `GlobalMemoryStatus` function, you must first set the length of the structure using the dwLength element. It seems kind of strange to be passing the length of something *inside* that something, but that's how it works! You determine the length of MEMORYSTATUS by simply using the `Len` function.

Following is a series of functions that retrieve individual values from the MEMORYSTATUS structure and return those values as Longs. The format of each function is the same, and only the specific element (or variable) of the structure is returned. Once again, you can refer to the SystemInfo program to see these functions in action.

```
Public Function GetTotalPhysicalMemory() As Long
    Dim ms As MEMORYSTATUS
    ms.dwLength = Len(ms)
    GlobalMemoryStatus ms
    GetTotalPhysicalMemory = ms.dwTotalPhys
End Function


Public Function GetAvailPhysicalMemory() As Long
    Dim ms As MEMORYSTATUS
    ms.dwLength = Len(ms)
    GlobalMemoryStatus ms
    GetAvailPhysicalMemory = ms.dwAvailPhys
End Function


Public Function GetTotalVirtualMemory() As Long
    Dim ms As MEMORYSTATUS
    ms.dwLength = Len(ms)
    GlobalMemoryStatus ms
    GetTotalVirtualMemory = ms.dwTotalVirtual
End Function


Public Function GetAvailVirtualMemory() As Long
    Dim ms As MEMORYSTATUS
    ms.dwLength = Len(ms)
    GlobalMemoryStatus ms
    GetAvailVirtualMemory = ms.dwAvailVirtual
End Function
```

Windows Version

The version of Windows that is running on your computer can allow your program to behave differently depending on the version name and number. The version information is stored in a structure called OSVERSIONINFO, which looks like this:

```
Private Type OSVERSIONINFO
    dwOSVersionInfoSize As Long
    dwMajorVersion As Long
    dwMinorVersion As Long
    dwBuildNumber As Long
    dwPlatformId As Long
    szCSDVersion As String * 128
End Type
```

The key function that returns this information is called GetVersionEx, and is simple enough to understand. Simply set the dwOSVersionInfoSize element to the length of the structure and then pass the OSVERSIONINFO variable to the function. This works on the same principle as the GlobalMemoryStatus function.

Following is a list of functions for identifying the name, version, and build of Windows running on a computer.

```
Public Function GetWindowsCore() As String
    Dim win As OSVERSIONINFO
    Dim ret As Long

    win.dwOSVersionInfoSize = Len(win)
    ret = GetVersionEx(win)

    Select Case win.dwPlatformId
        'Windows 3.1 core
        Case 0
            GetWindowsCore = "32"

        'Windows 95 core
        Case 1
            GetWindowsCore = "95"
```

```
                'Windows NT core
                Case 2
                    GetWindowsCore = "NT"
        End Select
End Function

Public Function GetWindowsName() As String
    Dim win As OSVERSIONINFO
    Dim ret As Long
    Dim lBuild As Long

    win.dwOSVersionInfoSize = Len(win)
    ret = GetVersionEx&(win)
    lBuild = GetWindowsBuild

    Select Case GetWindowsCore
        Case "32"
            GetWindowsName = "WIN32S"

        Case "95"
            If lBuild >= 3000 Then
                GetWindowsName = "WINDOWS ME"
            ElseIf lBuild >= 1998 Then
                GetWindowsName = "WINDOWS 98"
            Else
                GetWindowsName = "WINDOWS 95"
            End If

        Case "NT"
            If lBuild >= 3000 Then
                GetWindowsName = "WINDOWS XP"
            ElseIf lBuild >= 2000 Then
                GetWindowsName = "WINDOWS 2000"
            Else
                GetWindowsName = "WINDOWS NT"
            End If
    End Select
End Function
```

```
Public Function GetWindowsVersion() As String
    Dim win As OSVERSIONINFO
    Dim ret As Long

    win.dwOSVersionInfoSize = Len(win)
    ret = GetVersionEx&(win)
    GetWindowsVersion = win.dwMajorVersion & "." & win.dwMinorVersion
End Function

Public Function GetWindowsBuild() As Long
    Dim win As OSVERSIONINFO
    Dim ret As Long

    win.dwOSVersionInfoSize = Len(win)
    ret = GetVersionEx&(win)
    GetWindowsBuild = CLng(Trim(Str(win.dwBuildNumber And &HFFFF&)))
End Function
```

SUMMARY

This chapter introduced the Windows API and showed you how to use it to enhance Visual Basic, both in functionality and in performance. VB offers many features and is a highly versatile language. However, it is important to recognize that VB lacks some features needed for serious game development. You can certainly write a game using only the features built into VB, but to maximize the potential of your games, the Windows API is a necessity.

It is a given that DirectX will eclipse the Windows API functions in this book, but there might be times when you would rather just work with more traditional Windows functions like BitBlt and avoid DirectX for one reason or another. In such cases, it is important to have a fast library of functions for writing games without DirectX—this is where the Windows API comes in. It is truly a great way to enhance VB, as the benchmark programs demonstrated.

The next chapter goes a step further by showing you how to optimize VB even more, in order to get the most out of the language with as little overhead as possible. By using efficient variables and object-oriented features such as inheritance, and configuring projects for optimum speed, you can eke out every last ounce of horsepower available to VB and provide the means to create high-speed games with very little overhead.

CHAPTER 5

OPTIMIZING VISUAL BASIC WITH OBJECTS

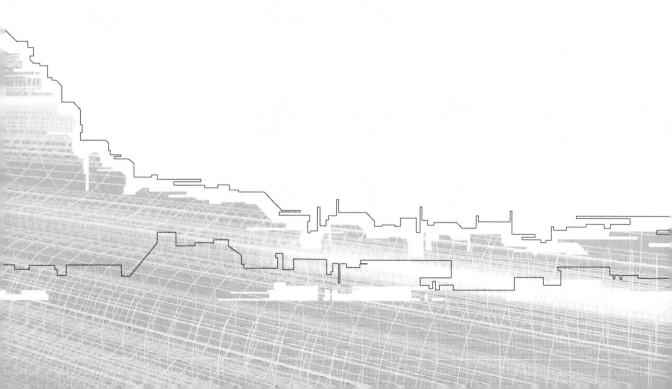

This chapter will help you get the absolute most out of Visual Basic by showing you some techniques for optimizing your programs. By following some simple techniques, you will get a lot more performance out of your code. In addition, there are some compiler options that you can set that also affect performance. I will show you how to optimize the compiler for speed while still maintaining stability. Along the way, I will also show you a sample program that demonstrates the difference between sloppy code and efficient code by benchmarking the differences in performance between the different variable data types.

To keep your programs running without interruption, you also need to take measures to handle errors that might occur when a program is running. I will explain the ins and outs of error handling and how and why you must trap all of the potential errors in a game.

Finally, I'll give you a crash course in object-oriented programming by introducing the basic concepts and showing you how the overall design of a game can be greatly influenced by a simple object-oriented design from the start.

This chapter covers the following topics:

- Designing for Efficiency
- Optimizing Visual Basic Code
- Keeping Track of Errors
- Setting Compiler Options
- Object-Oriented Programming

DESIGNING FOR EFFICIENCY

In Chapter 4, "Getting to Know the Windows API," I showed you how to drastically improve VB's graphics capabilities by tapping into Windows API functions like `SetPixel`, `LineTo`, and `Ellipse`, in addition to support functions like `GetTickCount`. These API functions gave you a glimpse of the capabilities of the Windows API, and how it can be used to speed up VB.

DirectX will add even more power to your game programming toolbox and will help speed up the sprite-handling code (which I will discuss in Chapter 8, "Supersonic Sprites"). In fact, DirectX does most of the difficult work for you by providing you with easy-to-use functions. However, it is not always clear what some of the DirectX functions do or how to set up the structures that they need. Custom DirectX classes will take care of the gritty details for you in later chapters, but you must consider how much overhead the game library adds to the code. After all, isn't it more important to get the highest frame rate possible, even at the expense of elegant code?

I would have to say no, not always.

Unless code is ridiculously bureaucratic—full of useless overhead and seldom-used features—you shouldn't worry about adding a level of wrapper code to a bunch of functions and structures that would be difficult to use on their own. The time required to pass one function call through another is a few nanoseconds, while the amount of time saved by readable code can be immense.

When you write code, think of the big picture and try not to get bogged down in the details of a single function. If a short snippet of code is problematic, it probably needs to be broken down into smaller, more manageable pieces. If you follow this technique, even the most complicated programming problem is manageable.

More importantly, the problem can be delegated. The strength of a well-designed object-oriented program is that it can be written and revised by more than one person. When you design a program with an object-oriented methodology, you are really describing how multiple components can be assembled to complete the program. This is a powerful programming technique when utilized correctly. If you design an object-oriented system for the sake of using objects and not to solve problems, then you are going about it for all the wrong reasons!

An object-oriented program is not a complicated program, although that is often what happens when hard-core C programmers get their hands on a C++ compiler. Instead of creating the solution to a problem, many programmers force a solution into their limited concept of it. My design paradigm of sorts is to just write straightforward and simple code. I believe in assembling simple solutions to conquer complex problems—and almost every game is a complex programming problem.

Forcing the Solution to Fit Your Mold

For example, suppose you want to draw random points on the screen, like the ChunkyPixels program from Chapter 3, "Visual Basic Programming in a Nutshell." It is a fairly simple program that could have been written several hundred thousand different ways, including the way I wrote it. At first glance, how would you do it?

Closed-Minded Solutions

C++ Solution. A hard-core C++ enthusiast will immediately design a Point class. This class will be awesome, filled with every conceivable private, public, and protected variable and function that you would ever possibly need. Better yet, a C++ programmer will design a Base_Point class and then extend it through inheritance into a Point class, which can then be extended to 3DPoint down the road. These functions will draw the point to any surface, retrieve the current point value, move the point around on the screen, change the color of the point, and clone the point into another point. There will also be several dozen variants of the Draw function, written to accept any conceivable data type imaginable, from an array index to a POINT API structure to a string containing comma-separated point values—all declared as Virtual so that the class can be enhanced down the road.

Assembly Solution. An Assembly programmer will immediately set to work encoding the memory locations of every video mode ever conceived (going back to the days of CGA graphics) and painstakingly writing the code to plot a pixel in any resolution and at any bit depth. The code will run extremely fast, because it will be optimized to use 32-bit registers, capable of holding a single 32-bit color value. Points are plotted directly into video memory with a single 4-byte burst, all in less than a single CPU clock cycle.

C Solution. A C programmer will create a library (LIB) module with several dozen functions, each of which is designed to manipulate a point in one way or another. This will include geometric translation and rotation, fractal generation, and every other 2-D mathematical operation you can imagine. All of this will be creatively crammed into a source code file only 30 lines long, thanks to single-character variable names.

Java Solution. A Java programmer will first start with the server application, which might be called Java Pixel Server, or JPS. The server will be able to handle 150 million points per second and will fully support multithreading. The client code will parse the server across a TCP/IP socket connection for a point value and then set up a queue of pixels that are received from the server. The highly optimized JIT (*Just-In-Time*) compiler will generate code that is capable of transmitting the entire back buffer for each screen refresh in real time, while still maintaining 30 frames per second. The real benefit to this solution is that it will run on almost any computer, including the popular Web browsers, without recompilation. Although the solution might have only called for the ability to draw a single point, the Java programmer will argue that all of the additional features would eventually be needed anyway, and then point out how neat it will be to host the pixel server on a mainframe.

Cobol Solution. A Cobol programmer will start by drawing the image of a video screen on print layout paper and then determining exactly where the pixel will be plotted. The code will describe the pixel and define exactly how many spaces will be required from the top and the left side of the screen in order to draw the pixel. The program will then be able to print out a version of the screen where the pixel is represented by an asterisk.

Linux Solution. A Linux programmer, using the GCC compiler, will borrow the code developed for the C++ Solution (above), and then announce a new open-source Point Graphics Library (PointGL) that conforms to the General Public License (GPL). The project will then be shared across all of the relevant newsgroups and programming Web sites, and interested coders will contribute their own ideas to PointGL. In time, several large companies will begin to support their own versions of PointGL, and wars will be fought over which version is the real version, while the original author maintains the PointGL core.

Visual Basic Solution. A Visual Basic programmer will likely start by designing an ActiveX custom control called Point. The control will have a resizable surface that represents the draw width of the point and properties for the Location and Color. The control might then be compiled and registered on an ActiveX transaction server for distributed Pointing. Point data will then be shared between multiple applications using XML (*Extensible Markup Language*). To draw multiple points, of course, all you would have to do is create a Point control array and use the Load command to launch a new point on the main form of the test program when you need it. (Ack!)

The Ideal Solution

Sarcasm and jest aside, the ideal solution to a problem is one that solves the problem with the least amount of effort and the greatest amount of efficiency. The wrong solution is one that takes advantage of the latest and greatest technology for the sole purpose of showing off that technology.

Figure 5.1 visually demonstrates the concept that forcing a solution to fit your mold—your potentially limited viewpoint, based on familiarity with a language or operating system—often leads to difficulty.

> **TIP**
>
> The ideal solution to a problem is the one that solves the problem with the least amount of effort and the greatest amount of efficiency.

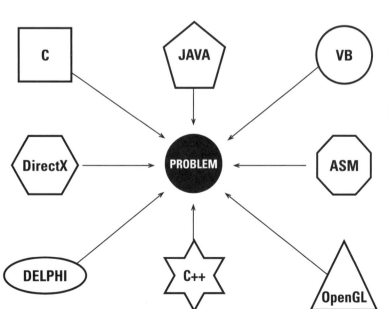

Figure 5.1

Always choose the best solution for a problem, regardless of your own preferences.

The reason there are so many different programming languages and libraries in the computer world is because every so often someone thinks of a new way to solve a problem more efficiently. It is a given that just about any programming language can be used—with varying amounts of effort—to solve just about any problem. Some languages are great for handling some problems and terrible for handling others.

For example, assembly language absolutely rocks for handling low-level stuff like the device drivers for video cards and sound cards, and for optimizing specific parts of a program. But using assembly to write a database program would be an absolute nightmare. It is just way too low-level for something like that, and I'm not sure it could even be done! (Even if you're the type who will take any dare, I still wouldn't do that to you!) At the same time, you certainly would not be able to write a video card device driver with Visual Basic. So, as you can see, there are some tradeoffs that offer no choice in the matter, while others do give you a choice.

I believe that every problem has an ideal solution. Sometimes the solution is not as sexy as another, just as some languages are not as sexy as others. SQL (*Structured Query Language*) comes to mind. This language has a singular purpose in that it is used for database programming. SQL is actually a pseudo-language that is recognized by database servers. You would not actually be able to write a whole application using SQL; it is merely a way to load and save data and do interesting things with it in the process. Now, given that SQL is the de facto standard for writing database queries, you should use it any time you need to work with a database. Using any other solution (such as XML) just because it is more interesting is foolish and foolhardy.

The C++ Language

At the other end of the spectrum is the original C++ language. Okay, look, I'm a huge fan of VB, and I use it every day. VB is my favorite language. I don't use C++ every day. But how can anyone deny that C++ is awesome? DirectX was written with C++. Visual Basic was written with C++ (gasp!). I'm not talking about all the extras that Microsoft stuffed into Visual C++. I'm talking about pure C++, the original language that was created by Bjarn Stoustrup. C++ is, without a doubt, the supermodel of programming languages.

After you're done writing a few killer games in VB, check out some of the other books in the Premier Press Game Development Series that focus on C++. I highly recommend *Multiplayer Game Programming* and *The Zen of Direct3D Game Programming*. If anything, you will find ways to enhance VB through components built using Visual C++.

When it comes to Visual Basic, I would abstract the concept outward a little and consider solutions within the language. (After all, the point of this book is to present programming solutions for game development with VB.) You have the intrinsic support within VB, the Windows API support, and then DirectX. Actually, there are two versions of DirectX supported by VB—DirectX 7.0 and DirectX 8.0. These two versions are sufficiently different that they could be considered separate solutions. DirectX 8.0 is a radical change in the architecture of DirectX and is not really compatible with earlier versions. Regardless, consider the type of game you would like to write and decide which way to go.

> **NOTE**
> Some of this discussion has revolved around game design, which is more fully discussed in the chapters that make up Part IV, "Complete Game Projects."

The Importance of Declaring Variables

The use of Windows API functions or DirectX is a waste of time if the rest of your VB code is slow and poorly written. VB is great in that it allows you to declare variables without a data type, like this:

```
Dim MyNumber
```

But this convenience comes at a cost. Undeclared variables default to the Variant data type, which is capable of treating the variable as any type, such as String, Long, Double, and Date, among others. Most likely, VB won't convert a Variant to a specific data type when you compile the program, because Variants are supposed to work no matter what value you assign them, and it is impossible for VB to determine ahead of time whether the variable will remain a specific data type or will need to be changed for new data that is encountered.

> **TIP**
> Think of a Variant as a late-bound variable.

Any time you declare a variable, be sure to specifically assign the data type to that variable. Most often, I use Longs when dealing with numbers, as opposed to Integers, because Longs can hold larger numbers and have about the same performance as Integers (and might even be faster in some cases). If you have come to VB from another language, such as C++, you might be tempted to declare the most efficient variable possible (such as Byte). However, I believe it is better to be consistent throughout the code by sticking to only a few data types. String, Long, and Byte are the most common variable types you will need for a game.

Proof of Concept: The SpeedTest Program

I suspect that you want some proof regarding the performance differences of variable types! I don't blame you. because you are a game programmer and you want to see something before you will believe it (as was the case the first time I heard about the graphics in *Homeworld*).

To satiate your endless craving for examples, I have written a short program that iterates through a series of tight loops (so tight that your PC will seem to freeze up momentarily) and shows the difference between using a Variant and using the other intrinsic data types. By running a test over and over again in a loop and then dividing the run time by the loop count, you can narrow down the time it takes to perform each operation, where it would be otherwise impossible to check. If you think about it, how would you calculate the time it takes to add two numbers in code? It would happen so fast that no timer could possibly trace it. So the solution is repetition and long loops, wrapped with calls to GetTickCount.

If you run through the loop many times, you can actually get back results in the *nanosecond* range (one-thousandth of a millisecond, equal to a billionth of a second!). If you're hoping to get some *picosecond* (trillionth of a second) results, better borrow some time on the supercomputer, ASCI White, because your PC is probably not up to the challenge.

This program, which is called SpeedTest, will use the GetTickCount API function to benchmark the time for each loop in the same manner as the programs in the last chapter. At the end of each loop, the resulting time is displayed for comparison. SpeedTest will be used at a few places in this chapter to test the relative performance of the data types and some various settings in VB, so I will refer to it often. The results are pretty exciting, and you will be surprised at the difference in speed after you learn how to optimize a VB project (in addition to the source code). Refer to Figure 5.2 for a glimpse of the SpeedTest program.

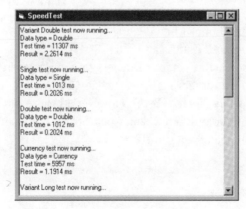

Figure 5.2

The SpeedTest program shows the performance of different variable types.

Creating the SpeedTest Program

This program is quite simple; it contains just a large TextBox on a form for displaying the results of the tests, which is a little more polite than spitting out Debug.Print lines. To get started, create a new project in the usual manner. Form1 should be included in the new project automatically. Add a single TextBox to the form (which will be called Text1) and resize the form and TextBox to a comfortable size. Change the following properties for Text1: MultiLine = True and ScrollBars = 2 - Vertical.

Now open the code window for SpeedTest and enter the following lines of code:

```vb
'===============================================================
' Visual Basic Game Programming With DirectX
' Chapter 5 : Optimizing Visual Basic With Objects
' SpeedTest Program Source Code
'===============================================================

Option Explicit
Option Base 0

'this function returns the system tick count in milliseconds
Private Declare Function GetTickCount Lib "kernel32" () As Long

'set this value higher for faster machines
Const GlobalMaxCount As Long = 5000

'global variables
Dim lLoop As Long
Dim lStartTime As Long
Dim lResult As Long
Dim dResult As Double


'===============================================================
' Form_Load
' Main startup routine for the program
'===============================================================
Private Sub Form_Load()
    Me.Caption = "SpeedTest"
    Me.Show
    Text1.Text = ""
    DoEvents
```

```
        'run the string tests
        TestStrings

        'run the integer data type tests
        TestIntegers

        'run the floating-point data type tests
        TestFloats
End Sub


'================================================================
' TestStrings
' Benchmarks the performance of the string data type
'================================================================
Private Sub TestStrings()
        Const LocalMaxCount As Long = 1000
        Dim String1 As Variant
        Dim String2 As String * 1024
        Dim String3 As String
        Dim lNum As Long
        Dim lChar As Long

        PrintText "Variant String test now running..."
        DoEvents
        lStartTime = GetTickCount
        'process one million characters
        For lLoop = 1 To GlobalMaxCount
            String1 = ""
            'add some characters to string
            For lChar = 1 To LocalMaxCount
                lNum = Random(255)
                String1 = String1 & Chr$(lNum)
            Next lChar
        Next lLoop
        lResult = GetTickCount - lStartTime
        PrintText "Data type = " & TypeName(String1)
        DisplayResults

        PrintText "Fixed-Length String test now running..."
        DoEvents
        lStartTime = GetTickCount
```

```
    'process one million characters
    For lLoop = 1 To GlobalMaxCount
        String2 = ""
        'add some characters to string
        For lChar = 1 To LocalMaxCount
            lNum = Random(255)
            String2 = String2 & Chr$(lNum)
        Next lChar
    Next lLoop
    lResult = GetTickCount - lStartTime
    PrintText "Data type = " & TypeName(String2)
    DisplayResults

    PrintText "Variable-Length String test now running..."
    DoEvents
    lStartTime = GetTickCount
    'process one million characters
    For lLoop = 1 To GlobalMaxCount
        String3 = ""
        'add some characters to string
        For lChar = 1 To LocalMaxCount
            lNum = Random(255)
            String3 = String3 & Chr$(lNum)
        Next lChar
    Next lLoop
    lResult = GetTickCount - lStartTime
    PrintText "Data type = " & TypeName(String3)
    DisplayResults
End Sub

'===================================================================
' TestIntegers
' Test the performance of integer data types
'===================================================================
Private Sub TestIntegers()
    Const LocalMaxCount As Long = 10000
    Dim Integer1 As Variant
    Dim Integer2 As Long
    Dim Integer3 As Integer
    Dim lNum As Long
```

```
PrintText "Variant Long test now running..."
DoEvents
lStartTime = GetTickCount
'process some Variants
For lLoop = 1 To GlobalMaxCount
    'start at large number to guarantee a Long
    Integer1 = 100000
    'increment variable by 1
    For lNum = 1 To LocalMaxCount
        Integer1 = Integer1 + 1
    Next lNum
Next lLoop
lResult = GetTickCount - lStartTime
PrintText "Data type = " & TypeName(Integer1)
DisplayResults

PrintText "Long test now running..."
DoEvents
lStartTime = GetTickCount
'process some Longs
For lLoop = 1 To GlobalMaxCount
    Integer2 = 0
    'increment variable by 1
    For lNum = 1 To LocalMaxCount
        Integer2 = Integer2 + 1
    Next lNum
Next lLoop
lResult = GetTickCount - lStartTime
PrintText "Data type = " & TypeName(Integer2)
DisplayResults

PrintText "Integer test now running..."
DoEvents
lStartTime = GetTickCount
'process some Integers
For lLoop = 1 To GlobalMaxCount
    Integer3 = 0
    'increment variable by 1
    For lNum = 1 To LocalMaxCount
        Integer3 = Integer3 + 1
    Next lNum
```

```
    Next lLoop
    lResult = GetTickCount - lStartTime
    PrintText "Data type = " & TypeName(Integer3)
    DisplayResults
End Sub


'==============================================================================
' TestFloats
' Test the performance of floating-point data types
'==============================================================================
Private Sub TestFloats()
    Const LocalMaxCount As Long = 10000
    Dim Float1 As Variant
    Dim Float2 As Single
    Dim Float3 As Double
    Dim Float4 As Currency
    Dim lNum As Long

    PrintText "Variant Double test now running..."
    DoEvents
    lStartTime = GetTickCount
    'process some Variants
    For lLoop = 1 To GlobalMaxCount
        'start at large number to guarantee a Double
        Float1 = 100000.1
        'increment variable by 1.5
        For lNum = 1 To LocalMaxCount
            Float1 = Float1 + 1.5
        Next lNum
    Next lLoop
    lResult = GetTickCount - lStartTime
    PrintText "Data type = " & TypeName(Float1)
    DisplayResults

    PrintText "Single test now running..."
    DoEvents
    lStartTime = GetTickCount
    'process some Singles
    For lLoop = 1 To GlobalMaxCount
        Float2 = 0
```

```
            'increment variable by 1.5
            For lNum = 1 To LocalMaxCount
                Float2 = Float2 + 1.5
            Next lNum
        Next lLoop
        lResult = GetTickCount - lStartTime
        PrintText "Data type = " & TypeName(Float2)
        DisplayResults

        PrintText "Double test now running..."
        DoEvents
        lStartTime = GetTickCount
        'process some Doubles
        For lLoop = 1 To GlobalMaxCount
            Float3 = 0
            'increment variable by 1.5
            For lNum = 1 To LocalMaxCount
                Float3 = Float3 + 1.5
            Next lNum
        Next lLoop
        lResult = GetTickCount - lStartTime
        PrintText "Data type = " & TypeName(Float3)
        DisplayResults

        PrintText "Currency test now running..."
        DoEvents
        lStartTime = GetTickCount
        'process some Doubles
        For lLoop = 1 To GlobalMaxCount
            Float4 = 0
            'increment variable by 1.5
            For lNum = 1 To LocalMaxCount
                Float4 = Float4 + 1.5
            Next lNum
        Next lLoop
        lResult = GetTickCount - lStartTime
        PrintText "Data type = " & TypeName(Float4)
        DisplayResults
End Sub
```

```
'===================================================================
' DisplayResults
' Displays the results of the last benchmark test
'===================================================================
Private Sub DisplayResults()
    PrintText "Test time = " & lResult & " ms"
    dResult = lResult / GlobalMaxCount
    PrintText "Result = " & dResult & " ms"
    PrintText ""
End Sub


'===================================================================
' Random
' Generate a random number from 0 to num using Rnd
'===================================================================
Public Function Random(ByVal num As Long) As Long
    Random = CLng(num * Rnd)
End Function


'===================================================================
' PrintText
' Add a line of text to the next line of the TextBox
'===================================================================
Private Sub PrintText(ByVal sText As String)
    Text1.Text = Text1.Text & sText & vbCrLf
End Sub
```

Benchmark Results

The SpeedTest program displays the results of each test in the TextBox, so you can copy the results out and paste them in a text file. The following listing shows the results for an unoptimized run of the program. I will refer to these results as a baseline for the other tests in this chapter. To interpret the results, just look at the data type and the result value and then compare that to other related values in the test.

For instance, compare the results of Single with Double or Long with Integer to see how these data types differ in performance. Later in this chapter, I will show you how you can modify the project settings to optimize the code (for instance, by turning off array bounds checking). I know this material is somewhat dull, but the alternative is cranking out game code without considering it. After all, as you well know, speed is everything in a game.

```
Variant String test now running...
Data type = String
Test time = 12871 ms
Result = 2.5742 ms

Fixed-Length String test now running...
Data type = String
Test time = 24593 ms
Result = 4.9186 ms

Variable-Length String test now running...
Data type = String
Test time = 12535 ms
Result = 2.507 ms

Variant Long test now running...
Data type = Long
Test time = 5525 ms
Result = 1.105 ms

Long test now running...
Data type = Long
Test time = 355 ms
Result = 0.071 ms

Integer test now running...
Data type = Integer
Test time = 415 ms
Result = 0.083 ms

Variant Double test now running...
Data type = Double
Test time = 5905 ms
Result = 1.181 ms

Single test now running...
Data type = Single
Test time = 1070 ms
Result = 0.214 ms
```

```
Double test now running...
Data type = Double
Test time = 1070 ms
Result = 0.214 ms

Currency test now running...
Data type = Currency
Test time = 3825 ms
Result = 0.765 ms
```

OPTIMIZING VISUAL BASIC CODE

Now that you have a simple but effective benchmark program (simple in that it only performs additions, but effective in that it runs quickly and calculates the time for each operation), I'll show you some techniques you can use to really speed up your code.

You have already learned that simple data types are more efficient than Variants, and some data types are much faster than others. For instance, no matter what the situation, integers will always be faster than floating-point numbers in Visual Basic. Sure, there are some cases where a highly advanced processor will have a faster FPU (*Floating-Point Unit*), but Visual Basic does not take advantage of such hardware, except possibly through the use of Windows API functions.

Now I will go over some fundamental optimizations that are critical for keeping a game running at top speed.

Stay Away from Variants

Under no circumstance should you ever use a Variant! Any time you declare a variable without a data type, Visual Basic treats that variable as a Variant. You can declare variables as Variants like this:

```
Dim Variable1
Dim Variable2 as Variant
```

The two variables, Variable1 and Variable2, will both be set up as Variants when the program is compiled. The Variant is a useful and powerful feature of VB and it does help to speed up development when you're building applications, particularly prototypes where you do not know exactly how the final program will operate. But as far as game programming goes, Variants will kill a game.

This is why I recommend that you stick to a few basic data types with which you are comfortable and keep your code consistent throughout. There might be cases where an Integer is indeed faster than a Long. If you are more comfortable using Integers, go ahead and use them. But you will run into overflow errors quite often because signed Integers are limited to 32,768 as a maximum value. In contrast, a Long has a maximum value in the billions.

> **NOTE**
>
> Another reason to avoid Variants like the plague is that VB.NET does not support them at all. The new language is strongly typed, in that you cannot declare a variable without a data type. If you plan to use VB.NET, you might as well get used to doing without Variants ahead of time.

Fast Strings, Slow Strings

Strings are particularly deadly to a game. Make sure you don't use too many Strings because it is a notoriously slow data type. Strings are fine for most uses, but take care any time you use a String inside a tight loop, because even touching a String in a loop could slow it down.

Displaying status information, like the frame rate or score, can't be avoided. But this information is displayed only once per frame (or even as slow as once per second), so there is no harm in using Strings as long as they do not adversely affect the game loop.

As the SpeedTest results show, also take care when declaring Strings. The fixed-length string (declared As String * n) is at least twice as slow as a variable-length string (declared As String).

Fast Longs, Faster Longs

Simple Longs are about twelve times (1,200 percent) faster than Variant Longs. Looking for an easy way to improve frame rates? Look for any accidental use of Variant, Single, Double, Currency, or any other data type where you intended to use a Long. VB will convert the value for you on-the-fly, which slows down the program, but does so automatically so you might not even be aware of it.

What happens when you assign a floating-point number to a Long? Most often this occurs when you assign a value that is derived from a division. In VB, there are two division operators, the forward slash (the "/" character) and the back slash (the "\" character). Traditional programming languages use the back slash for division, and VB follows suit. But VB also supports the forward slash when you're working with Integers and Longs, which is useful when you are interested in calculating the unrounded result along with the modulus. (The back slash division character automatically rounds up the result.)

Make sure you also use `Option Explicit` at the top of every source code file. Without this compiler directive, VB will default any variables automatically to Variant if they are not declared with a type. But `Option Explicit` does not catch variables that you declare without a type, only variables that are used before they are declared (if they are declared at all). I will cover `Option Explicit` in more detail later in this chapter.

Identifying Variables Using TypeName

The SpeedTest program uses a VB function called `TypeName` to display the data type used in each benchmark test and ensure that Variants are being used as intended. The `TypeName` function accepts a single parameter—the variable—and returns a string with the data type name. The data type names look exactly as you would expect (Long, String, Byte, and so on), and will even identify your own VB classes.

`TypeName` is a slow function as well, so you should only use it while debugging, or outside the game loop (which should run at quantum-level speed if possible). For reference, Table 5.1 shows the String values returned by the `TypeName` function.

Table 5.1 Variable Names Returned by TypeName

String Returned	Description
Object Type	System object or VB class name
Byte	Byte value
Integer	Integer
Long	Long integer
Single	Single-precision floating-point number
Double	Double-precision floating-point number
Currency	Currency value
Decimal	Decimal value
Date	Date value
String	String
Boolean	Boolean (true/false) value

Table 5.1 Continued

String Returned	Description
Error	Error value
Empty	Uninitialized variable
Null	Invalid variable
Object	Object
Unknown	Unknown variable
Nothing	Unreferenced object variable

Identifying Variables Using VarType

The VarType function is another useful debugging tool that will return a number representing the data type of a variable. It works in the same manner as TypeName. For your convenience, Table 5.2 shows the values of the data types returned by the VarType function.

The variable types will get even more interesting later in this chapter, when I explain how interface inheritance works. You can actually declare a variable As Object and then assign it to anything you want!

Procedures Versus Objects

C programmers often complain that object-oriented features add unnecessary overhead to a program and slow it down, when one could have written the same program just as easily without objects.

I completely disagree with that opinion. That is what you would call procedural code as opposed to object code. There's nothing quite as impressive as a well-designed object-oriented architecture behind a game—as long as it isn't overkill. It is simply wonderful to modify a game written with an OOP (*Object-Oriented Programming*) library, and it's easy to add new elements to the game as well.

Objects also allow for an unlimited amount of creativity as far as program organization and logic go. Suppose you write a function that expects a Sprite class as a parameter. You can then use interface inheritance (covered later in this chapter) to derive a new sub-class, and use the new class without modifying the function.

Table 5.2 Variable Data Types Returned by VarType

Constant	Value	Description
vbEmpty	0	Uninitialized variable
vbNull	1	Invalid variable
vbInteger	2	Integer
vbLong	3	Long integer
vbSingle	4	Single-precision floating-point number
vbDouble	5	Double-precision floating-point number
vbCurrency	6	Currency value
vbDate	7	Date value
vbString	8	String
vbObject	9	Object
vbError	10	Error value
vbBoolean	11	Boolean (true/false) value
vbVariant	12	Variant array
vbDataObject	13	Data access object
vbDecimal	14	Decimal value
vbByte	17	Byte value
vbUserDefinedType	36	Variant containing a structure (UDT)
vbArray	8192	Array

That is the key to object-oriented design—adding new classes without rewriting any of the existing code. It truly revolutionizes the way you write a game once you learn the power of OOP. The drawbacks—as far as overhead for using objects—are really negligible in VB. ActiveX controls are another matter. It is common practice to use an ActiveX control project as a placeholder for a class library. But in my experience, controls are really slow. Just accessing a property in a control adds a lot of overhead to a program, because VB must look up the reference to the control, then look up the reference to the property, and finally set or get the property value. Stick to regular classes and avoid controls at all costs in VB game programming, because controls are unwieldy, slow, and terrible!

If you come from a procedural background and do not feel comfortable with classes, you can still get along well in VB and even use the game library from this book, because once the game library is compiled and you have referenced it, the actual game code appears procedural. However, I would find it difficult to create a game library without the use of classes. A procedural library is definitely possible, and I encourage you to go that route if you are more comfortable with procedural code. However, you really can't beat the efficiency and power of OOP. I will go over the primary OOP features of VB later in this chapter.

The important thing is that you keep an open mind regarding the issue of procedural versus OOP. There are strengths and weaknesses in each architecture, but I believe the features in OOP far outweigh the limitations.

Passing Variables by Reference

A huge bottleneck most programs fall into is the amount of data that is passed from one function to another. Most of the time this data is just read by the destination function (meaning it is read-only), not actually modified. There are two ways you can pass a variable, by value (ByVal) and by reference (ByRef). Whenever you need to pass information from one function to another, be sure to pass variables by reference if possible, because it is much faster.

Passing variables by value causes all of the relevant data to be passed to the destination function, regardless of the size of that data. Passing arrays by value can be absolutely devastating to the performance of a program, and this is equally true of collections and objects as well. For simple data types (like String and Long), passing by value is the preferred method and is just as fast as passing by reference. To pass a variable by value, you use the ByVal keyword. Here is an example:

```
Public Function Random(ByVal num as Long) As Long
    Random = CLng(num * Rnd)
End Function
```

The Random function (which is something I wrote, not something built into VB) accepts a single parameter, num, as a Long passed by the value. This is the preferred method for a function of this type, because you want to be able to pass an actual number to the function. If you were to declare the Random function to accept a variable by reference, you would first have to declare a Long variable, set the variable to a number, and then pass it to the Random function so that the reference would be passed as expected. This is a waste of time, so simple data type parameters should be declared ByVal most of the time (which is the default if you leave out the ByVal or ByRef keyword).

There are many situations in which you would want to pass variables by reference using the ByRef keyword. Any time you need to pass an array, an object, or a user-defined type, you should pass it by reference. Otherwise, if you declare it by value, VB will make a byte-for-byte copy of the source data, which can be very time consuming when you're dealing with a lot of data or when it is performed in a loop. Just imagine how slow a game would be if you had to send the entire back buffer array to a blitter function, rather than just a reference to the array! A game like that would just not run at all.

> **NOTE**
> Passing a variable by reference in VB is very similar to passing a variable by reference in C++ using the ampersand (&) character.

ByRef simply passes a sort of pointer to the source data, so that when the destination (function, sub, or property) receives the reference to the object, it can modify the object directly through the reference. As far as the code is concerned, it is the same as passing by value. It is also more efficient, and the resulting changes are passed back to the calling function. In contrast, any changes made to data passed by value are discarded.

Here is an example of passing a variable by value and by reference:

```
Private Type POINT
    X As Long
    Y As Long
End Type

'passing a variable by value
Private Sub DrawPoint(ByVal MyPoint As POINT)
    Picture1.PSet (MyPoint.X, MyPoint.Y), RGB(255, 255, 255)
End Sub

'passing a variable by reference
Private Sub MovePoint(ByRef MyPoint As POINT, _
    ByVal X1 As Long, ByVal Y1 As Long)
    MyPoint.X = X1
    MyPoint.Y = Y1
End Sub

Private Sub Form_Load()
    Dim Point1 As POINT
    Point1.X = 100
    Point1.Y = 100
    DrawPoint Point1
    MovePoint Point1, 200, 200
    DrawPoint Point1
End Sub
```

Notice that the DrawPoint procedure uses ByVal for the MyPoint parameter, while the MovePoint routine uses ByRef for MyPoint. The result is that DrawPoint only uses the values in MyPoint, while MovePoint actually changes the values. This is an important distinction to remember. Not only do ByRef and ByVal affect performance, they also determine whether variables can be modified.

What happens when the first DrawPoint is called? A point should be drawn at the screen location (100,100). Then MovePoint is called, changing the values inside Point1. The second DrawPoint routine should then draw a point at (200,200), since the X and Y values have been changed.

At first glance it appears that MovePoint actually returns the variable back to Form_Load. In reality, the data inside Point1 was never actually sent to MovePoint in the first place; only a reference to Point1 was sent to MovePoint. This pointer-like behavior can be useful at times and is a powerful tool once mastered.

Variable Visibility

One of the most obvious tricks of C game programmers is to use globals to speed up program execution (a fancy phrase that relates to faster frame rates). What is a global? It is a variable that was declared, usually at the top of a source code file, and has scope—or visibility—throughout the program. In contrast, variables declared inside a function are only visible inside that function and are discarded when the function returns. Global variables retain their values throughout the entire run of the program and are only discarded when the program ends.

Global. The real benefit of globals is that they do not need to be declared while the program is running, which can be time consuming in the primary game loop. It is good to keep the scope of variables under control when they are only used by a single function, and it is also good to keep the number of globals to a minimum. But keep in mind that globals directly affect the size of the program in memory. Using numerous, large global variables can bloat a program unnecessarily.

The Global keyword in VB actually refers to project scope rather than module scope. When you declare a variable within a form, it will be visible only within that form, and in a limited fashion it is global only in the form's code module. Therefore, you cannot use the Global keyword in a form module, but only a code module.

Private. Declaring variables with the Private keyword causes them to retain visibility only within the current module. This is particularly useful for classes when you would like to hide the data in a class and provide accessors (properties, subs, or functions) to the data. This technique is called encapsulation, and will be discussed later in this chapter.

Public. Declaring variables with the Public keyword causes them to be visible to all modules in a project, and allows them to be read and modified from anywhere in a program. Public variables are similar to global variables, but globals are visible throughout the project while publics require that you use the module name with a period in front when accessing them from other modules.

For instance, if you have two forms in a project (Form1 and Form2) and you declare public variables in each, you can access the public variables with the dot operator like this: Form1.MyVariable and Form2.MyVariable. A global variable, on the other hand, would not need the dot operator or module name in front.

Friend. The `Friend` keyword is sort of a combination of public and private. Friend variables are visible within a project, but retain private visibility outside the project. Since global and public variables are visible outside a project (for instance, an ActiveX in-process server, such as the one that the game library will be built upon in Chapter 13, "Building the DirectX Game Library"), this is not always desirable. After all, there might be procedures in the game library that need to be able to see a variable in another module, but allowing code outside the project to modify such a variable could be disastrous to the program.

Friend variables are often overlooked during the development of a software project or game because many projects are built without foresight. Sure, there are a million ways to solve a programming problem, but looking ahead usually allows you to foresee the need for friend variables. This is one of the reasons why game design is such an important subject and will be covered later in the book in great detail, along with several full-blown games.

Writing Efficient Loops

The primary loop in a game is the engine that keeps it running in real time, tracking events, ticking off milliseconds for timing, animating the objects on the screen, and so on. Without the primary game loop, a game is really just an application!

As you can imagine—or might already know from experience—the primary game loop must run at absolute blazing, relativistic speed (or something like that). With any particular programming language, this means basically as fast as it can go, no holds barred. After everything is said and done, timing does come into play, and you must keep a game running at a stable frame rate. However, before the back buffer is blitted to the screen (thus marking the end of a single frame) there should be no limitation on the processing speed of the loop.

The primary loop must call all of the processes in a game (such as updating graphics, physics, collision detection, and artificial intelligence), and each of these processes suck the life out of the frame rate. There are a couple different types of loops that you can use in VB.

- **For...Next Loop**. This loop is great when you know exactly how many iterations you want to run through, but it isn't the best choice for a game loop because it has an ending point, and a game loop should be an endless loop.
- **Do Loop**. The Do loop has two different forms, using either the While or Until keywords. The loop condition can be tested either before or after the enclosed code. Performing the condition at the end of the loop ensures that the code will run at least

once. Performing the condition first means that the enclosed code might not run at all. The four forms of the Do loop are as follows:

```
Do While True
Loop

Do Until False
Loop

Do
Loop While True

Do
Loop Until False
```

Usually you will use a Boolean variable for the true/false test. That way, you can set the Boolean from anywhere in the program in order to end the program. Here is an example of what a primary game loop might look like:

```
Private Sub MainLoop()
    Static lNewTime As Long
    Do While bRunning
        lCounter = GetTickCount() - lStartTime
        If lCounter > lNewTime Then
            Process_Game_Loop
            lNewTime = lCounter + FrameRate
        End If
        DoEvents
    Loop
End Sub
```

Notice how much of the code involves timing! Keeping track of the timing within the game loop allows you to focus on more interesting things in the actual game (such as animation). There are also a few global variables shown in this game loop, which are declared elsewhere in the program.

Testing the Executable

One of the biggest mistakes you can make in VB is assuming that performance during interpreted runtime will be the same as the performance of the compiled executable. Nothing could be farther from the truth!

Compiled executables in VB have a lot of native executable code that speeds them up like crazy. Don't even bother timing a program running in the IDE! It's great for rapid development, but every once in a while you should compile the program and then run it from outside VB to see the actual performance. There are a lot of settings that affect the resulting compiled executable, and these settings are ignored until you compile the program into an executable.

KEEPING TRACK OF ERRORS

VB has an annoying habit of displaying error messages in the middle of a game even for the most trivial errors—if they are not handled. VB is a powerful compiler, but obviously it does not know the difference between a game and an application, so it just throws error messages all over the place, even when you have a high-speed game loop running.

That pretty much messes up a game, and the person playing it will probably become irritated. Therefore, it is critical that you handle all errors in a game and prevent VB from displaying any error messages. Here is an example of a simple error handler:

```
Private Sub Form_Load()
    'trap any errors that might occur
    On Error GoTo error_handler

    'do some stuff
    Debug.Print "Form_Load is running"

    'exit before error handler
    Exit Sub

error_handler:
    'take care of the error
    If HandleError(Err.Number) Then
        Resume Next
    End If
End Sub
```

The code following the error_handler label should be a call to the central error handling routine (or even class) that determines whether errors are critical or trivial. Only the most heinous error should bring down a game. This is called a crash, and it really harms the reputation of the game. Some errors result from hardware or operating system failure and cannot be helped. In the preceding code listing, if HandleError returns True, then the error was handled properly and the code can resume running following the line that generated the error (using the Resume Next statement).

Other errors, such as missing images or sound files for the game, should be detected at program startup, and an error message should be displayed before the game loop starts running. Even the most trivial operation can generate an error, so you should always trap errors using code similar to the preceding listing.

Using Option Explicit

The `Option Explicit` compiler directive should be present at the beginning of every source code module in a program because it enforces the declaration of variables. Even if you declare a variable without a type (which defaults to Variant), that is sufficient to satisfy the requirements of `Option Explicit`.

Of course, `Option Explicit` is completely voluntary and you can write programs without it. Your programs might even work flawlessly, if you have developed good programming habits. But why not take advantage of every opportunity that VB has to offer? `Option Explicit` might catch an elusive bug that could take hours to track down. I recommend that you avoid the possibility and simply use it.

Using Option Base N

The `Option Base N` compiler directive determines how arrays are handled in VB when you do not explicitly define the minimum value of an array. There are two versions: `Option Base 0` and `Option Base 1`.

For instance, the following array definition does not depend on `Option Base`, because it explicitly sets the range of the array:

```
Dim bBitmapBuffer(0 To 1023) As Byte
```

However, the following array definition *does* depend upon `Option Base`, because it includes only the size of the array, not the starting point:

```
Dim bBitmapBuffer(1024) As Byte
```

As an alternative, you can declare an array without any size at all and then use `ReDim` later to size the array to the needed value. This is a convenient feature that comes in handy when reading bitmap, wave, or other binary files. To keep things consistent, you can include the exact array size or simply use `Option Base` with the value (0 or 1) you prefer.

SETTING COMPILER OPTIONS

There are a number of compiler options that you can apply to a compiled executable to improve performance. To demonstrate how to use these settings, I will use the SpeedTest program that was developed earlier in this chapter.

Open the SpeedTest project and then select SpeedTest Properties from the Project menu, as shown in Figure 5.3.

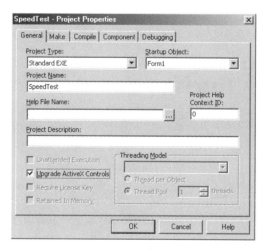

Figure 5.3

The Project Properties dialog box is used to set compiler options for optimizing a program.

Now select the Compile tab to bring up the compiler options, as shown in Figure 5.4.

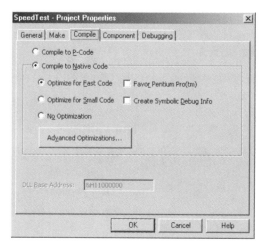

Figure 5.4

The Compile tab of the Project Properties dialog box, with specific compiler options

You will notice that there are two primary options in the Compile tab:

- **Compile to P-Code**. This option tells VB to compile P-code instead of native code, which is how programs were compiled prior to VB 5.0. For the life of me I don't know why this option is still present in the compiler options, because I can't think of any reason to use it. VB programs are not cross-platform compatible, so there is no reason to compile interpreted code (as you might with Java).

■ **Compile to Native Code**. This option tells VB to compile native executable code that includes 80 × 86 machine instructions up to the level of the Intel Pentium Pro processor (also known as the P6). While VB programs run just fine at this level of compilation, it is unfortunate that Microsoft has not included support for any of the newer processors and their advanced features (such as MMX and 3DNow!).

Compiling Native Code

When you have the Compile to Native Code option checked, there are three sub-options that you can select:

■ Optimize for Fast Code
■ Optimize for Small Code
■ No Optimization

Once again, this is a no-brainer, because I can't imagine a case where any option other than Optimize for Fast Code would be preferable. Imagine a scenario where a smaller executable would be better than a faster executable! Today, disk space is so plentiful that it is ludicrous to even consider such an option. Again, this is an obsolete option that Microsoft should have removed.

Compiling for Speed

If you click the Advanced Optimizations button, you will be presented with the Advanced Optimizations dialog box, shown in Figure 5.5.

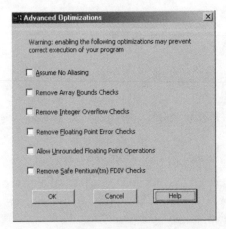

Figure 5.5

The Advanced Optimizations dialog box includes options for improving performance.

There are six optimizations that you can select in the Advanced Optimizations dialog box. If you have an error handler in every procedure in your game, go ahead and check all of these options because they will help to speed up your game. Some of these optimizations will not show up with the SpeedTest program because it just performs simple addition operations (no multiplication or division). A more advanced version of the SpeedTest program should probably include some advanced calculations to really push the program and get some more interesting results. Simple additions really don't push the code very hard, but they do show the differences among the variable types, which was the purpose for writing the program. The six optimizations are

- **Assume No Aliasing**. Aliasing is a technique for naming regions of memory with a single name rather than with multiple names. It affects how variables are handled when they are declared ByRef. This option allows the compiler to apply optimizations to variables through the use of registers and loop optimization.
- **Remove Array Bounds Checks**. Usually when an array is referenced, VB will check to make sure that the reference is within the bounds of the array. This is an error handling mechanism that is seldom found in other languages, and it slows down array handling significantly. This option disables array bounds checking, thus speeding up array-handling code. Just be sure that references stay within an array, or the program could crash.
- **Remove Integer Overflow Checks**. The default action of VB any time a value is assigned to an integer is to ensure that the value is within the range of the variable data type. Suffice it to say, with error-handling code kicking in every time an integer is accessed, the code runs a lot slower than is necessary. By carefully coding, you can avoid integer overflow yourself and speed up the code.
- **Remove Floating Point Error Checks**. This option is similar to the integer overflow check, but applies to floating-point numbers such as Singles and Doubles. This option also cancels error handling for division by zero; be sure to check for that in the code if you disable this option, because division by zero is often a critical error that will bring down a game.
- **Allow Unrounded Floating Point Operations**. This option allows the program to handle floating-point operations more efficiently through the direct use of registers, and reduces the amount of time spent copying floats into and out of memory. Comparisons of Single and Double numbers are also done at a higher precision. The only downside is that the comparison of seemingly equal floats might be seen as unequal due to the higher precision.
- **Remove Safe Pentium FDIV Checks**. This option removes the code that checks floating-point divisions for errors when running on Pentium processors, due to the infamous division bug in the early version of the processor. This is another option that is obsolete and should be removed. It speeds up the code slightly, so be sure to check this option. It is highly unlikely that a VB game will ever be run on an old Pentium with the division bug.

Comparing Optimization Differences

Table 5.3 shows a list of variable data types with columns of numbers that represent results from the SpeedTest program developed earlier in this chapter. The left-most column shows the results from the program compiled to P-code (ultra-slow), while the right-most column shows the results from the program compiled to native executable with all of the optimization options set (ultra-fast).

The difference with some of the values, such as Variant String, is not so great. But the difference with others, such as Long, is incredible! Just look at the difference between P-Code Long and Optimized Long in the table. The Optimized Long value is about 1,200 percent faster than P-Code Long, and 100 percent faster than unoptimized Native Long. Wow!

Figure 5.6 illustrates the data from Table 5.3 in a bar graph, which clearly shows the slowest and fastest data types.

Strangely, the option called Favor Pentium Pro seems to actually slow down the handling of some data types, while speeding up others. In particular, this option seems to handle variants better. Since the results might vary on some machines, you might want to try setting this option, finding a frame rate for your game, and comparing the result to the game compiled without this option. In general, however, I would recommend that you disable it. In my own experience, this option doesn't really help—it actually slows things down at times.

Table 5.3 Variable Type Performance Benchmark

Data Type	P-Code	Native	P6	P6-Opt	Optimized
Variant String	2.955	2.581	2.533	2.596	2.701
Fixed-Length String	5.104	4.991	4.826	4.860	4.888
Variable-Length String	2.645	2.515	2.480	2.429	2.475
Variant Long	1.826	1.104	1.142	1.043	1.043
Long	0.450	0.070	0.083	0.036	0.035
Integer	0.561	0.083	0.083	0.036	0.029
Variant Double	1.997	1.068	1.068	1.055	1.120
Single	0.532	0.213	0.212	0.095	0.095
Double	0.635	0.214	0.213	0.095	0.095
Currency	1.045	0.771	0.794	0.558	0.559

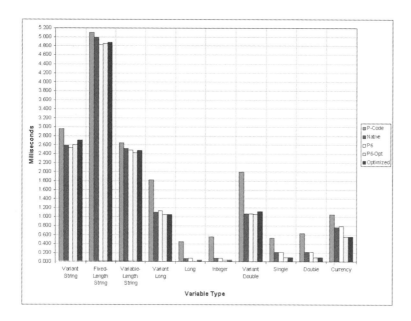

Figure 5.6

The performance differences between five versions of the SpeedTest program compiled with different options

OBJECT-ORIENTED PROGRAMMING

In this section, I will show you how to take advantage of the OOP features of VB through the use of properties and classes. If you are new to VB, or even if you have been using VB for years but you've never tapped these OOP features, this information will be helpful. Properties and classes alone will dramatically enhance your games. I will get into these features in much more detail in later chapters, and the game library itself is made up of classes. For this section, I will stick to basic concepts that might be useful for optimizing code.

I will cover VB's object-oriented features in detail in later chapters, especially Chapter 13, "Building the DirectX Game Library," which includes an extensive object-oriented library. Since Chapter 13 covers the subject in so much detail, I will just touch on the subject now and introduce the basic properties of OOP that will help you get started.

With that said, how about a short introduction to OOP? It is really a lot easier than you might expect, which is surprising when you consider how much work it can save you later when you develop a program with OOP.

Pure object-oriented programs treat everything as an object. Everything. For this reason, pure OOP is not such a great idea for game programming, because of the overhead! Every time you need to check the value of a simple integer variable, an object reference is required.

First, let's start at the beginning. The three primary properties that define an object-oriented program are

- Encapsulation
- Polymorphism
- Inheritance

Encapsulation

Encapsulation is a condition where data is hidden and cannot be manipulated directly. Only through specialized functions called *accessors* can private variables be modified. This protects the data from receiving invalid information, and allows it to be presented in a custom way. For example, suppose you have a class for handling a traffic light. The light might only have the values of red, yellow, or green. By encapsulating the functionality of a traffic light within a class, you have an opportunity to ensure that the light can only be changed to one of those three colors. An attempt to set the traffic light to purple, for instance, would fail. (Think software, not an actual traffic light.)

VB supports encapsulation through the use of properties. Properties are extremely useful and powerful, and allow you to write clean, solid code. Rather than using variables directly, you can set up a property that sets or gets a certain variable, or even an element of an array. I will show you how to use properties later in this chapter.

Polymorphism

Polymorphism is a feature in which a function can be written to return several different values or accept different sets of parameters. One common use of this feature is to return a different data type depending on a specific circumstance. For instance, in the traffic light analogy, you might write two versions of a function that returns the status of the light as either a string or a number, such as "Green" or "3" (the third color, with red and yellow being 1 and 2).

VB supports a limited form of polymorphism through the use of optional parameters and the variant return type, although these features pale in comparison to the OOP features of C++. Despite that, many programmers fail to even take advantage of the OOP features that VB supports! Remember, you can simulate almost any type of design through creative coding.

Inheritance

Inheritance is probably the best-known OOP feature. Inheritance enables you to set up foundation classes with functionality that will be shared across multiple child classes, allowing the program to work with those child classes through a common interface, even though they might differ in functionality.

For instance, you might declare a base Pet class with common features such as four legs, a tail, and a Speak function. You could then create a Dog and Cat class that inherits from Pet all of those features. A program could then work with Dog and Cat through the common Pet interface. Regardless of the type of Pet, each one would respond to the Speak function.

VB supports inheritance through the Implements keyword, which can be used to inherit the structure of a base class. This is a form of interface inheritance that does not actually incorporate runnable code from a base class, but only the abstract (functional) skeleton of the base class. This allows inherited classes to customize the implementation for multiple object types while maintaining a common interface that can be called with late binding (after compilation).

There are typically two forms of inheritance in computerdom—interface inheritance and implementation inheritance.

Interface Inheritance

Interface inheritance is a form of inheritance that is somewhat abstracted from real inheritance (see the "Implementation Inheritance" section below), in that the actual public objects in a class are not copied into a sub-class, but merely are provided as a template that must be followed in the sub-class. Also, the process is not handled automatically, and must be manually coded.

The Implements keyword allows VB classes to inherit the functionality of a parent class, but only at a single level (that is, only once). You cannot implement the functionality of a derived class in VB.

Implementation Inheritance

Implementation inheritance is what you might call *real* inheritance, where actual class public objects are implemented in sub-classes. VB does not support implementation inheritance, only the ability to inherit the structure of a parent class within another through the Implements keyword. Within the implementation inheritance, which is not supported by VB, there are two interesting sub-forms:

- **Single Inheritance**. Single inheritance occurs when one class inherits the functionality of another (parent) class and becomes a direct descendant (sub-class) with all of the public elements of the parent class. An example of single inheritance might be a car model (parent class) with several versions available (sub-classes). For instance, imagine a Ford Mustang, inherited into a Mustang GT and a Mustang Convertible. VB does not support single inheritance in the implementation category, but it does offer a form of abstract inheritance as mentioned previously.

- **Multiple Inheritance**. Multiple inheritance occurs when a new class inherits the functionality of several other classes. As you can imagine, there is a huge amount of potential with multiple inheritance, but an equal amount of complexity. This is where the C++ language really shines and pretty much blows away all other languages in the OOP arena. VB does not support multiple inheritance intrinsically, although you can emulate it with manual code (the hard way).

Classes

The primary OOP feature in VB is the class. A class in VB is defined as a single CLS file, and only one VB class can reside in a CLS file. VB classes are pretty easy to handle and do add a lot of power to a game. For instance, I'll show you in a later chapter how to build a Sprite class that takes care of all the details of loading and drawing sprites on the screen. I'm not going to delve into the subject in great detail here because it's a lot easier to show than it is to tell, and a lot of the code in later chapters really shows off the OOP features of VB. I'd rather just show you what can be done instead of trying to theorize at this point how to use classes.

Class Instancing

Class instancing has to do with the way a class can be used in a program. Instancing can be set through the class properties, and it determines how a class will behave during runtime. Here are the six instancing types available to a class. (Note that not all instancing values are available to all projects.)

1 - Private. Private classes are visible only within the current project and are not visible outside the project (through the usual type library). This instancing type should be used when you have a class that supports code in the current project, but might not be available in the program that uses the project, as in the case of an ActiveX DLL or EXE code library. This is also an effective way to distribute code libraries without giving away trade secrets, by putting the important code in a private class and then accessing that class through other means or not at all.

2 - PublicNotCreatable. This sets a class so that it cannot be created by another application using the `CreateObject` function or New operator. Instead, the current component must create the object internally, and provide outside sources with the object after it has already been created.

3 - SingleUse. This instancing type allows other applications to create objects from the class, but each new instance invokes a new copy of the ActiveX component in memory. It is not available to ActiveX DLL projects.

4 - GlobalSingleUse. This type is similar to SingleUse, but the properties and functions in the class can be used as if they are global in scope, and do not require that the class be first created. This is not available to ActiveX DLL projects.

5 - MultiUse. This is the most common form of instancing that you will encounter, and it is the one I recommend for most classes that you create. The current ActiveX component that is linked to your program can provide as many objects as are needed.

6 - GlobalMultiUse. This type is similar to GlobalSingleUse in that properties and functions have global scope. You do not need to create an instance of the class because one is created automatically. This is a great way to provide global user-defined types and constants to a game while keeping the source code hidden away in the game library.

Note that the default instancing for a standard EXE project is Private; for an ActiveX EXE or DLL, it is MultiUse; and for an ActiveX Control, it is PublicNotCreatable.

Global Classes

The GlobalMultiUse instancing type has some interesting properties that are useful in a game library. As the list of instancing types shows, you do not need to create an instance of a class with GlobalMultiUse instancing, because the instance is created automatically when the program starts.

GlobalMultiUse is only available to ActiveX EXE or DLL projects, not standard EXE or ActiveX control projects, because it affects how the class is instantiated.

The real power to GlobalMultiUse is that you can add a class to your game project with enumerations, constants, types, and other useful things, and all of these objects will be visible to your whole game. It allows you to keep the code clean without just duplicating code. The class approach is a much nicer way to handle it.

> **BUZZWORD**
> The word *instantiate* describes the process of creating an object out of a class definition. The class itself is like a blueprint for how the object will behave, while the object is the actual implementation of the class.

Properties

Properties are powerful constructs in VB that give programs incredible versatility. Properties are core to VB, giving the language most of its RAD (*Rapid Application Development*) capabilities. The ability to just set a few properties and then run a program is really the key to developing programs quickly in VB.

But properties are useful for much more than user interface design. Once you start using properties, you'll wonder how you ever managed to write programs without them! Properties have three different states that define how they are used. First, there is Let, which assigns a value to the property. Then there is Get, which returns the property value. Finally, there is Set, which assigns an object to the property.

Here is a sample property:

```
Public Property Let X(ByVal lNewValue As Long)
    lCurrentX = lNewValue
End Property

Public Property Get X() As Long
    X = lCurrentX
End Property
```

This property is simply called X and could be used to keep track of the X value of a pixel location. The Let procedure assigns the variable, lNewValue, to the property variable. But wait, what is the property variable?

That is the only drawback to properties. You must have a variable that holds the value of the property, because VB doesn't keep track of the value of the property for you. In a way, this is a blessing, since you control exactly how the value is handled. But in a way, it does lead to a large number of property variables. For this reason, it is a good idea to use properties extensively in classes, while not as often in code modules.

The really nice thing about properties is that once you set up a property and a local variable to keep track of the value, you can then use that property as if the Property Let and Property Get procedures are built into the variable. To the calling routine, a property looks just like a public variable, and that is the power of properties—allowing VB programs full support for the OOP feature called encapsulation, which was covered earlier in this chapter. Properties help to hide implementation from the calling routine and provide only an interface to the real data.

You can pass any kind of variable or object to or from a property. In addition to handling encapsulation, properties also allow you to incorporate polymorphism into your programs. A property can accept and return any kind of object, including variant. While it might be slower, you can use the TypeName function, covered earlier in this chapter, along with a Variant parameter to determine what type of value is being passed to the property, and then handle it accordingly.

Properties are absolutely my favorite feature of VB, and I will show you some interesting ways to use them in upcoming chapters.

SUMMARY

This chapter covered a lot of complicated material regarding optimization of VB code. I explained how some variable types are more efficient than others and showed you a program that performs a simple benchmark of the variable types to determine how fast they operate.

By performing a simple operation numerous times in a fast loop and then keeping track of the time, it is possible to see how fast each operation runs individually.

Following the coverage of data types, I explained how to set the compiler options in VB for maximum performance, and covered the advanced optimizations available with the compiler. Native executables run much faster than interpreted ones, so I demonstrated why you should compile and test your game projects from time to time and not rely solely upon the rapid development features of the VB IDE.

Finally, I introduced you to the object-oriented features of VB, including classes, properties, and the basic nature of an OOP program. VB truly has some excellent OOP features that can result in really powerful and efficient code when utilized properly.

Of course, these subjects are all geared toward getting the absolute most out of VB for writing games! Get ready for the next chapter, because you are finally going to jump into DirectX!

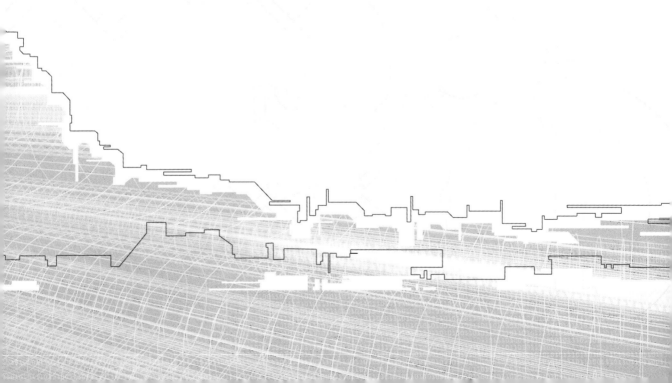

CHAPTER 6

SUPERCHARGING VISUAL BASIC WITH DIRECTX

ow, the last five chapters have been intense! But that's nothing compared to all the fun things you'll learn in this chapter! DirectX totally redefines the game programming experience in Visual Basic. I am going to introduce you to the basic concepts of DirectX in this chapter, including an overview of the components of DirectX 7.0 and DirectX 8.0. The differences between these versions (the two versions supported by VB at the time of this writing) are significant, so it is important to understand each one.

This chapter is an overview of DirectX, and includes a few sample programs to pique your interest. More in-depth DirectX programming will begin with Chapter 10, "Diving into DirectDraw," followed by additional DirectX components in successive chapters. In addition, Chapter 14, "DirectX Graphics and Direct3D," is a tutorial on 3-D programming with Direct3D using the new features of DirectX 8.0, and also includes a Direct3D-based sprite engine.

This chapter covers the following topics:

- Welcome to the Next Level
- The Grand Unified Theory of DirectX
- Visual Basic Support for DirectX
- Writing Some DirectX Code

WELCOME TO THE NEXT LEVEL

If you thought VB was fun, wait until you start doing DirectX with it! That's where the real fun begins. DirectX is so, well, *huge*! It handles so many details that it should come as no surprise that DirectX was designed just for writing games. Actually, that might have sounded strange a few years ago. Microsoft has become quite a player in the gaming industry in recent years.

Microsoft has started taking game development very seriously, which is evident in the VB support for DirectX. In fact, it's kind of funny to see the words "high-performance multimedia applications" tacked on to the end of Microsoft's own description of DirectX, because it is such a powerful gaming library, not an application library.

Next time you pick up a mainstream computer game magazine, flip to just about any random page and you are likely to see the word DirectX. In fact, pick up a console video game magazine and you will probably be able to find the term, given that there has been so much coverage of the Microsoft Xbox in the gaming media. (Xbox is a video game console powered by Windows 2000 and DirectX.) During the fall of 2001, the video game industry was a prime example of competition, with no fewer than four next-generation video game machines vying for consumer attention during the holiday season. I personally consider the Game Boy Advance sufficiently cool enough to be listed alongside the non-portable systems. Nintendo, Sony, and Sega have been duking it out for many years, constantly leapfrogging each other with technological advances in video game hardware, all in the name of home entertainment. But now, for the first time in a decade, an American company has dared to venture into an industry wholly dominated by Japan. It is a fascinating foray into the dynamics of pitting one economic giant against another in direct cutthroat competition.

The fact is that a proprietary Microsoft API (which is fondly known as DirectX) was created just to make Windows into a platform suitable for playing games. It has now become the most popular game programming API. DirectX has even accomplished something that was once considered impossible—bridging the gap between console and PC for cross-platform development. This factor does not necessarily mean that DirectX is the best

> **NOTE**
>
> Sega might be out of the hardware business now, but the Dreamcast has such a huge fan base that it will take many, many years before hardcore Sega fans will unplug their beloved Dreamcast machines; shelve the worn keyboard, mouse, and controllers; and permanently switch to another console. I, for one, was drawn to the Dreamcast because it is powered by Windows CE, the same operating system that drives Pocket PCs. With DirectX built in, the Dreamcast is even related to the Xbox.

graphics library; only that it is used in more products than any other due to the proliferation of Windows PCs. In the language of marketing, that means DirectX is the dominant game library, and game publishers will always target the largest audience possible.

> **BUZZWORD**
>
> A *Software Development Kit (SDK)* is a distribution of files that you install to your development PC. It provides the ability to write programs for a specific library, usually comprised of DLL or LIB files. An SDK is the development package that provides the means to use an API.

> **BUZZWORD**
>
> An *Application Programming Interface (API)* is the library of function calls that is made available after an SDK has been installed. This provides additional functionality to a development platform and extends the capabilities of programs written for that platform. The SDK must first be installed before the API is available for use.

Despite the difficulties of writing programs with earlier versions of DirectX (especially the unwieldy Direct3D), the latest incarnation of DirectX is a fundamental improvement over previous versions. DirectX 8.0 is now fully committed to 3-D game development, having shed the last vestiges of the 2-D realm. I personally enjoy writing 2-D games more than 3-D games, because I grew up playing arcade games like *Blasteroids*, *Heavy Barrel*, *Akari Warriors*, *Contra*, and *CyberBall*. I believe there will always be a market for 2-D games.

What Is DirectX?

The DirectX SDK is a library of routines that maximize the performance of 2-D and 3-D games, with full support of hardware-accelerated graphics and sound.

DirectX was developed by Microsoft to provide a set of low-level routines primarily for creating games, but also for creating high-performance multimedia programs. DirectX provides APIs for handling 2-D graphics, 3-D graphics, sound effects, music, input devices, and networking. The low-level hardware device drivers are developed both by Microsoft and by third-party hardware manufacturers (such as ATI, Nvidia, and Creative Labs). Without the device driver support of hardware manufacturers, DirectX would have never succeeded. Indeed, the saving grace of OpenGL has been persistent development and support of OpenGL drivers, without which the library would have been left behind in recent years. In the gaming world, device drivers pave the way for the success of new hardware, and provide a guaranteed upgrade path for new hardware many years after a hit game has been released (with *Half-Life* being the epitome of this argument).

> **NOTE**
>
> I will cover all of the DirectX components in greater detail in Part II, "The Nuts and Bolts of Game Development."

DirectX Game Development

The reason game developers love DirectX and OpenGL is because most graphics cards today include both DirectX and OpenGL drivers. Game publishers want to target the largest audience possible, and thus get the largest number of sales out of a game in the critical first three months after the game is released. To get the maximum return on a game, it must support a wide range of users, from hardcore gamers to beginners. Sure, there are many games that push the envelope and prompt great hordes of gamers to rush out and upgrade their PCs. But for the most part, games are written for the average PC, which usually includes hardware technology that is at least six months old.

For instance, at the time of this writing, the GeForce 3 chip is the hottest thing in the PC graphics arena (although the ATI Radeon is a strong competitor). This graphics chip is so far beyond current game technology that it will be a long time before any game comes close to pushing the limits of the GeForce 3. Most likely, games ported from Xbox to PC (such as *HALO*) will start to really take advantage of the advanced features of this graphics chip. Now, if a game development company decides to create a cutting-edge game that fully supports the GeForce 3 before the technology has really started to gain momentum, the critical first three months of game sales will probably not be very good. The game will almost certainly be guaranteed a longer shelf life due to cutting-edge features. However, most games are not developed for longevity, but rather for quick success.

First-person shooters, developed by companies like id Software (the creators of *Quake III Arena*) and Epic Games (the creators of *Unreal Tournament*), are usually responsible for harassing the silicon of aging computer hardware. In fact, you might find this hard to believe, but computers have actually heated up, smoked, caught fire, and even melted down as a result of people playing games on poorly built, highly overclocked PCs. Once in a while, a CPU will even explode, right on the motherboard! One might say that cutting-edge games often prompt hardware upgrades after careless overclockers destroy the unfortunate hardware.

NOTE

I can personally vouch for the foolhardiness of overclocking a PC, since I have ruined a processor by overclocking it by just ten percent. After a year or two, even a slightly under-cooled processor has the potential to fail. For this reason, I highly recommend that you avoid overclocking.

DirectX Versus OpenGL

I mentioned earlier that DirectX and OpenGL are the two most popular APIs supported by new hardware devices. Several attempts at standardizing the graphics hardware interface have come and gone in recent years, including attempts by 3dfx and S3 (neither of which are in the hardware business any longer).

As far as PC sound is concerned, Creative Labs has always been the most important player in town, having had an unusually long life out of the Sound Blaster franchise. I remember buying the very first Sound Blaster card for my old 386/33 PC. Before that time, I had been using Creative Labs' earlier product, the Game Blaster—an old rival of the popular Adlib card. For a while, Aureal seemed to be making headway with A3D-positional sound technology. But in the end, Creative Labs dominated the market with EAX technology.

When it comes to video cards, the market has experienced intense competition—the resulting technologies are an absolute testament to the success of a market economy with supply and demand, consumer power, and capitalism in general. What we have now in terms of graphics might not have seen the light of day were it not for the popularity of gaming and the need to constantly push the envelope of graphics technology. The capabilities of modern video cards rival those of large rendering workstations of the mid-1990s. It gives me a bit of a rush when I consider that modern PC flight simulators rival the military simulators of only a few years ago!

The real difference between DirectX and OpenGL is that DirectX is a complete API with components for handling input, sound, music, networking, and graphics. OpenGL has an equally complex suite of graphics functions, but it's just that—a graphics library. There is currently no VB support for OpenGL, but it is still a widely-used API for C and C++ graphics programming, and is supported by most games.

But what OpenGL does do, it does extremely well. More often than not, frame rates will be much higher in OpenGL than Direct3D for games that support both. DirectX is limited to Windows platforms (which includes the Windows-driven Xbox console), while OpenGL has been adopted by most of the industry as a professional-grade graphics rendering library.

DirectX Versus the Windows API

The real irony of the situation is that DirectX was first developed in the Stone Age of video hardware, before acceleration was the rule of the day. Now, everything is accelerated, including 2-D and 3-D graphics. Even the low-end PCs on the market have a standard graphics card that would have been considered high-end a few years ago, so assumptions can be made about the least common denominator as far as the graphics capability of PCs goes.

The core Windows API graphics routines—such as BitBlt—communicate directly with the video card device driver at the level of the hardware, which is what game programmers were looking for when DirectX was introduced. Now things have changed somewhat, and it is entirely possible to write games with the Windows API—simple games, at any rate. Of course, 3-D is out of the question. But a large number of games released are still locked in the realm of 2-D. Some take advantage of the special features in 3-D acceleration by basing the 2-D game engine on a 3-D surface, and then applying lighting and special effects. These capabilities are far beyond the Windows API. But a fair number of games can be developed with VB using the Windows API, with routines such as BitBlt for quickly drawing bitmaps and sprites to the screen.

Years ago, the only way to maximize performance in a game was through direct access to video memory, along with optimized code. Today, with Windows API and DirectX support for 2-D and 3-D acceleration, it is no longer necessary (or even desirable, in most cases) to modify video memory in order to get the best performance. Absolutely no amount of software wizardry will best the performance of a hardware blitter!

Chapter 13, "Building the DirectX Game Library," will show you how to develop the foundations of a game engine that can be reused from one game project to another, drastically reducing the time it takes to start each new game. The game library includes all of the Windows API and DirectX code developed in the book!

Installing DirectX for Visual Basic

There are several options available when installing the DirectX 8.0 SDK. There is the full-blown 140MB SDK installation, which includes everything, and then there are the partial installations. Generally, you will want to just install the whole whopping SDK and include everything whether

you need it or not (particularly the Visual C++ files). However, it is not necessary to install everything just for Visual Basic development. You do need the runtime library in order to actually test DirectX programs, but as for the SDK, you really only need the DirectX 8.0 for Visual Basic SDK, which is about 16MB is size. Take a look at Figure 6.1 to see what the DirectX 8 SDK for VB installer looks like.

> **TIP**
>
> Be sure to check out the latest and greatest downloads online at http://msdn.microsoft.com/downloads. Look for a topic called Graphics and Multimedia, and there you will find the latest DirectX SDK download page.

The DirectX SDK installation options are straight-forward and easy to understand. I recommend just accepting all of the default options.

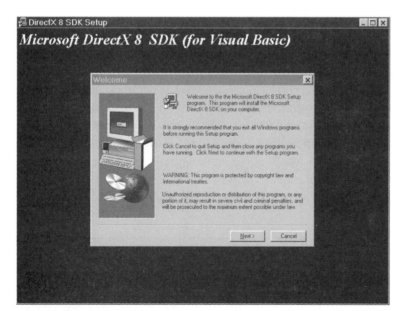

Figure 6.1

The DirectX 8 for Visual Basic SDK installer

THE GRAND UNIFIED THEORY OF DIRECTX

In this section, I am going to give you an overview of DirectX so you will know for certain exactly what DirectX can do. DirectX is pretty much all you need to write games for Windows. It includes all the functionality for nearly every game-programming feature you can imagine, all packaged nicely into a type library for use with VB! DirectX does not stop at providing a means to do speedy graphics; it also provides full-blown hardware support for sound cards, joysticks, the keyboard and mouse, 2-D and 3-D accelerators, and network cards.

In the old days of DOS game programming, you had to license a third-party graphics library if you wanted to get the most out of the video chipsets on the market—and there were a lot of them! Supporting all of the various video cards and sound cards in every game was a real nightmare, because none of these cards really followed any kind of standard. They were all out there trying to leapfrog each other in processing power and features, so the graphics card companies had no intention of supporting one another. Although an SVGA standard was agreed upon, the graphics card companies quickly expanded the standard to include new features, and the problems started all over again for game and graphics programmers. Were it not for DirectX, which provided a standard way of writing games for the most popular operating system in the world, games today might not be nearly as exciting. Or rather, standardized third-party libraries would have still been popular, along with hardware industry standards for implementing device drivers.

A Brief History of DirectX

The first version of DirectX was actually called the Game SDK, and was released soon after Windows 95. (Windows 95 provided absolutely no additional support for game programming other than an updated 32-bit Windows API, contrary to Microsoft's promises to game developers.) The Windows API is pretty good for programming games that run in a window, but it does not support exclusive access to the entire screen, or the ability to change the video mode. The Game SDK was a step in the right direction, solving both of the aforementioned problems. Using the Game SDK, a game programmer can leave Windows running in the background while setting any video mode—regardless of the current state of the Windows desktop. With the Game SDK, it was possible to use even small resolutions like 320 × 200—the old VGA favorite of DOS programmers.

The Game SDK might have gone through some changes before it was re-christened DirectX, but those changes were minor in comparison to the improvements made to DirectX by the time it reached version 3.0. This version finally defined the standard functionality of DirectDraw, the primary graphics API, and would remain largely unchanged until version 7.0.

Overview of DirectX

As a Visual Basic programmer, you are probably not very interested in the mechanics of how DirectX works. (I know that I'm not!) In the C++ world, DirectX is made up of COM (*Component Object Model*) interfaces, and this is where it really starts to get icky. While I *could* fully explain those components and give you a complete autopsy of DirectX, I just don't want to. Besides, there are so many books on the subject already; it would serve no purpose to put you to sleep by telling you about it. I would rather take a more hands-on approach to DirectX programming and leave the discussion of interfaces and COM to the C++ folks. (See Appendix E, "Recommended Reading" for more resources.)

DirectDraw

DirectDraw is the primary graphics library that handles low-level stuff like blitting images to a surface (such as the display screen). DirectDraw has been assimilated into DirectX Graphics (in DX8) along with Direct3D. However, even though DirectDraw no longer has a presence at the object level, it is still present in DirectX Graphics, handling the stream of pixels fired at it from Direct3D as the primary display. I will show you how to use DirectDraw in Chapter 10, "Diving into DirectDraw." While the DX8 runtime includes the interfaces for all previous versions of DirectX, the type library for VB provides only the latest objects directly related to DX8. For this reason, any DirectDraw code in this book will use the DX7 type library.

Direct3D

Direct3D is the rendering library that handles 3-D polygons and all of the advanced features required to create an advanced 3-D game. It handles things like texture mapping, alpha blending, mip-mapping, transformations, camera view, and lighting. Since Direct3D was given DirectDraw's job in DX8, even 2-D graphics must go through Direct3D. It might seem more complicated (and less efficient) to write a 2-D arcade game using Direct3D, but that is the way things are done in DX8. Don't worry, it's not too hard to draw sprites in Direct3D, because there is a support object called D3DX that helps out.

DirectSound

DirectSound handles multi-channel waveform output. You use DirectSound to play all of the digital music and sound effects in a game. It is surprisingly easy to load a wave and play it through DirectSound, as you will be pleasantly surprised to discover in later chapters. I cover DirectSound, DirectMusic, and DirectSound3D in Chapter 11, "Playing Sound and Music with DirectX Audio."

DirectInput

DirectInput takes care of all the input device support you will need in a game, and is particularly useful when you're working with advanced joysticks and driving wheels, which often come equipped with force feedback support. DirectInput helps by not only providing a standard interface to all of these input devices, but also providing a means to easily enumerate and access each input device in a system.

DirectPlay

DirectPlay is the networking component that allows you to add multiplayer support to a game. DirectPlay has a lot of features built in for supporting chat rooms and grouping players, along with the more traditional messaging. I will cover the Windows Sockets API in Chapter 16, "Multiplayer Programming with Windows Sockets," as well as DirectPlay in Chapter 17, "Network Programming with DirectPlay." It is valuable to understand socket programming in addition to DirectPlay (which abstracts packets and message handling). In Chapter 21, "Stellar War: Multiplayer Space Combat Game," I will show you how to build a complete multiplayer game.

What's New in DirectX 8.0?

DirectX 8.0 is a significant update to the DirectX API, featuring a much more streamlined set of functions that work together more closely and are more intuitive than in previous versions of DirectX. There are now only four primary components in DirectX:

- DirectX Graphics
- DirectX Audio
- DirectInput
- DirectPlay

A new DirectX Control Panel utility provides a central location for identifying DirectX components, with version information, driver and hardware supported features, and the ability to switch between debug and retail builds of the runtime library for development and testing.

DirectX Graphics

DirectX 8.0 has combined the two graphics libraries available in prior versions of DirectX, DirectDraw and Direct3D, into a single component called DirectX Graphics. This new component, which incorporates all of the features of both APIs, has been updated with support for all of the latest advances in graphics technology and 3-D acceleration, and fully supports the latest hardware innovations such as transform and lighting. I'll cover Direct3D in Chapter 14, "DirectX Graphics and Direct3D."

DirectX Audio

DirectX 8.0 has similarly integrated and enhanced the sound libraries of DirectX, DirectSound, and DirectMusic into a single component called DirectX Audio. At first, it does not seem to be any different than previous versions of DirectSound, until you start to look at how DirectMusic was integrated into the new library. In addition, DirectSound3D provides positional surround sound effects. I'll cover this subject in Chapter 11, "Playing Sound and Music with DirectX Audio."

DirectInput

DirectX 8.0 has not revolutionized DirectInput as it has other components, but there is a new feature in DirectInput called *action mapping*. This feature allows you to abstract the input devices so that the game can rely on simple commands rather than actual hardware devices. This version of DirectInput also fully supports force-feedback joysticks, driving wheels, and other accessories. I'll cover keyboard, mouse, and joystick input in Chapter 12, "Getting a Handle on User Input."

DirectPlay

DirectX 8.0 has provided considerable improvements to DirectPlay with additional multiplayer networking gaming capabilities (like support for voice chat) and greater ease-of-use for the programmer. I'll cover DirectPlay in Chapter 17, "Network Programming with DirectPlay."

VISUAL BASIC SUPPORT FOR DIRECTX

Before you can do any DirectX programming in VB, you must first reference the type library. But first, what exactly is a type library?

A *type library* is an interface that allows VB to access a COM object in Windows. Since DirectX is a COM object itself, a type library must first be created and then referenced before you will be able to write any DirectX programs in VB. Prior to DirectX 7.0, the only way to do any DirectX programming in VB was through third-party type libraries that industrious VB fans created. Fortunately, Microsoft created a type library for DirectX 7.0, which was the first version supported by VB.

> **NOTE**
>
> Drawing something as simple as a pixel is pretty easy using DirectDraw, but not so easy using Direct3D. So, to keep things simple, I'll just show you a sample DirectDraw program using DirectX 7.0, and I'll jump into DirectX Graphics later.

There are two versions of DirectX supported by VB, which means there are two DirectX type libraries for VB. The sample DirectX program presented in this section will demonstrate DirectDraw7, because this is what will be used for most of the 2-D graphics in later chapters.

2-D Overkill

Direct3D is overkill for doing 2-D games, which still comprise a large percentage of the gaming market. Just consider *Age of Kings* and other real-time strategy games that are built upon a 2-D graphics engine, and you will see the potential. You really do not need to go all-out with Direct3D to write classic-style arcade games, either. Believe it or not, classic games are still very popular! Some of the most fantastic 3-D titles don't do as well as some simple 2-D titles with incredible gameplay. This could be the reason why 2-D sprite-based Capcom games like *Street Fighter Alpha 3* seem to do so well, while at the same time there are amazing 3-D fighters like *Soul Calibur* and *Dead or Alive 2.* One would think that technology (graphics and sound) alone would determine success. After all, gamers usually want to see stuff that pushes their gaming hardware to the limits.

But this all really boils down to the fact that the ultimate deciding factor is gameplay, not graphics technology. I'm sure in the near future, gaming hardware will be able to render games as remarkable as the feature film, *Final Fantasy: The Spirits Within.* The Nvidia GeForce 3 is already approaching that level of graphics capability, with a programmable rendering pipeline in the chip itself. But in the meantime, I would like to justify the use of DirectDraw7 by the fact that it does a better job at handling 2-D games than DX8 (which is optimized for 3-D through DirectX Graphics). While I will still show you how to do 2-D with DX8 in a later chapter, the material is too complicated at this point and will be reserved for the advanced section of the book.

All Hail the Type Libraries!

The confusing thing about the two VB type libraries is that they are not backwards-compatible with older versions of DirectX (while the DirectX runtime *is* compatible with older versions). When you are writing code that directly references the DirectX API (for instance, with Visual C++), you have access to the entire API. But in VB, you have access to only those components that are included in the type library.

At first glance, it seems pretty obvious that you should be able to write code that uses DirectX 7.0 using the DirectX 8.0 library. Unfortunately, a type library is just an interface to the actual library, so things can be rearranged or left out as the authors of the type library wish. I'm not complaining! There are two type libraries provided for VB, so it is a simple matter to reference both of them as needed. Yes, it does work, and I highly recommend going this route for most 2-D games. I have found that some video cards do not support all of the features of Direct3D, including some of the sprite manipulation routines and blitters (included with D3DX and D3DXSprite, both of which are covered in Chapter 14, "DirectX Graphics and Direct3D"). There is also the general overhead of having everything in the game actually displayed on a 3-D surface!

Now imagine this scenario. Create a large 3-D surface, put a paddle at each end, send a ball sprite bouncing around, and depending on which half of the surface the camera is facing, you can create a two-player game out of it (using the multi-player code developed later in the book). So, as you can see, there are some pretty weird and some pretty cool things you can do with DirectX Graphics.

> **NOTE**
>
> In addition to DirectX Graphics and DirectX Sound, this book fully covers DirectDraw, DirectSound, DirectMusic, DirectInput, DirectPlay, and any other Direct-stuff that you might need to create a game.

Most of this book is dedicated to DirectX 8.0 programming with VB (although given the title of the book, I suppose that line is redundant). The majority of the code will be geared toward DirectX Graphics and DirectX Sound, the two primary components of DirectX 8.0. This is all fine and dandy for writing a modern game, but what if you are doing something along the lines of an arcade game, and you want to stick with 2-D graphics?

> **NOTE**
>
> There is a support class included with D3DX that helps in the transition from DirectDraw for developing 2-D sprite-based code with Direct3D. It automatically creates a 3-D surface on the screen with the proper ambient lighting.

Ouch. That does present a problem. DirectX 8.0 has integrated both DirectDraw and Direct3D into the DirectX Graphics and D3DX libraries. There is no DirectDrawSurface any longer! So, the easy solution for now is to simply use both type libraries together and combine DirectDraw7 with DirectSound8 and DirectInput8, and so on. Combining the two will work fine until I've had an opportunity to show you some of the advanced features of DirectX Graphics.

In fact, there is no reason why you can't continue to use this method to develop 2-D DirectX games with VB.

WRITING SOME DIRECTX CODE

Hey, you're about to write your first DirectX program with Visual Basic! If that doesn't get you excited, maybe you should go pick up an Access 2000 book and learn how to design a mailing list database program (just kidding).

Of course you're excited! DirectX is fun and we both love VB, so the ability to do DirectX programming in VB is something to really get worked up about! This program is actually not a graphics example, but rather just a program that creates the DirectX and DirectDraw objects and displays some information about your computer system. Another sample program after this one will actually use full screen mode and do something fun.

The GetInfo Program

The GetInfo program demonstrates how to reference the primary DirectX and DirectDraw objects, and displays some interesting information about the video hardware in your PC. The program is really short, so it's easy to pick out the parts of the program that call on the DirectX objects. Figure 6.2 shows the GetInfo program running.

Figure 6.2

The GetInfo program displays some properties provided by the DirectX objects.

Let's get started! First, create a new Standard EXE project in VB, with the usual default Form1 included. Grab a TextBox out of the Toolbox and add a single large TextBox control to Form1. The new control will be called Text1 by default—don't change the name. Now make sure Text1 is selected (by clicking it), and then look at the properties for Text1. Scroll down the list of properties until you find one called MultiLine. Set MultiLine = True. This allows you to add multiple lines of text to the control, and makes it into sort of a simple version of Notepad. Now set Scrollbars = 2 – Vertical.

Of course, you will also need to reference the DirectX library before this program will run! So let's take care of that little detail right now. Select the References item in the Project menu to bring up the list of objects referenced by this program, as shown in Figure 6.3. New projects will only have the standard VB objects listed. You can scroll down the list to locate the DirectX type library. For a quick jump, press the D key. Look for an item called DirectX 7 for Visual Basic Type Library and check it, then close the References dialog box.

Now that you have the project set up for DirectX, and the form is ready to go, enter the following lines of code into the code window for the GetInfo program.

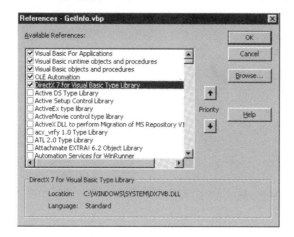

Figure 6.3

Referencing the DirectX 7 for Visual Basic Type Library

```
'==============================================================
' Visual Basic Game Programming With DirectX
' Chapter 6 : Supercharging Visual Basic With DirectX
' GetInfo Program Source Code
'==============================================================


Option Explicit
Option Base 0

'DirectX object
Dim DX As DirectX7

'DirectDraw object
Dim DD As DirectDraw7

'surface description type
Dim ddsd As DDSURFACEDESC2

'DirectDraw identification object
Dim ddi As DirectDrawIdentifier

'DirectDraw device enumeration object
Dim DDEnum As DirectDrawEnum

'DirectDraw capabilities structure
Dim ddsCaps As DDSCAPS2
```

```vb
'global variables
Dim r1 As RECT
Dim n As Long


'===============================================================
' Form_Load
' Main startup routine for the program
'===============================================================
Private Sub Form_Load()
    On Error GoTo error1

    'create the DirectX object
    Set DX = New DirectX7

    'create the DirectDraw object
    Set DD = DX.DirectDrawCreate("")

    'normal windowed program with current display settings
    DD.SetCooperativeLevel Me.hWnd, DDSCL_NORMAL

    'retrieve video card driver information
    Set ddi = DD.GetDeviceIdentifier(DDGDI_DEFAULT)
    PrintText "Video card : " & ddi.GetDescription
    PrintText "Driver : " & ddi.GetDriver
    PrintText "Major version : " & ddi.GetDriverVersion
    PrintText "Minor version : " & ddi.GetDriverSubVersion
    Set ddi = Nothing

    'retrieve the first display device
    Set DDEnum = DX.GetDDEnum()
    PrintText "Display device = " & DDEnum.GetDescription(1)
    Set DDEnum = Nothing

    'display amount of free video memory
    PrintText "Video memory = " & DD.GetFreeMem(ddsCaps)

    'retrieve information about the display mode
    DD.GetDisplayMode ddsd
    PrintText "Resolution : " & ddsd.lWidth & "x" & ddsd.lHeight
    PrintText "Color depth : " & ddsd.ddpfPixelFormat.lRGBBitCount
    PrintText "Pitch : " & ddsd.lPitch
```

```
    'delete some objects
    Set DD = Nothing
    Set DX = Nothing

    Exit Sub
error1:
    MsgBox "Error " & Err.Number & ": " & Err.Description, _
        vbOKOnly + vbExclamation, "GetInfo"
End Sub


'==========================================================================
' PrintText
' Add a line of text to the next line of the TextBox
'==========================================================================
Private Sub PrintText(ByVal msg As String)
    Text1.Text = Text1.Text & msg & vbCrLf
End Sub
```

Be sure to save the program before running it, in case there are any unhandled errors. This program doesn't change the video mode for full-screen handling, so it is less likely to cause a problem. But errors do often occur when writing DirectX programs, so it's a good idea to always save your project before running the program.

The Welcome Program

The next program I am going to show you how to write will actually use DirectDraw to create a primary surface, set up full-screen mode, and then display a welcome message to the display screen. Since this is the first full-screen DirectX program in the book, it follows the traditional method of sending a short greeting to you. The Welcome program is shown in Figure 6.4.

Setting Up the Project

If you were paying attention in the last section, then you probably already know how to reference the DirectX type library. But first, you need to create the VB project!

Fire up VB and create a new Standard EXE project (select New Project from the File menu). The new project will have a single form called Form1, as usual. Now select References from the Project menu and search for the reference called DirectX 7 for Visual Basic Type Library.

Figure 6.4

Welcome to DirectX!

Drop a check next to the type library and close the References dialog, just like you did in the last program. Your project is now powered by DirectX! (I hope that phrase doesn't violate any trademarks. Just in case, allow me to make it official: Everything even remotely related to DirectX is a trademark of Microsoft Corporation.)

In retrospect, it's kind of funny when you think about how much work it takes just to get to this point in Visual C++, if you have ever written a DirectX program with that language. Don't you just love VB? All it requires is a refer-

> **NOTE**
>
> If you reference the DirectX 8 for Visual Basic Type Library, you will not be able to access the DirectDraw class, which is only included in the DirectX 7.0 Type Library. You can reference both type libraries at the same time without any problem, if you wish.

ence in the Project menu, and off you go. To quote Steve Buscemi in the movie Armageddon: "This is so much fun it's freaky!"

Using the DirectX Object

Now you have a big, blank project with a powerful DirectX engine sitting behind the scenes, ready to go. What happens next? Well, the project is empty, after all, so let's put some code into it!

All of the DirectX code in VB must pass through the basic DirectX class, which is called DirectX7. To create a new DirectX7 object, you can declare it using code that looks something like this:

```
Dim DX As New DirectX7
```

You can also create the object like this, which is probably a better way to do it, since you can more easily trap any errors that might occur during object instantiation:

```
Dim DX As DirectX7
Set DX = New DirectX7
```

The DirectX7 object helps you manage all the other objects in the DirectX type library. With many of the objects, you can't simply declare them as new, the way you can declare the base DirectX7 object. Instead, many of these DirectX objects must be created by calling functions within the DirectX7 object, which is why you must start with DirectX7 in the first place!

Here is the code listing for the Welcome program. I'm not going to spend a lot of time explaining how everything works in this program, because that is all covered in Chapter 10, "Diving into DirectDraw." For now, just enjoy watching your first DirectX for VB program run and worry about how everything works later.

```
'=========================================================================
' Visual Basic Game Programming With DirectX
' Chapter 6 : Supercharging Visual Basic With DirectX
' Welcome Program Source Code
'=========================================================================

Option Explicit
Option Base 0

'Windows API declarations
Private Declare Function GetTickCount Lib "kernel32" () As Long

'program constants
Const SCREENWIDTH As Long = 640
Const SCREENHEIGHT As Long = 480
Const COLORDEPTH As Long = 16

'primary DirectX object
Dim dx As DirectX7

'primary DirectDraw object
Dim dd As DirectDraw7

'primary surface objects
Dim primary As DirectDrawSurface7
Dim ddsd As DDSURFACEDESC2
```

```
'global variables
Dim rPrim As RECT
Dim lLeft As Long
Dim lTop As Long



'===================================================================
' Form_Load
' Main startup routine for the program
'===================================================================
Private Sub Form_Load()
    'initialize DirectDraw
    InitDirectDraw

    Randomize GetTickCount

    'find the center of the screen
    lLeft = (ddsd.lWidth - TextWidth("Welcome to DirectX!")) / 2
    lTop = ddsd.lHeight / 2

    'clear the surface with a dark gray color
    primary.BltColorFill rPrim, RGB(Rnd * 30, Rnd * 30, Rnd * 30)

    Do While True
        'display welcome message in a random color
        primary.SetForeColor RGB(Rnd * 255 + 1, Rnd * 255 + 1, _
            Rnd * 255 + 1)
        primary.DrawText lLeft, lTop, "Welcome to DirectX!", False
        DoEvents
    Loop
End Sub


'===================================================================
' Form_KeyDown
' Triggered when a key is pressed
'===================================================================
Private Sub Form_KeyDown(KeyCode As Integer, Shift As Integer)
    Shutdown
End Sub
```

```
'===============================================================
' Form_Click
' Triggered when mouse button is clicked
'===============================================================
Private Sub Form_Click()
    Shutdown
End Sub


'===============================================================
' Init
' Initialize DirectDraw
'===============================================================
Private Sub InitDirectDraw()
    'create the DirectX object
    Set dx = New DirectX7

    'create the DirectDraw object
    Set dd = dx.DirectDrawCreate("")

    'indicate that we dont need to change display depth
    Call dd.SetCooperativeLevel(Me.hWnd, DDSCL_FULLSCREEN Or _
        DDSCL_ALLOWMODEX Or DDSCL_EXCLUSIVE)

    'set the display mode
    dd.SetDisplayMode SCREENWIDTH, SCREENHEIGHT, COLORDEPTH, 0, _
        DDSDM_DEFAULT

    'get the screen surface and create a back buffer too
    ddsd.lFlags = DDSD_CAPS
    ddsd.ddsCaps.lCaps = DDSCAPS_PRIMARYSURFACE

    'create the primary display surface
    Set primary = dd.CreateSurface(ddsd)
    primary.GetSurfaceDesc ddsd
    rPrim.Bottom = ddsd.lHeight
    rPrim.Right = ddsd.lWidth
End Sub


'===============================================================
' Shutdown
' Restore display and end the program
'===============================================================
```

```
Private Sub Shutdown()
    dd.RestoreDisplayMode
    dd.SetCooperativeLevel Me.hWnd, DDSCL_NORMAL
    Set primary = Nothing
    Set dd = Nothing
    Set dx = Nothing
    End
End Sub
```

PROMOTION!

You have now completed Part I, "Introducing Visual Basic and DirectX," thus demonstrating your dedication to the basics of game development. You have learned all about the Visual Basic language, the Windows API, and how to optimize your source code, and you've even written your first DirectDraw program.

You are hereby promoted to the rank of Apprentice Hacker, with all of the rights and privileges that come with the position. Use your new knowledge and skills wisely, and continue to push the envelope of Visual Basic gaming!

Here is a record of your progress so far:

1. **Newbie Gamer**
2. **Apprentice Hacker**
3. Skilled Programmer
4. Veteran Coder
5. Master Developer
6. Adept Game Designer

SUMMARY

This chapter introduced DirectX and explained the various components that make up DirectX 7.0 and DirectX 8.0. In the process, I compared DirectX with OpenGL and the Windows API, and included a little history of DirectX, including how it was developed, where it came from, and what prompted it to come into being.

I have only scratched the surface here, because it is not my intention to get into the details of the DirectX HAL and HEL, or any other acronyms that describe messy things that we VB programmers prefer to avoid. However, you might want to dig into the details yourself and learn all there is to know about DirectX in order to make your VB games as great as they can be. This book is focused on game development with hands-on tutorials for VB, so it does not cover DirectX in as much detail as you might find in a book dedicated to the subject.

For further study, I highly recommend you pick up *Multiplayer Game Programming* (Premier Press, Inc., 2001) by Todd Barron and *The Zen of Direct3D Game Programming* (Premier Press, Inc., 2001) by Peter Walsh. For a complete treatment of OpenGL, which was also mentioned in this chapter, be sure to read *OpenGL Game Programming* (Premier Press, Inc., 2001) by Kevin Hawkins and Dave Astle. These three books are also part of the Game Development series, and details can be found in Appendix E, "Recommended Reading."

PART II

THE NUTS AND BOLTS OF GAME DEVELOPMENT

Welcome to Part II of *Visual Basic Game Programming with DirectX.* Part II includes seven chapters that provide you with all the tools you need to create cutting-edge DirectX games with Visual Basic. These seven chapters will help you develop a toolbox of code that is necessary to get started working on a game.

Starting with bitmaps, Part II goes through the tricks and techniques of mastering the Windows API. It explains how to animate sprites, eliminate flicker with double buffering, and improve performance with dirty rectangles.

Part II also includes coverage of the most important components of DirectX, including DirectDraw, DirectSound, DirectSound3D, DirectMusic, and DirectInput. I think you will be surprised at what you can do with Visual Basic using DirectX with just these tools alone! The remaining DirectX libraries—Direct3D and DirectPlay—are covered in Part III, "Hardcore Game Programming."

Chapter 13, "Building the DirectX Game Library," summarizes all of Part II and bundles the game programming classes together into a single Visual Basic Game Library. You will be able to write a DirectX game by simply referencing this library or selecting from the large assortment of classes developed in Part II.

Part II includes the following chapters:

- Chapter 7: Break Out the Bitmaps
- Chapter 8: Supersonic Sprites
- Chapter 9: Let the Animation Begin
- Chapter 10: Diving into DirectDraw
- Chapter 11: Playing Sound and Music with DirectX Audio
- Chapter 12: Getting a Handle on User Input
- Chapter 13: Building the DirectX Game Library

CHAPTER 7

Break Out
the Bitmaps

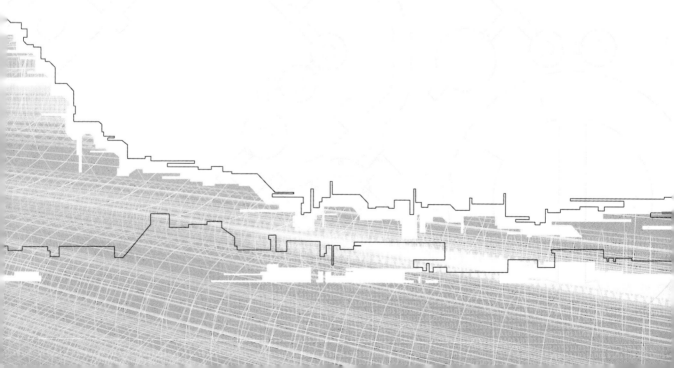

Bitmapped images are the core and substance of every game that is created, whether it is a 2-D vertical scrolling arcade game like the classics *1942* and *R-Type*, a flight simulator like *Jane's WWII Fighters* or *Iron Aces*, a first-person shooter like *Unreal Tournament* or *HALO: Combat Evolved*, or a real-time strategy game like *Age of Empires II* or *Empire Earth*. None of these games would amount to anything without the ability to load, manipulate, and display bitmap images.

Bitmaps are critical, the most important aspect of a game. Without the ability to load and display bitmaps of one form or another, you would be limited to vector graphics like points and lines, and games like the classic *Battlezone*. It should come as no surprise to learn that bitmap rendering is at the core of most graphics libraries, such as DirectDraw. Even a 3-D library must load and render textures—which are also bitmap images.

This chapter covers the subject of bitmaps in detail, showing you how to load and display Windows bitmap files. This chapter is very important because it lays the groundwork for the material that is covered in the next three chapters. The code in this chapter is the basis for most of the code that will follow, including advanced animation features like double buffering and dirty rectangles. You'll learn how to create memory bitmaps from scratch (for use as a double buffer, for instance), and also how to load bitmap files into memory.

This chapter covers the following topics:

- Basic Bitmap Handling (Using Visual Basic)
- All about Windows Bitmaps
- Advanced Bitmap Handling (Using Windows)
- Wrapping It All Up: The Bitmap Class

BASIC BITMAP HANDLING (USING VISUAL BASIC)

Visual Basic is quite limited when it comes to bitmap handling. Sure, there are the Image and PictureBox controls that can be very useful at times. But when it comes to loading numerous images and animating them on the screen, these controls are useless, because they are slow and consume a huge amount of memory.

In the past, I have tried to create a basic sprite engine using an array of PictureBox controls; trust me, the result was not pretty! There is a lot you can get away with by using this control, and you can even write games using PictureBox control arrays and the PaintPicture function. All you do is create the bitmaps for a game and then paste them into invisible controls on a form. Set a PictureBox control's AutoRedraw = True, so it will keep the bitmap in memory while it is invisible. (When AutoRedraw is enabled, the Image property holds a copy of the bitmap in memory—sort of an automatic double buffer built into PictureBox controls.) You can then use PaintPicture to display the image in a larger PictureBox (your main screen). Another option is to drop Image or Shape controls right smack inside the

> **TIP**
>
> **Keep use of the PictureBox control to a minimum, because it consumes a lot of resources.**

main Form or PictureBox and just move them using the Left and Top properties of the controls. I'll show you how to draw transparent bitmaps using these techniques later in the chapter, before you delve into more advanced methods.

How about Some Slow Shapes?

Here, let me show you what I'm talking about (since a source code listing is worth a thousand words, or something like that). Fire up a new project and name it Shapes. As with most of the programs in this book, you don't need to mess with the default form (which is always called Form1 in new projects). I prefer to do everything with code, even when controls are used. It's just more civilized that way!

For starters, this program will need a heading, followed by a Timer control and a Shape control:

```
'-------------------------------------------------------------------------
' Visual Basic Game Programming with DirectX
' Chapter 7: Break Out The Bitmaps
' Shapes Program Source Code File
'-------------------------------------------------------------------------

Option Explicit

Dim WithEvents timer1 As Timer
Dim shape1 As Shape
```

In case you were wondering, any time you declare a dynamic control that has events, you must use the WithEvents keyword. Note also that this doesn't work in code modules, only in forms. The reason you can't declare dynamic controls inside a class module is because controls only exist on forms. The really interesting thing about dynamic controls is that as soon as you declare the variable using WithEvents, the name of the control appears in the object drop-down list (along with Form1).

Now for the familiar `Form_Load` event. It is actually preferable to create dynamic controls inside the `Form_Activate` event, because `Form_Activate` is fired before `Form_Load` and it is usually better to have all of the dynamic controls ready to go before `Form_Load` comes along. But as long as controls are created before they are used, there is nothing wrong with creating them inside `Form_Load`. Here is the code listing for `Form_Load`:

```
Private Sub Form_Load()
    Randomize
    Form1.ScaleMode = 3
    Form1.AutoRedraw = False
    Form1.Caption = "Shapes"
    Form1.Show
    DoEvents

    'create the timer control
    Set timer1 = Controls.Add("VB.Timer", "timer1")
    timer1.Interval = 1
    timer1.Enabled = True

    'create the shape control
    Set shape1 = Controls.Add("VB.Shape", "shape1")
    ChangeShape
    shape1.Visible = True
End Sub
```

You must admit, that was more interesting than dragging controls onto the form. I personally think the GUI way is the hard way! There's just something sweet about a program that takes care of itself without human intervention. That reminds me, this is a great example to show the difference between early binding and late binding. When you create controls after the program has started running, that is late binding. Adding controls to a form during design time is early binding. You can tell the difference by looking in the Control Toolbox in VB. Only controls that are visible in the toolbox can be early bound (dropped onto a form).

But suppose you are linking in controls or objects at runtime, after the program has already been compiled? That calls for an interface, which is a powerful feature that allows you to add new components to a game after it has already been released to the public. For instance, suppose you want to create a really cool multiplayer galactic conquest game, and you want to frequently add new functionality to the game. Rather than recompile the whole program, you can just create new components using the interface the program uses and link the new features in through DLL files. Obviously the program would have to download new modules from the server, or you would have to ask users to download updates manually. But this functionality is extremely useful and allows for a huge amount of customization to a running game. If you noticed in the code listing for Form_Load above, there is a procedure call toward the end. The procedure is called ChangeShape. This procedure just sets the properties of the shape to random values to make the program more interesting.

```
Private Sub ChangeShape()
    shape1.BackStyle = Random(2)
    shape1.BorderStyle = 1
    shape1.BorderColor = RGB(Random(256), Random(256), Random(256))
    shape1.BorderWidth = 2
    shape1.DrawMode = Random(16) + 1
    shape1.FillColor = shape1.BorderColor
    shape1.FillStyle = Random(8)
    shape1.Shape = Random(5)
End Sub
```

ChangeShape is a pretty simple procedure, but you must take care when modifying it, because those properties are already being set at the maximum values (for instance, the FillStyle property). The Random function is actually not built into VB, and will be listed following the timer event below. (You will probably recognize this little function from previous chapters.) The easiest way to see what these properties do is to just run the program. But first, here's the code for the dynamic timer that was created earlier in the program. This timer is triggered at the fastest possible rate—one millisecond at a time. It probably doesn't actually run that fast, though. The timer control is a low-resolution timer and can't get anywhere near the performance needed for a real game. I decided to use a timer for this program to demonstrate how slow it is, compared to the programs presented later in this chapter. The Timer and Shape controls together make for a very slow demonstration. But that's okay, because it's always a good idea to keep your best stuff in reserve! I just want to set a base to which later programs might be compared.

Now, here is the listing for the timer1_Timer event.

```
Private Sub timer1_Timer()
    Static lMoveX As Long
    Static lMoveY As Long

    'initialize the movement variables
    If lMoveX = 0 Then lMoveX = 5
    If lMoveY = 0 Then lMoveY = 5

    'move the shape horizontally
    shape1.Left = shape1.Left + lMoveX
```

```
        If shape1.Left < 1 Then
            shape1.Left = 1
            lMoveX = Random(5) + 1
            ChangeShape
        ElseIf shape1.Left + shape1.Width > Form1.ScaleWidth Then
            shape1.Left = Form1.ScaleWidth - shape1.Width - 1
            lMoveX = Random(5) - 5
            ChangeShape
        End If

        'move the shape vertically
        shape1.Top = shape1.Top + lMoveY
        If shape1.Top < 1 Then
            shape1.Top = 1
            lMoveY = Random(5) + 1
            ChangeShape
        ElseIf shape1.Top + shape1.Height > Form1.ScaleHeight Then
            shape1.Top = Form1.ScaleHeight - shape1.Height - 1
            lMoveY = Random(5) - 5
            ChangeShape
        End If
End Sub
```

This is a pretty long piece of code just for a timer. Actually, this is the main loop of the program, and it is responsible for moving the shape. It also checks to make sure the shape stays within the bounds of the form. Also, any time the shape hits a wall, it is randomized using the ChangeShape procedure. Now a few support routines are required to finish off the program.

```
Private Function Random(ByVal lMax As Long) As Long
    Random = CLng(Rnd * lMax)
End Function

Private Sub Form_KeyDown(KeyCode As Integer, Shift As Integer)
    End
End Sub

Private Sub Form_MouseDown(Button As Integer, Shift As Integer, _
    X As Single, Y As Single)
    End
End Sub
```

The Random function just returns a random number using Rnd (which needs to be converted from a Single to a Long). The last two are events that make the program easier to use. You can press any key or click the form to end the program.

Now that the program is finished, press F5 to run it. The output from the Shapes program is shown in Figure 7.1.

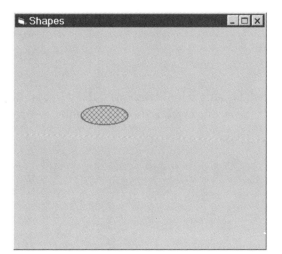

Figure 7.1

The Shapes program shows just how pathetic the Shape and Timer controls are!

The Budget Bitmap: Solid Images

Now for something that is a little more useful than the Shape control. Actually the Shape control could be used to create simple games, but vector-based games (using lines) are not nearly as much fun to play as raster-based games (using bitmaps). The Image control is a lightweight component that does not have a device context or window handle associated with it. This means that Images take up much less memory than the more powerful PictureBox. Images are fully capable of handling the needs of a simple card game or board game, for example.

How about if we take the Shapes program to the next level by using the Image control instead of a shape? The SolidImage program draws an image over a textured background, but is otherwise the same as the Shapes program. You will need to copy the background.bmp and image.bmp files from the CD-ROM (in \Sources\VB6\CH07\SolidImage) in order to run the SolidImage program. Additionally, all the graphics used throughout the book are collectively stored in a directory on the CD-ROM called \Bitmaps. You can refer to this directory any time you need a bitmap for one of the sample programs.

Since I fully explained the Shapes program earlier, and SolidImage is very similar to the Shapes program, I won't spend as much time on this one. Here is the declaration section of the program.

```
'----------------------------------------------------------------------
' Visual Basic Game Programming with DirectX
' Chapter 7: Break Out The Bitmaps
' SolidImage Program Source Code File
'----------------------------------------------------------------------


Option Explicit

Dim WithEvents timer1 As Timer
Dim image1 As Image
```

That should be pretty easy to understand, because it looks similar to the declaration section of the Shapes program. Now for the Form_Load event, which is used to initialize the program.

```
Private Sub Form_Load()
    Randomize
    Form1.ScaleMode = 3
    Form1.AutoRedraw = False
    Form1.Caption = "Solid Image"
    Form1.Picture = LoadPicture(App.Path & "\background.bmp")
    Form1.Show
    DoEvents

    'create the timer control
    Set timer1 = Controls.Add("VB.Timer", "timer1")
    timer1.Interval = 1
    timer1.Enabled = True

    'create the image control
    Set image1 = Controls.Add("VB.Image", "image1")
    image1.Picture = LoadPicture(App.Path & "\image.bmp")
    image1.Left = Random(Form1.ScaleWidth - image1.Width - 1)
    image1.Top = Random(Form1.ScaleHeight - image1.Height - 1)
    image1.Visible = True
End Sub
```

Did you notice the new LoadPicture function above in Form_Load? It looks like this:

```
Form1.Picture = LoadPicture(App.Path & "\background.bmp")
```

This single line of code loads a bitmap image from a disk and draws it on the form. Isn't that amazing? Some things are so easy to do in VB. I guess that is the greatest strength of the language—what it does, it does extremely well! Here is the code for the Timer event. It looks just like the code from the Shapes program, with the only difference being that every instance of "shape1" has been replaced with "image1."

```
Private Sub timer1_Timer()
    Static lMoveX As Long
    Static lMoveY As Long

    'initialize the movement variables
    If lMoveX = 0 Then lMoveX = 5
    If lMoveY = 0 Then lMoveY = 5

    'move the image horizontally
    image1.Left = image1.Left + lMoveX
    If image1.Left < 1 Then
        image1.Left = 1
        lMoveX = Random(5) + 1
    ElseIf image1.Left + image1.Width > Form1.ScaleWidth Then
        image1.Left = Form1.ScaleWidth - image1.Width - 1
        lMoveX = Random(5) - 5
    End If

    'move the image vertically
    image1.Top = image1.Top + lMoveY
    If image1.Top < 1 Then
        image1.Top = 1
        lMoveY = Random(5) + 1
    ElseIf image1.Top + image1.Height > Form1.ScaleHeight Then
        image1.Top = Form1.ScaleHeight - image1.Height - 1
        lMoveY = Random(5) - 5
    End If
End Sub
```

Okay, now for the support functions, which look the same here as they did in the Shapes program.

```
Private Function Random(ByVal lMax As Long) As Long
    Random = CLng(Rnd * lMax)
End Function
```

```
Private Sub Form_KeyDown(KeyCode As Integer, Shift As Integer)
    End
End Sub

Private Sub Form_MouseDown(Button As Integer, Shift As Integer, _
    X As Single, Y As Single)
    End
End Sub
```

Figure 7.2 shows the SolidImage program running.

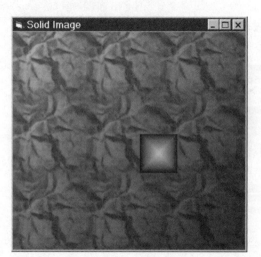

Figure 7.2

The SolidImage pro-gram shows how to use the Image control.

The Budget Bitmap: Transparent Images

Since you can't get inside an image, there is no way to draw an image transparently using the Windows API bitmap-drawing function, BitBlt. Instead, you must use the built-in bitmap-drawing function, PaintPicture. This function allows you to draw bitmaps transparently using the Picture property (which is the same process for drawing transparent bitmaps with BitBlt). Therefore, it is definitely possible to use images to create a game. While the Windows BitBlt function does not directly support the Picture property of an Image control, the VB PaintPicture function does! In order to draw an image transparently, you will first need to create a mask image that negates all of the transparent pixels in the source image, allowing the background to show through.

The mask is sort of like a negative version of the image that you would like to draw transparently. The mask (which is shown in Figure 7.3) is a black and white version of the source image.

Figure 7.3

The mask negates all transparent pixels in the source image.

Wherever there is a color pixel in the source image, there is a black pixel in the mask; on the other hand, all transparent pixels in the source image become white in the mask. The resulting mask can then be blitted to the screen using the vbSrcAnd ("logical and") operation, followed by the actual image using the vbSrcPaint ("logical paint") operation.

Figure 7.4 shows the result of applying vbSrcAnd between the mask and background images.

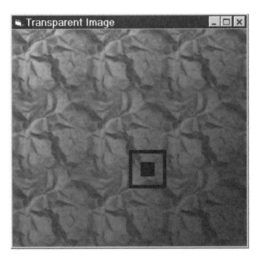

Figure 7.4

The mask blitted over the background using the vbSrcAnd operation

Notice how none of the white pixels in the mask showed up! Only the black pixels are displayed. This is the key to transparency—and the key to game programming in general. Here is what happens. The vbSrcAnd operation combines each of the pixels in the background with each of the pixels in the mask using a process that might look something like this:

```
For Y = 1 To MaskHeight
    For X = 1 To MaskWidth
        SourceColor = GetPixel(Background, X, Y)
        MaskColor = GetPixel(Mask, X, Y)
        NewColor = (SourceColor And MaskColor)
        SetPixel Background, X, Y, NewColor
    Next X
Next Y
```

This code would be way too slow in practice, and is meant only for illustration. The real blitting process involves a high-speed block memory copy using the vbSrcAnd operation. In the case of `BitBlt`, this is often handled by the video card's device driver and runs extremely fast. Even in VB, the `PaintPicture` blitting routine copies the entire block of memory in only a few processor cycles, and does not work on each pixel at a time. Since bit block transfers are integral to the Windows interface, blitting an entire back buffer to eliminate flickering is highly optimized. (This is what happens when AutoRedraw is set to True.)

Once the mask has been blitted using the vbSrcAnd operation, the source image is blitted to the same location using the vbSrcPaint operation. The vbSrcPaint operation combines pixels in the destination with the pixels in the source image. Figure 7.5 shows the result of blitting the source image using vbSrcPaint without the mask.

Figure 7.5

The source image blitted over the background, using the vbScrPaint operation

See how the source image still comes out transparent but looks like it has been blended into the background? This is the second key to game animation. When combined with the mask, the result is a fully rendered transparent image. Figure 7.6 shows the final result of combining the mask (using vbSrcAnd) with the source image (using vbSrcPaint). The result is that the black pixels from the transparent mask are combined with the solid pixels of the source image. Since the source image is blitted using vbSrcPaint (to eliminate the transparent pixels), the black pixels restore the source pixels to their original state.

Now for a program to demonstrate transparent blitting. The TransparentImage program is based on the SolidImage program, so the following listing should look familiar. The changes really just involve the use of the mask image. Here is the declaration section of the program:

Figure 7.6

The TransparentImage program shows you how to draw transparent bitmaps using the Image control.

```
'-----------------------------------------------------------------------
' Visual Basic Game Programming with DirectX
' Chapter 7: Break Out The Bitmaps
' TransparentImage Program Source Code File
'-----------------------------------------------------------------------


Option Explicit

Dim WithEvents timer1 As Timer
Dim image1 As Image
Dim mask1 As Image
```

The Form_Load event has also changed very little. At the bottom of the procedure, you will find the new lines of code that create the mask image. Note that AutoRedraw is now set to True. Since this program is using PaintPicture rather than moving the Image control (as in the SolidImage program), AutoRedraw keeps the display from flickering.

```
Private Sub Form_Load()
    Randomize
    Form1.ScaleMode = 3
    Form1.AutoRedraw = True
    Form1.Caption = "Transparent Image"
    Form1.Picture = LoadPicture(App.Path & "\background.bmp")
    Form1.Show
    DoEvents
```

```
        'create the timer control
        Set timer1 = Controls.Add("VB.Timer", "timer1")
        timer1.Interval = 1
        timer1.Enabled = True

        'create the image control
        Set image1 = Controls.Add("VB.Image", "image1")
        image1.Picture = LoadPicture(App.Path & "\image.bmp")
        image1.Left = Random(Form1.ScaleWidth - image1.Width - 1)
        image1.Top = Random(Form1.ScaleHeight - image1.Height - 1)
        image1.Visible = False

        'create the mask control
        Set mask1 = Controls.Add("VB.Image", "mask1")
        mask1.Picture = LoadPicture(App.Path & "\mask.bmp")
        mask1.Visible = False
End Sub
```

The Timer event has changed quite a bit in this program, because now the image and the mask must be blitted to the screen after the movement code is finished.

```
Private Sub timer1_Timer()
    Static lMoveX As Long
    Static lMoveY As Long

    'initialize the movement variables
    If lMoveX = 0 Then lMoveX = 5
    If lMoveY = 0 Then lMoveY = 5

    'move the image horizontally
    image1.Left = image1.Left + lMoveX
    If image1.Left < 1 Then
        image1.Left = 1
        lMoveX = Random(5) + 1
    ElseIf image1.Left + image1.Width > Form1.ScaleWidth Then
        image1.Left = Form1.ScaleWidth - image1.Width - 1
        lMoveX = Random(5) - 5
    End If

    'move the image vertically
    image1.Top = image1.Top + lMoveY
```

```
    If image1.Top < 1 Then
        image1.Top = 1
        lMoveY = Random(5) + 1
    ElseIf image1.Top + image1.Height > Form1.ScaleHeight Then
        image1.Top = Form1.ScaleHeight - image1.Height - 1
        lMoveY = Random(5) - 5
    End If

    'redraw the background image (the slow but easy way)
    Form1.Picture = LoadPicture(App.Path & "\background.bmp")

    'draw the mask bitmap
    Form1.PaintPicture mask1.Picture, image1.Left, image1.Top, _
        image1.Width, image1.Height, 0, 0, _
        image1.Width, image1.Height, vbSrcAnd

    'draw the image bitmap
    Form1.PaintPicture image1.Picture, image1.Left, image1.Top, _
        image1.Width, image1.Height, 0, 0, _
        image1.Width, image1.Height, vbSrcPaint
End Sub
```

Now for the support routines once again:

```
Private Function Random(ByVal lMax As Long) As Long
    Random = CLng(Rnd * lMax)
End Function

Private Sub Form_KeyDown(KeyCode As Integer, Shift As Integer)
    End
End Sub

Private Sub Form_MouseDown(Button As Integer, Shift As Integer, _
    X As Single, Y As Single)
    End
End Sub
```

When you run this program, notice how much smoother it looks. There is no more flickering because the Image control is not being physically moved around on the form. Rather, it remains hidden and is blitted to the form directly. AutoRedraw really slows down the program, but at least the display is flicker-free. This is definitely a step in the right direction! This level of transparent blitting is enough to get you started on a game right away. But hold on for a while, and I'll show you even more tricks. For example, how would you like to be able to load a bitmap directly into a Windows device context and then use the fast and powerful `BitBlt` function? Not only will I show you how to do that later in this chapter, I will also show you how to generate the mask image. That's right, you won't even have to create the mask yourself!

Now for a final note about transparency. There are some special effects you can create by using different combinations of the bitwise operation parameter. Try using vbSrcInvert on the mask and see what happens! It creates a ghosted image that might be useful for showing a cloaked spaceship. You can also draw the source image without the mask, using vbSrcPaint to get a merged image that is similar but not washed out in white. You can get some really interesting effects without manipulating any of the pixels. More importantly, you can perform some of these effects without redrawing any of your source bitmaps. Table 7.1 shows the blitting operations available to the `PaintPicture` procedure.

Graphics Heavyweight: The PictureBox Control

Not only does the PictureBox control have built-in drawing routines like PSet and Line, it is also capable of being a control container. This is one monstrous control, and is not even remotely usable as a means to store enough bitmaps in memory to be used in a game (as was the case with the lightweight Image control). The only thing a PictureBox is really useful for is acting as the destination drawing surface on a form. Think of the PictureBox as a big, heavy window that sits on a form, chock full of functionality. It is a heavyweight, ready to take on advanced image-handling chores. Not the sort of thing you want for storing sprites!

The PictureBox control exposes several new properties not found in Image. Most notably are the hDC and hWindow properties. With these two properties you can use a PictureBox with Windows functions like `BitBlt`. This control will be the focus of most of the graphics routines in this and the next few chapters. At the same time, PictureBox is similar to the Image control. Since both controls have a Picture property, they are interchangeable in that respect. They differ in the advanced properties mentioned previously (hDC and hWindow).

ALL ABOUT WINDOWS BITMAPS

In order to get the most out of something, you really do need to fully understand it. When it comes to code, taking someone else's word for it might be okay when you're in a hurry or when you're using a well-tested code library. But quite often in the development of a game you will come to a point where you need to do something differently. Without understanding how

Table 7.1 PaintPicture Raster Operations

Operation	Description
vbDstInvert	Inverts the destination bitmap.
vbMergeCopy	Combines the pattern and the source bitmap.
vbMergePaint	Combines the inverted source bitmap with the destination bitmap by using OR.
vbNotSrcCopy	Copies the inverted source bitmap to the destination.
vbNotSrcErase	Inverts the result of combining the destination and source bitmaps by using OR.
vbPatCopy	Copies the pattern to the destination bitmap.
vbPatInvert	Combines the destination bitmap with the pattern by using XOR.
vbPatPaint	Combines the inverted source bitmap with the pattern by using OR. Combines the result of this operation with the destination bitmap by using OR.
vbSrcAnd	Combines pixels of the destination and source bitmaps by using AND.
vbSrcCopy	Copies the source bitmap to the destination bitmap.
vbSrcErase	Inverts the destination bitmap and combines the result with the source bitmap by using AND.
vbSrcInvert	Combines pixels of the destination and source bitmaps by using XOR.
vbSrcPaint	Combines pixels of the destination and source bitmaps by using OR.

everything works, you are stuck using the routines provided to you (such as PaintPicture and BitBlt). How about a little clarification on what is going on behind the scenes with bitmaps?

Color Bit Depth

The most important factor to consider when working with bitmaps is the color depth of the images. The most common color depths include 8, 16, 24, and 32 bits. When referring to the number of colors in an image, you often refer to *bit depth*, since the number is representative of the bits, not the number of colors. To figure out how many colors are supported by the color depth (also referred to as *bits per pixel*, or BPP), use the following formula:

```
Total Colors = 2 ^ (Bit Depth)
```

In this formula, you take 2 to the power of the bit depth of the image (or video display). Table 7.2 shows the common bit depths, along with the total colors associated with each.

Another way to think of color depth is to consider the number of elements that make up each color. 8-bit color is limited to a maximum of 256 colors. 8-bit displays have a palette lookup table, while higher bit depths store the actual value of each color element within each pixel. For instance, 8-bit (palletized) displays use one byte for each pixel. 16-bit (high color) displays use two bytes per pixel, while 24-bit (true color) displays store three bytes per pixel. 24-bit color is not as common as 32-bit color because the formats both support the same number of colors, but 32-bit adds an additional channel (called the *alpha channel*) to each pixel. The alpha channel is used for translucency.

The important thing to consider with bit depth is performance. Most video displays are capable of accelerating the blitting routines at the device-driver level, and most new video cards today

Table 7.2 Common Color Bit Depths

Bit Depth	Number of Colors
8	256
12	4,096
16	65,536
24	16,777,216
32	4,294,967,296

have standardized the 32-bit display. It is usually best to support the widest audience possible when you're developing a game. By supporting only the latest technology you end up losing a large number of users who would otherwise have purchased and played your game. However, there will come a time when you will want to do away with code that supports older technologies to clean up the game engine and basically keep things simple.

When working with DirectX, there really is no problem switching from one display mode to another, because DirectDraw and Direct3D can handle any bit depth you throw at them. The real issue is with Windows GDI routines like BitBlt. Quite often higher bit depths will slow down a game without providing any real benefits. Unless you are specifically using the alpha channel for special effects, the extra byte required for every pixel in an image really does waste memory bandwidth and slow down the game.

I personally prefer to stick to 32-bit color in all of the graphics that I use, despite the alpha channel. 16-bit color is difficult to work with, because the three color components (red, green, and blue) must be packed into two bytes, which is a hassle. 24-bit color is not supported in as many graphics cards today, many of which offer either 16-bit or 32-bit color modes. Again, this is not an issue with DirectX, but I will show you how to tap into the memory buffer of a PictureBox and blit images directly to the screen in VB, and this requires familiarity with the subject.

Bitmap Structure

The Windows bitmap format has become a worldwide standard for image handling, due to the large number of Windows users on the planet. Windows bitmaps are most commonly uncompressed, but bitmaps can also be compressed. The compression algorithm is nowhere near the incredible results possible with JPG images. But the problem with JPG is that it alters the image in order to achieve higher compression levels. The bitmap format does not modify the image, which means it is *non-lossy*. A *lossy* compression algorithm, therefore, involves making changes to the image. The changes can be significant when dealing with an image consisting of many colors. Lossy compression usually works best with images that contain many similar colors, rather than many different colors.

For instance, shades of red may be compressed by breaking down the red hues into fewer colors. The result is an image nearly identical to the original, but capable of being highly compressed. This sort of compression is detrimental to game graphics, which is why it is better to use uncompressed image formats.

Game graphics are always meticulously created, and each pixel is very important because transparency is a factor. Therefore, you should not use a format such as JPG for game graphics. Probably the most common graphics format in the game industry is the Targa TGA format, but Windows bitmaps are also widely used in games. Figure 7.7 shows the structure of a bitmap file. Note that the color lookup table is only present in 8-bit bitmap images.

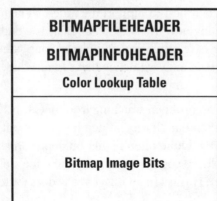

Figure 7.7

The structure of a bitmap file

The nice thing about bitmaps is that they look nearly the same in a disk file as they do in memory. When you load a bitmap file, the structure of the bits remains the same, so it is pretty easy to do a block read without a lot of code to decompress the image (as is the case with other formats). Fortunately, there is no need to write a custom bitmap reader because there is the LoadPicture function built into VB, and the LoadImage function built into the Windows API (which is covered later in this chapter). Once a bitmap has been loaded, however, it is important to be able to read the BITMAP structure, which looks like this:

```
Public Type BITMAP_STRUCT
    bmType As Long
    bmWidth As Long
    bmHeight As Long
    bmWidthBytes As Long
    bmPlanes As Integer
    bmBitsPixel As Integer
    bmBits As Long
End Type
```

You will encounter this structure later in the chapter, when I show you how to break into a PictureBox control's memory buffer. For now, just remember that this structure describes bitmaps in memory.

Bitmap File Header

The bitmap file header sits at the top of a bitmap file and describes the fun things that follow, such as the bitmap type and the offset in the file where the image bits begin. Why is it important to know this? I don't know; I just figured you might be curious! Actually, I'll show you how to read a bitmap header soon. The header of a bitmap starts with the BITMAPFILEHEADER structure, and is then followed by the BITMAPINFOHEADER structure. Here is what the bitmap file header looks like:

```
Public Type BITMAPFILEHEADER
    bfType As Integer
    bfSize As Long
    bfReserved1 As Integer
    bfReserved2 As Integer
    bfOffBits As Long
End Type
```

Bitmap Info Header

The bitmap info header follows the file header in the bitmap file, and describes the physical characteristics of the bitmap image (such as width and height).

```
Public Type BITMAPINFOHEADER
    biSize As Long
    biWidth As Long
    biHeight As Long
    biPlanes As Integer
    biBitCount As Integer
    biCompression As Long
    biSizeImage As Long
    biXPelsPerMeter As Long
    biYPelsPerMeter As Long
    biClrUsed As Long
    biClrImportant As Long
End Type
```

Reading the Bitmap Header

To show how the two bitmap file headers are used, I have written a short program that reads the headers from a bitmap file. The program is called GetBitmapInfo and is shown in Figure 7.8.

There are many cases where knowing the details of a bitmap would be helpful. For instance, if you want to make sure that only bitmaps of a specific bit depth are used, you could read the header for each image that your program uses and verify the bit depth. This might be handy if you allow the player to add his own mug shot to the game, for instance, but you want to require a

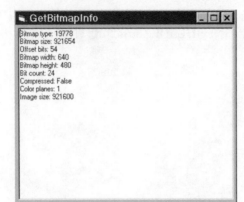

Figure 7.8

The GetBitmapInfo program reads a bitmap header and displays information about the image.

specific format. VB will convert the format to that used by the display in most cases, so this might not be needed, but it is nice to have the ability if you require it.

This is a Standard EXE program, using the default Form1 form in the project. Add a single TextBox to the form, and call it Text1. Resize the TextBox so that it fills the entire form and set a single property, MultiLine = True. This property allows the TextBox to display multiple lines of text.

Following is the listing for the GetBitmapInfo program. The listing is pretty short, so I don't think it requires a lot of explanation. If you have never used random-access files in VB, this program is a good example of how to open and read structures from a file.

GetBitmapInfo needs a bitmap image to read. You can use one of the bitmaps used earlier in the chapter or copy the bitmap.bmp file from the CD-ROM under the directory for this chapter (\Sources\VB6\CH07\GetBitmapInfo). You can actually use any bitmap image you want—the program should be able to read it.

```
'------------------------------------------------------------------
' Visual Basic Game Programming with DirectX
' Chapter 7: Break Out The Bitmaps
' GetBitmapInfo Program Source Code File
'------------------------------------------------------------------


Option Explicit

Private Type BITMAPFILEHEADER
    bfType As Integer
    bfSize As Long
    bfReserved1 As Integer
    bfReserved2 As Integer
```

```
        bfOffBits As Long
End Type


Private Type BITMAPINFOHEADER
    biSize As Long
    biWidth As Long
    biHeight As Long
    biPlanes As Integer
    biBitCount As Integer
    biCompression As Long
    biSizeImage As Long
    biXPelsPerMeter As Long
    biYPelsPerMeter As Long
    biClrUsed As Long
    biClrImportant As Long
End Type


Private Type BitmapStruct
    FileHeader As BITMAPFILEHEADER
    InfoHeader As BITMAPINFOHEADER
End Type


Dim bitmap As BitmapStruct
Dim filename As String
Dim filenum As Long

Private Sub PrintOut(ByVal msg As String)
    Text1.Text = Text1.Text & msg & vbCrLf
End Sub

Private Sub Form_Load()
    Form1.Caption = "GetBitmapInfo"

    'set the bitmap filename
    filename = App.Path & "\bitmap.bmp"

    'open the bitmap file
    filenum = FreeFile()
    Open filename For Random As #filenum _
        Len = Len(bitmap)
```

```
'read the bitmap header
Get #filenum, 1, bitmap

'close the file
Close #filenum

'see if bitmap file was valid
If Len(bitmap) = 0 Then
    PrintOut "Bitmap header is empty"
    Exit Sub
End If

'display bitmap information
PrintOut "Bitmap type: " & bitmap.FileHeader.bfType
PrintOut "Bitmap size: " & bitmap.FileHeader.bfSize
PrintOut "Offset bits: " & bitmap.FileHeader.bfOffBits
PrintOut "Bitmap width: " & bitmap.InfoHeader.biWidth
PrintOut "Bitmap height: " & bitmap.InfoHeader.biHeight
PrintOut "Bit count: " & bitmap.InfoHeader.biBitCount
PrintOut "Compressed: " & CBool(bitmap.InfoHeader.biCompression)
PrintOut "Color planes: " & bitmap.InfoHeader.biPlanes
PrintOut "Image size: " & bitmap.InfoHeader.biSizeImage
End Sub
```

Note how this program combined both the file header and info header into a single Type structure. This makes it really easy to load the structure and take a peek into the details of a bitmap without requiring more than a single line of code to read from the file (the Get statement).

ADVANCED BITMAP HANDLING (USING WINDOWS)

I don't know about you, but I'm pretty stoked already about the capabilities of VB for handling bitmaps! You have already seen how easy it is to load a bitmap using the LoadPicture function, and how easy it is to draw a transparent bitmap. This chapter could probably end right now based on just these features!

However, as is usually the case, there is always a faster way to do something in VB by tapping into the physics of the universe. (And, when working with VB, the universe is the Windows API.) In fact, that's a pretty good rule of thumb that you should remember: There is always a faster way to write code. I state this with confidence because progress is a scary thing. Just when you get the feeling that there are no more secrets in the universe, or that hard drive densities have reached the limit, or that compression has reached an unbelievable ratio…someone new comes along and shatters all the old records.

Loading Bitmaps into Memory

You have already seen how easy it is to load a bitmap into an Image control and then draw it transparently onto a form. But what if you don't want to use a control to load bitmaps? As the TransparentImage program showed, the Image control does not need to be visible, since the PaintPicture procedure just looks at the image's Picture property. Unlike the SolidImage program, which moved the actual control around the screen, the TransparentImage program kept the image hidden.

Given that factor, wouldn't it make more sense to avoid the overhead of the Image control altogether and just load a bitmap directly into a memory buffer? After all, Windows excels at bitmap handling, so there should be some way to tap into those advanced features from within VB.

Using LoadImage

Yes, there is a way! There is a really slick function called LoadImage that will not only load a bitmap file, but will also allocate memory and create a bitmap handle for you. Isn't the Windows API great? Here is what the LoadImage function looks like:

```
Private Declare Function LoadImage _
    Lib "user32" Alias "LoadImageA" ( _
    ByVal hInst As Long, _
    ByVal Filename As String, _
    ByVal un1 As Long, _
    ByVal Width As Long, _
    ByVal Height As Long, _
    ByVal opmode As Long _
) As Long
```

At first glance, this function can be intimidating. The important thing to remember when dealing with Windows functions is that they are pretty much self-contained, and therefore require a lot of parameters to handle many different options. The LoadImage function, for instance, will not only load a bitmap file, but will also resize it to any resolution you want! Quite often the extra parameters in Windows functions will be set to zero or null. Here is a sample of how to use the LoadImage function:

```
Dim hBitmap As Long
Const LR_LOADFROMFILE = &H10
hBitmap = LoadImage(0, Filename, 0, 0, 0, LR_LOADFROMFILE)
```

The LR_LOADFROMFILE parameter is a constant that tells LoadImage to load the bitmap from a file rather than from a resource.

Now, this function looks great, doesn't it? But what good is an hBitmap going to do anyone? As far as I know, there is no function that draws bitmaps based on a parameter that looks like hBitmap. That's true! The hBitmap variable is just a pointer to the image bits in memory. To really use the bitmap, you must first create a device context and associate it with the hBitmap.

Whoa, have I lost you? I hope not! I think this is really starting to get complicated though, so an example is in order. But before I show you how to use this new information, I need to explain how to create a device context. Trust me, it will all make sense soon enough.

Creating the Device Context

The key to gaining access to the high-speed blitting routines in Windows is through a device context. When you're using a PictureBox, it is pretty easy to do because the PictureBox control includes an hDC property that you can pass to functions like BitBlt. The problem with that method is the overhead required by the PictureBox control.

Now do you see why it is so important to be able to create a device context in memory and load a bitmap into it? To create a device context, you use the CreateCompatibleDC function, which looks like this:

```
Private Declare Function CreateCompatibleDC _
    Lib "gdi32" ( _
    ByVal hdc As Long__
) As Long
```

Not too complicated at all! See, all you do is pass a source device context to the function, and it returns a new device context that is compatible with the one you passed to it. When you want to refer to the display screen (the desktop) in Windows, you can simply pass a zero to this function, like this:

```
Dim hdcBitmap As Long
hdcBitmap = CreateCompatibleDC(0)
```

That's all there is to it. Are you surprised at how easy this is turning out to be? It is always pleasant to find a Windows function that is simple, since so many of them have a huge list of parameters.

Selecting a Bitmap Handle into a Device Context

Once the bitmap file has been loaded and the device context has been created, you must associate the bitmap with the device context. This makes the bitmap available to functions like BitBlt. To make the association, you use the SelectObject function, which looks like this:

```
Private Declare Function SelectObject _
    Lib "gdi32" ( _
    ByVal hdc As Long, _
    ByVal hObject As Long _
) As Long
```

As you can see from the parameters for SelectObject, the device context comes first, followed by the bitmap handle. Here is how you would use the SelectObject function:

```
lRes = SelectObject(hdcBitmap, hBitmap)
```

Notice that you can ignore the return value from SelectObject and just call it like a procedure.

Getting Down to Business: The Bitmap Loader

Putting all of this information together results in a function that loads a bitmap file into memory and creates a device context for the bitmap. This particular LoadBitmap function uses global variables for hBitmap and hdcBitmap. The result is that you can then use hdcBitmap with BitBlt to draw bitmaps to any destination device context (even to a PictureBox). The important thing to remember is to delete hBitmap and hdcBitmap after you are done with them, because Windows doesn't automatically delete them for you. Here is the code for the custom bitmap loader:

```
Public Function LoadBitmap(ByVal Filename As String) As Boolean
    LoadBitmap = False

    'load bitmap file into memory
    hBitmap = LoadImage(0, Filename, 0, 0, 0, LR_LOADFROMFILE)
    If hBitmap = 0 Then Exit Function

    'create a device context to hold the image
    hdcBitmap = CreateCompatibleDC(0)
    If hdcBitmap = 0 Then Exit Function

    'select the bitmap into the device context
    SelectObject hdcBitmap, hBitmap

    LoadBitmap = True
End Function
```

Loading a Bitmap Directly into a PictureBox Control

Okay, let's take a step back and try something a little different just for fun. I mentioned earlier that LoadImage can scale a bitmap to any resolution that you specify. So let's modify the LoadBitmap function to copy a bitmap directly into a PictureBox. Sure, this is almost the same as using the LoadPicture function, but there is a difference! The LoadImage function does a far better job at scaling the image than PaintPicture or BitBlt, which render blocky scaled images.

The only real difference between this version of the bitmap loader and the last one is that this version copies the bitmap directly into a PictureBox and then deletes the bitmap data from memory. Here is the function to load a bitmap into a PictureBox, with the bitmap automatically scaled to the width and height of the PictureBox:

```
Private Sub LoadBitmapIntoPicture(ByVal Filename As String, _
    ByVal pic As PictureBox)
    Dim wid As Long
    Dim hgt As Long

    'get the desired size in pixels
    wid = pic.ScaleX(pic.ScaleWidth, pic.ScaleMode, vbPixels)
    hgt = pic.ScaleY(pic.ScaleHeight, pic.ScaleMode, vbPixels)

    'get the bitmap handle from the file
    hBitmap = LoadImage(ByVal 0&, Filename, 0, _
        wid, hgt, LR_LOADFROMFILE)

    'create a device context to hold the image
    hdcBitmap = CreateCompatibleDC(0)

    'select the bitmap into the device context
    SelectObject hdcBitmap, hBitmap

    'copy the bitmap into picresult
    BitBlt pic.hdc, 0, 0, wid, hgt, hdcBitmap, 0, 0, vbSrcCopy

    'delete the device context and bitmap
    DeleteDC hdcBitmap
    DeleteObject hBitmap
End Sub
```

For reference, the DeleteDC and DeleteObject functions (which are used to delete hBitmap and hdcBitmap) look like this:

```
Private Declare Function DeleteDC _
    Lib "gdi32" ( _
    ByVal hdc As Long _
) As Long

Private Declare Function DeleteObject _
    Lib "gdi32" ( _
    ByVal hObject As Long _
) As Long
```

Creating Bitmaps from Scratch

Now you have learned how to load a bitmap file into memory and create a device context for it, which is required for drawing bitmaps in Windows. Now take the code a step further and learn how to actually create a memory bitmap from scratch. This is what LoadImage does for you, but I want to show you how to do it yourself. There are numerous uses for scratch bitmaps, not the least of which is as a double buffer for flicker-free animation!

Creating a bitmap involves some of the same code that was used to load a bitmap with LoadImage. The only difference is that now you must create the hBitmap rather than having it passed back from the LoadImage function. To create a bitmap, you must use the CreateCompatibleBitmap function, which looks like this:

```
Private Declare Function CreateCompatibleBitmap _
    Lib "gdi32" ( _
    ByVal hdc As Long, _
    ByVal nWidth As Long, _
    ByVal nHeight As Long _
) As Long
```

CreateCompatibleBitmap only needs a handle to the default device context, and then the width and height of the new bitmap to be created. The result is a new hBitmap pointer to the image in memory. You can call the function like this:

```
hBitmap = CreateCompatibleBitmap(hdcDest, 640, 480)
```

That's all there is to it! At this point, you can create a compatible device context using the CreateCompatibleDC function, and then associate the two objects with SelectObject (as explained earlier). To be thorough, here is a function that creates a memory bitmap from scratch:

```
Public Function CreateBitmap(ByVal hdcDest As Long, _
    ByVal lWidth As Long, ByVal lHeight As Long) As Boolean
    CreateBitmap = False

    'free up memory in case function is called twice
    If hdcBitmap <> 0 Then DeleteDC hdcBitmap

    'create DC compatible with drawing surface
    hdcBitmap = CreateCompatibleDC(hdcDest)
    If hdcBitmap = 0 Then Exit Function

    'free up memory in case function is called twice
    If hBitmap <> 0 Then DeleteObject hBitmap

    'create bitmap compatible with DC
    hBitmap = CreateCompatibleBitmap(hdcDest, lWidth, lHeight)
    If hBitmap = 0 Then Exit Function

    'associate the bitmap with the device context
    SelectObject hdcBitmap, hBitmap

    CreateBitmap = True
End Function
```

You could use this function to create a back buffer the same size as your display surface, such as a PictureBox on a form. The new back buffer would then be usable as if it were just another PictureBox or device context for functions like BitBlt. To display the back buffer, you would just blit the entire buffer to the display surface with a single call to BitBlt.

"B" Is for Blitting

I have brought up the BitBlt function on several occasions, so it is time to actually go over this Windows function and explain why it is so popular. There are two other related functions that are equally useful (TransparentBlt and StretchBlt), so I will go over those as well.

Using BitBlt

The BitBlt function was named after the process that it performs, which is called "bit-block transfer." This is a term used to describe the copying of large numbers of consecutive bits from one location in memory to another, as quickly as possible. The BitBlt function declaration looks like this:

```
Public Declare Function BitBlt Lib "gdi32" ( _
    ByVal hDestDC As Long, _
    ByVal X As Long, _
    ByVal Y As Long, _
    ByVal nWidth As Long, _
    ByVal nHeight As Long, _
    ByVal hSrcDC As Long, _
    ByVal xSrc As Long, _
    ByVal ySrc As Long, _
    ByVal dwRop As Long _
) As Long
```

My first piece of advice: Don't be intimidated by this list of parameters! This function is very easy to use and you will have no problem with it at all. These parameters, in summary, simply mean this: Copy a rectangular region (with a resolution of nWidth, nHeight) from source device context (starting at xSrc, ySrc) over to destination device context (at X, Y).

There are really just two groups of parameters in this function. The first group includes hDestDC, X, Y, nWidth, and nHeight. This describes the destination DC, the position to draw the image, and the image size.

The second group includes hSrcDC, xSrc, ySrc, and dwRop. This describes the source DC, the source position (usually 0,0) from which to copy, and the copy operation (usually SRCCOPY).

It is quite simple to use the BitBlt function. Consider it with the simplest possible scenario— two PictureBox controls. Suppose both PictureBox controls are exactly the same size, and you simply want to copy the contents of one into another. Now, you could just use the PaintPicture procedure—or better yet, just use this line of code:

```
Picture2.Picture = Picture1.Picture
```

This line of code could easily put BitBlt out of business, were it not for the fact that the Picture property does not work with a device context—absolutely essential for memory bitmap handling, which is all leading up to sprites in Chapter 8, "Supersonic Sprites."

Rather than cheat with the Picture properties, here is the code you would use to copy one PictureBox into another. However, there is one important consideration that I must mention first. This code assumes that the ScaleMode of both PictureBox controls has already been set to 3 - Pixel. If the ScaleMode is set to any other value, this code might not work. In practice, everything you do in VB graphics-wise should be in pixel mode. Now, here is that code I promised:

```
BitBlt Picture2.hDC, 0, 0, _
    Picture1.ScaleWidth, Picture1.ScaleHeight, _
    Picture1.hDC, 0, 0, vbSrcCopy
```

This call to BitBlt will copy the entire contents of Picture1 into Picture2. The beauty of this function is that you could just as easily blit the contents of a memory bitmap (identified by hdcBitmap) into Picture2, and vice versa.

Using StretchBlt

StretchBlt is very similar to BitBlt in functionality, but it has two extra parameters that define the width and height of the source region to be copied to the destination (which might not be the same size). StretchBlt scales the resulting image accordingly. The StretchBlt function looks like this:

```
Public Declare Function StretchBlt Lib "gdi32" ( _
    ByVal hdc As Long, _
    ByVal X As Long, _
    ByVal Y As Long, _
    ByVal nWidth As Long, _
    ByVal nHeight As Long, _
    ByVal hSrcDC As Long, _
    ByVal xSrc As Long, _
    ByVal ySrc As Long, _
    ByVal nSrcWidth As Long, _
    ByVal nSrcHeight As Long, _
    ByVal dwRop As Long _
) As Long
```

Normally, there is too great a performance hit when performing operations like scaling in real time. Most often, games will use varying image sizes to account for higher resolutions in the display (or the zoom feature in a game, as the case might be).

Using TransparentBlt

TransparentBlt is a function that handles transparent blitting automatically. Imagine that, a function that creates a mask on its own and then draws any bitmap you want—transparently! Actually, it is more likely that TransparentBlt just draws each pixel of the source bitmap and checks for transparency along the way, rather than using a mask. It is a pretty useful function. The only problem is that this function only made its debut with Windows 98; it is not available to Windows 95. This is probably not really a problem today, since Windows 95 is such an old operating system. But TransparentBlt is sufficiently unknown that you might not want to use it. The function is highly dependent upon the device driver that comes with the installed video card on a system, and performance will vary from one system to another. In other words, use at your own risk!

Here is what the `TransparentBlt` function looks like:

```
Public Declare Function TransparentBlt Lib "msimg32" ( _
    ByVal hdcDest As Long, _
    ByVal iXStartDest As Long, _
    ByVal iYStartDest As Long, _
    ByVal iWidthDest As Long, _
    ByVal iHeightDest As Long, _
    ByVal hdcSource As Long, _
    ByVal iXStartSrc As Long, _
    ByVal iYStartSrc As Long, _
    ByVal iWidthSrc As Long, _
    ByVal iHeightSrc As Long, _
    ByVal iTransparentColor As Long _
) As Long
```

This function is more like the `StretchBlt` function than `BitBlt`, because it lets you define the source and destination size of the region being blitted. Another interesting thing about `TransparentBlt` is the noticeable lack of a dwRop parameter, which is present in `BitBlt` and `StretchBlt` and determines the bitwise operation performed on the image. Instead, this function has an iTransparentColor parameter that you use to define the color key for the image. You can pass a color to the function using the RGB function. For an idea of how this support function works, check out the following line of code:

```
WhiteColor = RGB(255,255,255)
```

The key here is that `TransparentBlt` does not come from the same library as `BitBlt` and `StretchBlt`, which are both members of gdi32.dll. `TransparentBlt` is a member of msimg32.dll, the Microsoft Imaging library.

Due to the idiosyncrasies involved with this function, I prefer not to use it. `BitBlt` works just fine, and with this function I know exactly what is going on with the mask image. However, that should not deter you from using `TransparentBlt` for your own needs.

Accessing Bitmap Bits

What's the next step on the road to bitmap paradise? A useful feature might be to gain access to the actual bits that make up a bitmap image. One reason why this would be useful is the ability to modify the memory buffer that sits behind a PictureBox. That way, you are not confined to the drawing routines built into the control. This would also pave the way for subclassing the PictureBox into your own creation or providing the ability to generate a mask for transparent blitting.

Reading and setting the bits of a bitmap image is not a fast enough process to be performed in real time in the middle of a high-speed animation loop. But it is certainly a good way to tinker with the insides of a bitmap. You can do some fun things with bitmap bits. For instance, you could find out the device context of the program window and actually modify the default Windows Minimize, Maximize, and Close buttons.

GetBitmapBits and SetBitmapBits

The key to accessing a bitmap's memory buffer is a pair of functions called GetBitmapBits and SetBitmapBits. Now as the names infer, these functions retrieve and then replace the bits that make up a bitmap image. This is not actually a true method of reading and writing directly to the buffer, but rather a useful workaround.

The GetBitmapBits procedure looks like this:

```
Private Declare Function GetBitmapBits Lib "gdi32" ( _
    ByVal hBitmap As Long, _
    ByVal dwCount As Long, _
    lpBits As Any _
) As Long
```

Likewise, the SetBitmapBits function looks like this:

```
Private Declare Function SetBitmapBits Lib "gdi32" ( _
    ByVal hBitmap As Long, _
    ByVal dwCount As Long, _
    lpBits As Any _
) As Long
```

These functions both share the same set of parameters, which makes it easy to use them. The first parameter is a bitmap handle, hBitmap. Remember when I showed you how to create a bitmap using the CreateCompatibleBitmap function? Well, these functions use the handle returned by CreateCompatibleBitmap (as well as LoadImage).

The second parameter, dwCount, is the size of the image in bytes, while the lpBits parameter is a reference to an array that holds the bitmap bits.

The BitmapBits Program

What better way to demonstrate how to use GetBitmapBits and SetBitmapBits than through a real program? The BitmapBits program creates a PictureBox and then copies the bitmap bits of the PictureBox into a byte array. The program then loads a small bitmap image and draws it inside the PictureBox byte array. There are two different ways to draw the image—either solid or with transparency.

The BitmapBits program uses a new Windows function called CopyMemory, which looks like this:

```
Private Declare Sub CopyMemory _
    Lib "kernel32" Alias "RtlMoveMemory" ( _
    lpvDest As Any, _
    lpvSource As Any, _
    ByVal cbCopy As Long _
)
```

CopyMemory copies a source buffer into a destination buffer at the rate of 32 bits (4 bytes) at a time, which is significantly faster than any of the routines provided by VB. You can use CopyMemory for any purpose, to copy bytes from any array or memory buffer to another, and you will be guaranteed the fastest possible speed. Since this code was written to work with 32-bit color mode, where each pixel on the display requires four bytes, the CopyMemory function is perfect.

Now for the BitmapBits program listing. This listing is missing several types and Windows functions that have been listed already in this chapter, because I have refrained from re-listing the code. Just keep in mind when you try to compile this program that you will need to add a few things from this chapter in order to compile it.

First, think about the variable declarations section. The constant, bTrans, determines whether the source bitmap will be drawn with transparency. A single PictureBox resides on the main form, and it is declared WithEvents, which gives it life. The two bitmap bit arrays are BitmapBits and SourceBits, and are simply declared as empty arrays. Later in the program these arrays are redimensioned with the correct size to hold the bitmap bits for both the destination and source bitmaps.

All of the remaining code resides in the Form_Load event. Most of the code should be understandable, with the exception of possibly the main loop (Do While). The loop is really not all that hard to understand if you think about what is happening. There is one major loop that iterates through the rows of the destination PictureBox:

```
For cols = 1 To src.bmHeight
```

The real meat of this program lies in calculating the position of each pixel or row that is copied. When transparency is enabled, the program runs much slower, testing each pixel for transparency like this:

```
If SourceBits(srcIndex + 1) <> 0 Then
    CopyMemory BitmapBits(destIndex), _
        SourceBits(srcIndex), 4
End If
```

This snippet of code checks the current pixel in the source image for transparency, as shown in Figure 7.9.

If the pixel is not transparent, then `CopyMemory` is called to copy the four bytes of that 32-bit pixel to the destination. The solid rendering code is much simpler than the transparent rendering code. When drawing solid images, you do not have to worry about transparency. This is where you can see some serious performance gains, because it is possible to blast the image an entire line at a time rather than a pixel at a time. I have seen performance improve by a factor of 100 when transparency is not an issue. Figure 7.10 shows the BitmapBits program displaying solid images with transparency turned off.

Figure 7.9

The BitmapBits program, with transparency enabled

Figure 7.10

The BitmapBits program modifies the PictureBox memory buffer directly.

Here is the code that blasts an entire line of the source image to the destination:

```
CopyMemory BitmapBits(destIndex), _
    SourceBits(srcIndex), src.bmWidthBytes
```

Okay, enough theory! Here is the complete BitmapBits program listing.

```
'============================================================
' Visual Basic Game Programming with DirectX
' Chapter 7: Break Out The Bitmaps
' BitmapBits Program Source Code File
'============================================================


Option Explicit

'Windows API constants
Private Const LR_LOADFROMFILE = &H10

'Windows API structures
Private Type BITMAP
    bmType As Long
    bmWidth As Long
    bmHeight As Long
    bmWidthBytes As Long
    bmPlanes As Integer
    bmBitsPixel As Integer
    bmBits As Long
End Type

Private Declare Function GetObject _
    Lib "gdi32" Alias "GetObjectA" ( _
    ByVal hObject As Long, _
    ByVal nCount As Long, _
    lpObject As Any _
) As Long

Private Declare Function GetBitmapBits Lib "gdi32" ( _
    ByVal hBitmap As Long, _
    ByVal dwCount As Long, _
    lpBits As Any _
) As Long
```

```
Private Declare Function SetBitmapBits Lib "gdi32" ( _
    ByVal hBitmap As Long, _
    ByVal dwCount As Long, _
    lpBits As Any _
) As Long

Private Declare Function LoadImage Lib "user32" _
    Alias "LoadImageA" ( _
    ByVal hInst As Long, _
    ByVal Filename As String, _
    ByVal un1 As Long, _
    ByVal Width As Long, _
    ByVal Height As Long, _
    ByVal opmode As Long _
) As Long

Private Declare Function CreateCompatibleDC _
    Lib "gdi32" ( _
    ByVal hdc As Long _
) As Long

Private Declare Function SelectObject _
    Lib "gdi32" ( _
    ByVal hdc As Long, _
    ByVal hObject As Long _
) As Long

Private Declare Function DeleteDC Lib "gdi32" ( _
    ByVal hdc As Long _
) As Long

Private Declare Function DeleteObject Lib "gdi32" ( _
    ByVal hObject As Long _
) As Long

Private Declare Sub CopyMemory Lib "kernel32" _
    Alias "RtlMoveMemory" ( _
    lpvDest As Any, _
    lpvSource As Any, _
    ByVal cbCopy As Long _
)
```

```
Private Declare Function GetTickCount _
    Lib "kernel32" ( _
) As Long

'program constants
Const bTrans As Boolean = False

'program variables
Dim WithEvents Picture1 As PictureBox
Dim hBitmap As Long
Dim hdcBitmap As Long
Dim bmp As BITMAP
Dim BitmapSize As Long
Dim BitmapBits() As Byte
Dim src As BITMAP
Dim SourceSize As Long
Dim SourceBits() As Byte

Private Sub Form_Load()
    Dim X As Long
    Dim Y As Long
    Dim rows As Long
    Dim cols As Long
    Dim destIndex As Long
    Dim srcIndex As Long
    Dim iCount As Long
    Dim iStart As Long

    'set up the form
    Form1.Caption = "BitmapBits"
    Form1.ScaleMode = 3
    Form1.Show

    'create the PictureBox
    Set Picture1 = Controls.Add("VB.PictureBox", "picture1")
    Picture1.Left = 1
    Picture1.Top = 1
    Picture1.ScaleMode = 3
    Picture1.Width = Form1.ScaleWidth - 1
    Picture1.Height = Form1.ScaleHeight - 2
    Picture1.BackColor = RGB(0, 0, 0)
```

```
Picture1.AutoRedraw = True
Picture1.Visible = True

'read PictureBox bitmap bits
GetObject Picture1.Image, Len(bmp), bmp
BitmapSize = bmp.bmWidthBytes * bmp.bmHeight
ReDim BitmapBits(1 To BitmapSize)
GetBitmapBits Picture1.Image, BitmapSize, BitmapBits(1)

'load bitmap file
If Not LoadBitmap(App.Path & "\image.bmp") Then
    MsgBox "Image file, image.bmp, not found."
    Exit Sub
End If

'figure out the size of the bitmap file
GetObject hBitmap, Len(src), src
SourceSize = src.bmWidthBytes * bmp.bmHeight
ReDim SourceBits(1 To SourceSize)
GetBitmapBits hBitmap, SourceSize, SourceBits(1)

'display bitmap inside PictureBox repeatedly
Do While True
    'start counting the drawing time
    iStart = GetTickCount

    'draw bitmaps for one second
    Do Until GetTickCount > iStart + 1000
        X = Random(Picture1.ScaleWidth - 33)
        Y = Random(Picture1.ScaleHeight - 33)
        'process columns
        For cols = 1 To src.bmHeight
            If bTrans Then
                'process rows
                For rows = 1 To src.bmWidthBytes
                    destIndex = Y * _
                        bmp.bmWidthBytes + X * 4 + _
                        cols * bmp.bmWidthBytes + rows
                    srcIndex = cols * _
                        src.bmWidthBytes + rows
```

```
                        If SourceBits(srcIndex + 1) <> 0 Then
                            'assume this is a 32-bit image
                            CopyMemory BitmapBits(destIndex), _
                                SourceBits(srcIndex), 4
                        End If
                    Next rows
                Else
                    destIndex = Y * bmp.bmWidthBytes + X * _
                        4 + cols * bmp.bmWidthBytes
                    srcIndex = cols * src.bmWidthBytes
                    CopyMemory BitmapBits(destIndex), _
                        SourceBits(srcIndex), src.bmWidthBytes
                End If
            Next cols
            iCount = iCount + 1
            DoEvents
        Loop

        'copy bitmap bits into the PictureBox
        SetBitmapBits Picture1.Image, BitmapSize, BitmapBits(1)

        'display the draw time
        Debug.Print iCount & " images/second"
        iCount = 0
    Loop
End Sub

Private Sub Form_Unload(Cancel As Integer)
    DeleteDC hdcBitmap
    DeleteObject hBitmap
End Sub

Public Function LoadBitmap(ByVal Filename As String) As Boolean
    LoadBitmap = False

    'load bitmap file into memory
    hBitmap = LoadImage(0, Filename, 0, 0, 0, LR_LOADFROMFILE)
    If hBitmap = 0 Then Exit Function

    'create a device context to hold the image
    hdcBitmap = CreateCompatibleDC(0)
```

```
        If hdcBitmap = 0 Then Exit Function

        'select the bitmap into the device context
        SelectObject hdcBitmap, hBitmap

        LoadBitmap = True
End Function


Private Sub Form_Click()
        End
End Sub


Private Sub Form_KeyPress(KeyAscii As Integer)
        End
End Sub


Public Function Random(ByVal lNum As Long) As Long
        Random = CLng(lNum * Rnd)
End Function
```

WRAPPING IT ALL UP: THE BITMAP CLASS

Now let's package all of this newfound knowledge into a convenient class that you can use to easily load and display bitmaps. Since this is a complete class, I will not leave anything out; I will include all of the function declarations and constants so you will know for sure that this code will compile successfully into a bitmap class. In Chapter 13, "Building the DirectX Game Library," these function declarations will all be moved into a Declares.bas file along with the Windows API functions used in other classes developed in the book.

The bitmap class is kind of large and includes a whole bunch of features that are not immediately apparent. For instance, the class includes all of the drawing routines from earlier chapters for drawing lines, circles, rectangles, and text. These drawing routines will be needed in future chapters, because the bitmap class will be used as a double buffer as well as a sprite container.

This class will be called clsBitmap, and will eventually be part of the game library. In fact, clsBitmap and the sprite class developed in the next chapter will be used

> **NOTE**
> Notice that the bitmap class is called clsBitmap, while the filename is called Bitmap.cls.

to write two complete games later on, in Part IV, "Complete Game Projects." For now, you can just create a new project and add a class module to the project. (To do so, select Add Class Module from the Project menu.) When you have finished typing in the code, save the class as Bitmap.cls.

Here is the list of Windows functions and constants used by the class. This snippet of code should be at the top of the Bitmap.cls file. These declarations and constants will be moved to a common file in Chapter 13, "Building the DirectX Game Library," but for now they need to reside within the bitmap class itself.

```
'-----------------------------------------------------------------------
' Visual Basic Game Programming With DirectX
' Chapter 7 : Break Out The Bitmaps
' Bitmap Class Source Code File
'-----------------------------------------------------------------------


Option Explicit

Private Const BITSPIXEL = 12
Private Const LR_LOADFROMFILE = &H10

Public Type BITMAP_STRUCT
    bmType As Long
    bmWidth As Long
    bmHeight As Long
    bmWidthBytes As Long
    bmPlanes As Integer
    bmBitsPixel As Integer
    bmBits As Long
End Type

Private Type OSVERSIONINFO
    dwOSVersionInfoSize As Long
    dwMajorVersion As Long
    dwMinorVersion As Long
    dwBuildNumber As Long
    dwPlatformId As Long
    szCSDVersion As String * 128
End Type
```

```
Private Declare Function LoadImage _
    Lib "user32" Alias "LoadImageA" ( _
    ByVal hInst As Long, _
    ByVal Filename As String, _
    ByVal un1 As Long, _
    ByVal Width As Long, _
    ByVal Height As Long, _
    ByVal opmode As Long) As Long

Private Declare Function CreatePen _
    Lib "gdi32" ( _
    ByVal nPenStyle As Long, _
    ByVal nWidth As Long, _
    ByVal crColor As Long _
) As Long

Private Declare Function SetTextColor _
    Lib "gdi32" ( _
    ByVal hdc As Long, _
    ByVal crColor As Long _
) As Long

Private Declare Function TextOutA _
    Lib "gdi32" ( _
    ByVal hdc As Long, _
    ByVal X As Long, _
    ByVal Y As Long, _
    ByVal lpString As String, _
    ByVal nCount As Long _
) As Long

Private Declare Function SetBkMode _
    Lib "gdi32" ( _
    ByVal hdc As Long, _
    ByVal nBkMode As Long _
) As Long

Private Declare Function CreateCompatibleDC _
    Lib "gdi32" ( _
    ByVal hdc As Long _
) As Long
```

```vb
Private Declare Function CreateCompatibleBitmap _
    Lib "gdi32" ( _
    ByVal hdc As Long, _
    ByVal nWidth As Long, _
    ByVal nHeight As Long _
) As Long

Private Declare Function SelectObject _
    Lib "gdi32" ( _
    ByVal hdc As Long, _
    ByVal hObject As Long _
) As Long

Private Declare Function GetDeviceCaps _
    Lib "gdi32" ( _
    ByVal hdc As Long, _
    ByVal nIndex As Long _
) As Long

Private Declare Function GetDesktopWindow _
    Lib "user32" ( _
) As Long

Private Declare Function GetDC _
    Lib "user32" ( _
    ByVal hwnd As Long _
) As Long

Private Declare Function DeleteDC _
    Lib "gdi32" ( _
    ByVal hdc As Long _
) As Long

Private Declare Function DeleteObject _
    Lib "gdi32" ( _
    ByVal hObject As Long _
) As Long

Public Declare Function GetObjectW _
    Lib "gdi32" ( _
    ByVal hObject As Long, _
```

```
        ByVal nCount As Long, _
        lpObject As Any _
) As Long


Private Declare Function GetObjectA _
    Lib "gdi32" ( _
    ByVal hObject As Long, _
    ByVal nCount As Long, _
    lpObject As Any _
) As Long


Private Declare Function Ellipse _
    Lib "gdi32" ( _
    ByVal hdc As Long, _
    ByVal X1 As Long, _
    ByVal Y1 As Long, _
    ByVal X2 As Long, _
    ByVal Y2 As Long _
) As Long


Private Declare Function Polyline _
    Lib "gdi32" ( _
    ByVal hdc As Long, _
    lpPoint As POINT, _
    ByVal nCount As Long _
) As Long


Private Declare Function SetPixel _
    Lib "gdi32" ( _
    ByVal hdc As Long, _
    ByVal X As Long, _
    ByVal Y As Long, _
    ByVal crColor As Long _
) As Long


Private Declare Function MoveTo _
    Lib "gdi32" Alias "MoveToEx" ( _
    ByVal hdc As Long, _
    ByVal X As Long, _
```

```
    ByVal Y As Long, _
    lpPoint As POINT _
) As Long

Private Declare Function LineTo _
    Lib "gdi32" ( _
    ByVal hdc As Long, _
    ByVal X As Long, _
    ByVal Y As Long _
) As Long

Private Declare Function GetVersionEx _
    Lib "kernel32" Alias "GetVersionExA" ( _
    lpVersionInformation As OSVERSIONINFO _
) As Long

Private Declare Function BitBlt _
    Lib "gdi32" ( _
    ByVal hDestDC As Long, _
    ByVal X As Long, _
    ByVal Y As Long, _
    ByVal nWidth As Long, _
    ByVal nHeight As Long, _
    ByVal hSrcDC As Long, _
    ByVal xSrc As Long, _
    ByVal ySrc As Long, _
    ByVal dwRop As Long _
) As Long
```

There, that wasn't too bad. Now for the class global variables. You have already seen hdcBitmap and hBitmap, and BITMAP_STRUCT was explained earlier in the chapter.

```
Dim hdcBitmap As Long
Dim hBitmap As Long
Dim bmp As BITMAP_STRUCT
Dim pta(4) As Point
Private pt As Point
Dim hPen As Long
Dim hOldPen As Long
Dim ret As Long
```

Now for the class startup and shutdown procedures, which are called when the class is first created, and then when it is destroyed.

```
Private Sub Class_Initialize()
    Debug.Print "Bitmap_Initialize"
End Sub

Private Sub Class_Terminate()
    Debug.Print "Bitmap_Terminate"
    If hdcBitmap <> 0 Then DeleteDC hdcBitmap
    If hBitmap <> 0 Then DeleteObject hBitmap
End Sub
```

The next section of code for clsBitmap is a collection of properties for the class that expose some details about the bitmap that was either loaded from disk or created by the class. These properties include such useful values as Width and Height, and also provide a means to access the device context for the internal bitmap.

```
Public Property Get Width() As Long
    Width = bmp.bmWidth
End Property

Public Property Get Height() As Long
    Height = bmp.bmHeight
End Property

Public Property Get BitsPerPixel() As Long
    BitsPerPixel = bmp.bmBitsPixel
End Property

Public Property Get Planes() As Long
    Planes = bmp.bmPlanes
End Property

Public Property Get TypeNum() As Long
    TypeNum = bmp.bmType
End Property

Public Property Get WidthBytes() As Long
    WidthBytes = bmp.bmWidthBytes
End Property
```

```
Public Property Get hdc() As Long
    hdc = hdcBitmap
End Property

Public Property Get hWnd() As Long
    hWnd = hBitmap
End Property
```

Now for the bitmap drawing routine. This is probably the most used procedure of the class because it handles the blitting of the bitmap to a destination surface, such as a PictureBox. The procedure is deceptively short for all the functionality built into it. Since the class keeps track of the hdcBitmap variable and has access to the width and height of the image, the parameter list for Draw is really short. A generic Blt procedure is also included.

```
Public Sub Draw(ByVal X As Long, ByVal Y As Long, _
    ByVal hdcDest As Long)
    BitBlt hdcDest, X, Y, Width, Height, hdcBitmap, _
        0, 0, vbSrcCopy
End Sub

Public Sub Blt(ByVal hdcDest As Long, _
    ByVal Left As Long, ByVal Top As Long, _
    ByVal Right As Long, ByVal Bottom As Long)

    BitBlt hdcDest, Left, Top, Right - Left, Bottom - Top, _
        hdcBitmap, Left, Top, vbSrcCopy
End Sub
```

The Create function is similar to the CreateBitmap function presented earlier in the chapter, but now it makes a little more sense because the hBitmap and hdcBitmap variables are encapsulated inside the class, and you do not need to keep track of them as global variables. This also checks the version of Windows to make sure that the correct version of GetObject is called. There is a discrepancy between Windows 9x and Windows NT that causes a problem when GetObject is used, and this code gets around the problem.

```
Public Function Create(ByVal hdcDest As Long, _
    ByVal lWidth As Long, ByVal lHeight As Long) As Boolean
    Create = False

    'free up memory in case function is called twice
    If hdcBitmap <> 0 Then DeleteDC hdcBitmap
```

```
     'create DC compatible with drawing surface
     hdcBitmap = CreateCompatibleDC(hdcDest)
     If hdcBitmap = 0 Then Exit Function

     'free up memory in case function is called twice
     If hBitmap <> 0 Then DeleteObject hBitmap

     'create bitmap compatible with DC
     hBitmap = CreateCompatibleBitmap(hdcDest, lWidth, lHeight)
     If hBitmap = 0 Then Exit Function

     'associate the bitmap with the new DC
     SelectObject hdcBitmap, hBitmap

     'get bitmap info
     If GetWindowsCore = 1 Then
         'Win9x version
         GetObjectA hBitmap, Len(bmp), bmp
     Else
         'WinNT version
         GetObjectW hBitmap, Len(bmp), bmp
     End If

     Create = True
End Function
```

This Load function is almost identical to the LoadBitmap function presented earlier in the chapter, so it should require no explanation. The only difference is that this version now includes a call to GetObject and passes a structure variable called bmp. This is where the details of the bitmap are loaded into the class for retrieval through the properties. This functionality was covered earlier in the chapter, when I showed you how to read the header information of a bitmap. Since this function is so critical to the stability of the class, it includes some basic error handling.

While it is always a necessity to include minimal error handling in all of the code you write, I have not included much in the way of error handling in the sample code so far because it tends to make listings more complicated. The general rule, however, is to use error handling any time an error could cause the program to crash. The worst possible case is a dialog box appearing on the screen right in the middle of a game. To avoid that, trap errors and send them to a log file or just ignore them, unless the errors are absolutely critical.

Following the code listing for Load is the listing for LoadBitmapIntoPicture, which was discussed earlier in the chapter.

```
Public Function Load(ByVal Filename$) As Boolean
    On Error GoTo error1
    Load = False

    'get the bitmap handle from the file
    hBitmap = LoadImage(0, Filename, 0, 0, 0, LR_LOADFROMFILE)

    GetObject hBitmap, Len(bmp), bmp
    If hBitmap = 0 Or bmp.bmBitsPixel = 0 Or bmp.bmType = 0 Then
        Exit Function
    End If
    Debug.Print "Bitmap size: " & Len(bmp)

    'create a device context to hold the image
    hdcBitmap = CreateCompatibleDC(0)
    If hdcBitmap = 0 Then
        Exit Function
    End If

    'select the bitmap into the device context
    SelectObject hdcBitmap, hBitmap

    Load = True
error1:
    Exit Function
End Function

Private Sub LoadBitmapIntoPicture(ByVal Filename As String, _
    ByVal pic As PictureBox)
    Dim wid As Long
    Dim hgt As Long

    'get the desired size in pixels
    wid = pic.ScaleX(pic.ScaleWidth, pic.ScaleMode, vbPixels)
    hgt = pic.ScaleY(pic.ScaleHeight, pic.ScaleMode, vbPixels)

    'get the bitmap handle from the file
    hBitmap = LoadImage(ByVal 0&, Filename, 0, _
        wid, hgt, LR_LOADFROMFILE)
```

```
    'create a device context to hold the image
    hdcBitmap = CreateCompatibleDC(0)

    'select the bitmap into the device context
    SelectObject hdcBitmap, hBitmap

    'copy the bitmap into picresult
    BitBlt pic.hdc, 0, 0, wid, hgt, hdcBitmap, 0, 0, vbSrcCopy

    'delete the device context and bitmap
    DeleteDC hdcBitmap
    DeleteObject hBitmap
End Sub
```

Now for the additional code needed to complete the class. This includes DrawText, DrawEllipse, DrawRect, DrawPoint, DrawLine, and the support function called GetWindowsCore.

```
Public Sub DrawText(ByVal Left As Long, ByVal Top As Long, _
    ByVal sText As String, ByVal lColor As Long)
    Dim hPen As Long
    Dim hOldPen As Long

    hPen = CreatePen(0, 1, lColor)
    hOldPen = SelectObject(Me.hdc, hPen)

    SetTextColor hdcBitmap, lColor
    SetBkMode hdcBitmap, 1
    TextOutA hdcBitmap, Left, Top, sText, Len(sText)
    SelectObject hdcBitmap, hOldPen
    DeleteObject hPen
End Sub

Public Sub DrawEllipse(ByVal Left As Long, ByVal Top As Long, _
    ByVal Right As Long, ByVal Bottom As Long, ByVal Color As Long)
    hPen = CreatePen(0, 1, Color)
    hOldPen = SelectObject(hdcBitmap, hPen)
    Ellipse hdcBitmap, Left, Top, Right, Bottom
    SelectObject hdcBitmap, hOldPen
    DeleteObject hPen
End Sub
```

```
Public Sub DrawRect(ByVal Left As Long, ByVal Top As Long, _
    ByVal Right As Long, ByVal Bottom As Long, ByVal Color As Long)
    hPen = CreatePen(0, 1, Color)
    hOldPen = SelectObject(Me.hdc, hPen)
    pta(0).X = Left
    pta(0).Y = Top
    pta(1).X = Right
    pta(1).Y = Top
    pta(2).X = Right
    pta(2).Y = Bottom
    pta(3).X = Left
    pta(3).Y = Bottom
    pta(4).X = Left
    pta(4).Y = Top
    Polyline Me.hdc, pta(0), 5
    SelectObject Me.hdc, hOldPen
    DeleteObject hPen
End Sub

Public Sub DrawPoint(ByVal X As Long, ByVal Y As Long, _
    ByVal Color As Long, Optional ByVal hdcDest As Long = 0)
    ret = SetPixel(hdcDest, X, Y, Color)
End Sub

Public Sub DrawLine(ByVal Left As Long, ByVal Top As Long, _
    ByVal Right As Long, ByVal Bottom As Long, _
    ByVal Color As Long, Optional ByVal Width As Long = 1)
    hPen = CreatePen(0, Width, Color)
    hOldPen = SelectObject(Me.hdc, hPen)
    MoveTo Me.hdc, Left, Top, pt
    LineTo Me.hdc, Right, Bottom
    SelectObject Me.hdc, hOldPen
    DeleteObject hPen
End Sub

Public Function GetWindowsCore() As String
    Dim win As OSVERSIONINFO
    Dim ret As Long
    win.dwOSVersionInfoSize = Len(win)
    ret = GetVersionEx&(win)
    GetWindowsCore = win.dwPlatformId
End Function
```

SUMMARY

This chapter covered the subject of bitmaps in excruciating detail, exploring the structure of bitmaps, the header information, and the bits that make up the bitmap image. Along the way, I showed you how to animate shapes on the screen, draw solid and transparent images, and peek inside the memory buffer of a PictureBox with a program called BitmapBits.

Of course this chapter also covered the important subjects, like how to load a bitmap file, how to create a scratch bitmap in memory, how to draw bitmaps using Windows blitting functions, and also how to draw bitmaps directly to the bits inside a PictureBox.

This chapter was wrapped up with a functional bitmap class called clsBitmap that encapsulates all of the bitmap code developed in the chapter, providing an easy way to create, load, and draw bitmaps in a variety of ways. But that is only the beginning, because Chapter 8, "Supersonic Sprites," covers the fascinating subject of sprites. The next chapter will build upon all of the code developed in this chapter for handling bitmaps, and take it a step further with sprite routines for loading frames of animation and generating mask images.

CHAPTER 8

SUPERSONIC SPRITES

Sprites are usually small, transparent, animated objects that are the core elements of most games. Think of a sprite as a cartoon character in an animated movie like *Titan A.E.* or *Final Fantasy: The Spirits Within*. While these movies include a staggering amount of amazing computer-generated 3-D imagery, some on-screen images are actually drawn using standard animation techniques and overlaid on the 3-D generated backgrounds, which can be static backdrops or active scenes in motion.

> **NOTE**
>
> The sprite routines presented in this chapter build upon the source code for loading and drawing bitmaps from Chapter 7, "Break Out the Bitmaps."

To explain what this chapter is about, consider the definition of animation. Animation is the process of displaying pictures in rapid succession, each with a slightly different image, so that over a series of frames the appearance of motion is perceived. The key here is the word appearance. Sprites do not really "move" from one place to another on the screen or change shape. Rather, they are erased and redrawn in a new location (or with just a different frame) each time the screen is updated. The trick is flipping through the frames of animation fast enough to fool the human eye into thinking that motion is taking place, rather than images being drawn and erased over and over again. Sprite animation is actually very similar to cartoon animation.

The study of sprite animation is crucial to the mastery of game programming. No matter how powerful computer and video game hardware becomes, there will always be games that use sprites, despite the trend to move everything into the third dimension. Two-dimensional sprite-based games are among the most popular games on the market, including titles like *Age of Empires II*, *Diablo II*, *Panzer General III*, *Mech Commander*, and *The Operational Art of War*, among others. Mastery of sprite animation and all of the tricks and techniques involved is an important first step on the road to more advanced game development.

This chapter covers the following topics:

- What is a Sprite?
- Loading Animated Sprites
- Advanced Transparency
- Animating Sprites
- Putting It All Together: The Sprite Class
- Sprites in Action: Testing the Sprite Class
- Sprite Collision Detection

WHAT IS A SPRITE?

Since I don't want to leave you with a puzzled expression and more questions than answers, I'll start at the beginning and cover the basics of sprite animation. The reason is simple: No matter how many times I have read about sprites or written a sprite-based game, the subject never ceases to fascinate me, and I suspect most gamers feel the same way. Sprites are just plain fun to program. There are so many incredible things you can do once you understand how to program a sprite. That's right, a simple sprite! There is absolutely no need to jump into a complicated 3-D programming library like Direct3D when just simple transparent sprites will get the job done. Why, the possibilities for never before seen games are endless! It never fails: Every time I write a new sprite class or sprite engine, I always think of a new game that would be fun to play using this often-labeled *old school* programming model. Perhaps it comes from so many years of playing arcade games during the peak of the video game industry of the early 1990s.

Popular Sprite-Based Games

I vividly recall (even after all these years) pumping literally hundreds of quarters into *Street Fighter II*, a side-view fighting game for one or two players. After nearly six months of playing the game—and learning all the tricks by watching more adept players—I finally beat the game and became the so-called "world champion." I remember at that moment, all of the skills I had developed while playing with my favorite characters—Ken and Chun Li—had become finely tuned and synergistic. Rather than working out combos with the joystick and buttons, I was inside the character, performing actions without regard to what my hands were doing. That is what you might call the zen state of gaming, where you have attained such mastery of the game, you can nearly play with your eyes closed.

After completing *Street Fighter II*, I was then able to beat the game using only a couple of quarters rather than a couple of dollars. Of course, a year later I purchased the port of *Street Fighter II* for my Super Nintendo, and was very pleased with the quality of the game. It was very close to the original arcade game (although not necessarily worth the frightening price of $75.00 at the time!).

Achieving that level of mastery requires a certain amount of obsession and the desire to completely conquer something. Watching an adept player at the controls of a game is an experience in humility. Consider a martial arts master like Bruce Lee or Jackie Chan and watch the grace and speed at which they demonstrate their skill. Sure, most martial arts movies are highly-choreographed in order to avoid injury, particularly when using weapons such as knives or swords. But despite the choreography, one cannot watch a master without feeling a sense of wonder and awe.

Games such as *Street Fighter II* in the arcade (and *Doom* on the PC) are genre busters—games that set a new standard by raising the bar of technology and playability. Genre busters are always exciting because of the plethora of fun copycat games that are sure to follow (such as *Mortal Kombat* and *Primal Rage*).

Street Fighter II and other games in the fighting genre are all sprite-based games with sprite animation engines that display the movement frames for each character's fighting moves—which can number in the dozens or even hundreds. These games do not require 3-D hardware and do not feature a single polygon. Capcom is admired by many gamers for developing the greatest fighting game engine in the world. The recipe is so good that decade-old fighting games are still being ported to next-generation consoles like Sega Dreamcast and Sony Playstation 2, while far superior 3-D games like *Dead or Alive 3* and *Soul Calibur 2* are also available.

If you ever question what is more important—technology or playability—just consider the latest Zelda game for Game Boy Color. By following the same design paradigm from the mid-1980s, these old school games are outselling the latest Playstation 2 and Xbox titles. Technically, the game bits stored on a Game Boy cartridge take up less memory than a single textured 3-D character in a modern game (which might have hundreds of such characters stored on a CD-ROM or DVD-ROM). That is quite a testament to the importance of playability. But it also demonstrates that gamers are more than willing to sacrifice advanced technology for the portability afforded by handheld games.

My point is just this: Try not to get caught up in the hype of technology and 3-D graphics. Remember that gameplay is more important than any other factor! Sprites might be old school technology, but they are still used in modern games today and will continue to be used for years to come.

Static Sprites Versus Dynamic Sprites

Now, how about that definition of a sprite? If you actually look at any of the games I mentioned earlier, you can see that there are sprites all over the screen. In fact, you can't miss them! So, my definition of a sprite is this: A sprite is a transparent, animated, and moving object on the screen that is an active part of the gameplay.

The real difference between static and dynamic sprites is the amount of activity that a sprite performs. A completely non-moving, non-animated, non-transparent object such as a brick wall is not a sprite, but is rather a plain bitmap. You might want to use a sprite object to load and display the tiles of a brick wall, since tiles are most often stored as frames in a bitmap file. But the real definition of a sprite is an object that is an integral part of a game. Transparency is usually the telling attribute. Few objects in a game will move on the screen without transparency, so I would consider that a significant factor.

A static sprite, then, is a transparent object that moves on the screen and is an integral part of the game, but is not animated. A dynamic sprite differs only in that it is animated.

Basic Sprite Properties

Once you understand how sprites are used to create games, it is fairly straightforward to imagine what properties and functions a sprite will need in a game. This is where object-oriented code will really shine, because objects contain both the properties and functions internally. You will not need to include a code module with your game projects in order to use sprites, because the sprite class itself will be self contained (with the exception of reliance on the bitmap class that was created in Chapter 7, "Break Out the Bitmaps").

You might be wondering what any of this has to do with loading and drawing sprites. I have to admit, this sort of overhead (namely, talking about something before demonstrating it) seems to get off the subject of just drawing sprites on the screen. But what happens once you are able to do that? What differentiates a sprite from an ordinary bitmap? Without properties and functions to manipulate and handle the activities of a sprite, it is really nothing more than an array of bitmaps. That is not at all sufficient to write a game. The most interesting part of writing sprite code is plugging in all kinds of neat variables that will help to automate the sprite once it has been loaded and is ready to be blitted to the screen. In the case of sprite management, the over-head is really welcome and necessary. The idea is to create your universe so that it does not require too much micro-management.

You will probably find the need for even more sprite properties as you develop sprite-based games. Since the tendency is often to completely automate the sprite's activities and build a sort of engine to handle all the details, just remember that the sprites themselves should be rather lean. Additional functionality that relates to the bigger picture (such as limited sprite artificial intelligence) should be added to a sprite handler. The sprite itself should be thought of as a small person, with built-in capabilities (skills) and attributes (genes) that define the basic appearance and behavior of that person.

Now, here are some of the most common sprite properties, with a description of each.

Active Flag

The most important flag property of a sprite—with a flag being a true or false Boolean value—is the flag that tells whether the sprite is active (alive) or not. Since a game will have many sprites—usually hundreds, in fact—it is important to be able to differentiate between sprites that are currently active or inactive (dead) in the game.

Usually the sprite manager will iterate through all of the sprites in a huge array or collection and draw those sprites that are supposed to be visible on the screen. Obviously you do not want explosions to appear when there should be no explosion. For this reason, you must tell the sprite manager to ignore sprites that are not in use.

Transparent Flag

The transparency flag tells the sprite manager that this sprite should be drawn transparently, using a color key. The color key defines the RGB color that is *not* displayed when the sprite is drawn on the screen. When certain pixels in the sprite contain that color, they do not show up. The result is that background pixels will show through the sprite, making it appear transparent.

The actual process of drawing a transparent sprite involves merging the background and sprite pixels in creative ways (through two or more blitting operations), so that the end result is a transparent image. The transparency flag is important because not all sprites will need to be drawn transparently. Rather, some sprites might actually be background tiles that need to be drawn as solid blocks.

It is true that map tiles can be loaded as regular bitmaps, but it is usually more convenient to use a sprite to hold all of the tiles (using the animation frames rather than an array of tiles). The result is a clean way to handle tiles using the frame number, rather than a bitmap array. The same functionality could be handled with a bitmap array, but there is no need to do so when the sprite class is so convenient, even if tiles are not really sprites in the strictest sense of the word (since sprites are almost always rendered transparently). Any time you need to store numerous images in sequence for any reason, a sprite object is the way to go.

State

This property refers to the status of a sprite, usually called the sprite's *state of being*, so to speak. State is an important factor in gameplay because all sprites are moved on the screen based on the sprite handling code, which is discussed in Chapter 15, "Artificial and Simulated Intelligence." A simple sprite handler can use the state property to determine how to change the behavior of a sprite. For instance, suppose a sprite has five possible states:

- ATTACK
- DEFEND
- WANDER
- SEARCH
- FOLLOW

These state values help the sprite manager to move the sprite on a frame-by-frame basis. Note that a more *intelligent* sprite handler would actually coordinate all of the sprites in a game. The sprite manager is just the piece of code that draws, moves, and erases the sprites on the screen based on properties. The sprite handler is discussed in more detail later in this chapter, while a more advanced treatment of the subject is covered in Chapter 15.

Relative Position: CurrentX, CurrentY

The relative position of a sprite is the actual screen location in pixels, starting at the upper-left corner at 0,0. The horizontal position, which is maintained by a variable called CurrentX, and the vertical position, maintained by a variable called CurrentY, define exactly where the sprite is drawn and erased during each frame. This differs from the global position, which describes the position of the sprite in the *world* or *universe* of the game.

Global Position: GlobalX, GlobalY

The global position of a sprite is a large area of X, Y values that describe where the sprite is located in the game, which is often referred to as the game *universe* or *world*. The screen position can be considered a *snapshot* or *region* of the global game world. The GlobalX and GlobalY properties give a game much greater scope, since sprites can then move and act out simulated behavior on a much larger scale than is possible in the limited viewport of the screen. This is particularly true for scrolling arcade games and role-playing games, where the player sees only a small portion of the game world. By including a global position with each sprite, it is fairly easy to keep track of each sprite and determine when that sprite should actually be displayed on the screen.

Direction

The direction of a sprite *usually* defines which frame will be displayed when the sprite is drawn, but this is not always the case. Often a sprite can be traveling in a certain direction while facing in a completely different direction (as in a space combat game). Therefore, a separate property is used for the current frame. Despite this discrepancy, the number of frames usually equals the number of directions that a sprite can have. In the case of a role-playing game, direction will always equal the current frame, unless the game allows people and monsters to walk backward.

Direction is usually divided into discrete angles, and there are usually 8, 16, or 32 angles (or directions) that a sprite can face. The higher direction count means that many more frames of animation must be used, while a lower direction count requires far fewer frames, but gives a less realistic sense of motion.

Velocity: SpeedX, SpeedY

The velocity property is a set of variables that define the speed at which the sprite is traveling. These two variables, SpeedX and SpeedY, may or may not be closely related to the direction property. Often these values will directly affect the movement of the sprite, while the direction property is ignored.

The SpeedX variable affects the horizontal velocity of the sprite (left and right), while the SpeedY variable affects the vertical velocity (up and down). When the direction property is used instead of absolute velocity values, then a Select Case statement or a series of If…Then statements are required to determine how to update the sprite. For example, in a simple directional scheme that involves just eight degrees of motion, a sprite's velocity variables are updated based on the direction.

One of the problems with this velocity scheme is that diagonal directions usually end up being faster than horizontal or vertical directions. This sort of problem was solved by board game players with the invention of hexagonal game boards, where a step in any direction will result in close to the same distance. However, sprites do not move a space at a time, but rather by a specified number of pixels at a time, so a more clever method of movement is needed for more realistic motion. To simulate a more realistic method of sprite movement, you can use time delay variables such as movement rate and animation rate, which are covered next.

Movement Rate

The movement rate of a sprite is a time-delayed property that indicates how often a sprite's position should be updated, using the velocity variables. By using a delayed movement rate, it is then possible to use the more fluid values of –1 and 1 for the velocity variables and simply time all of the sprites based on movement rate (rather than absolute velocity). This keeps the animation speed down to a manageable level and allows you to create ultra-slow objects in the game, which would not be possible using straight velocity values alone.

Animation Rate

The animation rate of a sprite is also time delayed, like the movement rate, but it affects the timing of animation frames that are displayed. This property is distinct from the movement rate because the two separate properties allow for more complex (and realistic) sprite movement. Since movement and animation rates are not linked, you can have fast animation with slow movement, or slow animation with fast movement, and create some interesting effects. For instance, you might have blinking lights on a large spaceship that would otherwise not have much in the way of animation. By setting the animation rate to a higher value like 10, for instance, the lights will turn on and off at any interval that you need.

Erase Flag

The sprite erase flag indicates whether the sprite should be erased after each frame. Usually, the background image under a sprite is stored in a bitmap in the sprite class, which provides an easy means to erase the sprite by restoring the background image during the next frame. But this might not always be necessary, particularly when the background is rendered. When a background is static (meaning it does not change), it must be restored or the screen will fill with all of the previous locations where the sprite has been drawn. By erasing the sprite, the background is restored at each frame. But in a case where the background is rendered at each frame, such as in a scrolling arcade game, there is no need to keep track of the background under the sprite.

Current Frame

The current frame property keeps track of the sprite's current animation frame—the image that will be displayed the next time the sprite is drawn to the screen. The current frame should never exceed the frame count or be reduced to a negative value, or an array bounds error will occur in the bitmap array that stores the frames. When there is only one frame for a sprite (in which case the sprite has no animation), the current frame will be zero.

Frame Count

The frame count keeps track of the total number of animation frames that have been loaded into the sprite. This is a very useful variable because multiple animation sequences can be loaded into a sprite from multiple bitmap image sources, if desired. Each time a new frame is added to the sprite, the frame count is incremented. By keeping track of the sequence indexes, you can store multiple versions of the sprite images inside the same sequence (for instance, a normal plane and a damaged version of the plane).

Basic Sprite Functionality

The sprite properties look useful in theory, but really can't do much to get a game running without some functions built to use them. This is where the sprite functions come into play. The basic functionality of a sprite calls for the ability to load multiple frames of animation from one or more bitmap files, manage the frame number, and then draw and erase the sprite image based on the index in the animation array.

Load Frames

The basic bitmap class from Chapter 7, "Break Out the Bitmaps," included a function to load a bitmap image from a file and display it on the screen. Since sprites can consist of multiple frames of animation, a more advanced loading routine is needed—one that is capable of ripping frames out of a bitmap image and storing them in a bitmap array inside the sprite.

Generate Mask

Mask images are necessary for drawing sprites transparently. There are several ways to do this, but the most efficient way is to use the built-in Windows API blitting routine, which is called `BitBlt`. By first blitting a mask with the vbSrcAnd operation, and then blitting the sprite with vbSrcPaint, the sprite is drawn with transparency. Therefore, a routine to generate the mask based on the source image is needed.

Save Under

In order to erase the sprite after it has been drawn, the background under the sprite needs to be replaced over the sprite. To handle this functionality, the sprite will store a copy of the background before it is drawn to the screen.

Restore Under

The complement of the `Save Under` functionality, `Restore Under` effectively erases a sprite after it has been drawn (assuming the image under the sprite was first captured). This involves blitting the background image back over the sprite, bound to the precise dimensions of the sprite. This is the most efficient way to erase a sprite at every frame.

Draw Sprite

Naturally, a sprite needs a way to draw itself to the screen (or back buffer). As I explained in the description of the masking process earlier, the mask is first blitted with vbSrcAnd, followed by the sprite image with vbSrcPaint, to provide a transparent image. Of course, a sprite might not need transparency, so there is a flag to account for this possibility. When transparency is not needed, then the mask is ignored.

Next Frame

The easiest way to animate a sprite is to code the animation routine so that the frames can be looped with a simple function, which is what the `Next Frame` routine handles. When the frame counter exceeds the frame count, the counter should be looped back to zero.

Previous Frame

Likewise, the `Previous Frame` routine helps to animate a sprite by looping through the frames in the opposite direction. When the frame counter is less than zero, it is looped around to the last frame, and can then be decremented again using the `Previous Frame` routine.

Common Sprite Types

One of the most heated arguments I frequently have with fellow game developers concerns the need for a sprite engine to handle the chores of sprite management in a game. I have tried to develop several different types of sprite handlers; in each case, the overhead and number of conditions always made the sprite handler too complicated to be very useful. The problem is not that it is difficult to code a sprite engine. On the contrary, the basic functionality required to animate a sprite on the screen is a page of code or less. The problem is that, in a game, there are just too many instances where a specific sprite is handled differently than all the others. Coding the sprite engine to handle all the different types of sprites really ends up being a mess due to the number of custom conditions that must be handled.

One method I tried to use was creating a basic sprite class in VB, clsSprite, and then inheriting that class into multiple sub-classes, such as clsPlayerSprite, clsMapTileSprite, clsExplosionSprite, clsMissileSprite, and so forth. You get the idea, right? Well, by the time I finished coding all of these different sprites, I found that it actually took about twice as long as just coding the handler code within the main program! Not only that, all of these different sprite classes add unnecessary overhead to the program.

One appealing feature of a sprite engine is that you can have groups of sprites stored inside the sprite engine and classified by type. Then, any time you need to perform some operation on a group of sprites, simply request each sprite in the group, one at a time, before moving on to the next group. The real appeal of this concept is the ability to write sprite scripts and store them in data files, describing the behavior of each type of sprite. The sprite engine can then load a script and the images for a sprite, and the programmer does not need to interfere. Presto, instant sprites! There are psuedo-languages like Lua that were developed for this purpose. Here are some potential sprite types that could be supported by a theoretical sprite engine:

- **Enemy Units**. A group of sprites that includes the images of enemy units in a game—whether those units are enemy tanks, spaceships, or monsters—could be stored inside a sprite engine using this common group name.
- **Friendly Units**. All friendly units in the game might be stored in a sprite engine using this group name. Friendly units would be immune to player weapons (unless the game is very realistic), and might be controlled directly by the player, as in the case of a strategy game.
- **Projectiles**. This group includes all weapons that are fired, such as bullets, missiles, lasers, bombs, and so on. By grouping projectiles together in a common group, the sprite engine would be able to move and draw the projectiles automatically, and even process collisions with other sprites.

■ **Explosions**. Explosions might be grouped together and based on the type of projectile that generated the explosion, from a simple impact by a bullet to a thermonuclear mushroom. The sprite engine would possibly use a collision detection event to trigger an explosion based on the type of projectile that impacted an opposing sprite.

■ **Miscellaneous**. This group might include inanimate objects on the screen, such as destructible terrain in a war game (houses, trees, roads, and so on), clouds in the air, asteroids in space, or even birds flying by at random times.

Unfortunately, such attempts will usually fail or lead to overly complicated code (at least in my experience). Just imagine the amount of work it would require to write a script parser alone! When it comes to arcade games and role-playing games, there really is no better way to code sprites than to do so in the main program. Automating the sprite movement logic is really not a good solution. Trust me!

LOADING ANIMATED SPRITES

The basic bitmap loading routine that was developed in Chapter 7, "Break Out the Bitmaps," is great for loading background images and non-animated images for a game. But what about all this discussion of animated sprites? Surely if a sprite is animated, the game itself is not transforming the sprite as the game runs.

Of course not, although that is often the assumption that beginning programmers make. Although I will admit that as a beginner, my first impression was that a game actually loaded one image and created all the rest in an animation. In fact, I went so far as to write code (back in my Turbo Pascal days) to rotate sprites, not thinking of just using the graphics editor to do that job. The tendency to conserve disk space was a strong drive back in the old days, before even the first gigabyte hard drives had come along for consumers.

Today, memory and disk space is nearly expendable! In fact, let's just make that a rule: Never even consider the ramifications of using too much memory in your games. Memory is irrelevant in the face of creative expression. Don't worry about disk space or memory requirements when working on a game—within reason, of course.

However, lack of experience might lead to unnecessary waste. What I'm talking about is the tendency to share a bitmap image for multiple sprite animation sequences, or doing other things to cut down on memory use. Don't worry about it! Just crank out your graphics and put them all over the place when you are developing a game. If you store a single 16 × 16 sprite in a 1600 × 1200 bitmap image, maybe you should cut it down a little! But I suspect that you get the idea.

Back in the Old Days...

To put the subject of memory into perspective, I upgraded my old 386 back in 1991 with 8 MB of RAM (*Random Access Memory*) for about $300. I did this mainly so I could run the latest games by Sierra Online. *Space Quest III: The Pirates of Pestulon* was at one time the most enjoyable game I had ever played. But just imagine, there are *processors* today with 8 MB of internal cache alone. At the time of this writing, a one gigabyte stick of RAM is going for as little as $100. Astounding!

It's amazing to think that a one gig hard drive was considered unfillable, when today hundreds of megabytes of RAM are the norm, and a gig stick is only $100. I just can't fully express my awe at the computer industry. Unless you grew up in the 1980s and remember working with hardware back then, it is really difficult to relate. Then again, I suppose we will be saying the same thing about today's technology 10 years from now.

To get an idea, just multiply current tech values by 10 to see what the technology will be like a decade in the future. A household PC a decade from now will include one or two 20 gigahertz processors, five gigabytes of RAM, a terabyte (1,000 gigabyte) hard drive, and will still cost under $2,000.

The funny thing is, there will still be sprites. Very, *very* fast sprites!

Inheriting Functionality from the Bitmap Class

A sprite contains multiple images so it can be animated on the screen. The problem is, how do you store multiple images inside a single sprite? This is where I'll give you a little insight into things to come. A sprite is not very much fun without a class in VB, because all of this stuff—like the bitmaps that make up the sprite's animation sequence—is best kept tucked away inside the sprite class.

In the old days, when game programmers still wrote code with the obsolete language called C (I know I'm going to get a lot of flak for that one!), global variables and structs were used to keep track of sprites. As you can imagine, the code was messy. Today, the best way to write code is by combining data (variables, structures, arrays, and so on) with the procedures that manage that data. This is called object-oriented programming, and it is amazing how well it cleans up the source code for a game! Pure OOP languages (such as C++ and its descendants, Java and C#)

allow you to do some really amazing things with classes. But you can also create classes in VB that are just as useful.

Wait a second! I thought VB wasn't an object-oriented language?

VB *is* an object-oriented language, just like Turbo Pascal 6.0 was once a popular OOP language (as is its modern descendant, Delphi). Now, the key to making the most of a language is not to compare it with all others and bemoan what it lacks; rather, the key is to master a language so fully that you can do anything with it that can be done in any other language, regardless of the feature set.

You really do need to use the bitmap class to make sprites run smoothly. Otherwise, the sprite code will have to duplicate all of the bitmap code. Since VB doesn't support implementation inheritance (where inherited code actually runs automatically without the need to call it), the sprite class will have to call on a bitmap class to do some work. As it turns out, you really wouldn't want the sprite to directly inherit from a bitmap, because the sprite has to load a bitmap and rip animation frames out of it. (I have tried this route before in C++, and it is more difficult.) It makes more sense to just declare a bitmap variable inside the sprite and use it directly, rather than inheriting from it. The animation frames will then be loaded into an array of clsBitmap objects.

Creating the clsBitmap Array

Now, the images that make up a sprite's animation sequence are stored in an array of clsBitmap objects; call the array cbFrames. The cb stands for "class" and "bitmap" respectively, and makes it easy to identify the type of this array. This is just a personal naming preference of mine. All objects (which are instantiated class variables) in my code start with the character c, followed by one- or two-letter abbreviations of the class. It is more important to be consistent than to rigidly follow a coding standard—just be reasonable with your variable names so it is easy to identify what they are at first glance.

Here is how you would declare the bitmap array inside the sprite class:

```
Dim cbFrames() As clsBitmap
```

Notice that this array declaration does not show the size of the array inside the parentheses as you might expect. To keep things efficient, this array will be resized to whatever dimensions are needed when the frames are loaded, using the ReDim Preserve keywords (which redimension an array while preserving the elements already inside the array). This way, you can add frames to the array more than once, and it will appear as though new elements are appended to the end of the array.

Why would you not want to include the New operator with the declaration of a dynamically-sized array? Because there are no elements in the array to instantiate, and the New operator is only used when creating each individual element of the array.

Ripping Frames out of Tiled Bitmaps

The images that make up an animation sequence for a sprite could be stored as individual files in the game's directory, but that would mean that you must distribute several hundred images with the game—not such a great idea. The best way to store sprite images is inside a tiled bitmap image using a template, such as the one shown in Figure 8.1.

0	1	2	3	4	5	6	7
8	9	10	11	12	13	14	15
16	17	18	19	20	21	22	23
24	25	26	27	28	29	30	31

Figure 8.1

Animation frames stored inside a tiled bitmap help cut down the number of bitmap files that must be distributed with a game and make it easier to draw the animation artwork.

The key to ripping frames out of a bitmap and using them to create animation frames in a sprite is a function I have written, called LoadFrames. This function accepts six parameters, including the filename of the source bitmap file, the position in the bitmap to start grabbing frames, the dimensions of each frame, and the number of frames to rip out of the bitmap.

```
Public Function LoadFrames(ByVal sFilename As String, _
    ByVal lStartX As Long, ByVal lStartY As Long, _
    ByVal lWidth As Long, ByVal lHeight As Long, _
    ByVal lNumFrames As Long, _
    Optional bGenMasks As Boolean = True) As Boolean

    On Error GoTo error_out
    Dim cbSource As New clsBitmap
    Dim lFrame As Long
    Dim lCopyX As Long
    Dim lCopyY As Long
    Dim bFailed As Boolean

    LoadFrames = False

    'load the source bitmap file
    If Not cbSource.Load(sFilename) Then Exit Function
```

```
'copy each frame out of the source image
For lFrame = 0 To lNumFrames - 1
    'calculate the upper left corner
    'lCopyX = lStartX + lFrame * (lWidth + 1)
    lCopyX = lStartX + lFrame * lWidth
    lCopyY = lStartY
    'set the current frame
    lCurrentFrame = lFrameCount + lFrame
    'redimension the bitmap array to hold the new frame
    ReDim Preserve cbFrames(0 To lCurrentFrame)
    'instantiate the new sprite frame
    Set cbFrames(lCurrentFrame) = New clsBitmap
    'create the bitmap image based on sprite dimensions
    If Not cbFrames(lCurrentFrame).Create(cbSource.hdc, _
        lWidth, lHeight) Then
        LoadFrames = False
        Exit For
    End If
    'transfer frame from source image to sprite array
    If BitBlt(cbFrames(lCurrentFrame).hdc, 0, 0, _
        lWidth, lHeight, cbSource.hdc, lCopyX, lCopyY, _
        vbSrcCopy) = 0 Then
        LoadFrames = False
        Exit For
    End If
Next lFrame

'increment the frame count
lFrameCount = lFrameCount + lNumFrames

'generate masks
If bGenMasks Then
    'only gen masks if hardware support is false
    If Not HardwareTransparency Then
        If Not GenerateAllMasks() Then Exit Function
    End If
End If
```

```
        'successful operation
        Set cbSource = Nothing
        LoadFrames = True
        Exit Function
error_out:
End Function
```

The LoadFrames function starts by declaring some variables, including a bitmap for the source image. If the file is loaded successfully, the function iterates lNumFrames times to load all of the frames in the image. For each frame, it calculates the starting point, creates a new bitmap in the bitmap array, and then pastes the frame from the source bitmap into the new bitmap array element. The function is very straightforward and does not include any sophisticated frame-grabbing features, such as multiple rows. This was simply a design decision on my part to make it easier to understand.

After having written frame grabbers that can load multiple rows of a source image in a single call, I found that there were just too many parameters in the call to LoadFrames, thus causing the function to be difficult to use at this early point. In addition to the starting position and dimensions of the frames, with a multi-row frame grabber you must also pass the total number of tiles so the function can jump down to the next row automatically.

I believe this simplified version of LoadFrames is far easier and more pleasant to use. Further, the sprite itself keeps track of the frame counter, so if you need to load frames out of multiple rows into the same sprite, it is simply a matter of calling the function again with a new starting position. The vast majority of tiled bitmaps have animation sequences laid-out in a single row of a high-resolution image. One nice feature of this method is that you can create huge animation sequences and even load tiles from multiple images into a single sprite. You probably won't ever need to do that, but the functionality is there nonetheless.

Note that you will also use LoadFrames to load a single bitmap image into a sprite. To accomplish this feat, all you must do is set the starting positions equal to zero and the frame count equal to one.

ADVANCED TRANSPARENCY

What is a sprite without transparency? It is just a solid bitmap. But first, perhaps I should explain transparency. In the simplest of terms, when something is transparent, you can see through it. But there is a similar word called *translucency* that is often confused with transparency. When something is transparent, it is completely see-through. But when something is translucent, it is only partially see-through.

Transparency Versus Translucency

The level of translucency affects how much light passes through an object. Translucency is directly related to the subject of alpha blending, which is a feature available to 32-bit color images whereby there are four channels: Red, Green, Blue, and Alpha. Alpha describes how an image should be combined with the background. A fully translucent image will be completely merged with the background, while an image with no translucency will completely overwrite the background. This is one possible method of drawing transparent images, by setting a specific color in the image as translucent and then calling the `AlphaBlend` function.

Transparency differs from translucency in that it is an all-or-nothing attribute of a color. The transparent color is called the "color key." When the image is drawn with transparency enabled, all of the pixels in the image will be drawn except for the pixels with that color key. The result is a transparent image that does not completely block the background, but rather allows background pixels to show through the image. This process is absolutely essential for creating attractive games. The alternative is to have a completely black background (or any solid color, for that matter), which is not acceptable.

Transparent Background Tiles

Transparency is even necessary for the background in some games! Consider a hexagonal war game like *The Operational Art of War* by Norm Koger (the same freelance programmer who created *Stellar Crusade*, *Age of Rifles*, and *Conflict: Middle East*) or an isometric game like *Age of Empires II*. These games feature maps that are made up of tiles, and these tiles are oddly shaped, meaning there is transparency involved in drawing them. Figure 8.2 shows a simple illustration of how hex tiles can be assembled to create a hexagonal war game map.

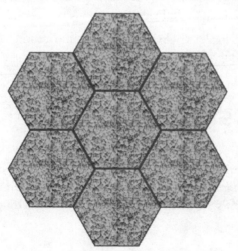

Figure 8.2

Transparent tiles are used to create a hexagonal war game map.

The same hexagonal map without the benefit of transparency would be totally unusable because the hex tiles would almost completely overlap each other, resulting in a very unpleasant background for a war game. The non-transparent hex map is shown in Figure 8.3.

Figure 8.3

The hex map as it would appear without the benefit of transparency

So, as you might have imagined, transparency is an essential feature for more aspects of a game than just the sprites! In fact, a hex map could be rendered with either bitmaps or sprites, depending on preference, although there might be map tiles that are animated (such as ocean tiles). In the case of animated tiles, you would want to use a sprite to handle hex tiles. The source hex tile is shown in Figure 8.4.

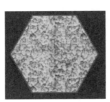

Figure 8.4

The hex tile bitmap uses a standard black color key for the transparent pixels.

Transparent Blitting Options

Your next question is probably, "How do I draw a transparent image?" There are several ways, one of which was demonstrated in Chapter 7, "Break Out the Bitmaps," where an Image control was drawn transparently using a mask image. Obviously, you are already aware that a mask is helpful for drawing transparent images. This tends to be the best method when working with standard VB Form and PictureBox drawing surfaces.

This chapter focuses on using mask images for high-speed transparent blitting (specifically, auto-generated masks). However, there are some alternatives to using masks that you might want to consider. Since DirectX handles transparency automatically, and later chapters will focus entirely on DirectX, I am not going to spend very much time on the subject here.

TIP

Have you ever wondered what to do if you actually need the color black in your image? There's an easy solution. Black has an RGB value of (0,0,0). Just use an RGB color that is (1,1,1). This color is indistinguishable from black to the naked eye, and will not be picked up as a transparent color.

The TransparentBlt Function

The Windows API actually provides a function called `TransparentBlt` that will draw a transparent image automatically. The function is pretty slow, so you probably would not want to use it in a high-speed game. However, a less-demanding game (one that is turn-based and doesn't require a high-speed loop) would probably work fine with the `TransparentBlt` function. For reference, here is what the function looks like:

```
Public Declare Function TransparentBlt _
    Lib "msimg32" ( _
    ByVal hdcDest As Long, _
    ByVal iXStartDest As Long, _
    ByVal iYStartDest As Long, _
    ByVal iWidthDest As Long, _
    ByVal iHeightDest As Long, _
    ByVal hdcSource As Long, _
    ByVal iXStartSrc As Long, _
    ByVal iYStartSrc As Long, _
    ByVal iWidthSrc As Long, _
    ByVal iHeightSrc As Long, _
    ByVal iTransparentColor As Long _
) As Long
```

Don't let the parameter list scare you off. It is grouped into two main parameters (source and destination) that include the device context; starting positions; dimensions; and in the case of the last parameter, the color key (the color that should be transparent).

`TransparentBlt` seems a logical function for drawing images transparently, but it is hobbled by a serious lack of performance, likely due to the fact that it is highly compatible across multiple displays and does not take advantage of any 2-D acceleration.

Tapping into Hardware Transparency Support

Most modern video cards include support for accelerated 2-D blitting in Windows. The common BitBlt function is used throughout the Windows user interface, so a hardware-accelerated version of the function will inherently speed up Windows and improve display quality. Why not tap into that functionality for speeding up the process of blitting images to the screen in a game as well? It is definitely something to consider; however, there are limitations to this otherwise appealing hardware support, as I will explain.

To draw an image using a hardware-accelerated version of BitBlt, you must tweak a few settings to tell Windows that you would like to tap into hardware transparent-blitting support. First and foremost, you must determine whether this support is available! You can check for hardware BitBlt acceleration by reading the device caps of the display hardware like this:

```
If (GetDeviceCaps(hdcDest, CAPS1) And C1_TRANSPARENT) Then
```

This function call determines whether the device context, hdcDest, supports transparency by including the CAPS1 and C1_TRANSPARENT constants. These values, along with a third constant called NEWTRANSPARENT that is also needed, are defined here:

```
Const CAPS1 = 94
Const C1_TRANSPARENT = &H1
Const NEWTRANSPARENT = 3
```

Now for the convoluted part of the scheme. You actually use the SetBkMode and SetBkColor functions to set the background drawing mode and drawing color before calling BitBlt to draw the image. You must then restore the original background values for the device context when you are finished. Here is what the function calls look like for setting up a destination device context for transparent blitting:

```
lOldMode = SetBkMode(hdcDest, NEWTRANSPARENT)
lOldColor = SetBkColor(hdcDest, RGB(0, 0, 0))
```

These two lines tell the Windows API to configure the background settings for transparent blitting based on a color key that is set to black. The actual call to BitBlt looks pretty normal after this has been done, and the blitting is simply performed with a bitwise vbSrcCopy operation (the normal solid blitting operation that runs at the fastest possible speed).

```
BitBlt hdcDest, X, Y, Width, Height, _
    cbFrames(lCurrentFrame).hdc, 0, 0, vbSrcCopy
```

This function call makes use of sprite properties like Width and Height, and draws the current element of the bitmap array. If the video card's device driver supports hardware 2-D blitting, then this single function call will render a transparent sprite, which could be a considerable bonus to the sprite engine. Following is a generic version of the DevBlt function:

```
Public Sub DevBlt(ByVal hdcDest As Long)
    Dim lOldColor As Long
    Dim lOldMode As Long

    'see if device driver supports transparent blitting
    If (GetDeviceCaps(hdcDest, CAPS1) And C1_TRANSPARENT) Then
        'configure for hardware transparent blitting
        lOldMode = SetBkMode(hdcDest, NEWTRANSPARENT)
        lOldColor = SetBkColor(hdcDest, RGB(0, 0, 0))
        'draw image using hardware transparent blit
        BitBlt hdcDest, X, Y, Width, Height, _
            cbFrames(lCurrentFrame).hdc, 0, 0, vbSrcCopy
        'restore background mode
        SetBkColor hdcDest, lOldColor
        SetBkMode hdcDest, lOldMode
    Else
        Debug.Print "Driver does not support transparency"
    End If
End Sub
```

DevBlt works when the hardware supports transparency, but that lack of certainty is a serious obstacle to embracing this method completely. You might want to set a flag in your program to check for hardware transparency support, and then use DevBlt if it is available. The sprite class, developed later in this chapter, will check to see whether hardware transparency is supported and make use of it if it is available. It is no longer a common feature provided by device drivers since the advent of DirectX, but older PCs might support hardware transparency.

Generating the Transparency Mask

Despite the added memory requirements for keeping track of a mask for every single sprite, the use of a mask is the best option for drawing transparently using BitBlt. Naturally, you will not need this functionality at all once you have made the leap to DirectX (see Chapter 10, "Diving into DirectDraw"). However, there is still a very strong need for this pre-DirectX code, since there are still cases where Windows GDI code may be preferable to DirectX. The ability to tap into the Windows API within a VB game project is a significant improvement over standard VB code.

There will be times when you might want to just whip together a prototype without having to get into DirectX. There are all kinds of reasons, in fact, why Windows GDI code is still useful, so a complete mastery of the subject will take you pretty far even without DirectX.

The transparency mask for the hex tile that was used to create the sample hexagonal war game map earlier in the chapter is shown in Figure 8.5.

Figure 8.5

The generated mask image for the hexagonal map tile, as it appears in memory after being generated

Transparency is absolutely essential for creating an attractive game, so what's the best way to create the mask image without manually drawing each one? The sprite code in this chapter so far has provided you with functionality for loading bitmap images into the animation frames of a sprite, so the next step involves generating the mask image in order to draw the sprite as fast as possible while retaining transparency. To accomplish this, the sprite will need to be able to get inside the bits of a bitmap. Fortunately, that is possible with the GetBitmapBits function, which was explained in Chapter 7, "Break Out the Bitmaps."

To generate a transparency mask, you must create a new clsBitmap object, copy the source image into the new mask image, and then copy the bitmap bits into a byte array. You can then iterate through each pixel of the image and determine whether that pixel contains the color key. If so, then the equivalent mask image pixel is set to white. Any pixels that contain colors other than the color key are set to black. Thus, the generated mask image is an inverted version of the source image. Here is how the bitmap bit array is declared:

```
Dim SourceBits() As Byte
```

SourceBits receives the image data from the GetBitmapBits function. Here are the two main loops that iterate through the pixels in the image and create the mask. Note that this code supports 16, 24, and 32-bit color images, but was intended only for 32 bits due to the way the byte index is incremented.

```
For cols = 0 To cbFrames(lFrame).Height - 1
    For rows = 0 To cbFrames(lFrame).Width - 1
        If SourceBits(index) = 0 And _
            SourceBits(index + 1) = 0 And _
            SourceBits(index + 2) = 0 Then
            CopyMemory SourceBits(index), C_WHITE, bNumBytes
```

```
        Else
            CopyMemory SourceBits(index), C_BLACK, bNumBytes
        End If
        index = index + bNumBytes
    Next rows
Next cols
```

The complete GenerateMask function listing follows. This function accepts a single parameter, which indicates the frame number in the sprite's bitmap array that should be used as the source for the mask generation. In a nutshell, this function adds a new element to the mask array, instantiates the new element, and then creates the bitmap inside that array element. Then the source frame is blitted into the mask, and the mask is copied into a byte array using GetBitmapBits. At this point, the function iterates through all of the pixels in the image, as explained earlier. The bitmap data is then copied back into the mask, at which point is it ready to be used. Note that the color constants, C_WHITE and C_BLACK, are assigned when the sprite class is created, and are private within the class.

```
Public Function GenerateMask(ByVal lFrame As Long) As Boolean
    Dim rows As Long
    Dim cols As Long
    Dim srcIndex As Long
    Dim index As Long
    Dim bNumBytes As Byte

    GenerateMask = False
    'make sure the bitmap array is not empty
    If lFrame < 0 Or lFrame > lFrameCount Then Exit Function
    'create the mask array
    ReDim Preserve cbMasks(0 To lFrameCount)
    'instantiate the mask frame
    Set cbMasks(lFrame) = Nothing
    Set cbMasks(lFrame) = New clsBitmap

    'make sure the source bitmap was already loaded
    If cbFrames(lFrame).hdc = 0 Then Exit Function
    If cbMasks(lFrame).hdc = 0 Then
        'create the mask bitmap
        If Not cbMasks(lFrame).Create(cbFrames(lFrame).hdc, _
            Width, Height) Then
            Exit Function
        End If
```

```
        End If
        'copy the source frame into the mask image
        BitBlt cbMasks(lFrame).hdc, 0, 0, Width, Height, _
            cbFrames(lFrame).hdc, 0, 0, vbSrcCopy
        'determine the size of the bitmap
        SourceSize = cbFrames(lFrame).WidthBytes * _
            cbFrames(lFrame).Height
        'create the bitmap bits array
        ReDim SourceBits(0 To SourceSize)
        'copy the source image into the array
        GetBitmapBits cbMasks(lFrame).hWnd, SourceSize, _
            SourceBits(0)

        'determine byte increment
        bNumBytes = ColorDepth \ 8
        index = 0
        'process each pixel in the source image
        For cols = 0 To cbFrames(lFrame).Height - 1
            For rows = 0 To cbFrames(lFrame).Width - 1
                'set mask pixel based on source pixel
                If SourceBits(index) = 0 And _
                    SourceBits(index + 1) = 0 And _
                    SourceBits(index + 2) = 0 Then
                    CopyMemory SourceBits(index), C_WHITE, _
                        bNumBytes
                Else
                    CopyMemory SourceBits(index), C_BLACK, _
                        bNumBytes
                End If
                index = index + bNumBytes
            Next rows
        Next cols
        'copy array back into source image
        SetBitmapBits cbMasks(lFrame).hWnd, SourceSize, SourceBits(0)
        GenerateMask = True
End Function
```

GenerateMask is an awesome function that really opens the door to true game development with VB. You can call this function any time you load a bitmap. But an additional function would be helpful to get the most out of this new code, one that generates all the masks automatically after the frames have been loaded. The new function, GenerateAllMasks, iterates through the bitmap array and calls GenerateMask for each frame. The source code for GenerateAllMasks is listed below.

```
Public Function GenerateAllMasks() As Boolean
    Dim lFrame As Long
    GenerateAllMasks = False
    For lFrame = 0 To lFrameCount - 1
        If Not (cbFrames(lFrame) Is Nothing) Then
            If cbFrames(lFrame).hdc > 0 Then
                GenerateMask lFrame
            End If
        End If
    Next lFrame
    GenerateAllMasks = True
End Function
```

Well, that about does it for sprite transparency. In the next few pages, I am going to show you how to use these features to actually write the sprite blitter.

Transparency and the Color Key

Once you have figured out how transparency works, the door is open for virtually unlimited new games that you can develop. This is one of the reasons why DirectX is such a powerful force in gaming—because it handles so many of the details for you. In the meantime, I need to show you how to use the mask and bitmap arrays to actually animate a sprite on the screen.

The color key is sort of a no-brainer, because most often it is just a solid black color with RGB values of (0,0,0). There might be cases where you would prefer to use a different color for the color key, so this factor should be a consideration. However, it is so easy to change the transparent color in a source image using floodfill tools that for now you should just assume the color key will be black. It is easier to work with black because all three color values are zero.

Writing Your Own Transparent Blitter

There are two operations required to draw a sprite with transparency. First, the mask is drawn using the bitwise vbSrcAnd operation. This causes the background pixels to merge with the mask, leaving a black outline on the background. This black outline becomes a placeholder for the non-transparent pixels in the source image, which is then blitted using vbSrcPaint. (This is equivalent to the XOR (*exclusive or*) operation.) Figure 8.6 shows the result of blitting just the masks.

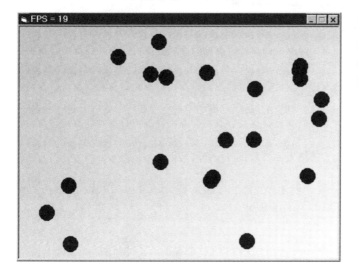

Figure 8.6

Blitting the mask paves the way for drawing a transparent sprite.

Blitting an image using vbSrcPaint alone results in an interesting blended copy of the image that can produce some spectacular special effects when combined with a creative use of colors. This method results in an image that features transparency, but the non-transparent pixels are *ghosted* over the background, as shown in Figure 8.7.

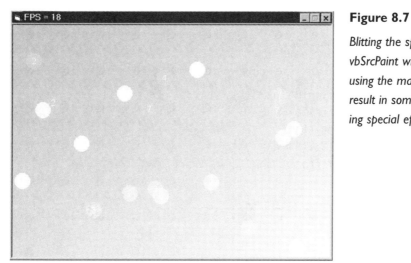

Figure 8.7

Blitting the sprite with vbSrcPaint without using the mask can result in some interesting special effects.

When combined, the ANDed mask and XORed image produce a transparent sprite, which was the goal from the beginning. So, let's get on with it!

Blitting the Mask

Blitting the mask using vbSrcAnd is pretty simple; it involves a single call to BitBlt, as follows:

```
'blit the mask using AND
BitBlt hdcDest, X, Y, Width, Height, _
    cbMasks(lCurrentFrame).hdc, 0, 0, vbSrcAnd
```

Blitting the Sprite

Likewise, a single call to BitBlt with vbSrcPaint is all that is required to blit the frame over the mask to complete the transparent blit operation:

```
'blit the image using XOR
BitBlt hdcDest, X, Y, Width, Height, _
    cbFrames(lCurrentFrame).hdc, 0, 0, vbSrcPaint
```

The Complete Transparent Blitter

Now for the complete sprite blitter. This function, which is called Draw, checks to see whether the Transparent property is true, and then draws the sprite. The Draw function listing follows.

```
Public Sub Draw(ByVal hdcDest As Long)
    If cbFrames(lCurrentFrame).hdc < 1 Then Exit Sub
    If Transparent Then
        'blit the mask using AND
        BitBlt hdcDest, X, Y, Width, Height, _
            cbMasks(lCurrentFrame).hdc, 0, 0, vbSrcAnd
        'blit the image using XOR
        BitBlt hdcDest, X, Y, Width, Height, _
            cbFrames(lCurrentFrame).hdc, 0, 0, vbSrcPaint
    Else
        'blit the image without transparency
        BitBlt hdcDest, X, Y, Width, Height, _
            cbFrames(lCurrentFrame).hdc, 0, 0, vbSrcCopy
    End If
End Sub
```

NOTE

A more complete version of Draw is included in the sprite class to make use of hardware transparency when available.

ANIMATING SPRITES

Congratulations! You are now knee-deep in sprite technology and have developed a fully functional transparent sprite blitter, complete with a mask generator and all the code to load frames out of a bitmap file. The only thing that remains is a way to actually animate the sprite! The functionality is already in the code that you have completed for drawing the correct animation frame, so the only thing remaining is a way to move the frame pointer forward or backward. In addition, it will be nice to add functionality for the animation rate (which allows some sprites to move slower or faster than others) that was discussed earlier in the chapter.

Keeping Track of Sprite Position

The sprite's position on the screen, as well as the current frame, animation rate, and other variables, are all present in the sprite class as properties. In some cases these properties are read-only, meaning that calling programs can only retrieve the value of the property and cannot change it. Read-write properties allow the calling program to both read and set the property value. However, property code may still validate the new value before allowing it to be set.

The sprite includes properties for directly manipulating the position of its X and Y values, as follows:

```
Public Property Let X(ByVal lNewValue As Long)
    lCurrentX = lNewValue
End Property

Public Property Get X() As Long
    X = lCurrentX
End Property

Public Property Let Y(ByVal lNewValue As Long)
    lCurrentY = lNewValue
End Property

Public Property Get Y() As Long
    Y = lCurrentY
End Property
```

Moving the Sprite on the Screen

In almost every case, a game will have an array of sprites (or a linked list, collection, or other construct). The game loop must process all of the sprites by erasing them, then moving and drawing them again in the new locations. Collision detection is also performed, to see whether any sprites have crashed into each other. (I'll talk more about this later in the chapter.)

What happens when a sprite is destroyed or killed in the game? It would be too difficult to take the sprite out of the array, so there is a simple solution to remove sprites from play—by using an Active property.

```
Public Property Get Active() As Boolean
    Active = bActive
End Property

Public Property Let Active(ByVal bNewValue As Boolean)
    bActive = bNewValue
End Property
```

Basically, each sprite in the game is tested to see if it is active; if not, it is ignored and the next sprite in the list is processed.

The process of actually moving a sprite involves looking at its X and Y values and modifying them based on its SpeedX and SpeedY values.

```
Public Property Get SpeedX() As Long
    SpeedX = lSpeedX
End Property

Public Property Let SpeedX(ByVal lNewValue As Long)
    lSpeedX = lNewValue
End Property

Public Property Get SpeedY() As Long
    SpeedY = lSpeedY
End Property

Public Property Let SpeedY(ByVal lNewValue As Long)
    lSpeedY = lNewValue
End Property
```

The MoveRate and AnimRate properties also come into play when the game must determine how to move the sprites. Here are those properties:

```
Public Property Let MoveRate(ByVal lNewValue As Long)
    lMoveRate = lNewValue
End Property

Public Property Get MoveRate() As Long
    MoveRate = lMoveRate
End Property

Public Property Let AnimRate(ByVal lNewValue As Long)
    lAnimRate = lNewValue
End Property

Public Property Get AnimRate() As Long
    AnimRate = lAnimRate
End Property
```

Each sprite will be erased and redrawn regardless of whether it has been moved or not. (This is necessary in order to allow other sprites to restore the background during an overlap.) So, to move a sprite during a single frame of animation, you would use code that looks like this:

```
Sprite.X = Sprite.X + Sprite.SpeedX
Sprite.Y = Sprite.Y + Sprite.SpeedY
```

Don't be fooled by the simplicity of this code! The SpeedX and SpeedY values could be positive or negative, resulting in a myriad of possible directions for the sprite.

Changing Frames

You can retrieve or set the current frame in use by the sprite by using the CurrentFrame property, which looks like this:

```
Public Property Get CurrentFrame() As Long
    CurrentFrame = lCurrentFrame
End Property

Public Property Let CurrentFrame(ByVal lNewValue As Long)
    If lNewValue >= 0 And lNewValue < lFrameCount Then
        lCurrentFrame = lNewValue
    End If
End Property
```

In addition, it would be helpful if the sprite itself provided an easy way to increment or decrement the current frame, based on the animation rate.

```
Public Sub NextFrame()
    If lAnimCount < lAnimRate Then
        lAnimCount = lAnimCount + 1
    Else
        lAnimCount = 0
        If lCurrentFrame < lFrameCount - 1 Then
            lCurrentFrame = lCurrentFrame + 1
        Else
            lCurrentFrame = 0
        End If
    End If
End Sub

Public Sub PrevFrame()
    If lAnimCount < lAnimRate Then
        lAnimCount = lAnimCount + 1
    Else
        lAnimCount = 0
        If lCurrentFrame > 0 Then
            lCurrentFrame = lCurrentFrame - 1
        Else
            lCurrentFrame = lFrameCount
        End If
    End If
End Sub
```

Notice how NextFrame and PrevFrame each check the current frame to determine whether it can be incremented or decremented, and then wrapped around if it exceeds either extreme. Were it not for these two functions, this code would have to be included in the game loop for each sprite. Since it is duplicated for every sprite in a game, it is nice to include this common functionality inside the sprite class instead.

Saving the Background Image

Drawing and animating a sprite is only useful if there is also a way to erase the sprite after it has been drawn. In the case of a scrolling or rendered background, this might not always be needed.

But most of the time, you will want some way to erase a sprite, which really involves restoring the background image underneath.

To facilitate this, the sprite class has two functions: SaveUnder and RestoreUnder. The SaveUnder procedure checks to see whether the private bitmap variable, cbUnder, has already been created; if not, it is created. After cbUnder has been created the first time SaveUnder is called, it will not need to be created again, and a simple BitBlt function call is all that is really needed to save the background image. Here is the listing for the SaveUnder function:

```
Public Sub SaveUnder(ByVal hdcDest As Long)
    If cbFrames(lCurrentFrame).hdc = 0 Or hdcDest = 0 Then Exit Sub
    If cbUnder.hdc = 0 Then
        If Not cbUnder.Create(hdcDest, Width, Height) Then
            Exit Sub
        End If
    End If
    BitBlt cbUnder.hdc, 0, 0, Width, Height, hdcDest, X, Y, vbSrcCopy
End Sub
```

Restoring the background image using RestoreUnder involves—as you might have guessed—blitting the bitmap image stored in cbUnder back to the background at the sprite's current position. The result is that the sprite is erased. This will work as long as you do not move the sprite before erasing it! It is important to remember the steps that must be followed in the game loop.

1. Erase the sprite.
2. Move the sprite.
3. Draw the sprite.

Here is the short listing for the RestoreUnder function:

```
Public Sub RestoreUnder(ByVal hdcDest As Long)
    If cbUnder.hdc = 0 Then Exit Sub
    BitBlt hdcDest, X, Y, Width, Height, cbUnder.hdc, 0, 0, vbSrcCopy
End Sub
```

PUTTING IT ALL TOGETHER: THE SPRITE CLASS

Now that you have all the tools for manipulating sprites, from loading frames to drawing and erasing the bitmap images, it's time to package it all up into a single class that contains all of the code needed to load and draw transparent sprites in a game.

Creating the Sprite Class Source Code

The new sprite class will need a home, so open a new Standard EXE project in VB (by selecting New Project from the File menu). Select Add Class Module from the Project menu in VB to add a new class to the project, and then type the following code into the new class. Be sure to name this class clsSprite and save it in a file called Sprite.cls. Alternatively, you can copy the sprite class right out of the chapter directory on the CD-ROM (\Sources\VB6\CH08\Classes).

First, add the Windows API declarations and the private variables that are needed by the sprite class, and then add `Class_Initialize` and `Class_Terminate`.

```
'------------------------------------------------------------------
' Visual Basic Game Programming With DirectX
' Chapter 8 : Supersonic Sprites
' Sprite Class Source Code File
'------------------------------------------------------------------


Option Explicit

'Windows API functions
Private Declare Function IntersectRect _
    Lib "user32" ( _
    lpDestRect As RECT_API, _
    lpSrc1Rect As RECT_API, _
    lpSrc2Rect As RECT_API _
) As Long

Private Declare Sub CopyMemory _
    Lib "kernel32" Alias "RtlMoveMemory" ( _
    lpvDest As Any, _
    lpvSource As Any, _
    ByVal cbCopy As Long _
)

Private Declare Function GetBitmapBits _
    Lib "gdi32" ( _
    ByVal hBitmap As Long, _
    ByVal dwCount As Long, _
    lpBits As Any _
) As Long
```

```
Private Declare Function SetBitmapBits _
    Lib "gdi32" ( _
    ByVal hBitmap As Long, _
    ByVal dwCount As Long, _
    lpBits As Any _
) As Long

Private Declare Function BitBlt _
    Lib "gdi32" ( _
    ByVal hDestDC As Long, _
    ByVal X As Long, _
    ByVal Y As Long, _
    ByVal nWidth As Long, _
    ByVal nHeight As Long, _
    ByVal hSrcDC As Long, _
    ByVal xSrc As Long, _
    ByVal ySrc As Long, _
    ByVal dwRop As Long _
) As Long

Private Declare Function GetDeviceCaps _
    Lib "gdi32" ( _
    ByVal hdc As Long, _
    ByVal nIndex As Long _
) As Long

Private Declare Function GetDesktopWindow _
    Lib "user32" ( _
) As Long

Private Declare Function GetDC _
    Lib "user32" ( _
    ByVal hWnd As Long _
) As Long

Private Declare Function SetBkMode _
    Lib "gdi32" ( _
    ByVal hdc As Long, _
    ByVal nBkMode As Long _
) As Long
```

```
Private Declare Function SetBkColor _
    Lib "gdi32" ( _
    ByVal hdc As Long, _
    ByVal crColor As Long _
) As Long

'Windows API structs
Private Type RECT_API
    Left As Long
    Top As Long
    Right As Long
    Bottom As Long
End Type

Private Type RGBQUAD
    Blue As Byte
    Green As Byte
    Red As Byte
    alpha As Byte
End Type

'Windows API constants
Private Const BITSPIXEL = 12
Private Const CAPS1 = 94
Private Const C1_TRANSPARENT = &H1
Private Const NEWTRANSPARENT = 3

'internal sprite variables
Dim cbFrames() As clsBitmap
Dim cbMasks() As clsBitmap
Dim cbUnder As New clsBitmap
Dim SourceBits() As Byte
Dim SourceSize As Long
Dim C_WHITE As RGBQUAD
Dim C_BLACK As RGBQUAD
Dim bUseMask As Boolean

'sprite properties
Private bActive As Boolean
Private bTransparent As Boolean
Private bHardwareTransBlit As Boolean
```

```
Private bErase As Boolean
Private lState As Long
Private lCurrentX As Long
Private lCurrentY As Long
Private lGlobalX As Long
Private lGlobalY As Long
Private lCurrentFrame As Long
Private lFrameCount As Long
Private lSpeedX As Long
Private lSpeedY As Long
Private lMoveRate As Long
Private lMoveCount As Long
Private lAnimRate As Long
Private lAnimCount As Long
Private lDirX As Long
Private lDirY As Long

Private Sub Class_Initialize()
    bActive = True
    bTransparent = False
    C_WHITE = Color32(255, 255, 255, 0)
    C_BLACK = Color32(0, 0, 0, 0)
    bUseMask = False

    'see if device driver supports transparent blitting
    bHardwareTransBlit = (GetDeviceCaps(GetDC(0), CAPS1) _
        And C1_TRANSPARENT)
End Sub

Private Sub Class_Terminate()
    On Local Error Resume Next
    Dim n As Long
    For n = 0 To lFrameCount - 1
        If Not (cbFrames(n) Is Nothing) Then
            Set cbFrames(n) = Nothing
        End If
        If bUseMask Then
            If Not (cbMasks(n) Is Nothing) Then
                Set cbMasks(n) = Nothing
            End If
        End If
```

```
        Next n
        ReDim cbFrames(0)
        ReDim cbMasks(0)
        If Not (cbUnder Is Nothing) Then Set cbUnder = Nothing
        ReDim SourceBits(0)
End Sub
```

Adding Sprite Properties

You have already seen most of the properties for the sprite class, but there are additional properties that have not been shown until now (including properties brought over from the bitmap class).

```
Public Property Let X(ByVal lNewValue As Long)
    lCurrentX = lNewValue
End Property

Public Property Get X() As Long
    X = lCurrentX
End Property

Public Property Let Y(ByVal lNewValue As Long)
    lCurrentY = lNewValue
End Property

Public Property Get Y() As Long
    Y = lCurrentY
End Property

Public Property Let GlobalX(ByVal lNewValue As Long)
    lGlobalX = lNewValue
End Property

Public Property Get GlobalX() As Long
    GlobalX = lGlobalX
End Property

Public Property Let GlobalY(ByVal lNewValue As Long)
    lGlobalY = lNewValue
End Property
```

```
Public Property Get GlobalY() As Long
    GlobalY = lGlobalY
End Property


Public Property Get SpeedX() As Long
    SpeedX = lSpeedX
End Property


Public Property Let SpeedX(ByVal lNewValue As Long)
    lSpeedX = lNewValue
End Property


Public Property Get SpeedY() As Long
    SpeedY = lSpeedY
End Property


Public Property Let SpeedY(ByVal lNewValue As Long)
    lSpeedY = lNewValue
End Property


Public Property Get DirX() As Long
    DirX = lDirX
End Property


Public Property Let DirX(ByVal lNewValue As Long)
    lDirX = lNewValue
End Property


Public Property Get DirY() As Long
    DirY = lDirY
End Property


Public Property Let DirY(ByVal lNewValue As Long)
    lDirY = lNewValue
End Property


Public Property Get Width() As Long
    Width = cbFrames(lCurrentFrame).Width
End Property
```

```vb
Public Property Get Height() As Long
    Height = cbFrames(lCurrentFrame).Height
End Property

Public Property Get Active() As Boolean
    Active = bActive
End Property

Public Property Let Active(ByVal bNewValue As Boolean)
    bActive = bNewValue
End Property

Private Property Get ColorDepth() As Long
    ColorDepth = GetDeviceCaps(GetDC(GetDesktopWindow), _
        BITSPIXEL)
End Property

Public Property Get CurrentFrame() As Long
    CurrentFrame = lCurrentFrame
End Property

Public Property Let CurrentFrame(ByVal lNewValue As Long)
    If lNewValue >= 0 And lNewValue < lFrameCount Then
        lCurrentFrame = lNewValue
    End If
End Property

Public Property Get hdc(Optional ByVal lFrame _
    As Long = -1) As Long
    If lFrame < 0 Then lFrame = lCurrentFrame
    hdc = cbFrames(lFrame).hdc
End Property

Public Property Get MaskDC(Optional ByVal lFrame _
    As Long = -1) As Long
    If lFrame < 0 Then lFrame = lCurrentFrame
    MaskDC = cbMasks(lFrame).hdc
End Property

Public Property Get Transparent() As Boolean
    Transparent = bTransparent
End Property
```

```vb
Public Property Let Transparent(ByVal bNewValue As Boolean)
    bTransparent = bNewValue
End Property


Public Property Get HardwareTransparency() As Boolean
    HardwareTransparency = bHardwareTransBlit
End Property


Public Property Let State(ByVal lNewValue As Long)
    lState = lNewValue
End Property


Public Property Get State() As Long
    State = lState
End Property


Public Property Let MoveRate(ByVal lNewValue As Long)
    lMoveRate = lNewValue
End Property


Public Property Get MoveRate() As Long
    MoveRate = lMoveRate
End Property


Public Property Let MoveCount(ByVal lNewValue As Long)
    lMoveCount = lNewValue
End Property


Public Property Get MoveCount() As Long
    MoveCount = lMoveCount
End Property


Public Property Let AnimRate(ByVal lNewValue As Long)
    lAnimRate = lNewValue
End Property


Public Property Get AnimRate() As Long
    AnimRate = lAnimRate
End Property
```

```
Public Property Let AnimCount(ByVal lNewValue As Long)
    lAnimCount = lNewValue
End Property

Public Property Get AnimCount() As Long
    AnimCount = lAnimCount
End Property
```

Adding Sprite Procedures

The procedures give life to the sprite class, providing the means to load bitmap images into the animation frames and all of the other routines that have been covered up to this point. These procedures have all been covered in the chapter already, so they should not need further explanation. Simply add the following code to the Sprite.cls file.

```
Public Sub NextFrame()
    If lAnimCount < lAnimRate Then
        lAnimCount = lAnimCount + 1
    Else
        lAnimCount = 0
        If lCurrentFrame < lFrameCount - 1 Then
            lCurrentFrame = lCurrentFrame + 1
        Else
            lCurrentFrame = 0
        End If
    End If
End Sub

Public Sub PrevFrame()
    If lAnimCount < lAnimRate Then
        lAnimCount = lAnimCount + 1
    Else
        lAnimCount = 0
        If lCurrentFrame > 0 Then
            lCurrentFrame = lCurrentFrame - 1
        Else
            lCurrentFrame = lFrameCount
        End If
    End If
End Sub
```

```vb
Public Sub SaveUnder(ByVal hdcDest As Long)
    If cbFrames(lCurrentFrame).hdc = 0 Or hdcDest = 0 Then Exit Sub
    If cbUnder.hdc = 0 Then
        If Not cbUnder.Create(hdcDest, Width, Height) Then Exit Sub
    End If
    BitBlt cbUnder.hdc, 0, 0, Width, Height, hdcDest, X, Y, vbSrcCopy
End Sub

Public Sub RestoreUnder(ByVal hdcDest As Long)
    If cbUnder.hdc = 0 Then Exit Sub
    BitBlt hdcDest, X, Y, Width, Height, cbUnder.hdc, 0, 0, vbSrcCopy
End Sub

Public Function LoadFrames(ByVal sFilename As String, _
    ByVal lStartX As Long, ByVal lStartY As Long, _
    ByVal lWidth As Long, ByVal lHeight As Long, _
    ByVal lNumFrames As Long, _
    Optional bGenMasks As Boolean = True) As Boolean

    On Error GoTo error_out
    Dim cbSource As New clsBitmap
    Dim lFrame As Long
    Dim lCopyX As Long
    Dim lCopyY As Long
    Dim bFailed As Boolean

    LoadFrames = False

    'load the source bitmap file
    If Not cbSource.Load(sFilename) Then Exit Function

    'copy each frame out of the source image
    For lFrame = 0 To lNumFrames - 1
        'calculate the upper left corner
        'lCopyX = lStartX + lFrame * (lWidth + 1)
        lCopyX = lStartX + lFrame * lWidth
        lCopyY = lStartY
        'set the current frame
        lCurrentFrame = lFrameCount + lFrame
        'redimension the bitmap array to hold the new frame
        ReDim Preserve cbFrames(0 To lCurrentFrame)
```

```
        'instantiate the new sprite frame
        Set cbFrames(lCurrentFrame) = New clsBitmap
        'create the bitmap image based on sprite dimensions
        If Not cbFrames(lCurrentFrame).Create(cbSource.hdc, _
            lWidth, lHeight) Then
            LoadFrames = False
            Exit For
        End If
        'transfer frame from source image to sprite array
        If BitBlt(cbFrames(lCurrentFrame).hdc, 0, 0, _
            lWidth, lHeight, cbSource.hdc, lCopyX, lCopyY, _
            vbSrcCopy) = 0 Then
            LoadFrames = False
            Exit For
        End If
    Next lFrame


    'increment the frame count
    lFrameCount = lFrameCount + lNumFrames


    'generate masks
    If bGenMasks Then
        'only gen masks if hardware support is false
        If Not HardwareTransparency Then
            If Not GenerateAllMasks() Then Exit Function
        End If
    End If


    'successful operation
    Set cbSource = Nothing
    LoadFrames = True
    Exit Function
error_out:
End Function

Public Sub Draw(ByVal hdcDest As Long)
    Dim lOldColor As Long
    Dim lOldMode As Long

    'make sure current frame is valid
    If cbFrames(lCurrentFrame).hdc < 1 Then Exit Sub
```

```vb
        'draw sprite with transparency?
        If Transparent Then
            'check for hardware transparent blitter
            If HardwareTransparency Then
                'configure for hardware transparent blitting
                lOldMode = SetBkMode(hdcDest, NEWTRANSPARENT)
                lOldColor = SetBkColor(hdcDest, RGB(0, 0, 0))

                'draw image using hardware transparent blit
                BitBlt hdcDest, X, Y, Width, Height, _
                    cbFrames(lCurrentFrame).hdc, 0, 0, vbSrcCopy

                'restore background mode
                SetBkColor hdcDest, lOldColor
                SetBkMode hdcDest, lOldMode
            Else
                'blit the mask using AND
                BitBlt hdcDest, X, Y, Width, Height, _
                    cbMasks(lCurrentFrame).hdc, 0, 0, vbSrcAnd
                'blit the image using XOR
                BitBlt hdcDest, X, Y, Width, Height, _
                    cbFrames(lCurrentFrame).hdc, 0, 0, vbSrcPaint
            End If
        Else
            'blit the image without transparency
            BitBlt hdcDest, X, Y, Width, Height, _
                cbFrames(lCurrentFrame).hdc, 0, 0, vbSrcCopy
        End If
End Sub

Public Function GenerateAllMasks() As Boolean
    On Error GoTo error1
    Dim lFrame As Long
    GenerateAllMasks = False
    For lFrame = 0 To lFrameCount - 1
        If Not (cbFrames(lFrame) Is Nothing) Then
            If cbFrames(lFrame).hdc <> 0 Then
                GenerateMask lFrame
            End If
        End If
    Next lFrame
```

```
    GenerateAllMasks = True
error1:
End Function

Public Function GenerateMask(ByVal lFrame As Long) As Boolean
    Dim rows As Long
    Dim cols As Long
    Dim srcIndex As Long
    Dim Index As Long
    Dim bNumBytes As Byte


    GenerateMask = False
    'make sure the bitmap array is not empty
    If lFrame < 0 Or lFrame > lFrameCount Then Exit Function
    'create the mask array
    ReDim Preserve cbMasks(0 To lFrameCount)
    'instantiate the mask frame
    Set cbMasks(lFrame) = Nothing
    Set cbMasks(lFrame) = New clsBitmap


    'make sure the source bitmap was already loaded
    If cbFrames(lFrame).hdc = 0 Then Exit Function
    If cbMasks(lFrame).hdc = 0 Then
        'create the mask bitmap
        If Not cbMasks(lFrame).Create(cbFrames(lFrame).hdc, _
            Width, Height) Then
            Exit Function
        End If
    End If
    'copy the source frame into the mask image
    BitBlt cbMasks(lFrame).hdc, 0, 0, Width, Height, _
        cbFrames(lFrame).hdc, 0, 0, vbSrcCopy
    'determine the size of the bitmap
    SourceSize = cbFrames(lFrame).WidthBytes * _
        cbFrames(lFrame).Height
    'create the bitmap bits array
    ReDim SourceBits(0 To SourceSize)
    'copy the source image into the array
    GetBitmapBits cbMasks(lFrame).hWnd, SourceSize, SourceBits(0)
```

```
        'determine byte increment (32-bit images work best)
        bNumBytes = ColorDepth \ 8
        Index = 0
        'process each pixel in the source image
        For cols = 0 To cbFrames(lFrame).Height - 1
            For rows = 0 To cbFrames(lFrame).Width - 1
                'set mask pixel based on source pixel
                If SourceBits(Index) = 0 And _
                    SourceBits(Index + 1) = 0 And _
                    SourceBits(Index + 2) = 0 Then
                    CopyMemory SourceBits(Index), C_WHITE, bNumBytes
                Else
                    CopyMemory SourceBits(Index), C_BLACK, bNumBytes
                End If
                Index = Index + bNumBytes
            Next rows
        Next cols
        'copy array back into source image
        SetBitmapBits cbMasks(lFrame).hWnd, SourceSize, SourceBits(0)
        bUseMask = True
        GenerateMask = True
End Function

Private Function Color32(ByVal bRed As Byte, ByVal bGreen As Byte, _
    ByVal bBlue As Byte, ByVal bAlpha As Byte) As RGBQUAD
    Color32.Blue = bBlue
    Color32.Green = bGreen
    Color32.Red = bRed
    Color32.alpha = bAlpha
End Function

Public Function Collided(ByRef OtherSprite As clsSprite) As Boolean
    Dim r1 As RECT_API
    Dim r2 As RECT_API
    Dim r3 As RECT_API

    'set up primary rect
    r1.Left = Me.X
    r1.Top = Me.Y
    r1.Right = r1.Left + Me.Width
    r1.Bottom = r1.Top + Me.Height
```

```
      'set up secondary rect
      r2.Left = OtherSprite.X
      r2.Top = OtherSprite.Y
      r2.Right = r2.Left + OtherSprite.Width
      r2.Bottom = r2.Top + OtherSprite.Height

      'check for collision
      Collided = CBool(IntersectRect(r3, r1, r2))
End Function
```

SPRITES IN ACTION: THE SPRITETEST PROGRAM

Take a look at Figure 8.8 to see the SpriteTest program in action. You might notice right away that the frame rate on this program is pretty slow—only 19 fps. This program is using a simple timer control for the game loop, so the frame rate pretty much tops out at 19 no matter how many sprites you use (although it will start to drop at around 30–40 sprites). Of course, this rate will vary on different PCs.

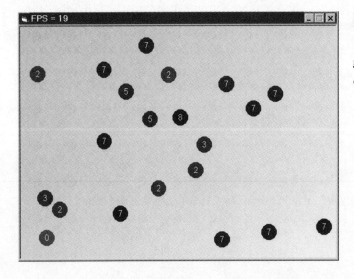

Figure 8.8

The SpriteTest program runs the sprite class through its paces.

Upon running the program, the next most significant thing you will notice is the terrible flicker! This program is as simple as possible; it just runs the sprite class through its paces without regard to speed or quality. Not only is this program slow, it is also not double buffered.

The SpriteTest program loads a series of frames from a file called shapes.bmp, which is shown in Figure 8.9. This file is really small, with only nine frames to the animation sequence, and the frames are only 32 × 32 pixels in size.

BUZZWORD

A *double buffer* (also called *back buffer*) is an image in memory with the same resolution as the screen, upon which all graphics routines will draw. Once all the drawing routines are done, the double buffer is quickly copied to the screen. The result is flicker-free, smooth animation.

Figure 8.9

The shapes.bmp file holds the animation frames for the SpriteTest program.

The important features this program tests are the animation rate and movement rate, both of which are properties of the sprite. These values are randomized when the program begins, so each sprite will animate a little differently than the others.

Feel free to experiment with different combinations of blitting operations in the sprite class by running the SpriteTest program. For example, you might want to see what happens when you turn off transparency (by setting Transparent = False), as shown in Figure 8.10.

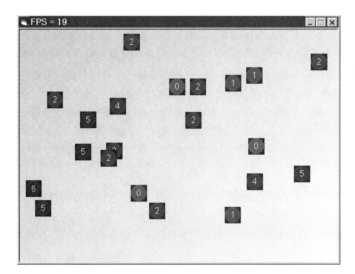

Figure 8.10

The SpriteTest program, running with transparency disabled

Building the SpriteTest Program

The SpriteTest program has a couple of dependencies. Obviously it will need the sprite class source code file, Sprite.cls, in the project. Otherwise the program will not be able to create the sprites. If you still have the project open from earlier when you added the sprite class, then you can use that program for SpriteTest. If not, then I'll go over it again.

First, you will need to run Visual Basic. (If it is already running, select New Project from the File menu.) I have shown you the New Project dialog box before, but Figure 8.11 shows it again for reference. This is the dialog box that appears when you run VB or start a new project.

Figure 8.11

The New Project dialog box shows all of the project types available in VB.

Select the default Standard EXE project and click OK to continue. The new project will have a single file called Form1.

Now, if the sprite class is not already in the project from earlier in this chapter, you will need to add it to the project. Select Add Class Module from the Project menu. (You can also right-click the project name in the Project Explorer and add a file using the menu that pops up.) The Add Class Module dialog box is shown in Figure 8.12. Click the Existing tab at the top, and locate the Sprite.cls file.

Don't forget! The sprite class needs the bitmap class from the last chapter in order to run! So you will need to also add the bitmap class to this project. Add the bitmap class in the same way that you added the sprite class, by using the Add Class Module dialog box and browsing for the file. When that is complete, you should have three files in the project: Bitmap.cls, Sprite.cls, and Form1.frm.

Alternatively, you can drag files from Windows Explorer onto the Project Explorer in VB to add those files to the project.

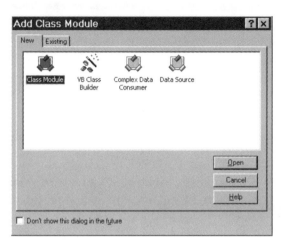

Figure 8.12

The Add Class Module dialog box allows you to add a new or existing class to the project.

The SpriteTest Source Code

You will enter the source code for SpriteTest in the code module for Form1. Double-click the Form1.frm file in the Project Explorer to open it, and then open the code window for the form. You can do this by either double-clicking somewhere on the form itself, or by selecting Code from the View menu. Type in this first section of code first, which includes the Windows API declarations and structures.

```
'-------------------------------------------------------------------------
' Visual Basic Game Programming With DirectX
' Chapter 8 : Supersonic Sprites
' SpriteTest Program Source Code
'-------------------------------------------------------------------------

Option Explicit

'Windows API functions
Private Declare Function GetClientRect _
    Lib "user32" (ByVal hWnd As Long, _
    lpRect As RECT) As Long

Private Declare Function ValidateRect _
    Lib "user32" (ByVal hWnd As Long, _
    lpRect As RECT) As Long

Private Declare Function GetTickCount _
    Lib "kernel32" () As Long
```

```
'Windows API structures
Private Type RECT
    Left As Long
    Top As Long
    Right As Long
    Bottom As Long
End Type
```

Hey, this program doesn't need very many Windows API functions, compared to previous programs! This will be a pattern with each new chapter as Windows API functionality is moved into classes like clsBitmap and clsSprite, hiding away the Windows routines and providing just an interface to a feature needed to write games.

Now for some constants, controls, and variables. In VB the tendency is usually to explain how to set up a form with all kinds of controls. But as you have found in the chapters up to this point, this is game programming! Controls are for database programs! As game developers, we just want to see some code, not a list of control properties that need to be set up. (For some reason, that reminds me of a great line by James Earl Jones in the movie *Sneakers*: "We are the United States government. We don't do that sort of thing!")

You will notice in the following listing that there are three controls in this program: Picture1, Timer1, and Timer2.

```
'constants
Const NUMSPRITES = 30

'controls used by program
Dim WithEvents Picture1 As PictureBox
Dim WithEvents Timer1 As Timer
Dim WithEvents Timer2 As Timer

'bitmaps and sprites
Dim cbBackgrnd As New clsBitmap
Dim csShapes(0 To NUMSPRITES) As clsSprite

'program variables
Dim lFrameCount As Long
Dim n As Long
```

The actual functionality of the SpriteTest program is shown in the remaining code listing. Note that the timers are responsible for the core functionality of the program.

```
Private Sub Form_Load()
    Randomize GetTickCount

    'set up the main form
    With Form1
        .AutoRedraw = False
        .BorderStyle = 1
        .ClipControls = False
        .KeyPreview = True
        .ScaleMode = 3
        .Width = 640 * Screen.TwipsPerPixelX
        .Height = 480 * Screen.TwipsPerPixelY
        .Show
    End With

    'create the main PictureBox control
    Set Picture1 = Controls.Add("VB.PictureBox", "Picture1")
    With Picture1
        .AutoRedraw = False
        .BorderStyle = 1
        .ClipControls = False
        .ScaleMode = 3
        .BackColor = RGB(0, 0, 0)
        .Left = 0
        .Top = 0
        .Width = Form1.ScaleWidth
        .Height = Form1.ScaleHeight
        .Visible = True
    End With

    'create the timer control
    Set Timer1 = Controls.Add("VB.Timer", "Timer1")
    Timer1.Interval = 1
    Timer1.Enabled = True

    'create the frame count timer
    Set Timer2 = Controls.Add("VB.Timer", "Timer2")
    Timer2.Interval = 1000
    Timer2.Enabled = True
```

```
    'load and draw the background image
    cbBackgrnd.Load App.Path & "\blueyellow640.bmp"
    cbBackgrnd.Draw 0, 0, Picture1.hdc

    'load and initialize the sprites
    For n = 0 To NUMSPRITES
        Set csShapes(n) = New clsSprite
        With csShapes(n)
            .Transparent = True
            If Not .LoadFrames(App.Path & _
                "\shapes.bmp", 1, 1, 32, 32, 9) Then
                MsgBox "Error loading shapes.bmp"
            End If

            .X = Random(Picture1.ScaleWidth - .Width - 1)
            .Y = Random(Picture1.ScaleHeight - .Height - 1)
            Do While .SpeedX = 0
                .SpeedX = Random(6) - 3
            Loop
            Do While .SpeedY = 0
                .SpeedY = Random(6) - 3
            Loop
            .AnimRate = Random(10) + 5
        End With
    Next n
End Sub

Private Sub Form_KeyDown(KeyCode As Integer, Shift As Integer)
    If KeyCode = 27 Then Picture1_Click
End Sub

Private Sub Form_Paint()
    Static r As RECT
    cbBackgrnd.Draw 0, 0, Picture1.hdc
    GetClientRect Picture1.hWnd, r
    ValidateRect Picture1.hWnd, r
End Sub

Private Sub Form_Terminate()
    Set cbBackgrnd = Nothing
```

```
    For n = 0 To NUMSPRITES
        Set csShapes(n) = Nothing
    Next n
End Sub

Private Sub Picture1_Click()
    Form1.Hide
    Unload Form1
End Sub

Private Sub Timer1_Timer()
    Static bFirst As Boolean

    'save under the first time
    If Not bFirst Then
        For n = 0 To NUMSPRITES
            csShapes(n).SaveUnder Picture1.hdc
        Next n
        bFirst = Not bFirst
    End If

    'restore image under the ball
    For n = 0 To NUMSPRITES
        csShapes(n).RestoreUnder Picture1.hdc
    Next n

    'move sprites to new locations
    For n = 0 To NUMSPRITES
        With csShapes(n)
            .X = .X + .SpeedX
            If .X > Picture1.ScaleWidth - .Width - 2 Then
                .X = Picture1.ScaleWidth - .Width - 1
                .SpeedX = -.SpeedX
            ElseIf .X < 2 Then
                .X = 2
                .SpeedX = -.SpeedX
            End If

            .Y = .Y + .SpeedY
```

```
            If .Y > Picture1.ScaleHeight - .Height - 2 Then
                .Y = Picture1.ScaleHeight - .Height - 1
                .SpeedY = -.SpeedY
            ElseIf .Y < 2 Then
                .Y = 2
                .SpeedY = -.SpeedY
            End If

            'increment the frame
            .NextFrame

            'save image under sprites
            .SaveUnder Picture1.hdc
        End With
    Next n

    'draw sprites
    For n = 0 To NUMSPRITES
        csShapes(n).Draw Picture1.hdc
    Next n

    'increment the frame count
    lFrameCount = lFrameCount + 1
End Sub

Private Sub Timer2_Timer()
    Form1.Caption = "FPS = " & lFrameCount
    lFrameCount = 0
End Sub

Public Function Random(ByVal lNum As Long) As Long
    Random = CLng(lNum * Rnd)
End Function
```

SPRITE COLLISION DETECTION

Collision detection is one of the most important aspects of sprite programming. Most of the action in a sprite-based game will depend on collisions between certain sprites on the screen. In a classic scrolling arcade game, collision is checked between the player's weapons and enemy ships (in a game such as *Space Invaders*), and likewise between the enemy weapons and the player. The most simplistic collision detection in a game is that which simply reports if a collision has occurred between a missile and a ship, and then blows up the ship.

But in a more complicated game, it is usually necessary to figure out which direction the sprites were traveling when they crashed into each other, in order to better model the physics of the collision. For example, consider the physics in play on a pool table when the cue ball has been hit. Balls on the table are bouncing off the walls and off each other, usually with a crashing cacophony of sound. How would you model a pool table? You can't just blow up a pool ball when it collides with another ball!

The situation is similar in a pinball game, where a little metal ball is rolling around, bumping into breakers and being whacked by the paddles (controlled by the player). This is another case where you can't just blow up the ball when it hits something! The physics of modeling a ball as it rolls around a curved surface are rather complicated, but I'm sure you can appreciate how a simple pinball game can be orders of magnitude more complex than even the most engaging shoot-em-up.

Detecting Sprite Collisions

The easiest way to detect a collision is by using a Windows API function called IntersectRect, which looks like this:

```
Private Declare Function IntersectRect _
    Lib "user32" (lpDestRect As RECT, _
    lpSrc1Rect As RECT, lpSrc2Rect As RECT) As Long
```

IntersectRect has three parameters, all of which are RECT structures. The RECT structure has been covered before, but here it is again for reference:

```
Private Type RECT
    Left As Long
    Top As Long
    Right As Long
    Bottom As Long
End Type
```

IntersectRect only really needs the last two parameters, which are the bounding rectangles around two sprites. But the first parameter is actually returned by IntersectRect with the union of the other two rectangles. This would be useful if you wanted to see how much the two sprites had intersected, but for now I would just ignore it and pass a filler variable.

The Collided function, which was included in the sprite class earlier in the chapter, accepts one sprite parameter. It then wraps a RECT variable around each of the two sprites (the internal class and the passed sprite), providing the bounding rectangles needed for IntersectRect. Collided simply returns true or false, based on the result of IntersectRect. The source code for the Collided function follows.

```
Public Function Collided(ByRef OtherSprite As clsSprite) As Boolean
    Dim r1 As RECT_API
    Dim r2 As RECT_API
    Dim r3 As RECT_API

    'set up primary rect
    r1.Left = Me.X
    r1.Top = Me.Y
    r1.Right = r1.Left + Me.Width
    r1.Bottom = r1.Top + Me.Height

    'set up secondary rect
    r2.Left = OtherSprite.X
    r2.Top = OtherSprite.Y
    r2.Right = r2.Left + OtherSprite.Width
    r2.Bottom = r2.Top + OtherSprite.Height

    'check for collision
    Collided = CBool(IntersectRect(r3, r1, r2))
End Function
```

Testing Sprite Collision

Now, how about a simple program to test sprite collision? I wrote a program called CollisionTest to show how the Collided function works, and it is shown in Figure 8.13. This program is based on the SpriteTest program that was written earlier in this chapter, so it will not require a complete rewrite.

There are only a few changes that must be made to the SpriteTest program to include the collision detection code, so I will list just the changes and leave it up to you to add them to the SpriteTest program on your own. I recommend that you first make a copy of the SpriteTest program directory.

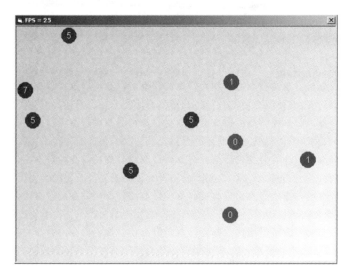

Figure 8. 13

The CollisionTest program demonstrates sprite collision as it might appear on a frictionless pool table. Notice how none of the sprites are overlapping, since they are bouncing off each other.

First, add the declaration for IntersectRect up at the top of the program, following the existing Windows API declarations. This program will also need a new structure called POINT. This structure makes it more convenient to work with point values, rather than needing two variables for X and Y positions. The changes are in bold text. If you have any problems modifying the program as explained, you can copy the CollisionTest program from the CD-ROM.

```
'-------------------------------------------------------------------------
' Visual Basic Game Programming With DirectX
' Chapter 8 : Supersonic Sprites
' CollisionTest Program Source Code
'-------------------------------------------------------------------------


'Windows API functions
Private Declare Function GetClientRect _
    Lib "user32" ( _
    ByVal hWnd As Long, _
    lpRect As RECT _
) As Long

Private Declare Function ValidateRect _
    Lib "user32" ( _
    ByVal hWnd As Long, _
    lpRect As RECT _
) As Long
```

```
Private Declare Function GetTickCount _
    Lib "kernel32" () As Long

Private Declare Function IntersectRect _
    Lib "user32" ( _
    lpDestRect As RECT, _
    lpSrc1Rect As RECT, _
    lpSrc2Rect As RECT _
) As Long

'Windows API structures
Private Type RECT
    Left As Long
    Top As Long
    Right As Long
    Bottom As Long
End Type

Private Type POINT
    X As Long
    Y As Long
End Type
```

Now skip down in the program listing to the Timer1_Timer event. This is the main game loop for
this program. It's not the fastest way to animate, but it makes the code simple and is easier to
demonstrate at this point. In Chapter 9, "Let the Animation Begin," I will show you how to write
a high-speed game loop (along with some other essential features, such as a double buffer). Since
Timer1_Timer is pretty short, I'll just list the entire event with the new code in bold text.

```
Private Sub Timer1_Timer()
    Static bFirst As Boolean
    Dim lSprite As Long
    Dim Center1 As POINT
    Dim Center2 As POINT

    'save under the first time
    If Not bFirst Then
        For n = 0 To NUMSPRITES
            csShapes(n).SaveUnder Picture1.hdc
        Next n
```

```
        bFirst = Not bFirst
End If


'restore image under the ball
For n = 0 To NUMSPRITES
    csShapes(n).RestoreUnder Picture1.hdc
Next n



'move sprites to new locations
For n = 0 To NUMSPRITES
    With csShapes(n)
        .X = .X + .SpeedX
        If .X > Picture1.ScaleWidth - .Width - 2 Then
            .X = Picture1.ScaleWidth - .Width - 1
            .SpeedX = -.SpeedX
        ElseIf .X < 2 Then
            .X = 2
            .SpeedX = -.SpeedX
        End If

        .Y = .Y + .SpeedY
        If .Y > Picture1.ScaleHeight - .Height - 2 Then
            .Y = Picture1.ScaleHeight - .Height - 1
            .SpeedY = -.SpeedY
        ElseIf .Y < 2 Then
            .Y = 2
            .SpeedY = -.SpeedY
        End If

        'check for sprite collisions
        For lSprite = 0 To NUMSPRITES
            If lSprite <> n Then
                If .Collided(csShapes(lSprite)) Then
                    'calculate center of primary sprite
                    Center1.X = .X + .Width / 2
                    Center1.Y = .Y + .Height / 2
                    'calculate center of secondary sprite
                    Center2.X = csShapes(lSprite).X + _
                        csShapes(lSprite).Width / 2
```

```
            Center2.Y = csShapes(lSprite).Y + _
                csShapes(lSprite).Height / 2

            'figure out which way the sprites collided
            If Center1.X <= Center2.X Then
                .SpeedX = -Random(6)
                csShapes(lSprite).SpeedX = Random(6)
                If Center1.Y <= Center2.Y Then
                    .SpeedY = -Random(6)
                    csShapes(lSprite).SpeedY = Random(6)
                Else
                    .SpeedY = Random(6)
                    csShapes(lSprite).SpeedY = -Random(6)
                End If
            Else
                .SpeedX = Random(6)
                csShapes(lSprite).SpeedX = -Random(6)
                If Center1.Y <= Center2.Y Then
                    .SpeedY = Random(6)
                    csShapes(lSprite).SpeedY = -Random(6)
                Else
                    .SpeedY = -Random(6)
                    csShapes(lSprite).SpeedY = Random(6)
                End If
            End If
        End If
    End If
Next lSprite

    'increment the frame
    .NextFrame

    'save image under sprites
    csShapes(n).SaveUnder Picture1.hdc
    End With
Next n

'draw sprites
```

```
    For n = 0 To NUMSPRITES
        csShapes(n).Draw Picture1.hdc
    Next n

    'increment the frame count
    lFrameCount = lFrameCount + 1
End Sub
```

The CollisionTest program might seem simple, but it actually demonstrates a powerful and absolutely critical feature of game programming, so it should not be overlooked. As you can see, collision detection does not need to be a complicated subject. The complexity of a collision test (such as the Collided function that is included with the sprite class) is based on the needs of each game. Most games will get by with this simple collision test, while other games will need a more precise collision test, possibly based on colliding pixels between two sprites (taking transparency into account). However, the key point is that *some* form of collision test is a requirement for most games.

SUMMARY

This chapter and the sprite class that was developed have significantly improved your game development toolbox by providing a comprehensive treatment of the subject of sprites, pushing the envelope of what can be accomplished with Visual Basic to the utter limit! Not only can you now load and display bitmaps, you can also load multiple tiles into a sprite and then animate it on the screen based on an animation rate and a movement rate. The result is a sprite class that contains all of the code needed to manipulate sprites, and it is all you need to write a complete game.

The sample programs in this chapter have been simplistic at the expense of performance in order to demonstrate the concepts presented herein. However, that is all about to end with Chapter 9, "Let the Animation Begin," which covers the techniques of writing high-speed game loops, double buffering, and even scrolling backgrounds commonly found in arcade games.

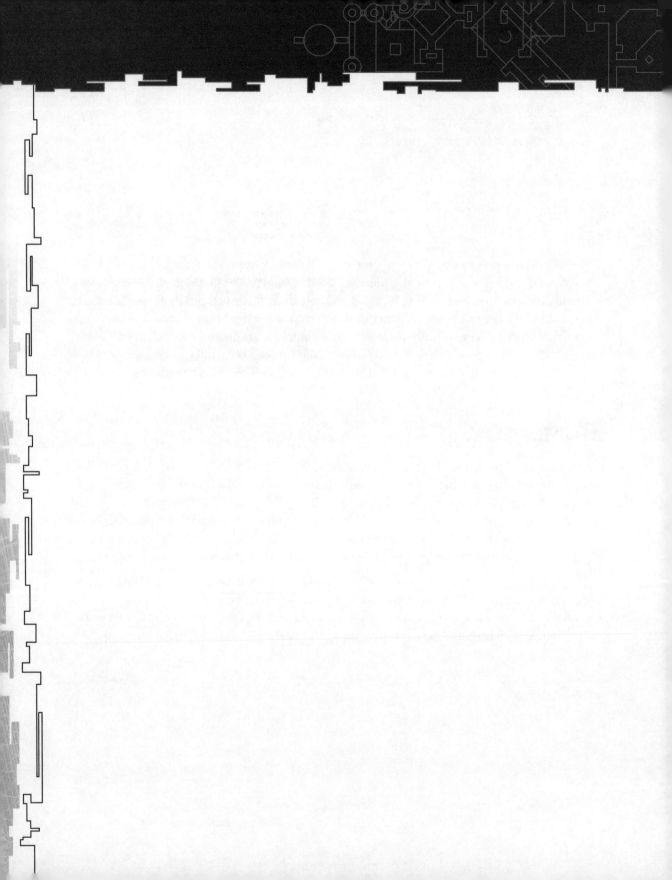

CHAPTER 9

LET THE ANIMATION BEGIN

Welcome to the animation chapter! In this chapter you will learn how to actually use the bitmaps and sprites that were covered in the last two chapters, making use of a high-speed game loop that does not need the Timer control. The game loop is really the engine that powers a game, and this chapter is all about writing and optimizing the game loop. Within this game loop are the background and sprite rendering code. In later chapters, additional functionality will be added to the game loop, such as keyboard, mouse, and joystick input, as well as playing sound effects and music.

In the following pages, I will show you how to draw static and rendered backgrounds (such as an arcade-style scrolling background), create flicker-free sprite animation using double buffering (with a bitmap image called the back buffer), and use dirty-rectangle updating (an advanced double buffering technique that draws only those portions of the game window that have changed since the last frame, thus speeding up the game).

This chapter covers the following topics:

- The High-Speed Animation Loop
- Using a Double Buffer to Eliminate Flicker
- Advanced Dirty-Rectangle Double Buffering
- Arcade-Style Vertical Scrolling

THE HIGH-SPEED ANIMATION LOOP

Regardless of the graphics subsystem used to render a game—whether it is Windows API, DirectDraw, Direct3D, or OpenGL—every game must have a main loop. This applies to old operating systems such as MS-DOS (which is poll-driven), as well as the latest version of Windows (which is event-driven).

In a modern event-driven game, the same resource events are actually sent to the game, so the game does not need to poll an input device at each interval of the game loop (as shown in Figure 9.1). This might seem like a much easier way to do it, but it does not eliminate the game loop. Even in an event-driven program, especially a game in which many

BUZZWORD

Event-driven is an architecture in which the operating system sends events when services become available. *Poll-driven* is an architecture in which the operating system must be polled for services.

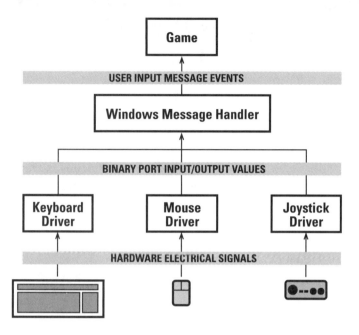

Figure 9.1

An event-driven, multi-tasking operating system like Windows uses a messaging system to communicate with hardware devices.

things might be happening at once, there must be a loop somewhere to actually do all the work. The fact that the operating system is event-driven is irrelevant in the context of the game loop.

In a classic poll-driven game, resources such as the keyboard, mouse, and joystick are polled for input at regular intervals by the game loop. At each frame, the polling determines whether an input device has sent a signal through a hardware port, at which point the game can take action based on that input (as shown in Figure 9.2).

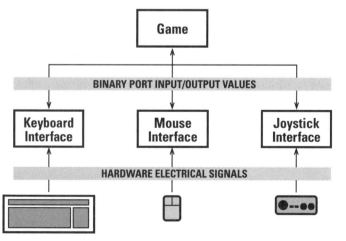

Figure 9.2

A non-multitasking operating system like MS-DOS uses a polling system at regular intervals to communicate with hardware devices and determine when data is available.

The job of a game library is quite often to provide a consistent interface for writing games on multiple platforms. A well-designed game library can then be compiled relatively easily on a PC, Mac, Dreamcast, Xbox, or even Pocket PC, just to name a few. Of course, some serious work that must be considered early on will be required with the different resolutions and image sizes, but such a thing is not only possible, it is done on a regular basis.

No More Timers!

One of the biggest problems with the Timer control in Visual Basic is that it is an interface to a low-resolution timer. This means that it only fires off a timer event after a set number of milliseconds have passed, with 18 milliseconds being common in some systems. To determine the maximum frame rate that is possible in a game loop, simply divide 1000 by the resolution of the timer (in milliseconds). Or, to make things easier, divide 1000 by the desired frame rate to get the maximum time available to your game loop for each frame.

If you are targeting a game that will run consistently at 60 frames per second (fps), then you must write a tight loop—1000 divided by 60 equals 16.67 milliseconds (ms). A far more realistic frame rate would be 30, which comes to 33.33 ms. While it is definitely possible to handle everything your game needs to do in only 33 ms, it would be difficult to fit it all into only 16 ms. Just think about all the things that must happen in a single frame.

1. Render the background or erase the sprites from the previous frame.
2. Move and animate all of the sprites to new locations based on movement rate.
3. Check all of the sprites for collisions.
4. Save the background image under each sprite (unless the background is rendered).
5. Draw the sprites at new positions.
6. Check for user input (keyboard, mouse, and joystick events).
7. Check the sound queue and start playing any new sound effects.
8. Apply artificial intelligence to computer-controlled players.
9. Send and receive network messages (in a multiplayer game).

When you consider that these tasks need not all be performed completely during each frame, the process is a little more manageable. See Figure 9.3 for an illustration of the game loop.

For example, the vast majority of the time there will be no user input events because human response is several orders of magnitude slower than the code running in a game loop. If your game runs at a steady 30 fps, that does not necessarily mean that you must synchronize the player's state with the other players in a multiplayer game during each frame. On the contrary, most players do not have that kind of bandwidth! Usually packets of data are sent and received at much slower intervals, such as ten times per second (or every 100 ms).

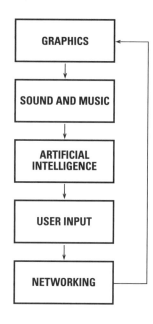

Figure 9.3

The primary game loop must call on each component of the game at a regularly timed interval to keep the game running smoothly.

Still, that leaves the graphics engine, sound and music, artificial intelligence, and user input, all of which must be handled during each frame. Obviously, the key is to optimize the graphics routines as much as possible and use the remaining clock ticks for everything else. In the old days, the graphics code was the whole game. Today, with DirectX and other libraries, that part of the equation has been simplified.

Creating a Fast Game Loop

Whether you are writing a flight simulator or a card game, you will need a game loop, and the faster the better. The game loop is a tight piece of code that kicks in after the game has finished loading all the resources and is ready to go. The game loop should then continue running incessantly until the game ends. The following is a snippet of code showing an actual game loop from one of the sample programs in this chapter.

```
Do While bRunning
    lCounter = GetTickCount - lStartTime
    If lCounter > lNewTime Then
        Game_Update lCounter
        lNewTime = lCounter + 1000 / MAXFRAMERATE
    End If
    DoEvents
Loop
```

At first glance, this code looks pretty simple, but then you might have noticed all the counter and timing variables mucking it up. This game loop is a Do . . . Loop construct, which is a looping mechanism similar to a For . . . Next loop, but with a conditional statement rather than a counting statement. This particular loop is endless: Do While True. Doesn't that seem like a strange bit of logic? When I saw this loop many years ago, my first thought was, "Do what, exactly?" Well, the answer to that question lies in the lines of code between the Do and the Loop statements.

In the first line, a variable called lCounter is set to GetTickCount – lStartTime. lStartTime is set elsewhere when the program starts. `GetTickCount` is a function that, as you might have guessed, returns the current clock tick. `GetTickCount` is not a high-resolution timer, but it gets the job done and is perfectly suitable for most games.

The next line checks to see whether a pre-determined number of milliseconds have passed since the last iteration through the loop. If enough time has passed, the `Game_Update` procedure is called, and the counter is incremented for the next frame. This procedure is where all the game code should be located, including user input, artificial intelligence, and graphics routines.

The game loop is deceptively simple, because the call to `Game_Update` might open up a plethora of code. It is therefore important to keep the code in `Game_Update` as tight as possible, avoiding loops and conditions when possible. Just remember that you only have a few milliseconds available, and you want to make the most of them.

USING A DOUBLE BUFFER TO ELIMINATE FLICKER

A double buffer is an exact duplicate of the display surface in memory. When all of the graphics routines draw to this double buffer, those routines run very quickly because system memory is usually faster than video memory. Although DDR (*Double Data Rate*) memory is now common on both video cards and motherboards, video memory was once much slower in older systems. Another benefit to using a double buffer is smooth, flicker-free animation.

Why would sprites otherwise flicker on the screen? The sample programs in Chapter 8, "Supersonic Sprites," did not use double buffering, so the images were being drawn, erased, and redrawn right on the screen in real time. When images are erased and redrawn, no matter how fast, there is a noticeable flicker to the display. The human eye can pick up this flicker even if it lasts only a few milliseconds, so there is no getting around it as long as the code is drawing directly to the screen. The solution is to draw to an off-screen buffer and then copy the buffer quickly to the screen all at once.

Frame Animation and Flicker

When you consider a typical television cartoon, each frame of the cartoon is drawn by hand—or rendered by a computer. The original frames are captured on film, with each frame slightly different than the last. The result is a cartoon in which little animated figures move on the screen and seem to interact. But taken individually, it is difficult to see exactly what is happening in a cartoon by looking at a single frame.

Sprite-based computer game animation is just like cartoon animation. There is a background image (which may be fixed or moving) with transparent objects that are drawn over the background. These transparent objects are changed slightly from one frame to the next and repositioned in small increments at each step, resulting in fluid motion. The trick is being able to do this in real time while the game is running, without the benefit of post-production editing that takes place in a television studio. All animation in a computer game is rendered from one moment to the next, and from one frame to the next, so there is no time to correct errors. If your code is not solid and thoroughly tested, a glitch will affect the player's impression of the game.

Often the difference between an expensive animated movie and a typical daily television cartoon is the amount of time spent on details, such as moving clouds in the sky, translucent water in a stream, birds flying in the distance, cycles of day and night, and multiple viewing angles for the characters. Computer-assisted and fully computer-rendered movies like *Titan A.E.* and *Final Fantasy: The Spirits Within* have so much detail that they are often more engaging than traditional films. (Why, you might ask, is this significant to the subject at hand? Computer animation studios like Industrial Light & Magic often recruit from the game development industry.)

Think of a secondary (double) buffer as the strip of film upon which an animated movie is rendered prior to viewing. Without the strip of film, the audience would be required to watch as each frame of the movie is assembled (disregarding the fact that computer-generated films require months or years to render).

The Benefits of Double Buffering

The trick to high-speed animation is to update the screen only when something has changed. If pure frame rate is your goal, you might want to have a static background or possibly a background that changes infrequently. But for visual appeal and the awe factor, a rendered background is much more impressive in a game.

The Challenge of Speed

Double buffering with a rendered background is significantly more challenging than with a static background, because you do not have the benefit of updating only the parts of the screen that have changed (a technique called *dirty-rectangle double buffering*, which is covered later in this chapter). A rendered background calls for a complete screen refresh at every single frame.

The Age-Old Question: Performance or Quality?

Double buffering may or may not improve the performance of a game, depending on the methods used. But there is no question that double buffering improves quality. In fact, double buffering is a given requirement that is usually taken for granted, like milk in a bowl of cereal. It is so commonplace that double buffer code is usually written and optimized early in a game's development and then pretty much ignored, with more important factors like artificial intelligence and multiplayer networking receiving most of the attention.

There was once a time when the graphics code was everything, and just getting double-buffered transparent sprites on the screen could be considered a game engine. Times have changed, and code that was once exciting and new is commonly forgotten like features on a new automobile. Remember when an air bag was an optional safety feature? Now many new automobiles have dual air bags, and even side-impact air bags.

You really must balance performance and quality to decide on a baseline for your game. You might allow users to disable or enable certain features to fine-tune the game on their own. Double buffering is one of those features that you must master. From that point forward, it will be an integral part of your game development arsenal.

Creating a Double Buffer

Hopefully you are already familiar with sprite animation. If you skipped the last two chapters, I would recommend that you go back and at least cover the main points, because this chapter builds upon code developed earlier.

The sprite class has a `Draw` procedure that blits the current frame to a destination device context using the `BitBlt` function. If transparency is enabled, the mask is first drawn with the vbSrcAnd method to invert the pixels on the destination. The sprite frame is then drawn with the vbSrcPaint method to draw the sprite transparently. Since the sprite code is already expecting to receive the destination as a parameter, it is simple to direct all blitting code to the double buffer instead. After everything has been updated, the double buffer can then be blitted directly to the screen.

To actually create the double buffer (which is also commonly referred to as a *back buffer*), you can use the bitmap class from Chapter 7, "Break Out the Bitmaps." This class is very convenient for creating the double buffer because it includes a `Create` function to create the bitmap in memory without needing to load an image. This memory bitmap will be the double buffer.

Here is the line of code that instantiates the double buffer variable:

```
Dim cbBackBuffer As New clsBitmap
```

When the program starts up (usually in Form_Load), you will want to create the memory bitmap by calling the Create function for the back buffer variable, and pass it the source hdc (which determines the format of the new memory bitmap), the width, and the height.

```
If Not cbBackBuffer.Create(Picture1.hdc, Picture1.ScaleWidth, _
    Picture1.ScaleHeight) Then
    MsgBox "Error creating back buffer"
    Shutdown
End If
```

Sending Graphics Output to the Double Buffer

As you can see, the functionality for creating a double buffer was already included in the bitmap class. Directing bitmaps, sprites, and other graphics-drawing routines to use the double buffer is also simple. Since every Windows drawing and blitting routine requires a surface, it is simply a matter of passing the surface of the double buffer rather than the PictureBox to drawing routines that are needed by the game.

The following lines of code show how simple it is to draw an array of sprites to the double buffer:

```
For n = 0 To NUMSPRITES
    csBall(n).Draw cbBackBuffer.hdc
Next n
```

The following line shows how to display the background image after loading it at the start of the program:

```
cbBackgrnd.Draw 0, 0, cbBackBuffer.hdc
```

Blitting the Back Buffer

Back in Chapter 7, "Break Out the Bitmaps," I showed you how to create, load, and draw bitmaps to the screen, and even included a sample program that used a pre-drawn mask to draw a transparent bitmap. This was the precursor to the mask-generating code and sprite code in the following chapter. Thanks to that earlier work, the code to actually draw the double buffer is just like the code to draw the sprites and the background image:

```
cbBackBuffer.Draw 0, 0, Picture1.hdc
```

As you can see, the double buffer is no different from any other bitmap, and the real usefulness of this class rests upon the hdc property (which is a handle to the device context, the surface that Windows uses for graphics output).

Testing the Double Buffer

To fully appreciate the difference that double buffering can make, I will walk you through a sample program that animates several rotating balls on the screen with a double buffer. This program is called—surprise!—DoubleBuffer, and is shown in Figure 9.4.

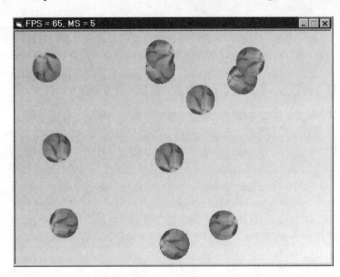

Figure 9.4

The animated sprites in this program are double buffered, resulting in smooth screen updates without flicker.

To create this program from scratch, start VB and create a new Standard EXE project. Add the Bitmap.cls and Sprite.cls files from the previous two chapters to the project. (In case you have forgotten, you can do this from the Project menu.) Name the new project DoubleBuffer.

Now, one small assumption that I often make is that you already have access to the graphics on the CD-ROM that came with this book. When you create the projects and type in the code listings manually—which is the best way to learn—you will need to create your own graphics or copy the original bitmaps off the CD-ROM. Figure 9.5 shows the source image for the animated ball that is used in the DoubleBuffer program. I rotated this ball at 22.5-degree intervals to come up with a total of 16 frames.

If you are not an expert VB programmer, going through the process of creating the projects and typing in the code is instructive. Just be sure to copy the bitmaps from the CD-ROM to your hard drive so you will be able to use them. For convenience, I have copied all of the graphics used in the book into a single directory on the CD-ROM called \Bitmaps. You can simply copy any bitmaps you need out of that directory. The animated ball is shown in Figure 9.6.

Figure 9.5

*The original artwork
for the animated ball
used in the
DoubleBuffer program*

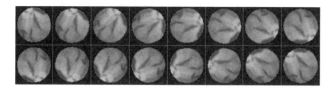

Figure 9.6

*The tiled bitmap of the
animated ball includes
16 frames.*

Open the code window for Form1 (the default file added to every new project) and type in the following lines of code. This first listing of code includes the Windows API functions and structures, program constants, program controls, and program variables.

> **TIP**
>
> **To make things easy, all background images and sample programs in this book run at 640 × 480 resolution, and the images are 32-bit bitmaps (which ensures that sprite masks can be generated properly). 24-bit images should be fine, although 16-bit images do not always turn out perfectly. To be safe, I recommend that you stick with 32-bit bitmaps.**

```
'-----------------------------------------------------------------
' Visual Basic Game Programming With DirectX
' Chapter 9 : Let The Animation Begin
' DoubleBuffer Source Code File
'-----------------------------------------------------------------

Option Explicit
Option Base 0

'Windows API functions and structures
Private Declare Function GetTickCount _
    Lib "kernel32" () As Long

Private Declare Function GetClientRect _
    Lib "user32" ( _
    ByVal hWnd As Long, _
    lpRect As RECT _
) As Long
```

```
Private Declare Function ValidateRect _
    Lib "user32" ( _
    ByVal hWnd As Long, _
    lpRect As RECT _
) As Long

Private Type RECT
    Left As Long
    Top As Long
    Right As Long
    Bottom As Long
End Type

'program constants
Const MAXFRAMERATE As Long = 120
Const NUMSPRITES As Long = 20

'program controls
Dim WithEvents Picture1 As PictureBox

'program variables
Dim cbBackgrnd As New clsBitmap
Dim cbBackBuffer As New clsBitmap
Dim csBall(NUMSPRITES) As clsSprite
Dim bRunning As Boolean
Dim n As Long
```

The next section of code for the DoubleBuffer program is the `Form_Load` event. This procedure runs at the very beginning of the program, so this is a good place to initialize the program and load the graphics. Pay attention to the section of code following the comment, "create the back buffer." This snippet of code actually creates the double buffer and prepares it for use in the program. Following that, the background image is loaded and then displayed on the double buffer. Then you will see the usual sprite-loading code and the game loop.

```
Private Sub Form_Load()
    Static lStartTime As Long
    Static lCounter As Long
    Static lNewTime As Long

    Randomize GetTickCount
    lStartTime = GetTickCount
    bRunning = True
```

```
'set up the main form
Form1.AutoRedraw = False
Form1.BorderStyle = 1
Form1.ClipControls = False
Form1.KeyPreview = True
Form1.ScaleMode = 3
Form1.Width = 640 * Screen.TwipsPerPixelX
Form1.Height = 480 * Screen.TwipsPerPixelY
Form1.Show

'create the PictureBox control for drawing
Set Picture1 = Controls.Add("VB.PictureBox", "Picture1")
Picture1.AutoRedraw = False
Picture1.BorderStyle = 1
Picture1.ClipControls = False
Picture1.ScaleMode = 3
Picture1.BackColor = RGB(0, 0, 0)
Picture1.Left = 0
Picture1.Top = 0
Picture1.Width = Form1.ScaleWidth
Picture1.Height = Form1.ScaleHeight
Picture1.Visible = True

'create the back buffer
If Not cbBackBuffer.Create(Picture1.hdc, Picture1.ScaleWidth, _
    Picture1.ScaleHeight) Then
    MsgBox "Error creating back buffer"
    Shutdown
End If

'load the background
If Not cbBackgrnd.Load(App.Path & "\blueyellow.bmp") Then
    MsgBox "Error loading background image"
    Shutdown
End If
cbBackgrnd.Draw 0, 0, cbBackBuffer.hdc

'load the animated ball sprites
For n = 0 To NUMSPRITES
    Set csBall(n) = New clsSprite
    csBall(n).Transparent = True
```

```
        'load the first row of animation
        If Not csBall(n).LoadFrames(App.Path & "\animball.bmp", _
            0, 0, 65, 64, 8) Then
            MsgBox "Error loading animball.bmp"
            Shutdown
        End If
        'load the second row of animation
        If Not csBall(n).LoadFrames(App.Path & "\animball.bmp", _
            0, 66, 65, 64, 8) Then
            MsgBox "Error loading animball.bmp"
            Shutdown
        End If

        'set up sprite's initial values
        InitSprite csBall(n)
    Next n

    'main game loop
    Do While bRunning
        lCounter = GetTickCount() - lStartTime
        If lCounter > lNewTime Then
            'update game display
            Game_Update lCounter
            'update frame count
            lNewTime = lCounter + 1000 / MAXFRAMERATE
        End If
        DoEvents
    Loop
End Sub
```

The next section of code in the DoubleBuffer program includes Form_Paint, Form_Unload, Form_KeyDown, Form_QueryUnload, and Picture1_Click. These support procedures help to keep the program running smoothly, as in the case of Form_Paint, which updates the screen properly when the program window has been minimized and restored or covered by another window.

Form_Unload frees up memory used by the classes in the program, including the sprites and double buffer. Picture1_Click and Form_KeyDown provide two easy ways to end the program—by either clicking the form or pressing the ESC key. Form_QueryUnload calls a cleanup procedure that prevents the program from ending before the cleanup code has had a chance to run. The Shutdown procedure is called by several others to close the form and end the program.

```
Private Sub Form_Paint()
    Dim r As RECT
    GetClientRect Picture1.hWnd, r
    ValidateRect Picture1.hWnd, r
    cbBackgrnd.Draw 0, 0, Picture1.hdc
End Sub

Private Sub Form_KeyDown(KeyCode As Integer, Shift As Integer)
    If KeyCode = 27 Then Shutdown
End Sub

Private Sub Form_QueryUnload(Cancel As Integer, UnloadMode As Integer)
    Shutdown
End Sub

Private Sub Picture1_Click()
    Shutdown
End Sub

Private Sub Shutdown()
    bRunning = False
    Form1.Hide
    Set cbBackgrnd = Nothing
    Set cbBackBuffer = Nothing
    For n = 0 To NUMSPRITES
        Set csBall(n) = Nothing
    Next n
    End
End Sub
```

The Game_Update procedure is the main animation routine in the program, and is called by the game loop in Form_Load. Game_Update includes the code to draw and erase the sprites, and to draw the double buffer to the screen at the end of each frame. Game_Update also includes some timing code that updates the caption of the program with the frame rate.

```
Private Sub Game_Update(ByVal MS As Long)
    Static bFirst As Boolean
    Static lCounter As Long
    Static lTimer As Long
    Static lStart As Long
    Dim n As Long
```

```
        'start counting milliseconds
        lStart = GetTickCount

        'save background images first time
        If Not bFirst Then
            For n = 0 To NUMSPRITES
                csBall(n).SaveUnder cbBackBuffer.hdc
            Next n
            bFirst = Not bFirst
        End If

        'restore background images
        For n = 0 To NUMSPRITES
            csBall(n).RestoreUnder cbBackBuffer.hdc
        Next n

        'move sprites
        For n = 0 To NUMSPRITES
            MoveSprite csBall(n)
            csBall(n).NextFrame
            csBall(n).SaveUnder cbBackBuffer.hdc
        Next n

        'draw sprites
        For n = 0 To NUMSPRITES
            csBall(n).Draw cbBackBuffer.hdc
        Next n

        'copy the back buffer to the screen
        cbBackBuffer.Draw 0, 0, Picture1.hdc

        'count the frames per second
        If MS > lTimer + 1000 Then
            lStart = GetTickCount - lStart
            Form1.Caption = "FPS = " & lCounter & ", MS = " & lStart
            lTimer = MS
            lCounter = 0
        Else
            lCounter = lCounter + 1
        End If
End Sub
```

The last listing of code for the DoubleBuffer program includes three procedures. `InitSprite` is used at program startup to set up each sprite with a random position, movement rate, and animation rate. The `MoveSprite` procedure is called by `Game_Update` to move each sprite and prevent it from moving beyond the edges of the screen. When a sprite reaches the edge, it is deflected and bounces away in the opposite direction. Finally, the `Random` function simply returns a random Long integer.

```
Public Sub InitSprite(ByRef sprite As clsSprite)
    sprite.Active = True
    sprite.Transparent = True
    sprite.CurrentFrame = 0
    sprite.X = Random(Picture1.ScaleWidth - _
        sprite.Width - 1)
    sprite.Y = Random(Picture1.ScaleHeight - _
        sprite.Height - 1)
    Do While sprite.SpeedX = 0
        sprite.SpeedX = Random(6) - 3
    Loop
    Do While sprite.SpeedY = 0
        sprite.SpeedY = Random(6) - 3
    Loop
    sprite.AnimRate = Random(10) + 1
    sprite.MoveRate = Random(10) + 1
End Sub

Public Sub MoveSprite(ByRef sprite As clsSprite)
    'update X position
    sprite.X = sprite.X + sprite.SpeedX
    If sprite.X > Picture1.ScaleWidth - sprite.Width - 2 Then
        sprite.X = Picture1.ScaleWidth - sprite.Width - 1
        sprite.SpeedX = -sprite.SpeedX
    ElseIf sprite.X < 2 Then
        sprite.X = 2
        sprite.SpeedX = -sprite.SpeedX
    End If

    'update Y position
    sprite.Y = sprite.Y + sprite.SpeedY
    If sprite.Y > Picture1.ScaleHeight - sprite.Height - 2 Then
        sprite.Y = Picture1.ScaleHeight - sprite.Height - 1
        sprite.SpeedY = -sprite.SpeedY
```

```
        ElseIf sprite.Y < 2 Then
            sprite.Y = 2
            sprite.SpeedY = -sprite.SpeedY
        End If
    End Sub

    Public Function Random(ByVal num As Long) As Long
        Random = CLng(num * Rnd)
    End Function
```

That's the end of the code listing for the DoubleBuffer program. Feel free to run the program now by pressing F5. Please be sure to turn off the Compile On Demand feature, or the program will run as interpreted code rather than compiled code, which is much slower! To disable this feature, go to the Tools menu and select Options, General, and then turn off Compile On Demand. If the code was typed in correctly, you should see several colorful balls on the screen, animating at random speeds. Since the sprites are double buffered, the animation should be smooth and flicker free.

One final note on double buffering. Bitmaps take up resources in Windows. When testing code that uses these resources, it is common for a program to terminate without properly releasing the resources. This could happen while debugging or during normal execution. In general, the `Shutdown` procedure will free those resources. But I have noticed at times that sprite frames will disappear. This is a result of resources being lost in Windows,

> **TIP**
>
> **Be sure to always free up resources before the program ends, because Windows resources are finite. If objects are not deleted after use, Windows will become unstable.**

causing the program to degrade each time it is run; it occasionally requires a reboot. Just be sure that your `Terminate` procedure deletes all of the objects in the program to avoid this problem.

ADVANCED DIRTY RECTANGLE DOUBLE BUFFERING

Now that you have learned how to create and use a double buffer, you are probably eager to get started on a game. Indeed, the tools developed so far are sufficient to create a prototype game, but there are more tricks that I would like to show you first. One such trick is called *dirty-rectangle double buffering*. This strange-sounding term refers to updating only those parts of the screen that change from one frame to the next. Since the entire screen is often not affected, it is wasteful to copy the entire double buffer to the screen every frame when only a fraction of the display has actually changed.

Why not leave those unaffected parts of the screen alone and simply update what has changed? Sounds logical enough, does it not? The theory of dirty rectangles might sound like something from a vacuum cleaner convention, but it is actually a powerful technique for speeding up a game.

Optimizing the Back Buffer Update Procedure

Using one or more dirty rectangles can drastically speed up a game. Consider a classic fixed-screen arcade game such as *Asteroids*, *Joust*, *Dig-Dug*, or *Space Invaders*. These games use a single screen with a static background (or no background at all). There is absolutely no reason why you would need to blast the entire back buffer to the screen every frame in a game like that, in which only a fraction of the actual screen has really changed. You do not want to go so far as to update the display based on each sprite individually, because that would kill performance. These classic arcade games did not even use transparent sprites, so they were probably not double buffered either, but the point is valid. Only the portion of the screen that encompasses all of the moving objects needs to be updated. This is called the *dirty rectangle*.

But there is one major drawback. Rendered backgrounds are not friendly to dirty rectangles. The point is to reduce the number of bytes being blasted from one surface to another, whether that is the double buffer, the screen, or a sprite. Fewer blitting operations result in a faster game. Therefore, when the background is rendered for every frame, and sprites are drawn over the background, there is no benefit to keeping track of a dirty rectangle, because the whole screen needs to be updated!

Understanding Dirty Rectangles

Now that you understand a little about what dirty rectangles can do, how about a description of what they are, how they can help, and how to create one? Dirty-rectangle double buffering, as I have referred to it, involves blitting only a portion of the back buffer to the screen, rather than the whole back buffer. This obviously saves time, because fewer pixels means faster frame rates.

Just do the math. Even if the dirty rectangle takes up 90 percent of a 640×480 screen, that is still 30,720 fewer pixels that must be displayed. Back in the old days of MS-DOS and VGA systems, that number of pixels would have equaled about half the screen! And if you count the actual bytes in a 32-bit display versus an old 8-bit VGA display, that is a savings of 122,880 bytes—or roughly the equivalent of two VGA buffers! Since blitting works directly with rectangular shapes, those pixels translate directly into increased frame rate.

However, 90 percent is a rather high number. Quite often the dirty rectangle will be significantly smaller. And yes, there is another possibility. By breaking the dirty rectangle into several small rectangles, you can achieve even greater performance (more on that in the next section).

Single Dirty Rectangle Double Buffering

The simplest form of dirty rectangle double buffering is a program that uses just a single rectangle. During the sprite animation loop, a RECT variable (which is a Windows API structure containing four Longs: Left, Top, Right, and Bottom) keeps track of the dimensions of the dirty rectangle. As each sprite is moved, the rectangle's bounds are expanded. The result is that after all the sprites have been processed, the RECT will hold the precise dimensions of the rectangle that must be updated on the back buffer.

Using a Single Dirty Rectangle

The DirtyRect program updates the dirty rectangle region of the double buffer by blitting that rectangular region directly to a PictureBox. To illustrate how the dirty rectangle is updated, the DrawDirtyRect procedure first blanks the PictureBox with all black so only the actual affected portion of the double buffer is displayed. This line of code should be commented out for production, but is useful while debugging a game.

```
Public Sub DrawDirtyRect()
    'blank the display surface for effect
    Picture1.BackColor = RGB(0, 0, 0)
    'draw back buffer clipped to dirty rectangle
    BitBlt Picture1.hdc, rDirty.Left, rDirty.Top, _
        rDirty.Right - rDirty.Left, rDirty.Bottom - rDirty.Top, _
        cbBackBuffer.hdc, rDirty.Left, rDirty.Top, vbSrcCopy
End Sub
```

The main game loop is actually where the dirty rectangle is reset, so Game_Update can assume that the rectangle is ready for use without initialization. The ResetDirtyRect procedure sets the rectangle's values to extremes so that even a single sprite will update it.

```
'main game loop
Do While bRunning
    lCounter = GetTickCount() - lStartTime
    If lCounter > lNewTime Then
        'reset the dirty rectangle
        ResetDirtyRect
        'update game display
        Game_Update lCounter
        'update frame count
        lNewTime = lCounter + 1000 / MAXFRAMERATE
    End If
    DoEvents
Loop
```

Game_Update iterates through the sprite array when erasing, moving, and drawing the sprites. After the sprites have been moved, the code to draw the sprites is executed. This is the best place to update the dirty rectangle.

```
'move sprites
For n = 0 To NUMSPRITES
    If csButterfly(n).Active Then
        MoveSprite csButterfly(n)
        ResizeDirtyRect csButterfly(n)
        CheckCollisions n
        csButterfly(n).NextFrame
    End If
Next n
```

Testing a Single Dirty Rectangle

Now it's time to create a sample program to demonstrate how to implement dirty rectangle double buffering. This new project will be called DirtyRect, and is located in the directory for this chapter on the CD-ROM. To create the program from scratch, create a new Standard EXE project and add the usual Bitmap.cls and Sprite.cls files to the project. Then open the code window for Form1 and enter the following code listing into the file.

Figure 9.7 shows what the DirtyRect program looks like while running. Notice the black border around the edge of the program window. I simply set the background color of the PictureBox to black just before blitting the dirty rectangle each frame to show exactly what the rectangle looks

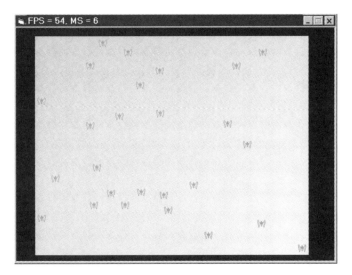

Figure 9.7

The DirtyRect program demonstrates how dirty rectangle double buffering works.

like. This produces a lot of flicker, but keep in mind that it is for testing purposes only. The line of code that blanks the background should be removed once you understand how it works.

The first section of code for the DirtyRect program includes the program header, Windows API functions and structures, program constants, program controls, and program variables. The only new code here that differs from the last program is the declaration of a variable called rDirty, which holds the dirty rectangle's dimensions.

```vb
'----------------------------------------------------------------------
' Visual Basic Game Programming With DirectX
' Chapter 9 : Let The Animation Begin
' DirtyRect Source Code File
'----------------------------------------------------------------------
Option Explicit
Option Base 0

'Windows API functions and structures
Private Declare Function GetTickCount _
    Lib "kernel32" () As Long

Private Declare Function GetClientRect _
    Lib "user32" ( _
    ByVal hWnd As Long, _
    lpRect As RECT _
) As Long

Private Declare Function ValidateRect _
    Lib "user32" ( _
    ByVal hWnd As Long, _
    lpRect As RECT _
) As Long

Private Declare Function IntersectRect _
    Lib "user32" ( _
    lpDestRect As RECT, _
    lpSrc1Rect As RECT, _
    lpSrc2Rect As RECT _
) As Long

Private Declare Function BitBlt _
    Lib "gdi32" ( _
```

```
        ByVal hDestDC As Long, _
        ByVal X As Long, _
        ByVal Y As Long, _
        ByVal nWidth As Long, _
        ByVal nHeight As Long, _
        ByVal hSrcDC As Long, _
        ByVal xSrc As Long, _
        ByVal ySrc As Long, _
        ByVal dwRop As Long _
    ) As Long

Private Type RECT
    Left As Long
    Top As Long
    Right As Long
    Bottom As Long
End Type

Private Type POINT
    X As Long
    Y As Long
End Type

'program constants
Const MAXFRAMERATE As Long = 100
Const NUMSPRITES As Long = 25

'program controls
Dim WithEvents Picture1 As PictureBox

'program variables
Dim cbBackgrnd As New clsBitmap
Dim cbBackBuffer As New clsBitmap
Dim csButterfly(NUMSPRITES) As clsSprite
Dim bRunning As Boolean
Dim rDirty As RECT
```

As usual, Form_Load is the startup procedure for the program, which initializes the program, loads the graphics, and starts the game loop running. Note that the dirty rectangle does not need to be initialized at this point. Only when the game loop starts does the dirty rectangle get reset.

```
Private Sub Form_Load()
    Static lStartTime As Long
    Static lCounter As Long
    Static lNewTime As Long
    Dim n As Long

    Randomize GetTickCount
    lStartTime = GetTickCount
    bRunning = True

    'set up the main form
    Form1.AutoRedraw = False
    Form1.BorderStyle = 1
    Form1.ClipControls = False
    Form1.KeyPreview = True
    Form1.ScaleMode = 3
    Form1.Width = 640 * Screen.TwipsPerPixelX
    Form1.Height = 480 * Screen.TwipsPerPixelY
    Form1.Show

    'create the PictureBox control for drawing
    Set Picture1 = Controls.Add("VB.PictureBox", "Picture1")
    Picture1.AutoRedraw = False
    Picture1.BorderStyle = 1
    Picture1.ClipControls = False
    Picture1.ScaleMode = 3
    Picture1.BackColor = RGB(0, 0, 0)
    Picture1.Left = 0
    Picture1.Top = 0
    Picture1.Width = Form1.ScaleWidth
    Picture1.Height = Form1.ScaleHeight
    Picture1.Visible = True

    'create the back buffer
    If Not cbBackBuffer.Create(Picture1.hdc, Picture1.ScaleWidth, _
        Picture1.ScaleHeight) Then
        MsgBox "Error creating back buffer"
        Shutdown
    End If
```

```
    'load the background
    If Not cbBackgrnd.Load(App.Path & "\blueyellow.bmp") Then
        MsgBox "Error loading blueyellow.bmp"
        Shutdown
    End If
    cbBackgrnd.Draw 0, 0, cbBackBuffer.hdc

    'load the animated ball sprites
    For n = 0 To NUMSPRITES
        Set csButterfly(n) = New clsSprite
        csButterfly(n).Transparent = True
        'load the first row of animation
        If Not csButterfly(n).LoadFrames(App.Path & "\butterfly.bmp", _
            0, 0, 16, 16, 1) Then
            MsgBox "Error loading butterfly.bmp"
            Shutdown
        End If

        'set up sprite's initial values
        InitSprite csButterfly(n)
    Next n

    'main game loop
    Do While bRunning
        lCounter = GetTickCount() - lStartTime
        If lCounter > lNewTime Then
            'reset the dirty rectangle
            ResetDirtyRect
            'update game display
            Game_Update lCounter
            'update frame count
            lNewTime = lCounter + 1000 / MAXFRAMERATE
        End If
        DoEvents
    Loop
End Sub
```

The support routines for DirtyRect include Form_Paint, which updates the game window when a refresh is needed; Form_QueryUnload, which is called when the user closes the program window; Form_Unload, which deletes the classes used by the program and frees up memory; Form_KeyDown, which ends the program when the ESC key is pressed; Picture1_Click, which ends the program when the game window is clicked; and Shutdown, which is called by the other procedures to end the program.

```
Private Sub Form_Paint()
    Dim r As RECT
    GetClientRect Picture1.hWnd, r
    ValidateRect Picture1.hWnd, r
    cbBackgrnd.Draw 0, 0, Picture1.hdc
End Sub

Private Sub Form_QueryUnload(Cancel As Integer, UnloadMode As Integer)
    Shutdown
End Sub

Private Sub Form_KeyDown(KeyCode As Integer, Shift As Integer)
    If KeyCode = 27 Then Shutdown
End Sub

Private Sub Picture1_Click()
    Shutdown
End Sub

Private Sub Shutdown()
    Dim n As Long
    bRunning = False
    Form1.Hide
    Set cbBackBuffer = Nothing
    Set cbBackgrnd = Nothing
    For n = 0 To NUMSPRITES
        Set csButterfly(n) = Nothing
    Next n
    End
End Sub
```

The Game_Update procedure is a little smarter than in previous programs, because it actually checks to see whether a sprite is active before doing anything with it. Previously, disabling a sprite by setting its Active property to false would not have affected the animation loop. Now there is a check at critical points in the Game_Update procedure to make sure only active sprites are being moved and displayed.

```vb
Private Sub Game_Update(ByVal MS As Long)
    Static bFirst As Boolean
    Static lCounter As Long
    Static lTimer As Long
    Static lStart As Long
    Dim n As Long

    'start counting milliseconds
    lStart = GetTickCount

    'save background images first time
    If Not bFirst Then
        For n = 0 To NUMSPRITES
            csButterfly(n).SaveUnder cbBackBuffer.hdc
        Next n
        bFirst = Not bFirst
    End If

    'restore background images
    For n = 0 To NUMSPRITES
        If csButterfly(n).Active Then
            csButterfly(n).RestoreUnder cbBackBuffer.hdc
        End If
    Next n

    'move sprites
    For n = 0 To NUMSPRITES
        If csButterfly(n).Active Then
            MoveSprite csButterfly(n)
            ResizeDirtyRect csButterfly(n)
            CheckCollisions n
            csButterfly(n).NextFrame
            csButterfly(n).SaveUnder cbBackBuffer.hdc
        End If
    Next n

    'draw sprites
    For n = 0 To NUMSPRITES
        If csButterfly(n).Active Then
            csButterfly(n).Draw cbBackBuffer.hdc
        End If
    Next n
```

```
    'draw the dirty rectangle
    DrawDirtyRect

    'count the frames per second
    If MS > lTimer + 1000 Then
        lStart = GetTickCount - lStart
        Form1.Caption = "FPS = " & lCounter & ", MS = " & lStart
        lTimer = MS
        lCounter = 0
    Else
        lCounter = lCounter + 1
    End If
End Sub
```

The InitSprite and MoveSprite procedures are exactly the same as they were in the DoubleBuffer program earlier. Basically, InitSprite is called to randomize the variables of a sprite, while MoveSprite is used to actually move a sprite on the screen.

```
Public Sub InitSprite(ByRef sprite As clsSprite)
    'initialize or reset the sprite
    sprite.Active = True
    sprite.Transparent = True
    sprite.CurrentFrame = 0

    'set the sprite's X,Y position
    sprite.X = Random(Picture1.ScaleWidth - _
        sprite.Width - 1)
    sprite.Y = Random(Picture1.ScaleHeight - _
        sprite.Height - 1)

    'set the sprite's X,Y speed
    Do While sprite.SpeedX = 0
        sprite.SpeedX = Random(6) - 3
    Loop
    Do While sprite.SpeedY = 0
        sprite.SpeedY = Random(6) - 3
    Loop

    'set the sprite's move and animation rates
    sprite.AnimRate = Random(10) + 1
    sprite.MoveRate = Random(10) + 1
End Sub
```

```
Public Sub MoveSprite(ByRef sprite As clsSprite)
    'update X position
    sprite.X = sprite.X + sprite.SpeedX
    If sprite.X > Picture1.ScaleWidth - sprite.Width - 2 Then
        sprite.X = Picture1.ScaleWidth - sprite.Width - 1
        sprite.SpeedX = -sprite.SpeedX
    ElseIf sprite.X < 2 Then
        sprite.X = 2
        sprite.SpeedX = -sprite.SpeedX
    End If

    'update Y position
    sprite.Y = sprite.Y + sprite.SpeedY
    If sprite.Y > Picture1.ScaleHeight - sprite.Height - 2 Then
        sprite.Y = Picture1.ScaleHeight - sprite.Height - 1
        sprite.SpeedY = -sprite.SpeedY
    ElseIf sprite.Y < 2 Then
        sprite.Y = 2
        sprite.SpeedY = -sprite.SpeedY
    End If
End Sub
```

This program has yet another feature that was lacking in the last program in this chapter—the ability to detect sprite collisions. This functionality was borrowed from Chapter 8, "Supersonic Sprites," and put into a new procedure called CheckCollisions. This procedure calls an additional function called Collided that returns true if the two passed sprites intersect on the screen. Collision detection slightly complicates this program and takes away from learning about dirty rectangles, but I figured it was worth the effort because I want you to become more familiar with collision detection with each new program.

CheckCollisions is not extremely reusable because it references the sprite array directly. If this procedure is ever moved into a class, it will need a new parameter with the sprite array passed to it by reference (a hint of things to come?). The procedure is pretty smart, though, at determining which side of a sprite was hit by another sprite. This functionality causes two sprites to deflect off each other realistically. The random elements help to disguise the simplicity of the physics here by sending the collided sprites off at random speeds, giving the impression that a real impact has occurred.

```
Public Sub CheckCollisions(ByRef lSpriteNum As Long)
    Dim Center1 As POINT
    Dim Center2 As POINT
    Dim lSprite As Long
```

```
'check all of the active sprites
For lSprite = 0 To NUMSPRITES
    If lSprite <> lSpriteNum Then
        With csButterfly(lSpriteNum)
            If .Collided(csButterfly(lSprite)) Then
                'calculate center of primary sprite
                Center1.X = .X + .Width / 2
                Center1.Y = .Y + .Height / 2
                'calculate center of secondary sprite
                Center2.X = csButterfly(lSprite).X + _
                    csButterfly(lSprite).Width / 2
                Center2.Y = csButterfly(lSprite).Y + _
                    csButterfly(lSprite).Height / 2

                'figure out which way the sprites collided
                'simulate momentum by deflecting sprites randomly
                If Center1.X <= Center2.X Then
                    'right side
                    .SpeedX = -Random(6)
                    csButterfly(lSprite).SpeedX = Random(6)
                    If Center1.Y <= Center2.Y Then
                        'bottom
                        .SpeedY = -Random(6)
                        csButterfly(lSprite).SpeedY = Random(6)
                    Else
                        'top
                        .SpeedY = Random(6)
                        csButterfly(lSprite).SpeedY = -Random(6)
                    End If
                Else
                    'left side
                    .SpeedX = Random(6)
                    csButterfly(lSprite).SpeedX = -Random(6)
                    If Center1.Y <= Center2.Y Then
                        'bottom
                        .SpeedY = Random(6)
                        csButterfly(lSprite).SpeedY = -Random(6)
                    Else
                        'top
                        .SpeedY = -Random(6)
                        csButterfly(lSprite).SpeedY = Random(6)
```

```
                    End If
                End If
            End If
        End With
    End If
    Next lSprite
End Sub
```

The code to handle the dirty rectangle follows, and is incorporated into three procedures. ResetDirtyRect is called at the beginning of each frame to set the rectangle to extreme values. This way, if there is at least one sprite being updated the rectangle will reflect the change. ResizeDirtyRect is passed a sprite reference, which it uses to resize the dirty rectangle. If the sprite is outside the current bounds then the bounds are expanded, up to but not exceeding the boundary of the game window. Finally, DrawDirtyRect does the grunt work of displaying the dirty rectangle to the screen at the end of a frame.

```
Public Sub ResetDirtyRect()
    'set dirty rectangle to extreme values
    rDirty.Left = 2000
    rDirty.Top = 2000
    rDirty.Right = 0
    rDirty.Bottom = 0
End Sub


Public Sub ResizeDirtyRect(ByRef spr As clsSprite)
    With spr
        'resize horizontal dirty rectangle
        If .X < rDirty.Left Then
            rDirty.Left = .X - 5
            If rDirty.Left < 0 Then rDirty.Left = 0
        ElseIf .X + .Width > rDirty.Right Then
            rDirty.Right = .X + .Width + 5
            If rDirty.Right > Picture1.ScaleWidth - 1 Then _
                rDirty.Right = Picture1.ScaleWidth - 1
        End If
        'resize vertical dirty rectangle
        If .Y < rDirty.Top Then
            rDirty.Top = .Y - 5
            If rDirty.Top < 0 Then rDirty.Top = 0
        ElseIf .Y + spr.Height > rDirty.Bottom Then
            rDirty.Bottom = .Y + .Height + 5
```

```
            If rDirty.Bottom > Picture1.ScaleHeight - 1 Then _
                rDirty.Bottom = Picture1.ScaleHeight - 1
        End If
    End With
End Sub

Public Sub DrawDirtyRect()
    'blank the display surface for effect
    Picture1.BackColor = RGB(0, 0, 0)

    'draw back buffer clipped to dirty rectangle
    BitBlt Picture1.hdc, rDirty.Left, rDirty.Top, _
        rDirty.Right - rDirty.Left, rDirty.Bottom - rDirty.Top, _
        cbBackBuffer.hdc, rDirty.Left, rDirty.Top, vbSrcCopy
End Sub
```

Last, but not least, is the trusty old Random function. This function converts the value returned by Rnd into a Long that is rounded up.

```
Public Function Random(ByVal lNum As Long) As Long
    Random = CLng(lNum * Rnd)
End Function
```

A single dirty rectangle will dramatically increase the frame rate of a game with a static background. Go ahead and run the program now to see a demonstration of dirty rectangle double buffering in action!

Now I will show you how to take the concept a step further by breaking it into four smaller dirty rectangles that are more efficient at updating images which would otherwise require a full screen refresh.

Using Multiple Dirty Rectangles

As if increasing the double buffer update speed was not enough, now I am going to show you yet another way to speed up this critical aspect of game programming. A single dirty rectangle is great for games with a lot of sprites at random locations on the screen, because a single rectangle is easy to handle.

But in some circumstances a single rectangle is wasteful, for instance when two sprites are located in opposite corners of the screen. A single huge rectangle would encompass most of the game window to include both sprites. A far more effective routine would handle the two opposing sprites separately with smaller dirty rectangles, which is what I am going to show you how to do next.

Encapsulating Dirty Rectangles

To make this process easier, I have created a class called clsDirtyRect (which will be covered shortly). Figure 9.8 shows a screenshot from the MultiRect program that I will walk you through next. As you can see from this figure, there are four distinct rectangles being updated on the screen, and each rectangle includes several sprites! Now do you see how this could be beneficial? Those four rectangles take up much less screen space than a single large rectangle encompassing all of the sprites.

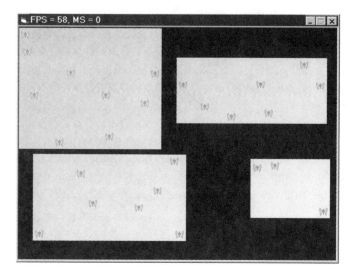

Figure 9.8

The MultiRect program demonstrates using multiple dirty rectangles to update the double buffer. This technique will speed up the rendering by an average of 10 percent.

Figure 9.9 shows another version of the MultiRect program, with only three of the quadrants being updated. This will occur when there are no sprites to be displayed in one of the four dirty rectangles.

The DirtyRect Class

Since multiple dirty rectangles require two arrays and a more complicated resizing routine, I have decided to put most of the dirty rectangle functionality into a class called clsDirtyRect. This class includes an Init procedure that sets up the quadrants based on a PictureBox reference that is passed to it.

The three dirty rectangle procedures from the last program (Reset, Resize, and Draw) are included in this class, and there is an additional function called PointInside that determines the quadrant where the sprite is located.

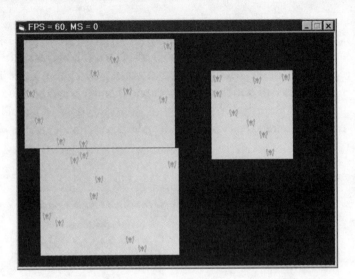

Figure 9.9

*When a quadrant has
no sprites, it is ignored
completely. Overlap
may occur to prevent
sprites from being
clipped between two
quadrants.*

An array of rectangles called rQuadrant holds the boundary information for each quadrant (which does not change), while an array of Boolean values called bQuadrant keeps track of which quadrants should be updated. In addition, an array called rDirty keeps track of the actual dirty rectangles. Each rectangle is bound by the corresponding rQuadrant RECT.

```
'-------------------------------------------------------------------
' Visual Basic Game Programming With DirectX
' Chapter 9 : Let The Animation Begin
' DirtyRect Class Source Code File
'-------------------------------------------------------------------

Option Explicit
Option Base 0

'Windows API functions and structures
Private Declare Function BitBlt _
    Lib "gdi32" ( _
    ByVal hDestDC As Long, _
    ByVal X As Long, _
    ByVal Y As Long, _
    ByVal nWidth As Long, _
    ByVal nHeight As Long, _
    ByVal hSrcDC As Long, _
    ByVal xSrc As Long, _
    ByVal ySrc As Long, _
```

```
        ByVal dwRop As Long _
) As Long

Private Type RECT_API
    Left As Long
    Top As Long
    Right As Long
    Bottom As Long
End Type

Private Type POINT
    X As Long
    Y As Long
End Type

'class constants
Const BORDER As Long = 5

'class variables
Dim rDirty(0 To 3) As RECT_API
Dim rQuadrant(0 To 3) As RECT_API
Dim bQuadrant(0 To 3) As Boolean
Dim n As Long

Public Sub Init(ByRef pic As PictureBox)
    'initialize quadrant 0
    rQuadrant(0).Left = pic.ScaleWidth / 2 - 2
    rQuadrant(0).Top = 0
    rQuadrant(0).Right = pic.ScaleWidth - 1
    rQuadrant(0).Bottom = pic.ScaleHeight / 2 + 2

    'initialize quadrant 1
    rQuadrant(1).Left = 0
    rQuadrant(1).Top = 0
    rQuadrant(1).Right = rQuadrant(0).Left + 4
    rQuadrant(1).Bottom = rQuadrant(0).Bottom

    'initialize quadrant 2
    rQuadrant(2).Left = 0
    rQuadrant(2).Top = rQuadrant(1).Bottom - 4
    rQuadrant(2).Right = rQuadrant(1).Right
    rQuadrant(2).Bottom = pic.ScaleHeight - 1
```

```
        'initialize quadrant 3
        rQuadrant(3).Left = rQuadrant(2).Right - 4
        rQuadrant(3).Top = rQuadrant(2).Top
        rQuadrant(3).Right = rQuadrant(0).Right
        rQuadrant(3).Bottom = rQuadrant(2).Bottom

End Sub

Public Sub Reset()
        'set dirty rectangles to extreme values
        For n = 0 To 3
            rDirty(n).Left = 2000
            rDirty(n).Top = 2000
            rDirty(n).Right = 0
            rDirty(n).Bottom = 0
            bQuadrant(n) = False
        Next n
End Sub

Public Sub Resize(ByRef spr As clsSprite, ByRef pic As Variant)
        Dim p As POINT
        Dim n As Long

        'grab sprite position
        p.X = spr.X
        p.Y = spr.Y

        'check all four quadrants
        For n = 0 To 3
            'figure out where sprite is located
            If PointInside(p, rQuadrant(n)) Then
                'yes, sprite is in this quadrant
                bQuadrant(n) = True

                With rDirty(n)
                    'see if sprite is beyond horizontal borders
                    If spr.X < .Left Then
                        .Left = spr.X - BORDER
                        If .Left < 0 Then .Left = 0
                    End If
```

```vb
                   If (spr.X + spr.Width) > rDirty(n).Right Then
                       .Right = spr.X + spr.Width + BORDER
                       If .Right > pic.ScaleWidth - 1 Then _
                           .Right = pic.ScaleWidth - 1
                   End If

                   'see if sprite is beyond vertical borders
                   If spr.Y < .Top Then
                       .Top = spr.Y - BORDER
                       If .Top < 0 Then .Top = 0
                   End If
                   If (spr.Y + spr.Height) > .Bottom Then
                       .Bottom = spr.Y + spr.Height + BORDER
                       If .Bottom > pic.ScaleHeight - 1 Then _
                           .Bottom = pic.ScaleHeight - 1
                   End If
               End With
               'found it, so stop checking
               Exit For
           End If
       Next n
End Sub

Public Sub Draw(ByRef hdcDest As Long, cbSource As clsBitmap)
    Dim n As Long
    'draw all four quadrants of the back buffer
    For n = 0 To 3
        'see if quadrant was used
        If bQuadrant(n) Then
            With rDirty(n)
                BitBlt hdcDest, .Left, .Top, _
                    .Right - .Left, .Bottom - .Top, _
                    cbSource.hdc, .Left, .Top, vbSrcCopy
            End With
        End If
    Next n
End Sub

Private Function PointInside(ByRef p As POINT, _
    ByRef r As RECT_API) As Boolean
```

```
        'see if point is inside rectangle
        PointInside = CBool(p.X > r.Left And _
            p.X < r.Right And p.Y > r.Top And _
            p.Y < r.Bottom)
End Function
```

Testing Multiple Dirty Rectangles

The MultiRect program is based on the DirtyRect program, so an entire listing is not necessary. Rather, I will show you what has changed to implement multiple dirty rectangle functionality by listing new source code with bold text and pointing out code that should be removed.

This might seem trivial, but the first thing you should do is make a copy of the DirtyRect program directory and start working on the sequel in a new directory. Add the DirtyRect.cls file to the project (from the class listing above). The first change is to the name of the program, which is simple enough.

```
'-----------------------------------------------------------------------
' Visual Basic Game Programming With DirectX
' Chapter 9 : Let The Animation Begin
' MultiRect Source Code File
'-----------------------------------------------------------------------
```

Now scroll down the listing a few lines to the "Windows API functions and structures" section of code, and delete the declaration for the BitBlt function. The resulting code should look something like this:

```
Option Explicit
Option Base 0

'Windows API functions and structures
Private Declare Function GetTickCount _
    Lib "kernel32" () As Long

Private Declare Function GetClientRect _
    Lib "user32" ( _
    ByVal hWnd As Long, _
    lpRect As RECT _
) As Long
```

```
Private Declare Function ValidateRect _
    Lib "user32" ( _
    ByVal hWnd As Long, _
    lpRect As RECT _
) As Long

Private Declare Function IntersectRect _
    Lib "user32" (lpDestRect As RECT, _
    lpSrc1Rect As RECT, lpSrc2Rect As RECT) As Long

'removed declaration of BitBlt

Private Type RECT
    Left As Long
    Top As Long
    Right As Long
    Bottom As Long
End Type

Private Type POINT
    X As Long
    Y As Long
End Type
```

Now scroll down to the program variables, add the clsDirtyRect variable, and remove the rDirty variable.

```
'program constants
Const MAXFRAMERATE As Long = 120
Const NUMSPRITES As Long = 25

'program controls
Dim WithEvents Picture1 As PictureBox

'program variables
Dim cbBackgrnd As New clsBitmap
Dim cbBackBuffer As New clsBitmap
Dim cdrRect As New clsDirtyRect
Dim csButterfly(NUMSPRITES) As clsSprite
Dim bRunning As Boolean
'Dim rDirty As RECT
```

Now scroll down to the Form_Load procedure and add the following two lines of code after the code that loads the background bitmap. There are no other changes to be made to Form_Load.

```
'load the background
If Not cbBackgrnd.Load(App.Path & "\blueyellow.bmp") Then
    MsgBox "Error loading blueyellow.bmp"
    Shutdown
End If
cbBackgrnd.Draw 0, 0, cbBackBuffer.hdc

'initialize the dirty rectangles
cdrRect.Init Picture1
```

Now scroll down to the Game_Update procedure and look for the section of code labeled "move sprites." Since the dirty rectangle routines have been moved into a class called clsDirtyRect, there is no longer a need for the related functions to reside in the main program. Change the "move sprite" code inside Game_Update as follows. (Only change the code that is highlighted in bold text.)

```
'move sprites
For n = 0 To NUMSPRITES
    If csButterfly(n).Active Then
        MoveSprite csButterfly(n)
        'ResizeDirtyRect csButterfly(n)
        cdrRect.Resize csButterfly(n), Picture1
        CheckCollisions n
        csButterfly(n).NextFrame
    End If
Next n
```

Scroll down further in Game_Update to the section called "draw the dirty rectangle" and change the code as follows. Delete the line that calls DrawDirtyRect, and add the cdrRect.Draw line. This snippet of code also makes a change due to the new clsDirtyRect class.

```
'draw the dirty rectangle
'DrawDirtyRect
Picture1.BackColor = RGB(0, 0, 0)
cdrRect.Draw Picture1.hdc, cbBackBuffer
```

TIP

Remember that the line that sets the Picture1.BackColor property to black is for illustrative purposes only and should be removed for production code. It shows off the dirty rectangles nicely, but should be commented out in production code.

You can now scroll down a few pages until you reach the code listings for the procedures ResetDirtyRect, ResizeDirtyRect, and DrawDirtyRect. These three procedures have been moved inside clsDirtyRect and are no longer needed by this program. Go ahead and delete these procedures or comment them out.

Once you have removed the last three procedures, you will be finished with the code changes for the MultiRect program. Be sure to change the name of the project. It is currently called DirtyRect. To differentiate this program from the one it was adapted from, change the project name to MultiRect. By compiling both programs into executable files (and following the project optimization techniques presented in Chapter 5, "Optimizing Visual Basic with Objects"), you can see the difference in performance from a single dirty rectangle to multiple dirty rectangles. Note that the change might not even be noticeable on ultra-fast PCs.

Just remember, multiple dirty rectangle double buffering is not always the best method to use in every game. In any game that uses a rendered background (such as the arcade-style vertical scroller presented in the next section), there is no need for a dirty rectangle at all, because the background is redrawn every frame. When working with a rendered background, sprite management is considerably simplified, since there is no need to save the background and erase the sprites.

ARCADE-STYLE VERTICAL SCROLLING

What would a chapter on animation be without some sort of arcade game to demonstrate? The ArcadeScroller program that I will walk you through in this last section of the chapter shows you how to create a scrolling background image like the one I have been talking about throughout this chapter. A scrolling background poses a few problems, namely performance. The background does not really scroll down as it appears, but rather is drawn tile by tile in the precise positions to assemble a background. Since this is such an intensive process, this particular program is not double buffered.

A double buffer will be needed to turn this into a full-blown game, but for now this program draws directly to the screen. On a slower video system you might notice slight tearing if the PC is not able to update the screen fast enough. This is basically a problem with vertical retrace, in that the screen starts to refresh before all of the tiles have been drawn, and a certain amount of overlap occurs. This is completely avoidable by using a double buffer, but that functionality will have to wait for the full-blown game upon which this ArcadeScroller program was based. Figure 9.10 shows the ArcadeScroller program in action.

If you find the ArcadeScroller program interesting, be sure to check out Chapter 20, "Warbirds 1944: Scrolling Shooter Game," for a complete arcade game based on the code developed here.

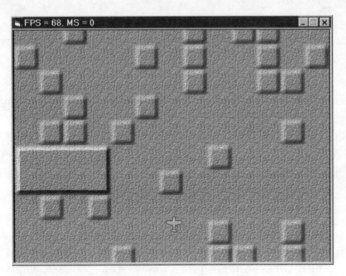

Figure 9.10

The ArcadeScroller program shows you how to scroll terrain down the screen to simulate motion for the airplane. A real arcade game would have enemy planes and tanks shooting at the player.

Creating a Random Scrolling Map

I tried several different methods to generate a tile-based terrain map in memory but continually ran into problems involving a sequence of tiles in a row not lining up correctly. So I finally decided to send random lines of the tilemap out to a file with a custom procedure called CreateRandomLevel. The level filename is passed to the procedure, along with the maximum number of rows and columns to be generated. This file can then be edited and reused, or it can just hold temporary tilemaps for each run of the program (which is the case with ArcadeScroller).

```
Public Sub CreateRandomLevel(ByVal sFilename As String, _
    ByVal lMaxCols As Long, ByVal lMaxRows As Long)
    Dim lTileArray() As Long
    Dim lFileNum As Long
    Dim rows As Long
    Dim cols As Long
    Dim lTile As Long
    Dim lWidth As Long
    Dim lHeight As Long
    Dim X As Long
    Dim Y As Long

    On Error GoTo error1
    'redimension tile array
    ReDim lTileArray(0 To lMaxCols + 5, 0 To lMaxRows + 5)
```

```
'create random tile values
For rows = 1 To lMaxRows
    For cols = 1 To lMaxCols
        lTile = Random(4)
        If lTile = 1 Then
            lTile = 9
        Else
            lTile = 0
        End If
        lTileArray(cols, rows) = lTile
    Next cols
Next rows

'place random tiles in larger virtual map
For lTile = 1 To 20
    lWidth = Random(3) + 1
    lHeight = Random(3) + 1
    X = Random(lMaxCols)
    Y = Random(lMaxRows)
    lTileArray(X, Y) = 7
    lTileArray(X, Y + lHeight) = 1
    lTileArray(X + lWidth, Y) = 5
    lTileArray(X + lWidth, Y + lHeight) = 3
    If lWidth = 3 Then
        lTileArray(X + 2, Y) = 6
        lTileArray(X + 2, Y + lHeight) = 2
    End If
    If lWidth >= 2 Then
        lTileArray(X + 1, Y) = 6
        lTileArray(X + 1, Y + lHeight) = 2
    End If
    If lHeight = 3 Then
        lTileArray(X, Y + 2) = 8
        lTileArray(X + lWidth, Y + 2) = 4
    End If
    If lHeight >= 2 Then
        lTileArray(X, Y + 1) = 8
        lTileArray(X + lWidth, Y + 1) = 4
    End If
Next lTile
```

```
    'write the tile values out to a file
    lFileNum = FreeFile()
    Open sFilename For Output As #lFileNum
    Write #lFileNum, lMaxCols; lMaxRows
    For rows = 1 To lMaxRows
        For cols = 1 To lMaxCols
            Write #lFileNum, lTileArray(cols, rows);
        Next cols
    Next rows

    Close #lFileNum
error1:
End Sub
```

Likewise, this program needed a way to load the tilemap data from the file into the array, and then to use that array to draw the terrain on the screen. The LoadLevel function handles this functionality by loading the filename passed to it. This function assumes that the scroller class variable, Scroller, is global.

```
Public Function LoadLevel(ByVal sFilename As String) As Boolean
    Dim numcols As Long
    Dim numrows As Long
    Dim rows As Long
    Dim cols As Long
    Dim lFileNum As Long
    Dim lTileValue As Long
    Dim sText As String
    Dim lLine As Long

    On Error GoTo error1
    LoadLevel = False

    'open level file and load tiles
    lFileNum = FreeFile()
    Open sFilename For Input As #lFileNum
    Input #lFileNum, numcols, numrows
    Scroller.InitTileMap numcols, numrows
    For rows = 0 To numrows - 1
        'load map tile values
        For cols = 0 To numcols - 1
            Input #lFileNum, lTileValue
```

```
        Scroller.SetTile cols, rows, lTileValue
      Next cols
    Next rows

    Close #lFileNum
    LoadLevel = True
error1:
End Function
```

Loading Tiles for the Map

The tiles for the scrolling terrain are stored in a file called maptiles.bmp, which is shown in Figure 9.11.

Figure 9.11

The map tiles are assembled in memory into a map that resembles terrain and forms the basis for the game. The tile images are then displayed based on the map values.

These tiles are simply loaded into a single sprite, which contains as many frames as needed to hold all of the tiles. Since the sprite frame index is sequential, it is convenient for displaying map tiles based on the tilemap values. The scroller class actually handles this functionality through a procedure called InitTileMap and a function called LoadTiles, both of which are listed below.

```
Public Sub InitTileMap(ByVal lCols As Long, ByVal lRows As Long)
    lNumColumns = lCols
    lNumRows = lRows
    ReDim lTiles(0 To lNumColumns, 0 To lNumRows)
    MajorScroll = lRows - lCols - 1
End Sub

Public Function LoadTiles(ByVal sFilename As String, _
    ByVal lStartX As Long, ByVal lStartY As Long, _
    ByVal lWidth As Long, ByVal lHeight As Long, _
    ByVal lNumFrames As Long) As Boolean
```

```
    On Error GoTo error1
    LoadTiles = False
    csTiles.LoadFrames sFilename, lStartX, lStartY, lWidth, _
        lHeight, lNumFrames
    csTiles.Transparent = False
    LoadTiles = True
error1:
End Function
```

Creating Terrain with Tiles

Once the map tiles have been loaded, and the tilemap values have been loaded from the created file, all that remains is a means to first draw the tiles, and then to scroll those tiles. This actually involves some tricky code because only a portion of the top row of tiles is displayed while scrolling is taking place.

There are two procedures in the scroller class to handle scrolling. The first procedure, DrawTiles, draws the partial lines of the first row based on the scroll position of the map, and then draws the full tiles for the rest of the map. The number of tiles drawn is based on the parameters passed to the procedure. Note that this partial display code calls BitBlt directly, rather than calling DrawTile. The second procedure, DrawTile, simply draws a single complete tile at the desired position on the screen.

```
Public Sub DrawTiles(ByVal lHorizTiles As Long, _
    ByVal lVertTiles As Long, ByVal hdcDest As Long)

    'draw the first row
    For cols = 0 To lHorizTiles - 1
        n = GetTile(cols, MajorScroll - 1)
        BitBlt hdcDest, _
            StartX + cols * TileWidth, 0, _
            TileWidth, MinorScroll, _
            GetTileDC(n), _
            0, 48 - MinorScroll, _
            vbSrcCopy
    Next cols

    'draw the remaining rows
    For rows = 0 To lVertTiles - 1
        For cols = 0 To lHorizTiles - 1
            DrawTile lStartX, cols, rows, hdcDest
```

```
        Next cols
    Next rows
End Sub


Public Sub DrawTile(ByVal lStartX As Long, ByVal lCol As Long, _
    ByVal lRow As Long, ByVal hdcDest As Long)
    Dim lTileValue As Long
    lTileValue = GetTile(lCol, MajorScroll + lRow)
    BitBlt hdcDest, lStartX + lCol * TileWidth, lRow * _
        TileHeight + MinorScroll, TileWidth, TileHeight, _
        csTiles.hdc(lTileValue), 0, 0, vbSrcCopy
End Sub
```

The Vertical Scroller Class

Okay, that should be enough information to get started. Seeing the actual code and being able to test the code while it is running is the best way to learn how a program works, so let's jump right in and write the VScroller class. This class will be used by the ArcadeScroller program later. Since I have already gone over the major procedures of this class, I will not explain the class in any more detail at this point. There are some additional class properties that I have not mentioned, but they are pretty easy to identify.

```
'-------------------------------------------------------------------
' Visual Basic Game Programming With DirectX
' Chapter 9 : Let The Animation Begin
' Vertical Scroller Class Source Code File
'-------------------------------------------------------------------


Option Explicit
Option Base 0


'Windows API functions and structures
Private Declare Function BitBlt Lib "gdi32" ( _
    ByVal hDestDC As Long, _
    ByVal X As Long, _
    ByVal Y As Long, _
    ByVal nWidth As Long, _
    ByVal nHeight As Long, _
    ByVal hSrcDC As Long, _
    ByVal xSrc As Long, _
```

```
        ByVal ySrc As Long, _
        ByVal dwRop As Long _
) As Long


Private Type RECT
    Left As Long
    Top As Long
    Right As Long
    Bottom As Long
End Type


'class variables
Private csTiles As New clsSprite
Private lTiles() As Long
Private lNumColumns As Long
Private lNumRows As Long
Private lMajorScroll As Long
Private lMinorScroll As Long
Private lStartX As Long
Private rows As Long
Private cols As Long
Private n As Long


Private Sub Class_Initialize()
    lNumColumns = 0
    lNumRows = 0
    lMajorScroll = 0
    lMinorScroll = 0
End Sub


Private Sub Class_Terminate()
    Set csTiles = Nothing
End Sub


Public Function GetTileDC(ByVal lTileNum As Long)
    GetTileDC = csTiles.hdc(lTileNum)
End Function


Public Property Get MajorScroll() As Long
    MajorScroll = lMajorScroll
End Property
```

```
Public Property Let MajorScroll(ByVal lNewValue As Long)
    lMajorScroll = lNewValue
End Property


Public Property Get MinorScroll() As Long
    MinorScroll = lMinorScroll
End Property


Public Property Let MinorScroll(ByVal lNewValue As Long)
    lMinorScroll = lNewValue
End Property


Public Property Get TileWidth() As Long
    TileWidth = csTiles.Width
End Property


Public Property Get TileHeight() As Long
    TileHeight = csTiles.Width
End Property


Public Property Get MaxTileCols()
    MaxTileCols = lNumColumns
End Property


Public Property Get MaxTileRows()
    MaxTileRows = lNumRows
End Property


Public Property Get StartX() As Long
    StartX = lStartX
End Property


Public Property Let StartX(ByVal lNewValue As Long)
    lStartX = lNewValue
End Property


Public Sub SetTile(ByVal lCol As Long, ByVal lRow As Long, _
    ByVal lTileValue As Long)
    lTiles(lCol, lRow) = lTileValue
End Sub
```

```
Public Function GetTile(ByVal lCol As Long, ByVal lRow As Long)
    GetTile = lTiles(lCol, lRow)
End Function

Public Sub InitTileMap(ByVal lCols As Long, ByVal lRows As Long)
    lNumColumns = lCols
    lNumRows = lRows
    ReDim lTiles(0 To lNumColumns, 0 To lNumRows)
    MajorScroll = lRows - lCols - 1
End Sub

Public Function LoadTiles(ByVal sFilename As String, _
    ByVal lStartX As Long, ByVal lStartY As Long, _
    ByVal lWidth As Long, ByVal lHeight As Long, _
    ByVal lNumFrames As Long) As Boolean

    On Error GoTo error1
    LoadTiles = False
    csTiles.LoadFrames sFilename, lStartX, lStartY, lWidth, _
        lHeight, lNumFrames
    csTiles.Transparent = False
    LoadTiles = True
error1:
End Function

Public Sub Scroll(ByVal lNumLines As Long)
    'handles scrolling one row
    MinorScroll = MinorScroll + lNumLines
    If MinorScroll > TileHeight - 1 Then
        MinorScroll = 0
        'handles scrolling entire screen
        MajorScroll = MajorScroll - 1
        If MajorScroll < 1 Then
            MajorScroll = lNumRows - lNumColumns - 1
        End If
    End If
End Sub

Public Sub DrawTiles(ByVal lHorizTiles As Long, _
    ByVal lVertTiles As Long, ByVal hdcDest As Long)
```

```
    'draw the first row
    For cols = 0 To lHorizTiles - 1
        n = GetTile(cols, MajorScroll - 1)
        BitBlt hdcDest, _
            StartX + cols * TileWidth, 0, _
            TileWidth, MinorScroll, _
            GetTileDC(n), _
            0, 48 - MinorScroll, _
            vbSrcCopy
    Next cols

    'draw the remaining rows
    For rows = 0 To lVertTiles - 1
        For cols = 0 To lHorizTiles - 1
            DrawTile lStartX, cols, rows, hdcDest
        Next cols
    Next rows
End Sub

Public Sub DrawTile(ByVal lStartX As Long, ByVal lCol As Long, _
    ByVal lRow As Long, ByVal hdcDest As Long)
    Dim lTileValue As Long
    lTileValue = GetTile(lCol, MajorScroll + lRow)
    BitBlt hdcDest, lStartX + lCol * TileWidth, lRow * _
        TileHeight + MinorScroll, TileWidth, TileHeight, _
        csTiles.hdc(lTileValue), 0, 0, vbSrcCopy
End Sub
```

Testing the Vertical Scroller

Now, how about a complete program to test the functionality of the VScroller class? Sounds like a good idea to me! This program will actually be fairly short because the important code is tucked away inside VScroller.cls. So what do you say about just jumping right in and getting started? Create a new Standard EXE project, like usual, and add the Bitmap.cls, Sprite.cls, and also the VScroller.cls files to the project. Name the project ArcadeScroller.

```
'-------------------------------------------------------------------
' Visual Basic Game Programming With DirectX
' Chapter 9 : Let The Animation Begin
' ArcadeScroller Source Code File
'-------------------------------------------------------------------
```

```
Option Explicit
Option Base 0

'Windows API functions
Private Declare Function GetTickCount _
    Lib "kernel32" () As Long

'program constants
Const MAXFRAMERATE As Long = 120

'program controls
Dim WithEvents Picture1 As PictureBox

'program variables
Dim Scroller As New clsVScroller
Dim csPlane As New clsSprite
Dim bRunning As Boolean

Private Sub Form_Load()
    Static lStartTime As Long
    Static lCounter As Long
    Static lNewTime As Long

    Randomize GetTickCount
    lStartTime = GetTickCount
    bRunning = True

    'set up the main form
    Form1.AutoRedraw = False
    Form1.BorderStyle = 1
    Form1.ClipControls = False
    Form1.KeyPreview = True
    Form1.ScaleMode = 3
    Form1.Width = 640 * Screen.TwipsPerPixelX
    Form1.Height = 480 * Screen.TwipsPerPixelY
    Form1.Show

    'create the PictureBox control for drawing
    Set Picture1 = Controls.Add("VB.PictureBox", "Picture1")
    Picture1.AutoRedraw = False
    Picture1.BorderStyle = 1
```

```
Picture1.ClipControls = False
Picture1.ScaleMode = 3
Picture1.BackColor = RGB(0, 0, 0)
Picture1.Left = 0
Picture1.Top = 0
Picture1.Width = Form1.ScaleWidth
Picture1.Height = Form1.ScaleHeight
Picture1.Visible = True

'create the scrolling terrain
CreateRandomLevel App.Path & "\level.dat", 13, 300
LoadLevel App.Path & "\level.dat"

If Not Scroller.LoadTiles(App.Path & "\maptiles.bmp", _
    1, 1, 48, 48, 10) Then
    MsgBox "Error loading maptiles.bmp"
    Picture1_Click
End If
Scroller.StartX = 2

'load the plane
csPlane.Transparent = True
If Not csPlane.LoadFrames(App.Path & "\fighter.bmp", _
    0, 0, 32, 32, 1) Then
    MsgBox "Error loading fighter.bmp"
    Picture1_Click
End If
csPlane.CurrentFrame = 1
csPlane.X = 320 - csPlane.Width / 2
csPlane.Y = Picture1.ScaleHeight - Picture1.ScaleHeight / 5

'main game loop
Do While bRunning
    lCounter = GetTickCount() - lStartTime
    If lCounter > lNewTime Then
        'update game display
        Game_Update lCounter
        'update frame count
        lNewTime = lCounter + 1000 / MAXFRAMERATE
    End If
```

```
            DoEvents
        Loop
    End Sub

    Private Sub Game_Update(ByVal MS As Long)
        Static lCounter As Long
        Static lTimer As Long
        Static lStart As Long

        'begin screen update timing
        lStart = GetTickCount

        'scroll the map
        Scroller.Scroll 1

        'draw the map tiles
        Scroller.DrawTiles 13, 10, Picture1.hdc

        'draw the plane
        csPlane.Draw Picture1.hdc

        'end screen update timing
        lStart = GetTickCount - lStart

        'display the frames per second
        If MS > lTimer + 1000 Then
            Form1.Caption = "FPS = " & lCounter & ", MS = " & lStart
            lTimer = MS
            lCounter = 0
        Else
            lCounter = lCounter + 1
        End If
    End Sub

    Public Sub CreateRandomLevel(ByVal sFilename As String, _
        ByVal lMaxCols As Long, ByVal lMaxRows As Long)
        Dim lTileArray() As Long
        Dim lFileNum As Long
        Dim rows As Long
        Dim cols As Long
        Dim lTile As Long
```

```
Dim lWidth As Long
Dim lHeight As Long
Dim X As Long
Dim Y As Long


On Error GoTo error1
'redimension tile array
ReDim lTileArray(0 To lMaxCols + 5, 0 To lMaxRows + 5)

'create random tile values
For rows = 1 To lMaxRows
    For cols = 1 To lMaxCols
        lTile = Random(4)
        If lTile = 1 Then
            lTile = 9
        Else
            lTile = 0
        End If
        lTileArray(cols, rows) = lTile
    Next cols
Next rows

'place random tiles in larger virtual map
For lTile = 1 To 20
    lWidth = Random(3) + 1
    lHeight = Random(3) + 1
    X = Random(lMaxCols)
    Y = Random(lMaxRows)
    lTileArray(X, Y) = 7
    lTileArray(X, Y + lHeight) = 1
    lTileArray(X + lWidth, Y) = 5
    lTileArray(X + lWidth, Y + lHeight) = 3
    If lWidth = 3 Then
        lTileArray(X + 2, Y) = 6
        lTileArray(X + 2, Y + lHeight) = 2
    End If
    If lWidth >= 2 Then
        lTileArray(X + 1, Y) = 6
        lTileArray(X + 1, Y + lHeight) = 2
    End If
```

```
            If lHeight = 3 Then
                lTileArray(X, Y + 2) = 8
                lTileArray(X + lWidth, Y + 2) = 4
            End If
            If lHeight >= 2 Then
                lTileArray(X, Y + 1) = 8
                lTileArray(X + lWidth, Y + 1) = 4
            End If
        Next lTile


        'write the tile values out to a file
        lFileNum = FreeFile()
        Open sFilename For Output As #lFileNum
        Write #lFileNum, lMaxCols; lMaxRows
        For rows = 1 To lMaxRows
            For cols = 1 To lMaxCols
                Write #lFileNum, lTileArray(cols, rows);
            Next cols
        Next rows

        Close #lFileNum
error1:
End Sub


Public Function LoadLevel(ByVal sFilename As String) As Boolean
        Dim lFileNum As Long
        Dim lTileValue As Long
        Dim numcols As Long
        Dim numrows As Long
        Dim rows As Long
        Dim cols As Long


        On Error GoTo error1
        LoadLevel = False

        'open level file and load tiles
        lFileNum = FreeFile()
        Open sFilename For Input As #lFileNum
        Input #lFileNum, numcols, numrows
```

```vb
    Scroller.InitTileMap numcols, numrows
    For rows = 0 To numrows - 1
        'load map tile values
        For cols = 0 To numcols - 1
            Input #lFileNum, lTileValue
            Scroller.SetTile cols, rows, lTileValue
        Next cols
    Next rows

    Close #lFileNum
    LoadLevel = True
error1:
End Function

Private Sub Picture1_Click()
    Shutdown
End Sub

Private Sub Form_QueryUnload(Cancel As Integer, _
    UnloadMode As Integer)
    Picture1_Click
End Sub

Private Sub Form_KeyDown(KeyCode As Integer, Shift As Integer)
    If KeyCode = 27 Then Picture1_Click
End Sub

Private Sub Shutdown()
    bRunning = False
    Set csPlane = Nothing
    Set Scroller = Nothing
    Form1.Hide
    End
End Sub

Public Function Random(ByVal lNum As Long) As Long
    Random = CLng(lNum * Rnd)
End Function
```

PROMOTION!

Congratulations, you have now completed an entire course on advanced Windows API graphics programming. The Windows API is a complicated and difficult subject that often seems counter-intuitive and illogical. The ability to skillfully wield device contexts and bitmap handles is no small feat, and is a terrific addition to your programming toolbox.

You are hereby promoted to the rank of *Skilled Programmer*, with all of the rights and privileges that come with the position. You now have the ability to write a game on your own. Use your new knowledge and skills wisely, and continue to push the envelope of Visual Basic gaming!

Here is a record of your progress so far:

1. **Newbie Gamer**
2. **Apprentice Hacker**
3. **Skilled Programmer**
4. Veteran Coder
5. Master Developer
6. Adept Game Designer

SUMMARY

Wow, this chapter was intense! Not only did you get a significant treatment of double buffering, you were even able to put together two advanced forms of double buffering using dirty rectangles to increase the speed. These are significant topics of advanced game development that you can now put to use.

This chapter also included a significant arcade-style scroller that demonstrated how to render the background of a game in real time. By loading a series of map tiles into a sprite for safe-keeping, the VScroller class is able to generate the background on the fly. This functionality is the basis for literally hundreds of games that have been written, from arcade shooters to role-playing games with scrolling backgrounds, and will be the basis for the game in Chapter 20, "Warbirds 1944: Scrolling Shooter Game."

CHAPTER 10

DIVING INTO DIRECTDRAW

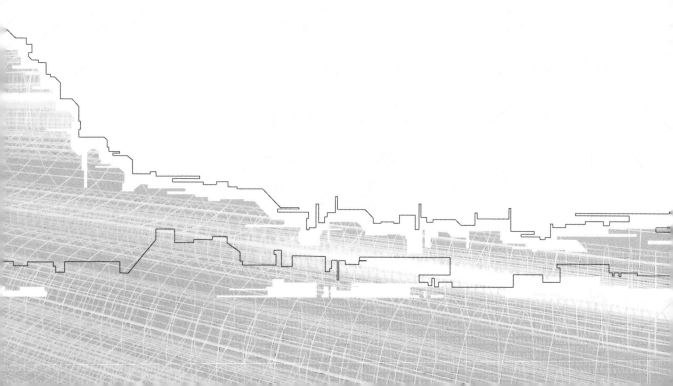

elcome to the next level of Visual Basic game development with DirectDraw. This is the next step in the quest for graphics and multimedia power with VB. DirectX 7.0 is the last traditional DirectX version that based graphics output on DirectDraw. DirectX 8.0 has integrated DirectDraw and Direct3D into a new component called DirectX Graphics. By not supporting existing code bases, game libraries and engines must be rewritten to support the latest features in DirectX 8.0. However, that is precisely the reason behind the change; by doing away with legacy DirectX code (which dated back to 1995), the new library can take advantage of the latest graphics hardware, and doesn't need to worry about supporting older systems.

This chapter is an introduction to DirectDraw, which is a natural step toward DirectX 8.0 programming (see Chapter 14, "DirectX Graphics and Direct3D"). This chapter will teach you how to create windowed and full-screen DirectDraw programs and DirectDraw surfaces. It will also show you how to load bitmap images directly into a surface, and how to write a new set of classes that encapsulate this functionality for ease of use. This chapter is a hands-on study of the subject, with emphasis on the important aspects of DirectDraw and on what is needed to get a game running. For an in-depth reference to DirectDraw or any other DirectX library, see Appendix E, "Recommended Reading," for a list of recommended books.

This chapter covers the following topics:

- The Basics of DirectDraw
- Supporting DirectDraw with DirectX 7.0
- DirectDraw Surfaces
- Double Buffering with DirectDraw
- Drawing Bitmaps and Sprites
- Testing DirectDraw in Windowed Mode
- Encapsulating DirectDraw
- Testing DirectDraw in Full-Screen Mode

THE BASICS OF DIRECTDRAW

By learning, understanding, and then using DirectDraw in this chapter, you will quickly see how it changes every assumption about games and graphics in VB. Simply put, DirectDraw is awesome. The sample programs later in this chapter clearly show the immense power of this code library.

But I would like to emphasize that this chapter is not an in-depth reference of DirectDraw architecture. There are plenty of books on the market that cover the inner details of how DirectDraw works. My goal with this chapter is to show what DirectDraw can do, not necessarily how it goes about doing it. This hands-on approach should help you get up to speed as quickly as possible by understanding the important aspects of developing games with DirectDraw.

> **NOTE**
>
> To demonstrate the raw power of DirectDraw, later in this chapter you will have the opportunity to write a program capable of drawing 500 transparent sprites, double-buffered at 1600×1200, running at a decent frame rate.

The Low-Down on DirectDraw

DirectDraw is simple and straightforward, and was clearly influenced and directed by game developers. When you're working with DirectDraw, there is much less bureaucracy than with the Windows API. There is no longer a need to create a mask image for transparency because DirectDraw uses a simple color key to identify the transparent color in an image. There are no more device contexts, pens, brushes, or handles. There are just graphics surfaces and drawing routines. It is basically assumed that the video card supports hardware blitting at the device driver level. Otherwise, DirectDraw wouldn't be able to achieve such terrific frame rates.

DirectDraw has the built-in functionality you need to load and display solid and transparent bitmaps. Solid bitmaps are commonly used for background images, while transparent bitmaps usually make up the foreground images (which are called sprites).

Reinvent the Wheel or Buy Some New Tires?

One of the nice things about an object-oriented game library is that you can rewrite the library to support new technologies. I have not gone over a formal game library yet (see Chapter 13, "Building the DirectX Game Library"), since the programs so far have been built with custom classes. While it might make sense to convert the existing clsBitmap and clsSprite classes from earlier chapters (which focused on the Windows API), this really is not practical for DirectDraw, which is far more powerful. Instead of trying to write a new DirectDraw class that is compatible with earlier code, I will simply show you some new classes that are specifically geared to take advantage of DirectDraw features. It will be up to you to decide which way to go later on—Windows API, DirectDraw, or Direct3D.

Chapter 14, "DirectX Graphics and Direct3D," will give you a third option for writing games, but it is not necessarily superior to DirectDraw in all cases. Direct3D is great for writing 3-D games, as well as 2-D games with special effects like colored lighting. But DirectDraw is still the easiest and fastest way to write a traditional 2-D game.

I want to give you as many alternatives as possible, and not simply focus on my favorite graphics solution. I must admit that prior to writing this chapter, I spent far too much time working with VB controls and Windows API code (and functions like BitBlt). I'm sure that by the end of this chapter, you will wholeheartedly embrace DirectDraw as I have.

SUPPORTING DIRECTDRAW WITH DIRECTX 7.0

DirectX 7.0 was the first version of DirectX that officially supported VB; ironically, it was also the last version that supported DirectDraw. However, DX7 demonstrated Microsoft's dedication to VB programmers. DirectX is a library that fully supports games written for older versions of the library, and this is accomplished simply by renaming the components in later versions. A game written for a DirectDraw4 object will still run even when the DirectDraw7 object has been installed, because that older component is still present in the newer library.

This is how it works in theory, but that theory does not necessarily apply to VB, which lives in an alternate universe from Visual C++ (the native language of DirectX). While VB fully supports DirectX 7.0 and DirectX 8.0, it is limited to the viewport provided by the type library.

That brings up a good point. What is a type library?

DirectX7 Type Library

A type library (in my own words) is an interface that lets VB programs communicate with Visual C++ components like DirectX. These components are compiled as COM objects, and must be registered in your system before use. Since VB does not have a way to link in a lib file (which is how Visual C++ works), it must interface directly with the COM object through a type library. If VB had the ability to link the lib file for DirectDraw, it would have no need for a type library. This is just the way VB was designed, and one of the reasons why it is much more popular than Visual C++.

To see the complete list of type libraries available to VB, select References from the Project menu to bring up the References dialog, as shown in Figure 10.1.

> **BUZZWORD**
>
> A *type library* is an interface that lets VB programs communicate with COM components, such as DirectX.

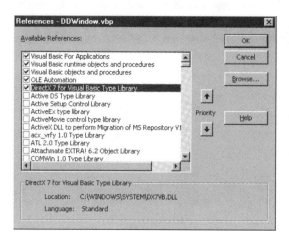

Figure 10.1

Referencing the DirectX7 for Visual Basic Type Library

Referencing a Type Library in Visual Basic

Now, you are probably wondering how you use the DirectX type library in VB. First, you must install the DirectX SDK. It is always a good idea to check online for new versions of software, since *service pack* and *service release* are public relations terms that really mean "assortment of bug fixes." For example, at the time of this writing, DirectX 8.1 is available. This new version no doubt includes bug fixes as well as new features, such as support for new video cards. Sure, you can get along fine without the latest and greatest, but it is a good idea to stay up to date.

Most of the sample programs in this book have been verified to run under Windows 95, and you can even install DirectX 8.1 on a Windows 95 machine!

> **TIP**
>
> **Be sure to download and install the latest service pack for Visual Basic, which is Service Pack 5 (SP5) at the time of this writing.**

However, many hardware vendors have stopped supporting Windows 95, preferring to put resources on writing drivers for Windows 2000 and Windows XP. This is but one example of the industry's drive for constant evolution, driven primarily by constant consumer demand.

You should be familiar with how to set up a DirectX project in VB from Chapter 6, "Supercharging Visual Basic with DirectX." If you skipped over that chapter, I recommend you go back and read it first, because that chapter covers the history and basics of the DirectX API in more detail than is touched upon here.

Retaining Backward Compatibility

As I started to explain earlier, the type library for DirectX is limited to only those features supported by that version, and no others. If you reference the DX8 type library, you will not automatically gain access to the DX7 objects. I know this is unfortunate, but it is how the DirectX type libraries were written. To remedy the situation, when you need to support both versions of DirectX (for instance, when you are using DirectDraw7 and DirectSound8 in the same program), you can simply reference both type libraries and then get to work.

> **NOTE**
>
> DirectDraw is the only component of DX7 that is covered in this book. All other DirectX components (such as DirectSound, DirectInput, and Direct3D) are part of DX8.

What about DirectX 8.0?

This chapter is but a stepping stone on the path to DX8, and specifically DirectX Graphics programming. However, that does not undermine the importance or usability of DirectDraw7, which is an extremely powerful and easy-to-use graphics library, and is still the core graphics engine behind DX8. It is vitally important that you understand the roots of traditional DirectX programming before you jump into the radical new DirectX Graphics. Not only will this provide you with a base of information from which to draw upon, it will also provide some appreciation for the new features of DX8, and how much effort was put into it. Increased power and functionality usually come at the cost of simplicity, but the time invested in learning how to use it will be time well spent.

2-D Versus 3-D Surfaces

DirectDraw can have many different surfaces for things like the screen, double buffer, and even individual sprites. DirectX Graphics, on the other hand, which is the graphics component of DX8, does not use flat surfaces mapped directly to the screen, like those found in DirectDraw. Rather, visible DX8 surfaces are all located in 3-D space. When you need to have just a plain flat screen for a 2-D game, you must create a surface, set up ambient lighting, and then face the camera directly toward the surface. Fortunately, there is a support class called D3DXSprite that helps to solve some of these problems. It is covered in Chapter 14, "DirectX Graphics and Direct3D."

Most of the functionality that was re-written for DX8 was optimized for 3-D video cards, including the new generation of video cards that handle transform and lighting inside the 3-D chip itself. (Previously, the programmer handled that.) The fact is, a $79 video card today would have cost tens of thousands of dollars in equivalent gear a decade ago. So it is natural for DX8 to do away with legacy code and support the latest hardware.

Hardware Support for DirectX

In fact, that turnstile is starting to rotate in both directions, with hardware manufacturers like Nvidia now adding DirectX support right inside the silicon chips. This should come as no surprise when you consider that an Nvidia chip like the GeForce 3 powers the graphics subsystem in the Microsoft Xbox video game console.

DirectX Graphics is a highly evolved and advanced graphics development library, and it can be somewhat intimidating at first. By picking up DirectDraw and using it within VB first, you will have a much easier time adjusting to DirectX Graphics in later chapters. In fact, this is the only chapter dedicated to DirectX 7.0. All subsequent chapters focus upon DirectX 8.0 components, including DirectSound, DirectInput, and Direct3D.

DIRECTDRAW SURFACES

The basis of a DirectDraw program is a DirectDrawSurface7 object. This object includes all the capability that is needed to create a primary display buffer for the screen, a secondary double buffer for animation, and individual surface buffers for all of the images in a game. In addition, these surfaces all come pre-loaded with drawing and blitting routines, so there is no need to use the Windows API and no need to write custom code.

Creating the DirectX and DirectDraw Objects

Before you can start using DirectDraw, you must first create a DirectX7 object, because this object is used to create the DirectDraw7 object. Consider the following lines of code:

```
Dim objDX As New DirectX7
Dim objDD As DirectDraw7
Set objDD = objDX.DirectDrawCreate("")
```

As you can see, the DirectX7 object has a member function called `DirectDrawCreate` that actually creates the DirectDraw7 object and then returns a reference to the object. At this point, objDX is no longer needed, since objDD is the primary DirectDraw object. You really only need DirectX7 to set up DirectDraw7 in the first place.

Creating a DirectDraw Surface

A DirectDrawSurface7 object must be created by calling one of the member functions for creating surfaces in DirectDraw7. There are three primary functions in DirectDraw for creating surfaces, and these functions are covered in the following sections.

The CreateSurface Function

The CreateSurface function can be used to create a DirectDraw surface in memory. This is the function you will use to create the primary display surface, which is located in video memory, as well as secondary drawing surfaces for game images.

The CreateSurface function looks like this:

```
CreateSurface( _
    dd As DDSURFACEDESC2 _
) As DirectDrawSurface7
```

As you can see from the function declaration, CreateSurface returns a DirectDrawSurface7 object. The sole parameter, a DDSURFACEDESC2 variable, holds the settings that define how the surface should be created, such as width and height.

To create a surface, first declare a variable of type DirectDrawSurface7, and another variable of type DDSURFACEDESC2:

```
Dim ddSurface As DirectDrawSurface7
Dim ddsd As DDSURFACEDESC2
```

Once you have set up the variables, you can create the object. Assuming that you have already created a DirectDraw7 object called objDD, the code might look like this:

```
Set ddSurface = objDD.CreateSurface(ddsd)
```

Of course, the DDSURFACEDESC2 variable must be set up prior to calling the CreateSurface function. This variable must be set up differently in order to create the primary display surface, the double buffer, and the images in a game.

Creating the Primary Display Surface

To create the primary display surface, you would use the following lines of code to set the DDSCAPS_PRIMARYSURFACE option and then call CreateSurface:

```
ddsd.ddsCaps.lCaps = DDSCAPS_PRIMARYSURFACE
ddsd.lWidth = 640
ddsd.lHeight = 480
Set ddSurface = objDD.CreateSurface(ddsd)
```

Creating the Double Buffer Surface

To create secondary surfaces, such as a double buffer or game sprites, you would set up the surface with a parameter called DDSCAPS_OFFSCREENPLAIN, as shown in the following lines of code:

```
ddsd.lFlags = DDSD_CAPS Or DDSD_WIDTH Or DDSD_HEIGHT
ddsd.ddsCaps.lCaps = DDSCAPS_OFFSCREENPLAIN
ddsd.lWidth = lWidth
ddsd.lHeight = lHeight
Set ddSurface = objDD.CreateSurface(ddsd)
```

The ddsd.lFlags variable tells the CreateSurface function what to actually look at in the ddsd structure. This saves time because the structure is big. In this code snippet, the lFlags variable tells CreateSurface to look at the device caps (a default option that is always required), the width, and the height, but no other features.

After the ddsd.lFlags variable has been properly set up, you then fill the structure with the appropriate values. In this case, it involves only setting the width and height of the image.

The CreateSurfaceFromFile Function

The CreateSurfaceFromFile function is extremely useful for loading bitmap images directly into a DirectDraw surface. Without this function, you would be required to load a bitmap, open up the memory buffer of a surface, and then copy the bitmap bits into the surface—in other words, the hard way.

The CreateSurfaceFromFile function declaration looks like this:

```
CreateSurfaceFromFile( _
    file As String, _
    dd As DDSURFACEDESC2 _
) As DirectDrawSurface7
```

Unlike CreateSurface, you do not need to fill a ddsd structure prior to calling CreateSurfaceFromFile. Rather, the function itself fills the structure when the bitmap image is loaded. This function is so easy to use that it doesn't need much more explanation. I will show you how to actually put it to use in the DDWindow program later in this chapter.

The CreateSurfaceFromResource Function

If you prefer to use resources instead of files for storing game graphics, then you will find the CreateSurfaceFromResource function useful. It is similar to CreateSurfaceFromFile in functionality, but obviously it reads a bitmap out of a program resource rather than a file.

My personal preference is to avoid using resources, but that is only because I have always been fascinated with downloadable add-ons for games, and it seems like that would be fairly difficult when using resources.

The CreateSurfaceFromResource function declaration looks like this:

```
CreateSurfaceFromResource( _
    file As String, _
    resName As String, _
    ddsd As DDSURFACEDESC2 _
) As DirectDrawSurface7
```

Blitting with DirectDraw Surfaces

The DirectDrawSurface7 object includes several blitters. For this reason (and to keep things simple), I will not cover direct video buffer access. The built-in DirectDraw blitters are already so fast that there is no practical need to modify surface memory directly. It is highly unlikely—in fact, I would go so far as to state that it is impossible—to write a blitter in VB that is faster than the built-in functions.

Therefore, I will cover the built-in blitting functions and then show you how to use them later in this chapter. Of the five blitters available to a DirectDrawSurface7 object, you will find that only two are really useful, and only one is capable of rendering transparent images on-the-fly.

The Blt Function

The primary blitter for a DirectDraw surface is simply called Blt. This function is versatile in that it supports scaling to arbitrary rectangle sizes on the destination, providing a means to perform some interesting special effects.

The Blt function looks like this:

```
Blt( _
    destRect As RECT, _
    ddS As DirectDrawSurface7, _
    srcRect As RECT, _
    flags As CONST_DDBLTFLAGS _
) As Long
```

> **TIP**
>
> Blt is the most important function available to a surface, because it is the only blitter capable of drawing images transparently with a color key.

When using Blt, make sure that you do not inadvertently resize the surface when blitting, because this slows down the drawing process. While frame rates will still be extremely fast, calling Blt with source and destination rectangles that do not match will result in a time-consuming scaling process. The easiest way to avoid this problem is to simply pass vbNull to the source and destination RECT parameters, thus forcing Blt to copy directly from source to destination using the image dimensions.

The BltFast Function

BltFast is a hard-core blitting function that simply copies the source directly to the destination without regard to clipping, which is fabulous for double buffers! Therefore, if you assign a clipping object to the destination and then blit an image that is too big to that destination, BltFast will return an error message. BltFast will take advantage of a hardware blitter if one is available for maximum 2-D performance, but it is not capable of drawing transparent images; it is only capable of drawing solid images (such as double buffers) quickly.

Here is the function declaration for BltFast:

```
BltFast( _
    dx As Long, dy As Long, _
    ddS As DirectDrawSurface7, _
    srcRect As RECT, _
    trans As CONST_DDBLTFASTFLAGS _
) As Long
```

The BltColorFill Function

BltColorFill is a very handy function for quickly clearing the screen with a specified color. The function also works with any other surface, including the double buffer. If you happen to be writing a game that uses a solid color for the background (such as black), then BltColorFill is a great function to use for clearing regions of the background.

The BltColorFill function declaration looks like this:

```
BltColorFill( _
    destRect As RECT, _
    fillvalue As Long _
) As Long
```

The BltFx Function

The BltFx function can be used for special effects programming, such as modifying the resulting image through source or destination raster operations or through alpha blending, among other techniques. I will not be covering BltFx, since it is not used often for common game-programming tasks (and is somewhat beyond the scope of this chapter). However, you might need to perform some advanced pixel manipulation that is not possible with the other blitting functions, so BltFx might be worth looking into for such cases.

The function declaration for BltFx looks like this:

```
BltFx( _
    destRect As RECT, _
    ddS As DirectDrawSurface7, _
    srcRect As RECT, _
    flags As CONST_DDBLTFLAGS, _
    BltFx As DDBLTFX _
) As Long
```

The BltToDC Procedure

The BltToDC procedure is a strange hybrid that allows you to blit a DirectDrawSurface7 object to a standard Windows device context. As the name implies, this procedure does not return a value (where normally a function would return an error code).

Obviously this function was not intended for writing games using a combination of both Windows API and DirectDraw, but is rather a support procedure that might be useful when porting a Windows API game to DirectDraw (as unlikely as that may sound), as a possible backup solution in the event that a DirectDraw primary surface cannot be created on a target system, or perhaps as a means to transfer a surface to a device context for printing. There are few good uses for this procedure when working on a game, so I will not be covering BltToDC beyond this brief summary.

The BltToDC procedure looks like this:

```
BltToDC( _
    hdc As Long, _
    srcRect As RECT, _
    destRect As RECT _
)
```

Transparency and the Color Key

DirectDraw surfaces have built-in support for blitting transparently with the Blt function. This is accomplished by referring to a color key for the transparent color when drawing the image. It is all done behind the scenes. You simply tell a surface to use a particular color key, and from that point forward, the pixels in a source image that equal the color key will not be copied to the destination.

A color key can be applied to a destination, including the primary surface and the double buffer surface. But more commonly, a color key is used in conjunction with a foreground image like a sprite with a source key (instead of a destination key).

To assign a color key to a surface, you must first create the color key variable:

```
Private ddcColorKey As DDCOLORKEY
```

Then you are free to set the value of the color key to the desired color. To do this, you simply set the low and high values of the color key. (Unfortunately, the color key does not support a simple RGB format.) The easiest way to create a color key is to use the color black. This is most often the transparent color used in source images, but you can use any color you want for the color key. I recommend using black, which has a value of (0,0). This is the easiest color to specify using the low/high format.

```
ddcColorKey.low = 0
ddcColorKey.high = 0
```

Finally, you call the SetColorKey procedure to set the transparent color to a surface. From that point forward, any calls to the Blt function will result in transparency. To change the color key, you must set up a different set of low and high values and set the color key again. Here is a sample of how to use SetColorKey:

```
ddSurface.SetColorKey DDCKEY_SRCBLT, ddcColorKey
```

DOUBLE BUFFERING WITH DIRECTDRAW

I introduced you to double buffering back in Chapter 9, "Let the Animation Begin," which included a sample double-buffered program using Windows API code along with the clsBitmap and clsSprite classes.

Double buffering works in exactly the same way in DirectDraw as it does in Windows API code, and the back buffer (as the double buffer is often referred to) is just like any other surface in memory.

As I explained in the last chapter, the double buffer is absolutely essential for a smooth-running game with fluid, flicker-free animation.

Creating the Double Buffer

Fortunately, you can use the same code to create the double buffer that you would use to create the background image or the sprites in a game. To create a double buffer, you simply use the CreateSurface function, as explained earlier. But first you must declare a variable to hold the double buffer, along with a variable for the DDSURFACEDESC2 and RECT structures:

```
Dim ddBackBuffer As DirectDrawSurface7
Private ddsdBackBuffer As DDSURFACEDESC2
Dim rBackBuffer As RECT
```

Now that the variables are taken care of, let's get right down to business and create the double buffer. This code sets up the double buffer so it is ready for use. You will then be able to draw surfaces onto the double buffer, and draw the double buffer on the screen in similar fashion.

```
ddsdBackBuffer.lFlags = DDSD_CAPS Or DDSD_WIDTH Or DDSD_HEIGHT
ddsdBackBuffer.ddsCaps.lCaps = DDSCAPS_OFFSCREENPLAIN
ddsdBackBuffer.lWidth = 640
ddsdBackBuffer.lHeight = 480
Set ddBackBuffer = ddraw.CreateSurface(ddsdBackBuffer)
rBackBuffer.Bottom = ddsdBackBuffer.lHeight
rBackBuffer.Right = ddsdBackBuffer.lWidth
```

Blitting the Double Buffer

Video memory in a DirectDraw program is called the primary surface, and you can treat it like any other DirectDraw surface. The only real difference is that the primary surface is set up using the DDSCAPS_PRIMARYSURFACE option. Here is a code snippet borrowed from the DDWindow program, which is covered later in the chapter.

```
'set up primary display surface
ddraw.SetCooperativeLevel Picture1.hWnd, DDSCL_NORMAL
ddsdScreen.lFlags = DDSD_CAPS
ddsdScreen.ddsCaps.lCaps = DDSCAPS_PRIMARYSURFACE
ddsdScreen.lWidth = SCREENWIDTH
ddsdScreen.lHeight = SCREENHEIGHT
Set ddScreen = ddraw.CreateSurface(ddsdScreen)
'set surface rectangle
rScreen.Bottom = ddsdScreen.lHeight
rScreen.Right = ddsdScreen.lWidth
```

Now that you see how to set up the primary surface, it might start to make sense how you would copy the double buffer to the screen. Quite simply, you can use the ddScreen surface's Blt function. Note that when you're working with a windowed program, you must return to the rectangle of the program window before drawing the double buffer. Here is the code that draws the double buffer:

```
objDX.GetWindowRect Picture1.hWnd, rScreen
ddScreen.Blt rScreen, ddBackBuffer, rBackBuffer, _
    DDBLT_WAIT
```

DRAWING BITMAPS AND SPRITES

The DirectDraw equivalent to clsBitmap (from Chapter 7, "Break Out the Bitmaps") is the DirectDraw surface. I will show you how to encapsulate a DirectDrawSurface into a class later in this chapter. For now, just assume that blitting a sprite is similar to blitting the double buffer. The destination of a sprite should be the double buffer, and the optional parameter is simply a method to tell that surface to draw the sprite transparently with a color key (that was supposedly assigned already).

To draw a sprite using DirectDraw, you must set up a rectangle that includes the sprite's position, width, and height. Recall that the double buffer was drawn using a rectangle as well. That rectangle did not need to be updated every time because the double buffer does not move. To retrieve the sprite's dimensions, you simply access the ddsdSprite structure and refer to the lWidth and lHeight values. The code looks something like this:

```
rTemp.Left = SpriteX
rTemp.Top = SpriteY
rTemp.Right = SpriteX + ddsdSprite.lWidth
rTemp.Bottom = SpriteY + ddsdSprite.lHeight
ddBackBuffer.Blt rTemp, ddSprites(n), rSprite, _
    DDBLT_WAIT Or DDBLT_KEYSRC
```

Note that rSprite was set up when the sprite was first loaded. The critical thing to note in this snippet of code is the option called DDBLT_KEYSRC. Without this option in the parameter for Blt, the sprite will not be drawn transparently. This option tells the ddBackBuffer surface to draw the image using the color key.

TESTING DIRECTDRAW IN WINDOWED MODE

Now it's time to put all this good theory into practice with a sample program. This first program, called DDWindow, shows how to set up a DirectDraw program to run in a window (as opposed to running full-screen, which is covered next). DDWindow includes everything that a traditional game needs to run, including transparent sprites, a double buffer, and a background image. By studying this program and using it as a template, you should be able to adapt it to any game project you want. Refer to Figure 10.2 to see the DDWindow program in action.

The source code for this program is located in the code module for Form1. To get started working on this project, you will need to create a new project in VB. Make it a Standard EXE project, and name it DDWindow. There are two bitmap files needed by this program. The first, called

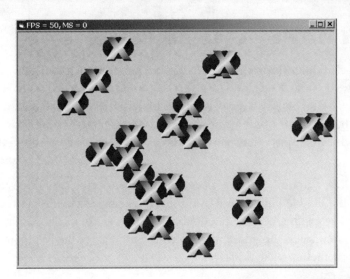

Figure 10.2

The DDWindow program demonstrates all the basics for using DirectDraw.

blueyellow.bmp, is a 640 × 480 background image, and has been used in most of the earlier chapters as well. The second bitmap file is directx.bmp, which is a 64 × 64 sprite. You can copy these files from the CD-ROM (in the \Bitmaps directory), or you can create the images yourself using a program like Paint Shop Pro.

> **NOTE**
>
> **If you want to change the resolution of the program to something other than 640 × 480, you will need to create a new background image with precisely the same resolution, or the background will not display correctly.**

DDWindow Source Code

If you have created the DDWindow project, then you are ready to start typing in the code for the program. This first section of code includes the usual basics like program constants and controls, and also includes the DirectX and DirectDraw objects, in addition to DirectDraw surfaces and related variables.

```
'-----------------------------------------------------------------
' Visual Basic Game Programming With DirectX
' Chapter 10 : Diving Into DirectDraw
' DDWindow Source Code File
'-----------------------------------------------------------------

Option Explicit
Option Base 0
```

```
'Windows API functions and structures
Private Declare Function GetTickCount _
    Lib "kernel32" () As Long

'program constants
Const SCREENWIDTH As Long = 640
Const SCREENHEIGHT As Long = 480
Const MAXFRAMERATE As Long = 100
Const NUMSPRITES As Long = 30

'program controls
Dim WithEvents Picture1 As PictureBox

'DirectDraw variables
Dim objDX As DirectX7
Dim ddraw As DirectDraw7
Dim objDDClip As DirectDrawClipper
Private ddcKey As DDCOLORKEY

'primary display surface variables
Dim ddScreen As DirectDrawSurface7
Private ddsdScreen As DDSURFACEDESC2
Private rScreen As RECT

'double buffer variables
Dim ddBackBuffer As DirectDrawSurface7
Private ddsdBackBuffer As DDSURFACEDESC2
Dim rBackBuffer As RECT

'background image variables
Dim ddBackground As DirectDrawSurface7
Private ddsdBackground As DDSURFACEDESC2
Dim rBackground As RECT

'sprite variables
Dim ddSprites(NUMSPRITES) As DirectDrawSurface7
Dim SpriteX(NUMSPRITES) As Long
Dim SpriteY(NUMSPRITES) As Long
Dim SpeedX(NUMSPRITES) As Long
Dim SpeedY(NUMSPRITES) As Long
```

```
Private ddsdSprite As DDSURFACEDESC2
Dim rSprite As RECT

'program variables
Dim rTemp As RECT
Dim bRunning As Boolean
Dim n As Long
```

The next section of code is the listing for Form_Load, the startup procedure for the program. Form_Load is really the key to this entire program, since it not only creates and loads the graphics and DirectX objects, it also includes the main game loop. Hopefully, most of the code found in Form_Load will look familiar to you from previous chapters, but there is a lot of new code to set up the DirectX objects.

```
Private Sub Form_Load()
    Static lStartTime As Long
    Static lCounter As Long
    Static lNewTime As Long

    bRunning = True
    Randomize GetTickCount

    'set up the main form
    With Form1
        .Width = SCREENWIDTH * Screen.TwipsPerPixelX
        .Height = SCREENHEIGHT * Screen.TwipsPerPixelY
        .AutoRedraw = False
        .ClipControls = False
        .KeyPreview = True
        .ScaleMode = 3
        .BorderStyle = 1
        .Show
    End With

    'create the PictureBox control
    Set Picture1 = Controls.Add("VB.PictureBox", "Picture1")
    With Picture1
        .AutoRedraw = False
        .BorderStyle = 1
        .ClipControls = False
        .ScaleMode = 3
```

```
        .BackColor = RGB(0, 0, 0)
        .Left = 0
        .Top = 0
        .Width = Form1.ScaleWidth
        .Height = Form1.ScaleHeight
        .Visible = True
End With

'create the DirectX object
Set objDX = New DirectX7

'create the DirectDraw object
Set ddraw = objDX.DirectDrawCreate("")

'set up primary display surface
ddraw.SetCooperativeLevel Picture1.hWnd, DDSCL_NORMAL
ddsdScreen.lFlags = DDSD_CAPS
ddsdScreen.ddsCaps.lCaps = DDSCAPS_PRIMARYSURFACE
ddsdScreen.lWidth = SCREENWIDTH
ddsdScreen.lHeight = SCREENHEIGHT
Set ddScreen = ddraw.CreateSurface(ddsdScreen)

'set surface rectangle
rScreen.Bottom = ddsdScreen.lHeight
rScreen.Right = ddsdScreen.lWidth

'create the clipper object
Set objDDClip = ddraw.CreateClipper(0)
objDDClip.SetHWnd Picture1.hWnd
ddScreen.SetClipper objDDClip

'create the back buffer
ddsdBackBuffer.lFlags = DDSD_CAPS Or DDSD_WIDTH Or DDSD_HEIGHT
ddsdBackBuffer.ddsCaps.lCaps = DDSCAPS_OFFSCREENPLAIN
ddsdBackBuffer.lWidth = SCREENWIDTH
ddsdBackBuffer.lHeight = SCREENHEIGHT
Set ddBackBuffer = ddraw.CreateSurface(ddsdBackBuffer)
rBackBuffer.Bottom = ddsdBackBuffer.lHeight
rBackBuffer.Right = ddsdBackBuffer.lWidth
```

```
'load the background image
ddsdBackground.lFlags = DDSD_CAPS Or DDSD_WIDTH Or DDSD_HEIGHT
ddsdBackground.ddsCaps.lCaps = DDSCAPS_OFFSCREENPLAIN
ddsdBackground.lWidth = SCREENWIDTH
ddsdBackground.lHeight = SCREENHEIGHT
Set ddBackground = ddraw.CreateSurfaceFromFile(App.Path & _
    "\blueyellow.bmp", ddsdBackground)
rBackground.Bottom = ddsdBackground.lHeight
rBackground.Right = ddsdBackground.lWidth
ddBackBuffer.BltFast 0, 0, ddBackground, rBackground, _
    DDBLTFAST_WAIT

'set up the sprite information
ddsdSprite.lFlags = DDSD_CAPS Or DDSD_WIDTH Or DDSD_HEIGHT
ddsdSprite.ddsCaps.lCaps = DDSCAPS_OFFSCREENPLAIN
ddsdSprite.lWidth = 64
ddsdSprite.lHeight = 64
ddcKey.low = 0
ddcKey.high = 0

'load the sprites
For n = 0 To NUMSPRITES
    Set ddSprites(n) = ddraw.CreateSurfaceFromFile(App.Path & _
        "\directx.bmp", ddsdSprite)
    rSprite.Bottom = ddsdSprite.lHeight
    rSprite.Right = ddsdSprite.lWidth
    SpriteX(n) = Random(SCREENWIDTH - ddsdSprite.lWidth)
    SpriteY(n) = Random(SCREENHEIGHT - ddsdSprite.lHeight)
    Do Until SpeedX(n) <> 0
        SpeedX(n) = Random(6) - 3
    Loop
    Do Until SpeedY(n) <> 0
        SpeedY(n) = Random(6) - 3
    Loop
    ddSprites(n).SetColorKey DDCKEY_SRCBLT, ddcKey
Next n

'main game loop
Do While bRunning
    lCounter = GetTickCount - lStartTime
```

```
            If lCounter > lNewTime Then
                'update game display
                Game_Update lCounter
                'update frame count
                lNewTime = lCounter + 1000 / MAXFRAMERATE
            End If
            DoEvents
        Loop
End Sub
```

The next section of code includes some program events like Form1_Click, as well as the support functions Shutdown and Random. Shutdown is of particular interest because it actually restores the video display back to normal, and then hides Form1 and frees up memory used by the program.

```
Private Sub Form_KeyDown(KeyCode As Integer, Shift As Integer)
    If KeyCode = 27 Then Shutdown
End Sub


Private Sub Form_QueryUnload(Cancel As Integer, _
    UnloadMode As Integer)
    Shutdown
End Sub


Private Sub Form1_Click()
    Shutdown
End Sub


Private Sub Picture1_Click()
    Shutdown
End Sub


Private Sub Shutdown()
    bRunning = False
    ddraw.RestoreDisplayMode
    ddraw.SetCooperativeLevel Picture1.hWnd, DDSCL_NORMAL
    Form1.Hide
    Unload Form1
    Set ddraw = Nothing
    Set objDX = Nothing
End Sub
```

```
Public Function Random(ByVal num&) As Long
    Random = CLng(num * Rnd)
End Function
```

Finally, the Game_Update procedure is called by the game loop to update the primary display. This includes moving the sprites, drawing the background image, displaying the frame rate, and drawing the double buffer to the screen.

```
Public Sub Game_Update(ByVal MS As Long)
    Static lTimer As Long
    Static lStart As Long
    Static lCounter As Long

    'start counting draw time
    lStart = GetTickCount

    'erase sprites
    For n = 0 To NUMSPRITES
        rTemp.Left = SpriteX(n)
        rTemp.Top = SpriteY(n)
        rTemp.Right = rTemp.Left + ddsdSprite.lWidth
        rTemp.Bottom = rTemp.Top + ddsdSprite.lHeight
        ddBackBuffer.BltFast SpriteX(n), SpriteY(n), ddBackground, _
            rTemp, DDBLTFAST_WAIT
    Next n

    'move and draw the sprites
    For n = 0 To NUMSPRITES
        'update X position
        SpriteX(n) = SpriteX(n) + SpeedX(n)
        If SpriteX(n) < 1 Then
            SpeedX(n) = -SpeedX(n)
            SpriteX(n) = 1
        ElseIf SpriteX(n) + ddsdSprite.lWidth > SCREENWIDTH Then
            SpeedX(n) = -SpeedX(n)
            SpriteX(n) = SCREENWIDTH - ddsdSprite.lWidth - 1
        End If

        'update Y position
        SpriteY(n) = SpriteY(n) + SpeedY(n)
```

```
        If SpriteY(n) < 1 Then
            SpeedY(n) = -SpeedY(n)
            SpriteY(n) = 1
        ElseIf SpriteY(n) + ddsdSprite.lHeight > SCREENHEIGHT Then
            SpeedY(n) = -SpeedY(n)
            SpriteY(n) = SCREENHEIGHT - ddsdSprite.lHeight - 1
        End If

        'draw the sprite
        rTemp.Left = SpriteX(n)
        rTemp.Top = SpriteY(n)
        rTemp.Right = SpriteX(n) + ddsdSprite.lWidth
        rTemp.Bottom = SpriteY(n) + ddsdSprite.lHeight
        ddBackBuffer.Blt rTemp, ddSprites(n), rSprite, _
            DDBLT_WAIT Or DDBLT_KEYSRC
    Next n

    'copy double buffer to the screen
    objDX.GetWindowRect Picture1.hWnd, rScreen
    ddScreen.Blt rScreen, ddBackBuffer, rBackBuffer, DDBLT_WAIT

    'count the frames per second
    If MS > lTimer + 1000 Then
        lStart = GetTickCount - lStart
        Form1.Caption = "FPS = " & lCounter & ", MS = " & lStart
        lTimer = MS
        lCounter = 0
    Else
        lCounter = lCounter + 1
    End If
End Sub
```

I hope this program was easy enough to follow because in the next section, I am going to jump right into encapsulating the DirectDraw code into classes. As you have seen, there are several steps involved just to draw a sprite with DirectDraw, so it would naturally be easier to move this common code into a class. If you don't have a good grasp of DirectDraw at this point, I recommend that you go back and review before moving on, because I will pick up the pace for the second half of the chapter.

ENCAPSULATING DIRECTDRAW

The source code for DDWindow is useful because it demonstrates how to write a DirectDraw program in VB with just simple, straightforward code. But the fact is, that code was messy and would get even worse in a complete game. What is really needed is a way to strip out the redundant DirectDraw code and stuff it in a class that can be easily reused.

I have created three classes to make DirectDraw easier to handle. The first class, clsDirectDraw7, encapsulates the main DirectX7 and DirectDraw7 objects. The DirectDraw7 class includes the primary display surface and the clipper, and provides an easy means to copy a double buffer to the primary display.

The second class, clsDDSurface7, encapsulates the DirectDrawSurface7 object and includes the ddsd and rectangle structures for easy access.

The third class in this chapter, clsDDSprite7, encapsulates the functionality of a sprite for DirectDraw and makes use of clsDDSurface7 to hold the sprite frames, which were clsBitmap objects in previous chapters. This sprite class really opens up DirectDraw for gaming, hiding the details of loading and blitting surfaces, and allowing you to focus on just writing the game.

Following the source code listings for these three classes is a sample program called DDFullscreen that shows how to use the new classes to write a full-screen DirectDraw program. I'm not going to spend as much time explaining all of the source code that follows because it is almost exactly the same as the code for the DDWindow program, only divided into classes. If you get lost, just refer back to the DDWindow program to see where the code in these classes came from.

The clsDirectDraw7 Class

The clsDirectDraw7 class includes the DirectX7 object because that object is not needed for anything more elaborate than creating the DirectDraw7 object at this point. Was that a tongue twister? Normally it might make sense to give DirectX7 a class of its own, but it is just not necessary. It is actually common to include more than one copy of the main DirectX object whenever needed in individual classes.

This first section of code for clsDirectDraw7 includes the class variables, the `Class_Initialize` and `Class_Terminate` procedures, and the `Startup` and `Shutdown` procedures. Pay close attention to `Startup`, because this procedure includes some new code for telling DirectDraw to enter exclusive full-screen mode.

```
'--------------------------------------------------------------------
' Visual Basic Game Programming With DirectX
' Chapter 10 : Diving Into DirectDraw
' DirectDraw7 Class Source Code File
'--------------------------------------------------------------------
Option Explicit
Option Base 0

'class variables
Dim objDX As DirectX7
Dim objDD As DirectDraw7
Dim cddsScreen As clsDDSurface7
Dim objDDClip As DirectDrawClipper
Dim rScreen As DxVBLib.RECT
Dim hSourccWindow As Long

Private Sub Class_Initialize()
    'create the DirectX7 object
    Set objDX = New DirectX7
    'create the DirectDraw object
    Set objDD = objDX.DirectDrawCreate("")
End Sub

Private Sub Class_Terminate()
    Set objDD = Nothing
    Set objDX = Nothing
End Sub

Public Function Startup(ByVal hWnd As Long, ByVal lWidth As Long, _
    ByVal lHeight As Long, ByVal lBPP As Long, _
    ByVal bFullscreen As Boolean) As Boolean

    hSourceWindow = hWnd
    If bFullscreen Then
        'set the color depth
        objDD.SetCooperativeLevel hWnd, DDSCL_FULLSCREEN Or _
            DDSCL_EXCLUSIVE
        If lBPP < 1 Or lBPP > 32 Then lBPP = 32
        'set the display mode
        objDD.SetDisplayMode lWidth, lHeight, lBPP, 0, DDSDM_DEFAULT
```

```
        Else
            'windowed mode
            objDD.SetCooperativeLevel hWnd, DDSCL_NORMAL
        End If

        'set up the primary display surface
        Set cddsScreen = New clsDDSurface7

        'create the primary display surface
        Startup = cddsScreen.Create(objDD, lWidth, lHeight, True)
        If Startup Then
            'create the clipper object
            Set objDDClip = objDD.CreateClipper(0)

            'assoiciate the window handle with the clipper
            objDDClip.SetHWnd hSourceWindow

            'clip blitting routines to the window
            cddsScreen.Surface.SetClipper objDDClip
        End If
End Function

Public Sub Shutdown()
    objDD.RestoreDisplayMode
    objDD.SetCooperativeLevel hSourceWindow, DDSCL_NORMAL
End Sub
```

The next section of code includes a procedure called Draw that can be used to copy a double buffer to the primary display. A related property called ScreenRect returns the internal RECT structure that can be used as the destination rectangle for displaying the double buffer.

Also included are two properties that are absolutely essential. DXObj and DDObj return references to the DirectX7 and DirectDraw7 objects that are created inside this class. Without these object references, it is impossible for you to use any of the features of these objects that were not exposed by the class. It would be a ridiculous effort to duplicate all of the functionality of the DirectX7 and DirectDraw7 objects, so these object references will solve that problem nicely.

```
Public Sub Blt(ByRef ddsSource As DirectDrawSurface7, _
    ByRef srcRect As DxVBLib.RECT)
    cddsScreen.Blt ScreenRect, ddsSource, srcRect
End Sub
```

```
Public Sub Draw(ByRef cddsSource As clsDDSurface7, _
    ByRef srcRect As DxVBLib.RECT)
    cddsScreen.Blt ScreenRect, cddsSource.Surface, srcRect
End Sub

Public Property Get DXObj() As DirectX7
    Set DXObj = objDX
End Property

Public Property Get ddObj() As DirectDraw7
    Set ddObj = objDD
End Property

Public Property Get ScreenRect() As DxVBLib.RECT
    objDX.GetWindowRect hSourceWindow, rScreen
    ScreenRect = rScreen
End Property
```

The clsDDSurface7 Class

The clsDDSurface7 class encapsulates the functionality of the DirectDrawSurface7 object and includes the DDSURFACEDESC2 and RECT structures that are needed when working with a surface. This class also includes a DDCOLORKEY structure for transparent blitting.

This class does not expose all the functionality of a DirectDrawSurface7 object, but it does include all the functionality needed to create a primary surface, a double buffer, and game images, along with the ability to blit these images to any other surface with or without transparency. In case you do want to tap into more advanced features, the surface object is exposed through a property.

The first section of code for clsDDSurface7 includes the class variables, the Create function, and the Load function. The Create function is used to create a surface in memory for a double buffer or any other purpose. The Load function is used to load a bitmap image directly into a surface.

```
'--------------------------------------------------------------------
' Visual Basic Game Programming With DirectX
' Chapter 10 : Diving Into DirectDraw
' DDSurface7 Class Source Code File
'--------------------------------------------------------------------
Option Explicit
Option Base 0
```

```vb
'class variables
Private ddSurface As DirectDrawSurface7
Private ddsd As DDSURFACEDESC2
Private rSurface As DxVBLib.RECT
Private ddcColorKey As DDCOLORKEY

Public Function Create(ByRef objDD As DirectDraw7, _
    ByVal lWidth As Long, ByVal lHeight As Long, _
    Optional bPrimary As Boolean = False) As Boolean
    Create = False
    On Error GoTo create_error

    If bPrimary Then
        'create the primary display surface
        ddsd.lFlags = DDSD_CAPS
        ddsd.ddsCaps.lCaps = DDSCAPS_PRIMARYSURFACE
    Else
        'create a normal surface
        ddsd.lFlags = DDSD_CAPS Or DDSD_WIDTH Or DDSD_HEIGHT
        ddsd.ddsCaps.lCaps = DDSCAPS_OFFSCREENPLAIN
    End If

    'set surface resolution
    ddsd.lWidth = lWidth
    ddsd.lHeight = lHeight

    'create the requested surface
    Set ddSurface = objDD.CreateSurface(ddsd)

    'set transparent color to black
    ddcColorKey.low = 0
    ddcColorKey.high = 0
    ddSurface.SetColorKey DDCKEY_SRCBLT, ddcColorKey

    'set surface rectangle
    rSurface.Bottom = ddsd.lHeight
    rSurface.Right = ddsd.lWidth
    Create = True
create_error:
End Function
```

```
Public Function Load(ByRef ddraw As clsDirectDraw7, _
    ByVal sFilename As String) As Boolean

    Load = False
    On Error GoTo load_error

    'create surface and load bitmap
    Set ddSurface = ddraw.ddObj.CreateSurfaceFromFile(sFilename, ddsd)
    If ddSurface Is Nothing Then Exit Function

    'set transparent color to black
    ddcColorKey.low = 0
    ddcColorKey.high = 0
    ddSurface.SetColorKey DDCKEY_SRCBLT, ddcColorKey

    'set surface rectangle
    rSurface.Bottom = ddsd.lHeight
    rSurface.Right = ddsd.lWidth
    Load = True
load_error:
End Function
```

The next section of code includes the blitting procedures and some useful properties. Included is the standard Blt, BltFast, BltColorFill, DrawText, and a new procedure called BltTrans that includes the appropriate transparency options in the call to Blt. The properties include Width and Height, the Surface object directly from the DirectDrawSurface7 object, and the surface rectangle.

```
Public Sub Blt(ByRef dstRect As DxVBLib.RECT, _
    ByRef ddsSource As DirectDrawSurface7, _
    ByRef srcRect As DxVBLib.RECT)
    ddSurface.Blt dstRect, ddsSource, srcRect, DDBLT_WAIT
End Sub

Public Sub BltTrans(ByRef dstRect As DxVBLib.RECT, _
    ByRef ddsSource As DirectDrawSurface7, _
    ByRef srcRect As DxVBLib.RECT)
    ddSurface.Blt dstRect, ddsSource, srcRect, DDBLT_WAIT Or _
        DDBLT_KEYSRC
End Sub
```

```
Public Sub BltFast(ByVal X As Long, ByVal Y As Long, _
    ByRef ddsSource As DirectDrawSurface7, _
    ByRef srcRect As DxVBLib.RECT)
    ddSurface.BltFast X, Y, ddsSource, srcRect, DDBLTFAST_WAIT
End Sub

Public Sub BltColorFill(ByVal lColor As Long)
    ddSurface.BltColorFill rSurface, lColor
End Sub

Public Sub DrawText(ByVal X As Long, ByVal Y As Long, _
    ByVal sText As String)
    ddSurface.DrawText X, Y, sText, False
End Sub

Public Property Get Surface() As DirectDrawSurface7
    Set Surface = ddSurface
End Property

Public Property Get SurfaceRect() As DxVBLib.RECT
    SurfaceRect = rSurface
End Property

Public Property Get Width() As Long
    Width = ddsd.lWidth
End Property

Public Property Get Height() As Long
    Height = ddsd.lHeight
End Property
```

The clsDDSprite7 Class

Okay, finally something that looks familiar, a sprite class! The clsDDSprite7 class includes the
functionality needed to take surface management to the next level, encapsulating the basic sprite
properties to move an object around on the screen transparently. This sprite class differs from
the clsSprite class in previous chapters because it doesn't store the background internally.
Instead, it's up to you to erase the sprite using the background surface. However, clsDDSprite7 is
extremely fast at both loading and drawing sprites. You have the option of loading directly from a

file or loading from an existing surface. Obviously, this significantly speeds up the initialization time of the program when a lot of sprites are using the same source image.

The first section of code includes the class variables, property variables, `Initialize`, `Terminate`, and the actual public properties of the class.

```
'-----------------------------------------------------------------
' Visual Basic Game Programming With DirectX
' Chapter 10 : Diving Into DirectDraw
' DDSprite7 Class Source Code File
'-----------------------------------------------------------------
Option Explicit
Option Base 0

'class variables
Dim ddraw As clsDirectDraw7
Dim ddsSource As clsDDSurface7
Dim SourceSize As Long

'class property variables
Dim bActive As Boolean
Dim bTransparent As Boolean
Dim bErase As Boolean
Dim lState As Long
Dim lCurrentX As Long
Dim lCurrentY As Long
Dim lGlobalX As Long
Dim lGlobalY As Long
Dim lCurrentFrame As Long
Dim lFrameCount As Long
Dim lSpeedX As Long
Dim lSpeedY As Long
Dim lMoveRate As Long
Dim lMoveCount As Long
Dim lAnimRate As Long
Dim lAnimCount As Long
Dim lAnimDir As Long
Dim lDirX As Long
Dim lDirY As Long

'program variables
Dim bLoadFromFile As Boolean
```

```
Dim lFramesPerRow As Long
Dim lWidth As Long
Dim lHeight As Long

Private Sub Class_Initialize()
    bActive = True
    bTransparent = True
    bLoadFromFile = False
End Sub

Private Sub Class_Terminate()
    'avoid deleting any references
    If bLoadFromFile Then
        Set ddsSource = Nothing
    End If
End Sub

Public Property Let X(ByVal lNewValue As Long)
    lCurrentX = lNewValue
End Property

Public Property Get X() As Long
    X = lCurrentX
End Property

Public Property Let Y(ByVal lNewValue As Long)
    lCurrentY = lNewValue
End Property

Public Property Get Y() As Long
    Y = lCurrentY
End Property

Public Property Let GlobalX(ByVal lNewValue As Long)
    lGlobalX = lNewValue
End Property

Public Property Get GlobalX() As Long
    GlobalX = lGlobalX
End Property
```

```vb
Public Property Let GlobalY(ByVal lNewValue As Long)
    lGlobalY = lNewValue
End Property


Public Property Get GlobalY() As Long
    GlobalY = lGlobalY
End Property


Public Property Get SpeedX() As Long
    SpeedX = lSpeedX
End Property


Public Property Let SpeedX(ByVal lNewValue As Long)
    lSpeedX = lNewValue
End Property


Public Property Get SpeedY() As Long
    SpeedY = lSpeedY
End Property


Public Property Let SpeedY(ByVal lNewValue As Long)
    lSpeedY = lNewValue
End Property


Public Property Get Width() As Long
    Width = lWidth
End Property


Public Property Get Height() As Long
    Height = lHeight
End Property


Public Property Get Active() As Boolean
    Active = bActive
End Property


Public Property Let Active(ByVal bNewValue As Boolean)
    bActive = bNewValue
End Property
```

```
Public Property Get CurrentFrame() As Long
    CurrentFrame = lCurrentFrame
End Property

Public Property Let CurrentFrame(ByVal lNewValue As Long)
    If lNewValue >= 0 And lNewValue < lFrameCount Then
        lCurrentFrame = lNewValue
    End If
End Property

Public Property Get Transparent() As Boolean
    Transparent = bTransparent
End Property

Public Property Let Transparent(ByVal bNewValue As Boolean)
    bTransparent = bNewValue
End Property

Public Property Let State(ByVal lNewValue As Long)
    lState = lNewValue
End Property

Public Property Get State() As Long
    State = lState
End Property

Public Property Let MoveRate(ByVal lNewValue As Long)
    lMoveRate = lNewValue
End Property

Public Property Get MoveRate() As Long
    MoveRate = lMoveRate
End Property

Public Property Let MoveCount(ByVal lNewValue As Long)
    lMoveCount = lNewValue
End Property

Public Property Get MoveCount() As Long
    MoveCount = lMoveCount
End Property
```

```vb
Public Property Let AnimRate(ByVal lNewValue As Long)
    lAnimRate = lNewValue
End Property

Public Property Get AnimRate() As Long
    AnimRate = lAnimRate
End Property

Public Property Let AnimCount(ByVal lNewValue As Long)
    lAnimCount = lNewValue
End Property

Public Property Get AnimCount() As Long
    AnimCount = lAnimCount
End Property

Public Property Let AnimDir(ByVal lNewValue As Long)
    lAnimDir = lNewValue
End Property

Public Property Get AnimDir() As Long
    AnimDir = lAnimDir
End Property

Public Property Get DirX() As Long
    DirX = lDirX
End Property

Public Property Let DirX(ByVal lNewValue As Long)
    lDirX = lNewValue
End Property

Public Property Get DirY() As Long
    DirY = lDirY
End Property

Public Property Let DirY(ByVal lNewValue As Long)
    lDirY = lNewValue
End Property
```

The next section of code for clsDDSprite includes Create, NextFrame, PrevFrame, Draw, LoadFromFile, and LoadFromSurface. Create must be called before anything else or the sprite class will complain, because Create sets the local reference to the DirectDraw7 object. The frame routines should be familiar from clsSprite, which was developed earlier. LoadFromFile loads a bitmap file into a surface object, while LoadFromSurface simply creates a reference to an existing surface. Note that it doesn't actually create a new surface, so you will need to ensure that you keep that original surface in memory as long as the sprite needs it.

```
Public Sub Create(ByRef ddObj As clsDirectDraw7)
    'set local reference to DirectDraw
    Set ddraw = ddObj
End Sub

Public Sub NextFrame()
    If lAnimCount < lAnimRate Then
        lAnimCount = lAnimCount + 1
    Else
        lAnimCount = 0
        If lCurrentFrame < lFrameCount - 1 Then
            lCurrentFrame = lCurrentFrame + 1
        Else
            lCurrentFrame = 0
        End If
    End If
End Sub

Public Sub PrevFrame()
    If lAnimCount < lAnimRate Then
        lAnimCount = lAnimCount + 1
    Else
        lAnimCount = 0
        If lCurrentFrame > 0 Then
            lCurrentFrame = lCurrentFrame - 1
        Else
            lCurrentFrame = lFrameCount - 1
        End If
    End If
End Sub

Public Sub Draw(ByRef ddsDest As clsDDSurface7)
    Dim srcRect As DxVBLib.RECT
    Dim dstRect As DxVBLib.RECT
```

```
    'set the source rect
    srcRect.Left = (lCurrentFrame Mod lFramesPerRow) * lWidth
    srcRect.Top = (lCurrentFrame \ lFramesPerRow) * lHeight
    srcRect.Right = srcRect.Left + lWidth
    srcRect.Bottom = srcRect.Top + lHeight

    'set the dest rect
    dstRect.Left = lCurrentX
    dstRect.Top = lCurrentY
    dstRect.Right = lCurrentX + lWidth
    dstRect.Bottom = lCurrentY + lHeight

    'draw the sprite
    ddsDest.BltTrans dstRect, ddsSource.Surface, srcRect
End Sub

Public Function LoadFromFile(ByVal sFilename As String, _
    ByVal lSprWidth As Long, ByVal lSprHeight As Long, _
    ByVal lNumCols As Long, ByVal lNumFrames As Long) As Boolean

    LoadFromFile = False
    If ddraw Is Nothing Then Exit Function

    'create surface object
    Set ddsSource = Nothing
    Set ddsSource = New clsDDSurface7

    'load bitmap file into a surface
    If Not ddsSource.Load(ddraw, sFilename) Then Exit Function

    'set the starting position
    lCurrentX = 0
    lCurrentY = 0

    'set the width and height of the sprite
    lWidth = lSprWidth
    lHeight = lSprHeight

    'set the column count and frame count
    lFramesPerRow = lNumCols
    lFrameCount = lNumFrames
```

```
        bLoadFromFile = True
        LoadFromFile = True
End Function

Public Function LoadFromSurface(ByRef ddsOther As clsDDSurface7, _
    ByVal lSprWidth As Long, ByVal lSprHeight As Long, _
    ByVal lNumCols As Long, ByVal lNumFrames As Long) As Boolean

        LoadFromSurface = False
        If ddraw Is Nothing Then Exit Function

        'copy surface from an existing surface
        Set ddsSource = ddsOther
        If ddsSource Is Nothing Then Exit Function

        'set the starting position
        lCurrentX = 0
        lCurrentY = 0

        'set the width and height of the sprite
        lWidth = lSprWidth
        lHeight = lSprHeight

        'set the column count and frame count
        lFramesPerRow = lNumCols
        lFrameCount = lNumFrames

        LoadFromSurface = True
End Function
```

TESTING DIRECTDRAW IN FULL-SCREEN MODE

The performance difference from 640×480 to 1600×1200 is only a matter of a few frames per second, demonstrating that DirectDraw has a high-end limit that is not being pushed hard enough by this code. To demonstrate the real power of DirectDraw, it is best to enter full-screen mode. The primary benefit of going into full-screen mode is that you can select any valid resolution that you want to use, including non-standard resolutions. Full-screen mode provides the best performance, and there is the added benefit of pushing Windows into the background and gaining exclusive use of the graphics and sound systems of the PC.

This final section of the chapter includes a sample program called DDFullscreen that shows not only how to enter full-screen and exclusive

> **TIP**
>
> When using DirectDraw in full-screen mode, you must remove the border from the form. Unfortunately, this can't be done in code because BorderStyle is a read-only property. Set BorderStyle = 0 - None any time you are using DirectDraw in full-screen mode.

modes, but also how to use the new DirectDraw classes: clsDirectDraw7, clsDDSurface7, and clsDDSprite. Figure 10.3 shows DDFullscreen running with a resolution of 640 × 480.

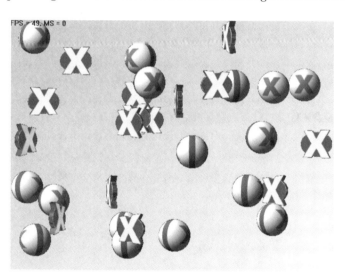

Figure 10.3

The DDFullscreen program shows off the capabilities of the DirectDraw classes in full-screen mode.

This is a versatile program, allowing you to change the constants at the top of the program listing (such as SCREENWIDTH and SCREENHEIGHT). Figure 10.4 shows the same program running at the astounding resolution of 1600 × 1200. Even at this high resolution, and with double buffering enabled, the program is still showing a very high frame rate. Later, I will show you a shot of the program running with even more outrageous settings.

A Simple Mistake Spells Disaster

I would like to point out a potential problem ahead of time, because it is so significant. There is a single setting that will drastically affect the performance of a DirectDraw program. Normally, when creating a DirectDraw surface, which the clsDDSurface7 class now handles automatically,

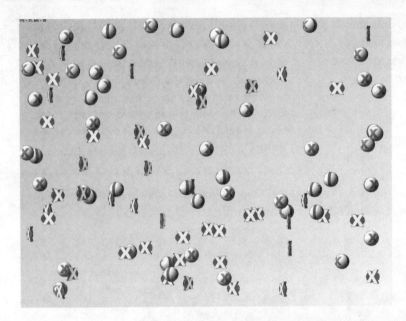

Figure 10.4

DirectDraw performs exceptionally well, even at ultra-high resolutions like 1600 × 1200.

you will want to use the option called DDSCAPS_OFFSCREENPLAIN. However, one of my first mistakes when working on the DDFullscreen program was to include the option called DDSCAPS_SYSTEMMEMORY.

This is a terrible mistake. Take a look at Figure 10.5 for an example of how slowly the program runs (even at 640 × 480) when this option is being used.

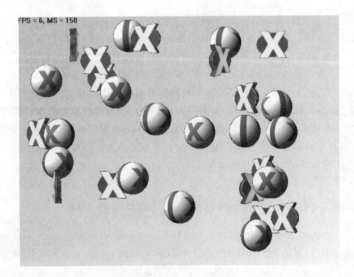

Figure 10.5

A single option in the creation of the primary display wreaks havoc on DirectDraw performance.

By all means, use a DirectDraw feature if it looks promising, but avoid that option at all costs because it forces surface data to reside in system memory, rather than the ultra-fast video memory. Copying the surfaces from system to video memory over and over again causes performance to completely flatten out. If you ever notice that your DirectDraw game is running unusually slowly after you make recent changes to a setting, be sure to verify that some new feature is not affecting performance. Figure 10.6 shows the same program that was shown before, only this time, the option that forced surfaces to reside in system memory has been removed.

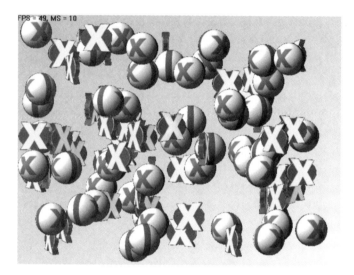

Figure 10.6

A properly initialized DirectDraw primary display surface can achieve extraordinary frame rates with Visual Basic.

DDFullscreen Source Code

Now for the source code you have been waiting for! The DDFullscreen program is a full-featured DirectDraw demonstration program that utilizes the new DirectDraw classes that were created earlier in this chapter.

This first section of code includes the all-important program constants that I mentioned before, along with program variables and Form_Load, which initializes the program and starts the game loop running.

```
'-------------------------------------------------------------------
' Visual Basic Game Programming With DirectX
' Chapter 10 : Diving Into DirectDraw
' DDFullscreen Source Code File
'-------------------------------------------------------------------
Option Explicit
Option Base 0
```

```vb
'Windows API functions and structures
Private Declare Function GetTickCount _
    Lib "kernel32" () As Long

'program constants
Const FULLSCREEN As Boolean = True
Const SCREENWIDTH As Long = 640
Const SCREENHEIGHT As Long = 480
Const COLORDEPTH As Long = 32
Const MAXFRAMERATE As Long = 80
Const NUMSPRITES As Long = 100
Const BGFILENAME = "blueyellow640.bmp"

'program controls
Dim WithEvents Picture1 As PictureBox

'primary DirectDraw object
Dim ddraw As clsDirectDraw7

'DirectDraw surfaces
Dim cddsBackground As clsDDSurface7
Dim cddsBackBuffer As clsDDSurface7
Dim cdsSprite(NUMSPRITES) As clsDDSprite7

'program variables
Dim bRunning As Boolean
Dim lastX As Long
Dim lastY As Long
Dim fps As Long
Dim n As Long
Dim lWindowHandle As Long
Dim sFrameRate As String
Dim rTemp As RECT

Private Sub Form_Load()
    Static lStartTime As Long
    Static lCounter As Long
    Static lNewTime As Long

    'set up the main form
    Form1.Width = SCREENWIDTH * Screen.TwipsPerPixelX
```

```
Form1.Height = SCREENHEIGHT * Screen.TwipsPerPixelY
Form1.AutoRedraw = False
Form1.ClipControls = False
Form1.KeyPreview = True
Form1.ScaleMode = 3

'create the PictureBox control for drawing
Set Picture1 = Controls.Add("VB.PictureBox", "Picture1")
Picture1.AutoRedraw = False
Picture1.BorderStyle = 1
Picture1.ClipControls = False
Picture1.ScaleMode = 3
Picture1.BackColor = RGB(0, 0, 0)
Picture1.Left = 0
Picture1.Top = 0
Picture1.Width = Form1.ScaleWidth
Picture1.Height = Form1.ScaleHeight
Picture1.Visible = Not FULLSCREEN

Form1.Show
If FULLSCREEN Then
    lWindowHandle = Form1.hWnd
Else
    lWindowHandle = Picture1.hWnd
End If

'create primary DirectDraw object
Set ddraw = New clsDirectDraw7
If Not ddraw.Startup(lWindowHandle, SCREENWIDTH, _
    SCREENHEIGHT, COLORDEPTH, FULLSCREEN) Then
    MsgBox "Error creating DirectDraw primary display surface"
    Shutdown
End If

'create back buffer
Set cddsBackBuffer = New clsDDSurface7
If Not cddsBackBuffer.Create(ddraw.ddObj, SCREENWIDTH, _
    SCREENHEIGHT) Then
    MsgBox "Error creating back buffer surface"
    Shutdown
End If
```

```
'load the background image
Set cddsBackground = New clsDDSurface7
If Not cddsBackground.Load(ddraw, App.Path & "\" & _
    BGFILENAME) Then
    MsgBox "Error loading blueyellow.bmp"
    Shutdown
End If


'load new sprite class
For n = 0 To NUMSPRITES
    Set cdsSprite(n) = New clsDDSprite7
    With cdsSprite(n)
        .Create ddraw
        If (n Mod 2) = 0 Then
            'even sprites load rotating_sphere
            If Not .LoadFromFile(App.Path & _
                "\rotating_sphere.bmp", 64, 64, 8, 32) Then
                MsgBox "Error loading rotating_sphere.bmp"
                Shutdown
            End If
        Else
            'odd sprites load rotating_x
            If Not .LoadFromFile(App.Path & _
                "\rotating_x.bmp", 64, 64, 10, 30) Then
                MsgBox "Error loading rotating_sphere.bmp"
                Shutdown
            End If
        End If
        .X = Random(SCREENWIDTH - .Width)
        .Y = Random(SCREENHEIGHT - .Height)
        Do Until .SpeedX <> 0
            .SpeedX = Random(6) - 3
        Loop
        Do Until .SpeedY <> 0
            .SpeedY = Random(6) - 3
        Loop
        .CurrentFrame = Random(30)
    End With
Next n
```

```
        'draw the background image
        cddsBackBuffer.BltFast 0, 0, cddsBackground.Surface, _
            cddsBackground.SurfaceRect

        bRunning = True
        sFrameRate = "FPS"

        'main game loop
        Do While bRunning
            lCounter = GetTickCount() - lStartTime
            If lCounter > lNewTime Then
                'update game display
                Game_Update lCounter
                'update frame count
                lNewTime = lCounter + 1000 / MAXFRAMERATE
            End If
            DoEvents
        Loop
End Sub
```

The next section of code includes some familiar program events, such as Form_KeyDown, as well as the common Shutdown and Random routines. Following these is the Game_Update procedure that actually does all of the work to animate the sprites on the screen with transparency. Again, this is all pretty much repeat material from the DDWindow program, only it is easier to follow because much of the code has been encapsulated within classes.

```
Private Sub Form_KeyDown(KeyCode As Integer, Shift As Integer)
    If KeyCode = 27 Then Shutdown
End Sub

Private Sub Form_QueryUnload(Cancel As Integer, UnloadMode As Integer)
    Shutdown
End Sub

Private Sub Form1_Click()
    Shutdown
End Sub

Private Sub Picture1_Click()
    Shutdown
End Sub
```

```vb
Private Sub Shutdown()
    bRunning = False
    ddraw.Shutdown
    Form1.Hide
    Unload Form1
End Sub

Public Function Random(ByVal lNum As Long) As Long
    Random = CLng(lNum * Rnd)
End Function

Public Sub Game_Update(ByVal MS As Long)
    Static lTimer As Long
    Static lStart As Long
    Static lCounter As Long

    'start counting milliseconds
    lStart = GetTickCount

    'erase the status line
    rTemp.Left = 0
    rTemp.Top = 0
    rTemp.Right = 300
    rTemp.Bottom = 20
    cddsBackBuffer.BltFast 0, 0, cddsBackground.Surface, rTemp

    'erase sprites
    For n = 0 To NUMSPRITES
        rTemp.Left = cdsSprite(n).X
        rTemp.Top = cdsSprite(n).Y
        rTemp.Right = rTemp.Left + cdsSprite(n).Width
        rTemp.Bottom = rTemp.Top + cdsSprite(n).Height
        cddsBackBuffer.BltFast cdsSprite(n).X, cdsSprite(n).Y, _
            cddsBackground.Surface, rTemp
    Next n

    'move and draw sprites
    For n = 0 To NUMSPRITES
        With cdsSprite(n)
            .X = .X + .SpeedX
```

```
            If .X < 1 Then
                .SpeedX = -.SpeedX
                .X = 1
            ElseIf .X + .Width > SCREENWIDTH Then
                .SpeedX = -.SpeedX
                .X = SCREENWIDTH - .Width - 1
            End If

            .Y = .Y + .SpeedY
            If .Y < 1 Then
                .SpeedY = -.SpeedY
                .Y = 1
            ElseIf .Y + .Height > SCREENHEIGHT Then
                .SpeedY = -.SpeedY
                .Y = SCREENHEIGHT - .Height - 1
            End If

            .NextFrame

            .Draw cddsBackBuffer
        End With
    Next n

    'display status line
    cddsBackBuffer.DrawText 0, 0, sFrameRate

    'copy back buffer to the screen
    ddraw.Draw cddsBackBuffer, cddsBackBuffer.SurfaceRect

    'count the frames per second
    If MS > lTimer + 1000 Then
        lStart = GetTickCount - lStart
        sFrameRate = "FPS = " & lCounter & ", MS = " & lStart
        Form1.Caption = sFrameRate
        lTimer = MS
        lCounter = 0
    Else
        lCounter = lCounter + 1
    End If
End Sub
```

Scaling the DirectDraw Primary Surface

By all means, tinker with the DDFullscreen program to see what kind of fun effects you can produce. One of the most rewarding aspects of computer programming is trying out new things, the results of which you cannot predict. That's why it's called "computer science," after all. It is exciting to try something weird with a program and see what bizarre special effects result. This is how many new technologies are discovered, by pure curiosity and tinkering.

One such result of tinkering that I experienced involved setting the program to run in full-screen mode and then setting Form1 so that it is resizable. I was surprised to find that rather than running in exclusive mode as expected, the program scaled itself to the borders of the program window. By resizing the window, I was able to scale the program in any direction (as shown in Figure 10.7).

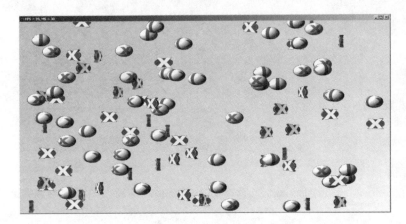

Figure 10.7

By setting the DDFullscreen program to run in full-screen mode, and then setting the form to resizable, the program window becomes scalable in any direction.

Centering on a Single Sprite

Another result of tinkering is shown in Figure 10.8. While working on the DDFullscreen program, I inadvertently passed the wrong rectangle to a Blt call, and the display zoomed in on a single sprite. It was fascinating, watching the sprite zoom quickly past other sprites and then rebound off the edges of the screen, with the background image whirring by. To recreate this problem, simply pass the source rectangle for a sprite in the destination rectangle parameter to Draw. The results are entertaining!

Pushing DirectDraw to the Limits!

Now for the grand finale of this chapter. To fully illustrate how incredible DirectDraw is, take a look at Figure 10.9, which shows the DDFullscreen program running at maximum resolution (at

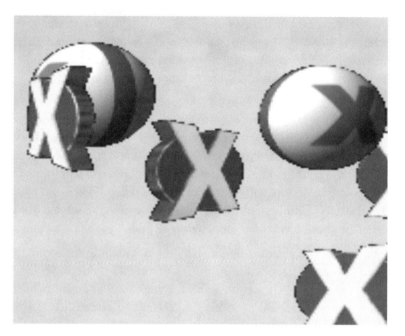

Figure 10.8

Tinkering with DirectDraw blitting rectangles can produce some entertaining special effects.

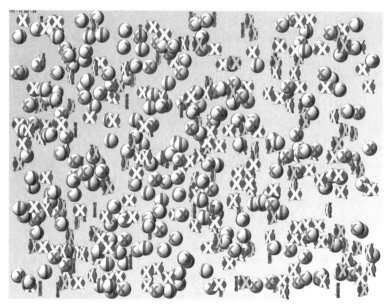

Figure 10.9

500 transparent sprites at 1600 × 1200, double buffered, and it still runs!

least on my PC). In this figure, there are 500 sprites (yes, five hundred!) being drawn transparently on a double-buffered screen at 1600 × 1200, in 32-bit color mode. Surprisingly enough, the system was able to handle the memory requirements of this pressure test, thanks to the efficient storage of the source images. The frame rate even at this staggering resolution and number of sprites is still surprisingly good.

I was so astonished at this result that I debugged the program line-by-line to verify that it was working properly (and not skipping any sprites). By testing the program with varying numbers of sprites, you can see how it becomes incrementally slower with each additional sprite. At a certain point the program will not be able to run due to memory requirements, but I will admit to having set it to 2,000 sprites at one point. Unfortunately, screen corruption occurred because the program ran out of memory and started blitting random memory locations to the screen. To avoid this problem, additional error checking code would need to be added to the program.

You can duplicate the settings I used in this example by changing the constants at the top of the program. What does this version of the program demonstrate? That graphics rendering code is no longer the most processor-intensive process in a game. With this high level of performance—on a mid-level system—there are plenty of cycles left for other aspects of the game, such as artificial intelligence and multiplayer networking.

SUMMARY

This chapter was an entertaining romp through the features of DirectDraw. I hope that if you come away with anything from this chapter, it is a deep appreciation for what DirectDraw and DirectX in general provide for Visual Basic game development. The levels of performance that I have demonstrated with the sample programs in this chapter conclusively show that VB is a capable language that is fully suited to developing professional games.

In the chapters that follow, I will expand upon the code developed in this chapter by including support for DirectSound in Chapter 11, "Playing Sound and Music with DirectX Audio," and support for DirectInput in Chapter 12, "Getting a Handle on User Input." Following those two chapters, I will show you how to wrap all of these classes and everything you have learned into a single comprehensive game library in Chapter 13, "Building the DirectX Game Library."

Very soon you will have all the tools you need to write professional games with VB! In the meantime, I encourage you to fast forward to Chapter 20, "Warbirds 1944: Scrolling Shooter Game," which is a game developed with the DirectDraw techniques presented in this chapter.

CHAPTER 11

PLAYING SOUND
AND MUSIC
WITH DIRECTX
AUDIO

In years past, programming sound and music for games was an enormous task. Custom sound code was usually too difficult to write due to the conflicting standards among the various sound cards in the industry. Today, that is no longer a problem, because there is now a single dominant hardware maker and a single dominant sound library. While some might argue the point, I believe that Creative Labs has the sound card market wrapped up with the Sound Blaster Live! family. At the same time, the complicated audio driver industry has been eclipsed by the incredibly versatile and powerful DirectX Audio library.

This chapter is a quick jaunt through the various components of DirectX Audio, with several small programs to demonstrate how to use DirectSound, DirectSound3D, and DirectMusic in a Visual Basic program. This chapter is by no means a reference for DirectX Audio, and only touches upon some of the advanced subjects (like environmental effects). For an in-depth study of the advanced features of DirectX Audio, see Appendix E, "Recommended Reading," for a list of recommended reference books.

This chapter covers the following topics:

- Introduction to DirectX Audio
- Programming Music
- Programming 3-D Positional Sound
- Encapsulating DirectX Audio
- Putting It All Together: The SoundTest Program

INTRODUCTION TO DIRECTX AUDIO

Welcome to the sound and music chapter! Audio is always such a fun subject to explore because sound effects and music have such an impact on impression and influence our opinions of games so strongly. What is a game without sound? It is nothing more than a technology demo. Sound is absolutely essential for the success of any game, no matter how large or small.

I remember the sound card war of the early 1990s, when several competing companies took on Creative Labs to produce a dominant sound card. This was about the time when multimedia was the next big thing and buzzwords like "edutainment" started to be overused in marketing and by the press. Although CD-ROMs were technically available as far back as 1988, I searched through the entire Comdex in 1992 and couldn't find one. It just goes to show how young the multimedia industry really is.

Accessing DirectX Audio Components in Visual Basic

DirectX Audio is made up of the DirectSound, DirectSound3D, and DirectMusic components, each of which is comprised of several more components. To gain access to DirectX Audio, you simply reference the DirectX 8 for Visual Basic Type Library in the Project References dialog box for your VB project. The DirectX type library is huge, providing access to absolutely everything in DirectX 8.0 with a single reference.

Using the DirectX Audio Components

DirectX Audio is an enormously complex library for playing, recording, and manipulating sounds of numerous types, from simple mono wave files to multi-sample audio segments to MIDI files. DirectX Audio can be used to write more than just games! This library is capable of handling just about any audio programming need.

DirectSound

DirectSound is the main component of DirectX Audio, and the one used most often in games. This component is capable of mixing wave sound buffers in real time.

DirectSound3D

DirectSound3D is a support component that works with DirectSound to provide real-time 3-D positional audio processing. DirectX 8.0 fully supports accelerated sound hardware, and DirectSound3D is the component which takes advantage of that.

DirectMusic

DirectMusic is now a much more powerful component than in past versions of DirectX, because it seems that DirectMusic performance and audio path objects are the main focus of the DirectX Audio system, which may eclipse DirectSound in the same way that DirectX Graphics eclipsed DirectDraw.

PROGRAMMING AMBIENT SOUND

Now, if you are going into this chapter with a desire to grab some code and use it in a game right away, you will most likely be pleased with the sample programs in this chapter. Rather than theorize about sound hardware and waveforms, how about if I just jump right in and show you how to play some cool sounds to spruce up your game projects? That's exactly what I'm going to show you in this section—how to get started programming DirectDraw right away. Figure 11.1 shows an illustration of a waveform.

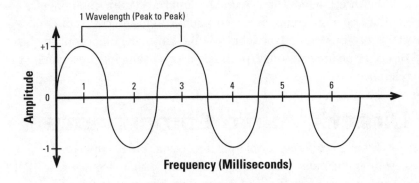

Figure 11.1

This illustration of a sine wave shows that a waveform is a function of frequency versus amplitude.

Understanding Ambient Sound

Ambient sound is a term that I borrowed from ambient light, a concept that you might already understand. Just look at a light bulb in a light fixture on the ceiling. The light emitted by the bulb pretty much fills the room, unless you are in a very large room that is not well-lit. When light permeates a room, it is said to be ambient; that is, the light does not seem to have a source.

Contrast this idea with directional light and you will get the idea behind ambient sound. By ambient sound I am referring to sound that appears to have no direction or source. Ambient sound is emitted by speakers uniformly, without any positional effects. This is the common type of sound that is generated by most games. (At least, that is the case in most older games—the tendency with modern games is to use positional sound.)

The DirectX Audio component that handles ambient sound is called DirectSound8. DirectSound is the primary sound mixer for DirectX. While the new version is technically called DirectX Audio, it really boils down to using the individual components of DirectX 8.0. DirectSound8 is one such component, capable of mixing and playing multi-channel wave sound buffers.

Creating the DirectSound8 Object

In order to use DirectSound, you must first create a standard DirectX8 object, which is then used to create DirectSound. You can declare the objects like this:

```
Dim objDX As New DirectX8
Dim objDS As DirectSound8
```

Once the objects have been declared, you can then instantiate them like this:

```
Set objDX = New DirectX8
Set objDS = objDX.DirectSoundCreate("")
```

As you can see, the DirectSound object is returned by the `DirectSoundCreate` function. Like all of the major components, DirectSound is initialized and returned by the main DirectX8 object.

Creating the DirectSoundSecondaryBuffer8 Object

The next step to playing sound with DirectSound involves creating a buffer to hold a waveform that is loaded from a wave file. The object that holds the wave is called DirectSoundSecondaryBuffer8. I know this is a large name to have to learn, but it will be second nature to you in time. To create a DirectSound buffer object, you must first declare it in the variable declarations section of the program:

```
Dim Sound1 As DirectSoundSecondaryBuffer8
```

There is no need to `New` the object because it is returned by the wave loader function, which is called `CreateSoundBufferFromFile`. This function returns an object of type—yep, you guessed it—DirectSoundSecondaryBuffer8. (I promise, I won't make you endure that object name much longer.) `CreateSoundBufferFromFile` is a member of the main DirectSound8 object, and can be called like this:

```
Set Sound1 = objDS.CreateSoundBufferFromFile("filename.wav", dsBuf)
```

Mixing Waves with DirectSound8

Strangely enough, the DirectSoundSecondaryBuffer8 object itself is responsible for playing the wave buffer. This is something that you must get used to, after working with Windows API functions and other code that is not object-oriented. A library like DirectSound8 typically has support objects rather than numerous support functions to do all of the work.

To play back a wave sound that has been loaded into a buffer, you simply use the `Play` procedure:

```
Sound1.Play DSBPLAY_DEFAULT
```

There is another option that you can use when calling the `Play` procedure. The DSBPLAY_DEFAULT constant tells the object to just play the wave once and then stop. But another constant called DSBPLAY_LOOPING tells the object to loop the sound, playing it over and over until stopped.

The AmbientSound Program

The AmbientSound program demonstrates how to create and initialize the DirectSound8 object, load a couple of wave files into DirectSound buffers, and then play the waves with automatic mixing support. Since there is not much to this program other than the simple form, I will not bother with a screenshot.

To create this program, simply start a new Standard EXE project and enter the following lines of code into the code window for Form1. The source code will do the rest. This program is a simple demonstration of how to use DirectSound. To see how to create 3-D positional sound output, refer to the PositionalSound program later in this chapter.

```
'-------------------------------------------------------------------
' Visual Basic Game Programming With DirectX
' Chapter 11 : Playing Sound and Music With DirectX Audio
' AmbientSound Source Code File
'-------------------------------------------------------------------
Option Explicit
Option Base 0

'program controls
Dim WithEvents Command1  As CommandButton
Dim WithEvents Command2 As CommandButton

'program variables
Dim objDX As New DirectX8
Dim objDS As DirectSound8
Dim Sound1 As DirectSoundSecondaryBuffer8
Dim Sound2 As DirectSoundSecondaryBuffer8
```

The Form_Load procedure sets up the form and creates the buttons that let you play the sounds in this program. Form_Load also initializes the DirectX and DirectSound objects and then loads the two wave files.

```
Private Sub Form_Load()
    'set up the main form
    Form1.Caption = "AmbientSound"
    Form1.KeyPreview = True
    Form1.Visible = True

    'add the first button to the form
    Set Command1 = Controls.Add("VB.CommandButton", "Command1")
```

```
    Command1.Caption = "Halleleuia"
    Command1.Left = 45
    Command1.Top = 30
    Command1.Width = 250
    Command1.Height = 70
    Command1.Visible = True

    'add the second button to the form
    Set Command2 = Controls.Add("VB.CommandButton", "Command2")
    Command2.Caption = "Punch"
    Command2.Left = 45
    Command2.Top = 130
    Command2.Width = 250
    Command2.Height = 70
    Command2.Visible = True

    'create the DirectX8 object
    Set objDX = New DirectX8

    'create the DirectSound8 object
    Set objDS = objDX.DirectSoundCreate("")
    If Err.Number <> 0 Then
        MsgBox "Error creating DirectSound object"
        Shutdown
    End If

    'set the priority level for DirectSound
    objDS.SetCooperativeLevel Me.hWnd, DSSCL_PRIORITY

    'load the wave files
    Set Sound1 = LoadSound(App.Path & "\halleleuia.wav")
    Set Sound2 = LoadSound(App.Path & "\punch.wav")
End Sub
```

The next three procedures are simple user interface routines. Form_KeyDown causes the program to end if you hit ESC, while the two button click events play the wave files.

```
Private Sub Form_KeyDown(KeyCode As Integer, Shift As Integer)
    If KeyCode = 27 Then Shutdown
End Sub
```

```
Private Sub Command1_Click()
    'play the halleleuia sound
    PlaySound Sound1, False, False
End Sub

Private Sub Command2_Click()
    'play the punch sound
    PlaySound Sound2, False, False
End Sub
```

Now for the LoadSound function. You were probably expecting this to be a two-pager, but it is actually quite simple to load a wave file with DirectSound. First, set up a DSBUFFERDESC structure and tell it that the sound buffer will be a simple static buffer (in other words, there will be no special effects applied to the sound). Next, the CreateSoundBufferFromFile function (a member of DirectSound8) loads and returns the wave file into a DirectSoundSecondaryBuffer8 reference variable. Once this is done, the wave file is ready to be played.

```
Public Function LoadSound(ByVal sFilename As String) _
    As DirectSoundSecondaryBuffer8
    Dim dsBuf As DSBUFFERDESC

    'set up sound buffer for normal playback
    dsBuf.lFlags = DSBCAPS_STATIC

    'load wave file into DirectSound buffer
    Set LoadSound = objDS.CreateSoundBufferFromFile(sFilename, dsBuf)
    If Err.Number <> 0 Then
        MsgBox "Error loading sound file: " & sFilename
        Shutdown
    End If
End Function
```

Now for the PlaySound procedure. This is also surprisingly short and easy to understand, because the DirectSound buffer object does all the work. This version of PlaySound (yes, there will be others in the chapter) first checks to see whether the bCloseFirst parameter wants it to first terminate any sound currently playing in that buffer. Then it checks to see if the bLoopSound parameter determines whether the sound will be played back continuously in a loop (in which case the only way to stop it is to call PlaySound again with the bCloseFirst parameter set to True).

```
Public Sub PlaySound(ByRef Sound As DirectSoundSecondaryBuffer8, _
    ByVal bCloseFirst As Boolean, ByVal bLoopSound As Boolean)
```

```
    'stop currently playing waves?
    If bCloseFirst Then
        Sound.Stop
        Sound.SetCurrentPosition 0
    End If

    'loop the sound?
    If bLoopSound Then
        Sound.Play DSBPLAY_LOOPING
    Else
        Sound.Play DSBPLAY_DEFAULT
    End If
End Sub
```

Finally, the Shutdown procedure stops sound playback, deletes objects from memory, and then ends the program.

```
Private Sub Shutdown()
    'stop sound playback
    Sound1.Stop
    Sound2.Stop

    'delete DirectX Audio objects
    Set objDX = Nothing
    Set objDS = Nothing

    'delete waves
    Set Sound1 = Nothing
    Set Sound2 = Nothing

    End
End Sub
```

Now run the program by pressing F5. What do you think of your first experience with DirectSound? It wasn't too bad after all, now was it? Next I'll show you how to play some music.

PROGRAMMING MUSIC

DirectMusic and DirectSound were once separate components of DirectX, along with DirectSound3D. Now these components are integrated into DirectX Audio. What does this mean for DirectX programmers? Basically, these components are still around, and there is not really a component called DirectX Audio. It is just a name that describes the three main components (and their support objects).

DirectMusic is ridiculously complicated when you consider that all it really needs to do is provide a sound and music mixer. Instead, DirectMusic suffers from feature glut in an attempt to provide a multitude of audio features in DirectX Audio. You could literally run a professional music studio with DirectX Audio, because it includes some incredibly advanced new features. However, by avoiding most of the unnecessary features of DirectX Audio and by just focusing on what is needed for a game, the code is much easier to manage.

> **NOTE**
> If you would like to delve into the advanced features of DirectX Audio, pick up one or more references that are listed in Appendix E, "Recommended Reading." Entire volumes have been written about each component of DirectX.

Understanding DirectMusic Audio Paths

One important factor that you should remember is that DirectMusic does not have an audio gain feature, meaning that volume is maxed-out by default. The only option for modifying volume is to reduce the volume of a music sequence. Volume is expressed in hundredths of a decibel and will always be a negative value. If you want to restore volume to maximum, set the volume to zero. This might seem like a strange way to control volume, but just remember that DirectMusic cannot amplify sound.

A DirectMusic audio path is an object that controls the output of a single channel. Any changes made to that channel affect all sound operations that are routed through the channel, such as wave, MIDI, or segment playback.

MIDI Versus Wave Music

Why would anyone consider using MIDI today when it is far more exciting to go with digital background music, such as MP3? The reason is primarily due to performance and size. A very long MIDI sequence might take up only a few hundred kilobytes, while a lengthy digital sample will require multiple megabytes per minute. While digital music provides the best quality and is the most impressive way to handle background music, there are advantages to using MIDI.

One of the main advantages is the sheer number of public domain MIDI files available on the Internet. There are literally thousands of songs that can be freely used in a game, as long as those songs are not copyrighted. In contrast, digital music must be composed and recorded (or licensed by the original composer or musician).

Playing Background Music

Even the simplest game needs some form of background music, or it is difficult for the player to remain interested in the game. Remember the golden rule of gaming: Any game without sound and music is just a technology demo. It is absolutely essential that you spend some of your development time on a game working on the music and sound effects. In fact, it is probably a good idea to do so during development. As the game takes shape, so should the sounds and music.

Background music should reflect what is going on in the game, and can even be used to evoke the emotions of the player. Consider a scene where a beloved game character dies. Upbeat music would spoil the mood, while dark and menacing background music would fill the player with feelings of remorse and sorrow (or perhaps even anger).

Keep this in mind when working on sections of a game, and try to have different background sequences for different circumstances. Victory should be rewarded with upbeat music, while menacing or dangerous situations should be accompanied by low-beat, low-tempo songs that reinforce the natural emotions that will arise in such a circumstance.

The DirectMusic Program

The DirectMusic program (not a very creative name, I know) is very simple, so that nothing takes away from the code to load and play a music sequence. Basically, this program creates the various objects needed to get a MIDI file loaded and playing without any bells or whistles.

The key objects in this program include DirectMusicLoader8, DirectMusicPerformance8, DirectMusicSegment8, DirectMusicSegmentState8, and DirectMusicAudioPath8. (See, I warned you that DirectMusic was needlessly complicated.) To make things easier, I have created a couple of classes that take care of these objects internally and just provide a means to load and play a MIDI file. In the meantime, I'll show you how to do it with regular code.

You might be surprised by how easy it is to actually load a MIDI file, considering the long list of objects listed above. But here is all you need to do to load a MIDI file into a DirectMusic segment:

```
Set dmSeg = dmLoader.LoadSegment(sFile)
dmSeg.SetStandardMidiFile
dmSeg.Download dmPath
```

Surprised? I sure was the first time I came across this code. It is similarly easy to play the MIDI sequence (which is loaded into the segment object):

```
Set dmSegState = dmPerf.PlaySegmentEx(dmSeg, 0, 0, Nothing, dmPath)
```

This function, PlaySegmentEx, is all that is required to play a MIDI file once it has been loaded into a segment.

Now, I'm a firm believer in the concept that practice makes perfect. So, without further ado, here is the listing for the DirectMusic program. Like the AmbientSound program earlier, this program is a simple Standard EXE project, and you can type the code into the code window for Form1.

```
'-------------------------------------------------------------------
' Visual Basic Game Programming With DirectX
' Chapter 11 : Playing Sound and Music With DirectX Audio
' DirectMusic Source Code File
'-------------------------------------------------------------------
Option Explicit
Option Base 0

'Windows API functions and structures
Private Declare Function GetTickCount _
    Lib "kernel32" () As Long

'main DirectX object
Dim objDX As New DirectX8

'DirectMusic loader object
Private dmLoader As DirectMusicLoader8

'DirectMusic performance object
Private dmPerf As DirectMusicPerformance8

'DirectMusic segment object
Private dmSeg As DirectMusicSegment8

'DirectMusic segment state object
Private dmSegState As DirectMusicSegmentState8

'DirectMusic audio path object
Private dmPath As DirectMusicAudioPath8

'DirectMusic audio parameters
Dim dmA As DMUS_AUDIOPARAMS
```

The Form_Load procedure initializes DirectX8 and the DirectMusic objects used in this program. Notice how the DirectX object is needed to create all of the other objects. Next the audio path is created, the MIDI file is loaded into memory, and then PlayMusic is called.

```
Private Sub Form_Load()
    'set up line-by-line error checking
    On Local Error Resume Next

    'create the DirectX object
    Set objDX = New DirectX8

    'create the DirectMusic loader object
    Set dmLoader = objDX.DirectMusicLoaderCreate
    If Err.Number <> 0 Then
        MsgBox "Error creating DirectMusic loader object"
        Shutdown
    End If

    'create the DirectMusic performance object
    Set dmPerf = objDX.DirectMusicPerformanceCreate
    If Err.Number <> 0 Then
        MsgBox "Error creating DirectMusic performance object"
        Shutdown
    End If

    'initialize DirectMusic
    dmPerf.InitAudio Me.hWnd, DMUS_AUDIOF_ALL, dmA
    If Err.Number <> 0 Then
        MsgBox "Error initializing DirectMusic audio system"
        Shutdown
    End If

    'create the DirectMusic audio path object
    Set dmPath = dmPerf.CreateStandardAudioPath( _
        DMUS_APATH_DYNAMIC_3D, 64, True)

    If Err.Number <> 0 Then
        MsgBox "Error creating DirectMusic audio path object"
        Shutdown
    End If
```

```
    'load the MIDI file
    If Not LoadMusic(App.Path & "\symphony.rmi") Then
        MsgBox "Error loading music file symphony.rmi"
        Shutdown
    End If

    'print some music information to the immediate window
    Debug.Print "Length: " & dmSeg.GetLength
    Debug.Print "Name: " & dmSeg.GetName
    Debug.Print "Repeats: " & CBool(dmSeg.GetRepeats)
    Debug.Print "Clock time: " & dmPerf.GetClockTime
    Debug.Print "Music time: " & dmPerf.GetMusicTime
    Debug.Print "Latency time: " & dmPerf.GetLatencyTime

    PlayMusic
End Sub
```

There is only one user interface support procedure in this program. That's because this is sort of a dumb program. Don't get me wrong—this program does a lot as far as the music playback goes, but it sort of ignores the user, and that's not usually the best way to go in a VB program. But this is just a demo, and the code is simple this way.

```
Private Sub Form_QueryUnload(Cancel As Integer, UnloadMode As Integer)
    Shutdown
End Sub
```

Now for the LoadMusic function! Okay, maybe it's not really all that exciting. But this function does a lot more work than the LoadSound function in the AmbientSound program. First, the function determines whether a MIDI sequence is already playing by checking to see if dmSeg has been initialized. If a sequence has already been loaded, it is removed from memory. Then the MIDI file is loaded by the LoadSegment function (which is a member of DirectMusicLoader8). Okay, now the song is ready to be played, right?

Wrong! For some reason, DirectMusic forces you to download the segment into an audio path for playback. I think that should have been included in the LoadSegment function, but for some reason the authors of DirectMusic chose to put the file loader into a separate object (and for the life of me, I do not know why).

```
Public Function LoadMusic(sFile As String) As Boolean
    On Local Error Resume Next
    LoadMusic = False
    If Len(sFile) = 0 Then Exit Function
```

```
    'remove any existing segment
    If Not (dmSeg Is Nothing) Then
        dmSeg.Unload dmPath
        Set dmSeg = Nothing
    End If

    'load the MIDI file
    Set dmSeg = dmLoader.LoadSegment(sFile)
    If Err.Number <> 0 Then Exit Function
    dmSeg.SetStandardMidiFile

    'download the music segment
    dmSeg.Download dmPath
    If Err.Number <> 0 Then Exit Function

    'success
    LoadMusic = True
End Function
```

PlayMusic and StopMusic include the functionality to play and stop playback of a MIDI file (or any other type of sound that is loaded). It seems confusing with so many objects, until you see which object is actually calling the PlaySegmentEx function to start playback. It is called by the performance object, with the segment and audio path objects included as parameters. This sort of makes sense if you think of the audio path as the destination for the music playback, while the segment is the source of the music.

```
Private Sub PlayMusic()
    If dmSeg Is Nothing Then Exit Sub
    Set dmSegState = dmPerf.PlaySegmentEx(dmSeg, 0, 0, Nothing, dmPath)
End Sub

Private Sub StopMusic()
    If dmSeg Is Nothing Then Exit Sub
    dmPerf.StopEx dmSeg, 0, 0
End Sub
```

As usual, the Shutdown procedure cleans up the program by deleting objects, freeing up memory, and then ending the program.

```
Private Sub Shutdown()
    'stop music playback
    If Not (dmPerf Is Nothing) Then
        dmPerf.StopEx dmSeg, 0, 0
        dmPerf.CloseDown
    End If

    'delete DirectMusic objects
    Set dmLoader = Nothing
    Set dmSeg = Nothing
    Set dmPath = Nothing
    Set dmPerf = Nothing
    Set objDX = Nothing

    End
End Sub
```

All finished! Now run the program. If you receive a strange error message, that is usually just DirectMusic complaining that the MIDI file was not found. Be sure to copy the MIDI file (which is called symphony.rmi for this program) from the CD-ROM to your project directory, or just search the Web for one of your favorite tunes. If all goes well, you should hear Beethoven tickling the virtual keys.

PROGRAMMING 3-D POSITIONAL SOUND

Positional and environmental sound is a fascinating subject, and I wish I had more time to spend on it than just this small part of the chapter. Indeed, an entire book could be written about this subject alone.

Positional sound first started to become popular with first-person shooters like *Doom*, which actually included a working positional sound mixer! The ability to sense where a sound is coming from is a fascinating feature in a game, and is capable of affecting multiple emotions in the player.

The ability to program positional sound was once (and actually still is) an extremely complicated subject involving some heavy mathematics. It was a feature that once set some games apart from the rest, something that was often bragged about by developers. But now positional sound is built into DirectSound3D, so you do not need to know anything about how it works in order to use it!

That's great news, wouldn't you agree? Now for a little tutorial on 3-D sound.

Understanding 3-D Sound

Positional 3-D sound involves tricking the ears into hearing a sound as if it is coming from a certain direction, while in reality the sounds are simply being coerced into complex patterns and played back through simple speakers or headphones.

My first experience with positional sound absolutely freaked me out! I was listening to Stephen King's audio book, *The Mist*, not realizing that it was one of the first to feature positional sound encoding on a cassette tape. I was lying on my living room couch when I started to hear sounds coming from the back room. Then the sounds seemed to be coming from the kitchen, and then from all around. This really excited me, and to this day I have been fascinated by the subject of 3-D sound. I believe it is a subject that has still not come into its own (and hopefully will receive more attention in future games and audio productions).

Positional sound is created either with a DSP (*Digital Signal Processor*) in real time, or with an expensive studio sound mixer. The latter was used to create *The Mist*, while the former is now available in most modern sound cards, and is fully supported by DirectX 8.0. To take advantage of 3-D positional sound in your games, all you need to do is learn how to use the DirectSound3D object. It is surprisingly easy to use, attached to the regular DirectSound object after a wave has been loaded.

Applying Positional Sound to a Sound Buffer

Positional sound requires that you define the position of the source using a simple structure that contains an X, Y, and Z value. But first you must set up the DirectSound3DBuffer object. When setting up a DirectSound buffer for normal ambient playback, you will generally use the DSBCAPS_STATIC constant, like this:

```
dsBuf.lFlags = DSBCAPS_STATIC
```

But in order to support positional sound, this option must be set to support 3-D sound and volume:

```
dsBuf.lFlags = DSBCAPS_CTRL3D Or DSBCAPS_CTRLVOLUME
dsBuf.guid3DAlgorithm = GUID_DS3DALG_HRTF_LIGHT
```

After loading the wave file with the `CreateSoundBufferFromFile` function, you can then create the DirectSound3DBuffer object and attach it to the sound buffer:

```
Set ds3dBuffer = LoadSound.GetDirectSound3DBuffer
ds3dBuffer.SetConeAngles DS3D_MINCONEANGLE, 100, DS3D_IMMEDIATE
ds3dBuffer.SetConeOutsideVolume -400, DS3D_IMMEDIATE
```

Obviously there are a lot of options available for the SetConeAngles and SetConeOutsideVolume procedures, but I have just skimmed over them in order to get something functional. Again, recommendations for detailed coverage of some DirectX Audio features can be found in Appendix E, "Recommended Reading."

The PositionalSound Program

To demonstrate how to use 3-D positional sound in practice, rather than just in theory, I've written a program called PositionalSound. This program features two wave files: Halleleuia.wav and Punch.wav. These sounds are then played at a random position in DirectSound3D space to demonstrate how the process works. It is surprisingly easy to set the X,Y,Z values of the sound source and then play the sound normally.

Note that positional sound only works with monaural sound files. If you load a stereo wave file into a sound buffer, the positional sound effects might not work (unless the sound driver is capable of converting the wave). You can see this firsthand by running the PositionalSound program and trying the Halleleuia.wav sound, which is stereo. It will sound like an ambient sound every time, while the Punch.wav sound is positioned randomly around the listener. Some sounds cards are capable of handling stereo waves, while others are not.

Following is the source code for the PositionalSound program. You will notice that this program is similar to the AmbientSound program, but includes the new DirectSound3D objects and code. I have set key lines of code (those that differ from the AmbientSound program) in bold text so they will be easily identifiable. Go ahead and click each of the buttons in the program multiple times to hear the sounds played as if from different positions around the room. Each time you play one of the sounds, it will seem to be coming from a different location.

```
'--------------------------------------------------------------
' Visual Basic Game Programming With DirectX
' Chapter 11 : Playing Sound and Music With DirectX Audio
' PositionalSound Source Code File
'--------------------------------------------------------------
Option Explicit
Option Base 0

'Windows API functions and structures
Private Declare Function GetTickCount _
    Lib "kernel32" () As Long

'program controls
Dim WithEvents Command1  As CommandButton
Dim WithEvents Command2 As CommandButton
```

```
'DirectSound objects
Dim objDX As New DirectX8
Dim objDS As DirectSound8

'3-D positional variables
Dim ds3dBuffer As DirectSound3DBuffer8
Dim vPos As D3DVECTOR

'DirectSound wave buffers
Dim Sound1 As DirectSoundSecondaryBuffer8
Dim Sound2 As DirectSoundSecondaryBuffer8
```

The Form_Load procedure initializes the form and creates the two buttons used to play back the waves. After creating the DirectX and DirectSound objects, Form_Load then loads the wave files into memory.

```
Private Sub Form_Load()
    Randomize GetTickCount

    'set up the main form
    Form1.Caption = "PositionalSound"
    Form1.KeyPreview = True
    Form1.Visible = True

    'add the first button to the form
    Set Command1 = Controls.Add("VB.CommandButton", "Command1")
    Command1.Caption = "Halleleuia"
    Command1.Left = 45
    Command1.Top = 30
    Command1.Width = 250
    Command1.Height = 70
    Command1.Visible = True

    'add the second button to the form
    Set Command2 = Controls.Add("VB.CommandButton", "Command2")
    Command2.Caption = "Punch"
    Command2.Left = 45
    Command2.Top = 130
    Command2.Width = 250
    Command2.Height = 70
    Command2.Visible = True
```

```
    'create the DirectX8 object
    Set objDX = New DirectX8

    'create the DirectSound8 object
    Set objDS = objDX.DirectSoundCreate("")
    If Err.Number <> 0 Then
        MsgBox "Error creating DirectSound object"
        Shutdown
    End If

    'set the priority level for DirectSound
    objDS.SetCooperativeLevel Me.hWnd, DSSCL_PRIORITY

    'load the wave files
    Set Sound1 = LoadSound(App.Path & "\halleleuia.wav")
    Set Sound2 = LoadSound(App.Path & "\punch.wav")
End Sub
```

Now for the user interface procedures. Form_KeyDown simply detects when the ESC key is pressed, and ends the program by calling Shutdown. The two button click events are similar, assigning random values to the X,Y,Z elements in the D3DVECTOR structure before playing the sound with PlaySound.

```
Private Sub Form_KeyDown(KeyCode As Integer, Shift As Integer)
    If KeyCode = 27 Then Shutdown
End Sub

Private Sub Command1_Click()
    'play the halleleuia sound
    vPos.x = Random(10) - 5
    vPos.y = Random(10) - 5
    vPos.z = Random(10) - 5
    PlaySound Sound1, True, False, vPos
End Sub

Private Sub Command2_Click()
    'play the punch sound
    vPos.x = Random(10) - 5
    vPos.y = Random(10) - 5
    vPos.z = Random(10) - 5
    PlaySound Sound2, True, False, vPos
End Sub
```

```
Public Function Random(ByVal lNum As Long) As Long
    Random = CLng(lNum * Rnd)
End Function
```

This version of LoadSound differs from the one found in the AmbientSound program in that it sets up the buffer for positional playback. After loading the wave into memory, the DirectSound3D object is created and assigned to the sound buffer. The result is that DirectSound3D will process the sound before it is sent out to DirectSound for playback. You might think of DirectSound3D as middleware that intercepts the wave output and tweaks the bits for positional sound.

```
Public Function LoadSound(ByVal sFilename As String) _
    As DirectSoundSecondaryBuffer8
    Dim dsBuf As DSBUFFERDESC

    'set up sound buffer for positional playback
    dsBuf.lFlags = DSBCAPS_CTRL3D Or DSBCAPS_CTRLVOLUME
    dsBuf.guid3DAlgorithm = GUID_DS3DALG_HRTF_LIGHT

    'load wave file into a DirectSound buffer
    Set LoadSound = objDS.CreateSoundBufferFromFile(sFilename, dsBuf)
    If Err.Number <> 0 Then
        MsgBox "Error loading sound file: " & sFilename
        Shutdown
    End If

    'set the position
    Set ds3dBuffer = LoadSound.GetDirectSound3DBuffer
    ds3dBuffer.SetConeAngles DS3D_MINCONEANGLE, 100, DS3D_IMMEDIATE
    ds3dBuffer.SetConeOutsideVolume -400, DS3D_IMMEDIATE
End Function
```

This PlaySound procedure is similar to the one in the AmbientSound program, except for a new line of code in the middle. This is a call to SetPosition, which tells DirectSound3D how to manipulate the sound to make it appear to come from a position somewhere around the listener.

```
Public Sub PlaySound(ByRef Sound As DirectSoundSecondaryBuffer8, _
    ByVal bCloseFirst As Boolean, ByVal bLoopSound As Boolean, _
    ByRef vPos As D3DVECTOR)

    'stop currently playing waves?
    If bCloseFirst Then
```

```
            Sound.Stop
            Sound.SetCurrentPosition 0
        End If

        'set the position
        ds3dBuffer.SetPosition vPos.x, vPos.y, vPos.z, DS3D_IMMEDIATE

        'loop the sound?
        If bLoopSound Then
            Sound.Play DSBPLAY_LOOPING
        Else
            Sound.Play DSBPLAY_DEFAULT
        End If
End Sub
```

The Shutdown procedure deletes objects, frees up memory, and ends the program.

```
Private Sub Shutdown()
    'stop sound playback
    Sound1.Stop
    Sound2.Stop

    'delete DirectX Audio objects
    Set objDX = Nothing
    Set objDS = Nothing
    Set ds3dBuffer = Nothing

    'delete waves
    Set Sound1 = Nothing
    Set Sound2 = Nothing

    End
End Sub
```

Now you should be able to run the program. What do you think of the positional playback? If the sound output is poor in quality, or if it does not sound like it is positional at all, it might be possible that your sound card does not support DirectSound3D. More likely it was a simple typo that caused the problem.

Now for some support code to put all of this new audio functionality into classes so it will be easy to reuse the code.

ENCAPSULATING DIRECTX AUDIO

DirectSound, DirectMusic, and DirectSound3D are fairly easy to use, as the previous programs have demonstrated. However, daily use of this code would result in a game project that is difficult to manage, and objects that are easy to miss when freeing up memory. Therefore, to make it easier to use DirectX Audio, I have created four new classes to encapsulate the functionality of the four primary objects in this chapter.

The DirectSound8 Class

The clsDirectSound8 class includes all of the key code developed in the AmbientSound program, encapsulated so it is easy to include in new projects (such as the games at the end of the book). Following is the code listing for the clsDirectSound8 class. Be sure to save this code in a file called DirectSound8.cls, and include it in any new project you create that needs sound. You can also copy this class from the chapter directory on the CD-ROM to your hard drive.

This is a fairly short class because it just incorporates the major objects needed to get DirectSound up and running. The clsDSWave8 class that follows will actually include the functionality to load and play waves.

```
'----------------------------------------------------------------------
' Visual Basic Game Programming With DirectX
' Chapter 11 : Playing Sound and Music With DirectX Audio
' clsDirectSound8 Source Code File
'----------------------------------------------------------------------
Option Explicit
Option Base 0

Dim objDX As New DirectX8
Dim objDS As DirectSound8

Private Sub Class_Terminate()
    Set objDS = Nothing
    Set objDX = Nothing
End Sub

Public Property Get DSObj() As DirectSound8
    Set DSObj = objDS
End Property
```

```
Public Property Get DXObj() As DirectX8
    Set DXObj = objDX
End Property

Public Sub Startup(ByRef lWindowHandle As Long)
    'create the DirectX8 object
    Set objDX = New DirectX8

    'create the DirectSound8 object
    Set objDS = objDX.DirectSoundCreate("")

    'set the priority level for DirectSound
    objDS.SetCooperativeLevel lWindowHandle, DSSCL_PRIORITY
End Sub
```

The DSWave8 Class

The clsDSWave8 class encapsulates the functionality of a DirectSound wave buffer, and includes functions to load and play waves. This class works closely with the clsDirectSound8 class that was covered earlier, so be sure to include both classes in any new game project that needs to support sound.

```
'--------------------------------------------------------------------
' Visual Basic Game Programming With DirectX
' Chapter 11 : Playing Sound and Music With DirectX Audio
' clsDSWave8 Source Code File
'--------------------------------------------------------------------
Option Explicit
Option Base 0

'DirectSound objects
Dim dsBuffer As DirectSoundSecondaryBuffer8
Dim ds3dBuffer As DirectSound3DBuffer8

'DirectSound structures
Dim format As WAVEFORMATEX
Dim dsBuf As DSBUFFERDESC
Dim vPos As D3DVECTOR
```

```
'program variables
Dim bInterrupt As Boolean
Dim bLooping As Boolean
Dim bPositional As Boolean
```

The Class_Initialize and Class_Terminate procedures set up some local variables and free up resources, respectively. Class_Terminate also calls StopSound in case sound playback is still in progress when the class terminates.

```
Private Sub Class_Initialize()
    bInterrupt = False
    bLooping = False
    bPositional = False
End Sub

Private Sub Class_Terminate()
    StopSound
    Set ds3dBuffer = Nothing
    Set dsBuffer = Nothing
End Sub
```

If you worked through the DirectDraw chapter earlier (Chapter 10, "Diving into DirectDraw"), you might be familiar with the object variables. Basically, DSBObj is a property of clsDSWave8 that gives other classes in your project access to the internal DirectSoundSecondaryBuffer8 object. This is to accommodate functionality that I have not foreseen and is automatically included in the class. This is generally a good idea when wrapping a class around a library that is likely to be updated regularly (as is the case with DirectX).

```
Public Property Get DSBObj() As DirectSoundSecondaryBuffer8
    Set DSBObj = dsBuffer
End Property

Public Property Set DSBObj(ByRef dssbNewValue _
    As DirectSoundSecondaryBuffer8)
    Set dsBuffer = dssbNewValue
End Property
```

The class variables for clsDSWave8 provide some internal information about the wave buffer, such as frequency, channels, bits per sample, and size of the buffer.

```
Public Property Get Interrupt() As Boolean
    Interrupt = bInterrupt
End Property

Public Property Let Interrupt(ByVal bNewValue As Boolean)
    bInterrupt = bNewValue
End Property

Public Property Get Looping() As Boolean
    Looping = bLooping
End Property

Public Property Let Looping(ByVal bNewValue As Boolean)
    bLooping = bNewValue
End Property

Public Property Get Positional() As Boolean
    Positional = bPositional
End Property

Public Property Let Positional(ByVal bNewValue As Boolean)
    bPositional = bNewValue
End Property

Public Property Get Frequency() As Long
    Frequency = dsBuffer.GetFrequency
End Property

Public Property Get Channels() As Long
    dsBuffer.GetFormat format
    Channels = format.nChannels
End Property

Public Property Get Samples() As Long
    dsBuffer.GetFormat format
    Samples = format.lSamplesPerSec
End Property

Public Property Get BitsPerSample() As Long
    dsBuffer.GetFormat format
    BitsPerSample = format.nBitsPerSample
End Property
```

```
Public Property Get Size() As Long
    dsBuffer.GetFormat format
    Size = format.nSize
End Property
```

SetPosition is the procedure that tells DirectSound3D where the sound source should be located in the spherical region around the listener, using the D3DVECTOR values X,Y, and Z.

```
Public Sub SetPosition(ByVal X As Long, ByVal Y As Long, _
    ByVal Z As Long)
    vPos.X = X
    vPos.Y = Y
    vPos.Z = Z
End Sub
```

Okay, here we are back at the LoadSound function again. This version is a little different from the one found in the AmbientSound and PositionalSound programs earlier, because it now looks to the class properties to determine whether 3-D positional sound should be used. The properties are great because they keep the number of parameters for the function down to a minimum.

```
Public Function LoadSound(ByRef objDS As clsDirectSound8, _
    ByVal sFilename As String)
    If bPositional Then
        'set buffer parameters to accept positional data
        dsBuf.lFlags = DSBCAPS_CTRL3D Or DSBCAPS_CTRLVOLUME
        dsBuf.guid3DAlgorithm = GUID_DS3DALG_HRTF_LIGHT
    Else
        'set buffer parameter for normal playback
        dsBuf.lFlags = DSBCAPS_STATIC
    End If

    'load wave file into DirectSound buffer
    Set dsBuffer = Nothing
    Set dsBuffer = objDS.DSObj.CreateSoundBufferFromFile(sFilename, _
        dsBuf)

    'set positional sound environment
    If bPositional Then
        Set ds3dBuffer = Nothing
```

```
            Set ds3dBuffer = dsBuffer.GetDirectSound3DBuffer
            ds3dBuffer.SetConeAngles DS3D_MINCONEANGLE, 100, _
                DS3D_IMMEDIATE
            ds3dBuffer.SetConeOutsideVolume -400, DS3D_IMMEDIATE
        End If
End Function
```

The last procedure of this class is PlaySound. This version does not even have any parameters because the information is now available in the class properties. This procedure checks to see whether the sound should be interrupted and whether positional sound is being used. PlaySound then calls the Play procedure of DirectSoundSecondaryBuffer8 to actually output the wave.

Likewise, StopSound terminates any sound that is still in the buffer.

```
Public Sub PlaySound()
    'stop currently playing waves?
    If bInterrupt Then
        StopSound
    End If

    'set position of sound source
    If bPositional Then
        ds3dBuffer.SetPosition vPos.X, vPos.Y, vPos.Z, DS3D_IMMEDIATE
    End If

    'loop the sound?
    If bLooping Then
        dsBuffer.Play DSBPLAY_LOOPING
    Else
        dsBuffer.Play DSBPLAY_DEFAULT
    End If
End Sub

Public Sub StopSound()
    dsBuffer.Stop
    dsBuffer.SetCurrentPosition 0
End Sub
```

Keep this class and the last one handy, because I will show you how to use them in a program later.

The DirectMusic8 Class

Like the DirectSound classes, there are two new classes for DirectMusic as well. The first class is clsDirectMusic8, but it is significantly more complex than the one-page listing for clsDirectSound8 earlier. The DirectMusic8 class contains the DirectMusicPerformance8 and DirectMusicAudioPath8 objects. Later, I will introduce you to another function that manages the MIDI sequence.

```
'------------------------------------------------------------------
' Visual Basic Game Programming With DirectX
' Chapter 11 : Playing Sound and Music With DirectX Audio
' clsDirectMusic8 Source Code File
'------------------------------------------------------------------
Option Explicit
Option Base 0

'main DirectX object
Dim objDX As New DirectX8

'DirectMusic performance object
Private dmPerf As DirectMusicPerformance8

'DirectMusic audio path object
Private dmPath As DirectMusicAudioPath8

'DirectMusic audio parameters
Dim dmA As DMUS_AUDIOPARAMS
```

The class initialization and termination procedures automatically create and then delete objects used in the class, respectively.

```
Private Sub Class_Initialize()
    'create the DirectX object
    Set objDX = New DirectX8
End Sub

Private Sub Class_Terminate()
    'stop music playback
    If Not (dmPerf Is Nothing) Then
        dmPerf.CloseDown
    End If
```

```
        'delete DirectMusic objects
        Set dmPath = Nothing
        Set dmPerf = Nothing
        Set objDX = Nothing
End Sub
```

Now for the properties! I always enjoy working with properties because they simplify the code enormously. Just look at some of the object names and function calls inside these properties. Were it not for this class and its properties, you would have to look up the references for these functions and procedures the hard way. That's one of the greatest benefits of wrapping untamed code inside a class.

```
Public Property Let Volume(ByVal lNewValue As Long)
    If lNewValue <= 0 Then
        dmPath.SetVolume lNewValue, 0
    End If
End Property

Public Property Get ClockTime() As Long
    ClockTime = dmPerf.GetClockTime
End Property

Public Property Get MusicTime() As Long
    MusicTime = dmPerf.GetMusicTime
End Property

Public Property Get LatencyTime() As Long
    LatencyTime = dmPerf.GetLatencyTime
End Property

Public Property Get DXObj() As DirectX8
    Set DXObj = objDX
End Property
```

I'm sure you will recall seeing an object variable earlier in this chapter. The object variables for clsDirectMusic8 are called DMPerfObj and DMPathObj, and are used by the SoundTest program later in this chapter.

```
Public Property Get DMPerfObj() As DirectMusicPerformance8
    Set DMPerfObj = dmPerf
End Property
```

```
Public Property Get DMPathObj() As DirectMusicAudioPath8
    Set DMPathObj = dmPath
End Property
```

The Startup function is something of a standard in the classes I have created thus far, so I have decided to keep using it any time a class needs to be initialized. It's too bad this isn't VB.NET code, or the Startup code could simply be put into the class constructor instead. Of course, VB.NET adds its own complexity to the mix, so it's just as well.

```
Public Function Startup(ByVal lWindowHandle As Long) As Boolean
    On Local Error Resume Next
    Startup = False

    'create the DirectMusic performance object
    Set dmPerf = objDX.DirectMusicPerformanceCreate
    If Err.Number <> 0 Then Exit Function

    'initialize DirectMusic
    dmPerf.InitAudio lWindowHandle, DMUS_AUDIOF_ALL, dmA
    If Err.Number <> 0 Then Exit Function

    'create the DirectMusic audio path object
    Set dmPath = dmPerf.CreateStandardAudioPath( _
        DMUS_APATH_DYNAMIC_3D, 64, True)

    If Err.Number <> 0 Then Exit Function
    Startup = True
End Function
```

The DMSequence8 Class

The clsDMSequence8 class supports the DirectMusic class (which is called clsDirectMusic8) by providing an easy interface for loading and playing a MIDI sequence from an .rmi or .mid file. This class incorporates the DirectMusicLoader8, DirectMusicSegment8, and DirectMusicSegmentState8 objects, and also includes a local reference of clsDirectMusic8.

There is no Class_Initialize for this class, although there is a Class_Terminate procedure that deletes the aforementioned objects from memory when the class terminates.

```
'-------------------------------------------------------------------
' Visual Basic Game Programming With DirectX
' Chapter 11 : Playing Sound and Music With DirectX Audio
' clsDMSequence8 Source Code File
'-------------------------------------------------------------------
Option Explicit
Option Base 0

'local reference to clsDirectMusic8
Private dmusic As clsDirectMusic8

'DirectMusic loader object
Private dmLoader As DirectMusicLoader8

'DirectMusic segment object
Private dmSeg As DirectMusicSegment8

'DirectMusic segment state object
Private dmSegState As DirectMusicSegmentState8

Private Sub Class_Terminate()
    Set dmLoader = Nothing
    Set dmSeg = Nothing
    Set dmSegState = Nothing
End Sub
```

The clsDMSequence8 class includes several properties for returning the length and name of the segment, the looping property, and the playing property (which returns true if a sequence is currently playing). Note that if you try to use these properties before first loading a MIDI file, you will get runtime errors, because these properties don't check the validity of the dmSeg object.

```
Public Property Get Length() As Long
    Length = dmSeg.GetLength
End Property

Public Property Get Name() As String
    Name = dmSeg.GetName
End Property

Public Property Get Looping() As Boolean
    Looping = CBool(dmSeg.GetRepeats)
End Property
```

```
Public Property Let Looping(ByVal bNewValue As Boolean)
    dmSeg.SetRepeats (CLng(bNewValue))
End Property

Public Property Get Playing() As Boolean
    Playing = dmusic.DMPerfObj.IsPlaying(dmSeg, dmSegState)
End Property
```

The LoadMusic function loads a MIDI file into memory and sets up the objects needed to play the sequence through the clsDirectMusic8 class, which actually keeps track of the performance and audio path objects. This version of LoadMusic is similar to the one found in the DirectMusic program, although it includes some code that was handled elsewhere in that program (such as the code to create the loader).

```
Public Function LoadMusic(ByRef dm As clsDirectMusic8, _
    ByVal sFile As String) As Boolean
    On Local Error Resume Next
    LoadMusic = False
    If Len(sFile) = 0 Then Exit Function

    'set reference to clsDirectMusic8 object
    Set dmusic = dm
    If Err.Number <> 0 Then Exit Function

    'create the DirectMusic loader object
    Set dmLoader = Nothing
    Set dmLoader = dmusic.DXObj.DirectMusicLoaderCreate
    If Err.Number <> 0 Then Exit Function

    'remove existing segment
    If Not (dmSeg Is Nothing) Then
        dmSeg.Unload dmusic.DMPathObj
        Set dmSeg = Nothing
    End If

    'load the MIDI file
    Set dmSeg = dmLoader.LoadSegment(sFile)
    If Err.Number <> 0 Then Exit Function
    dmSeg.SetStandardMidiFile
```

```
    'download the music segment
    dmSeg.Download dmusic.DMPathObj
    If Err.Number <> 0 Then Exit Function

    'success
    LoadMusic = True
End Function
```

The PlayMusic and StopMusic procedures are just like the ones found in the DirectMusic program. Each procedure checks to make sure the segment exists before calling the appropriate function to play or stop playback.

```
Public Sub PlayMusic()
    If dmSeg Is Nothing Then Exit Sub
    Set dmSegState = dmusic.DMPerfObj.PlaySegmentEx( _
        Seg, 0, 0, Nothing, dmusic.DMPathObj)
End Sub

Public Sub StopMusic()
    If dmSeg Is Nothing Then Exit Sub
    dmusic.DMPerfObj.StopEx dmSeg, 0, 0
End Sub
```

Putting It All Together: The SoundTest Program

Now I'm going to show you how to put the classes to work in a real program called SoundTest. This program has three buttons:

- Halleleuia
- Punch
- Music

Pressing either of the first two buttons results in a wave being played with positional information. Pressing the third button alternates between playing and stopping the MIDI sequence.

Running the SoundTest Program

Figure 11.2 shows the SoundTest program running. Since this is an audio demonstration, there is not much to see in the screenshot, but this program shows just a sample of what you can accomplish with DirectX Audio!

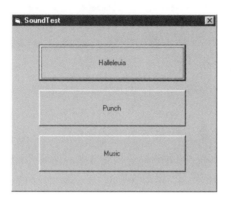

Figure 11.2

The SoundTest program demonstrates mixing MIDI music with positional sound effects.

SoundTest Source Code

The SoundTest source code relies heavily on the four support classes that were developed earlier:

- clsDirectSound8
- clsDSWave8
- clsDirectMusic8
- clsDMSequence8

Be sure to add these four class files to the project before you type in the source code for SoundTest. As usual, you can enter this code in the code window for Form1. To get this program to compile, be sure to reference the DirectX 8 for Visual Basic Type Library in the Project References dialog box.

```
'------------------------------------------------------------------------
' Visual Basic Game Programming With DirectX
' Chapter 11 : Playing Sound and Music With DirectX Audio
' SoundTest Source Code File
'------------------------------------------------------------------------
Option Explicit
Option Base 0

'program controls
Dim WithEvents Command1 As CommandButton
Dim WithEvents Command2 As CommandButton
Dim WithEvents Command3 As CommandButton

'DirectSound objects
Dim dsound As clsDirectSound8
```

```
Dim Sound1 As clsDSWave8
Dim Sound2 As clsDSWave8

'DirectMusic objects
Dim dmusic As clsDirectMusic8
Dim Music1 As clsDMSequence8
```

The Form_Load procedure sets up the form and adds the three buttons to it. Then the objects are initialized and the wave and MIDI files are loaded into memory. Hopefully this code is already familiar to you. If it seems confusing, you might want to review the chapter again to get a better understanding of what is happening. I'm sure it will not be difficult to follow, however, because the classes make the code very easy to read.

```
Private Sub Form_Load()
    On Local Error Resume Next

    'set up the main form
    Form1.Caption = "SoundTest"
    Form1.KeyPreview = True
    Form1.Visible = True

    'add the first button to the form
    Set Command1 = Controls.Add("VB.CommandButton", "Command1")
    Command1.Caption = "Halleleuia"
    Command1.Left = 45
    Command1.Top = 30
    Command1.Width = 250
    Command1.Height = 60
    Command1.Visible = True

    'add the second button to the form
    Set Command2 = Controls.Add("VB.CommandButton", "Command2")
    Command2.Caption = "Punch"
    Command2.Left = 45
    Command2.Top = 105
    Command2.Width = 250
    Command2.Height = 60
    Command2.Visible = True
```

```
    'add the third button to the form
    Set Command3 = Controls.Add("VB.CommandButton", "Command3")
    Command3.Caption = "Music"
    Command3.Left = 45
    Command3.Top = 180
    Command3.Width = 250
    Command3.Height = 60
    Command3.Visible = True

    'create the DirectSound object
    Set dsound = New clsDirectSound8
    dsound.Startup Form1.hWnd

    'load the first wave file
    Set Sound1 = New clsDSWave8
    Sound1.Positional = True
    Sound1.Interrupt = True
    Sound1.LoadSound dsound, App.Path & "\halleleuia.wav"

    'load the second wave file
    Set Sound2 = New clsDSWave8
    Sound2.Positional = True
    Sound2.Interrupt = True
    Sound2.LoadSound dsound, App.Path & "\punch.wav"

    'create the DirectMusic object
    Set dmusic = New clsDirectMusic8
    If Not dmusic.Startup(Form1.hWnd) Then
        MsgBox "Error initializing DirectMusic"
        Shutdown
    End If

    'load MIDI file
    Set Music1 = New clsDMSequence8
    If Not Music1.LoadMusic(dmusic, App.Path & "\symphony.rmi") Then
        MsgBox "Error loading music file symphony.rmi"
        Shutdown
    End If
End Sub
```

The user interface events include Form_KeyDown and click events for the three buttons. The first two buttons set up the position of the sound source and then play back a wave, while the third button starts or stops the MIDI sequence playing.

```
Private Sub Form_KeyDown(KeyCode As Integer, Shift As Integer)
    If KeyCode = 27 Then Shutdown
End Sub


Private Sub Command1_Click()
    'play the halleleuia sound
    Sound1.SetPosition Random(10) - 5, Random(10) - 5, Random(10) - 5
    Sound1.PlaySound
End Sub


Private Sub Command2_Click()
    'play the punch sound
    Sound2.SetPosition Random(10) - 5, Random(10) - 5, Random(10) - 5
    Sound2.PlaySound
End Sub


Private Sub Command3_Click()
    If Music1.Playing Then
        'stop music if already playing
        Music1.StopMusic
    Else
        'set volume to random value
        dmusic.Volume = Random(5000) * -1
        'start music if not already playing
        Music1.PlayMusic
    End If
End Sub
```

Finally, there are two support routines in the SoundTest program. Random is an old friend, having made an appearance in most of the chapters thus far. Shutdown is also becoming popular, because it does a fine job of cleaning up the program before it ends.

```
Public Function Random(ByVal lNum As Long) As Long
    Random = CLng(lNum * Rnd)
End Function
```

```
Private Sub Shutdown()
    'stop sound playback
    Sound1.StopSound
    Sound2.StopSound
    Music1.StopMusic

    'delete objects
    Set Sound1 = Nothing
    Set Sound2 = Nothing
    Set dsound = Nothing
    Set Music1 = Nothing
    Set dmusic = Nothing
    End
End Sub
```

Now run the program and try it out. You might want to start and stop the music several times until it is audible (or, as the case may be, not too loud), because the volume is random. While the music is playing, try playing the wave sounds at the same time. The sounds should be played back at random positions around the listener.

SUMMARY

Well, that about sums up the subject of DirectX Audio. This chapter included an introduction to DirectSound, DirectMusic, and DirectSound3D, and several sample programs to show you how to use these components. Sound effects and music are extremely important in a game, and this chapter has tackled the subject—if not thoroughly, at least functionally.

At this point you should have a formidable collection of code for writing games with Visual Basic. Bitmaps, masks, sprites, double buffers, dirty rectangles, and now sound and music. The collection of game programming classes is growing, and you should be able to write a complete DirectX game at this point. I don't know about you, but I think that's pretty exciting.

But guess what…if you thought the previous subjects were cool, wait until you turn the page and see what comes next. Keyboard, mouse, and joystick support—woo hoo!

CHAPTER 12

GETTING A
HANDLE ON
USER INPUT

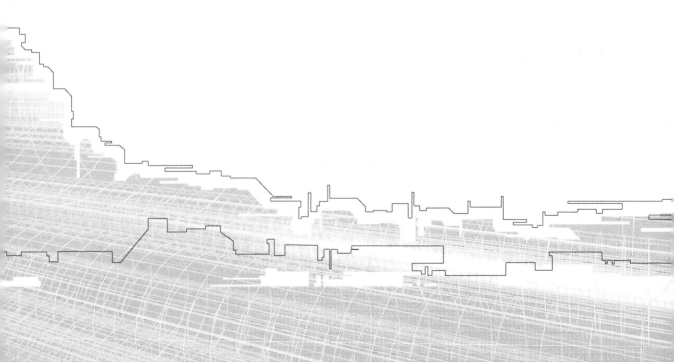

In years past, programming sound and music for games was an enormous task, with custom sound code or expensive third-party sound libraries being the solution for many games. Today, DirectX is the dominant game development library in the world and with it comes DirectInput, a comprehensive library for programming input devices such as the keyboard, mouse, and joystick.

This chapter explores DirectInput in detail, providing all the code you will need to handle the user input for a game written with Visual Basic. From a simple keyboard interface to multi-button mouse routines to an advanced joystick handler with support for digital buttons and analog inputs, this chapter will give you all the tools to handle the user input needs of any game.

This chapter covers the following topics:

- Why User Input is Important
- Choosing the Best Input Device for a Game
- Introduction to DirectInput
- Programming the Keyboard
- Programming the Mouse
- Programming the Joystick

WHY USER INPUT IS IMPORTANT

User input is critical to developing a fun game. After all, what is a game without user input? Something like that is called a technology demo. In this chapter, I will demonstrate how to acquire the keyboard, mouse, and joystick for exclusive use in a game using DirectInput (a component of DirectX).

What about Built-In Visual Basic Support?

Visual Basic has built-in support for detecting mouse and keyboard events, but provides no support for game controllers, such as flight sticks and gamepads. It is definitely possible to write a game without joystick support by using just the standard events that are part of a VB form. However, joysticks are becoming more popular as games are ported from advanced, next-generation video game consoles like the Sony Playstation 2 and Microsoft Xbox, both of which feature multi-function controllers with digital and analog inputs.

Since VB provides no support for joysticks (which seems strange since TRS-80 BASIC umpteen years ago even included joystick support), and Windows API routines are not geared to support the latest game controllers, I am just going to focus on DirectInput, which is a highly-evolved and advanced game input library. After writing sample programs to test the keyboard, mouse, and joystick with DirectInput, I will provide you with a class to handle each device individually. This will allow you, for instance, to write a normal Visual Basic program with joystick support. It is definitely possible to pick and choose DirectX components and use whatever you need. There is no requirement that you use DirectDraw or Direct3D just because you are supporting DirectInput in a program.

DirectInput Support

The most significant benefit to using DirectInput for keyboard, mouse, and joystick input in a game is that there is no need to use a VB form to detect input events (at least for the keyboard and mouse). There is also the additional problem of transforming mouse movement events into a full-screen DirectX program, which might be running in a completely different resolution than the Windows desktop (which is where the VB form is located). Obviously, if you track a mouse click somewhere on the primary form in a game, and the game is actually running at 640×480 (for example), the mouse input events probably will not even show up. (Or more likely, such events will have to be converted to the resolution being used by DirectX.)

CHOOSING THE BEST INPUT DEVICE FOR A GAME

Different types of games are suited for different input devices. RTS (*Real-Time Strategy*) games are not well suited for joysticks because such games involve detailed control (often called "micro-management") over the game that is only possible with the mouse.

The keyboard and mouse combination is the absolute best solution for FPS (*First-Person Shooter*) games like *Quake III*, *Unreal Tournament*, and *Counter-Strike*. Controllers with dual analog sticks are also great for FPS games (such as *HALO*). You can use an advanced PC joystick (like the Logitech WingMan RumblePad USB that is featured in this chapter) in an FPS game, but you probably will not score anywhere near the level of a player who is adept with a keyboard and mouse. The reason? A joystick is a single device. Even with multiple analog sticks and digital buttons, a joystick does not have the precision of a mouse pointer on the screen for targeting. The ability to quickly run, jump, and crouch by pressing closely-coupled keys on the keyboard, along with aiming and firing with a mouse, simply cannot be beat.

It is vitally important that you consider the best form of user input for any game you develop, and then optimize the game for that form of input. Of course you must also provide an alternative means of input for those players who are not adept with your own favorite devices. No matter the argument, you must provide for the three primary forms of input—keyboard, mouse, and joystick. Supporting more exotic input devices (like driving wheels) is then much easier, since DirectInput abstracts such devices into looking like one of the three primary devices (as shown in Figure 12.1).

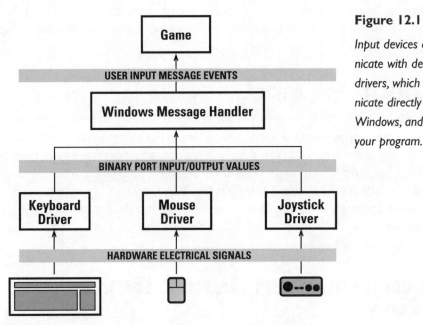

Figure 12.1

Input devices commu-nicate with device drivers, which commu-nicate directly with Windows, and on to your program.

Understanding Keyboard Input

Keyboards have been around since the 1950s—the dawn of the computer revolution. Supporting a keyboard might seem like a given until you actually start to consider how the keyboard should be utilized in a game. The keyboard is always available, while other devices like joysticks are not. Therefore, regardless of your input device of choice, you must support a keyboard in every game, at least minimally.

Most games provide a means to quickly end the game by pressing a simple key combination. This has been somewhat lacking in games of late, but is a feature I highly recommend. Back in the MS-DOS days, it was common for games to use Alt+X, Alt+Q, Ctrl+X, or Ctrl+Q to end the game.

No matter how awesome you think your game is, and no matter if you believe that users will just leave your game running nonstop, you must realize that some players will try out the game and then uninstall it five minutes later with utmost urgency. Player tastes vary widely. There are some players who think *Quake III* is the worst game ever, while at the same time believing that *Wolfenstein 3-D* was the best game ever.

DirectX usually runs in full screen mode, so you should provide a quick method to end the game in a hurry; be sure to use a common key combination. In addition to the combinations listed, the F10 key is often an end game key as well.

Understanding Mouse Input

The mouse is another user input device that has been around for decades, and must be considered required hardware—something you can count on being present in a computer system. Building a game entirely around mouse input is acceptable, as long as basic keyboard functionality is provided as a supplement for power users.

It is often tedious to use a mouse for absolutely everything in a game when shortcut keys may also be used. Power users demand it, so it is a good idea to provide at least minimal keyboard support, even if you plan to target the mouse as the primary means of input for your game. I don't know anyone who uses a joystick to play *Age of Empires II* (in fact, I'm sure the game does not support a joystick), but it would be novel to support everything in the games you develop, as a matter of course.

Understanding Joystick Input

Joysticks have become extremely popular forms of game input in recent years, again due to the proliferation of consoles in the world. With gaming at the top of software development in the computer industry, and also the primary sales point for hardware companies, it is easy to understand how joysticks have become so popular. Quite often a game will be ported from a console (such as the Xbox) to the PC (or vice versa), with the natural result that a game controller will be the primary form of input for the game.

Most consoles now support a keyboard and mouse accessory in addition to the main game controllers, but marketing in the game industry has clearly shown that the vast majority of gamers end up using only what comes in the box, and seldom purchase additional accessories for a video game system.

Joysticks with force feedback are now quite popular, and add an enormous new element to gameplay. One or more simple motors in the controller generate the feedback. Dual-motor force feedback joysticks have the added advantage of being able to simulate impacts coming from any position around the player.

Introduction to DirectInput

DirectInput is the component of DirectX responsible for providing a common interface to user input devices, which allows the programmer to write code for a standard input device category that will then work with any existing or future device. Like the other components of DirectX (such as DirectDraw, Direct3D, DirectSound, and so on), DirectInput is included when you install the DirectX runtime library. If you have not yet installed DirectX 8.0, refer to Chapter 6, "Supercharging Visual Basic with DirectX."

DirectInput does use a callback procedure (called `DirectXEvent8_DXCallback`) for mouse and joystick input, but even these devices must be polled before the callback runs. In order to support this callback procedure you must implement an interface called DirectXEvent8 like this:

```
Implements DirectXEvent8
```

Implementing this interface allows your program to use the procedure for handling DirectInput events. However, there is an alternative way to handle mouse and joystick events—by polling the devices directly. Since callback routines can be difficult to manage, especially in a pre-compiled library, you will need this alternative method in order to create the keyboard, mouse, and joystick classes later in the chapter.

Device Abstraction with DirectInput

DirectInput provides a common interface to literally hundreds of different input devices that might be installed on a system. In the past, a game programmer would have needed to write a custom interface for each device separately (or license an expensive third-party library). DirectInput is free, as is every component of DirectX. Microsoft does not charge royalties to use DirectX, and that's a beautiful thing. But most of us tend to take it for granted now, since Microsoft provides so many software products for free.

One common way to abstract code is to wrap it in a class. Previous chapters have included classes for the major sections of code to make it easier to use that code in new programs. DirectInput uses a callback procedure to report the status of DirectInput devices, making it difficult to wrap the code in a class. However, there is a way you can poll DirectInput devices instead of relying on a callback procedure, thus making it possible to encapsulate DirectInput.

Enumerating Input Devices

Most books and tutorials on DirectX (including the documentation that comes with DirectX) suggest that you enumerate the devices on a system before using them. The reasoning behind this is that DirectX components will detect all installed devices on a system, and it is then up to you to determine which device to use.

In every case I have seen, the default device is the correct one. Is there really a need to enumerate the keyboard and mouse? Of course not! I follow the same logic with joystick code. The only important thing to consider in a Visual Basic game is that a joystick exists. If there are additional game controllers in a system, they are simply ignored.

Adding Joystick Support

You might be surprised at how easy it is to capture a joystick device and then use it in a game. I will walk you through a sample program called JoystickTest that includes just standard DirectInput code (no classes). Most of the code in a joystick handler involves doing something with joystick events after they have been received. Indeed, most of the code for the JoystickTest program is user interface code.

Encapsulating DirectInput

The DirectInput8 object is required to create the input device handlers (for the keyboard, mouse, and joystick). The following class, which is called clsDirectInput8, encapsulates the DirectX8 and DirectInput8 objects, and will be needed later in the chapter when I show you how to encapsulate the input devices.

```
'-------------------------------------------------------------------
' Visual Basic Game Programming With DirectX
' Chapter 12 : Getting a Handle on User Input
' DirectInput8 Class Source Code File
'-------------------------------------------------------------------
Option Explicit
Option Base 0

Dim objDX As New DirectX8
Dim objDI As DirectInput8

Private Sub Class_Terminate()
    Set objDI = Nothing
    Set objDX = Nothing
End Sub

Public Property Get DIObj() As DirectInput8
    Set DIObj = objDI
End Property
```

```
Public Property Get DXObj() As DirectX8
    Set DXObj = objDX
End Property

Public Sub Startup(ByRef lWindowHandle As Long)
    'create the DirectX8 object
    Set objDX = New DirectX8
    'initialize DirectInput
    Set objDI = objDX.DirectInputCreate()
End Sub
```

PROGRAMMING THE KEYBOARD

The keyboard is definitely the easiest device to program with DirectInput, because it just provides an event when a key is pressed or released. Multiple, simultaneous key presses are supported, allowing you to move a character (or space ship, for example) while shooting. Some games are naturally easier to control with a keyboard when a joystick is not available. Most arcade games do not work well with a mouse. There is a natural tendency to use two hands in an arcade game, which is most likely brought about by arcade or console experience.

The arrow keys and spacebar have been used in countless games as the primary means of user input. In a typical example like *Asteroids*, the left and right arrow keys would be used to rotate the ship. The up arrow key would be used to apply thrust to move the ship. The spacebar would be a good candidate for firing a weapon. If you like *Asteroids*, be sure to check out the game in Chapter 21, "Stellar War: Multiplayer Space Combat Game."

The keyboard is a multi-use input device. With the ability to detect multiple key presses at the same time using DirectInput, the keyboard is a great choice for many types of games, even high-speed arcade games and first-person shooters.

Using Intrinsic Keyboard Events

Visual Basic provides simple keyboard events associated with a form. These events are triggered serially—that is, one at a time. A fast-paced game needs keyboard events to trigger in parallel so that multiple keys can be pressed at the same time. Since this is not possible with simple keyboard events that are provided by VB, it is not a recommended method of input for a game.

Although it is not as good as DirectInput, there might be cases where you would prefer to use the intrinsic keyboard events for a simple game (or a game that does not use the keyboard for primary input).

Detecting Key Press Events

There are three keyboard events associated with a form:

- KeyPress
- KeyDown
- KeyUp

The KeyPress event is similar to KeyDown, but returns the ASCII code for the key rather than the key code (which is returned by the other two keyboard events).

> **BUZZWORD**
> **ASCII (American Standard Code for Information Interchange)** is a common format for storing characters.

The following code snippet shows what the KeyPress event looks like in the code module for a VB form:

```
Private Sub Form_KeyPress(KeyAscii As Integer)
End Sub
```

Within the KeyPress event, you will normally use a Select…End Select statement to scan the ASCII codes for a particular key (such as A, B, C, and so on). The ASCII codes for lowercase letters differ from the ASCII code for uppercase letters, and ASCII codes do not reflect the physical key that was pressed on the keyboard.

KeyDown and KeyUp

Now for the KeyDown and KeyUp events:

```
Private Sub Form_KeyDown( _
    KeyCode As Integer, _
    Shift As Integer _
)

Private Sub Form_KeyUp( _
    KeyCode As Integer, _
    Shift As Integer _
)
```

These events are actually more useful than KeyPress because you have the actual scan code, which is more useful than the ASCII code of a character. The keyboard scan code lets you pick up the non-ASCII keys like Ctrl, Alt, Backspace, and so on.

KeyDown and KeyUp might seem like just the ticket for a keyboard handler, but unfortunately these events do not handle multiple keys well. You might be able to work around the serial nature of these events by remembering which keys have been pressed (but not yet released). Since every KeyDown event will be followed by a KeyUp event, you can simply keep track of a key state array, and as long as a specific key has not yet been turned off (with the KeyUp event), then you can assume it is still pressed.

Obviously it would be better to not have to keep track of key states in the program. What is the alternative? DirectInput to the rescue!

Detecting DirectInput Keyboard Events

DirectInput uses a callback procedure for mouse and joystick events but not for keyboard events, so programming the keyboard with DirectInput is fairly easy. There are four primary objects and structures needed to handle the keyboard:

```
Dim dx8 As New DirectX8
Dim dinput As DirectInput8
Dim diDevice As DirectInputDevice8
Dim diState As DIKEYBOARDSTATE
```

The DirectInput8 object handles the creation of DirectInputDevice8 objects through the CreateDevice function, which is called like this:

```
'create an interface to the keyboard
Set diDevice = dinput.CreateDevice("GUID_SysKeyboard")
```

The GUID_SysKeyboard string is an identifier that tells DirectInput to create a device interface to the system keyboard. After that is done, you must describe the properties of the keyboard device and then acquire it for exclusive use in your program:

```
diDevice.SetCommonDataFormat DIFORMAT_KEYBOARD
diDevice.SetCooperativeLevel Me.hWnd, DISCL_BACKGROUND Or _
    DISCL_NONEXCLUSIVE
diDevice.Acquire
```

The SetCommonDataFormat procedure provides this device object with an identifier that describes a keyboard. SetCooperativeLevel tells the device to acquire input for a specific program window. Finally, the Acquire procedure acquires the keyboard for exclusive use in your program.

Detecting Key Presses

In order to detect keyboard events, you must read the keyboard status with a procedure called GetDeviceStateKeyboard, which returns data inside a DIKEYBOARDSTATE variable:

```
'get the list of pressed keys
diDevice.GetDeviceStateKeyboard diState
```

Once you have filled the diState structure with the state of all the keys, you can then check for keys that are being pressed. There is a single member of diState called key that holds the status of every key on the keyboard as a byte. The definition of the key array follows:

```
key(0 To 255) As Byte
```

To scan the keyboard, you can simply iterate through this key array and see whether each element of the array is alive (in which case the value will be something other than zero). Most keyboards have 101 keys or fewer, so it seems logical that you might not need to scan every single element of this array. Unfortunately, the key codes do not map sequentially in this array, but are scattered throughout it. Most of the consecutive keys (A, B, C, and so on) are sequential in the array, but many other keys (such as Page Up, Page Down, Home, and End) appear toward the end of the array.

Therefore, in order to scan the entire keyboard, you will need to loop through the entire array. The following snippet of code scans through the keys and displays to the Immediate window the scan code of each key that is currently being pressed:

```
'scan the entire list for pressed keys
For n = 0 To 255
    If diState.Key(n) <> 0 Then
        Debug.Print "Key " & n & " was pressed"
    End If
Next
```

Detecting Key Releases

Detecting key releases is not such a simple task. DirectInput's keyboard handler only updates the key array when a key has been pressed, but no event is triggered when a key is actually released. The only thing you can do is check for keys that are currently being pressed, and which keys are not being pressed. DirectInput does provide a nice and simple means to check the status of the keys, but it does not complicate the process any more than that with events.

Fortunately, most games do not care if a key has been released, only if it has been pressed. Consider a *Breakout*-style game where you must move a paddle across the bottom of the screen to deflect a moving ball, with the goal of clearing out all of the blocks on the level (such as the game in Chapter 19, "Block Attack: Classic Arcade Game"). Why would you need to detect key release events?

The source code for a *Breakout*-style game would really only care about the left or right arrow keys for moving the paddle left or right. While you are holding down a key, the paddle will move in that direction. As soon as you release the key, the movement stops. It might seem like an event has occurred, but really nothing has happened. This is a passive type of event, rather than an active event. This might be thought of as being intrusive to your program, because it is forcing you to see an event. It works well, and that is one of the key design factors for most of the DirectX components.

Testing Keyboard Input

To demonstrate how to write a keyboard handler using DirectInput, I will walk you through a sample program called KeyboardTest. This simple program includes a ListBox control that shows the keys that are currently being pressed. Figure 12.2 shows the KeyboardTest program running.

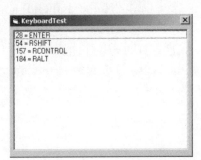

Figure 12.2

The KeyboardTest program shows how DirectInput can detect multiple key presses.

The first section of the KeyboardTest program includes declarations for API functions, program user interface controls, and program variables.

```
'-------------------------------------------------------------------
' Visual Basic Game Programming With DirectX
' Chapter 12 : Getting A Handle On User Input
' KeyboardTest Source Code File
'-------------------------------------------------------------------
Option Explicit
Option Base 0
```

```
'Windows API functions and structures
Private Declare Function GetTickCount _
    Lib "kernel32" () As Long

'program user interface controls
Dim WithEvents List1 As ListBox

'program variables
Dim dx8 As New DirectX8
Dim dinput As DirectInput8
Dim diDevice As DirectInputDevice8
Dim diState As DIKEYBOARDSTATE
Dim sKeyNames(255) As String
Dim bRunning As Boolean
```

The next section of code for KeyboardTest includes Form_Load and Form_QueryUnload. Form_Load sets up the form and creates a ListBox control to hold the keyboard events. Next, Form_Load initializes DirectInput, creates an interface to the keyboard object, sets up the KeyNames array, and then starts the main loop running.

```
Private Sub Form_Load()
    Static lStartTime As Long
    Static lCounter As Long
    Static lNewTime As Long

    'set up the form
    Form1.Caption = "KeyboardTest"
    Form1.ScaleMode = 3
    Form1.BorderStyle = 1
    Form1.KeyPreview = True
    Form1.Show

    'create the list control
    Set List1 = Controls.Add("VB.ListBox", "List1")
    List1.Left = 5
    List1.Top = 5
    List1.Width = Form1.ScaleWidth - 10
    List1.Height = Form1.ScaleHeight - 10
    List1.Visible = True
```

```
    'initialize DirectInput
    Set dinput = dx8.DirectInputCreate()
    If Err.Number <> 0 Then
        MsgBox "Error creating DirectInput object"
        End
    End If

    'create an interface to the keyboard
    Set diDevice = dinput.CreateDevice("GUID_SysKeyboard")
    diDevice.SetCommonDataFormat DIFORMAT_KEYBOARD
    diDevice.SetCooperativeLevel Me.hWnd, DISCL_BACKGROUND Or _
        DISCL_NONEXCLUSIVE
    diDevice.Acquire

    'initialize the keyboard value array
    InitKeyNames

    'main game loop
    bRunning = True
    Do While bRunning
        lCounter = GetTickCount() - lStartTime
        If lCounter > lNewTime Then
            Check_Keyboard
            lNewTime = lCounter + 20
        End If
        DoEvents
    Loop
End Sub

Private Sub Form_QueryUnload(Cancel As Integer, UnloadMode As Integer)
    Shutdown
End Sub
```

The next two procedures in the program listing are Check_Keyboard and Shutdown. The
Check_Keyboard procedure, which is called from Form_Load by the game loop, retrieves the keyboard state array and then scans the array for active keys, which it then adds to the ListBox to
show all the keys currently being pressed. Shutdown is a standard procedure in the sample programs so far, and simply cleans up before ending the program.

```
Private Sub Check_Keyboard()
    Dim n As Long

    'display pressed keys in the listbox
    List1.Clear

    'get the list of pressed keys
    diDevice.GetDeviceStateKeyboard diState

    'scan the entire list for pressed keys
    For n = 0 To 255
        If diState.Key(n) <> 0 Then
            List1.AddItem n & " = " & sKeyNames(n)
        End If
    Next

    'check for ESC key
    If diState.Key(1) > 0 Then Shutdown
End Sub

Private Sub Shutdown()
    bRunning = False
    Form1.Hide
    diDevice.Unacquire
    Set diDevice = Nothing
    Set dinput = Nothing
    Set dx8 = Nothing
    End
End Sub
```

The InitKeyNames procedure sets up a string array with the names of the keys. Since DirectInput provides actual key codes for the physical location of keys (rather than scan codes or ASCII codes), this program will be useful to you any time you need to check the code of a particular key. See, this is a multipurpose program. In addition to teaching you how to program DirectInput, this program is also a useful keyboard code utility.

```
Public Sub InitKeyNames()
    sKeyNames(1) = "ESC"
    sKeyNames(2) = "1"
    sKeyNames(3) = "2"
```

```
sKeyNames(4) = "3"
sKeyNames(5) = "4"
sKeyNames(6) = "5"
sKeyNames(7) = "6"
sKeyNames(8) = "7"
sKeyNames(9) = "8"
sKeyNames(10) = "9"
sKeyNames(11) = "0"
sKeyNames(12) = "-"
sKeyNames(13) = "="
sKeyNames(14) = "BACKSPACE"
sKeyNames(15) = "TAB"
sKeyNames(16) = "Q"
sKeyNames(17) = "W"
sKeyNames(18) = "E"
sKeyNames(19) = "R"
sKeyNames(20) = "T"
sKeyNames(21) = "Y"
sKeyNames(22) = "U"
sKeyNames(23) = "I"
sKeyNames(24) = "O"
sKeyNames(25) = "P"
sKeyNames(26) = "["
sKeyNames(27) = " ]"
sKeyNames(28) = "ENTER"
sKeyNames(29) = "LCTRL"
sKeyNames(30) = "A"
sKeyNames(31) = "S"
sKeyNames(32) = "D"
sKeyNames(33) = "F"
sKeyNames(34) = "G"
sKeyNames(35) = "H"
sKeyNames(36) = "J"
sKeyNames(37) = "K"
sKeyNames(38) = "L"
sKeyNames(39) = ";"
sKeyNames(40) = "'"
sKeyNames(41) = "`"
sKeyNames(42) = "LSHIFT"
sKeyNames(43) = "\"
sKeyNames(44) = "Z"
```

```
sKeyNames(45) = "X"
sKeyNames(46) = "C"
sKeyNames(47) = "V"
sKeyNames(48) = "B"
sKeyNames(49) = "N"
sKeyNames(50) = "M"
sKeyNames(51) = ","
sKeyNames(52) = "."
sKeyNames(53) = "/"
sKeyNames(54) = "RSHIFT"
sKeyNames(55) = "NUMPAD*"
sKeyNames(56) = "LALT"
sKeyNames(57) = "SPACE"
sKeyNames(58) = "CAPSLOCK"
sKeyNames(59) = "F1"
sKeyNames(60) = "F2"
sKeyNames(61) = "F3"
sKeyNames(62) = "F4"
sKeyNames(63) = "F5"
sKeyNames(64) = "F6"
sKeyNames(65) = "F7"
sKeyNames(66) = "F8"
sKeyNames(67) = "F9"
sKeyNames(68) = "F10"
sKeyNames(69) = "NUMLOCK"
sKeyNames(70) = "SCRLLOCK"
sKeyNames(71) = "NUMPAD7"
sKeyNames(72) = "NUMPAD8"
sKeyNames(73) = "NUMPAD9"
sKeyNames(74) = "NUMPAD-"
sKeyNames(75) = "NUMPAD4"
sKeyNames(76) = "NUMPAD5"
sKeyNames(77) = "NUMPAD6"
sKeyNames(78) = "NUMPAD+"
sKeyNames(79) = "NUMPAD1"
sKeyNames(80) = "NUMPAD2"
sKeyNames(81) = "NUMPAD3"
sKeyNames(82) = "NUMPAD0"
sKeyNames(83) = "NUMPAD."
sKeyNames(87) = "F11"
sKeyNames(88) = "F12"
```

```
        sKeyNames(86) = "F13"
        sKeyNames(84) = "F14"
        sKeyNames(85) = "F15"
        sKeyNames(156) = "NUMPADENTER"
        sKeyNames(157) = "RCONTROL"
        sKeyNames(91) = "NUMPAD,"
        sKeyNames(181) = "NUMPAD/"
        sKeyNames(183) = "SYSRQ"
        sKeyNames(184) = "RALT"
        sKeyNames(199) = "HOME"
        sKeyNames(200) = "UP"
        sKeyNames(201) = "PAGE UP"
        sKeyNames(203) = "LEFT"
        sKeyNames(205) = "RIGHT"
        sKeyNames(207) = "END"
        sKeyNames(208) = "DOWN"
        sKeyNames(209) = "PAGE DN"
        sKeyNames(210) = "INSERT"
        sKeyNames(211) = "DELETE"
        sKeyNames(219) = "LWIN"
        sKeyNames(220) = "RWIN"
        sKeyNames(221) = "APPS"
        sKeyNames(116) = "PAUSE"
End Sub
```

Well, that's the end of the KeyboardTest program. Run the program; if all goes well, you should be able to press and hold multiple keys, and the program will list those keys (along with DirectInput keyboard scan codes) in the ListBox.

Classing Up the Keyboard

The KeyboardTest program was fairly simple and should have been easy to understand. But with so much keyboard interface code in the main program, the code listing can get long and complicated during the development of a game. The keyboard handler must be associated directly with a form (actually a window handle). Therefore, it would be handy to have a class that encapsulates the keyboard handler, providing methods to initialize and then read the keyboard by wrapping the DirectInput keyboard handler code within a class.

The following listing is the source code for the clsDIKeyboard8 class.

```
'-----------------------------------------------------------------------
' Visual Basic Game Programming With DirectX
' Chapter 12 : Getting A Handle On User Input
' DIKeyboard8 Class Source Code File
'-----------------------------------------------------------------------
Option Explicit
Option Base 0

'class events
Public Event KeyDown(ByVal lKey As Long)

'local references
Dim dinput As clsDirectInput8

'class variables
Dim diDev_Keyboard As DirectInputDevice8
Dim diState_Keyboard As DIKEYBOARDSTATE
Dim sKeyNames(255) As String

Public Sub Startup(ByRef di As clsDirectInput8, _
    ByVal hWindowHandle As Long)
    'create reference to DirectInput object
    Set dinput = di

    'create an interface to the keyboard
    Set diDev_Keyboard = dinput.DIObj.CreateDevice("GUID_SysKeyboard")

    diDev_Keyboard.SetCommonDataFormat DIFORMAT_KEYBOARD
    diDev_Keyboard.SetCooperativeLevel hWindowHandle, _
        DISCL_BACKGROUND Or DISCL_NONEXCLUSIVE
    diDev_Keyboard.Acquire

    'initialize the key name array
    InitKeyNames
End Sub

Public Sub Check_Keyboard()
    Dim n As Long

    'make sure the keyboard handler is running
    If diDev_Keyboard Is Nothing Then Exit Sub
```

```
    'get the list of pressed keys
    diDev_Keyboard.GetDeviceStateKeyboard diState_Keyboard

    'scan the entire list for pressed keys
    For n = 0 To 255
        If diState_Keyboard.Key(n) > 0 Then
            RaiseEvent KeyDown(n)
        End If
    Next
End Sub

Public Sub Shutdown()
    On Local Error Resume Next

    'release the keyboard
    If Not (diDev_Keyboard Is Nothing) Then
        diDev_Keyboard.Unacquire
        Set diDev_Keyboard = Nothing
    End If
End Sub

Public Property Get KeyName(ByVal lKey As Long) As String
    KeyName = sKeyNames(lKey)
End Property
```

Now, the only thing remaining to complete the keyboard class is the InitKeyNames procedure, which was listed earlier at the end of the KeyboardTest program. Since the procedure is so long, I won't list it again here. Paste the InitKeyNames procedure to the bottom of the keyboard class and then the class will be complete!

PROGRAMMING THE MOUSE

Mouse handling is second only to keyboard handling in simplicity, because of the way DirectInput has abstracted mouse motion. But first, I'd like to show you what VB provides before jumping into mouse handling with DirectInput.

The standard VB form includes six mouse events, each of which might be useful in a game. Here is the list of events related to the mouse (not including the OLE events, which are related to embedded objects on a VB form, and are not covered here):

- Form_Click
- Form_DblClick
- Form_DragDrop
- Form_DragOver
- Form_MouseDown
- Form_MouseUp

Detecting Mouse Movement

You can track mouse movement on a form by using the Form_MouseDown, Form_MouseMove, and Form_MouseUp events. These three events provide all the information you need to detect button presses and mouse movement, along with the status of the Shift key (which is usually not needed in a game). For most simple games, these three events work great.

Here is the declaration for the Form_MouseDown event:

```
Private Sub Form_MouseDown( _
    Button As Integer, _
    Shift As Integer, _
    X As Single, _
    Y As Single _
)
```

This is the declaration for the Form_MouseUp event:

```
Private Sub Form_MouseUp( _
    Button As Integer, _
    Shift As Integer, _
    X As Single, _
    Y As Single _
)
```

And finally, here is the declaration for the Form_MouseMove event:

```
Private Sub Form_MouseMove( _
    Button As Integer, _
    Shift As Integer, _
    X As Single, _
    Y As Single _
)
```

Using DirectInput to Handle Mouse Input

DirectInput abstracts the mouse events specifically for game programming, providing relative motion values for the mouse rather than absolute values. For instance, when tracking the mouse with DirectInput, if you move the mouse slowly to the right, the mouse X position will be a small number (usually less than five), but that number will not increase. When you stop moving the mouse, the X motion will return to zero.

Likewise, moving the mouse to the left will generate a negative X motion, which returns to zero when you stop moving the mouse. The process works in the same manner for vertical Y motion. The fascinating aspect of the DirectInput mouse handler is that the faster you move the mouse, the higher the X and Y motion values will be.

Just think for a minute how great this is in a game. Suppose you are writing a block-bashing game where the player controls a paddle at the bottom of the screen. By looking at the mouse motion values, you can move the paddle left or right using the mouse motion values directly—that is, without having to massage the numbers first. If you were to use the VB events like Form_MouseMove, you would have to convert the absolute position of the mouse into a relative motion value by keeping track of the mouse with a static or global variable. DirectInput handles that automatically.

> **TIP**
>
> When you stop moving the mouse, DirectInput reports the mouse motion values as zero for both the **X** and **Y** axes.

Which brings up a question. How do you figure out where the mouse is located on the screen without absolute values? The answer is that you must track the mouse pointer just like you would move a sprite on the screen. You have to make sure the pointer doesn't go off the edge of the screen, and you update the pointer position based on the mouse's motion. The hardware mouse cursor is displayed by default, so it is up to you to create a cursor using a simple sprite and display it. You also have to keep track of the absolute position of the cursor, which is why a sprite would be a good solution. I should point out that if you do capture the mouse using DirectInput, the default hardware cursor is not displayed.

> **TIP**
>
> One thing to keep in mind is that you should draw the mouse cursor after you have finished drawing all the other objects in the game so the mouse cursor will always appear on top of the other images in the game.

Now, I'm going to assume you are becoming more familiar with the DirectInput objects, so I won't cover the base objects again. I'll just explain how to set up the mouse object and track the mouse events.

Mouse Movement

The mouse handler requires the use of a callback procedure called `DirectXEvent8_DXCallback`, which is required when you include the DirectXEvent8 interface in the program. You can do that by including a single line of code at the top of the program:

```
Implements DirectXEvent8
```

That line of code tells your program to use a specific interface that DirectX understands (and which allows DirectX to send events directly into a VB program). In order to track mouse movement, you will need to look at the `DirectXEvent8_DXCallback` procedure. I will be talking about this procedure in more detail later in this chapter, so I am only going to skim over it at this point. What I am more interested in showing you is how to call mouse events from within the callback procedure.

There are two DirectInput constants that you need to look for inside the callback procedure when you read the mouse's relative position. These constants are DIMOFS_X and DIMOFS_Y.

Here is how you might write the code to detect mouse movement:

```
Case DIMOFS_X
    lMouseX = lMouseX + diDeviceData(n).lData
    Debug.Print "MouseX = " & lMouseX

Case DIMOFS_Y
    lMouseY = lMouseY + diDeviceData(n).lData
    Debug.Print "MouseY = " & lMouseY
```

This code will make more sense with all of the supporting code that goes along with it. However, it does demonstrate how the mouse movement values are relative. Look how the lMouseX and lMouseY variables are updated—they are incremented by the mouse motion, rather than set directly to it! That is the key to converting relative mouse motion to absolute mouse position.

Mouse Buttons

The mouse button events are reported by DirectInput with the `DIMOFS_BUTTONx` events. Simply replace the "x" at the end of the constant with 0–7 to detect up to seven different button press and release events.

Here is how you would write the code to detect the primary mouse button press and release events:

```
Case DIMOFS_BUTTON0
    If diDeviceData(n).lData > 0 Then
        Debug.Print "Button 1 pressed"
    Else
        Debug.Print "Button 1 released"
    End If
```

I know this snippet of code doesn't make much sense without the Select…End Select statements wrapped around it, but I'll show you the whole procedure soon enough. Note that the button events are based on zero for the first button.

Testing Mouse Input

Now to put all of this fragmented knowledge into a cohesive program. The MouseTest program is interesting in that it is a windowed program that captures the mouse. When DirectInput captures the mouse, it hides the mouse cursor. The result is that there is no way to click anywhere on the screen while this program is running. Rather, mouse events are completely captured by the MouseTest program, including mouse movement and button click events.

Figure 12.3 shows the MouseTest program running with Button1 and Button3 pressed. Only a few mouse models have more than three buttons (such as the Microsoft IntelliMouse Explorer).

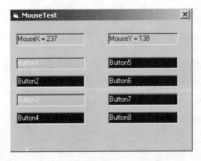

Figure 12.3

The MouseTest program shows how DirectInput makes it easy to handle mouse events.

The MouseTest program is a Standard EXE project with a reference to the DirectX 8 for Visual Basic Type Library. This first section of code includes the user interface controls, the DirectX objects and structures, and the program variables.

```
'----------------------------------------------------------------
' Visual Basic Game Programming With DirectX
' Chapter 12 : Getting A Handle On User Input
' MouseTest Source Code File
'----------------------------------------------------------------
```

```
Option Explicit
Option Base 0

Implements DirectXEvent8

'program controls
Dim WithEvents lblMouseX As Label
Dim WithEvents lblMouseY As Label
Dim WithEvents lblButton1 As Label
Dim WithEvents lblButton2 As Label
Dim WithEvents lblButton3 As Label
Dim WithEvents lblButton4 As Label
Dim WithEvents lblButton5 As Label
Dim WithEvents lblButton6 As Label
Dim WithEvents lblButton7 As Label
Dim WithEvents lblButton8 As Label

'DirectX objects and structures
Public dx As New DirectX8
Public di As DirectInput8
Public diDev As DirectInputDevice8
Dim didevstate As DIMOUSESTATE

'program constants and variables
Const BufferSize = 10
Public EventHandle As Long
Public Drawing As Boolean
Public Suspended As Boolean
```

The Form_Load event sets up the program and starts it running. First, the user interface is set up, and then the DirectInput and mouse objects are created. Next, the mouse device properties are set and the event handler is created (which activates the callback procedure). Finally, the mouse device is acquired for exclusive use.

The Form_KeyDown event simply checks for the ESC key, at which point it will end the program. The Shutdown procedure is called by other routines to actually clean up and then end the program.

```
Private Sub Form_Load()
    'set up the user interface
    Setup_Form
```

```
        'create the DirectInput object
        Set di = dx.DirectInputCreate

        'create the mouse object
        Set diDev = di.CreateDevice("guid_SysMouse")

        'configure DirectInputDevice to support the mouse
        Call diDev.SetCommonDataFormat(DIFORMAT_MOUSE)
        Call diDev.SetCooperativeLevel(Form1.hWnd, _
            DISCL_FOREGROUND Or DISCL_EXCLUSIVE)

        'set properties for the mouse device
        Dim diProp As DIPROPLONG
        diProp.lHow = DIPH_DEVICE
        diProp.lObj = 0
        diProp.lData = BufferSize
        Call diDev.SetProperty("DIPROP_BUFFERSIZE", diProp)

        'create mouse callback event handler
        EventHandle = dx.CreateEvent(Form1)
        diDev.SetEventNotification EventHandle

        'acquire the mouse
        diDev.Acquire
End Sub

Private Sub Form_KeyDown(KeyCode As Integer, Shift As Integer)
    If KeyCode = 27 Then Shutdown
End Sub

Private Sub Shutdown()
    On Local Error Resume Next
    dx.DestroyEvent EventHandle
    Set diDev = Nothing
    Set di = Nothing
    Set dx = Nothing
    End
End Sub
```

Mouse_Move, Mouse_ButtonDown, and Mouse_ButtonUp are three events that are called from within the callback procedure to report mouse activity. The SetButton procedure is a user interface support routine that sets the background color of the labels on the form.

```
Public Sub Mouse_Move(ByVal X As Long, ByVal Y As Long)
    lblMouseX.Caption = "MouseX = " & X
    lblMouseY.Caption = "MouseY = " & Y
End Sub


Public Sub Mouse_ButtonDown(ByVal lButton As Long)
    Debug.Print "Button " & lButton & " down"
    SetButton lButton, RGB(0, 255, 0)
End Sub


Public Sub Mouse_ButtonUp(ByVal lButton As Long)
    Debug.Print "Button " & lButton & " up"
    SetButton lButton, RGB(0, 0, 0)
End Sub


Public Sub SetButton(ByVal lButton As Long, ByVal lColor As Long)
    Select Case lButton
        Case 1
            lblButton1.BackColor = lColor
        Case 2
            lblButton2.BackColor = lColor
        Case 3
            lblButton3.BackColor = lColor
        Case 4
            lblButton4.BackColor = lColor
        Case 5
            lblButton5.BackColor = lColor
        Case 6
            lblButton6.BackColor = lColor
        Case 7
            lblButton7.BackColor = lColor
        Case 8
            lblButton8.BackColor = lColor
    End Select
End Sub
```

`DirectXEvent8_DXCallback` is the callback procedure that reports the mouse events. This procedure shows the complete mouse-handling code that I briefly touched upon earlier, and actually calls the mouse events that were shown above.

```
Private Sub DirectXEvent8_DXCallback(ByVal eventid As Long)
    Dim diDeviceData(1 To BufferSize) As DIDEVICEOBJECTDATA
    Static lMouseX As Long
    Static lMouseY As Long
    Static lOldSeq As Long
    Dim n As Long

    'loop through events
    For n = 1 To diDev.GetDeviceData(diDeviceData, 0)
        Select Case diDeviceData(n).lOfs
            Case DIMOFS_X
                lMouseX = lMouseX + diDeviceData(n).lData
                If lMouseX < 0 Then lMouseX = 0
                If lMouseX >= Form1.ScaleWidth Then
                    lMouseX = Form1.ScaleWidth - 1
                End If

                If lOldSeq <> diDeviceData(n).lSequence Then
                    Debug.Print diDeviceData(n).lData
                    Mouse_Move lMouseX, lMouseY
                    lOldSeq = diDeviceData(n).lSequence
                Else
                    lOldSeq = 0
                End If

            Case DIMOFS_Y
                lMouseY = lMouseY + diDeviceData(n).lData
                If lMouseY < 0 Then lMouseY = 0
                If lMouseY >= Form1.ScaleHeight Then
                    lMouseY = Form1.ScaleHeight - 1
                End If

                If lOldSeq <> diDeviceData(n).lSequence Then
                    Mouse_Move lMouseX, lMouseY
                    lOldSeq = diDeviceData(n).lSequence
                Else
                    lOldSeq = 0
                End If
```

```
Case DIMOFS_BUTTON0
    If diDeviceData(n).lData > 0 Then
        Mouse_ButtonDown 1
    Else
        Mouse_ButtonUp 1
    End If

Case DIMOFS_BUTTON1
    If diDeviceData(n).lData > 0 Then
        Mouse_ButtonDown 2
    Else
        Mouse_ButtonUp 2
    End If

Case DIMOFS_BUTTON2
    If diDeviceData(n).lData > 0 Then
        Mouse_ButtonDown 3
    Else
        Mouse_ButtonUp 3
    End If

Case DIMOFS_BUTTON3
    If diDeviceData(n).lData > 0 Then
        Mouse_ButtonDown 4
    Else
        Mouse_ButtonUp 4
    End If

Case DIMOFS_BUTTON4
    If diDeviceData(n).lData > 0 Then
        Mouse_ButtonDown 5
    Else
        Mouse_ButtonUp 5
    End If

Case DIMOFS_BUTTON5
    If diDeviceData(n).lData > 0 Then
        Mouse_ButtonDown 6
    Else
        Mouse_ButtonUp 6
    End If
```

```
            Case DIMOFS_BUTTON6
                If diDeviceData(n).lData > 0 Then
                    Mouse_ButtonDown 7
                Else
                    Mouse_ButtonUp 7
                End If

            Case DIMOFS_BUTTON7
                If diDeviceData(n).lData > 0 Then
                    Mouse_ButtonDown 8
                Else
                    Mouse_ButtonUp 8
                End If


        End Select
    Next n
End Sub
```

Finally, the Setup_Form procedure is a support routine that sets up the user interface and is called by Form_Load to make the code easier to follow in that procedure. Setup_Form simply sets up the main form of the program and then adds the label controls to the form. These controls are used to provide visual feedback when mouse events occur.

```
Private Sub Setup_Form()
    'set up the form
    Form1.Caption = "MouseTest"
    Form1.ScaleMode = 3
    Form1.Show


    'set up user interface controls
    Set lblMouseX = Controls.Add("VB.Label", "lblMouseX")
    lblMouseX.Left = 10
    lblMouseX.Top = 20
    lblMouseX.Width = 120
    lblMouseX.Height = 20
    lblMouseX.BorderStyle = 1
    lblMouseX.Visible = True

    Set lblMouseY = Controls.Add("VB.Label", "lblMouseY")
    lblMouseY.Left = 170
    lblMouseY.Top = 20
```

```
lblMouseY.Width = 120
lblMouseY.Height = 20
lblMouseY.BorderStyle = 1
lblMouseY.Visible = True

Set lblButton1 = Controls.Add("VB.Label", "lblButton1")
lblButton1.Left = 10
lblButton1.Top = 60
lblButton1.Width = 120
lblButton1.Height = 20
lblButton1.BorderStyle = 1
lblButton1.Caption = "Button1"
lblButton1.BackColor = RGB(0, 0, 0)
lblButton1.ForeColor = RGB(255, 255, 255)
lblButton1.Visible = True

Set lblButton2 = Controls.Add("VB.Label", "lblButton2")
lblButton2.Left = 10
lblButton2.Top = 90
lblButton2.Width = 120
lblButton2.Height = 20
lblButton2.BorderStyle = 1
lblButton2.Caption = "Button2"
lblButton2.BackColor = RGB(0, 0, 0)
lblButton2.ForeColor = RGB(255, 255, 255)
lblButton2.Visible = True

Set lblButton3 = Controls.Add("VB.Label", "lblButton3")
lblButton3.Left = 10
lblButton3.Top = 120
lblButton3.Width = 120
lblButton3.Height = 20
lblButton3.BorderStyle = 1
lblButton3.Caption = "Button3"
lblButton3.BackColor = RGB(0, 0, 0)
lblButton3.ForeColor = RGB(255, 255, 255)
lblButton3.Visible = True

Set lblButton4 = Controls.Add("VB.Label", "lblButton4")
lblButton4.Left = 10
lblButton4.Top = 150
```

```
lblButton4.Width = 120
lblButton4.Height = 20
lblButton4.BorderStyle = 1
lblButton4.Caption = "Button4"
lblButton4.BackColor = RGB(0, 0, 0)
lblButton4.ForeColor = RGB(255, 255, 255)
lblButton4.Visible = True

Set lblButton5 = Controls.Add("VB.Label", "lblButton5")
lblButton5.Left = 170
lblButton5.Top = 60
lblButton5.Width = 120
lblButton5.Height = 20
lblButton5.BorderStyle = 1
lblButton5.Caption = "Button5"
lblButton5.BackColor = RGB(0, 0, 0)
lblButton5.ForeColor = RGB(255, 255, 255)
lblButton5.Visible = True

Set lblButton6 = Controls.Add("VB.Label", "lblButton6")
lblButton6.Left = 170
lblButton6.Top = 90
lblButton6.Width = 120
lblButton6.Height = 20
lblButton6.BorderStyle = 1
lblButton6.Caption = "Button6"
lblButton6.BackColor = RGB(0, 0, 0)
lblButton6.ForeColor = RGB(255, 255, 255)
lblButton6.Visible = True

Set lblButton7 = Controls.Add("VB.Label", "lblButton7")
lblButton7.Left = 170
lblButton7.Top = 120
lblButton7.Width = 120
lblButton7.Height = 20
lblButton7.BorderStyle = 1
lblButton7.Caption = "Button7"
lblButton7.BackColor = RGB(0, 0, 0)
lblButton7.ForeColor = RGB(255, 255, 255)
lblButton7.Visible = True
```

```
    Set lblButton8 = Controls.Add("VB.Label", "lblButton8")
    lblButton8.Left = 170
    lblButton8.Top = 150
    lblButton8.Width = 120
    lblButton8.Height = 20
    lblButton8.BorderStyle = 1
    lblButton8.Caption = "Button8"
    lblButton8.BackColor = RGB(0, 0, 0)
    lblButton8.ForeColor = RGB(255, 255, 255)
    lblButton8.Visible = True
End Sub
```

That's the end of the MouseTest program. Go ahead and run it now. Remember that you can end the program by hitting the ESC key, since the mouse is not visible while the program is running. You can move the mouse around and press buttons to see how the program reports mouse input.

Classing Up the Mouse

The mouse handler can be encapsulated into a class for convenience and for the benefit of reducing the amount of code in the main source code listing for a game. While the MouseTest program used a callback procedure, the clsDIMouse8 class provides a cleaner and more programmer-friendly version of the mouse handler that is polled rather than event driven.

This mouse handler class is actually a lot simpler than the event-driven handler in the MouseTest program. A single procedure called Check_Mouse polls the mouse input device for status information. If the mouse is currently being moved, or if any mouse buttons are being pressed, Check_Mouse will fire off custom events that your program will then receive. These events are not part of a single, large callback procedure, but rather take the form of custom events that are more intuitive.

Here is the list of events provided by the mouse handler class:

- MouseMove
- MouseDown
- MouseUp

The source code listing for clsDIMouse8 follows. Simply type the code into a new Class Module and save it with the name DIMouse8.cls.

```vb
'--------------------------------------------------------------------------
' Visual Basic Game Programming With DirectX
' Chapter 12: Getting A Handle On User Input
' DIMouse8 Class Source Code File
'--------------------------------------------------------------------------
Option Explicit
Option Base 0

'class events
Public Event MouseMove(ByVal X As Long, ByVal Y As Long)
Public Event MouseDown(ByVal lButton As Long)
Public Event MouseUp(ByVal lButton As Long)

'local references
Dim dinput As clsDirectInput8

'class variables
Public diDev_Mouse As DirectInputDevice8
Dim diState As DIMOUSESTATE
Public MouseEvents As Long
Private lMouseX As Long
Private lOldX As Long
Private lMouseY As Long
Private lOldY As Long
Private lOldButtons(0 To 3) As Long
Dim bRelativeMotion As Boolean
Dim n As Long

Private Sub Class_Initialize()
    bRelativeMotion = True
End Sub

Private Sub Class_Terminate()
    Shutdown
End Sub

Public Property Get RelativeMotion() As Boolean
    RelativeMotion = bRelativeMotion
End Property
```

```vb
Public Property Let RelativeMotion(ByVal bNewValue As Boolean)
    bRelativeMotion = bNewValue
End Property

Public Sub Startup(ByRef di As clsDirectInput8, ByVal hWindow As Long)
    'create reference to DirectInput object
    Set dinput = di

    'create the mouse object
    Set diDev_Mouse = dinput.DIObj.CreateDevice("guid_SysMouse")

    'configure DirectInputDevice to support the mouse
    Call diDev_Mouse.SetCommonDataFormat(DIFORMAT_MOUSE)
    Call diDev_Mouse.SetCooperativeLevel(hWindow, _
        DISCL_FOREGROUND Or DISCL_EXCLUSIVE)

    'acquire the mouse
    diDev_Mouse.Acquire
End Sub

Public Sub Check_Mouse(ByVal lScreenWidth As Long, _
    ByVal lScreenHeight As Long)
    'get mouse status
    diDev_Mouse.GetDeviceStateMouse diState

    'get mouse position
    lMouseX = lMouseX + diState.lX
    If lMouseX < 0 Then lMouseX = 0
    If lMouseX >= lScreenWidth Then
        lMouseX = lScreenWidth - 1
    End If

    lMouseY = lMouseY + diState.lY
    If lMouseY < 0 Then lMouseY = 0
    If lMouseY >= lScreenHeight Then
        lMouseY = lScreenHeight - 1
    End If

    'raise event if mouse has moved
    If lMouseX <> lOldX Or lMouseY <> lOldY Then
```

```
        If bRelativeMotion Then
            RaiseEvent MouseMove(diState.lX, diState.lY)
        Else
            RaiseEvent MouseMove(lMouseX, lMouseY)
        End If
        lOldX = lMouseX
        lOldY = lMouseY
    End If


    'check for button events
    For n = 0 To 3
        If diState.Buttons(n) <> lOldButtons(n) Then
            If diState.Buttons(n) = 0 Then
                RaiseEvent MouseUp(n)
            Else
                RaiseEvent MouseDown(n)
            End If
            lOldButtons(n) = diState.Buttons(n)
        End If
    Next n

End Sub

Public Sub Shutdown()
    On Local Error Resume Next
    'release the mouse
    If Not (diDev_Mouse Is Nothing) Then
        diDev_Mouse.Unacquire
        Set diDev_Mouse = Nothing
        'dx8.DestroyEvent MouseEvents
    End If
End Sub
```

Programming the Joystick

What is a fast-paced arcade game without joystick support? Joysticks are suitably named because they add an enormous amount of fun factor to a game that is suited for a joystick. Some games are obviously not designed to support a joystick (such as a real-time strategy game like

Dark Reign II). But there are a great many games that are designed to use a joystick, and such games are difficult to play with a keyboard or mouse.

Joysticks range in price from five-dollar gamepads to $200 flight sticks with throttle and pedal controls. The best option is usually something closer to the low-end of the pricing spectrum, since there are some very nice joysticks and gamepads available—with force feedback—for a very affordable price. There are also devices that are difficult to categorize and fall somewhere between a joystick and a mouse.

The Microsoft Strategic Commander is one such device. This controller was designed for strategy games, with X and Y axes for scrolling the game map, while the player uses the mouse to manipulate units in the game. The Strategic Commander also includes a multi-

> **TIP**
>
> Providing joystick support in a game is a decision that you should make early in the design process, because the game should be optimized for the preferred input device early in development.

tude of programmable buttons that can invoke macros in a game. For example, most mouse commands in a real-time strategy game include keyboard shortcuts. By programming a sequence of keys into a macro for a button on the Strategic Commander, you could program a single button to perform a complicated task (such as building a new tank in the factory). The Strategic Commander allows you to store such macros in a profile that can be saved and recalled for different games.

Using DirectInput to Program a Joystick

Joystick support in the past was made available primarily through functionality that was built into MS-DOS and Windows, or through custom joystick code. DirectInput dramatically simplifies joystick programming, and makes it relatively easy to support a wide variety of joysticks with a single code base.

The key to programming a joystick with DirectInput lies with two objects called DirectInputDevice8 and DirectInputEnumDevices, as well as a structure called DIDEVCAPS. These three components provide the functionality to write a joystick handler.

```
Dim diDev As DirectInputDevice8
Dim diDevEnum As DirectInputEnumDevices8
Dim joyCaps As DIDEVCAPS
```

Reading the List of Game Controllers

The first thing you need to do is retrieve a list of available game controllers that are attached to the computer using a DirectInput function called GetDIDevices:

```
'enumerate the game controllers
Set diDevEnum = di.GetDIDevices(DI8DEVCLASS_GAMECTRL, _
    DIEDFL_ATTACHEDONLY)
```

You can then use the diDevEnum variable to see if a joystick is available:

```
If diDevEnum.GetCount = 0 Then
    MsgBox "No joystick could be found"
End If
```

Creating the Joystick Device Object

Once you have determined that a joystick is available, the next step is to create the joystick object, which is a DirectInputDevice8 object. While DirectInput supports multiple joysticks, I will only show you how to work with the primary joystick attached to the computer, because things get messy when you're trying to support multiple joysticks. Here is the code to create the joystick object:

```
'create the joystick object
Set diDev = di.CreateDevice(diDevEnum.GetItem(1).GetGuidInstance)
diDev.SetCommonDataFormat DIFORMAT_JOYSTICK
diDev.SetCooperativeLevel Me.hWnd, DISCL_BACKGROUND Or _
    DISCL_NONEXCLUSIVE
```

The DirectXEvent8 Callback Procedure

The next step to writing a joystick handler is to set up the event handler and the callback procedure. The event handler is actually returned by the primary DirectX object, rather than the DirectInput object. Any VB program that needs to provide joystick support through DirectInput will need to implement the DirectX event object at the top of the program source code:

```
Implements DirectXEvent8
```

The actual callback procedure looks like this:

```
Private Sub DirectXEvent8_DXCallback(ByVal eventid As Long)
End Sub
```

To return the event handle for the joystick callback procedure, you can use the DirectX `CreateEvent` function. You then pass the value to the DirectInputDevice8 procedure, which is called `SetEventNotification`. The code looks like this:

```
'create an event handler for the joystick
EventHandle = dx.CreateEvent(Me)
'ask for notification of events
diDev.SetEventNotification EventHandle
```

Detecting Joystick Motion

The key to reading joystick events in the `DirectXEvent8_DXCallback` procedure is a procedure called `GetDeviceStateJoystick` (which is a member of DirectInputDevice8). The procedure calls look like this:

```
'retrieve joystick status
Dim js As DIJOYSTATE
diDev.GetDeviceStateJoystick js
```

The DIJOYSTATE structure is filled with status information by this procedure, and this is where you need to look for joystick events. (I can't help but laugh every time I see "DIJOYSTATE," because it sounds like it's referring to an emotional state.) This structure will contain values for the analog axes, the directional pad (D-pad), the buttons, and sliders. To check on the analog motion of the joystick, you can pick up the values for X and Y (with an additional value for the Z axis if you need it). In addition, there is an equivalent RX, RY, and RZ for an alternate analog stick (such as the second stick on a PlayStation 2 Dual-Shock controller, which is available on some PC gamepads now).

Handling Joystick Buttons

The buttons are read from the same DIJOYSTATE structure. Since joysticks come in various shapes and sizes, with anywhere from one to more than twenty buttons, the button values are stored inside DIJOYSTATE as an enumeration (which looks like an array, for all practical purposes). The number of buttons on a joystick is stored in the DIDEVCAPS structure, and is called lButtons. Since the button array is zero-based, you will want to use lButtons – 1 when processing the buttons. Here is a code snippet that checks the status of all the buttons on a joystick:

```
For n = 0 To joyCaps.lButtons - 1
    If js.Buttons(n) = 0 Then
        Debug.Print "Button " & n & " was released"
    Else
```

```
        Debug.Print "Button " & n & " was pressed"
    End If
Next n
```

Handling Joystick Directional Pads

The directional pad is standard equipment on gamepads (note the name), but is not usually found on flight sticks. The DIJOYSTATE structure keeps track of the directional pad buttons in a separate array from the buttons, and this array is called POV (which means "point of view"), since the D-pad is often used for movement.

Programming the POV buttons is similar to programming regular buttons. The strange thing about the D-pad support, however, is that DirectInput treats it as an array itself and returns the values of the D-pad as if they are analog input buttons rather than digital buttons (hence, the reason why POV was separated from the buttons). I have personally never seen a joystick or gamepad with two or more D-pads, so I'm not sure why there is an array of POVs available. (Perhaps the DirectInput team has aspirations that the library will be used on real military vehicles with all kinds of different controls?)

In the following code, note that I'm just using POV(0) to read the default directional pad. If you can think of a reason to program multiple D-pads, then you have either been given an experimental, high-tech joystick with dual D-pads, or you are some kind of freak (just kidding). Really, though, I think there are some advanced joysticks that treat the POV inputs as additional sliders, like for those nightmarishly realistic flight simulators that require you to set the fuel intake valves and the diameter of the thrust nozzles manually, among other features (the likes of which only a turbofan engine mechanic would understand).

Now, back to the subject at hand. Here is the code to read the D-pad:

```
If js.POV(0) = -1 Then
    Debug.Print "D-pad is centered"
Else
    Debug.Print "D-pad = " & js.POV(0)
End If
```

Testing Joystick Input

Now I will walk you through the process of creating a program that handles a joystick with DirectInput. Figure 12.4 shows the JoystickTest program running. Note the two PictureBox controls that show the position of the analog inputs. The regular buttons and POV buttons are also shown highlighted.

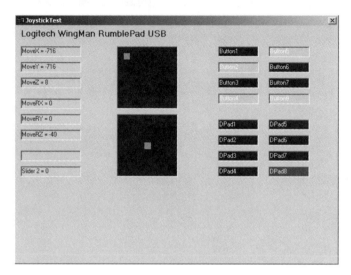

Figure 12.4

The JoystickTest program shows you how DirectInput makes it easy to program a joystick handler.

Now for the JoystickTest project and source code. This, like every other project in the book, requires a single Standard EXE project with a single form, and a reference to the DirectX 8 for Visual Basic Type Library. (Recall that some programs will use the DirectX 7 type library any time DirectDraw is needed.) This program uses a lot of controls, but the controls are all created and set up with source code, so you do not need to do anything with the format design time (hallelujah!).

The first part of the program includes the extensive list of user interface controls, along with the DirectX events and objects, and the program variables.

```
'-------------------------------------------------------------------
' Visual Basic Game Programming With DirectX
' Chapter 12 : Getting A Handle On User Input
' JoystickTest Source Code File
'-------------------------------------------------------------------
Option Explicit
Option Base 0

Implements DirectXEvent8

'program user interface controls
Dim WithEvents lblJoystick As Label
Dim WithEvents picAxis1 As PictureBox
Dim WithEvents picAxis2 As PictureBox
Dim WithEvents lblMoveX As Label
```

```
Dim WithEvents lblMoveY As Label
Dim WithEvents lblMoveZ As Label
Dim WithEvents lblMoveRX As Label
Dim WithEvents lblMoveRY As Label
Dim WithEvents lblMoveRZ As Label
Dim WithEvents lblSlider1 As Label
Dim WithEvents lblSlider2 As Label
Dim WithEvents lblButton1 As Label
Dim WithEvents lblButton2 As Label
Dim WithEvents lblButton3 As Label
Dim WithEvents lblButton4 As Label
Dim WithEvents lblButton5 As Label
Dim WithEvents lblButton6 As Label
Dim WithEvents lblButton7 As Label
Dim WithEvents lblButton8 As Label
Dim WithEvents lblDPad1 As Label
Dim WithEvents lblDPad2 As Label
Dim WithEvents lblDPad3 As Label
Dim WithEvents lblDPad4 As Label
Dim WithEvents lblDPad5 As Label
Dim WithEvents lblDPad6 As Label
Dim WithEvents lblDPad7 As Label
Dim WithEvents lblDPad8 As Label

'DirectX objects and structures
Dim dx As New DirectX8
Dim di As DirectInput8
Dim diDev As DirectInputDevice8
Dim diDevEnum As DirectInputEnumDevices8
Dim joyCaps As DIDEVCAPS

'keep track of analog stick motion
Dim Analog(1 To 2) As D3DVECTOR

'program variables
Dim running As Boolean
Dim lMoveRX As Long
Dim lMoveRY As Long
Dim EventHandle As Long
```

The `Form_Load` event sets up the user interface for the JoystickTest program, creates the DirectInput object, initializes the joystick (by calling `Joystick_Init`), and then starts a small program loop running. `Form_KeyDown` and `Form_QueryUnload` are long-time favorites that should now be part of your game-programming dictionary.

```
Private Sub Form_Load()
    On Local Error Resume Next

    'set up the user interface
    Setup_Form

    'create the DirectInput object
    Set di = dx.DirectInputCreate()
    If Err.Number <> 0 Then
        MsgBox "Error creating DirectInput object"
        Shutdown
    End If

    'enumerate the game controllers
    Set diDevEnum = di.GetDIDevices(DI8DEVCLASS_GAMECTRL, _
        DIEDFL_ATTACHEDONLY)
    If Err.Number <> 0 Then
        MsgBox "Error enumerating game controllers"
        Shutdown
    End If

    'check for the presence of a joystick
    If diDevEnum.GetCount = 0 Then
        MsgBox "No joystick could be found"
        Shutdown
    End If

    'initialize the joystick
    Joystick_Init

    'main polling loop
    running = True
    Do While running
        DoEvents
        diDev.Poll
    Loop
End Sub
```

```
Private Sub Form_KeyDown(KeyCode As Integer, Shift As Integer)
    If KeyCode = 27 Then Shutdown
End Sub

Private Sub Form_QueryUnload(Cancel As Integer, UnloadMode As Integer)
    Shutdown
End Sub
```

The Joystick_Init procedure sets up the joystick object, creates the callback procedure event, sets the analog stick ranges, and acquires the joystick for exclusive use by the program. Then the procedure retrieves the joystick properties and displays some interesting information to the Immediate window with Debug.Print statements.

```
Private Sub Joystick_Init()
    On Local Error Resume Next

    'see if joystick was already acquired
    If Not diDev Is Nothing Then
      diDev.Unacquire
    End If

    'create the joystick object
    Set diDev = Nothing
    Set diDev = di.CreateDevice(diDevEnum.GetItem(1).GetGuidInstance)
    diDev.SetCommonDataFormat DIFORMAT_JOYSTICK
    diDev.SetCooperativeLevel Me.hWnd, DISCL_BACKGROUND Or _
        DISCL_NONEXCLUSIVE

    'create an event handler for the joystick
    EventHandle = dx.CreateEvent(Me)

    'ask for notification of events
    diDev.SetEventNotification EventHandle

    'set the analog response range
    SetAnalogRanges -1000, 1000

    'acquire joystick for exclusive use
    diDev.Acquire
```

```
        'manually poll joystick first time
        DirectXEvent8_DXCallback 0

        'retrieve joystick information
        diDev.GetCapabilities joyCaps

        'display information about the joystick
        lblJoystick.Caption = diDevEnum.GetItem(1).GetInstanceName
        Debug.Print diDevEnum.GetItem(1).GetInstanceName
        Debug.Print "Number of axes: " & joyCaps.lAxes
        Debug.Print "Number of buttons: " & joyCaps.lButtons
        Debug.Print "Device type: " & joyCaps.lDevType
        Debug.Print "Driver version: " & joyCaps.lDriverVersion
        Debug.Print "Time resolution: " & joyCaps.lFFMinTimeResolution
        Debug.Print "Sample period: " & joyCaps.lFFSamplePeriod
        Debug.Print "Firware revision: " & joyCaps.lFirmwareRevision
        Debug.Print "Hardware revision: " & joyCaps.lHardwareRevision
        Debug.Print "Number of POVs: " & joyCaps.lPOVs
End Sub
```

The SetAnalogRanges procedure is used to set up the range of motion for the analog stick (which would be the primary analog input for a flight stick, or maybe an analog thumb stick on a gamepad). SetAnalogRanges uses two structures: DIPROPLONG and DIPROPRANGE. Rather than delve into the details of these structures, I'll just show you how to use them.

The analog range is the range of values returned when you move the stick, and can be as small or as large as you like (within reason). While you might be more comfortable with a range of, say, 0 – 10000, I prefer to use a negative range for left or up, and a positive range for right or down on the analog stick. So, I have set up the range in the JoystickTest program for -1000 to 1000.

SetAnalogRanges also configures the joystick object's dead zone and saturation zone. The dead zone is the space at dead center that does not generate movement events, and should be a very small value. The saturation zone is the area of motion that is active, and thus generates events.

```
Private Sub SetAnalogRanges(ByVal lMin As Long, ByVal lMax As Long)
    Dim DiProp_Dead As DIPROPLONG
    Dim DiProp_Range As DIPROPRANGE
    Dim DiProp_Saturation As DIPROPLONG
    On Local Error Resume Next
```

```
    'set range for all axes
    With DiProp_Range
        .lHow = DIPH_DEVICE
        .lMin = lMin
        .lMax = lMax
    End With
    'set the property
    diDev.SetProperty "DIPROP_RANGE", DiProp_Range

    'set deadzone for X and Y axes to 5 percent
    With DiProp_Dead
        .lData = (lMax - lMin) / 5
        .lHow = DIPH_BYOFFSET
        .lObj = DIJOFS_X
        diDev.SetProperty "DIPROP_DEADZONE", DiProp_Dead
        .lObj = DIJOFS_Y
        diDev.SetProperty "DIPROP_DEADZONE", DiProp_Dead
    End With

    'set saturation zone for X and Y axes to 95 percent
    With DiProp_Saturation
        .lData = (lMax - lMin) * 0.95
        .lHow = DIPH_BYOFFSET
        .lObj = DIJOFS_X
        diDev.SetProperty "DIPROP_SATURATION", DiProp_Saturation
        .lObj = DIJOFS_Y
        diDev.SetProperty "DIPROP_SATURATION", DiProp_Saturation
    End With
End Sub
```

The next section of code in the JoystickTest program includes the joystick events that are called by the callback procedure. These joystick events are just normal procedures in the program at this point, but will be made an integral part of the game library in Chapter 13, "Building the DirectX Game Library." The only complicated piece of code in this section involves an array called Analog, which was declared at the top of the program as a D3DVECTOR (which was just a convenient structure to use). The Analog array simply holds the values of the analog sticks, and is used to draw the green block in the analog display PictureBox controls.

```
Private Sub Joystick_AnalogMove(ByVal lNum As Long, _
    ByRef vAnalog As D3DVECTOR)
    Analog(lNum).x = vAnalog.x + 1000
```

```
        Analog(lNum).y = vAnalog.y + 1000
        Analog(lNum).z = vAnalog.z
        If lNum = 1 Then
            lblMoveX.Caption = "Analog1.X = " & vAnalog.x
            lblMoveY.Caption = "Analog1.Y = " & vAnalog.y
            lblMoveZ.Caption = "Analog1.Z = " & vAnalog.z
            Update_PicAxis1 Analog(1)
        Else
            lblMoveRX.Caption = "Analog2.X = " & vAnalog.x
            lblMoveRY.Caption = "Analog2.Y = " & vAnalog.y
            lblMoveRZ.Caption = "Analog2.Z = " & vAnalog.z
            Update_PicAxis2 Analog(2)
        End If
End Sub

Private Sub Joystick_SliderMove(ByVal lSlider As Long, _
    ByVal lValue As Long)
    If lSlider = 1 Then
        lblSlider1.Caption = "Slider 1 = " & lValue
    Else
        lblSlider2.Caption = "Slider 2 = " & lValue
    End If
End Sub

Private Sub Joystick_ButtonDown(ByVal lButton As Long)
    SetButton lButton, RGB(0, 255, 0)
End Sub

Private Sub Joystick_ButtonUp(ByVal lButton As Long)
    SetButton lButton, RGB(0, 0, 0)
End Sub

Private Sub Joystick_DPAD(ByVal lButton As Long)
    Dim n As Long
    'reset the labels
    For n = 0 To 7
        SetDPAD n, RGB(0, 0, 0)
    Next n
    'show which DPAD button was pressed
    SetDPAD lButton, RGB(0, 0, 255)
End Sub
```

Now for the callback procedure that I have been promoting throughout this section of the chapter. The `DirectXEvent8_DXCallback` procedure was implemented as an interface at the top of the program with the `Implements` keyword. Remember earlier when I covered the `CreateEvent` function? That function was passed the window handle for the JoystickTest program, which is actually the Form1.hWnd property. When you tell the event to look at this form, it calls the `DXCallback` procedure automatically. Therefore, if you don't include the procedure in the source code listing, you will get a compile-time error.

I have already covered most of the key ingredients for this procedure, so I will not focus on the details again. One important factor to consider, however, is how this procedure fires off the joystick events. Regardless of the state of the joystick, these events are being called. That's not a good way to do it in a real game, because there will be several hundred joystick events per second, even when nothing has changed! A much better method—and the method that is used by the game library in Chapter 13—is to keep track of the state of each value that is passed to the joystick events, and then only fire off an event if the value has actually changed.

```
Private Sub DirectXEvent8_DXCallback(ByVal eventid As Long)
    Static Analog1 As D3DVECTOR
    Static Analog2 As D3DVECTOR
    Dim js As DIJOYSTATE
    Dim n As Long
    On Local Error Resume Next

    'retrieve joystick status
    diDev.GetDeviceStateJoystick js
    If Err.Number = DIERR_NOTACQUIRED Or _
        Err.Number = DIERR_INPUTLOST Then
        diDev.Acquire
        Exit Sub
    End If

    'fire off any joystick analog movement events
    For n = 1 To 8
        Select Case n
            Case 1
                Analog1.x = js.x
                'Joystick_MoveX js.x
                Joystick_AnalogMove 1, Analog1
            Case 2
                'Joystick_MoveY js.y
                Analog1.y = js.y
                Joystick_AnalogMove 1, Analog1
```

```
            Case 3
                'Joystick_MoveZ js.z
                Analog1.z = js.z
                Joystick_AnalogMove 1, Analog1
            Case 4
                'Joystick_MoveRX js.rx
                Analog2.x = js.rx
                Joystick_AnalogMove 2, Analog2
            Case 5
                'Joystick_MoveRY js.ry
                Analog2.y = js.ry
                Joystick_AnalogMove 2, Analog2
            Case 6
                'Joystick_MoveRZ js.rz
                Analog2.z = js.rz
                Joystick_AnalogMove 2, Analog2
            Case 7
                Joystick_SliderMove 1, js.slider(0)
            Case 8
                Joystick_SliderMove 2, js.slider(1)
        End Select
    Next n

    'fire off any button events
    For n = 0 To joyCaps.lButtons - 1
        Select Case js.Buttons(n)
            Case 0
                Joystick_ButtonUp n
            Case Else
                Joystick_ButtonDown n
        End Select
    Next

    'fire off any direction-pad button events
    If js.POV(0) = -1 Then
        Joystick_DPAD -1
    Else
        Joystick_DPAD js.POV(0) / 4500
    End If
End Sub
```

The next section of code for the JoystickTest program includes some support routines to update the user interface. The SetButton and SetDPAD procedures update the label controls with a bright color when a button is pressed, and set the color back to black when the button is released.

The Update_PicAxis1 and Update_PicAxis2 procedures display the small green squares in the analog event PictureBox controls to reflect the position of the joystick for those two devices (if available).

The Shutdown procedure, as usual, cleans up the objects, frees up memory, and ends the program.

```
Private Sub SetButton(ByVal lButton As Long, ByVal lColor As Long)
    Select Case lButton
        Case 0
            lblButton1.BackColor = lColor
        Case 1
            lblButton2.BackColor = lColor
        Case 2
            lblButton3.BackColor = lColor
        Case 3
            lblButton4.BackColor = lColor
        Case 4
            lblButton5.BackColor = lColor
        Case 5
            lblButton6.BackColor = lColor
        Case 6
            lblButton7.BackColor = lColor
        Case 7
            lblButton8.BackColor = lColor
    End Select
End Sub

Private Sub SetDPAD(ByVal lButton As Long, ByVal lColor As Long)
    Select Case lButton
        Case 0
            lblDPad1.BackColor = lColor
        Case 1
            lblDPad2.BackColor = lColor
        Case 2
            lblDPad3.BackColor = lColor
        Case 3
            lblDPad4.BackColor = lColor
```

```
        Case 4
            lblDPad5.BackColor = lColor
        Case 5
            lblDPad6.BackColor = lColor
        Case 6
            lblDPad7.BackColor = lColor
        Case 7
            lblDPad8.BackColor = lColor
    End Select
End Sub

Private Sub Update_PicAxis1(ByRef Analog As D3DVECTOR)
    picAxis1.Cls
    picAxis1.Line (Analog.x - 100, Analog.y - 100)-(Analog.x + 100, _
        Analog.y + 100), RGB(255, 0, 0), BF
End Sub

Private Sub Update_PicAxis2(ByRef Analog As D3DVECTOR)
    picAxis2.Cls
    picAxis2.Line (Analog.x - 100, Analog.y - 100)-(Analog.x + 100, _
        Analog.y + 100), RGB(255, 0, 0), BF
End Sub

Private Sub Shutdown()
    running = False
    dx.DestroyEvent EventHandle
    If Not diDev Is Nothing Then diDev.Unacquire
    Set diDev = Nothing
    Set di = Nothing
    Set dx = Nothing
    End
End Sub
```

The Setup_Form procedure initializes the user interface by setting the form size to 640 × 480. Since the user interface controls are all created at runtime, this procedure is lengthy. However, the code is very simple and just involves creating controls and setting properties.

```
Private Sub Setup_Form()
    'set up the form
    Form1.ScaleMode = 3
    Form1.Width = 640 * Screen.TwipsPerPixelX
```

```
Form1.Height = 480 * Screen.TwipsPerPixelY
Form1.KeyPreview = True
Form1.Caption = "JoystickTest"
Form1.Show
DoEvents

'set up primary analog PictureBox
Set picAxis1 = Controls.Add("VB.PictureBox", "picAxis1")
picAxis1.BackColor = RGB(0, 0, 0)
picAxis1.BorderStyle = 1
picAxis1.ScaleMode = 3
picAxis1.Left = 200
picAxis1.Top = 40
picAxis1.Width = 120
picAxis1.Height = 120
picAxis1.ScaleLeft = 0
picAxis1.ScaleWidth = 2000
picAxis1.ScaleTop = 0
picAxis1.ScaleHeight = 2000
picAxis1.Visible = True

'set up secondary analog PictureBox
Set picAxis2 = Controls.Add("VB.PictureBox", "picAxis2")
picAxis2.BackColor = RGB(0, 0, 0)
picAxis2.BorderStyle = 1
picAxis2.ScaleMode = 3
picAxis2.Left = 200
picAxis2.Top = 170
picAxis2.Width = 120
picAxis2.Height = 120
picAxis2.ScaleLeft = 0
picAxis2.ScaleWidth = 2000
picAxis2.ScaleTop = 0
picAxis2.ScaleHeight = 2000
picAxis2.Visible = True

'set up analog stick event labels
Set lblJoystick = Controls.Add("VB.Label", "lblJoystick")
lblJoystick.Left = 10
lblJoystick.Top = 5
lblJoystick.FontBold = True
```

```
lblJoystick.Font.Size = 12
lblJoystick.AutoSize = True
lblJoystick.Visible = True

Set lblMoveX = Controls.Add("VB.Label", "lblMoveX")
lblMoveX.Left = 10
lblMoveX.Top = 40
lblMoveX.Width = 120
lblMoveX.Height = 20
lblMoveX.BorderStyle = 1
lblMoveX.Visible = True

Set lblMoveY = Controls.Add("VB.Label", "lblMoveY")
lblMoveY.Left = 10
lblMoveY.Top = 70
lblMoveY.Width = 120
lblMoveY.Height = 20
lblMoveY.BorderStyle = 1
lblMoveY.Visible = True

Set lblMoveZ = Controls.Add("VB.Label", "lblMoveZ")
lblMoveZ.Left = 10
lblMoveZ.Top = 100
lblMoveZ.Width = 120
lblMoveZ.Height = 20
lblMoveZ.BorderStyle = 1
lblMoveZ.Visible = True

Set lblMoveRX = Controls.Add("VB.Label", "lblMoveRX")
lblMoveRX.Left = 10
lblMoveRX.Top = 140
lblMoveRX.Width = 120
lblMoveRX.Height = 20
lblMoveRX.BorderStyle = 1
lblMoveRX.Visible = True

Set lblMoveRY = Controls.Add("VB.Label", "lblMoveRY")
lblMoveRY.Left = 10
lblMoveRY.Top = 170
lblMoveRY.Width = 120
lblMoveRY.Height = 20
```

```
lblMoveRY.BorderStyle = 1
lblMoveRY.Visible = True

Set lblMoveRZ = Controls.Add("VB.Label", "lblMoveRZ")
lblMoveRZ.Left = 10
lblMoveRZ.Top = 200
lblMoveRZ.Width = 120
lblMoveRZ.Height = 20
lblMoveRZ.BorderStyle = 1
lblMoveRZ.Visible = True

Set lblSlider1 = Controls.Add("VB.Label", "lblSlider1")
lblSlider1.Left = 10
lblSlider1.Top = 240
lblSlider1.Width = 120
lblSlider1.Height = 20
lblSlider1.BorderStyle = 1
lblSlider1.Visible = True

Set lblSlider2 = Controls.Add("VB.Label", "lblSlider2")
lblSlider2.Left = 10
lblSlider2.Top = 270
lblSlider2.Width = 120
lblSlider2.Height = 20
lblSlider2.BorderStyle = 1
lblSlider2.Visible = True

'set up button event controls
Set lblButton1 = Controls.Add("VB.Label", "lblButton1")
lblButton1.Left = 400
lblButton1.Top = 40
lblButton1.Width = 80
lblButton1.Height = 20
lblButton1.BorderStyle = 1
lblButton1.Caption = "Button1"
lblButton1.BackColor = RGB(0, 0, 0)
lblButton1.ForeColor = RGB(255, 255, 255)
lblButton1.Visible = True

Set lblButton2 = Controls.Add("VB.Label", "lblButton2")
lblButton2.Left = 400
```

```
lblButton2.Top = 70
lblButton2.Width = 80
lblButton2.Height = 20
lblButton2.BorderStyle = 1
lblButton2.Caption = "Button2"
lblButton2.BackColor = RGB(0, 0, 0)
lblButton2.ForeColor = RGB(255, 255, 255)
lblButton2.Visible = True

Set lblButton3 = Controls.Add("VB.Label", "lblButton3")
lblButton3.Left = 400
lblButton3.Top = 100
lblButton3.Width = 80
lblButton3.Height = 20
lblButton3.BorderStyle = 1
lblButton3.Caption = "Button3"
lblButton3.BackColor = RGB(0, 0, 0)
lblButton3.ForeColor = RGB(255, 255, 255)
lblButton3.Visible = True

Set lblButton4 = Controls.Add("VB.Label", "lblButton4")
lblButton4.Left = 400
lblButton4.Top = 130
lblButton4.Width = 80
lblButton4.Height = 20
lblButton4.BorderStyle = 1
lblButton4.Caption = "Button4"
lblButton4.BackColor = RGB(0, 0, 0)
lblButton4.ForeColor = RGB(255, 255, 255)
lblButton4.Visible = True

Set lblButton5 = Controls.Add("VB.Label", "lblButton5")
lblButton5.Left = 500
lblButton5.Top = 40
lblButton5.Width = 80
lblButton5.Height = 20
lblButton5.BorderStyle = 1
lblButton5.Caption = "Button5"
lblButton5.BackColor = RGB(0, 0, 0)
lblButton5.ForeColor = RGB(255, 255, 255)
lblButton5.Visible = True
```

```
Set lblButton6 = Controls.Add("VB.Label", "lblButton6")
lblButton6.Left = 500
lblButton6.Top = 70
lblButton6.Width = 80
lblButton6.Height = 20
lblButton6.BorderStyle = 1
lblButton6.Caption = "Button6"
lblButton6.BackColor = RGB(0, 0, 0)
lblButton6.ForeColor = RGB(255, 255, 255)
lblButton6.Visible = True

Set lblButton7 = Controls.Add("VB.Label", "lblButton7")
lblButton7.Left = 500
lblButton7.Top = 100
lblButton7.Width = 80
lblButton7.Height = 20
lblButton7.BorderStyle = 1
lblButton7.Caption = "Button7"
lblButton7.BackColor = RGB(0, 0, 0)
lblButton7.ForeColor = RGB(255, 255, 255)
lblButton7.Visible = True

Set lblButton8 = Controls.Add("VB.Label", "lblButton8")
lblButton8.Left = 500
lblButton8.Top = 130
lblButton8.Width = 80
lblButton8.Height = 20
lblButton8.BorderStyle = 1
lblButton8.Caption = "Button8"
lblButton8.BackColor = RGB(0, 0, 0)
lblButton8.ForeColor = RGB(255, 255, 255)
lblButton8.Visible = True

'set up direction-pad event controls
Set lblDPad1 = Controls.Add("VB.Label", "lblDPad1")
lblDPad1.Left = 400
lblDPad1.Top = 180
lblDPad1.Width = 80
lblDPad1.Height = 20
lblDPad1.BorderStyle = 1
lblDPad1.Caption = "DPad1"
```

```
lblDPad1.BackColor = RGB(0, 0, 0)
lblDPad1.ForeColor = RGB(255, 255, 255)
lblDPad1.Visible = True

Set lblDPad2 = Controls.Add("VB.Label", "lblDPad2")
lblDPad2.Left = 400
lblDPad2.Top = 210
lblDPad2.Width = 80
lblDPad2.Height = 20
lblDPad2.BorderStyle = 1
lblDPad2.Caption = "DPad2"
lblDPad2.BackColor = RGB(0, 0, 0)
lblDPad2.ForeColor = RGB(255, 255, 255)
lblDPad2.Visible = True

Set lblDPad3 = Controls.Add("VB.Label", "lblDPad3")
lblDPad3.Left = 400
lblDPad3.Top = 240
lblDPad3.Width = 80
lblDPad3.Height = 20
lblDPad3.BorderStyle = 1
lblDPad3.Caption = "DPad3"
lblDPad3.BackColor = RGB(0, 0, 0)
lblDPad3.ForeColor = RGB(255, 255, 255)
lblDPad3.Visible = True

Set lblDPad4 = Controls.Add("VB.Label", "lblDPad4")
lblDPad4.Left = 400
lblDPad4.Top = 270
lblDPad4.Width = 80
lblDPad4.Height = 20
lblDPad4.BorderStyle = 1
lblDPad4.Caption = "DPad4"
lblDPad4.BackColor = RGB(0, 0, 0)
lblDPad4.ForeColor = RGB(255, 255, 255)
lblDPad4.Visible = True

Set lblDPad5 = Controls.Add("VB.Label", "lblDPad5")
lblDPad5.Left = 500
lblDPad5.Top = 180
lblDPad5.Width = 80
```

```
        lblDPad5.Height = 20
        lblDPad5.BorderStyle = 1
        lblDPad5.Caption = "DPad5"
        lblDPad5.BackColor = RGB(0, 0, 0)
        lblDPad5.ForeColor = RGB(255, 255, 255)
        lblDPad5.Visible = True

        Set lblDPad6 = Controls.Add("VB.Label", "lblDPad6")
        lblDPad6.Left = 500
        lblDPad6.Top = 210
        lblDPad6.Width = 80
        lblDPad6.Height = 20
        lblDPad6.BorderStyle = 1
        lblDPad6.Caption = "DPad6"
        lblDPad6.BackColor = RGB(0, 0, 0)
        lblDPad6.ForeColor = RGB(255, 255, 255)
        lblDPad6.Visible = True

        Set lblDPad7 = Controls.Add("VB.Label", "lblDPad7")
        lblDPad7.Left = 500
        lblDPad7.Top = 240
        lblDPad7.Width = 80
        lblDPad7.Height = 20
        lblDPad7.BorderStyle = 1
        lblDPad7.Caption = "DPad7"
        lblDPad7.BackColor = RGB(0, 0, 0)
        lblDPad7.ForeColor = RGB(255, 255, 255)
        lblDPad7.Visible = True

        Set lblDPad8 = Controls.Add("VB.Label", "lblDPad8")
        lblDPad8.Left = 500
        lblDPad8.Top = 270
        lblDPad8.Width = 80
        lblDPad8.Height = 20
        lblDPad8.BorderStyle = 1
        lblDPad8.Caption = "DPad8"
        lblDPad8.BackColor = RGB(0, 0, 0)
        lblDPad8.ForeColor = RGB(255, 255, 255)
        lblDPad8.Visible = True
End Sub
```

That's the end of the JoystickTest program. Give it a spin and see what happens. If you have a joystick plugged in, you should see the program window appear. If not, you will get an error message telling you that a joystick could not be found.

Classing Up the Joystick

Despite the complexity of the JoystickTest program, most of the code in that program is for the user interface. The actual code to handle joystick events is much more manageable. Like the keyboard and mouse before it, the joystick handler can also be encapsulated within a class and polled for activity. Events that are triggered by the joystick device are forwarded on to the main program through custom events and the RaiseEvent procedure, which is a native VB feature.

The joystick handler class provides the following events:

- AnalogMove
- SliderMove
- ButtonDown
- ButtonUp
- DPAD

Now for the source code for the joystick handler class, which is called clsDIJoystick8. You will want to type this code into a Class Module and save it as DIKeyboard8.cls.

```
'------------------------------------------------------------------------
' Visual Basic Game Programming With DirectX
' Chapter 12 : Getting A Handle On User Input
' DIJoystick8 Class Source Code File
'------------------------------------------------------------------------
Option Explicit
Option Base 0

'class events
Public Event AnalogMove(ByVal lNum As Long, ByVal X As Long, _
    ByVal Y As Long, ByVal Z As Long)
Public Event SliderMove(ByVal lSlider As Long, ByVal lValue As Long)
Public Event ButtonDown(ByVal lButton As Long)
Public Event ButtonUp(ByVal lButton As Long)
Public Event DPAD(ByVal lButton As Long)

'local references
Dim dinput As clsDirectInput8
```

```
'joystick handler variables
Public diDev As DirectInputDevice8
Dim diDevEnum As DirectInputEnumDevices8
Dim diState As DIJOYSTATE
Dim joyCaps As DIDEVCAPS

'class variables
Dim lOldButtons(0 To 12) As Long
Dim lOldPOV As Long
Dim Analog1 As D3DVECTOR
Dim OldAnalog1 As D3DVECTOR
Dim Analog2 As D3DVECTOR
Dim OldAnalog2 As D3DVECTOR
Dim lOldSlider(0 To 1) As Long
Dim n As Long

Public Function Startup(ByRef di As clsDirectInput8, _
    ByVal hWindow As Long) As Boolean
    Startup = False

    'create reference to DirectInput object
    Set dinput = di

    'enumerate the game controllers
    Set diDevEnum = dinput.DIObj.GetDIDevices(DI8DEVCLASS_GAMECTRL, _
        DIEDFL_ATTACHEDONLY)
    If Err.Number <> 0 Then
        MsgBox "Error enumerating game controllers"
        Shutdown
    End If

    'check for the presence of a joystick
    If diDevEnum.GetCount = 0 Then
        Exit Function
    End If

    'see if joystick was already acquired
    If Not diDev Is Nothing Then
      diDev.Unacquire
    End If
```

```
    'create the joystick object
    Set diDev = Nothing
    Set diDev = dinput.DIObj.CreateDevice(diDevEnum.GetItem(1). _
        GetGuidInstance)
    diDev.SetCommonDataFormat DIFORMAT_JOYSTICK
    diDev.SetCooperativeLevel hWindow, DISCL_BACKGROUND Or _
        DISCL_NONEXCLUSIVE

    'ask for notification of events
    'diDev.SetEventNotification JoyEvent

    'set the analog response range
    SetAnalogRanges -1000, 1000

    'acquire joystick for exclusive use
    diDev.Acquire

    'retrieve joystick information
    diDev.GetCapabilities joyCaps
    Debug.Print diDevEnum.GetItem(1).GetInstanceName
    Debug.Print "Number of axes: " & joyCaps.lAxes
    Debug.Print "Number of buttons: " & joyCaps.lButtons
    Debug.Print "Device type: " & joyCaps.lDevType
    Debug.Print "Driver version: " & joyCaps.lDriverVersion
    Debug.Print "Time resolution: " & joyCaps.lFFMinTimeResolution
    Debug.Print "Sample period: " & joyCaps.lFFSamplePeriod
    Debug.Print "Firware revision: " & joyCaps.lFirmwareRevision
    Debug.Print "Hardware revision: " & joyCaps.lHardwareRevision
    Debug.Print "Number of POVs: " & joyCaps.lPOVs
    Startup = True
End Function

Public Sub Check_Joystick()
    On Error Resume Next
    'retrieve joystick status
    diDev.GetDeviceStateJoystick diState
    If Err.Number = DIERR_NOTACQUIRED Or _
        Err.Number = DIERR_INPUTLOST Then
        diDev.Acquire
        Exit Sub
    End If
```

```
'fire off any joystick analog movement events
For n = 1 To 8
    Select Case n
        Case 1
            If Analog1.X <> diState.X Then
                Analog1.X = diState.X
                RaiseEvent AnalogMove(0, diState.X, diState.Y, _
                    diState.Z)
            End If
        Case 2
            If Analog1.Y <> diState.Y Then
                Analog1.Y = diState.Y
                RaiseEvent AnalogMove(0, diState.X, diState.Y, _
                    diState.Z)
            End If
        Case 3
            If Analog1.Z <> diState.Z Then
                Analog1.Z = diState.Z
                RaiseEvent AnalogMove(0, diState.X, diState.Y, _
                    diState.Z)
            End If
        Case 4
            If Analog2.X <> diState.rx Then
                Analog2.X = diState.rx
                RaiseEvent AnalogMove(1, diState.X, diState.Y, _
                    diState.Z)
            End If
        Case 5
            If Analog2.Y <> diState.ry Then
                Analog2.Y = diState.ry
                RaiseEvent AnalogMove(1, diState.X, diState.Y, _
                    diState.Z)
            End If
        Case 6
            If Analog2.Z <> diState.rz Then
                Analog2.Z = diState.rz
                RaiseEvent AnalogMove(1, diState.X, diState.Y, _
                    diState.Z)
            End If
```

```
            Case 7
                If lOldSlider(0) <> diState.slider(0) Then
                    lOldSlider(0) = diState.slider(0)
                    RaiseEvent SliderMove(1, diState.slider(0))
                End If
            Case 8
                If lOldSlider(1) <> diState.slider(1) Then
                    lOldSlider(1) = diState.slider(1)
                    RaiseEvent SliderMove(2, diState.slider(1))
                End If
        End Select
    Next n

    'fire off any button events
    For n = 0 To joyCaps.lButtons - 1
        If diState.Buttons(n) <> lOldButtons(n) Then
            If diState.Buttons(n) = 0 Then
                RaiseEvent ButtonUp(n)
            Else
                RaiseEvent ButtonDown(n)
            End If
            lOldButtons(n) = diState.Buttons(n)
        End If
    Next n

    'fire off any direction-pad button events
    If diState.POV(0) <> lOldPOV Then
        If diState.POV(0) = -1 Then
            RaiseEvent DPAD(-1)
        Else
            RaiseEvent DPAD(diState.POV(0) / 4500)
        End If
        lOldPOV = diState.POV(0)
    End If
End Sub

Public Sub Shutdown()
    On Local Error Resume Next
    'release the joystick
```

```
        If Not (diDev Is Nothing) Then
            diDev.Unacquire
            Set diDev = Nothing
        End If

        If Not (diDevEnum Is Nothing) Then
            Set diDevEnum = Nothing
        End If
End Sub

Private Sub SetAnalogRanges(ByVal lMin As Long, ByVal lMax As Long)
    Dim DiProp_Dead As DIPROPLONG
    Dim DiProp_Range As DIPROPRANGE
    Dim DiProp_Saturation As DIPROPLONG
    On Local Error Resume Next

    'set range for all axes
    With DiProp_Range
        .lHow = DIPH_DEVICE
        .lMin = lMin
        .lMax = lMax
    End With
    'set the property
    diDev.SetProperty "DIPROP_RANGE", DiProp_Range

    'set deadzone for X and Y axes to 5 percent
    With DiProp_Dead
        .lData = (lMax - lMin) / 5
        .lHow = DIPH_BYOFFSET
        .lObj = DIJOFS_X
        diDev.SetProperty "DIPROP_DEADZONE", DiProp_Dead
        .lObj = DIJOFS_Y
        diDev.SetProperty "DIPROP_DEADZONE", DiProp_Dead
    End With

    'set saturation zone for X and Y axes to 95 percent
    With DiProp_Saturation
        .lData = (lMax - lMin) * 0.95
        .lHow = DIPH_BYOFFSET
        .lObj = DIJOFS_X
```

```
        diDev.SetProperty "DIPROP_SATURATION", DiProp_Saturation
        .lObj = DIJOFS_Y
        diDev.SetProperty "DIPROP_SATURATION", DiProp_Saturation
    End With
End Sub
```

That's the end of the source code for the joystick handler class. At this point, you should have four classes to support DirectInput programming:

- clsDirectInput8
- clsDIKeyboard8
- clsDIMouse8
- clsDIJoystick8

Keep these classes handy, because in Chapter 13, "Building the DirectX Game Library," I will show you how to integrate them into an ActiveX DLL project, along with all the other classes up to this point.

SUMMARY

This chapter has covered the fascinating subject of user input with DirectInput, a component of DirectX. While Visual Basic has rudimentary user input events that are available with a form, these events pale in comparison to what is provided with DirectInput. In addition to covering the keyboard and mouse, this chapter explored how to read the analog controls and digital buttons on a joystick.

User input is such a critical part of a game that it deserves adequate attention during the design of the game. It is important that you consider what the optimum input device will be for a game and then optimize the game for that particular device while still supporting other devices as an option.

While DirectInput provides a means to support input through a callback procedure, it is more useful to poll the user input devices directly and then encapsulate the DirectInput code inside classes for convenience and reuse.

CHAPTER 13

Building the
DirectX Game
Library

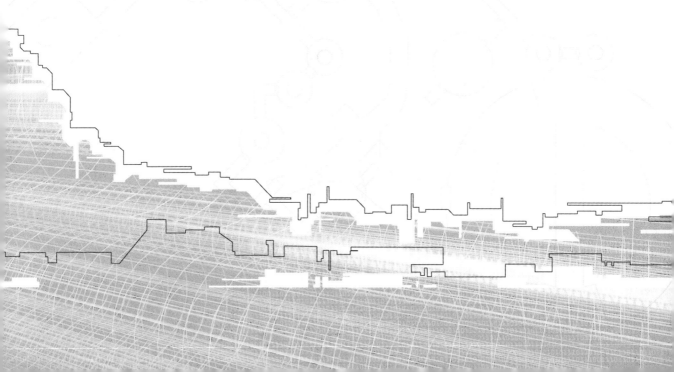

There comes a time in the development life cycle of a game where the project reaches critical mass and begins to really take off. Up to this point in the book, most of the work has been in the development of the game engine—the part of the game that handles the mundane chores of timing, loading graphics and sounds, animating objects on the screen, handling double buffering, and completing other processes necessary to build a game.

Once that work is done and a rudimentary version of the game is up and running, critical mass kicks in and you get a lot more bang for every additional line of code. I somewhat dislike the word synergy, but it does describe what happens at this point in the development of a game. All of the code components begin to work together and become the physical universe for a game.

What does that make you, the programmer—the architect of this game universe? The implications are intriguing: You are the creator of your own little universe!

The nice thing is, at the point where the game engine is functional, you can relax and take a break, throw a party, and blow off a little tension, because the hardest part of the job is done. From that point forward, the focus of development is on refining the high-level requirements, such as artificial intelligence, game physics, special effects, and the storyline. (These topics are the bane of the game designer from that point forward. Just be ready to re-write the entire engine if the designer is not happy with it!)

The game engine itself should be generic enough that it can be used over and over for each new game project, with improvements and additions refining the engine with each completed game. In the case of the game library developed in this book, I will use the classes from this point forward for sample programs, including the full-blown games in Part IV, "Complete Game Projects."

This chapter is about taking all of the fundamental processes in a typical game and packaging them up in an easy-to-use library that will empower the core functionality of many games to come. Indeed, the game engine—which I have called the Visual Basic Game Library, or VBGL for short—will provide power for most of the programs in this book by leveraging the phenomenal DirectX API (which I covered in the last three chapters).

This chapter covers the following topics:

- Developing the Game Library
- Communicating through Events

- Creating the VBGL Project
- Testing the Visual Basic Game Library

DEVELOPING THE GAME LIBRARY

Early in the development of this library, I was planning to build two complete game libraries. The first would include only Windows API functionality, with a pretty cool graphics library. (Check out Chapter 9, "Let the Animation Begin," for some high-performance graphics without DirectX.) The problem with this approach is that with a complete DirectX library available—one that is capable of running in windowed or full-screen mode—what's the point of a separate Windows API library that pales in comparison to the DirectX library?

I think the idea was to provide support for earlier versions of the compiler (with a library based entirely on the Windows API), or perhaps to provide a means to write games for low end systems. I quickly dropped the whole idea of building two libraries after I realized that the first one would be useless with the second one available! Rather, the single DirectX library will contain everything covered up to this point, including classes developed in future chapters, as summarized below:

- Direct3D: clsDirect3D8, clsD3DTriangle8, clsD3DRectangle8, clsD3DSprite8
- DirectDraw: clsDirectDraw7, clsDDSurface7, clsDDSprite7
- DirectMusic: clsDirectMusic8, clsDMSequence8
- DirectInput: clsDirectInput8, clsDIKeyboard8, clsDIMouse8, clsDIJoystick8
- DirectSound: clsDirectSound8, clsDSWave8
- Sprite Control: clsFuzzyEngine, clsFESpriteControl, clsGeneticEngine, clsGESpriteControl, clsStateEngine, clsStateEntity, clsSESpriteControl
- Windows API: clsBitmap, clsSprite, clsDirtyRect, clsVScroller
- Windows Sockets API: clsClientSocket, clsServerSocket

The result is that this chapter takes all of the code and classes from the first half of the book and packages it all up into a single ActiveX DLL, an in-process (inproc) server, as Microsoft has called it. You will then be able to tap into this library as an interface between your game and DirectX with very little overhead (negative effect on performance).

> **TIP**
>
> Using this library, you can write a game based on DirectDraw 7, while still supporting DirectX 8 components such as DirectX Audio.

Why Do You Need a Game Library?

I know that there are many programmers who shun game libraries and would rather use pure code that does not have a convenience layer. That is precisely why I have covered all of the subjects up to this point largely without a game library, and have only provided convenient classes after discussing how to write the code directly. In every case, there have been sample programs to demonstrate the subject (such as DirectDraw surfaces back in Chapter 10, "Diving into DirectDraw") prior to building the convenience class (which was called clsDirectDraw7, as you might recall).

The Visual Basic Game Library (VBGL) contains all of the classes developed up to this point for supporting Windows API functions and DirectX (and some that haven't been covered yet). The library supports both DX7 and DX8 at the same time, although DirectDraw is the only component from DX7 in the library. This does provide the potential for some interesting games. For example, you can write a standard VB game using PictureBox and Image controls, and at the same time, support DirectInput and DirectSound. Perhaps you might like to use the Windows animation classes (clsBitmap, clsSprite, and clsDirtyRect) along with DirectSound for a low-end game, such as the arcade game presented in Chapter 19, "Block Attack: Classic Arcade Game."

Benefits of a Self-Contained Library

One of the benefits of writing a game library is the ability to reuse the components of the library without recompiling the source code for those components. Once you have a comprehensive library at your disposal, you can create functional, working prototype games very quickly.

The game library presented in this chapter is not strictly necessary for developing games with the classes in this book. You could write an entire game—or several games, for that matter—just by including the classes directly in your game projects. If that is your preference, then by all means use that method. However, if you are more inclined to use a self-contained library that provides everything you need to develop a game, and you are not likely to modify the original source code for the library, then you might prefer to pre-compile the library and reference it in your game projects as an ActiveX DLL.

One of the nice things about the VB environment is that you can easily change the type of a project by selecting Properties from the Project menu. Figure 13.1 shows the Project Properties dialog box, with the Project Type drop-down menu visible.

Note the four options for the project type:

- Standard EXE
- ActiveX EXE
- ActiveX DLL
- ActiveX Control

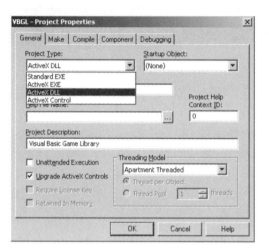

Figure 13.1

The Project Properties dialog box allows you to change the settings for a project.

The VBGL project in this chapter will be an ActiveX DLL project. But you also have the option of converting this project into an ActiveX EXE project. What is the difference, you might ask?

An ActiveX DLL project runs in process, which means it is loaded into the memory space shared by the main program. An ActiveX EXE project runs out of process, which means it is loaded separately into memory and may be shared by multiple programs.

You are free to use either type of shared library for the Visual Basic Game Library. I do recommend compiling it as an ActiveX DLL, which often runs faster and is more stable than an ActiveX EXE.

Distributing the Game Library

Once you have assembled everything you need inside the ActiveX DLL project, you will need to distribute that DLL with your game when you package it up for others (either in demo form, as a shareware game, or perhaps even as a commercial product). The DLL can be registered on another computer automatically with the Visual Basic Package & Deployment Wizard, which is a tool that will build an installation file set out of your project.

Although I am not going to provide a detailed explanation of how to use the deployment tool, I will at least point you in the right direction. You can run the program from the Start menu by looking in the Microsoft Visual Studio 6.0 folder, followed by Microsoft Visual Studio 6.0 Tools. It is in that sub-menu that you should find the Package & Deployment Wizard. The program is very easy to use, although you will definitely need to familiarize yourself with it by building a few sample installers. Be sure to add all of the graphics, sounds, and data files for your game to the install file set before building it.

COMMUNICATING THROUGH EVENTS

The classes in the game library communicate with your main program through custom events that are fired off with the `RaiseEvent` procedure. Before using an event, you must declare it. Here is a sample event from the clsDIKeyboard8 class:

```
Public Event KeyDown(ByVal lKey As Long)
```

Notice the `Public Event` keywords that prefix the declaration for this event. This tells VB to compile the class with an active event process that is visible to calling programs.

Generating Events

To generate an event, you use the `RaiseEvent` procedure. The event that you would like to raise must have been declared at the top of the source code listing with `Public Event`, as previously explained. Here is a sample line of code that shows how to raise an event:

```
RaiseEvent KeyDown(lKeyCode)
```

Notice how this event is called like a function, with surrounding parentheses. Event parameters are optional; you are free to create events that have no parameters. This is useful when all you need to do is notify the main program that something has happened, such as an error. In general, it is a good idea to provide at least one parameter to an event.

Keeping Track of Events

When you need to receive events in the main program, you must declare a class variable using the `WithEvents` keyword. This tells VB to accept events from the class. Here is an example of how you would declare a variable to receive events:

```
Dim WithEvents Keyboard As clsDIKeyboard8
```

The Keyboard variable is so named because it will prefix the `KeyDown` event. I prefer to ignore coding standards when it comes to event handling and callbacks, in the interest of more attractive source code. Here is what the `KeyDown` event looks like in the main program:

```
Private Sub Keyboard_KeyDown(ByVal lKey As Long)
    'handle DirectInput keyboard events here
End Sub
```

CREATING THE VBGL PROJECT

The main project for the Visual Basic Game Library can be either an ActiveX DLL or ActiveX EXE, although I would recommend the former for performance reasons. If the library has problems, it is safer to have it running out of the current process (out in its own memory space, in the case of an ActiveX EXE). But once you have written and tested the game library to a certain degree, it should be safe to use in process.

Selecting the Project Type

To create the project, fire up VB and select ActiveX DLL for the project type, as shown in Figure 13.2.

Figure 13.2

The New Project dialog box allows you to select the type of project you want to create.

The new ActiveX DLL project will be empty, except for a single file called Class1. The default file for a DLL project is a Class Module, since most DLL projects include at least one class. Figure 13.3 shows the Project Explorer window with the default class that was added to the project.

Figure 13.3

The Project Explorer shows the default file added to a new ActiveX DLL project.

Configuring the Properties for VBGL

Now that you have a sample DLL project, rename Project1 to VBGL. Select VBGL Properties from the Project menu. The Project Properties dialog is shown again in Figure 13.4; this time, notice the field called Project Description.

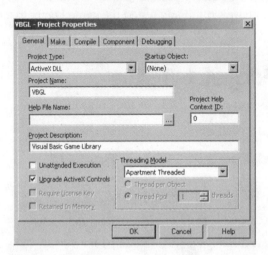

Figure 13.4

The Project Properties dialog box is where you change the project description.

Change the description to Visual Basic Game Library. This is the name of the component, as it will appear in the References when you are ready to create a sample game using the pre-compiled library. Save the new project as VBGL.vbp.

Adding Files to the Game Library

The VBGL project is empty, except for the default Class1 file. Right-click the file and remove it. You are going to want to retrieve the class files for the previous chapters and add those files to the new VBGL project. The easiest way to add a file to a VB project is to drag the file from Windows Explorer to the VB Project Explorer window.

Due to the amount of source code developed at this point, I am not going to re-list the source code for the classes again in this chapter. However, I would like you to take note of a few changes. Since the class files are now part of the VBGL project, there is no longer a need to have Windows API function and structure definitions inside each individual class.

Following is the complete list of classes that you will need to add to the library (also shown in Figure 13.5). Although new classes will be added in future chapters, I have included all of the classes in the project on the CD-ROM (under \Sources\VB6\CH13\VBGL).

- clsBitmap
- clsDDSprite
- clsDDSurface7
- clsDIJoystick8
- clsDIKeyboard8
- clsDIMouse8
- clsDirectDraw7
- clsDirectInput8
- clsDirectMusic8
- clsDirectSound8
- clsDirtyRect
- clsDMSequence8
- clsDSWave8
- clsSprite
- clsVScroller

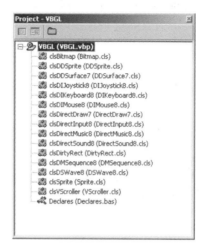

Figure 13.5

The Project Explorer window shows all the classes that make up the Visual Basic Game Library.

The Declares.bas Module

In addition to these classes, you will need a single code module called Declares.bas that holds the Windows API functions and declarations. To build this file, simply open each of the class files and cut any Windows API code from the top of the source code and paste the code into Declares.bas. If you prefer to leave the classes alone (self-contained), feel free to do so. However, moving all the Windows API code out of the classes and into a code module cleans up the code.

The complete game library on the CD-ROM features classes with all of the Windows API calls stripped out, since they are all available in the Declares.bas file. If you simply include this file in all of your game projects, you won't have any problems with missing structs, constants, or function calls. You will probably notice that the RECT struct has been renamed to RECT_API. This is to keep it from conflicting with the version of RECT that is included in the DirectX type libraries. Here is the final version of Declares.bas:

```
'-------------------------------------------------------------------
' Visual Basic Game Programming With DirectX
' Chapter 13 : Building The DirectX Game Library
' Game Library Declares Module
'-------------------------------------------------------------------
Option Explicit
Option Base 0
```

```
'Windows API constants
Public Const BITSPIXEL = 12
Public Const SYSTEM_FONT = 13
Public Const LR_LOADFROMFILE = &H10
Public Const CAPS1 = 94
Public Const C1_TRANSPARENT = &H1
Public Const NEWTRANSPARENT = 3


'Windows API structures
Public Type OSVERSIONINFO
    dwOSVersionInfoSize As Long
    dwMajorVersion As Long
    dwMinorVersion As Long
    dwBuildNumber As Long
    dwPlatformId As Long
    szCSDVersion As String * 128
End Type


Public Type BITMAP_STRUCT
    bmType As Long
    bmWidth As Long
    bmHeight As Long
    bmWidthBytes As Long
    bmPlanes As Integer
    bmBitsPixel As Integer
    bmBits As Long
End Type


Public Type RECT_API
    Left As Long
    Top As Long
    Right As Long
    Bottom As Long
End Type


Public Type POINT
    X As Long
    Y As Long
End Type
```

```
Public Type RGBQUAD
    Blue As Byte
    Green As Byte
    Red As Byte
    alpha As Byte
End Type


'Windows API functions
Public Declare Function BitBlt _
    Lib "gdi32" ( _
    ByVal hDestDC As Long, _
    ByVal X As Long, _
    ByVal Y As Long, _
    ByVal nWidth As Long, _
    ByVal nHeight As Long, _
    ByVal hSrcDC As Long, _
    ByVal xSrc As Long, _
    ByVal ySrc As Long, _
    ByVal dwRop As Long _
) As Long


Public Declare Sub CopyMemory _
    Lib "kernel32" Alias "RtlMoveMemory" ( _
    lpvDest As Any, _
    lpvSource As Any, _
    ByVal cbCopy As Long _
)


Public Declare Function CreateCompatibleBitmap _
    Lib "gdi32" ( _
    ByVal hdc As Long, _
    ByVal nWidth As Long, _
    ByVal nHeight As Long _
) As Long


Public Declare Function CreateCompatibleDC _
    Lib "gdi32" ( _
    ByVal hdc As Long _
) As Long
```

```
Public Declare Function CreatePen _
    Lib "gdi32" ( _
    ByVal nPenStyle As Long, _
    ByVal nWidth As Long, _
    ByVal crColor As Long _
) As Long

Public Declare Function DeleteDC _
    Lib "gdi32" ( _
    ByVal hdc As Long _
) As Long

Public Declare Function DeleteObject _
    Lib "gdi32" ( _
    ByVal hObject As Long _
) As Long

Public Declare Function Ellipse _
    Lib "gdi32" ( _
    ByVal hdc As Long, _
    ByVal X1 As Long, _
    ByVal Y1 As Long, _
    ByVal X2 As Long, _
    ByVal Y2 As Long _
) As Long

Public Declare Function GetBitmapBits _
    Lib "gdi32" ( _
    ByVal hBitmap As Long, _
    ByVal dwCount As Long, _
    lpBits As Any _
) As Long

Public Declare Function GetClientRect _
    Lib "user32" ( _
    ByVal hWnd As Long, _
    lpRect As RECT_API _
) As Long
```

```vb
Public Declare Function GetDC _
    Lib "user32" ( _
    ByVal hWnd As Long _
) As Long

Public Declare Function GetDesktopWindow _
    Lib "user32" ( _
) As Long

Public Declare Function GetDeviceCaps _
    Lib "gdi32" ( _
    ByVal hdc As Long, _
    ByVal nIndex As Long _
) As Long

Public Declare Function GetObjectA _
    Lib "gdi32" ( _
    ByVal hObject As Long, _
    ByVal nCount As Long, _
    lpObject As Any _
) As Long

Public Declare Function GetObjectW _
    Lib "gdi32" ( _
    ByVal hObject As Long, _
    ByVal nCount As Long, _
    lpObject As Any _
) As Long

Public Declare Function GetStockObject _
    Lib "gdi32" ( _
    ByVal nIndex As Long _
) As Long

Public Declare Function GetPixel _
    Lib "gdi32" ( _
    ByVal hdc As Long, _
    ByVal X As Long, _
    ByVal Y As Long _
) As Long
```

```
Public Declare Function GetTickCount _
    Lib "kernel32" ( _
) As Long

Public Declare Function GetVersionEx _
    Lib "kernel32" Alias "GetVersionExA" ( _
    lpVersionInformation As OSVERSIONINFO _
) As Long

Public Declare Function IntersectRect _
    Lib "user32" ( _
    lpDestRect As RECT_API, _
    lpSrc1Rect As RECT_API, _
    lpSrc2Rect As RECT_API _
) As Long

Public Declare Function LineTo _
    Lib "gdi32" ( _
    ByVal hdc As Long, _
    ByVal X As Long, _
    ByVal Y As Long _
) As Long

Public Declare Function LoadImage _
    Lib "user32" Alias "LoadImageA" ( _
    ByVal hInst As Long, _
    ByVal Filename As String, _
    ByVal un1 As Long, _
    ByVal Width As Long, _
    ByVal Height As Long, _
    ByVal opmode As Long _
) As Long

Public Declare Function MoveTo _
    Lib "gdi32" Alias "MoveToEx" ( _
    ByVal hdc As Long, _
    ByVal X As Long, _
    ByVal Y As Long, _
    lpPoint As POINT _
) As Long
```

```
Public Declare Function Polyline _
    Lib "gdi32" ( _
    ByVal hdc As Long, _
    lpPoint As POINT, _
    ByVal nCount As Long _
) As Long


Public Declare Function SelectObject _
    Lib "gdi32" ( _
    ByVal hdc As Long, _
    ByVal hObject As Long _
) As Long


Public Declare Function SetBkColor _
    Lib "gdi32" ( _
    ByVal hdc As Long, _
    ByVal crColor As Long _
) As Long


Public Declare Function SetBkMode _
    Lib "gdi32" ( _
    ByVal hdc As Long, _
    ByVal nBkMode As Long _
) As Long


Public Declare Function SetBitmapBits _
    Lib "gdi32" ( _
    ByVal hBitmap As Long, _
    ByVal dwCount As Long, _
    lpBits As Any _
) As Long


Public Declare Function SetPixel _
    Lib "gdi32" ( _
    ByVal hdc As Long, _
    ByVal X As Long, _
    ByVal Y As Long, _
    ByVal crColor As Long _
) As Long
```

```
Public Declare Function SetTextColor _
    Lib "gdi32" ( _
    ByVal hdc As Long, _
    ByVal crColor As Long _
) As Long

Public Declare Function TextOutA _
    Lib "gdi32" ( _
    ByVal hdc As Long, _
    ByVal X As Long, _
    ByVal Y As Long, _
    ByVal lpString As String, _
    ByVal nCount As Long _
) As Long

Public Declare Function TextOutW _
    Lib "gdi32" ( _
    ByVal hdc As Long, _
    ByVal X As Long, _
    ByVal Y As Long, _
    ByVal lpString As String, _
    ByVal nCount As Long _
) As Long

Public Declare Function ValidateRect _
    Lib "user32" ( _
    ByVal hWnd As Long, _
    lpRect As RECT_API _
) As Long
```

Compiling the Game Library

Once you have typed in the code for the Declares.bas file and have added the classes to the library, you can compile the ActiveX DLL. The first thing you need to do is build the project to get an initial VBGL.dll file, in order to set the version compatibility. Open the File menu and select Make VBGL.dll to build the project. If you encounter any syntax errors, they are likely from the Declares.bas file, since the classes should have already been tested in earlier chapters (with the exception of the DirectInput classes, which were not tested).

If all else fails, you can copy the project off the CD-ROM, but I recommend you try to build the library on your own first. Once you are able to create the VBGL.dll file, then you can set the version compatibility (which is necessary when recompiling the project multiple times).

Bring up the Project Properties once again, and click the Component tab. Select the option called Binary Compatibility and type VBGL.dll into the filename field, as shown in Figure 13.6.

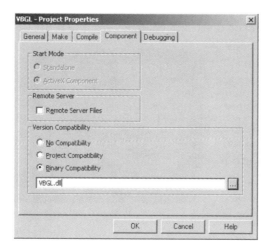

Figure 13.6

Setting the Version Compatibility option with the Project Properties dialog box

Setting the Version Compatibility option allows you to make changes to the source code and recompile the library without affecting programs that already use the library. For example, suppose you release a game that relies on the VBGL.dll file. Soon after, you discover a bug in some new code you added to the library, and you need to release a patch. Without the Binary Compatibility option set, you would have to release a whole new executable for the game, in addition to the new VBGL.dll, because the existing game would not know how to reference the new game library.

Any time you recompile an ActiveX DLL project, VB automatically registers the component in the Windows Registry. Binary compatibility keeps the existing class identifier for the component so that existing code doesn't fail after a new compile. This way, you can compile the game, and then make minor changes to the game library without recompiling the game. This is an excellent way to upgrade a game after it has been released.

A frequent error message is associated with this potential problem. If you ever get a Run-Time Error '429': ActiveX Component Can't Create Object error, you know that the game library is incompatible with the existing program due to a compatibility failure.

TESTING THE VISUAL BASIC GAME LIBRARY

To show how easy it is to use the game library, I have converted four sample programs from earlier chapters. I'm not listing the source code for these programs here, because they are quite lengthy. You can load the projects from the CD-ROM under the directory for this chapter. The reason is that these programs have not been drastically changed to support the game library. In several cases, all I did was remove the classes and recompile the sample programs with a reference to VBGL.

> **NOTE**
>
> Any time you add a new class to the library, be sure to change the Instancing property of the class to 5 - Multiuse. The default instancing of 1 - Private prevents classes from being used in the calling program.

Before compiling these new programs to test the game library, be sure to compile the game library into a VBGL.dll file. This registers the component in the Windows Registry, which is mandatory before you open any projects that require it. Of course, by now you should be familiar with the Project References dialog box for adding components to a game, since you have used the DirectX type libraries in earlier chapters. The game library will appear in the References dialog box as well.

The DoubleBuffer2 Program

Figure 13.7 shows the DoubleBuffer2 test program. Recall that this program does not use DirectDraw, but instead uses the Windows API code developed in earlier chapters.

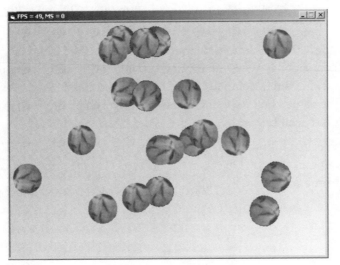

Figure 13.7

DoubleBuffer2 was modified with only a few source code changes to support the Visual Basic Game Library.

The CollisionTest2 Program

Figure 13.8 shows the CollisionTest2 program, which was adapted from an earlier program that showed how to detect sprite collisions.

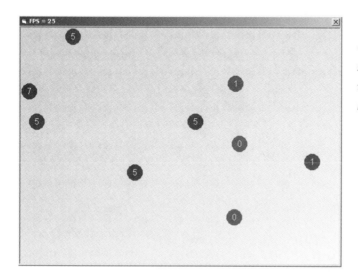

Figure 13.8

CollisionTest2 shows sprite collision detection using the game library.

The DDFullscreen2 Program

Figure 13.9 shows a screenshot from the DDFullscreen2 program, which is a full-screen DirectDraw sample program, also from an earlier chapter. This program shows how to use the DirectDraw class that is now built into the game library.

The JoystickTest2 Program

The last program that I adapted to demonstrate the game library is JoystickTest2, shown in Figure 13.10. This program does not use the callback procedure like the original JoystickTest program did, but instead now uses the polling code in the clsDIJoystick8 class.

SUMMARY

This chapter summarized all of the code developed to this point, and assembled all of the game development classes into a single library called Visual Basic Game Library. By compiling this project into a code library, you have the ability to develop prototype games quickly and easily with a minimum amount of code. To make use of the game library in a VB program, you can simply

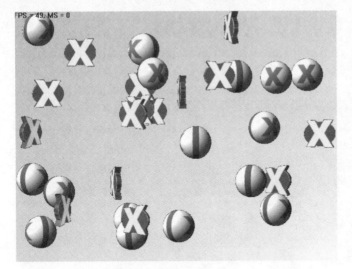

Figure 13.9

DDFullscreen2 shows how to write a full-screen DirectDraw program using the game library, and was simply adapted from an earlier program.

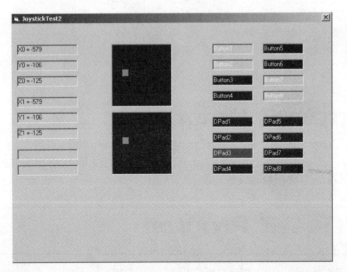

Figure 13.10

The JoystickTest2 program shows how to use the game library to support a joystick with DirectInput.

select the library from the list of Project References, at which point all of the classes in the library will become available to your program.

Now that Part II is completed and you have a complete game library at your disposal, why not take a break from learning and work on a game of your own design? If you need inspiration, feel free to skip ahead to Part IV, "Complete Game Projects," and check out one of the games presented at the end of the book. It is always a good idea to take a break now and then from serious programming and have some fun working on a real game.

Part III

Advanced
Game
Programming
Techniques

Welcome to Part III of *Visual Basic Game Programming with DirectX*. Part III includes five chapters that cover the following advanced topics: 3-D game programming with Direct3D (including coverage of sprite surfaces in 3-D); simulating artificial intelligence with game state, instinctive response, genetic programming, and simple neural networks; adding realism by employing simple physics to game objects; multiplayer networking with TCP/IP sockets and DirectPlay; and game theory and design.

The subjects in Part III are considered power-user subjects because they push the specifications of a game, while not necessarily filling a crucial role. The subject of 3-D alone fills volumes. Most games require some type of computer opponent, which is where a study of artificial intelligence is useful. Multiplayer programming is important in the online world today. Plus, it is always helpful to discuss game design now and then.

My favorite subject is multiplayer programming. Designing a game with multiplayer support opens up a whole new world for the game and makes even a simple arcade game explosively fun! Part III includes coverage of both the Windows Sockets API and DirectPlay.

Part III includes the following chapters:

- Chapter 14: DirectX Graphics and Direct3D
- Chapter 15: Artificial and Simulated Intelligence
- Chapter 16: Multiplayer Programming with Windows Sockets
- Chapter 17: Network Programming with DirectPlay
- Chapter 18: Effective Game Design Techniques

CHAPTER 14

DirectX Graphics and Direct3D

This chapter covers the new DirectX Graphics component that was introduced in DirectX 8.0. DirectX Graphics combines DirectDraw and Direct3D into a single, seamless graphics rendering library. Literally dozens of books have been written on the subject of Direct3D, so this chapter will only scratch the surface. I hope to at least give you the basics that will allow you to tap into the fascinating world of Direct3D and show you how to draw 3-D objects with enough detail to build 3-D games. This chapter also provides an important section on developing a 3-D sprite engine using alpha blended 3-D textures, which is pretty exciting. This chapter basically gives you just what you need to write Direct3D games, whether they are based on sprites or 3-D objects.

This chapter covers the following topics:

- What's the Deal with 3-D Games?
- Introduction to DirectX Graphics
- 3-D Graphics Programming with Direct3D
- Sprite Programming with Direct3D

WHAT'S THE DEAL WITH 3-D GAMES?

As I started working on this chapter, I came to something of a dilemma. This book has been, up to this point, entirely focused on building 2-D games. The dilemma was in the decision of how to cover 3-D without making the material seem irrelevant in the context of previous chapters. What is needed—and what this chapter covers—is a basic theory of the subject with functional source code for drawing sprites with Direct3D, as well as the source code and classes for a 3-D engine.

Drawing sprites on a Direct3D surface will provide a means to completely support DirectX 8, without the need to use DirectDraw. There are some advantages to a sprite-based game that is rendered on a Direct3D surface, such as the ability to rotate and scale the sprite with ease. Like previous chapters, this one is a hands-on tutorial of the subject. I prefer to sacrifice some theory and just show you how to do things. Check out Figure 14.1 for a sample of what is to come later in this chapter.

The 3-D engine in this chapter is perfect for writing simple 3-D games, because it doesn't get into any of the complicated subjects normally found in a full-blown tutorial of Direct3D. To make the subject easier to understand, I do not cover lighting, materials, or any mathematics (like trigonometry or matrix calculations). Instead, the 3-D engine in this chapter will use ambient

Figure 14.1

The Cube3D program draws a rotating, textured cube over a tiled floor, using the classes developed in this chapter.

lighting. Not only will this give your games a much better frame rate, it will cut down on an enormous amount of overhead that must first be covered.

If you're like me, you would rather build a complete 3-D game first and then add advanced features to it later, rather than get bogged down in all kinds of advanced 3-D techniques that only take away from the learning experience. If you have ever wanted to just jump in and write a quick Direct3D game, but have been intimidated by other books and tutorials, then you will be pleasantly surprised by the content of this chapter, which just sticks to the basics.

TIP

Think of the code in this chapter as the Nintendo 64 of 3-D engines—something that was built for pure fun, at the expense of more advanced features.

NOTE

If you are an advanced programmer who would like to delve into advanced Direct3D, I can recommend some excellent books that you will find tremendously helpful. For a list of recommended books on the subject, see Appendix E, "Recommended Reading."

The decision to skip these subjects was a necessary one, because they are far beyond the scope of this book. After all, a hundred pages on 3-D graphics theory would be wasteful when such information is readily available in books that specifically cover the subject. My goal is to give you enough information to build a solid 3-D engine that can be used to write some cool games, while leaving it open for improvement should you wish to enhance the 3-D engine with more advanced features. If you are intimidated by C++ code and COM then fear not, because the DirectX type library mimics the C++ function calls closely. Porting a section of Direct3D code from Visual C++ to Visual Basic is not difficult to do.

Since I am equally focused on building a 2-D engine with Direct3D, as well as building a 3-D engine, this chapter will cover the material that would normally require a whole book. However, earlier in the book I showed you some advanced techniques for creating sprites using the Windows API and functions like `BitBlt`. That lesson did not necessarily include a detailed treatment of Windows API programming (which is often offensive to VB programmers—just kidding). Visual Basic inherently hides all of the messy details that you have to work out yourself in Visual C++, so it is natural to treat Direct3D similarly by avoiding the messy details and just covering what you will need to build a game.

I have elaborated so much on this because I want to emphasize the point: Writing a fun game is more important than writing a technically advanced game. The bargain shelves at computer stores are full of games that feature technically sophisticated 3-D engines that power cruddy games.

Just take a look at *Half-Life*, for instance (not in the context of a cruddy game, but in gameplay versus game engine). The *Half-Life* engine was based on code from *Quake* and *Quake II*, with considerable revision. The *Half-Life* engine comes with a software development kit that allows talented programmers to write "mods" (custom games written with an existing API) for the engine. In effect, you can build your own game without having to write your own 3-D engine. The *Half-Life* engine and SDK make it possible for newcomers in the gaming industry to come up with some very cool mods like *Counter-Strike* and *Day of Defeat*.

At the same time, there are mods being created for *Unreal Tournament* and *Quake III*, but they are nowhere near as popular as *Half-Life* mods (at least at the time of this writing), despite being more recent. *Half-Life* has what I would describe as a simple physics model that is more down-to-earth than other games, most likely because it features more realistic scenarios and weapons in the game (while more technically advanced engines like *Quake III* are geared for sci-fi scenarios, in my experience).

Game Engines Are All the Rage

Now, back to the subject at hand. The goal of this chapter is to build a Nintendo 64-style 3-D engine. No embellishments, no bells or whistles, just a fast and easy-to-use 3-D engine. *Mario 64* was a landmark 3-D game, setting all kinds of precedents before 3-D gaming even hit the PC market in full force. In fact, *Tomb Raider* could have been an N64 game, since it originally debuted on the ultra low-end PlayStation (the specs of which are startling, considering the game base).

My all-time favorite N64 game is *Goldeneye 007*, based on the James Bond movie. (The follow-up game, *Perfect Dark*, was even better.) The scope of games like these is startlingly within your grasp, once you have come up with a basic 3-D engine. In fact, I think you would be surprised by what you can come up with, given the investment of time. I would absolutely love to base an entire book on just building a single 3-D game like *Goldeneye*.

> **TIP**
>
> If you would like to build an advanced 3-D game with all the trimmings, without requiring a lot of programming skill, check out an awesome product called DarkBASIC, available at http://www.darkbasic.com.

Hardware Acceleration

Today, hardware 3-D acceleration is all over the place, from ultra high-end custom-built gaming rigs to bargain basement low-end budget systems. Only older PCs and some notebook computers lack even rudimentary 3-D hardware, so you can assume that a decent 3-D card is available on a target machine and ignore software rendering altogether.

Video cards have come a long way in just a few short years. I remember when the hottest cards on the market were boasting Windows acceleration, as if fast 2-D was an afterthought. But today, the market is incredible, and has been pushed constantly forward by computer games. Yes, believe it or not, the entire computer industry today has game developers to thank for computer sales.

Sure, there are figures that tie large percentages of sales to business purchases and leases. But the fact remains that gaming is the driving force in the computer industry today. If you are an aspiring game programmer, then you have a much better chance of landing a job with a game studio than in previous years. Technical know-how with computer graphics coding is a sure way to keep yourself gainfully employed.

A Note about Consoles

I am strongly influenced by all the console games that I have played over the years. I think that PC games are, on average, about ten times more complicated than console games. But there is an amazing appeal to a game you just pop into the CD-ROM tray (or cartridge slot), grab a controller, and go at it. PC games are so annoying! You know the routine where you have to install the game, which usually requires at least the latest version of DirectX (and possibly other APIs, such as those required to play on some of the online networks).

In comparison, I can log on to a *Quake III* server and begin playing with my Dreamcast in a matter of minutes. Then I can switch to *Unreal Tournament* or *Soldier of Fortune* without the need to install these games. Once installed, some PC games are a pain to remove from your system as well. I realize that PCs do not have fixed specifications like consoles, so they require more attention. But my point is just that consoles are so much easier to play with, you know?

The last time I played the Dreamcast version of *Gauntlet Legends* with three of my friends, we had an incredible time. This is one of the rare games that allows four players to play cooperatively to solve each level of the game. On the PC, I enjoy death-matching with friends at LAN parties, but those events are always so hardcore. (If you have ever been to a LAN tournament, you know what I mean.) Console gaming with a few friends beats out any LAN party I've ever attended.

Given the subject of this book, I'm assuming that you are primarily a PC game fan, rather than a hardcore console gamer. Most gamers fall into one category or the other, but usually not both (in an avid fashion).

One of the misnomers in the gaming press is the use of the word "bit," which is somewhat frustrating. Console makers want to promote their hardware as being several generations ahead of what it really is. But for all practical intents and purposes, all current video game consoles have a 32-bit central processor. That means that the overly hyped PlayStation 2 and Xbox consoles are not any more advanced than a typical Windows PC. Sure, the hardware is all custom, as are the games, but these machines are not 64-bit or 128-bit or even 256-bit machines like they claim. What those higher bit values represent is the graphics capability of the console, the data bus, and other factors. But these machines do not truly have 128-bit or 256-bit registers in the CPU, as you might think from the marketing propaganda.

Sega Dreamcast

The Dreamcast was a landmark video game machine that ushered in the fourth-generation console market. This console came equipped with both the Sega game libraries and also a DirectX 6.0-enabled version of Windows CE 3.0 (the same operating system that powers Pocket PCs).

I think it is pretty clear that Microsoft used the experience to move ahead with the Xbox, after working with Sega on the Dreamcast. While Windows CE pales in comparison to the Windows 2000 core that is built into the Xbox, the two consoles share a common heritage through DirectX.

Despite the less-impressive specs on the Dreamcast, it has a killer selection of games, and it is also the most affordable fourth-generation console on the market today. While the PS2 is still looking for a killer game to promote the console, the Dreamcast has at least a dozen such games (like *Shenmue* and *Soul Calibur*).

Microsoft Xbox

The Microsoft Xbox was an epiphany waiting to happen. Americans have been out of the video game console business since Atari went kaput, after a valiant attempt with the Jaguar and Lynx game machines. Given that DirectX is the dominant API used to write games for PCs, it was inevitable that Microsoft would put together a computer that is custom designed to power games.

The Xbox is Microsoft's most highly anticipated, highly marketed, successful product launch in the company's history. The Xbox was even bigger than the Windows 95 launch.

The Xbox is powered by an optimized Windows 2000 core operating system, with all of the user interface, virtual memory, device driver, and other pieces stripped out of it. With a 733-megahertz processor, a custom version of the GeForce 3 graphics processor, double data rate (DDR) memory, a hard drive, DVD-ROM drive, and Ethernet adapter, the Xbox really blows away other consoles.

Think of the Xbox as a hardware implementation of DirectX 8.0 (and yes, it is DX8 and not DX9, because the hardware specs for Xbox were fixed in early 2000). It is pretty exciting when you think about it. Imagine not worrying about the millions of different PCs that your game normally has to support, each with different video cards, sound cards, and the like. When writing games for Xbox, there is a single, standard hardware spec for the machine that game developers can count on (and optimize for), along with a single, comprehensive DirectX API. Windows PC game developers can get into Xbox development in a fraction of the time it takes to learn the PS2 or GameCube development kits.

The bottom line is that by learning Direct3D, you might be able to market yourself for Xbox development, if that is something you would like to do.

INTRODUCTION TO DIRECTX GRAPHICS

I am one of many programmers who stumbled upon the latest version of Direct3D and then found it difficult to go back to the old 2-D way of things. The fact is, once you start playing around with Direct3D and discover how easy it is to build basic 3-D games (with the potential to add more advanced features later), you will likely also find it difficult to go back to 2-D game coding. There is a short learning curve, and it helps a lot if you've had experience with other 3-D libraries in the past.

The Basics of 3-D Graphics

The most basic element of a 3-D engine is the vertex. In comparison to the real universe, a vertex is like an atom. As you might already know, atoms are made up of three basic parts: protons, neutrons, and electrons. Atomic theory is what has made computers possible, because computers run on electricity.

> **NOTE**
> Contrary to popular belief, electrons do not travel at the speed of light. Therefore, just slap the next person who tells you that e-mail travels at light speed, because it doesn't! Broadcast television and radio signals travel at the speed of light, but not the cable or telephone networks, which are based on electricity.

In case you were sleeping through this particular subject in high school, electricity is simply a flow of electrons from the *negative* pole to the *positive* pole. That seems odd when you first think about it, because it seems like the positive pole of a car battery is more, well, scary, than the negative pole (know what I mean?). Touching the negative post on a battery never seems to do anything. But if you happen to be wearing chain mail armor and you brush against the positive pole, that battery gets medieval on you. It is true, though, that electrons pass from negative to positive (and they do the passing with a vengeance).

It's All about the Polygons, Baby

So, what do 3-D graphics have to do with car batteries? Back to the components of an atom. Like an atom, a vertex has three parts: X, Y, and Z. These three values are the glue that holds together the 3-D realm. Now, there is a whole heck of a lot of mathematics involved too, but that is just too icky for my taste, so let's not get into it, okay?

A polygon is made up of three or more vertex points (or vertices). Take a look at Figure 14.2 for an illustration of a simple triangle made up of three vertices.

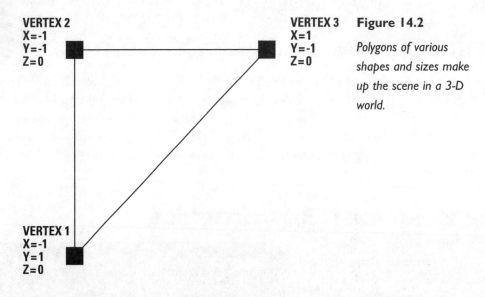

VERTEX 2
X=-1
Y=-1
Z=0

VERTEX 3
X=1
Y=-1
Z=0

VERTEX 1
X=-1
Y=1
Z=0

Figure 14.2

Polygons of various shapes and sizes make up the scene in a 3-D world.

Creating a 3-D scene involves the use of many, many vertex points, all tied together into polygons, which are combined into an object (also called a *mesh*). Therefore, the 3-D chip in your computer really only sees X,Y,Z values, not polygons. The 3-D hardware just fills in the empty space between those vertices to create the image (in something called the *pixel fill rate*). That's basically all there is to 3-D graphics, the manipulation of vertices (which causes motion) and the filling in of polygons that are made up of three or more vertices.

Direct3D includes all the functionality you will ever need to render the objects in a 3-D game. You do not need a degree in mathematics to use Direct3D. However, learning to use an advanced rendering program like 3D Studio Max would be beneficial, as would the ability to load 3-D scenes into a program.

Making the Leap from DirectDraw

Mastery of DirectX once included both DirectDraw and Direct3D, but that has changed with DX8, which has incorporated DirectDraw into the Direct3DSurface8 object (among others). Performance aside, it is entirely up to you whether you would like to build a game on a 2-D or 3-D foundation, because DX8 can handle it either way. (As the Sprite3D program will demonstrate later, a game can be based on both.)

Drawing 2-D Sprites on 3-D Surfaces

Now, there are three completely different ways to draw sprites with Direct3D. Trust me, you will lose no sleep over the lack of DirectDraw in the new DirectX Graphics library. First, there is the Direct3DSurface8 object, which has close ties to the now-obsolete DirectDraw. In fact, Direct3DSurface8 is the descendant of DirectDraw. Since I've already covered DirectDraw in detail, why bother learning the new version of it when something more interesting is available?

We're working in three dimensions now, since this is the modern way of things. (I just hope no one comes up with a 4-D graphics library with quantum pixels that translate through time rather than across the screen.)

The secret to twenty-first century sprites is the Direct3DTexture8 object—the very same object used to add texture mapping to polygons in a full 3-D game. Now imagine the possibilities with an alpha-blended rectangle containing a sprite. If you have algorithmic Tourette's Syndrome (my own term) that causes you to burst forth with expletives every time you think about solving math problems, then I'll spell it out for you in simple terms: The result is a 3-D transparent sprite. The only thing cooler than a 3-D sprite would have to be commercial space travel.

3-D sprites are very cool, because you can do anything with them in 3-D space and treat them like any other textured polygon. While advanced lighting techniques are beyond the scope of this book, 3-D sprites are affected by dynamic, colored lighting just like other polygons.

But it gets even better. The Direct3DX utility library comes with a basic sprite handler that encapsulates all of this 3-D sprite functionality into a simple-to-use interface called D3DXSprite. Of course, you can always use alpha blended textures and write your own complete Direct3D sprite handler. But it turns out that D3DXSprite is really cool, and provides all the support for sprite handling that you will need. I'll show you how to create 3-D sprites in the next section, after I've had a chance to explain the whole 3-D rendering process.

The Left-Handed System

All of the code in this chapter is based on the left-handed system of rendering 3-D graphics. What this means is simply that the Z direction goes *into the screen*, rather than *out of the screen* toward you. If you hold up your left hand, palm up, your thumb will point to the left. The palm of your hand represents the X-axis. Point your fingers up and they represent the Y-axis. On the flip side, a right-handed 3-D system is similar to the left-handed system, but the Z-axis is reversed. The importance of this is really only related to perspective and the way vertices are handled.

Transformations

Direct3D makes it easy to perform matrix transformations to the objects in a scene. The confusing part is how Direct3D manipulates the scene. At first it seems inefficient, but in order to rotate, translate, or scale an object, you work directly with the world matrix for the entire scene. After you have transformed a 3-D object (such as a triangle, cube, or "mech"), you set the world matrix back to the identity matrix, which centers everything at the origin at 0,0,0. From that point, you can transform the next object in the scene, and so on until all of the 3-D objects have been rotated, translated, or scaled.

Translation

Translation is how you move a vertex in 3-D space using matrix mathematics. This simply means that any time you want to move an object in the X,Y, or Z direction, it must be translated by a matrix. The routine to move a 3-D object is D3DXMatrixTranslation, and it looks like this:

```
D3DXMatrixTranslation matTranslate, 10, -20, 30
```

In this procedure call, a matrix called matTranslate is created mathematically, with the values required to move a 3-D object 10 units on the X-axis, -20 units on the Y-axis, and 30 units on the Z-axis. Before Direct3D (and other 3-D APIs) came along, game programmers had to write all their own code to perform matrix calculations. Thanks to Direct3D, it only requires about two lines of code to move a 3-D object.

Rotation

Rotation is how you twist an object in 3-D space using matrix math. The important thing to remember about rotation is that it is based on the origin at 0,0,0. If you move an object (by translating it) to a new position and then apply a rotation value to it, that object will rotate around the origin, rather than twisting as you might expect. So it's important to keep an object at 0,0,0 when you need to rotate it, and then move it to where you need it. The procedures to rotate a 3-D object are D3DXMatrixRotationX, D3DXMatrixRotationY, and D3DXMatrixRotationZ, and can be called like this:

```
D3DXMatrixRotationX matRotateX, 10
D3DXMatrixRotationY matRotateY, 20
D3DXMatrixRotationZ matRotateZ, 30
```

Normally you will not pass an explicit value to rotation procedures, but rather you will keep track of the rotation values in separate variables. Otherwise, the object will only rotate to those specific angles and sit there. In other words, the angles you pass are not additive, but absolute.

Scaling

Scaling is how you resize an object in 3-D space using matrix calculations. The scale of an object can be a fractional part of 1.0 (to decrease the size) or a multiple of 1.0 (to increase the size). The procedure to perform scaling on a 3-D object is D3DXMatrixScaling, and can be called like this:

```
D3DXMatrixScaling matScale, fScaleX, fScaleY, fScaleZ
```

This procedure fills the matrix called matScale with the rotation values passed for the X, Y, and Z axes. Using this procedure, you can squeeze, squish, expand, or flatten a 3-D object however you like, because all of the vertices in the object that is rendered with the scaling matrix are scaled together.

3-D GRAPHICS PROGRAMMING WITH DIRECT3D

Direct3D is a powerful graphics rendering API that is also easy to use, which is almost unheard of in the graphics and games industry. Direct3D makes it relatively easy to program a 3-D game by providing a minimum amount of functionality that will get you up and running, while at the same time providing some amazing advanced features. The trick, in my opinion, to writing a cool 3-D game is to build the entire game first, and then add any special effects that you want later. At least that way you have a complete game to show off, and you have an opportunity to improve it as you learn new aspects of Direct3D.

The Flexible Vertex Format

The FVF (*Flexible Vertex Format*) was designed to allow as much flexibility as possible for the rendering pipeline of Direct3D. Rather than including every possible field directly in the structure, you define a vertex identifier that tells Direct3D what to expect from the vertex structure. Here is a simple form of the vertex identifier that tells Direct3D to expect a simple vertex structure with XYZ values, along with a color value.

```
Const D3DFVF_MYVERTEX = (D3DFVF_XYZ Or D3DFVF_DIFFUSE)
```

The vertex structure that goes with the identifier looks like this:

```
Private Type VERTEX_TYPE
    x As Single
    y As Single
    z As Single
    Color As Long
End Type
```

Later on in the chapter, I will show you how to define a vertex structure for adding textures to the polygons.

Creating a Vertex Buffer

Once you have defined the vertex identifier and structure, you are free to fill in the vertex values and then create the vertex buffer. Direct3D allows you to send as few or as many polygons as needed to it at a time for rendering. If you want to define individual polygons or an entire scene in a single vertex array, Direct3D will have no trouble rendering the polygons. To draw a simple triangle, here's a structure that declares three vertices:

```
Private Type TRIANGLE_TYPE
    v1 As VERTEX_TYPE
    v2 As VERTEX_TYPE
    v3 As VERTEX_TYPE
End Type
```

Now you simply declare a variable of type TRIANGLE_TYPE along with a vertex buffer variable, and you will soon be in business:

```
Dim poly As TRIANGLE_TYPE
Dim poly_vb As Direct3DVertexBuffer8
```

Creating Vertices for the Triangle

In order to create a triangle, you must supply the vertices that make up that triangle. Using the TRIANGLE_TYPE structure, you could create a triangle with code that looks like this:

```
poly.v1 = CreateVertex(-1, -1, 0, C_BLUE)
poly.v2 = CreateVertex(1, -1, 0, C_GREEN)
poly.v3 = CreateVertex(-1, 1, 0, C_GREEN)
```

Once you have created the triangle, the next step is to tell Direct3D about it. You must plug the TRIANGLE_TYPE into a vertex buffer that Direct3D can understand. The following code does just that:

```
Dim vbData As Direct3DVertexBuffer8
Dim vert(0 To 2) As VERTEX

'create the D3D vertex buffer
Set vbData = d3ddevice.CreateVertexBuffer( _
    Len(poly), 0, D3DFVF_MYVERTEX, D3DPOOL_DEFAULT)

'fill the vertex buffer with the triangle data
D3DVertexBuffer8SetData vbData, 0, Len(poly), 0, poly
```

In case you were wondering, the CreateVertex function looks like this:

```
Private Function CreateVertex(ByVal x As Single, _
    ByVal y As Single, ByVal z As Single, _
    ByVal Color As Long) As VERTEX_TYPE
    CreateVertex.x = x
    CreateVertex.y = y
    CreateVertex.z = z
    CreateVertex.Color = Color
End Function
```

Rendering the Scene

There are six short steps to rendering a scene with Direct3D:

1. **Clear the Back Buffer.** First, you need to clear the back buffer to prepare it for the next rendering process. Because Direct3D handles double buffering, there is no need to erase objects individually. You simply clear out the back buffer.

   ```
   'clear the back buffer
   d3dDevice.Clear 0, ByVal 0, D3DCLEAR_TARGET, C_BLACK, 1, 0
   ```

2. **Start Rendering.** Second, you tell the Direct3D device object to start rendering.

   ```
   'start rendering
   d3dDevice.BeginScene
   ```

3. **Set the Source Vertex Buffer.** Third, you set the source vertex buffer where Direct3D should retrieve the vertices for the objects to be rendered. This can be a single triangle or an entire scene made up of thousands of polygons!

```
'set source vertex buffer
d3dDevice.SetStreamSource 0, poly_vb, Len(poly.v1)
```

4. **Draw the Triangle.** Fourth, you tell Direct3D to draw the triangle using the vertex buffer that was assigned in the previous step. Repeat steps 3 and 4 as many times as necessary, including all related transformations, to render the entire scene.

```
'draw the triangle
d3dDevice.DrawPrimitive D3DPT_TRIANGLELIST, 0, 1
```

5. **Stop Rendering.** Fifth, you tell Direct3D to stop the rendering process. At this point, all of the output is sitting on the back buffer.

```
'stop rendering
d3dDevice.EndScene
```

6. **Copy Back Buffer to the Screen.** Sixth, you tell Direct3D to copy the back buffer to the screen.

```
'copy the back buffer to the screen
d3dDevice.Present ByVal 0, ByVal 0, 0, ByVal 0
```

What Is the Matrix?

The Matrix was a very cool movie starring Keanu Reaves that did sort of deal with 3-D graphics. The fantastic idea that a computer program is capable of sending output directly into the human brain, thus accessing the nervous system directly, is quite a challenging concept and sort of defeats all of the code presented in this chapter. However, as far as computer graphics go, matrixes are used all over the place to transform 3-D objects in the scene.

The World Transformation

The world transformation matrix holds the entire 3-D environment and determines how that environment is rendered. The world matrix is what you use to translate, rotate, and scale objects in the scene, either individually or as a whole. Here is some sample code that shows how to transform the world matrix:

```
Dim matWorld As D3DMATRIX
D3DXMatrixIdentity matWorld
d3ddevice.SetTransform D3DTS_WORLD, matWorld
```

The View Transformation

The view transformation matrix relates to the camera position and the direction that the camera is pointing, which defines the view of the 3-D environment on the screen. Here is some sample code that shows how to transform the view matrix (which positions the camera):

```
Dim matView As D3DMATRIX
D3DXMatrixLookAtLH matView, vecSource, vecTarget, vecUp
d3ddevice.SetTransform D3DTS_VIEW, matView
```

The Projection Transformation

The projection transformation matrix defines how the view is displayed on the screen with the proper perspective. This causes objects in the distance to appear in the right place based on the resolution of the screen. The following code shows how to transform the projection matrix:

```
Dim matProj As D3DMATRIX
D3DXMatrixPerspectiveFovLH matProj, PI / 4, 0.7, 1, 1000
d3ddevice.SetTransform D3DTS_PROJECTION, matProj
```

The Triangle3D Program

The Triangle3D program demonstrates how to put all of the techniques from the past few pages into practice with an actual Direct3D program. This program (like all of those that follow in this chapter) is a Standard EXE project, with a reference to the DirectX 8 for Visual Basic Type Library. When you have created the new project in Visual Basic, name this program Triangle3D. The program draws a single rectangle using diffuse color blending, and then rotates the triangle about the X and Y axes. Figure 14.3 shows what the program looks like while running.

The first section of code for the Triangle3D program includes the constants, structures, and variable declarations for the program.

```
'-------------------------------------------------------------------
' Visual Basic Game Programming With DirectX
' Chapter 14 : DirectX Graphics and Direct3D
' Triangle3D Source Code File
'-------------------------------------------------------------------

Option Explicit
Option Base 0
```

Figure 14.3

The Triangle3D program shows the basics of programming Direct3D.

```
'Windows API functions and structures
Private Declare Function GetTickCount _
    Lib "kernel32" () As Long

'colors
Const C_WHITE As Long = &HFFFFFF
Const C_GRAY As Long = &H111111
Const C_RED As Long = &HFF0000
Const C_GREEN As Long = &H1FF00
Const C_BLUE As Long = &H1FF
Const C_BLACK As Long = &H0

'custom flexible vertex format
Const D3DFVF_MYVERTEX = (D3DFVF_XYZ Or D3DFVF_DIFFUSE)

'some number I found one time
Const PI = 3.141592654

'custom vertex type representing a point on the screen
Private Type VERTEX_TYPE
    x As Single
    y As Single
    z As Single
```

```
        Color As Long
End Type

Private Type TRIANGLE_TYPE
    v1 As VERTEX_TYPE
    v2 As VERTEX_TYPE
    v3 As VERTEX_TYPE
End Type

Dim bRunning As Boolean
Dim lFrameRate As Long
Dim sFrameRate As String

Dim dx As New DirectX8
Dim d3d As Direct3D8
Dim d3dDevice As Direct3DDevice8
Dim d3dx As D3DX8
Dim poly1 As TRIANGLE_TYPE
Dim poly1_vb As Direct3DVertexBuffer8

Dim matProj As D3DMATRIX
Dim matWorld As D3DMATRIX
Dim matView As D3DMATRIX
Dim vecCameraSource As D3DVECTOR
Dim vecCameraTarget As D3DVECTOR

Dim matRotateX As D3DMATRIX
Dim matRotateY As D3DMATRIX
Dim fRotateX As Single
Dim fRotateY As Single
```

Next in line is Form_Load, followed by Form_KeyDown, Form_Unload, and Shutdown. Form_Load sets up the main form (since this program runs in a window, not full screen), initializes Direct3D, initializes the scene, and then starts the game loop running. Form_KeyDown includes code for the up and down arrow keys, which cause the view to zoom in and out, along with support for the Escape key, which ends the program. Form_Unload simply calls Shutdown, which deletes objects and ends the program.

```
Private Sub Form_Load()
    Static lStartTime As Long
    Static lCounter As Long
    Static lNewTime As Long
```

```vb
        'set up the main form
        Form1.Caption = "Triangle3D"
        Form1.AutoRedraw = False
        Form1.BorderStyle = 1
        Form1.ClipControls = False
        Form1.KeyPreview = True
        Form1.ScaleMode = 3
        Form1.Width = Screen.TwipsPerPixelX * 652
        Form1.Height = Screen.TwipsPerPixelY * 510
        Form1.Show

        'initialize Direct3D
        If Not InitD3D(Me.hWnd) Then
            MsgBox "Error initializing Direct3D"
            Shutdown
        End If

        'initialize the scene
        If Not SetupScene() Then
            MsgBox "Error initializing vertex buffer"
            Shutdown
        End If

        bRunning = True
        lFrameRate = 60

        'main game loop
        Do While bRunning
            lCounter = GetTickCount() - lStartTime
            If lCounter > lNewTime Then
                RenderScene lCounter
                lNewTime = lCounter + 1000 / lFrameRate
            End If
            DoEvents
        Loop
End Sub

Private Sub Form_KeyDown(KeyCode As Integer, Shift As Integer)
    Debug.Print KeyCode
    Select Case KeyCode
```

```
        Case 38
            vecCameraSource.z = vecCameraSource.z - 1
            D3DXMatrixLookAtLH matView, vecCameraSource, _
                vecCameraTarget, CreateVector(0, 1, 0)
            d3dDevice.SetTransform D3DTS_VIEW, matView
        Case 40
            vecCameraSource.z = vecCameraSource.z + 1
            D3DXMatrixLookAtLH matView, vecCameraSource, _
                vecCameraTarget, CreateVector(0, 1, 0)
            d3dDevice.SetTransform D3DTS_VIEW, matView
        Case 27
            Shutdown
    End Select
End Sub


Private Sub Form_Unload(Cancel As Integer)
    Shutdown
End Sub


Private Sub Shutdown()
    Set poly1_vb = Nothing
    Set d3dx = Nothing
    Set d3dDevice = Nothing
    Set d3d = Nothing
    Set dx = Nothing
    End
End Sub
```

The InitD3D function initializes Direct3D with the values that cause the program to run in a window with the current display mode. The function creates a new Direct3D device with support for hardware 3-D rendering.

```
Private Function InitD3D(hWnd As Long) As Boolean
    On Local Error Resume Next

    'create the D3D object
    Set d3d = dx.Direct3DCreate()
    If d3d Is Nothing Then Exit Function

    Set d3dx = New D3DX8
    If d3dx Is Nothing Then Exit Function
```

```
    'get the current display mode
    Dim mode As D3DDISPLAYMODE
    d3d.GetAdapterDisplayMode D3DADAPTER_DEFAULT, mode

    'fill in the type structure used to create the device
    Dim d3dpp As D3DPRESENT_PARAMETERS
    d3dpp.hDeviceWindow = Form1.hWnd
    d3dpp.Windowed = 1
    d3dpp.BackBufferWidth = Form1.ScaleWidth
    d3dpp.BackBufferHeight = Form1.ScaleHeight
    d3dpp.BackBufferFormat = mode.Format
    d3dpp.BackBufferCount = 1
    d3dpp.SwapEffect = D3DSWAPEFFECT_COPY_VSYNC
    d3dpp.MultiSampleType = D3DMULTISAMPLE_NONE
    d3dpp.AutoDepthStencilFormat = D3DFMT_D32

    Set d3dDevice = d3d.CreateDevice(D3DADAPTER_DEFAULT, _
        D3DDEVTYPE_HAL, Form1.hWnd, _
        D3DCREATE_SOFTWARE_VERTEXPROCESSING, d3dpp)
    If d3dDevice Is Nothing Then
        MsgBox "Error creating Direct3D device"
        Shutdown
    End If

    'turn on ambient lighting
    d3dDevice.SetRenderState D3DRS_AMBIENT, True
    'turn off z-buffering
    d3dDevice.SetRenderState D3DRS_ZENABLE, False
    'turn off backface removal
    d3dDevice.SetRenderState D3DRS_CULLMODE, D3DCULL_NONE
    'turn off hardware lighting
    d3dDevice.SetRenderState D3DRS_LIGHTING, False

    InitD3D = True
End Function
```

The SetupScene function is called from Form_Load to initialize the scene, which includes setting up the camera position, setting the view and projection matrixes, and creating the vertices and vertex buffer for the triangle.

```
Private Function SetupScene() As Boolean
    vecCameraSource.x = 0
    vecCameraSource.y = 0
    vecCameraSource.z = 5

    vecCameraTarget.x = 0
    vecCameraTarget.y = 0
    vecCameraTarget.z = 0

    'set up the camera view matrix
    D3DXMatrixLookAtLH matView, vecCameraSource, vecCameraTarget, _
        CreateVector(0, 1, 0)
    'use the camera view for the viewport
    d3dDevice.SetTransform D3DTS_VIEW, matView

    'set up the projection matrix (pi/4 = radians)
    D3DXMatrixPerspectiveFovLH matProj, PI / 4, 1, 1, 100
    'tell device to use the projection matrix
    d3dDevice.SetTransform D3DTS_PROJECTION, matProj
    'set vertex shader
    d3dDevice.SetVertexShader D3DFVF_MYVERTEX

    'set up poly1
    poly1.v1 = CreateVertex(-1, -1, 0, C_BLUE)
    poly1.v2 = CreateVertex(1, -1, 0, C_GREEN)
    poly1.v3 = CreateVertex(-1, 1, 0, C_GREEN)

    'create vertex buffer for poly1
    Set poly1_vb = d3dDevice.CreateVertexBuffer(Len(poly), 0, _
        D3DFVF_MYVERTEX, D3DPOOL_DEFAULT)
    If poly1_vb Is Nothing Then Exit Function
    D3DVertexBuffer8SetData poly1_vb, 0, Len(poly1), 0, poly1
    SetupScene = True
End Function
```

The RenderScene procedure is the engine, so to speak, of the program. RenderScene processes the six steps of the rendering pipeline for Direct3D and looks very similar to the steps that were presented earlier, with the exception of the code that rotates the triangle. That section of code actually does require a little more explanation. Matrix math is great—it is fast and easy to use. But you can only apply a single matrix to Direct3D at a time. Therefore, you must multiply two matrixes together to get a third matrix. In this case, matRotateX and matRotateY are multiplied together with the D3DXMatrixMultiply procedure, with the result fed into matWorld. Once the matrix multiplication is finished, the world matrix is transformed within Direct3D.

```
Public Sub RenderScene(ByVal MS As Long)
    Static lTimer As Long
    Static lStart As Long
    Static lCounter As Long
    Static fTheta As Single

    'start counting milliseconds
    lStart = GetTickCount
    If d3dDevice Is Nothing Then Exit Sub

    'clear the back buffer
    d3dDevice.Clear 0, ByVal 0, D3DCLEAR_TARGET, C_BLACK, 1#, 0

    'begin rendering
    d3dDevice.BeginScene

    'rotate the triangle
    fTheta = fTheta + PI / 40
    D3DXMatrixRotationX matRotateX, fTheta / 2
    D3DXMatrixRotationY matRotateY, fTheta
    D3DXMatrixMultiply matWorld, matRotateX, matRotateY
    d3dDevice.SetTransform D3DTS_WORLD, matWorld

    'set source vertex buffer and draw the triangle
    d3dDevice.SetStreamSource 0, poly1_vb, Len(poly1.v1)
    d3dDevice.DrawPrimitive D3DPT_TRIANGLELIST, 0, 1

    'stop rendering
    d3dDevice.EndScene

    'copy the back buffer to the screen
    d3dDevice.Present ByVal 0, ByVal 0, 0, ByVal 0

    'count the frames per second
    If MS > lTimer + 1000 Then
        lStart = GetTickCount - lStart
        sFrameRate = "FPS = " & lCounter & ", MS = " & lStart
```

```
        Debug.Print sFrameRate
        lTimer = MS
        lCounter = 0
    Else
        lCounter = lCounter + 1
    End If
End Sub
```

The last two routines in the program are support routines. `CreateVertex` is a function that returns a VERTEX_TYPE structure that is filled in with parameters that are passed to the function. `CreateVector` is similar to `CreateVertex`, but returns a simple D3DVECTOR instead.

```
Private Function CreateVertex(ByVal x As Single, _
    ByVal y As Single, ByVal z As Single, _
    ByVal Color As Long) As VERTEX_TYPE
    CreateVertex.x = x
    CreateVertex.y = y
    CreateVertex.z = z
    CreateVertex.Color = Color
End Function

Private Function CreateVector(x As Single, y As Single, _
    z As Single) As D3DVECTOR
    CreateVector.x = x
    CreateVector.y = y
    CreateVector.z = z
End Function
```

The Rectangle3D Program

The Rectangle3D program is nearly identical to the Triangle3D program, so there is nothing new to learn here. The only difference is that Rectangle3D uses two triangles! Couldn't be much simpler than that, right? I recommend that you make a copy of the directory for the Triangle3D program, and then use the copy for the Rectangle3D program. Figure 14.4 shows the program in action.

The following sections of code are just snippets of the Rectangle3D program, showing the subtle changes that have been made to the Triangle3D program to make it work with two triangles. First, you will want to change the name of the program in the comment section at the top of the program.

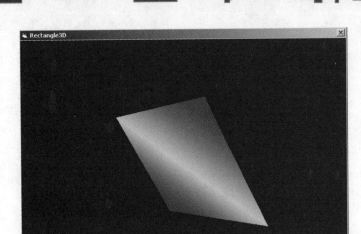

Figure 14.4

The diffuse rectangle rotates around the X and Y axes with a blend of colors rather than a texture.

```
'-------------------------------------------------------------------
' Visual Basic Game Programming With DirectX
' Chapter 14 : DirectX Graphics and Direct3D
' Rectangle3D Source Code File
'-------------------------------------------------------------------


Option Explicit
Option Base 0

'Windows API functions and structures
Private Declare Function GetTickCount Lib "kernel32" () As Long
```

Following that, add two new variables for poly2 in the variable declaration section at the top of the program.

```
Dim poly1 As TRIANGLE_TYPE
Dim poly1_vb As Direct3DVertexBuffer8

Dim poly2 As TRIANGLE_TYPE
Dim poly2_vb As Direct3DVertexBuffer8
```

The next changes involve the Form_Load and Shutdown procedures. The only change that needs to be made to Form_Load is to rename the caption of the program Rectangle3D. Shutdown now includes a line that deletes the second vertex buffer before the program ends.

```vb
Private Sub Form_Load()
    Static lStartTime As Long
    Static lCounter As Long
    Static lNewTime As Long

    'set up the main form
    Form1.Caption = "Rectangle3D"
    Form1.AutoRedraw = False
    Form1.BorderStyle = 1
    Form1.ClipControls = False
    Form1.KeyPreview = True
    Form1.ScaleMode = 3
    Form1.Width = Screen.TwipsPerPixelX * 652
    Form1.Height = Screen.TwipsPerPixelY * 510
    Form1.Show

    'initialize Direct3D
    If Not InitD3D(Me.hWnd) Then
        MsgBox "Error initializing Direct3D"
        Shutdown
    End If

    'initialize the scene
    If Not SetupScene() Then
        MsgBox "Error initializing vertex buffer"
        Shutdown
    End If

    bRunning = True
    lFrameRate = 60

    'main game loop
    Do While bRunning
        lCounter = GetTickCount() - lStartTime
        If lCounter > lNewTime Then
            RenderScene lCounter
            lNewTime = lCounter + 1000 / lFrameRate
        End If
        DoEvents
    Loop
End Sub
```

```
Private Sub Shutdown()
    Set poly1_vb = Nothing
    Set poly2_vb = Nothing
    Set d3dx = Nothing
    Set d3dDevice = Nothing
    Set d3d = Nothing
    Set dx = Nothing
    End
End Sub
```

The next section of code includes the SetupScene function, with additional code to initialize the second triangle. The initialization code is just like the code for the first triangle.

```
Private Function SetupScene() As Boolean
    vecCameraSource.x = 0
    vecCameraSource.y = 0
    vecCameraSource.z = 5

    vecCameraTarget.x = 0
    vecCameraTarget.y = 0
    vecCameraTarget.z = 0

    'set up the camera view matrix
    D3DXMatrixLookAtLH matView, vecCameraSource, vecCameraTarget, _
        CreateVector(0, 1, 0)
    'use the camera view for the viewport
    d3dDevice.SetTransform D3DTS_VIEW, matView

    'set up the projection matrix (pi/4 = radians)
    D3DXMatrixPerspectiveFovLH matProj, PI / 4, 1, 1, 100
    'tell device to use the projection matrix
    d3dDevice.SetTransform D3DTS_PROJECTION, matProj
    'set vertex shader
    d3dDevice.SetVertexShader D3DFVF_MYVERTEX

    'set up poly1
    poly1.v1 = CreateVertex(-1, -1, 0, C_BLUE)
    poly1.v2 = CreateVertex(1, -1, 0, C_GREEN)
    poly1.v3 = CreateVertex(-1, 1, 0, C_GREEN)
```

```
    'create vertex buffer for poly1
    Set poly1_vb = d3dDevice.CreateVertexBuffer(Len(poly1), _
        0, D3DFVF_MYVERTEX, D3DPOOL_DEFAULT)
    If poly1_vb Is Nothing Then Exit Function
    D3DVertexBuffer8SetData poly1_vb, 0, Len(poly1), 0, poly1

    'set up poly2
    poly2.v1 = CreateVertex(-1, 1, 0, C_GREEN)
    poly2.v2 = CreateVertex(1, -1, 0, C_GREEN)
    poly2.v3 = CreateVertex(1, 1, 0, C_BLUE)

    'create vertex buffer for poly2
    Set poly2_vb = d3dDevice.CreateVertexBuffer(Len(poly2), _
        0, D3DFVF_MYVERTEX, D3DPOOL_DEFAULT)
    If poly2_vb Is Nothing Then Exit Function
    D3DVertexBuffer8SetData poly2_vb, 0, Len(poly2), 0, poly2

    SetupScene = True
End Function
```

The last section of code in the Rectangle3D program involves the RenderScene procedure. Right below the code that rendered the triangle in the Triangle3D program is the code for rendering the second triangle, and this code looks very similar.

```
Public Sub RenderScene(ByVal MS As Long)
    Static lTimer As Long
    Static lStart As Long
    Static lCounter As Long
    Static fTheta As Single

    'start counting milliseconds
    lStart = GetTickCount
    If d3dDevice Is Nothing Then Exit Sub

    'clear the back buffer
    d3dDevice.Clear 0, ByVal 0, D3DCLEAR_TARGET, C_BLACK, 1, 0

    'begin rendering
    d3dDevice.BeginScene
```

```
'rotate the triangle
fTheta = fTheta + PI / 40
D3DXMatrixRotationX matRotateX, fTheta / 2
D3DXMatrixRotationY matRotateY, fTheta
D3DXMatrixMultiply matWorld, matRotateX, matRotateY
d3dDevice.SetTransform D3DTS_WORLD, matWorld

'set source vertex buffer and draw triangle
d3dDevice.SetStreamSource 0, poly1_vb, Len(poly1.v1)
d3dDevice.DrawPrimitive D3DPT_TRIANGLELIST, 0, 1

'draw the second triangle
d3dDevice.SetStreamSource 0, poly2_vb, Len(poly2.v1)
d3dDevice.DrawPrimitive D3DPT_TRIANGLELIST, 0, 1

'stop rendering
d3dDevice.EndScene

'copy the back buffer to the screen
d3dDevice.Present ByVal 0, ByVal 0, 0, ByVal 0

'count the frames per second
If MS > lTimer + 1000 Then
    lStart = GetTickCount - lStart
    sFrameRate = "FPS = " & lCounter & ", MS = " & lStart
    Debug.Print sFrameRate
    lTimer = MS
    lCounter = 0
Else
    lCounter = lCounter + 1
End If
End Sub
```

Moving on to Textures

Texture mapping is really the key to creating great 3-D games, because without textures a 3-D object is just a shaded single-color monstrosity. I remember playing some 3-D shaded polygon games back in the old days, like *4D Sports Boxing* and *4D Sports Tennis*. (I guess the 4D part was a marketing thing.) Texturing does add some complexity to the situation, but luckily it is easy to learn. Once you have picked up the concept of texture coordinates, you can apply the code to create texture coordinates to new polygons without having to work it out ever again—now that's what I call code reuse!

Understanding Texture Coordinates

Texture coordinates define how a texture will be drawn over a polygon, and can get very complicated if you don't plan ahead. Texture coordinates represent a position on the source texture with the U and V values of the vertex structure. (I'll get to that next.) The UV pair holds a value for the X and Y position in the source texture, oddly enough as a decimal from 0.0 to 1.0. A value of 0.0 for the X position represents the left edge, while a 0.0 for the Y position represents the top of the texture. Therefore, to position the top-left corner of the texture you would refer to it as 0.0,0.0, as shown in Figure 14.5.

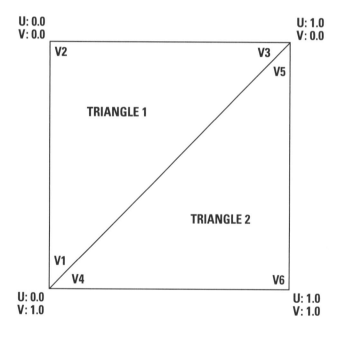

Figure 14.5

Texture coordinates for a rectangle

The New Vertex Format

To accommodate the UV pair required for texture mapping, a new flexible vertex format is needed, as follows:

```
Private Type VERTEX
    vecPos As D3DVECTOR
```

```
    vecNorm As D3DVECTOR
    u As Single
    v As Single
End Type
```

Note that the X,Y,Z values have been put into a D3DVECTOR structure, which is more convenient. This FVF includes a vector for the normal of the vertex, which is related to lighting. While this is needed for the textured format, it is not used in this chapter. However, I have included the normalization vector so that it will be easy to add lighting to the scene, should you wish to add lighting on your own. The new vertex identifier looks like this:

```
Const D3DFVF_MYVERTEX = (D3DFVF_XYZ Or D3DFVF_TEX1 _
    Or D3DFVF_NORMAL)
```

Rendering a Textured Polygon

The rendering pipeline for Direct3D is kind of strange when it comes to texturing. It seems to me that it would be more logical to assign the textures first, during initial setup. However, Direct3D requires you to assign each texture on-the-fly, during the rendering process. Basically, if you have an FVF that was set up to accept a texture (with a UV pair), then all you need to render a texture-mapped polygon is the texture itself. You assign the texture using the SetTexture procedure, like this:

```
d3ddevice.SetTexture 0, d3dtTexture
```

If you would like to render a polygon without a texture, you can set up the texture value like this:

```
d3ddevice.SetTexture 0, Nothing
```

Of course, before you can render a textured polygon, you first need to load the texture image! There are two ways to load a texture—using the CreateTextureFromFile procedure or the CreateTextureFromFileEx procedure. Here is what the first one looks like:

```
Set d3dtTexture = d3dx.CreateTextureFromFile(d3ddevice, sFilename)
```

Likewise, the second form of the texture-loading procedure might be called like this:

```
Set d3dtTexture = d3dx.CreateTextureFromFileEx(d3d.Device, _
    sFilename, D3DX_DEFAULT, D3DX_DEFAULT, D3DX_DEFAULT, _
    0, D3DFMT_UNKNOWN, D3DPOOL_MANAGED, D3DX_FILTER_POINT, _
    D3DX_FILTER_POINT, &HFF000000, ByVal 0, ByVal 0)
```

Whoa, what's the deal with that one? The second form of the texture-loading routine accommodates a lot more features. The most important feature is involving the alpha channel, which

CreateTextureFromFileEx is capable of handling. Ignore all of the parameters and just focus on the third from the last parameter, which is &HFF000000. This is the hex value for black, or RGB(0,0,0). The difference, however, is that CreateTextureFromFileEx uses this color to fill in the alpha channel for each pixel in the texture, so that all black pixels are left transparent.

This alpha-blending trick is actually the key to drawing transparent sprites later in the chapter!

The Cube3D Program

The Cube3D program (shown in Figure 14.6) is somewhat inefficient because it draws about twice as many vertex points as necessary. I wanted to keep the program simple and work with only triangle lists, because I believe it is far easier to understand how to program 3-D by using complete triangles—at least in the beginning.

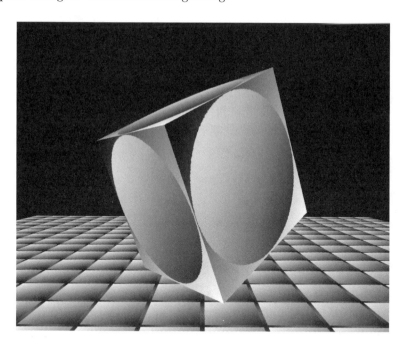

Figure 14.6

The Cube3D program, with the camera zoomed in close to the rotating cube

A far more efficient way to render is to use a triangle strip instead of a triangle list, as shown in Figure 14.7. In a triangle strip, you only need to define the first two starting vertices, and then each additional vertex that you add to the vertex buffer results in a whole new triangle (using the two previous vertices along with the new one). This way, you can create basic 3-D geometry more easily, and it is rendered more quickly.

TRIANGLE LIST

TRIANGLE STRIP

Figure 14.7

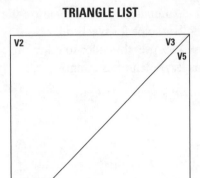 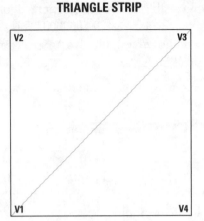

A triangle list compared to a triangle strip

The Cube3D program allows you to move the camera position on all three of the axes (X, Y, and Z) using the arrow keys and the page up/down keys. The program starts zoomed close to the rotating cube. If you would like to zoom out, press the down arrow key (see Figure 14.8).

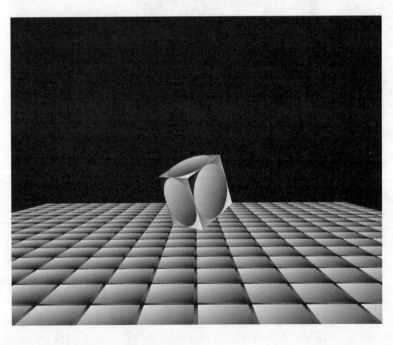

Figure 14.8

The rotating cube is zoomed further out in this scene.

The Cube3D program incorporates some new classes that I will help you create. You will want to copy these classes from the chapter directory on the CD-ROM. If you are creating the project from scratch, which I recommend, then you will want to simply create a new Class Module (from the Project menu in VB) for each class. The clsDirect3D class encapsulates some of the initialization for Direct3D, along with the Direct3DDevice8 object. The clsD3DTriangle8 class encapsulates the code, array, and vertex buffer for creating a triangle. The clsD3DRectangle8 class similarly encapsulates the functionality needed to create and render textured rectangles made up of two triangles.

The clsDirect3D8 Class

The clsDirect3D8 class encapsulates the main components of Direct3D, making it easier to initialize and set up Direct3D for rendering. This class includes the Direct3DDevice8 object, which is referenced by a property called Device and used extensively in the Cube3D program.

Take notice of the properties that return device capabilities. I've included the most useful properties, but you might want to browse the D3DCAPS8 object if you need any more detailed information about the Direct3D device. Here are the results that these properties returned on my Dell laptop equipped with an ATI Mobility-M4:

```
MaxPrimitiveCount = 65535
MaxActiveLights = -1
MaxTextureWidth = 1024
MaxTextureHeight = 1024
```

The result for the active lights simply means that there are no hardware lights active in the program (which is as it should be, given that I have not created any lights). The max texture width and height is pretty good for a mobile 3-D chip, but is probably common in all modern cards (particularly those with advanced texture compression built into the silicon). I recall that some of the early 3-D cards were limited to a texture size of 256×256.

I was actually tempted to plug the transformation matrixes into this class, but then decided against it, because it is important to not encapsulate everything. The transformation matrixes probably do not change while a program is running, but it is nice to have direct access to the code that initializes the projection, view, and world matrixes.

Now, go ahead and type this code into a file called Direct3D8.cls with the name of clsDirect3D8, and include it in the Cube3D project.

```
'----------------------------------------------------------------
' Visual Basic Game Programming With DirectX
' Chapter 14 : DirectX Graphics and Direct3D
' clsDirect3D8 Class Source Code File
'----------------------------------------------------------------
```

```vb
Option Explicit
Option Base 0

'define the flexible vertex format for textured polygons
Const D3DFVF_MYVERTEX = (D3DFVF_XYZ Or D3DFVF_TEX1 Or D3DFVF_NORMAL)

Dim dx As New DirectX8
Dim d3d As Direct3D8
Dim d3dDevice As Direct3DDevice8

Dim mode As D3DDISPLAYMODE
Dim d3dpp As D3DPRESENT_PARAMETERS
Dim caps As D3DCAPS8

Private Sub Class_Terminate()
    Set d3dDevice = Nothing
    Set d3d = Nothing
    Set dx = Nothing
End Sub

Public Function Startup(ByVal hWnd As Long, ByVal lWidth As Long, _
    ByVal lHeight As Long, _
    ByVal bFullscreen As Boolean) As Boolean
    On Local Error GoTo startup_error

    Startup = False

    'create the D3D object
    Set d3d = dx.Direct3DCreate()
    If d3d Is Nothing Then Exit Function

    'get the current display mode
    d3d.GetAdapterDisplayMode D3DADAPTER_DEFAULT, mode

    'fill in the type structure used to create the device
    Dim d3dpp As D3DPRESENT_PARAMETERS
    d3dpp.hDeviceWindow = Form1.hWnd
    d3dpp.BackBufferWidth = lWidth
    d3dpp.BackBufferHeight = lHeight
    d3dpp.BackBufferFormat = mode.Format
    d3dpp.BackBufferCount = 1
```

```
d3dpp.SwapEffect = D3DSWAPEFFECT_COPY_VSYNC
d3dpp.MultiSampleType = D3DMULTISAMPLE_NONE
d3dpp.AutoDepthStencilFormat = D3DFMT_D32

'set windowed or fullscreen mode
If bFullscreen Then
    d3dpp.Windowed = 0
Else
    d3dpp.Windowed = 1
End If


'create the D3D device with hardware 3D support
Set d3dDevice = d3d.CreateDevice(D3DADAPTER_DEFAULT, D3DDEVTYPE_HAL, _
    Form1.hWnd, D3DCREATE_SOFTWARE_VERTEXPROCESSING, d3dpp)
If d3dDevice Is Nothing Then Exit Function


'set vertex shader
d3dDevice.SetVertexShader D3DFVF_MYVERTEX

'turn off z-buffering
d3dDevice.SetRenderState D3DRS_ZENABLE, 0

'turn on ambient lighting
d3dDevice.SetRenderState D3DRS_AMBIENT, True

'turn off hardware lighting
d3dDevice.SetRenderState D3DRS_LIGHTING, False

'turn on counter-clockwise backface removal
d3dDevice.SetRenderState D3DRS_CULLMODE, D3DCULL_CCW

'turn on alpha blending to support transparent textures
Device.SetRenderState D3DRS_SRCBLEND, D3DBLEND_SRCALPHA
Device.SetRenderState D3DRS_DESTBLEND, D3DBLEND_INVSRCALPHA
Device.SetRenderState D3DRS_ALPHABLENDENABLE, 1

'retrieve device capabilities
Device.GetDeviceCaps caps

Startup = True
Exit Function
```

```
startup_error:
    Startup = False
End Function

Public Property Get Device() As Direct3DDevice8
    Set Device = d3dDevice
End Property

Public Property Get RefreshRate() As Long
    RefreshRate = mode.RefreshRate
End Property

Public Property Get DisplayMode() As Long
    DisplayMode = mode.Format
End Property

Public Property Get MaxPrimitiveCount() As Long
    MaxPrimitiveCount = caps.MaxPrimitiveCount
End Property

Public Property Get MaxActiveLights()
    MaxActiveLights = caps.MaxActiveLights
End Property

Public Property Get MaxTextureWidth()
    MaxTextureWidth = caps.MaxTextureWidth
End Property

Public Property Get MaxTextureHeight()
    MaxTextureHeight = caps.MaxTextureHeight
End Property

Public Sub Clear(ByVal lColor As Long)
    If Device Is Nothing Then Exit Sub
    Device.Clear 0, ByVal 0, D3DCLEAR_TARGET, lColor, 1#, 0
End Sub

Public Sub BeginScene()
    Device.BeginScene
End Sub
```

```
Public Sub EndScene()
    Device.EndScene
End Sub

Public Sub Present()
    'copy the back buffer to the screen
    Device.Present ByVal 0, ByVal 0, 0, ByVal 0
End Sub
```

The clsD3DTriangle8 Class

The clsD3DTriangle8 class encapsulates the vertex struct, the vertex array, the vertex buffer, and the texture for rendering a triangle. Type the code into a file called D3DTriangle8.cls and include it in the Cube3D project. The Cube3D program does not explicitly use this class, but it will be handy later on.

```
'-------------------------------------------------------------------
' Visual Basic Game Programming With DirectX
' Chapter 14 : DirectX Graphics and Direct3D
' clsD3DTriangle8 Class Source Code File
'-------------------------------------------------------------------

Option Explicit
Option Base 0

'describe the features in the flexible vertex format
Const D3DFVF_MYVERTEX = (D3DFVF_XYZ Or D3DFVF_TEX1 Or D3DFVF_NORMAL)

'custom vertex type representing a point on the screen
Private Type VERTEX
    vecPos As D3DVECTOR
    vecNorm As D3DVECTOR
    u As Single
    v As Single
End Type

'local reference to D3D object
Dim d3d As clsDirect3D8

'd3dx is used to load textures
Dim d3dx As New D3DX8
```

```
'vertex information
Dim vert(0 To 2) As VERTEX

'vertex buffer
Dim vbData As Direct3DVertexBuffer8

'texture object
Dim d3dtTexture As Direct3DTexture8
Dim bUseTexture As Boolean

Private Sub Class_Terminate()
    Set vbData = Nothing
    Set d3dtTexture = Nothing
    Set d3dx = Nothing
End Sub

Public Sub Create(ByRef d3dObj As clsDirect3D8)
    'set reference to D3D object
    Set d3d = d3dObj

    'create the D3D vertex buffer
    Set vbData = d3d.Device.CreateVertexBuffer(VertexSize * 3, _
        0, D3DFVF_MYVERTEX, D3DPOOL_DEFAULT)

    'make sure triangle data is valid
    If vbData Is Nothing Then Exit Sub

    'fill the vertex buffer with the triangle data
    D3DVertexBuffer8SetData vbData, 0, VertexSize * 3, 0, vert(0)

    bUseTexture = False
End Sub

Public Function LoadTexture(ByVal sFilename As String) As Boolean
    LoadTexture = False
    Set d3dtTexture = d3dx.CreateTextureFromFile(d3d.Device, _
        sFilename)
    If d3dtTexture Is Nothing Then Exit Function
    LoadTexture = True
    bUseTexture = True
End Function
```

```vb
Public Sub Draw()
    If d3d Is Nothing Then Exit Sub

    'texture must be assigned for each triangle before rendering
    If bUseTexture Then
        d3d.Device.SetTexture 0, d3dtTexture
    Else
        d3d.Device.SetTexture 0, Nothing
    End If

    'set source vertex buffer for rendering
    d3d.Device.SetStreamSource 0, vbData, VertexSize

    'draw the triangle
    d3d.Device.DrawPrimitive D3DPT_TRIANGLELIST, 0, 1

End Sub

Public Sub SetVertex(ByVal lVert As Long, ByVal x As Single, _
    ByVal y As Single, ByVal z As Single, _
    ByVal u As Single, ByVal v As Single)
    If lVert < 0 Or lVert > 2 Then Exit Sub
    vert(lVert).vecPos.x = x
    vert(lVert).vecPos.y = y
    vert(lVert).vecPos.z = z
    vert(lVert).vecNorm.x = 0
    vert(lVert).vecNorm.y = 0
    vert(lVert).vecNorm.z = 1
    vert(lVert).u = u
    vert(lVert).v = v
End Sub

Public Sub SetPosition(ByVal lVert As Long, ByVal x As Single, _
    ByVal y As Single, ByVal z As Single)
    vert(lVert).vecPos.x = x
    vert(lVert).vecPos.y = y
    vert(lVert).vecPos.z = z
End Sub

Public Sub SetNormal(ByVal lVert As Long, ByVal x As Single, _
    ByVal y As Single, ByVal z As Single)
```

```
      vert(lVert).vecNorm.x = x
      vert(lVert).vecNorm.y = y
      vert(lVert).vecNorm.z = z
End Sub

Public Sub SetTexturePos(ByVal lVert As Long, ByVal u As Single, _
      ByVal v As Single)
      vert(lVert).u = u
      vert(lVert).v = v
End Sub

Public Property Get VertexSize() As Long
      VertexSize = Len(vert(0))
End Property
```

The clsD3DRectangle8 Class

The clsD3DRectangle8 class is similar to the triangle class, but it includes two triangles and is capable of mapping a single texture across both of them. This class is the workhorse of the 3-D engine you are building in this chapter, and is great for creating things like the floor, walls, or any other object in a game, whether the object is small or large.

Once you have a working rectangle class that combines two triangles to render a textured image, the triangle class becomes somewhat useless. It would have been nice to build the rectangle out of two already-coded triangle classes, but that would have been inefficient because the triangle class loads a texture itself, and I want the rectangle to load a single texture that wraps over both triangles in the vertex buffer.

If you are building a more complex 3-D object, such as an automobile that has a lot of curves, then you will want to base that object on triangles rather than rectangles. In that sense, the triangle class is more useful in large numbers.

Save the code for this class in a file called D3DRectangle8.cls, and include it in the Cube3D project.

```
'-------------------------------------------------------------------
' Visual Basic Game Programming With DirectX
' Chapter 14 : DirectX Graphics and Direct3D
' clsD3DRectangle8 Class Source Code File
'-------------------------------------------------------------------
```

```vb
Option Explicit
Option Base 0


'describe the features in the flexible vertex format
Const D3DFVF_MYVERTEX = (D3DFVF_XYZ Or D3DFVF_TEX1 Or D3DFVF_NORMAL)


'custom vertex type representing a point on the screen
Private Type VERTEX
    vecPos As D3DVECTOR
    vecNorm As D3DVECTOR
    u As Single
    v As Single
End Type


Dim vert(0 To 5) As VERTEX
Dim vbData As Direct3DVertexBuffer8
Dim d3dtTexture As Direct3DTexture8
Dim d3dx As New D3DX8
Dim d3d As clsDirect3D8
Dim bUseTexture As Boolean

Private Sub Class_Terminate()
    Set vbData = Nothing
    Set d3dtTexture = Nothing
    Set d3dx = Nothing
End Sub

Public Sub Create(ByRef d3dObj As clsDirect3D8)
    'set reference to D3D object
    Set d3d = d3dObj

    'create the D3D vertex buffer
    Set vbData = d3d.Device.CreateVertexBuffer(VertexSize * 6, _
        0, D3DFVF_MYVERTEX, D3DPOOL_DEFAULT)

    'make sure triangle data is valid
    If vbData Is Nothing Then Exit Sub

    'fill the vertex buffer with the triangle data
    D3DVertexBuffer8SetData vbData, 0, VertexSize * 6, 0, vert(0)
```

```
        bUseTexture = False
    End Sub


    Public Function LoadTexture(ByVal sFilename As String, _
        Optional ByVal bAlpha As Boolean = False) As Boolean
        LoadTexture = False
        bUseTexture = False

        If Not bAlpha Then
            'load regular texture
            Set d3dtTexture = d3dx.CreateTextureFromFile(d3d.Device, _
                sFilename)
        Else
            'load texture with alpha color set to black
            Set d3dtTexture = d3dx.CreateTextureFromFileEx(d3d.Device, _
                sFilename, D3DX_DEFAULT, D3DX_DEFAULT, D3DX_DEFAULT, _
                0, D3DFMT_UNKNOWN, D3DPOOL_MANAGED, D3DX_FILTER_POINT, _
                D3DX_FILTER_POINT, &HFF000000, ByVal 0, ByVal 0)
        End If

        If d3dtTexture Is Nothing Then Exit Function
        LoadTexture = True
        bUseTexture = True
    End Function

    Public Sub Draw()
        If d3d Is Nothing Then Exit Sub

        'texture must be set for each redraw
        If bUseTexture Then
            d3d.Device.SetTexture 0, d3dtTexture
        Else
            d3d.Device.SetTexture 0, Nothing
        End If

        'set source vertex buffer for rendering
        d3d.Device.SetStreamSource 0, vbData, VertexSize

        'draw the scene
        d3d.Device.DrawPrimitive D3DPT_TRIANGLELIST, 0, 2
    End Sub
```

```vb
Public Sub SetDefaultVertices()
    'set up the vertices for two triangles
    SetVertex 0, 1, -1, 0, -1, 1
    SetVertex 1, 1, 1, 0, -1, 0
    SetVertex 2, -1, 1, 0, 0, 0
    SetVertex 3, 1, -1, 0, -1, 1
    SetVertex 4, -1, 1, 0, 0, 0
    SetVertex 5, -1, -1, 0, 0, 1
End Sub

Public Sub SetVertex(ByVal lVert As Long, ByVal x As Single, _
    ByVal y As Single, ByVal z As Single, _
    ByVal u As Single, ByVal v As Single)
    If lVert < 0 Or lVert > 5 Then Exit Sub
    vert(lVert).vecPos.x = x
    vert(lVert).vecPos.y = y
    vert(lVert).vecPos.z = z
    vert(lVert).vecNorm.x = 0
    vert(lVert).vecNorm.y = 0
    vert(lVert).vecNorm.z = 1
    vert(lVert).u = u
    vert(lVert).v = v
End Sub

Public Sub SetPosition(ByVal lVert As Long, ByVal x As Single, _
    ByVal y As Single, ByVal z As Single)
    vert(lVert).vecPos.x = x
    vert(lVert).vecPos.y = y
    vert(lVert).vecPos.z = z
End Sub

Public Sub SetNormal(ByVal lVert As Long, ByVal x As Single, _
    ByVal y As Single, ByVal z As Single)
    vert(lVert).vecNorm.x = x
    vert(lVert).vecNorm.y = y
    vert(lVert).vecNorm.z = z
End Sub

Public Sub SetTexturePos(ByVal lVert As Long, ByVal u As Single, _
    ByVal v As Single)
    vert(lVert).u = u
```

```
        vert(lVert).v = v
End Sub

Public Property Get VertexSize() As Long
    VertexSize = Len(vert(0))
End Property
```

The Cube3D Source Code

The Cube3D program demonstrates all of the topics covered in the chapter to this point, and makes use of the classes just written. The classes make it easier to program Direct3D, because they take care of repetitive sections of code that would otherwise be found in the main program listing. Cube3D is similar to other sample programs in the book, with a main loop that calls a rendering procedure. Now, without further ado, here is the source code for the program.

```
'-------------------------------------------------------------------
' Visual Basic Game Programming With DirectX
' Chapter 14 : DirectX Graphics and Direct3D
' Cube3D Source Code File
'-------------------------------------------------------------------

Option Explicit
Option Base 0

'Windows API functions and structures
Private Declare Function GetTickCount Lib "kernel32" () As Long

'define some useful colors
Const C_WHITE As Long = &HFFFFFF
Const C_GRAY As Long = &H111111
Const C_RED As Long = &HFF0000
Const C_GREEN As Long = &H1FF00
Const C_BLUE As Long = &H1FF
Const C_BLACK As Long = &H0

Const PI As Single = 3.141592654

'define the Direct3D object
Dim d3d As New clsDirect3D8
```

```
'define the floor and cube objects
Dim Cube(0 To 5) As clsD3DRectangle8
Dim floor As clsD3DRectangle8

'define matrixes
Dim matProj As D3DMATRIX
Dim matView As D3DMATRIX
Dim matWorld As D3DMATRIX
Dim matRotateX As D3DMATRIX
Dim matRotateY As D3DMATRIX
Dim matTranslate As D3DMATRIX

'define the camera
Dim vecCameraSource As D3DVECTOR
Dim vecCameraTarget As D3DVECTOR

'program variables
Dim bRunning As Boolean
Dim lFrameRate As Long
Dim sFrameRate As String
Dim fTheta As Single
Dim fRotate As Single
```

The quality of the display at 640 × 480 is not very good, due to the small size of the cube (which is only one unit in diameter). To improve the display, you could enlarge the cube using a scaling matrix or by modifying the vertices of the cube. But a far easier way to improve the quality of the display is to simply increase the resolution of the program. I have found that 1024 × 768 looks good, while 1280 × 1024 and 1600 × 1200 both look fantastic! You can change the resolution of the program by modifying the line of code in Form_Load, where the call to Startup is made.

```
Private Sub Form_Load()
    Static lStartTime As Long
    Static lCounter As Long
    Static lNewTime As Long

    'set up the main form
    Form1.Caption = "Cube3D"
    Form1.AutoRedraw = False
    Form1.BorderStyle = 1
    Form1.ClipControls = False
    Form1.KeyPreview = True
```

```
        Form1.ScaleMode = 3
        Form1.Width = Screen.TwipsPerPixelX * 652
        Form1.Height = Screen.TwipsPerPixelY * 510
        Form1.Show

        'initialize Direct3D
        If Not d3d.Startup(Form1.hWnd, 640, 480, True) Then
            MsgBox "Error initializing Direct3D"
            Shutdown
        End If
        'set up the 3D scene
        If Not SetupScene() Then
            MsgBox "Error setting up the 3D scene"
            Shutdown
        End If

        bRunning = True
        lFrameRate = 60
        fTheta = 0
        fRotate = PI / 45

        'start main game loop
        Do While bRunning
            lCounter = GetTickCount() - lStartTime
            If lCounter > lNewTime Then
                RenderScene lCounter
                lNewTime = lCounter + 1000 / lFrameRate
            End If
            DoEvents
        Loop
End Sub

Private Sub Form_KeyDown(KeyCode As Integer, Shift As Integer)
    Debug.Print KeyCode
    Select Case KeyCode
        Case 38 'up arrow
            vecCameraSource.z = vecCameraSource.z - 1
            D3DXMatrixLookAtLH matView, vecCameraSource, _
                vecCameraTarget, CreateVector(0, 1, 0)
            d3d.Device.SetTransform D3DTS_VIEW, matView
```

```
            Case 40 'down arrow
                vecCameraSource.z = vecCameraSource.z + 1
                D3DXMatrixLookAtLH matView, vecCameraSource, _
                    vecCameraTarget, CreateVector(0, 1, 0)
                d3d.Device.SetTransform D3DTS_VIEW, matView
            Case 37 'right arrow
                vecCameraSource.x = vecCameraSource.x + 1
                D3DXMatrixLookAtLH matView, vecCameraSource, _
                    vecCameraTarget, CreateVector(0, 1, 0)
                d3d.Device.SetTransform D3DTS_VIEW, matView
            Case 39 'left arrow
                vecCameraSource.x = vecCameraSource.x - 1
                D3DXMatrixLookAtLH matView, vecCameraSource, _
                    vecCameraTarget, CreateVector(0, 1, 0)
                d3d.Device.SetTransform D3DTS_VIEW, matView
            Case 33 'page up
                vecCameraSource.y = vecCameraSource.y + 1
                D3DXMatrixLookAtLH matView, vecCameraSource, _
                    vecCameraTarget, CreateVector(0, 1, 0)
                d3d.Device.SetTransform D3DTS_VIEW, matView
            Case 34 'page down
                vecCameraSource.y = vecCameraSource.y - 1
                D3DXMatrixLookAtLH matView, vecCameraSource, _
                    vecCameraTarget, CreateVector(0, 1, 0)
                d3d.Device.SetTransform D3DTS_VIEW, matView
            Case 27 'escape
                Shutdown
        End Select
    End Sub

Private Sub Form_Unload(Cancel As Integer)
    Shutdown
End Sub

Private Sub Shutdown()
    Dim n As Long
    Set d3d = Nothing
    Set floor = Nothing
    For n = 0 To 5
        Set Cube(n) = Nothing
    Next n
```

```
        End
End Sub

Function SetupScene() As Boolean
      vecCameraSource.x = 0
      vecCameraSource.y = 0.3
      vecCameraSource.z = 46

      vecCameraTarget.x = 0
      vecCameraTarget.y = 0
      vecCameraTarget.z = 0

      'set up the camera view matrix
      D3DXMatrixLookAtLH matView, vecCameraSource, vecCameraTarget, _
          CreateVector(0, 1, 0)

      'use the camera view for the viewport
      d3d.Device.SetTransform D3DTS_VIEW, matView

      'set up the projection matrix (for perspective)
      D3DXMatrixPerspectiveFovLH matProj, PI / 4, 0.7, 1, 1000

      'tell device to use the projection matrix
      d3d.Device.SetTransform D3DTS_PROJECTION, matProj

      'create the floor
      Set floor = New clsD3DRectangle8
      floor.SetVertex 0, 50, -10, 50, -20, 20
      floor.SetVertex 1, 50, -10, -50, -20, 0
      floor.SetVertex 2, -50, -10, -50, 0, 0
      floor.SetVertex 3, 50, -10, 50, -20, 20
      floor.SetVertex 4, -50, -10, -50, 0, 0
      floor.SetVertex 5, -50, -10, 50, 0, 20
      floor.Create d3d
      floor.LoadTexture App.Path & "\floor.bmp"

      'create the six sides of the cube
      Set Cube(0) = New clsD3DRectangle8
      Cube(0).SetDefaultVertices
      Cube(0).SetPosition 0, 1, -1, 1        'bottom left
```

```
Cube(0).SetPosition 1, 1, 1, 1        'top left
Cube(0).SetPosition 2, -1, 1, 1       'top right
Cube(0).SetPosition 3, 1, -1, 1       'bottom left
Cube(0).SetPosition 4, -1, 1, 1       'top right
Cube(0).SetPosition 5, -1, -1, 1      'bottom right
Cube(0).Create d3d
Cube(0).LoadTexture App.Path & "\cube.bmp"

Set Cube(1) = New clsD3DRectangle8
Cube(1).SetDefaultVertices
Cube(1).SetPosition 0, -1, -1, 1
Cube(1).SetPosition 1, -1, 1, 1
Cube(1).SetPosition 2, -1, 1, -1
Cube(1).SetPosition 3, -1, -1, 1
Cube(1).SetPosition 4, -1, 1, -1
Cube(1).SetPosition 5, -1, -1, -1
Cube(1).Create d3d
Cube(1).LoadTexture App.Path & "\cube.bmp"

Set Cube(2) = New clsD3DRectangle8
Cube(2).SetDefaultVertices
Cube(2).SetPosition 0, -1, -1, -1
Cube(2).SetPosition 1, -1, 1, -1
Cube(2).SetPosition 2, 1, 1, -1
Cube(2).SetPosition 3, -1, -1, -1
Cube(2).SetPosition 4, 1, 1, -1
Cube(2).SetPosition 5, 1, -1, -1
Cube(2).Create d3d
Cube(2).LoadTexture App.Path & "\cube.bmp"

Set Cube(3) = New clsD3DRectangle8
Cube(3).SetDefaultVertices
Cube(3).SetPosition 0, 1, -1, -1
Cube(3).SetPosition 1, 1, 1, -1
Cube(3).SetPosition 2, 1, 1, 1
Cube(3).SetPosition 3, 1, -1, -1
Cube(3).SetPosition 4, 1, 1, 1
Cube(3).SetPosition 5, 1, -1, 1
Cube(3).Create d3d
Cube(3).LoadTexture App.Path & "\cube.bmp"
```

```
    Set Cube(4) = New clsD3DRectangle8
    Cube(4).SetDefaultVertices
    Cube(4).SetPosition 0, 1, 1, 1
    Cube(4).SetPosition 1, 1, 1, -1
    Cube(4).SetPosition 2, -1, 1, -1
    Cube(4).SetPosition 3, 1, 1, 1
    Cube(4).SetPosition 4, -1, 1, -1
    Cube(4).SetPosition 5, -1, 1, 1
    Cube(4).Create d3d
    Cube(4).LoadTexture App.Path & "\cube.bmp"

    Set Cube(5) = New clsD3DRectangle8
    Cube(5).SetDefaultVertices
    Cube(5).SetPosition 0, -1, -1, 1
    Cube(5).SetPosition 1, -1, -1, -1
    Cube(5).SetPosition 2, 1, -1, -1
    Cube(5).SetPosition 3, -1, -1, 1
    Cube(5).SetPosition 4, 1, -1, -1
    Cube(5).SetPosition 5, 1, -1, 1
    Cube(5).Create d3d
    Cube(5).LoadTexture App.Path & "\cube.bmp"

    SetupScene = True
End Function

Public Sub RenderScene(ByVal MS As Long)
    Static lTimer As Long
    Static lStart As Long
    Static lCounter As Long
    Static fLighting As Single
    Static lDir As Long
    Dim n As Long

    'start counting milliseconds
    lStart = GetTickCount

    d3d.Clear C_BLACK

    'start rendering
    d3d.BeginScene
```

```
    'set world matrix to origin
    SetIdentity

    'draw the tiled floor
    floor.Draw

    'rotate the cube about the X and Y axes
    fTheta = fTheta + fRotate
    D3DXMatrixRotationX matRotateX, fTheta / 2
    D3DXMatrixRotationY matRotateY, fTheta
    D3DXMatrixTranslation matTranslate, 0, 0, 40
    D3DXMatrixMultiply matWorld, matRotateX, matRotateY
    D3DXMatrixMultiply matWorld, matWorld, matTranslate
    d3d.Device.SetTransform D3DTS_WORLD, matWorld

    'draw the cube
    For n = 0 To 5
        Cube(n).Draw
    Next n

    'stop rendering
    d3d.EndScene

    'draw the back buffer to the screen
    d3d.Present

    'count the frames per second
    If MS > lTimer + 1000 Then
        lStart = GetTickCount - lStart
        sFrameRate = "FPS = " & lCounter & ", MS = " & lStart
        Debug.Print sFrameRate
        lTimer = MS
        lCounter = 0
    Else
        lCounter = lCounter + 1
    End If
End Sub

Public Sub SetIdentity()
    'set default position, scale, and rotation
    D3DXMatrixIdentity matWorld
```

```
    d3d.Device.SetTransform D3DTS_WORLD, matWorld
End Sub

Function CreateVector(x As Single, y As Single, z As Single) As D3DVECTOR
    CreateVector.x = x
    CreateVector.y = y
    CreateVector.z = z
End Function
```

The AlphaBlend3D Program

The AlphaBlend3D program is based on Cube3D and only involves a few changes to the code from Cube3D to implement. Basically, the functionality for alpha blending with a texture is already present in the clsD3DRectangle8 class, so the only thing you need to do is enable alpha blending when loading a texture for a rectangle. Figure 14.9 shows the program with transparency not yet enabled.

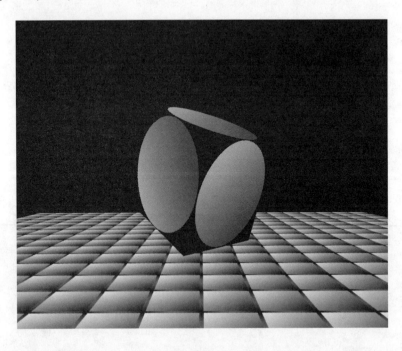

Figure 14.9

The AlphaBlend3D program, showing the circle texture with transparency disabled

This simple alpha blending technique demonstrates how easy it is to render transparent images with Direct3D, and paves the way to understanding how the 3-D sprite class in the next section works. Figure 14.10 shows the AlphaBlend3D program with transparency enabled.

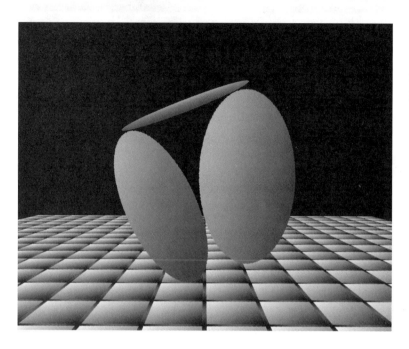

Figure 14.10

The AlphaBlend3D program, with transparency enabled

The first section of code that needs to be changed is just the comment at the top of the source code listing.

```
'----------------------------------------------------------------------
' Visual Basic Game Programming With DirectX
' Chapter 14 : DirectX Graphics and Direct3D
' AlphaBlend3D Source Code File
'----------------------------------------------------------------------
```

The next section of code is actually just a single line from Form_Load that changes the caption of the form.

```
'set up the main form
Form1.Caption = "AlphaBlend3D"
```

The next code change is located in the SetupScene function. Since there are so many changes, I have listed the entire function. Basically, by passing a value of True to the LoadTexture procedure calls, you enable alpha blending!

```
Private Function SetupScene() As Boolean
    vecCameraSource.x = 0
    vecCameraSource.y = 10
    vecCameraSource.z = 80
```

```
        vecCameraTarget.x = 0
        vecCameraTarget.y = 0
        vecCameraTarget.z = 0

        'set up the camera view matrix
        D3DXMatrixLookAtLH matView, vecCameraSource, vecCameraTarget, _
            CreateVector(0, 1, 0)

        'use the camera view for the viewport
        d3d.Device.SetTransform D3DTS_VIEW, matView

        'set up the projection matrix (for perspective)
        D3DXMatrixPerspectiveFovLH matProj, PI / 4, 0.7, 1, 1000

        'tell device to use the projection matrix
        d3d.Device.SetTransform D3DTS_PROJECTION, matProj

        'create the floor
        Set floor = New clsD3DRectangle8
        floor.SetVertex 0, 50, -10, 50, -20, 20
        floor.SetVertex 1, 50, -10, -50, -20, 0
        floor.SetVertex 2, -50, -10, -50, 0, 0
        floor.SetVertex 3, 50, -10, 50, -20, 20
        floor.SetVertex 4, -50, -10, -50, 0, 0
        floor.SetVertex 5, -50, -10, 50, 0, 20
        floor.Create d3d
        floor.LoadTexture App.Path & "\floor.bmp"

        'create the six sides of the cube
        Set Cube(0) = New clsD3DRectangle8
        Cube(0).SetDefaultVertices
        Cube(0).SetPosition 0, 1, -1, 1       'bottom left
        Cube(0).SetPosition 1, 1, 1, 1        'top left
        Cube(0).SetPosition 2, -1, 1, 1       'top right
        Cube(0).SetPosition 3, 1, -1, 1       'bottom left
        Cube(0).SetPosition 4, -1, 1, 1       'top right
        Cube(0).SetPosition 5, -1, -1, 1      'bottom right
        Cube(0).Create d3d
        Cube(0).LoadTexture App.Path & "\circle.bmp", True
```

```
Set Cube(1) = New clsD3DRectangle8
Cube(1).SetDefaultVertices
Cube(1).SetPosition 0, -1, -1, 1
Cube(1).SetPosition 1, -1, 1, 1
Cube(1).SetPosition 2, -1, 1, -1
Cube(1).SetPosition 3, -1, -1, 1
Cube(1).SetPosition 4, -1, 1, -1
Cube(1).SetPosition 5, -1, -1, -1
Cube(1).Create d3d
Cube(1).LoadTexture App.Path & "\circle.bmp", True


Set Cube(2) = New clsD3DRectangle8
Cube(2).SetDefaultVertices
Cube(2).SetPosition 0, -1, -1, -1
Cube(2).SetPosition 1, -1, 1, -1
Cube(2).SetPosition 2, 1, 1, -1
Cube(2).SetPosition 3, -1, -1, -1
Cube(2).SetPosition 4, 1, 1, -1
Cube(2).SetPosition 5, 1, -1, -1
Cube(2).Create d3d
Cube(2).LoadTexture App.Path & "\circle.bmp", True


Set Cube(3) = New clsD3DRectangle8
Cube(3).SetDefaultVertices
Cube(3).SetPosition 0, 1, -1, -1
Cube(3).SetPosition 1, 1, 1, -1
Cube(3).SetPosition 2, 1, 1, 1
Cube(3).SetPosition 3, 1, -1, -1
Cube(3).SetPosition 4, 1, 1, 1
Cube(3).SetPosition 5, 1, -1, 1
Cube(3).Create d3d
Cube(3).LoadTexture App.Path & "\circle.bmp", True


Set Cube(4) = New clsD3DRectangle8
Cube(4).SetDefaultVertices
Cube(4).SetPosition 0, 1, 1, 1
Cube(4).SetPosition 1, 1, 1, -1
Cube(4).SetPosition 2, -1, 1, -1
Cube(4).SetPosition 3, 1, 1, 1
Cube(4).SetPosition 4, -1, 1, -1
```

```
    Cube(4).SetPosition 5, -1, 1, 1
    Cube(4).Create d3d
    Cube(4).LoadTexture App.Path & "\circle.bmp", True

    Set Cube(5) = New clsD3DRectangle8
    Cube(5).SetDefaultVertices
    Cube(5).SetPosition 0, -1, -1, 1
    Cube(5).SetPosition 1, -1, -1, -1
    Cube(5).SetPosition 2, 1, -1, -1
    Cube(5).SetPosition 3, -1, -1, 1
    Cube(5).SetPosition 4, 1, -1, -1
    Cube(5).SetPosition 5, 1, -1, 1
    Cube(5).Create d3d
    Cube(5).LoadTexture App.Path & "\circle.bmp", True

    SetupScene = True
End Function
```

Sprite Programming with Direct3D

Programming a sprite handler with Direct3D code might seem like a challenge at first. After all, Direct3D was not designed to draw 2-D bitmaps. However, with a little effort, the power of Direct3D gives a sprite (based on Direct3D) significant advantages over earlier technologies (such as Windows API sprites and DirectDraw sprites). The one thing you will find most noticeable about the Sprite3D program is that the sprites are scaled randomly, with some spectacular results. Some of the sprites are scaled very small, while others are huge. Of course, if you don't want to mess with scaling at all, you can simply leave the default ScaleX and ScaleY at 1.0. But where's the fun in that?

The Sprite3D Program

Actually, there's a very real and powerful advantage to being able to scale sprites on-the-fly. Right away, it gives me the idea that an entire game can be zoomed in and out by setting a global scaling value that affects all of the sprites in the game. There is also the very cool possibility of adding more variety to a game by using a single sprite size throughout all of the source artwork for a game (such as 64×64), and then scaling the sprites according to the game specs. For instance, rather than drawing a large boss character at the end of a level, just scale a normal-sized enemy to three times normal size and there you go!

Transparent Sprites

Transparency is almost an afterthought to an advanced API like Direct3D, so that is not really an issue that you need to worry about. In Direct3D, transparency is actually accomplished through alpha blending. Basically, there are options that you can set when loading the source bitmap for a sprite that tell Direct3D to set the alpha bit for the source image, thus making black the transparent color (as has been the standard throughout this book).

Rather than code a bunch of support routines like in previous chapters, I simply created properties that allow you to modify the sprite variables yourself. So, rather than having a NextFrame procedure for incrementing the current frame, I thought it would be better to just provide direct access to the lCurrentFrame variable through a property. However, if you found the two previous sprite classes (namely, clsSprite and clsDDSprite7) more useful with those built-in routines, then I encourage you to modify the sprite class in this chapter, clsD3DSprite8, however you see fit.

Relative Performance

Of course, the frame rate of a sprite engine built upon Direct3D will not be anywhere near as fast as a DirectDraw sprite engine, because there is a huge amount of overhead involved in rendering the 3-D scene along with the sprites. If you are building a tile-based arcade game or something similar to that, then you might want to consider just using DirectDraw instead of Direct3D. The 3-D sprite engine is very cool, and allows you to incorporate special effects that are not possible in a 2-D game. Just having a 3-D background with subtle animation can have a huge impact on a game that is visually boring (such as *Tetris*).

Figure 14.11 shows the Sprite3D program running at 1600 × 1200, with 200 sprites on the screen, running at about 20 fps. Increasing the sprite count to 300 seemed to kill the program; it still ran, but the 3-D rendering took a nosedive. So it appears that using Direct3D to render sprites does achieve some good results—and keep in mind that these sprites were rendered with scaling enabled, which adds a significant performance hit.

If your monitor is capable of hitting 1600 × 1200, then bump the program up to that resolution and check it out. If you want to get more sprites into the scene, then you might try using smaller sprites. 64 × 64 is a pretty good, average size, but smaller sprites will result in more of them. Just consider that four 32 × 32 sprites will fill a single 64 × 64 sprite. Plus, when loading directly off an existing texture (as opposed to loading a new texture), there is just a very small memory footprint for each new sprite.

> **TIP**
>
> To see the frame rate, you will need to look at the Immediate window in VB while the program is running, because this program (like the others in this chapter) simply outputs frame rate information with Debug.Print.

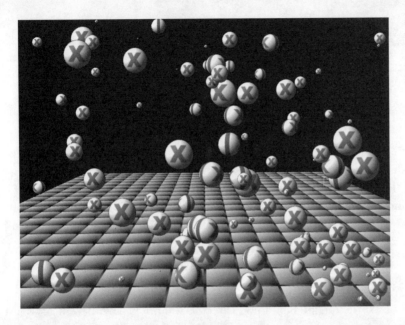

Figure 14.11

The Sprite3D program running at 1600 × 1200

Figure 14.12 shows the program running at 1280 × 1024, but with a huge MAXSCALE setting of 5.0. The scale will be a random value from 0.0 to 5.0 with this setting, as the figure shows. The huge scaling factor caused the frame rate to drop by 25 percent.

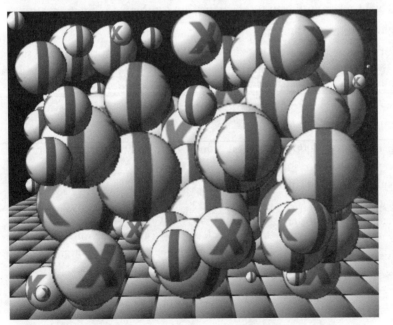

Figure 14.12

Manipulating the scaling can produce some funny results that might prove useful later.

As is the case with most video cards, some resolutions are significantly faster than others (disregarding the obvious fact that fewer pixels are being manipulated). Some cards just really blaze at 640×480, while others tear up the screen at 800×600. Figure 14.13 shows the program running at 640×480, with 100 sprites and a MAXSCALE value of 2.0. The program ran at around 50 fps with these settings.

Figure 14.13

Reducing the resolution and scaling gives the program a huge boost in performance.

One interesting thing that I found with the Sprite3D program is that Direct3D handles the back buffer automatically, so there is no need to save and restore the background under each sprite, as was the case with the Windows API and DirectDraw programs in earlier chapters. The Present procedure copies the back buffer to the screen, so the opportunity exists if you would like to write your own back buffer blitter, but I'm sure that the DirectX team has already optimized this code as much as humanly possible.

The clsD3DSprite8 Class

Now, to be consistent, I have written a class that encapsulates the functionality of drawing sprites in the middle of the Direct3D rendering process. In case you were wondering, this code is using the D3DXSprite object, along with a regular Direct3DTexture8 object for the source bitmap. This sprite class is similar to those in previous chapters (clsSprite and clsDDSprite7), and is actually somewhat simpler than the earlier attempts. This sprite class allows you to load a texture directly from a bitmap file on disk, or you have the option of grabbing sprite frames out of an already-loaded texture (which is a powerful and memory-saving option). Save the code for this class in a file called D3DSprite8.cls and include it in the Sprite3D project.

```
'--------------------------------------------------------------
' Visual Basic Game Programming With DirectX
' Chapter 14 : DirectX Graphics and Direct3D
' clsD3DSprite8 Class Source Code File
'--------------------------------------------------------------


Option Explicit
Option Base 0

'Direct3D objects
Dim spr As D3DXSprite
Dim d3dtSpr As Direct3DTexture8
Dim d3dx As New D3DX8
Dim d3d As clsDirect3D8

'sprite manipulation variables
Dim vecScale As D3DVECTOR2
Dim vecRot As D3DVECTOR2
Dim vecTrans As D3DVECTOR2
Dim sprRect As RECT
Dim fRotation As Single

'sprite properties
Dim lWidth As Long
Dim lHeight As Long
Dim lFramesPerRow As Long
Dim lFrameCount As Long
Dim lCurrentFrame As Long
Dim lSpeedX As Long
Dim lSpeedY As Long
Dim lDirX As Long
Dim lDirY As Long
Dim bLoadFromFile As Boolean

Private Sub Class_Terminate()
    Set spr = Nothing
    'don't delete any references
    If bLoadFromFile Then
        Set d3dtSpr = Nothing
    End If
```

```
    Set d3dx = Nothing
End Sub

Public Sub Create(ByRef d3dObj As clsDirect3D8)
    'set local reference to Direct3D
    Set d3d = d3dObj
    'create the sprite object
    Set spr = d3dx.CreateSprite(d3d.Device)
End Sub

Public Sub LoadFromFile(ByVal sFilename As String, _
        ByVal lSprWidth As Long, ByVal lSprHeight As Long, _
        ByVal lNumCols As Long, ByVal lNumFrames As Long)

    'load the source bitmap file into a texture
    Set d3dtSpr = d3dx.CreateTextureFromFileEx(d3d.Device, _
        sFilename, D3DX_DEFAULT, D3DX_DEFAULT, 1, 0, _
        D3DFMT_UNKNOWN, D3DPOOL_MANAGED, D3DX_FILTER_NONE, _
        D3DX_FILTER_NONE, &HFF000000, ByVal 0, ByVal 0)

    'set the column and frame count
    lFramesPerRow = lNumCols
    lFrameCount = lNumFrames

    'set the starting position
    X = 0
    Y = 0

    'set the starting scale values
    vecScale.X = 1
    vecScale.Y = 1

    'set the width and height of each frame
    lWidth = lSprWidth
    lHeight = lSprHeight

    'set the starting rotation value
    fRotation = 0
    bLoadFromFile = True
End Sub
```

```
Public Sub LoadFromTexture(ByRef d3dtSprite As Direct3DTexture8, _
    ByVal lSprWidth As Long, ByVal lSprHeight As Long, _
    ByVal lNumCols As Long, ByVal lNumFrames As Long)

    'load texture from another texture
    Set d3dtSpr = d3dtSprite

    'set the column and frame count
    lFramesPerRow = lNumCols
    lFrameCount = lNumFrames

    'set the starting position
    X = 0
    Y = 0

    'set the starting scale values
    vecScale.X = 1
    vecScale.Y = 1

    'set the width and height of each frame
    lWidth = lSprWidth
    lHeight = lSprHeight

    'set the starting rotation value
    fRotation = 0

    bLoadFromFile = False
End Sub

Public Sub Draw()
    'save the current rendering state
    spr.Begin

    'set the source rect
    sprRect.Left = (lCurrentFrame Mod lFramesPerRow) * lHeight
    sprRect.Top = (lCurrentFrame \ lFramesPerRow) * lWidth
    sprRect.Right = sprRect.Left + lWidth
    sprRect.bottom = sprRect.Top + lHeight

    'draw the sprite
    spr.Draw d3dtSpr, sprRect, vecScale, vecRot, _
        fRotation, vecTrans, &HFFFFFFFF
```

```vb
    'restore the rendering state
    spr.End
End Sub

Public Property Get X() As Long
    X = vecTrans.X
End Property

Public Property Let X(ByVal lNewValue As Long)
    vecTrans.X = lNewValue
End Property

Public Property Get Y() As Long
    Y = vecTrans.Y
End Property

Public Property Let Y(ByVal lNewValue As Long)
    vecTrans.Y = lNewValue
End Property

Public Property Get ScaleX() As Single
    ScaleX = vecScale.X
End Property

Public Property Let ScaleX(ByVal fNewValue As Single)
    vecScale.X = fNewValue
End Property

Public Property Get ScaleY() As Single
    ScaleY = vecScale.Y
End Property

Public Property Let ScaleY(ByVal fNewValue As Single)
    vecScale.Y = fNewValue
End Property

Public Property Get Width() As Long
    Width = lWidth
End Property
```

```
Public Property Get Height() As Long
    Height = lHeight
End Property


Public Property Get TotalFrames() As Long
    TotalFrames = lFrameCount
End Property


Public Property Get CurrentFrame() As Long
    CurrentFrame = lCurrentFrame
End Property


Public Property Let CurrentFrame(ByVal lNewValue As Long)
    lCurrentFrame = lNewValue
End Property


Public Property Get SpeedX() As Long
    SpeedX = lSpeedX
End Property


Public Property Let SpeedX(ByVal lNewValue As Long)
    lSpeedX = lNewValue
End Property


Public Property Get SpeedY() As Long
    SpeedY = lSpeedY
End Property


Public Property Let SpeedY(ByVal lNewValue As Long)
    lSpeedY = lNewValue
End Property


Public Property Get DirX() As Long
    DirX = lDirX
End Property


Public Property Let DirX(ByVal lNewValue As Long)
    lDirX = lNewValue
End Property
```

```
Public Property Get DirY() As Long
    DirY = lDirY
End Property

Public Property Let DirY(ByVal lNewValue As Long)
    lDirY = lNewValue
End Property
```

The Sprite3D Source Code

The Sprite3D program is very similar to the other Direct3D programs in this chapter. It includes a tiled floor to help give some depth (and prove that it is indeed a 3-D program). It still allows you to move the camera around the 3 D environment with the arrow keys and page up/down. Simply type this code into the code module for Form1 in the Sprite3D project. One final note: If you want your sprites to be displayed exactly, without scaling, then you will want to set the ScaleX and ScaleY properties to 1.0.

```
'--------------------------------------------------------------------
' Visual Basic Game Programming With DirectX
' Chapter 14 : DirectX Graphics and Direct3D
' Sprite3D Source Code File
'--------------------------------------------------------------------

Option Explicit
Option Base 0

'Windows API functions and structures
Private Declare Function GetTickCount _
    Lib "kernel32" () As Long

'define some useful background-clearing colors
Const C_WHITE As Long = &HFFFFFF
Const C_GRAY As Long = &H111111
Const C_RED As Long = &HFF0000
Const C_GREEN As Long = &H1FF00
Const C_BLUE As Long = &H1FF
Const C_BLACK As Long = &H0
Const PI As Single = 3.141592654
```

```
'program constants
Const SCREENWIDTH As Long = 640
Const SCREENHEIGHT As Long = 480
Const NUMSPRITES As Long = 30
Const MAXSCALE As Single = 2

'define the DirectX objects
Dim d3d As New clsDirect3D8
Dim d3dx As New D3DX8
Dim floor As New clsD3DRectangle8

Dim d3dtSpr As Direct3DTexture8
Dim sprites(0 To NUMSPRITES) As clsD3DSprite8

'define matrixes
Dim matProj As D3DMATRIX
Dim matView As D3DMATRIX
Dim matWorld As D3DMATRIX
Dim matRotateX As D3DMATRIX
Dim matRotateY As D3DMATRIX
Dim matTranslate As D3DMATRIX

'define the camera
Dim vecCameraSource As D3DVECTOR
Dim vecCameraTarget As D3DVECTOR

'program variables
Dim bRunning As Boolean
Dim lFrameRate As Long
Dim sFrameRate As String

Private Sub Form_Load()
    Static lStartTime As Long
    Static lCounter As Long
    Static lNewTime As Long

    Randomize GetTickCount
    lFrameRate = 60
```

```
    'set up the main form
    Form1.Caption = "Sprite3D"
    Form1.AutoRedraw = False
    Form1.BorderStyle = 1
    Form1.ClipControls = False
    Form1.KeyPreview = True
    Form1.ScaleMode = 3
    Form1.Width = Screen.TwipsPerPixelX * (SCREENWIDTH + 12)
    Form1.Height = Screen.TwipsPerPixelY * (SCREENHEIGHT + 30)
    Form1.Show

    'initialize Direct3D
    If Not d3d.Startup(Form1.hWnd, SCREENWIDTH, SCREENHEIGHT, _
        True) Then
        MsgBox "Error initializing Direct3D"
        Shutdown
    End If

    'set up the 3D scene
    If Not SetupScene() Then
        MsgBox "Error setting up the 3D scene"
        Shutdown
    End If

    'initialize the sprites
    InitSprites

    'start main game loop
    bRunning = True
    Do While bRunning
        lCounter = GetTickCount() - lStartTime
        If lCounter > lNewTime Then
            RenderScene lCounter
            lNewTime = lCounter + 1000 / lFrameRate
        End If
        DoEvents
    Loop
End Sub

Private Sub Form_KeyDown(KeyCode As Integer, Shift As Integer)
    Select Case KeyCode
```

```
            Case 38 'up arrow
                vecCameraSource.z = vecCameraSource.z - 1
                D3DXMatrixLookAtLH matView, vecCameraSource, _
                    vecCameraTarget, CreateVector(0, 1, 0)
                d3d.Device.SetTransform D3DTS_VIEW, matView
            Case 40 'down arrow
                vecCameraSource.z = vecCameraSource.z + 1
                D3DXMatrixLookAtLH matView, vecCameraSource, _
                    vecCameraTarget, CreateVector(0, 1, 0)
                d3d.Device.SetTransform D3DTS_VIEW, matView
            Case 37 'right arrow
                vecCameraSource.X = vecCameraSource.X + 1
                D3DXMatrixLookAtLH matView, vecCameraSource, _
                    vecCameraTarget, CreateVector(0, 1, 0)
                d3d.Device.SetTransform D3DTS_VIEW, matView
            Case 39 'left arrow
                vecCameraSource.X = vecCameraSource.X - 1
                D3DXMatrixLookAtLH matView, vecCameraSource, _
                    vecCameraTarget, CreateVector(0, 1, 0)
                d3d.Device.SetTransform D3DTS_VIEW, matView
            Case 33 'page up
                vecCameraSource.Y = vecCameraSource.Y + 1
                D3DXMatrixLookAtLH matView, vecCameraSource, _
                    vecCameraTarget, CreateVector(0, 1, 0)
                d3d.Device.SetTransform D3DTS_VIEW, matView
            Case 34 'page down
                vecCameraSource.Y = vecCameraSource.Y - 1
                D3DXMatrixLookAtLH matView, vecCameraSource, _
                    vecCameraTarget, CreateVector(0, 1, 0)
                d3d.Device.SetTransform D3DTS_VIEW, matView
        Case 27 'escape
            Shutdown
    End Select
End Sub

Private Sub Form_Unload(Cancel As Integer)
    Shutdown
End Sub

Private Sub Shutdown()
    Dim n As Long
```

```
        Set d3d = Nothing
        Set floor = Nothing
        For n = 0 To NUMSPRITES
            Set sprites(n) = Nothing
        Next n
        End
End Sub

Function SetupScene() As Boolean
        'set the camera source
        vecCameraSource.X = 0
        vecCameraSource.Y = 10
        vecCameraSource.z = 80

        'set the camera's target
        vecCameraTarget.X = 0
        vecCameraTarget.Y = 0
        vecCameraTarget.z = 0

        'set up the camera view matrix
        D3DXMatrixLookAtLH matView, vecCameraSource, vecCameraTarget, _
            CreateVector(0, 1, 0)

        'use the camera view for the viewport
        d3d.Device.SetTransform D3DTS_VIEW, matView

        'set up the projection matrix (for perspective)
        D3DXMatrixPerspectiveFovLH matProj, PI / 4, 0.7, 1, 1000

        'tell device to use the projection matrix
        d3d.Device.SetTransform D3DTS_PROJECTION, matProj

        'create the floor
        floor.SetVertex 0, 50, -10, 50, -20, 20
        floor.SetVertex 1, 50, -10, -50, -20, 0
        floor.SetVertex 2, -50, -10, -50, 0, 0
        floor.SetVertex 3, 50, -10, 50, -20, 20
        floor.SetVertex 4, -50, -10, -50, 0, 0
        floor.SetVertex 5, -50, -10, 50, 0, 20
        floor.Create d3d
        floor.LoadTexture App.Path & "\floor.bmp"
```

```
       'display the device caps
       Debug.Print "MaxPrimitiveCount = " & d3d.MaxPrimitiveCount
       Debug.Print "MaxActiveLights = " & d3d.MaxActiveLights
       Debug.Print "MaxTextureWidth = " & d3d.MaxTextureWidth
       Debug.Print "MaxTextureHeight = " & d3d.MaxTextureHeight

       SetupScene = True
End Function
```

The InitSprites procedure is the only major routine in the Sprite3D program that is new, while the rest of the code for this program was borrowed from Cube3D and AlphaBlend3D. InitSprites creates the first sprite by loading a texture from a bitmap file, to demonstrate how to use the LoadFromFile and LoadFromTexture routines. The sprite movement code should be familiar from earlier chapters, since I based the Direct3D sprite class on code that was developed earlier in the book.

```
Public Sub InitSprites()
    Dim n As Long

    'initialize the first sprite
    'this shows loading the texture from a bitmap file
    Set sprites(0) = New clsD3DSprite8
    With sprites(0)
        .Create d3d

        'load this sprite's frames from a bitmap file
        .LoadFromFile App.Path & "\rotating_sphere.bmp", _
            64, 64, 8, 32

        .CurrentFrame = Random(60)
        .SpeedX = Random(4) + 1
        .SpeedY = Random(4) + 1
        .DirX = Random(3) - 1
        .DirY = Random(3) - 1
    End With

    'load the texture to use for remaining sprites
    Set d3dtSpr = d3dx.CreateTextureFromFileEx(d3d.Device, _
        App.Path & "\rotating_sphere.bmp", D3DX_DEFAULT, _
        D3DX_DEFAULT, 1, 0, D3DFMT_UNKNOWN, D3DPOOL_MANAGED, _
```

```
            D3DX_FILTER_NONE, D3DX_FILTER_NONE, &HFF000000, _
            ByVal 0, ByVal 0)

        'initialize the remaining sprites
        'shows loading from a texture rather than a file
        For n = 1 To NUMSPRITES
            Set sprites(n) = New clsD3DSprite8
            With sprites(n)
                .Create d3d
                .LoadFromTexture d3dtSpr, 64, 64, 8, 32
                .X = Random(SCREENWIDTH - 64)
                .Y = Random(SCREENHEIGHT - 64)
                .ScaleX = CSng(Random(MAXSCALE * 10) / 10)
                .ScaleY = .ScaleX
                .CurrentFrame = Random(60)
                .SpeedX = Random(6) + 1
                .SpeedY = Random(6) + 1
                Do While .DirX = 0
                    .DirX = Random(3) - 1
                Loop
                Do While .DirY = 0
                    .DirY = Random(3) - 1
                Loop
            End With
        Next n
End Sub
```

The RenderScene procedure should look familiar from the Cube3D program, but it now includes
a large chunk of code in the middle for moving and drawing the sprites. This code is pretty common by now, and simply increments the sprite's X and Y values based on SpeedX, SpeedY, DirX,
and DirY. Note, however, that since Direct3D is doing the hard work of drawing the back buffer,
there is no need to save and restore the background under the sprites.

```
Public Sub RenderScene(ByVal MS As Long)
    Static lTimer As Long
    Static lStart As Long
    Static lCounter As Long
    Static fLighting As Single
    Static lDir As Long
    Dim n As Long
```

```
'start counting milliseconds
lStart = GetTickCount

'clear the D3D back buffer
d3d.Clear C_BLACK

'start rendering
d3d.BeginScene

'set world matrix to origin
SetIdentity

'draw the tiled floor
floor.Draw

'move and draw the sprites
For n = 0 To NUMSPRITES
    With sprites(n)
        'update X position
        .X = .X + .SpeedX * .DirX
        If .X > SCREENWIDTH - .Width * .ScaleX Then
            .X = SCREENWIDTH - .Width * .ScaleX
            .DirX = -1
        ElseIf .X < 0 Then
            .X = 0
            .DirX = 1
        End If

        'update Y position
        .Y = .Y + .SpeedY * .DirY
        If .Y > SCREENHEIGHT - .Height * .ScaleY Then
            .Y = SCREENHEIGHT - .Height * .ScaleY
            .DirY = -1
        ElseIf .Y < 0 Then
            .Y = 0
            .DirY = 1
        End If

        'update the sprite frame
        .CurrentFrame = .CurrentFrame + 1
```

```vb
            If .CurrentFrame > .TotalFrames - 1 Then
                .CurrentFrame = 0
            End If

            'draw the sprite
            .Draw
        End With
    Next n

    'stop rendering
    d3d.EndScene

    'draw the back buffer to the screen
    d3d.Present

    'count the frames per second
    If MS > lTimer + 1000 Then
        lStart = GetTickCount - lStart
        sFrameRate = "FPS = " & lCounter & ", MS = " & lStart
        Debug.Print sFrameRate
        lTimer = MS
        lCounter = 0
    Else
        lCounter = lCounter + 1
    End If
End Sub

Public Sub SetIdentity()
    'set default position, scale, and rotation
    D3DXMatrixIdentity matWorld
    d3d.Device.SetTransform D3DTS_WORLD, matWorld
End Sub

Function CreateVector(X As Single, Y As Single, z As Single) _
    As D3DVECTOR
    CreateVector.X = X
    CreateVector.Y = Y
    CreateVector.z = z
End Function
```

```
Public Function Random(ByVal lNum As Long) As Long
    Random = CLng(Rnd * lNum)
End Function
```

Promotion!

Very impressive! You have now mastered DirectSound, DirectMusic, DirectInput, and Direct3D. By understanding the basics of 3-D graphics, you are on your way to building completely immersive games. 3-D programming is, without a doubt, the most difficult subject in the whole field of game programming. Not only that, you have found a way to manipulate 3-D space in such a way that you are able to draw sprites using Direct3D. These powerful new skills are most impressive, indeed.

You are hereby promoted to the rank of *Veteran Coder*, with all of the rights and privileges that come with the position. You now have the ability to build complete 2-D and 3-D games with sound, music, and even joystick input. Use your new knowledge and skills wisely, and continue to push the envelope of Visual Basic gaming!

Here is a record of your progress so far:

1. **Newbie Gamer**
2. **Apprentice Hacker**
3. **Skilled Programmer**
4. **Veteran Coder**
5. Master Developer
6. Adept Game Designer

Summary

Well, that's about all I have to say on the matter of Direct3D. This chapter was a lot of fun because it included a lot of new information. First, I gave you a crash course in 3-D graphics, followed by an introduction to Direct3D, and then I showed you how the Direct3D rendering pipeline works. After discussing vertex structures and alpha blending, I showed you some classes that make the whole Direct3D experience more productive. Finally, I showed you how to build a Direct3D sprite engine.

CHAPTER 15

Artificial and Simulated Intelligence

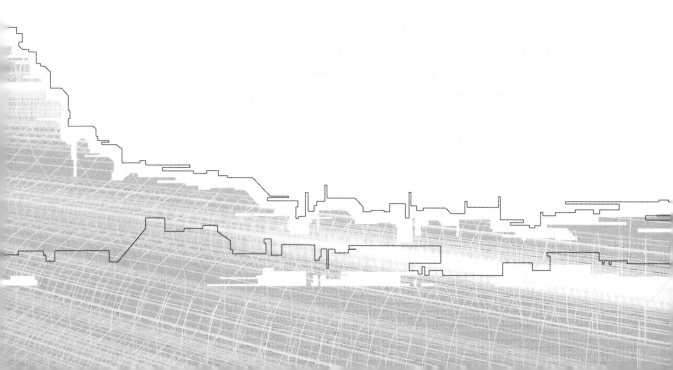

The subject of artificial (and simulated) intelligence is vast and incredibly complex. Recent advances in computer technology for simulating intelligence at both the hardware and software levels have produced thinking machines that would have stunned researchers of years past. And yet, every time a new advancement is made in artificial intelligence research, the bar is raised and the standard by which true intelligence is measured is pushed up, up, up to higher—and apparently unachievable—levels.

This chapter discusses the subject of artificial intelligence as it relates to game programming—and that's it. There are no theories presented in this chapter that are not backed up by sample code. Since I recognize the importance of providing working and usable code, the samples presented herein are working demonstrations of the topics being covered. Each major topic includes a reusable class that can be plugged into a game and immediately used, in conjunction with existing classes such as clsSprite. Since this is a hands-on crash course in artificial intelligence, the tone will be casual, and the topics will be functional. I'm not covering anything that required research into the subject. I am simply explaining these topics as I understand them.

The goal is to provide games with enough smarts to make them fun and challenging—but not by starting a global thermonuclear war, as in the movie *War Games,* or by creating an intelligent Terminator. Although, wouldn't it be scary to create a game in which your opponent seems to be alive? When it comes to game development, the appearance of intelligence is enough to create a fun and challenging game.

This chapter covers the following topics:

- What is Artificial Intelligence?
- Intelligent Computer Player Control
- Creating Smart Opponents

WHAT IS ARTIFICIAL INTELLIGENCE?

Artificial intelligence is sort of a loaded phrase, since it can mean so little and it can mean so much. Most often, the phrase is misused to mean game logic. Left to the popular media, the process of just moving a sprite around the screen is called AI. A more realistic description of the subject is *simulated situational intelligence.* Taken apart, this phrase describes the process of simulating computer intelligence surrounding specific situations or events. In other words, the computer is smart when it comes to one thing, but dumb when it comes to everything else.

Computers are brilliant idiots, to put it bluntly. Take a machine that can crunch billions of numbers per second, but can't understand a simple question like "How are you?" In this sense, computers are somewhat autistic, although the analogy doesn't quite fit. Computers must be told not only how to do everything, but also when to do things. After you describe to the computer how to do one thing, it is completely helpless at accomplishing a similar task in which a few variables have changed.

Imagine one of Isaac Asimov's robots from his many popular robot novels, which may have looked to the esteemed author very much like C-3PO, as envisioned by George Lucas. Robots are primarily gears and motors, with something like a brain controlling it all. When such a robot is invented one day, it will be primarily a task for engineers rather than AI researchers. So let's stick to pure software models here.

The Definition of Life

"To truly understand someone—even an enemy—is to love them. Therefore, it is always wise to understand a question before trying to come up with an answer," (Sarek, *Star Trek IV: The Voyage Home*). The question of this chapter is: What is the definition of life, and what does that have to do with game programming?

How would you describe life and intelligence? After all, isn't a grasshopper alive? Insects are indeed living creatures with limited intelligence, and understanding the smallest life forms helps to understand the larger ones. Insects have all the smarts they need to find food, avoid danger, and reproduce. In a nutshell, that is the meaning of life. Everything else is just fluff.

What Is Consciousness?

Marvin Minsky is an esteemed AI researcher who has contributed much to the subject. Minsky once suggested that a machine will be intelligent when it can engage in believable and natural conversation with a human. That test for AI has been passed already, so what can be used to judge intelligence?

What if AI is already among us?

Let us pause a moment for that to properly sink in. The definitions of life need not apply so strictly to a machine without a connection to the real world. The universe of the machine is one in which simulacrum rules. Do you really need to run barefoot across a grassy field to know what grass is? Wind might be difficult to explain, but do you need to feel it blowing against your face to understand it?

Cyberspace: The Machine Universe

Cyberspace is a term that was invented by William Gibson—the author of the sci-fi novel *Neuromancer*. We humans far too often insist that human experience defines life and intelligence. When you think about it, 99 percent of our experience is through our senses, not through pure thought. We actually spend very little time during the course of a day just thinking. Most of a day is spent taking care of basic needs and working for a living.

In contrast, a computer is all thought, with no senses. So what sense does it make to judge computer intelligence by human standards? It is a problem we humans share, and it is called anthropomorphism—giving human traits to non-human things. You are probably familiar with the word *morph*. Morphing software is fun, allowing you to take one picture and morph it into another. Well, *anthros* is a word that means human. Taken together, anthros and morph become "to transform into a human."

We name our pets with cute names and try to teach them to speak and perform human-like tasks, because deep down we are creative and wish to create something like us. To anthropomorphize something is to try to make it human, even when doing so makes no sense. It is somewhat frightening to think that this is going on subconsciously, where most people do not realize it. Now do you see why aliens have hesitated to make contact with us after all these years?

The Birth of AI

Conventional means to judge AI are now irrelevant, since machine intelligence will not come about through a simple source code listing. And how could it? I can't believe that early AI researchers believed that a source code file could spontaneously come to life and start speaking to them. That makes about as much sense as drawing a picture of a butterfly and then waiting for it to fly away.

More than likely, AI is already among us, but we do not yet recognize it. In fact, it is a sure bet. The Internet changed the world, and most of us now chat online or at least exchange e-mail. How many times have you sent an e-mail to someone without even realizing that the response was sent back by an intelligent computer?

More chilling still: How do you know that your online chat buddy is human?

The market economy drives the point into us that if something is not for sale, it might not exist. AI is not yet for sale. We don't see advertisements for AI, so we believe it has not yet been developed. Mistake? I believe AI is here; we simply do not recognize it for what it is! AI is like electricity, like the phone system, like automobiles, and like automated grocery checkout lines. We have been desensitized to AI, now taking it for granted through small advances. But take a step back, think back a decade…and consider what is missing.

Agent Smith from the movie *The Matrix* told Morpheus that the human race became extinct when we allowed computers to do all our thinking for us. We have grown so used to our automated society that we no longer remember the past. When is the last time you remember paying cash for gasoline, or watching a cashier run a credit card through an imprint machine? That was common before instant-approval online ATM networks were developed. But here's an even more significant question: Do you remember the world before video games were invented? After all, video games predate the PC.

More Power to the Machines

Trends are often marked by important dates that changed something about normal life. In the computer industry, there have been five revolutions—or rather, generations—of computing. I like to think of the evolution of computers on my own terms, because popular educational texts seem to limit the history of computers entirely to hardware. Therefore, the following paragraphs are not contemporary teaching, but are simply my own estimation of events.

First Generation: Hard-Wired

The first generation computer was mechanical in nature, with the earliest computers being built to perform census calculations for the government at the beginning of the 20th century. This type of computer was not programmable, but hard-wired, and was used to calculate the trajectory of artillery shells in World War I.

Second Generation: Electro-Mechanical

The second-generation computer was electro-mechanical, with newly invented vacuum tubes that replaced some of the gears and levers in the all-mechanical computers. These faster, programmable computers were much more powerful than mechanical computers, and allowed England to crack Germany's Enigma code, which was a turning point in World War II. (For an excellent treatment of the subject, see the movie *U-571*.)

Third Generation: Electrical

The third generation computer was electrical, with vacuum tubes providing the means to perform calculations and store information entirely in memory. Although this type of computer was as large as a warehouse, it was entirely digital, as are modern computers today. For that reason, this might be considered the first true generation of "digital" computers.

Fourth Generation: Transistor

The fourth generation computer was brought upon by the invention of the transistor. The transistor is a solid-state device capable of storing a simple on or off state, and is faster and more reliable than a vacuum tube. Transistor computers might have filled an entire room—or part of a room—rather than an entire warehouse. For example, the popular PDP-11 was a transistor computer.

Fifth Generation: Microprocessor

The fifth generation computer features an incredibly complex microprocessor with millions of transistors stored on a single silicon chip. The modern microprocessor can execute billions of instructions per second, providing the capability to design advanced 3-D games with graphics that would have required a rendering farm (a network of graphics-rendering computers) a decade earlier.

Sixth Generation: ?

The sixth generation computer, not yet realized (or not yet recognized), emphasizes multi-processing and massive networking capabilities. This computer of the future is powered by numerous and extremely powerful microprocessors, all working in tandem. This generation is also marked by hardware that links multiple computers across high-speed network lines.

The Machines are Running the Asylum

The sixth generation computer network provides the environment that AI needs to develop. As we delegate more and more processing to automated systems within the massive global network, the system will continue to learn and grow. Rather than acting as a catalyst, the slow evolution of the system will spawn an intelligence that is self-aware.

What happens after that is anyone's guess. Imagine the universe to a machine of trillions of bits of information flying in every direction—very much like wind. AI doesn't necessarily understand everything that is going on in the system. It is simply aware that it is there, and is feeding back on itself in a continual loop that is the engine of artificial life.

Large, powerful, dangerous, frightening, cunning, or deadly? Not at all. Anything that monstrous would decompile, fall apart, dissolve in its own chaos, or not be recognizable.

Artificial Life

No, I believe that a life form in such an environment is small, insignificant, and unaware of the world outside the network—the world where humans live—but very clearly and unmistakably alive. How would such a creature come to be? I will discuss the four states of awareness later in the chapter to answer that question.

The speculation that AI is already among us but is not recognizable is a fascinating idea that is difficult to prove or disprove. After all, how do you track an unrecognizable program on the Internet when it does not follow any standards or protocols, but simply goes where it wants, unaware of the mechanics of its universe? The creature would have no eyes, ears, or any of our familiar senses. Rather, it might sense information flowing from one direction to another, like a fish in a stream. Since bits are nothing but ones and zeros, the AI would not see information from the real world, such as pictures, Web sites, bank transactions, weather reports, or satellite video feeds. It would have absolutely no way to understand that virtual wind is actual data!

The Virtual Universe

Instead, it would feel the flow of this information. Our amazing technology has the means to send information to a specific destination on the Internet using a packet header with an IP (*Internet Protocol*) address and a home return address. But imagine that to our AI creature, a packet of data is like a cup of water poured into a river. By starting to see the universe of such a creature, without requiring that it have our senses—in other words, without applying anthropomorphic attributes—you start to see how such a life form might exist.

Imagine if our universe was a simulacrum, and reality was nothing more than impulses sent to the brain. What would be real, and how would you learn to trust your sense of reality? Can you imagine some machine running the universe around you? Likewise, an AI would not know anything about the structure of the universe. Packets of data on the Internet, to a networked AI, are akin to quantum particles in our universe. To at least an early AI, such things are incomprehensible.

Spiritual Machines

Ray Kurzweil wrote an awe-inspiring book called *The Age of Spiritual Machines* (Penguin, 2000), which is summarized in detail at http://www.penguinputnam.com/static/packages/us/kurzweil. The book is a follow-up of his previous work, *The Age of Intelligent Machines* (MIT Press, 1992). The premise of this book is that machines will not only match human intellect in the near future, but they will actually exceed us, and we will embrace technology and extend ourselves to keep up with the machines.

At what point will we start to recognize—much less acknowledge—the existence of AI? Will we first communicate with an artificial entity as an alien being or as our technological offspring? Compelling questions are not often easy to answer.

INTELLIGENT COMPUTER PLAYER CONTROL

I hope my view of the subject of AI has piqued your interest a little. It is clearly a fascinating subject, seemingly without bounds, which makes it difficult to focus on AI techniques just to improve a game, when AI seems to be such a vast concept. Commercial games have not even scratched the surface of real AI, so the term is not really suitable in the context of game programming. However, I will try to explain the difference.

Game AI is more relevant when you think of it as simulated intelligence, or SI. As I explained earlier, SI is usually situational, based on a small set of variables, and incapable of reacting to new events. While this is not intelligence in the true sense of the word, it conveys meaning when used in the context of a game, since most gamers are familiar with the term *game AI.* Just remember that it is not the same as the computer science discipline that studies artificial intelligence for more lofty goals than entertainment.

The Study of Behavior and Emotion

Since we're now clear that game AI is just a familiar term that really describes simulated intelligence, let's jump into the subject of behavior and emotion and try to understand how to present the appearance of intelligence in a game—which is the goal of this chapter.

Responding to Stimulus

There are two primary ways in which we respond to stimuli:

1. Active (Conscious) Response
2. Passive (Unconscious) Response

The first, active response, is a conscious reaction to a situation or event in day-to-day life. The second response to stimuli is passive, which is an unconscious reaction to an unforeseen event. For instance, if someone pulls out in front of you on the road and causes you to slam on your brakes, your unconscious response is to hit the brakes, while your active response is usually a feeling of anger.

The Influence of Emotional State

Understanding the basic human emotions is helpful when designing a computer opponent in a game. Whether the action in a game is obsequious or threatening, the computer opponent should respond appropriately. Often in real-time games, the action is so fast paced that there is little time to focus on the emotional state of the entities in the game. Such games usually involve shooting first and asking questions later!

What if a game entity did show an emotional response to the player's actions? What if characters in a game were able to demonstrate a form of friendship with each other, and what if they were to respond violently (or compassionately) when friends are attacked? This type of response can be developed by keeping track of the state of each entity in a game. The dynamics of entities interacting with each other through various states (like happiness, anger, affection, respect, and other emotions) can seem quite complex, and yet be fairly easy to develop with code.

The Impact of Change

The important factor to consider in game AI is the impact of change on entities in the game. Without some form of stimulus, characters normally should not change their activities (unless you are able to program boredom into your computer players). Only through a change in the environment should game entities change. This might sound like a simple concept at first, but consider how profound it is if game entities are not pre-programmed (or *scripted*) to perform actions in the game.

Rather, suppose that game characters follow a simple set of rules that are based on game state and internal emotional states. Suddenly a simple activity becomes profoundly complicated— exponentially so when multiple characters are interacting. A rules-based AI system that uses state to determine action is definitely an easy way to handle game AI, and provides fairly good results.

CREATING SMART OPPONENTS

This section is devoted to describing and then building three constructs of artificial intelligence in an attempt to better understand the subject, and also to developing routines that will actually be useful in a game. The three subjects of AI covered here are as follows.

- **State Machines (Logical Thought)**. The next step beyond simple reactive control of a game object is to pre-program different modules that can be plugged into a game object to affect its behavior. This is similar to hard-coding the object's behavior, but adds an additional dimension of being able to change behavior by changing the control program associated with the object. One of the best and most popular methods of controlling game objects is to treat them as finite state machines.
- **Fuzzy Logic (Probabilistic Thought)**. The most straightforward use of fuzzy logic can enhance the functionality of state machines by remembering previous states and making simple logical decisions by treating logical operations as continuous (or analog) rather than discrete (or digital), with the result that some solutions are not completely true. While a state machine is capable of making only immediate decisions, fuzzy logic allows a game object to consider alternatives to the most obvious course of action and make new decisions based on the results of previous decisions.

■ **Genetic Algorithms (Adaptive Thought).** Since it is impossible to predict every possible situation in a dynamic environment, it is necessary to extend the functionality of fuzzy logic state machines by providing a game object with the ability to solve problems through adaptive reasoning. One of the most well-known methods of adaptation is called a *genetic algorithm*, so named because it involves simulating vast numbers of small entities that are actually bred to solve problems.

State Machines (Logical Thought)

In general, a computer is a state machine itself, with an operating system that has an initial state and processes data based on state. Likewise, programs are state machines, featuring an initial state and operating on logical instructions based on input and providing a result as an output. A brain cell—which is called a *neuron*—is also a state machine; it accepts input, processes data, and provides output. So, as you can see, the definition of a state machine is broad in scope.

Definition of a Finite State Machine

A finite state machine can be described as an object with a fixed number of initial states, a set of possible inputs, processes that operate on the input (also called *state transition functions*), and a set of possible outputs. By applying a simple state machine to each sprite in a game, and then by providing those sprites with simple rules to follow, you have the ability to create sprites that operate without being programmed in advance.

Artificial Neural Networks

The epitome of advanced artificial intelligence is the "neural network," named after the structure of the human brain. A biological neural network is an extremely powerful construct made up of billions of individual neurons, like a vast network of inter-connected state machines. While the logic of a state machine might be represented as a chain of individual links, a neural network functions on a much higher level by propagating inputs and outputs throughout the network of neurons, with the added ability of reorganizing itself. This self-organization might be the basis of conscious thought. The study of neural networks is so far beyond the scope of this book that I could not possibly begin to scratch the surface of it in only part of one chapter. An artificial neural network is actually not needed to write a game, and I'm sure you will find that the three subjects covered in this chapter are sufficient for most game projects.

Suppose you have a simple ball sprite that needs to travel inside the boundary of the computer screen. The logic for the ball sprite might be to simply bounce off each wall of the screen and that's it. You could easily program this functionality into the ball in advance, but wouldn't it be way cooler to give the ball a simple state engine and then provide it with some rules to follow instead?

Imagine how this type of functionality would affect the game loop. You would no longer need to process each sprite manually within the game loop. Rather, you could simply tell each sprite to "do its thing" each time through the loop. Once you had assigned the logic to a sprite, you would no longer need to worry about it. Sure, the logic is pre-programmed, but the sprite itself is generic and can be programmed with as many state engines as you care to develop. It is the state engine that must be pre-programmed, not the sprite. To program a state engine for a bouncing ball, you might pass the screen boundaries to the state engine and then assign it to the sprite, thus causing the sprite to bounce off the edges of the screen automatically.

Really advanced state machines encroach on the subject of neural networks and other AI concepts. For the sake of simplicity, I will only examine a simplistic state machine and show how it can be used to automate the activities of sprites.

Keeping Track of Game State

The state of the overall game, as well as the state of each object in the game, should influence the thinking of game AI, in order to provide a more challenging opponent. Game states might include the player's position, rate of movement, direction, attack and defense values, and other factors. By simply comparing these various states with a game entity, the AI in a game can simulate basic behavioral patterns.

The StateEngine Class

The state engine works by keeping track of a rule value, a test value, and the desired state by which the two variables should be compared. A procedure called Process can then be invoked to perform the comparison, after which the result can be determined by looking at the Result property (which shows the current state of the object). The state engine uses just three simple forms of logic:

- Equals
- Greater Than
- Less Than

A test for equality is not strictly needed, since equality can be proven if both greater than and less than fail (thus, the two values being compared are equal). But I found it convenient to include the test for equality in the state engine's logic.

The following lines of code make up the StateEngine class. You will want to save this code in a file called StateEngine.cls, and give it a name of clsStateEngine.

```
'-------------------------------------------------------------------
' Visual Basic Game Programming With DirectX
' Chapter 15 : Artificial and Simulated Intelligence
' StateEngine Class Source Code File
'-------------------------------------------------------------------
Option Explicit
Option Base 0

Public Enum STATES
    Equal = 0
    GreaterThan = 1
    LessThan = 2
End Enum

Dim eState As STATES
Dim lRuleValue As Long
Dim lTestValue As Long
Dim bResult As Boolean

Public Property Get State() As STATES
    State = eState
End Property

Public Property Let State(ByVal eNewValue As STATES)
    eState = eNewValue
End Property

Public Property Get RuleValue() As Long
    RuleValue = lRuleValue
End Property

Public Property Let RuleValue(ByVal lNewValue As Long)
    lRuleValue = lNewValue
End Property

Public Property Get TestValue() As Long
    TestValue = lTestValue
End Property
```

```
Public Property Let TestValue(ByVal lNewValue As Long)
    lTestValue = lNewValue
End Property

Public Property Get Result() As Boolean
    Result = bResult
End Property

Public Property Let Result(ByVal bNewValue As Boolean)
    bResult = bNewValue
End Property

Public Sub Process()
    Select Case eState
        Case Equal
            Result = (TestValue = RuleValue)
        Case GreaterThan
            Result = (TestValue > RuleValue)
        Case LessThan
            Result = (TestValue < RuleValue)
    End Select
End Sub
```

The StateEntity Class

To really make a state engine useful, there needs to be a controlling class that holds an array of
StateEngine objects. Since that object is so simple, it is capable of keeping track of only a single
logical state. The controlling class will be useful for assigning multiple states to a logical test,
which is where the true power of a state engine comes into play.

Any time you need to keep track of multiple states that must all be true in order to regard
the object as valid, you will want to use a StateEntity object. A state entity can have a virtually
unlimited number of links in the chain of logic. To add a new link to the chain, you call the
AddLink procedure. You can then set the rule and test values using SetRule and SetTest, use
CheckLink to test the validity of a link, or call ProcessChain to test the state of the object.

The source code for clsStateEntity is presented below. Be sure to save this code in a file called
StateEntity.cls.

```vb
'-------------------------------------------------------------------
' Visual Basic Game Programming With DirectX
' Chapter 15 : Artificial and Simulated Intelligence
' StateEntity Class Source Code File
'-------------------------------------------------------------------
Option Explicit
Option Base 0

Dim engine() As clsStateEngine
Dim lNumLinks As Long
Dim lValue As Long
Dim bResult As Boolean
Dim lCurrentLink As Long

Public Property Get Value() As Long
    Value = lValue
End Property

Public Property Let Value(ByVal lNewValue As Long)
    lValue = lNewValue
End Property

Public Property Get Result() As Boolean
    Result = bResult
End Property

Public Property Let Result(ByVal bNewValue As Boolean)
    bResult = bNewValue
End Property

Public Property Get CurrentLink() As Long
    CurrentLink = lCurrentLink
End Property

Public Property Let CurrentLink(ByVal lNewValue As Long)
    If lNewValue >= 0 And lNewValue < lNumLinks Then
        lCurrentLink = lNewValue
    End If
End Property
```

```
Public Sub AddLink(ByVal eState As STATES, ByVal lRule As Long, _
    ByVal lTest As Long)
    ReDim Preserve engine(lNumLinks)
    Set engine(lNumLinks) = New clsStateEngine
    engine(lNumLinks).State = eState
    engine(lNumLinks).RuleValue = lRule
    engine(lNumLinks).TestValue = lTest
    lNumLinks = lNumLinks + 1
    lCurrentLink = lNumLinks
End Sub


Public Sub SetRule(ByVal lLink As Long, ByVal lValue As Long)
    If lLink >= 0 And lLink < lNumLinks Then
        engine(lLink).RuleValue = lValue
    End If
End Sub


Public Sub SetTest(ByVal lLink As Long, ByVal lValue As Long)
    If lLink >= 0 And lLink < lNumLinks Then
        engine(lLink).TestValue = lValue
    End If
End Sub


Public Sub ProcessChain()
    Dim n As Long
    For n = 0 To lNumLinks - 1
        lCurrentLink = n
        Result = CheckLink(lCurrentLink)
        If Not Result Then Exit For
    Next n
End Sub


Public Function CheckLink(ByVal lLink As Long) As Boolean
    If lLink >= 0 And lLink < lNumLinks Then
        engine(lLink).Process
        CheckLink = engine(lLink).Result
    Else
        CheckLink = False
    End If
End Function
```

The SESpriteControl Class

To demonstrate how to use the state classes presented earlier, I have written a class called SESpriteControl, which keeps track of a sprite on the screen and prevents it from moving past the boundaries of the screen by bouncing the sprite off the edges. This is a small class, and it demonstrates how you can add varied functionality to the sprites in a game to reduce the amount of logic code in the game.

```
'-------------------------------------------------------------------
' Visual Basic Game Programming With DirectX
' Chapter 15 : Artificial and Simulated Intelligence
' SESpriteControl Class Source Code File
'-------------------------------------------------------------------


Option Explicit
Option Base 0

'class variables
Dim seControl As clsStateEntity

Public Sub SetBounds(ByVal lLeft As Long, ByVal lTop As Long, _
    ByVal lRight As Long, ByVal lBottom As Long)

    Set seControl = Nothing
    Set seControl = New clsStateEntity
    seControl.AddLink GreaterThan, lLeft, 0
    seControl.AddLink GreaterThan, lTop, 0
    seControl.AddLink LessThan, lRight, 0
    seControl.AddLink LessThan, lBottom, 0
End Sub

Public Property Get Result() As Boolean
    Result = seControl.Result
End Property

Public Function CheckLink(ByVal lLink As Long) As Boolean
    CheckLink = seControl.CheckLink(lLink)
End Function
```

```
Public Sub UpdatePosition(ByRef sprite As clsDDSprite7)
    sprite.X = sprite.X + sprite.SpeedX
    sprite.Y = sprite.Y + sprite.SpeedY
End Sub

Public Sub CheckBounds(ByRef sprite As clsDDSprite7)
    'update state engine with sprite position
    seControl.SetTest 0, sprite.X
    seControl.SetTest 1, sprite.Y
    seControl.SetTest 2, sprite.X
    seControl.SetTest 3, sprite.Y

    'process state engine
    seControl.ProcessChain

    'bounce sprite off wall if test failed
    If Not seControl.Result Then
        Select Case seControl.CurrentLink
            Case 0, 2
                sprite.SpeedX = sprite.SpeedX * -1
            Case 1, 3
                sprite.SpeedY = sprite.SpeedY * -1
        End Select
    End If
End Sub
```

The StateMachine Program

Now for the state machine test program! This program uses the three classes (clsStateEngine, clsStateEntity, and clsSESpriteControl) to move a DirectDraw sprite around the screen in windowed mode. Most of the code in the StateMachine program was borrowed from the DDWindowed program from Chapter 10, "Diving into DirectDraw." It basically sets up DirectDraw, creates the back buffer, loads the background and sprite images, and handles the game loop.

Programming the State Engine

The code that is actually related to the state machine is fairly short. Here is the code that initializes the state machine (found in Form_Load):

```
'initialize the state machine
scBounce.SetBounds 5, 20, SCREENWIDTH - 70, SCREENHEIGHT - 70
```

In the DDWindowed program, all sprite control was handled in the Game_Update procedure. Now, sprite control is handled by the SESpriteControl class, with the following lines of code:

```
'update sprite position
scBounce.UpdatePosition ball
'run the sprite control state machine
scBounce.CheckBounds ball
If scBounce.Result Then
    lFrameRate = 120
Else
    lFrameRate = 1
End If
```

Running the StateMachine Program

As the code shows, the StateMachine program pauses for a few seconds (which is accomplished by setting lFrameRate = 1) each time the sprite hits one of the four edges of the screen, in order to show the state of the sprite at that moment. Figures 15.1 through 15.4 show the four different sprite states that are automatically handled by the state engine when the sprite hits one of the four edges of the screen.

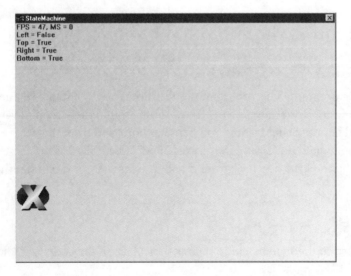

Figure 15.1

Sprite state changes as the sprite hits the left wall in the StateMachine program.

Figure 15.2

Sprite state changes as the sprite hits the top wall in the StateMachine program.

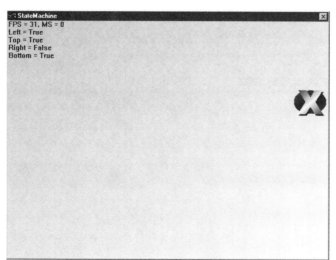

Figure 15.3

Sprite state changes as the sprite hits the right wall in the StateMachine program.

Building the StateMachine Program

Create a new Standard EXE project in VB and call it StateMachine. Add the three class files you created earlier in the chapter, along with the DirectDraw classes (or reference the Visual Basic Game Library in the Project References dialog). Figure 15.5 shows the Project Explorer with the files you will need for this program.

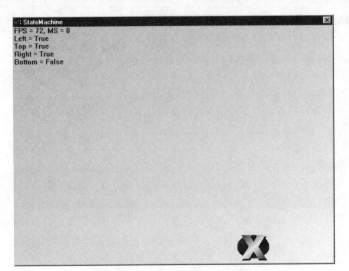

Figure 15.4

Sprite state changes as the sprite hits the bottom wall in the StateMachine program.

Figure 15.5

The Project Explorer, showing the files needed to compile the StateMachine program

```
'-----------------------------------------------------------------
' Visual Basic Game Programming With DirectX
' Chapter 15 : Artificial and Simulated Intelligence
' StateMachine Source Code File
'-----------------------------------------------------------------

Option Explicit
Option Base 0

'Windows API functions and structures
Private Declare Function GetTickCount Lib "kernel32" () As Long

'program constants
Const SCREENWIDTH As Long = 640
Const SCREENHEIGHT As Long = 480
```

```
'program objects
Dim ddraw As New clsDirectDraw7
Dim cddsBackground As New clsDDSurface7
Dim cddsBackBuffer As New clsDDSurface7
Dim ball As New clsDDSprite7
Dim scBounce As New clsSESpriteControl

'program variables
Dim bRunning As Boolean
Dim n As Long
Dim sFrameRate As String
Dim lFrameRate As Long
Dim rTemp As dxvblib.RECT

Private Sub Form_Load()
    Static lStartTime As Long
    Static lCounter As Long
    Static lNewTime As Long

    'initialize the state machine
    scBounce.SetBounds 5, 20, SCREENWIDTH - 70, SCREENHEIGHT - 70

    'set up the main form
    Form1.Caption = App.Title
    Form1.Width = SCREENWIDTH * Screen.TwipsPerPixelX
    Form1.Height = SCREENHEIGHT * Screen.TwipsPerPixelY
    Form1.AutoRedraw = False
    Form1.ClipControls = False
    Form1.KeyPreview = True
    Form1.ScaleMode = 3
    Form1.Show

    'create primary DirectDraw object
    If Not ddraw.Startup(Form1.hWnd, SCREENWIDTH, _
        SCREENHEIGHT, 0, False) Then
        MsgBox "Error creating DirectDraw primary display surface"
        Shutdown
    End If
```

```
'create back buffer
If Not cddsBackBuffer.Create(ddraw.DDObj, _
    SCREENWIDTH, SCREENHEIGHT) Then
    MsgBox "Error creating back buffer surface"
    Shutdown
End If


'load the background image
If Not cddsBackground.Load(ddraw, App.Path & _
    "\blueyellow640.bmp") Then
    MsgBox "Error loading blueyellow.bmp"
    Shutdown
End If


'load the sprite
With ball
    .Create ddraw
    If Not .LoadFromFile(App.Path & "\directx.bmp", 64, 64, 1, 1) Then
        MsgBox "Error loading directx.bmp"
        Shutdown
    End If
    .X = Random(SCREENWIDTH - .Width)
    .Y = Random(SCREENHEIGHT - .Height)
    Do Until .SpeedX <> 0
        .SpeedX = Random(8) - 4
    Loop
    Do Until .SpeedY <> 0
        .SpeedY = Random(8) - 4
    Loop
End With

'draw the background image
cddsBackBuffer.BltFast 0, 0, cddsBackground.Surface, _
    cddsBackground.SurfaceRect

bRunning = True
lFrameRate = 120
sFrameRate = "FPS"
```

```vb
    'main game loop
    Do While bRunning
        lCounter = GetTickCount() - lStartTime
        If lCounter > lNewTime Then
            Game_Update lCounter
            lNewTime = lCounter + 1000 / lFrameRate
        End If
        DoEvents
    Loop

End Sub

Private Sub Form_KeyDown(KeyCode As Integer, Shift As Integer)
    If KeyCode = 27 Then Shutdown
End Sub

Private Sub Form_QueryUnload(Cancel As Integer, UnloadMode As Integer)
    Shutdown
End Sub

Private Sub Form1_Click()
    Shutdown
End Sub

Private Sub Shutdown()
    'stop game loop
    bRunning = False
    ddraw.Shutdown

    'delete objects
    Set ddraw = Nothing
    Set cddsBackground = Nothing
    Set cddsBackBuffer = Nothing
    Set ball = Nothing
    Set scBounce = Nothing

    'end program
    Form1.Hide
    End
End Sub
```

```vb
Public Function Random(ByVal num As Long) As Long
    Random = CLng(num * Rnd)
End Function

Public Sub Game_Update(ByVal MS As Long)
    Static lTimer As Long
    Static lStart As Long
    Static lCounter As Long

    'start counting milliseconds
    lStart = GetTickCount

    'erase sprite
    rTemp.Left = ball.X
    rTemp.Top = ball.Y
    rTemp.Right = rTemp.Left + ball.Width
    rTemp.Bottom = rTemp.Top + ball.Height
    cddsBackBuffer.BltFast ball.X, ball.Y, _
        cddsBackground.Surface, rTemp

    'update sprite position
    scBounce.UpdatePosition ball

    'run the sprite control state machine
    scBounce.CheckBounds ball
    If scBounce.Result Then
        lFrameRate = 120
    Else
        lFrameRate = 1
    End If

    'draw the sprite
    ball.Draw cddsBackBuffer

    'print status messages
    rTemp.Left = 1
    rTemp.Top = 1
    rTemp.Right = 160
    rTemp.Bottom = 100
```

```
cddsBackBuffer.BltFast 5, 20, cddsBackground.Surface, rTemp
cddsBackBuffer.DrawText 5, 20, sFrameRate
cddsBackBuffer.DrawText 5, 35, "Left = " & scBounce.CheckLink(0)
cddsBackBuffer.DrawText 5, 50, "Top = " & scBounce.CheckLink(1)
cddsBackBuffer.DrawText 5, 65, "Right = " & scBounce.CheckLink(2)
cddsBackBuffer.DrawText 5, 80, "Bottom = " & scBounce.CheckLink(3)

'copy back buffer to the screen
ddraw.Draw cddsBackBuffer, cddsBackBuffer.SurfaceRect

'count the frames per second
If MS > lTimer + 1000 Then
    lStart = GetTickCount - lStart
    sFrameRate = "FPS = " & lCounter & ", MS = " & lStart
    lTimer = MS
    lCounter = 0
Else
    lCounter = lCounter + 1
End If
End Sub
```

Fuzzy Logic (Probabilistic Thought)

Fuzzy logic is an extension of Boolean logic (which consists of simple true or false results) that provides a means to handle values between absolutely true and absolutely false. There is no specific theory or algorithm that describes how fuzzy logic should operate. Rather, it is a concept that applies to all logical operations. By thinking of problems in terms of continuous (fuzzy) results rather than specific (discrete) ones, a fuzzy system is able to solve logical problems that are difficult or impossible for Boolean logic to solve.

Discrete Versus Fuzzy

Suppose you have built a highly advanced robot car that is able to drive by itself. How does the robot car know when a streetlight is red, yellow, or green? The most obvious answer is by comparing the colors. But what if there was a glare due to bright sunlight, or what if a streetlight was really old and the bulbs were no longer clearly illuminated? If a robot car looked for a specific color, it might confuse green for yellow and cause an automobile accident in a busy intersection. Figure 15.6 is a diagram of a discrete logic process.

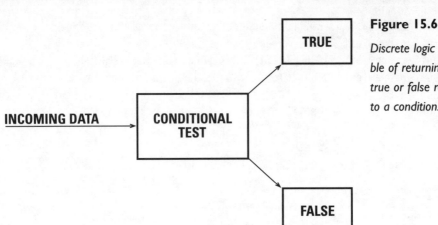

Figure 15.6

Discrete logic is capable of returning only a true or false response to a condition.

The solution to the problem is to program the robot car to see a range of colors rather than discrete colors, and then make a decision based on uncertainty. Fuzzy logic provides a means to solve the streetlight problem, like any other logic problem, without a complete set of input variables, which allows for a lot of flexibility. Figure 15.7 is a diagram of a fuzzy logic process.

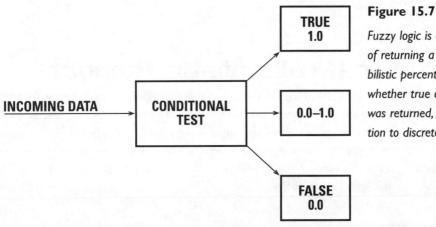

Figure 15.7

Fuzzy logic is capable of returning a probabilistic percentage of whether true or false was returned, in addition to discrete results.

Fuzzy Functions

One interesting way to test fuzzy theory is to write a program with fuzzy variables rather than discrete variables. The Variant data type appears to have some fuzzy properties, because it determines what type of data type to use on-the-fly. Obviously you wouldn't want every variable in a program to be fuzzy, because precision is needed for things like loading bitmap images and blitting graphics to the screen. But on a higher level—concerning program flow and sprite movement—the use of fuzzy variables might provide the means to write a compelling game.

Take a look at the Process procedure from the StateEngine class (earlier in the chapter), which uses discrete tests to determine the state of an object:

```
Public Sub Process()
    Select Case eState
        Case Equal
            Result = (TestValue = RuleValue)
        Case GreaterThan
            Result = (TestValue > RuleValue)
        Case LessThan
            Result = (TestValue < RuleValue)
    End Select
End Sub
```

Note how the test for equality is performed:

```
Result = (TestValue = RuleValue)
```

This is a simple logical statement that reads like this: "If TestValue equals RuleValue, then Result equals true, else Result equals false." An easier logical statement to understand is one that tests for inequality, since the test is more obvious:

```
Result = (value > 100)
```

This statement reads as follows: "If value is greater than 100, then Result equals true, else Result equals false."

To "fuzzify" this last logical statement, you would still perform the logical test; but rather than returning a specific true or false value, the test would return a probability of truth as a value between zero and one (inclusive). That is the key to understanding fuzzy logic. Here is an example of a fuzzified version of the equality test, using a minimum and maximum range rather than a discrete value:

```
If value < minimum Then
    Result = 0
ElseIf value >= minimum and value <= maximum Then
    Result = (value - minimum) / (maximum - minimum)
ElseIf value > maximum Then
    Result = 1
End If
```

The fuzzy version of the logic statement uses a floating-point data type (like Single) rather than a Boolean variable, because the fuzzy result is a probability value between zero and one. Here is how you would read the snippet of code: "If value is less than minimum, then Result is zero; but if value is within the range, then Result is the value minus the minimum, divided by the range; finally, if value is greater than the maximum, then Result is one." Here is the code snippet with actual numbers to make it easier to understand:

```
If value < 10 Then
    Result = 0
ElseIf value >= 10 and value <= 15 Then
    Result = (value - 10) / (15 - 10)
ElseIf value > 15 Then
    Result = 1
End If
```

Does that seem to make more sense? If you plug in a number for value, such as 12, the value is calculated as described in the code snippet below.

```
Result = (12 - 10) / (15 - 10)
Result = 2 / 5
Result = 0.4
```

Now, how do you interpret what Result = 0.4 means? Think of it as a probability, and then use that probability to teach your game objects how to behave. If there is a threshold variable, it would be easy to use fuzzy logic to determine when a value is close to the minimum or maximum threshold, and then trigger some form of response. You might interpret Result = 0.4 as something like this: "Result is close to the halfway point, but favors the minimum value."

Using Fuzzy Logic for Sprite Control

The cool thing about fuzzy logic is that it doesn't break existing code, such as that developed earlier for the state engine. You might think of fuzzy logic, then, as a sort of infinite state machine, since there are an infinite number of decimals in a probability.

For example, rather than performing a discrete check on whether a sprite has reached the edge of the screen, how about passing the position of the sprite to a fuzzy function that returns a probability of whether the sprite has reached the edge? The cool thing about handling game logic like this is that your game is able to run smoothly when unexpected things happen—things that you could not possibly have pre-programmed in advance. A program that uses discrete logic will be absolutely baffled when a new situation arises that it was not programmed to handle. True and False are so limited in comparison to a fuzzy value!

Can you think of any cool ways to use fuzzy logic to improve the state machine that was developed earlier? I sure can! How about a fuzzy function that compares a sprite's position with the boundaries of the screen, and then changes the speed of the sprite to correspond with the distance? With such a function in place, the sprite position would be reported as a value between zero and one, rather than with discrete coordinates on the screen! For example, if the sprite is dead center on the screen, then Result(X) = 0.5, and Result(Y) = 0.5. Of course, actual blitting code will use discrete pixel-level precision; only general sprite motion will be manipulated by fuzzifying the sprite handler.

The FuzzyEngine Class

To make things easier, I have created a class to handle the basic fuzzy logic engine for a sprite handler. If it looks familiar, it is because FuzzyEngine was based on the StaticEngine class! The only difference is between the two lines in the Process procedure and the result (which now returns a Single instead of a Boolean). Name this new class clsFuzzyEngine, and save it in a file called FuzzyEngine.cls.

```
'-----------------------------------------------------------------------
' Visual Basic Game Programming With DirectX
' Chapter 15 : Artificial and Simulated Intelligence
' FuzzyEngine Class Source Code File
'-----------------------------------------------------------------------
Option Explicit
Option Base 0

Dim lMinimum As Long
Dim lMaximum As Long
Dim lTestValue As Long
Dim fResult As Single

Public Property Get Minimum() As Long
    Minimum = lMinimum
End Property

Public Property Let Minimum(ByVal lNewValue As Long)
    lMinimum = lNewValue
End Property

Public Property Get Maximum() As Long
    Maximum = lMaximum
End Property
```

```
Public Property Let Maximum(ByVal lNewValue As Long)
    lMaximum = lNewValue
End Property

Public Property Get TestValue() As Long
    TestValue = lTestValue
End Property

Public Property Let TestValue(ByVal lNewValue As Long)
    lTestValue = lNewValue
End Property

Public Property Get Result() As Single
    Result = fResult
End Property

Public Property Let Result(ByVal fNewValue As Single)
    fResult = fNewValue
End Property

Public Sub Process()
    If lTestValue <= lMinimum Then
        fResult = 0
    ElseIf lTestValue >= lMaximum Then
        fResult = 1
    Else
        fResult = Round((lTestValue - lMinimum) / _
            (lMaximum - lMinimum), 2)
    End If
End Sub
```

The FESpriteControl Class

The fuzzy engine sprite control class is similar to the one developed for the state engine, but there is no intermediary class like FuzzyEntity. Instead, FESpriteControl uses two fuzzy engines to keep track of the horizontal and vertical position of a sprite.

```
'-------------------------------------------------------------
' Visual Basic Game Programming With DirectX
' Chapter 15: Artificial and Simulated Intelligence
' FESpriteControl Class Source Code File
'-------------------------------------------------------------
```

```
Option Explicit
Option Base 0

'class variables
Dim feHoriz As clsFuzzyEngine
Dim feVert As clsFuzzyEngine

Public Property Get ResultH() As Single
    ResultH = feHoriz.Result
End Property

Public Property Get ResultV() As Single
    ResultV = feVert.Result
End Property

Public Sub SetBounds(ByVal lLeft As Long, ByVal lTop As Long, _
    ByVal lRight As Long, ByVal lBottom As Long)

    Set feHoriz = Nothing
    Set feHoriz = New clsFuzzyEngine
    feHoriz.Minimum = lLeft
    feHoriz.Maximum = lRight

    Set feVert = Nothing
    Set feVert = New clsFuzzyEngine
    feVert.Minimum = lTop
    feVert.Maximum = lBottom
End Sub

Public Sub UpdatePosition(ByRef sprite As clsDDSprite7)
    sprite.X = sprite.X + sprite.SpeedX * sprite.DirX
    sprite.Y = sprite.Y + sprite.SpeedY * sprite.DirY
End Sub

Public Sub CheckBounds(ByRef sprite As clsDDSprite7)
    'process horiz position
    feHoriz.TestValue = sprite.X
    feHoriz.Process
```

```
        Select Case feHoriz.Result
            Case 0, 1
                'change direction
                sprite.DirX = sprite.DirX * -1
            Case Else
                'slow down
                sprite.SpeedX = 11 - ResultH * 10
        End Select

        'process vert position
        feVert.TestValue = sprite.Y
        feVert.Process
        Select Case feVert.Result
            Case 0, 1
                'change direction
                sprite.DirY = sprite.DirY * -1
            Case Else
                'slow down
                sprite.SpeedY = 11 - ResultV * 10
        End Select
End Sub
```

The FuzzyLogic Program

Okay, now for a demonstration program! The FuzzyLogic program uses the clsFuzzyEngine and clsFESpriteControl classes to move a sprite around on the screen. The sprite's velocity is based on the resolution of the game window and the position of the sprite on the screen. These two factors provide for some amazing control over how the sprite moves, as shown in Figure 15.8.

When the sprite approaches the right or bottom edges of the screen, it will speed up while avoiding the actual edges (most of the time, anyway).

Running the FuzzyLogic Program

Figure 15.9 shows the sprite near the bottom-right corner of the screen. Note the Horiz, Vert, and Speed values, which show the status of the sprite.

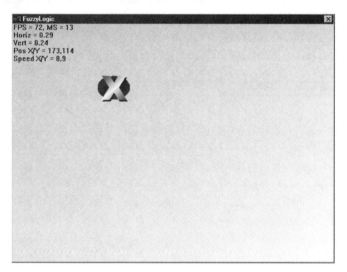

Figure 15.8

The FuzzyLogic program shows how fuzzy data can create dynamic and fluid sprite movement.

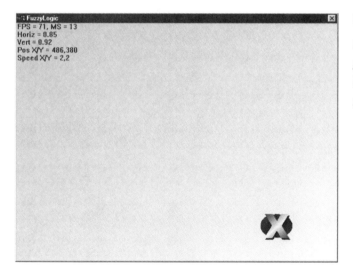

Figure 15.9

In the FuzzyLogic program, the screen resolution affects the sprite's velocity.

Building the FuzzyLogic Program

The FuzzyLogic program is similar to the StateMachine program, running in a window while being powered by DirectDraw. Figure 15.10 shows the Project Explorer with the list files needed to compile the program.

Figure 15.10

The Project Explorer shows the files needed to compile the FuzzyLogic program.

```vb
'------------------------------------------------------------------
' Visual Basic Game Programming With DirectX
' Chapter 15 : Artificial and Simulated Intelligence
' FuzzyLogic Source Code File
'------------------------------------------------------------------

Option Explicit
Option Base 0

'Windows API functions and structures
Private Declare Function GetTickCount Lib "kernel32" () As Long

'program constants
Const SCREENWIDTH As Long = 640
Const SCREENHEIGHT As Long = 480

'program objects
Dim ddraw As New clsDirectDraw7
Dim cddsBackground As New clsDDSurface7
Dim cddsBackBuffer As New clsDDSurface7
Dim ball As New clsDDSprite7
Dim scBounce As New clsFESpriteControl

'program variables
Dim bRunning As Boolean
Dim n As Long
Dim sFrameRate As String
Dim lFrameRate As Long
Dim rTemp As DxVBLib.RECT
```

```
Private Sub Form_Load()
    Static lStartTime As Long
    Static lCounter As Long
    Static lNewTime As Long

    Randomize GetTickCount

    'initialize the state machine
    scBounce.SetBounds 10, 20, SCREENWIDTH - 70, SCREENHEIGHT - 70

    'set up the main form
    Form1.Caption = App.Title
    Form1.Width = SCREENWIDTH * Screen.TwipsPerPixelX
    Form1.Height = SCREENHEIGHT * Screen.TwipsPerPixelY
    Form1.AutoRedraw = False
    Form1.ClipControls = False
    Form1.KeyPreview = True
    Form1.ScaleMode = 3
    Form1.Show

    'create primary DirectDraw object
    If Not ddraw.Startup(Form1.hWnd, SCREENWIDTH, _
        SCREENHEIGHT, 0, False) Then
        MsgBox "Error creating DirectDraw primary display surface"
        Shutdown
    End If

    'create back buffer
    If Not cddsBackBuffer.Create(ddraw.DDObj, _
        SCREENWIDTH, SCREENHEIGHT) Then
        MsgBox "Error creating back buffer surface"
        Shutdown
    End If

    'load the background image
    If Not cddsBackground.Load(ddraw, App.Path & _
        "\blueyellow640.bmp") Then
        MsgBox "Error loading blueyellow.bmp"
        Shutdown
    End If
```

```
        'load the sprite
        With ball
            .Create ddraw
            If Not .LoadFromFile(App.Path & "\directx.bmp", 64, 64, 1, 1) Then
                MsgBox "Error loading directx.bmp"
                Shutdown
            End If
            .X = Random(SCREENWIDTH - .Width)
            .Y = Random(SCREENHEIGHT - .Height)
            Do Until .SpeedX <> 0
                .SpeedX = Random(8) - 4
            Loop
            Do Until .SpeedY <> 0
                .SpeedY = Random(8) - 4
            Loop
            .DirX = 1
            .DirY = 1
        End With

        'draw the background image
        cddsBackBuffer.BltFast 0, 0, cddsBackground.Surface, _
            cddsBackground.SurfaceRect

        bRunning = True
        lFrameRate = 120
        sFrameRate = "FPS"

        'main game loop
        Do While bRunning
            lCounter = GetTickCount() - lStartTime
            If lCounter > lNewTime Then
                Game_Update lCounter
                lNewTime = lCounter + 1000 / lFrameRate
            End If
            DoEvents
        Loop

End Sub
```

```
Private Sub Form_KeyDown(KeyCode As Integer, Shift As Integer)
    If KeyCode = 27 Then Shutdown
End Sub


Private Sub Form_QueryUnload(Cancel As Integer, UnloadMode As Integer)
    Shutdown
End Sub


Private Sub Form1_Click()
    Shutdown
End Sub


Private Sub Shutdown()
    'stop game loop
    bRunning = False
    ddraw.Shutdown

    'delete objects
    Set ddraw = Nothing
    Set cddsBackground = Nothing
    Set cddsBackBuffer = Nothing
    Set ball = Nothing
    Set scBounce = Nothing

    'end program
    Form1.Hide
    End
End Sub


Public Function Random(ByVal num&) As Long
    Random = CLng(num * Rnd)
End Function


Public Sub Game_Update(ByVal MS As Long)
    Static lTimer As Long
    Static lStart As Long
    Static lCounter As Long

    'start counting milliseconds
    lStart = GetTickCount
```

```
'erase sprite
rTemp.Left = ball.X
rTemp.Top = ball.Y
rTemp.Right = rTemp.Left + ball.Width
rTemp.Bottom = rTemp.Top + ball.Height
cddsBackBuffer.BltFast ball.X, ball.Y, _
    cddsBackground.Surface, rTemp

'update sprite position
scBounce.UpdatePosition ball

'run the sprite control state machine
scBounce.CheckBounds ball

'draw the sprite
ball.Draw cddsBackBuffer

'print status messages
rTemp.Left = 1
rTemp.Top = 1
rTemp.Right = 160
rTemp.Bottom = 100
cddsBackBuffer.BltFast 5, 20, cddsBackground.Surface, rTemp
cddsBackBuffer.DrawText 5, 20, sFrameRate
cddsBackBuffer.DrawText 5, 35, "Horiz = " & scBounce.ResultH
cddsBackBuffer.DrawText 5, 50, "Vert = " & scBounce.ResultV
cddsBackBuffer.DrawText 5, 65, _
    "Pos X/Y = " & ball.X & "," & ball.Y
cddsBackBuffer.DrawText 5, 80, _
    "Speed X/Y = " & ball.SpeedX & "," & ball.SpeedY

'copy back buffer to the screen
ddraw.Draw cddsBackBuffer, cddsBackBuffer.SurfaceRect

'count the frames per second
If MS > lTimer + 1000 Then
    lStart = GetTickCount - lStart
    sFrameRate = "FPS = " & lCounter & ", MS = " & lStart
    lTimer = MS
    lCounter = 0
```

```
        Else
            lCounter = lCounter + 1
        End If
End Sub
```

Genetic Algorithms (Adaptive Thought)

A GA (*Genetic Algorithm*) is a method of solving problems through adaptive reasoning and the inter-action of a multitude of individual objects. The idea behind the genetic branch of artificial intelli-gence is that most problems can't be anticipated, and thus, solutions can't be pre-programmed. Therefore, a solution might be bred over numerous generations to solve a problem in a more nat-ural way—one that simulates a biological system's ability to adapt to new situations.

Instincts

A genetic algorithm (which I prefer to call an *adaptive engine*) treats a software object like a strand of DNA (*Deoxyribonucleic Acid*—the building block of life). DNA-based computing and molecular computing is a huge subject, and I will be able to give it only a brief summary in this chapter. But the basic concepts are fairly easy to grasp and can be used in a game without too much effort. Granted, without a solid tutorial on genetic algorithms, this treatment of the subject will be limited, but I hope you will find it useful for your game projects.

Evolving Solutions

The key to adapting software to solve a problem is through simulated mutation and reproduction within a group of similar objects. A common genetic algorithm can be applied to numerous types of problems, but I have chosen to focus on using a genetic algorithm to control the motion of a sprite on the screen, in order to show how GA can be applied directly in a game. Solving mazes is a common demonstration of GA, and such algorithms can be applied to pathfinding and other game AI problems (which are beyond the scope of this book).

The GeneticEngine Class

The key to writing the genetic engine sprite handler is a class called GeneticEngine. Don't be intimidated by the name! This is actually a very small and simple class that just keeps track of an array of genes, and might be thought of as the double helix that forms DNA. It is simple in struc-ture, but powerful in function. To set a specific trait, you can call the SetGene procedure with an index parameter. Likewise, to read a trait, you call the GetGene function with an index parameter. Call this new class clsGeneticEngine and save it in a file called GeneticEngine.cls.

```
'-----------------------------------------------------------------
' Visual Basic Game Programming With DirectX
' Chapter 15 : Artificial and Simulated Intelligence
' GeneticEngine Class Source Code File
'-----------------------------------------------------------------
Option Explicit
Option Base 0

Const MAXGENES As Long = 100
Dim genes(0 To MAXGENES) As Double

Public Sub SetGene(ByVal lGeneNum As Long, ByVal lGeneValue As Double)
    If lGeneNum >= 0 And lGeneNum < MAXGENES Then
        genes(lGeneNum) = lGeneValue
    End If
End Sub

Public Function GetGene(ByVal lGeneNum As Long) As Double
    If lGeneNum >= 0 And lGeneNum < MAXGENES Then
        GetGene = genes(lGeneNum)
    End If
End Function
```

The GESpriteControl Class

The GESpriteControl class is an abstracted version of the GeneticEngine class, using familiar mnemonics for a sprite that are mapped to the array of genes in the genetic engine. This class also includes procedures to reset and mutate a genetic sprite. Granted, these procedures limit the class somewhat to a specific role in the sample program that follows, but the class might be useful as a base class for building new game routines that need a genetic engine. You will want to call this new class clsGESpriteControl and save it in a file called GESpriteControl.cls.

```
'-----------------------------------------------------------------
' Visual Basic Game Programming With DirectX
' Chapter 15 : Artificial and Simulated Intelligence
' GESpriteControl Class Source Code File
'-----------------------------------------------------------------
Option Explicit
Option Base 0
```

```
Const CDIRX As Long = 0
Const CDIRY As Long = 1
Const CRATEX As Long = 2
Const CRATEY As Long = 3
Const CACTIVE As Long = 4
Const CCOUNTX As Long = 5
Const CCOUNTY  As Long = 6
Const CPOSX As Long = 7
Const CPOSY As Long = 8
Const CMOVECOUNT As Long = 9
Const CMOVERATE As Long = 10


Dim geGenes As New clsGeneticEngine

Public Property Get DirX() As Double
    DirX = geGenes.GetGene(CDIRX)
End Property


Public Property Let DirX(ByVal lNewValue As Double)
    geGenes.SetGene CDIRX, lNewValue
End Property


Public Property Get DirY() As Double
    DirY = geGenes.GetGene(CDIRY)
End Property


Public Property Let DirY(ByVal lNewValue As Double)
    geGenes.SetGene CDIRY, lNewValue
End Property


Public Property Get RateX() As Double
    RateX = geGenes.GetGene(CRATEX)
End Property


Public Property Let RateX(ByVal lNewValue As Double)
    geGenes.SetGene CRATEX, lNewValue
End Property


Public Property Get RateY() As Double
    RateY = geGenes.GetGene(CRATEY)
End Property
```

```
Public Property Let RateY(ByVal lNewValue As Double)
    geGenes.SetGene CRATEY, lNewValue
End Property

Public Property Get Active() As Boolean
    Active = (geGenes.GetGene(CACTIVE) = 1)
End Property

Public Property Let Active(ByVal bNewValue As Boolean)
    If bNewValue Then
        geGenes.SetGene CACTIVE, 1
    Else
        geGenes.SetGene CACTIVE, 0
    End If
End Property

Public Property Get CountX() As Double
    CountX = geGenes.GetGene(CCOUNTX)
End Property

Public Property Let CountX(ByVal lNewValue As Double)
    geGenes.SetGene CCOUNTX, lNewValue
End Property

Public Property Get CountY() As Double
    CountY = geGenes.GetGene(CCOUNTY)
End Property

Public Property Let CountY(ByVal lNewValue As Double)
    geGenes.SetGene CCOUNTY, lNewValue
End Property

Public Property Get PosX() As Double
    PosX = geGenes.GetGene(CPOSX)
End Property

Public Property Let PosX(ByVal lNewValue As Double)
    geGenes.SetGene CPOSX, lNewValue
End Property
```

```
Public Property Get PosY() As Double
    PosY = geGenes.GetGene(CPOSY)
End Property

Public Property Let PosY(ByVal lNewValue As Double)
    geGenes.SetGene CPOSY, lNewValue
End Property

Public Property Get MoveCount() As Double
    MoveCount = geGenes.GetGene(CMOVECOUNT)
End Property

Public Property Let MoveCount(ByVal lNewValue As Double)
    geGenes.SetGene CMOVECOUNT, lNewValue
End Property

Public Property Get MoveRate() As Double
    MoveRate = geGenes.GetGene(CMOVERATE)
End Property

Public Property Let MoveRate(ByVal lNewValue As Double)
    geGenes.SetGene CMOVERATE, lNewValue
End Property

Public Sub Mutate(ByVal lStartX As Long, ByVal lStartY As Long)
    Active = True
    PosX = lStartX
    PosY = lStartY
    MoveCount = 0
    CountX = 0
    CountY = 0
    MoveRate = MoveRate + Mutator
    RateX = RateX + Mutator
    RateY = RateX + Mutator
End Sub

Public Sub Reset(ByVal lStartX As Long, ByVal lStartY As Long)
    Active = True
    MoveCount = 0
    PosX = lStartX
    PosY = lStartY
```

```
        DirX = Random(3) - 1
        DirY = Random(3) - 1
        CountX = 0
        CountY = 0
        MoveRate = 1 + Random(10)
        RateX = 1 + Random(10)
        RateY = 1 + Random(10)
End Sub

Public Function Mutator() As Double
        Mutator = CDbl((Random(10) - 5) / 10)
End Function

Public Function Random(ByVal lMax As Double) As Double
        Random = CDbl(lMax * Rnd)
End Function
```

The AdaptiveBugs Program

I wrote a program called AdaptiveBugs to demonstrate the genetic engine that was implemented in the two classes that were developed earlier. The goal of this program is to generate a species of bugs that move toward a goal on the screen (marked by an exit sign). This could be a food source or anything that the bugs need to survive. The trick is to mutate a bug that moves neither too slowly nor too quickly, but rather just fast enough and in just the right direction to reach the exit without moving past the edge of the screen.

Running the AdaptiveBugs Program

Okay, I admit that the artwork for the bugs could use a little work. Feel free to redo the bug.bmp image to your liking. Figures 15.11 to 15.13 show three screenshots of the program running at later and later generations in the mutation process (specifically, 1, 10, and 24 generations).

The initial variables for the bugs are as follows:

1. Move rate is between 0 and 100.
2. Horizontal direction is left, stationary, or right.
3. Vertical direction is up, stationary, or down.
4. Horizontal speed ranges are from 0 to 3.
5. Vertical speed ranges are from 0 to 3.
6. All bugs start at the same location for each new generation.

The program runs for a variable number of frames and then mutates a new generation of bugs. Each new generation starts out at the same location on the screen (the starting position) in order to validate the genetic algorithm. If the bugs were to start out at a new location from one generation to the next, it would cause the bugs to behave in a completely random way, and the simulation would not work at all. Figure 15.14 shows the start of a potentially successful "species."

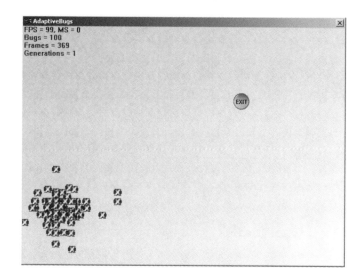

Figure 15.11

The first generation of adaptive bugs is completely random and chaotic.

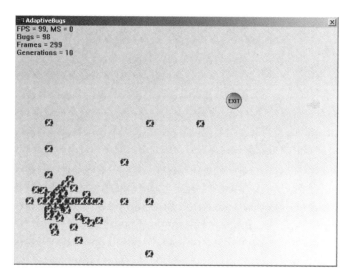

Figure 15.12

The tenth generation of adaptive bugs already shows progress at reaching the goal.

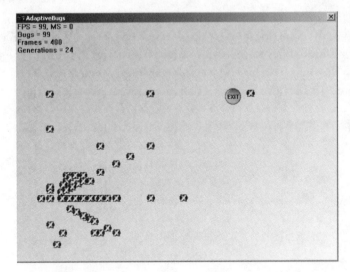

Figure 15.13

By the 24th generation, a stream of adaptive bugs has reached the goal.

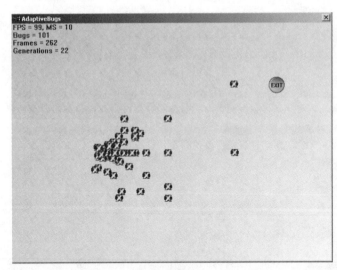

Figure 15.14

The start of another successful mutation! The bugs are altering their course to target the goal.

At the end of each generation, half of the bugs (those closest to the exit) are mated to form a new set of offspring with a combination of genes from each of the two parents. The other half of the bugs (those farthest from the exit) will die. In addition, random new bugs are introduced to add an element of chaos to the simulation. (After all, a completely closed environment is unrealistic.) Therefore, at the start of each new generation, there will be the same number of bugs. Figure 15.15 shows the species of the current run in the 41st generation.

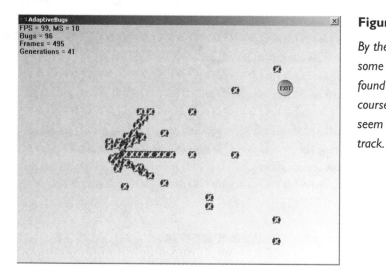

Figure 15.15

By the 41st generation, some of the bugs have found a possible course, while others seem to be way off track.

Here are the rules that govern how the bugs behave in the environment:

1. If frame count exceeds limit, then mutate a new generation.
2. If move rate is zero, then the bug dies.
3. If horizontal and vertical speeds are both zero, then the bug dies.
4. If move count exceeds move rate, then move the bug.
5. If the bug moves off the screen, then the bug dies.

The resolution (that is, the decimal precision) of this program is somewhat limited because I wanted to get results more quickly. Figure 15.16 shows a highly developed species at the 90th generation.

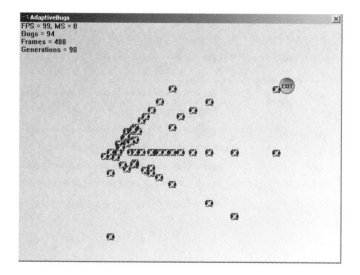

Figure 15.16

After 90 generations, some of the bugs have reached the goal.

To properly run the simulation, it would be better to set the mutator to a much smaller value (on the order of a hundredth or thousandth of a percent). The resulting figures show the lack of precision in the program as it is now. By improving the decimal precision of the variables, you can achieve a much more natural and accurate display (although it will have to run for hours before providing any results). Lower precision

NOTE
Genetic algorithms will usually come up with quick, but not necessarily ideal, solutions. Do not expect all of the bugs to reach the goal. This is generally how an ecosystem works.

allows the program to run faster, while higher precision provides better accuracy (as shown in Figure 15.17).

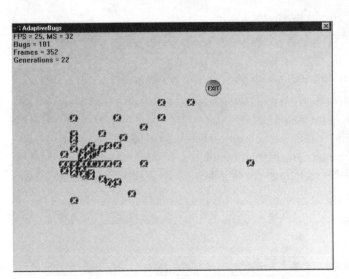

Figure 15.17

By increasing decimal precision in the mutator, the AdaptiveBugs program is much more accurate. Notice that the frame rate is lower than in previous figures.

Building the AdaptiveBugs Program

The AdaptiveBugs program is kind of lengthy due to two long procedures called ProcessGeneration and MutateBugs. The important functionality for handling genetic sprites was locked away in the clsGeneticEngine and clsGESpriteControl classes, but the program is more of a complete simulation than the programs developed earlier in this chapter. The list of files needed to compile this program is shown in Figure 15.18.

Figure 15.18

The Project Explorer shows the files needed to compile the AdaptiveBugs program.

```
'------------------------------------------------------------------
' Visual Basic Game Programming With DirectX
' Chapter 15: Artificial and Simulated Intelligcncc
' AdaptiveBugs Source Code File
'------------------------------------------------------------------
Option Explicit
Option Base 0

'Windows API functions and structures
Private Declare Function GetTickCount _
    Lib "kernel32" () As Long

'program constants
Const SCREENWIDTH As Long = 640
Const SCREENHEIGHT As Long = 480
Const MAXFRAMERATE As Long = 120
Const NUMBUGS As Long = 100
Const FRAMESPERGEN As Long = 500

'program objects
Dim ddraw As New clsDirectDraw7
Dim cddsBackground As New clsDDSurface7
Dim cddsBackBuffer As New clsDDSurface7
Dim ddsBug As New clsDDSprite7
Dim bugs(0 To NUMBUGS) As clsGESpriteControl
Dim newbugs(0 To NUMBUGS) As clsGESpriteControl
Dim ddsExit As New clsDDSprite7
```

```
'program variables
Dim bRunning As Boolean
Dim lStartX As Long
Dim lStartY As Long
Dim sFrameRate As String
Dim lFrameRate As Long
Dim lBugCount As Long
Dim lFrameCount As Long
Dim lGenCount As Long
Dim rTemp As DxVBLib.RECT

Private Sub Form_Load()
    Static lStartTime As Long
    Static lCounter As Long
    Static lNewTime As Long
    Dim n As Long

    'set up the main form
    Form1.Caption = App.Title
    Form1.Width = SCREENWIDTH * Screen.TwipsPerPixelX
    Form1.Height = SCREENHEIGHT * Screen.TwipsPerPixelY
    Form1.AutoRedraw = False
    Form1.ClipControls = False
    Form1.KeyPreview = True
    Form1.ScaleMode = 3
    Form1.Show

    'set starting values
    Randomize GetTickCount
    lStartX = 20 + Random(SCREENWIDTH / 4)
    lStartY = SCREENHEIGHT / 4 + Random(SCREENHEIGHT / 2)

    'create primary DirectDraw object
    If Not ddraw.Startup(Form1.hWnd, SCREENWIDTH, _
        SCREENHEIGHT, 0, False) Then
        MsgBox "Error creating DirectDraw primary display surface"
        Shutdown
    End If

    'create back buffer
    If Not cddsBackBuffer.Create(ddraw.DDObj, _
```

```
    SCREENWIDTH, SCREENHEIGHT) Then
    MsgBox "Error creating back buffer surface"
    Shutdown
End If


'load the background image
If Not cddsBackground.Load(ddraw, App.Path & _
    "\blueyellow640.bmp") Then
    MsgBox "Error loading blueyellow640.bmp"
    Shutdown
End If


'load the bug sprite
ddsBug.Create ddraw
If Not ddsBug.LoadFromFile(App.Path & "\bug.bmp", 16, 16, 1, 1) Then
    MsgBox "Error loading bug.bmp"
    Shutdown
End If


'initialize the bugs
For n = 0 To NUMBUGS
    Set newbugs(n) = New clsGESpriteControl
    Set bugs(n) = New clsGESpriteControl
    bugs(n).Reset lStartX, lStartY
Next n


'load the exit sprite
ddsExit.Create ddraw
If Not ddsExit.LoadFromFile(App.Path & "\exit.bmp", 32, 32, 1, 1) Then
    MsgBox "Error loading exit.bmp"
    Shutdown
End If
'position exit in right side of screen
ddsExit.X = SCREENWIDTH / 2 + Random(SCREENWIDTH / 2 - 64)
ddsExit.Y = Random(SCREENHEIGHT / 2 - 64)


'draw the background image
cddsBackBuffer.BltFast 0, 0, cddsBackground.Surface, _
    cddsBackground.SurfaceRect
```

```
        bRunning = True
        lFrameRate = MAXFRAMERATE
        sFrameRate = "FPS"
        lGenCount = 1

        'main game loop
        Do While bRunning
            lCounter = GetTickCount() - lStartTime
            If lCounter > lNewTime Then
                Game_Update lCounter
                lNewTime = lCounter + 1000 / lFrameRate
            End If
            DoEvents
        Loop

End Sub

Private Sub Form_KeyDown(KeyCode As Integer, Shift As Integer)
    If KeyCode = 27 Then Shutdown
End Sub

Private Sub Form_QueryUnload(Cancel As Integer, UnloadMode As Integer)
    Shutdown
End Sub

Private Sub Form1_Click()
    Shutdown
End Sub
Private Sub Shutdown()
    'stop game loop
    bRunning = False
    ddraw.Shutdown

    'delete objects
    Set ddraw = Nothing
    Set cddsBackground = Nothing
    Set cddsBackBuffer = Nothing
    Set ddsBug = Nothing
    Set ddsExit = Nothing
```

```
    'end program
    Form1.Hide
    End
End Sub


Public Function Distance(ByVal X1 As Double, ByVal Y1 As Double, _
    ByVal X2 As Double, ByVal Y2 As Double) As Long
    Distance = CLng(Sqr((X2 - X1) * (X2 - X1) + (Y2 - Y1) * (Y2 - Y1)))
End Function


Public Function Random(ByVal num&) As Long
    Random = CLng(num * Rnd)
End Function


Public Sub Game_Update(ByVal MS As Long)
    Static lTimer As Long
    Static lStart As Long
    Static lCounter As Long
    Dim n As Long

    'start counting milliseconds
    lStart = GetTickCount

    'erase status messages
    rTemp.Left = 1
    rTemp.Top = 1
    rTemp.Right = 160
    rTemp.Bottom = 80
    cddsBackBuffer.BltFast 5, 20, cddsBackground.Surface, rTemp

    'erase the exit sprite
    EraseSprite ddsExit

    'erase bug sprites
    For n = 0 To NUMBUGS
        If bugs(n).Active Then
            ddsBug.X = bugs(n).PosX
            ddsBug.Y = bugs(n).PosY
            EraseSprite ddsBug
        End If
    Next n
```

```
        'update bug sprites
        ProcessGeneration

        'draw the exit sprite
        ddsExit.Draw cddsBackBuffer

        'draw the bug sprites
        For n = 0 To NUMBUGS
            If bugs(n).Active Then
                ddsBug.X = bugs(n).PosX
                ddsBug.Y = bugs(n).PosY
                ddsBug.Draw cddsBackBuffer
            End If
        Next n

        'display status messages
        cddsBackBuffer.DrawText 5, 20, sFrameRate
        cddsBackBuffer.DrawText 5, 35, "Bugs = " & lBugCount
        cddsBackBuffer.DrawText 5, 50, "Frames = " & lFrameCount
        cddsBackBuffer.DrawText 5, 65, "Generations = " & lGenCount

        'copy back buffer to the screen
        ddraw.Draw cddsBackBuffer, cddsBackBuffer.SurfaceRect

        'count the frames per second
        If MS > lTimer + 1000 Then
            lStart = GetTickCount - lStart
            sFrameRate = "FPS = " & lCounter & ", MS = " & lStart
            lTimer = MS
            lCounter = 0
        Else
            lCounter = lCounter + 1
        End If
    End Sub

Private Sub EraseSprite(ByRef sprite As clsDDSprite7)
    rTemp.Left = sprite.X
    rTemp.Top = sprite.Y
    rTemp.Right = rTemp.Left + sprite.Width
    rTemp.Bottom = rTemp.Top + sprite.Height
    cddsBackBuffer.BltFast sprite.X, sprite.Y, cddsBackground.Surface, rTemp
End Sub
```

The ProcessGeneration procedure (which is called by Game_Update) requires a little explanation. First, there is a mutation counter that keeps track of the frame count, which determines when a new generation occurs (at which point the MutateBugs procedure is called). Next, the bugs are all moved based on the X and Y movement rates and directions. If the sprite moves outside the boundary of the screen, it is deactivated (which is a polite way of saying that the bug was stupid and fell off a steep cliff!).

```
Private Sub ProcessGeneration()
    Dim n As Long

    'increment mutation counter
    lFrameCount = lFrameCount + 1
    If lFrameCount > FRAMESPERGEN Then
        lGenCount = lGenCount + 1
        lFrameCount = 0
        MutateBugs
    End If

    'move the bugs
    lBugCount = 0
    For n = 0 To NUMBUGS
        With bugs(n)
            If .MoveRate = 0 Then .Active = False
            If .RateX = 0 And .RateY = 0 Then .Active = False
            If .Active Then
                lBugCount = lBugCount + 1
                'update movement
                .MoveCount = .MoveCount + 1
                If .MoveCount > .MoveRate Then
                    .MoveCount = 0
                    'update X
                    .CountX = .CountX + 1
                    If .CountX > .RateX Then
                        .CountX = 0
                        .PosX = .PosX + .DirX
                        If .PosX < 0 Or .PosX > SCREENWIDTH Then
                            .Active = False
                        End If
                    End If
                    'update Y
                    .CountY = .CountY + 1
```

```
                    If .CountY > .RateY Then
                        .CountY = 0
                        .PosY = .PosY + .DirY
                        If .PosY < 0 Or .PosY > SCREENHEIGHT Then
                            .Active = False
                        End If
                    End If
                End If
            End If
        End With
    Next n
End Sub
```

The MutateBugs procedure is called by ProcessGeneration any time a new generation is supposed
to be bred. MutateBugs tries to provide the species with a means to survive by weeding out any
individuals that stray too far off the path. The distance formula is used to determine how far each
of the bugs is from the goal; it then uses the closest and farthest bugs to make that determination
(the cutoff percentage is 90). After that, any bugs that are still alive are mutated, while any bugs
that died in the previous generation are reset. This introduces a random element into the simulation that keeps the gene pool from growing stagnant.

```
Private Sub MutateBugs()
    Dim fFurthest As Double
    Dim fClosest As Double
    Dim fDist As Double
    Dim fCutoff As Double
    Dim lClosestBug As Long
    Dim n As Long

    'clear the screen
    cddsBackBuffer.BltFast 0, 0, _
        cddsBackground.Surface, cddsBackground.SurfaceRect

    'find closest and farthest bugs
    fClosest = 999
    fFurthest = 0
    For n = 0 To NUMBUGS
        If bugs(n).Active Then
            fDist = Distance(ddsExit.X, ddsExit.Y, bugs(n).PosX, bugs(n).PosY)
```

```
            If fDist < fClosest Then
                fClosest = fDist
                lClosestBug = n
                Debug.Print "Closest bug = " & lClosestBug
            End If
            If fDist > fFurthest Then fFurthest = fDist
        End If
        DoEvents
    Next n

    'calculate the cutoff point
    fCutoff = fFurthest * 0.9

    'mix up the bug species' gene pool
    For n = 0 To NUMBUGS
        With bugs(n)
            fDist = Distance(ddsExit.X, ddsExit.Y, .PosX, .PosY)
            .Active = (fDist < fCutoff)
            If .Active Then
                bugs(n).Mutate lStartX, lStartY
            Else
                bugs(n).Reset lStartX, lStartY
            End If
        End With
        DoEvents
    Next n
End Sub
```

SUMMARY

This chapter delved into the fascinating subject of artificial intelligence (which often should be referred to as simulated intelligence). It presented a short history of AI and how it is related to the computer industry, and then covered three sub-branches of AI—state machines, fuzzy logic, and genetic algorithms. Along the way, several new classes were introduced (such as clsStateEngine, clsFuzzyEngine, and clsGeneticEngine), providing a means to quickly and easily add some simple AI processes to a game. Along with the classes, each subject also included a sample program for demonstration.

The study of artificial intelligence is as complicated as any advanced calculus course. Like many primers, this chapter attempted to introduce you to these subjects, and is by no means a complete guide. The goal of this chapter was to build simple sprite control routines by studying basic AI concepts.

CHAPTER 16

MULTIPLAYER PROGRAMMING WITH WINDOWS SOCKETS

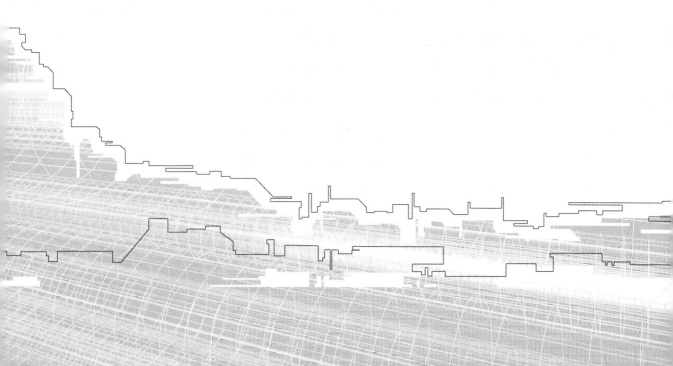

elcome to the first chapter on multiplayer programming! This is the first chapter in a two-part series on multiplayer programming, covering the hardcore and often difficult subject of Windows sockets (Winsock for short). Socket programming is the basis for every Internet program in existence, including Web browsers, FTP (*File Transfer Protocol*) clients, IRC (*Internet Relay Chat*) clients, and instant messaging clients. Chapter 17, "Network Programming with DirectPlay," covers the DirectX solution for multiplayer programming.

Everything on the Internet is built with sockets, regardless of the brand of computer or operating system. This chapter teaches you how to program this ultra low-level language of computer networking. But rather than dig into the complicated details of networking, I will simply show you how to write code to use it. As in previous chapters, this one focuses on practical solutions rather than just theory.

This chapter covers the following topics:

- Essentials of Multiplayer Programming
- Programming Windows Sockets
- Creating the SocketChat Program

ESSENTIALS OF MULTIPLAYER PROGRAMMING

Multiplayer game programming has a long history that stretches back to the earliest bulletin board systems in the 1970s. While some boards had multiple phone lines (and multiple modems) that allowed users to chat with each other, by far the most prevalent form of gaming took place on a turn-by-turn basis, in which players would log on to the board, play several turns for the day, and then wait until the next day to play the game again (after all the other players had done the same). This style of online gaming is similar to "play by e-mail," which is common in turn-based games like chess, and very popular with strategy wargamers.

However, gamers today demand immediate feedback to their actions, which calls for real-time game programming. For all practical purposes, there is absolutely no distinction between playing a game over a LAN and playing a game over the Internet. The protocols and source code are the same. The only difference is that LAN gaming is usually much faster than Internet gaming.

The term *online game*, however, is usually reserved for Internet gaming, and generally means that players from around the world can play together as if they lived in the same town.

Physical Connections

Before you can start coding a multiplayer game, you first need a way to test it. You might be surprised at how easy this is. In reality, you can test the client and server programs on the very same development PC, because TCP/IP doesn't really care where the source or destination addresses are physically located.

Where is Internet service going today? Just take a look at the latest gaming consoles to hit the market in 2001 and 2002. Neither the Sony PlayStation 2 nor the Nintendo GameCube come equipped with multiplayer hardware. Even the older Sega Dreamcast came with a 56k modem, and Scga still has a thriving online network for Dreamcast users. Some Dreamcast games, like *Quake III Arena*, are even marginally compatible with the PC version of the game. There is even a broadband adapter for the Dreamcast (although it was offered only through Sega's Web site for a limited time).

The Microsoft Xbox, however, comes factory-equipped with a 10Base-T LAN port that is compatible with standard networking equipment like cables, routers, and hubs, and supports online multiplayer gameplay out of the box. Why the disparity? Well, given that Dreamcast is powered by Windows CE, and Xbox is powered by Windows 2000, it is no wonder. Microsoft has been an Internet proponent for many years. The Japanese market is just not as "wired" as the American market. The Xbox will likely surprise a great many gamers in the Far East.

Dial-Up Modem Connections

In the old days, bulletin boards allowed players to log in through a phone line and play games directly on the board. Today, many gamers still use the phone lines for gaming, but they do so through an Internet service provider, such as America Online (AOL), Microsoft Network (MSN), or a local provider. Obviously, you need a modem to log on to the Internet through a dial-up service provider. Most games today still work fine with a modem connection, but performance is usually less than satisfactory due to the slow speed of analog phone lines.

Local Area Network Connections

The LAN and Ethernet were such great inventions. I have had some great times at LAN parties, hanging out with friends, making new friends, and fragging them all in the process. LAN parties are popular because the games run extremely fast over a local area network, which runs at 10 or 100 megabits per second. Compare that to only a few kilobits over a phone line (or even the meager 1–3 megabits with broadband connections), and it is clear why LAN parties are so much fun. Quite simply, lag is not an issue at a LAN party like it is on the Internet. But by far the most enjoyable part of a LAN party is interacting with others while sharing a favorite pastime. To participate in a LAN party, you need a PC with a LAN card (preferably a 100-megabit card).

Broadband Connections

Broadband is a great alternative to modem gaming and LAN parties because it provides decent bandwidth over the Internet, allowing games to run at an acceptable rate. The lag will be much higher than at a LAN party, but it is usually quite acceptable considering the alternative of going back to a dial-up modem. Broadband companies are currently struggling for dominance in the industry, with cable modem companies competing with DSL (*Digital Subscriber Line*) companies. The competition is interesting because cable modem providers are typically the same companies that provide cable television, thus they use the existing lines. Similarly, DSL is operated by telephone companies using the existing telephone networks. To gain access to the Internet through broadband, you need a PC with a LAN card.

Multiplayer Games: The Next Generation

One game in particular comes to mind after mentioning these subjects, and that is *HALO: Combat Evolved*. This is an Xbox game developed by Bungie (the same folks who created the *Myth* series for the PC). Without reservation, I think *HALO* is the most beautiful, gripping, white-knuckled, phenomenal game I have ever played. I bought a Microsoft Xbox console just for this game, but then found that several other Xbox games were fun too. Basically, *HALO* is a ring-world, reminiscent of Larry Niven—a massive metal construction thousands of miles in diameter, with a life-supporting landscape on the inner side of the ring (as shown in Figure 16.1).

While Niven's ringworld actually had a diameter the size of Earth's orbit around the sun (on the order of 180 million miles), it was a limited version and more practical type of a Dyson sphere. HALO is much smaller and orbits a gas giant planet (sort of like a ring*moon*, perhaps?). But that is just the setting for this revolutionary game. An alien race called the Covenant has been wiping out human civilization, one planet at a time. As the game's main character (see Figure 16.2), you are known only by your rank: Master Chief, a genetically engineered cyborg with built-in AI that helps you crack alien computer systems. You are stranded on HALO with a bunch of gear, weaponry, and marines, and your goal is to defeat the Covenant forces that have tried to take over HALO. Along the way, you discover the true nature of HALO, and thus the plot unfolds.

Figure 16.1

HALO: Combat Evolved *takes place on a ringworld.*

Figure 16.2

The main character of HALO *is a genetically enhanced cyborg named Master Chief.*

The reason I have brought up this game is because it is not only the best single-player game I have ever played, it is also the most intense multiplayer game I have played (and the two-player, split-screen, cooperative mode is simply amazing). You can connect up to four Xbox consoles with the built-in 10Base-T port (using your own network hub and cabling), and play deathmatch-style games like Capture the Flag and King of the Hill.

The background story, use of vehicles and alien weaponry, and stunning visuals all help *HALO* to outpace PC games like *Quake III Arena* and *Unreal Tournament*. As Figure 16.3 shows, *HALO* is truly combat evolved, and is the new standard for first-person shooters.

Figure 16.3

HALO *features many different weapons and vehicles that you can use to fight Covenant forces.*

Internet Protocols

Without a doubt, the TCP/IP protocol is now the world standard protocol for networking everything from PCs to game consoles to Pocket PCs to home security systems. The protocol of the future is TCP/IP, until something better comes along (which will no doubt need to be compatible with TCP/IP to make it in the marketplace).

Transport Control Protocol/Internet Protocol

The transport control protocol (TCP) and Internet protocol (IP) is a software layer that sits between the network driver and the socket library. The PC version is called Windows Sockets API, or Winsock API, and is compatible with the Berkley socket standard for UNIX (which *was* the Internet in the early days). TCP/IP is a live connection protocol that requires both sides of the socket to maintain the connection in order to communicate. If either side ends the session, the connection is lost. TCP/IP packets are guaranteed, so you can be reasonably certain that if you send data to a socket server, it will arrive at its destination. If a socket is unable to reach the destination, it is possible that the packet will be forever lost, but in most cases that involves a lost connection anyway.

A socket is simply an open port on a particular IP address that waits for a connection request from a client computer. The physical location of the IP address is irrelevant to the socket, so it might be on a computer 10,000 miles away, on another computer on the LAN, or even on the same PC.

Universal Datagram Packet Protocol

The universal datagram packet (UDP) protocol is similar to IP, but does not guarantee delivery. UDP is therefore faster than TCP/IP at delivering messages, because response codes are not needed. This is a good way to transmit broadcast messages to a large number of players in a massively multiplayer game, for instance. Rather than requiring an established connection, UDP messages sort of establish the connection as they are received. This doesn't mean that just anyone can write a UDP program to flood your computer with messages, because you must still have a server running on the specific port and written to understand the incoming message. UDP is not the best protocol for a game, because there is no way to guarantee that all players receive player moves. Sure, you could add in your own response codes, but it would not be worth the effort when TCP/IP is available.

PROGRAMMING WINDOWS SOCKETS

The Windows Sockets API includes functions that are "blocking," which means that nothing else can happen in that program thread until the socket receives some kind of response from the other end. This is a serious problem in a game, which has to run smoothly. The alternative is to run socket commands in a separate thread. That is where things get messy with Visual Basic. But there is an alternative to multithreaded programming, as I will explain later.

The Winsock API

As I have shown you in previous chapters, when it comes to the Windows API, there is practically nothing that you can't do with Visual Basic. However, one of the things that I try to avoid is the dreaded callback function. You had a little exposure to callbacks in Chapter 12, "Getting a Handle on User Input," when I explained how DirectInput can either be programmed to use a callback or can be polled. Without a doubt, polling is a preferred method when interfacing VB to Windows API or DirectX components, because it gives you ultimate control over how those processes run. Need to pause the game? Great, just turn off polling for a while. But when dealing with callbacks, it can get messy. I suppose you could just test a condition inside the callback that prevents any code from running if the game is paused, but the fact remains that something is out there, sending stuff to your program, and doing so without your intervention.

Game programmers who were skilled in the MS-DOS era are probably more comfortable with polled software, and shudder at event-driven callbacks. Imagine if MS-DOS had decided to interrupt your game to tell you something, rather than the other way around?

Have you ever had a computer virus? Most computer professionals have encountered several viruses in their careers, and cleaning out viruses is a way of life for corporate IT departments (thanks to less-than-savvy users). It seems to me that the general fear that is caused by a virus is the uncertainty of having a rogue program running in your computer. To a programmer, that uncertainty is lurking nearby when dealing with callback functions. You just never know when timing or program state is going to cause a callback to fail and crash the program. Well-written code will get around this, but game code is a complicated business and it is often difficult to see the results of cutting-edge tricks, all in the name of the deity known as frame rate.

The Winsock Control

If you are new to Visual Basic, I'm sure you were drawn to the language because of its simplicity. If you are an experienced VB coder, I'm sure you have found over time that often the best way to write code is to avoid many of the ease-of-use pitfalls that Microsoft built into VB. Those features make the language amazingly easy for a beginner, but over time become difficult and unwieldy. That is, of course, the path I have taken throughout this book—ignoring the get-rich-quick tricks and focusing on long-term investments. As an analogy, that means treating VB as a programming language and not a drag-and-drop GUI paint program.

The Winsock Control is a fabulous exception to the rule when it comes to game programming. I'm sure that this control has been dismissed far too easily in the past, because I have not seen much done with it. The first thing that I notice when talking to game programmers is that they immediately jump into DirectPlay, never having written a Winsock program! I always wonder how someone will comprehend everything that is going on under the hood, so to speak, without first learning how to do something the hard way.

Okay, I am contradicting myself a bit now. Back in Chapter 14, "DirectX Graphics and Direct3D," I immediately jumped into Direct3D coding without explaining how it all works. I admit it, my bad. But I did explain that most game developers do the same thing. What is the point in writing your own 3-D library when Direct3D and OpenGL are available? What is the point in learning how to apply texture mapping to a polygon when Direct3D lets you do the same thing in only a few lines of code? It's all about efficiently using your time and avoiding the temptation to reinvent the wheel. Back in the old days of game programming, most games were written from scratch to try to push the envelope of gaming. But today, the technology has reached critical mass and is now supporting itself, so game developers can focus on gameplay, artificial intelligence, physics, multiplayer, and other game aspects.

Message Handling

The key to multiplayer game programming is understanding how messages are handled in a socket connection. Basically, you can send any type of information you want from the client to the server, and vice versa. It is completely up to you to decide how to work with that information once it has been received. This is not necessarily the case when you're programming with DirectPlay, which abstracts the process for you and provides a common interface for different types of communication. When working with sockets, you are in complete control of what information passes between the client and server.

Rather than go into a long discourse on the theory of networking and socket programming, with a listing of the various procedure and function calls with parameters lists, I'm going to just show you how to create a chat program. The program will actually be made up of a socket server and a chat client that connects to the server. To chat with multiple people, simply run the SocketServer.exe program on your PC, send the SocketChat.exe program to a few friends, provide them with the IP address of the PC running the SocketServer, and then try sending messages back and forth. Learn by example—that is my motto.

CREATING THE SOCKETCHAT PROGRAM

The SocketChat program shows you how to link multiple clients to a socket server and allow them to send messages to each other. When the socket server receives a chat message, it forwards the message to all the clients in a broadcast. This is the basis for a multiplayer game.

The ability to update the server with player data (in the form of messages) and have the server broadcast that data to all the other clients allows you to build any type of game, including real-time games. By using small packets of data, such as 128 bytes, the server is able to keep track of numerous players without a problem. Figure 16.4 shows the server for the chat program.

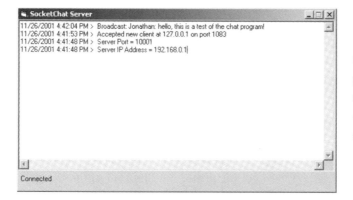

Figure 16.4

The socket server for the chat program displays broadcast messages and server events in the server log.

The object of the SocketChat program, shown in Figure 16.5, is to provide a simple interface to the socket library using several Winsock controls to provide multiple connections for a socket server. This will allow you to connect, in theory, up to 255 players in a single game before requiring a new instance of the socket server. This is due to a limitation on the number of controls in a control array, which is how the multiplayer element is accomplished.

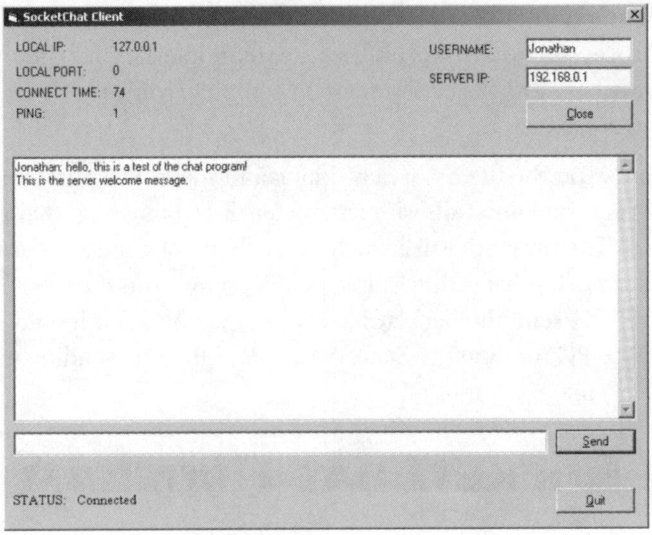

Figure 16.5

The SocketChat client program displays server messages, including messages that you type, which are broadcast to all connected clients.

Common Components

Eventually, the code from this chapter will make its way into the game library that was started back in Chapter 13, "Building the DirectX Game Library." So the idea is to build reusable classes that can be plugged into the library and then easily used in future games.

The Socket Event Form (frmLink)

The Winsock control needs a home before it will do its work, so that calls for a form. The form can be added to the game library down the road, along with the socket classes, so once the game library has been recompiled with the socket code, you will be able to write multiplayer games fairly easily by simply referencing the VBGL. Both the socket server and client classes will share the form.

I have called the form frmLink, since it contains both of the client and server Winsock controls, as well as the link control array. Beneath the form is some code that generates events for any class that invokes a new instance of frmLink using the WithEvents keyword. The settings of the form are completely irrelevant; so don't worry about doing anything with it. All you need to do with this form is add three Winsock controls to it.

But wait! First, you need to reference the Winsock control, in order to have it show up in the Control Toolbox. Go to the Projects menu and select Components, as shown in Figure 16.6. Scroll down the list until you find Microsoft Winsock Control 6.0. Check the control and then close the dialog box to continue.

Figure 16.6

The Components dialog box shows the ActiveX controls that are available.

Figure 16.7 shows the form as it appears in the VB form editor. Note that I have added labels to the form to show the names of the Winsock controls.

Figure 16.7

The frmLink form contains the Winsock controls needed to write the client and server classes.

The labels are for illustration only and are not necessary. Besides the client and server controls, a the third Winsock control is an array called "link." To create a control array, you plunk down a control and then set the Index property of the control to zero. This automatically sets it up as a control array. I would have much preferred to create these controls in source code (as in previous programs) because it is easy to list and doesn't require much explanation, unlike setting up a form in VB. But it is not possible to use the Controls.Add function to create a control array. You can create a normal control, as usual, but the Index property that you need to set in order to establish a control array must be set during design time. If you try to set Index = 0 during runtime, the compiler will generate the error message shown in Figure 16.8. The workaround is to simply add the Winsock controls to the form during design time and then move on.

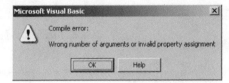

Figure 16.8

This error message explains why it is not possible to create a control array during runtime.

Here is the source code for the frmLink form. This short source code listing is the basis for an entire multiplayer socket game. Can you believe that? It doesn't seem like much, does it? Well, actually, the socket classes that follow will access the properties of the Winsock controls directly, rather than doing everything through events. The events in frmLink are directly passed on to any form or class that instantiates it, so the bulk of the socket code will be found in the client and server socket classes.

```vb
'-----------------------------------------------------------------------
' Visual Basic Game Programming With DirectX
' Chapter 16 : Multiplayer Programming With Windows Sockets
' frmLink Source Code File
'-----------------------------------------------------------------------

Option Explicit
Option Base 0

'public events passed on by the Winsock controls
Public Event SocketError(ByVal lIndex As Long, ByVal lNumber As Long, _
    ByVal sDescription As String)
Public Event ConnectionClosed(ByVal lIndex As Long)
Public Event ServerConnectionRequest(ByVal lRequestID As Long)
Public Event ClientDataArrival(ByVal lTotalBytes As Long, _
    ByVal sData As String)
Public Event DataArrival(ByVal lIndex As Long, _
    ByVal lTotalBytes As Long, ByVal sData As String)

'the sole tcpClient event
Private Sub tcpClient_DataArrival(ByVal lTotalBytes As Long)
    Dim sIncoming As String
    tcpClient.GetData sIncoming, vbString
    RaiseEvent ClientDataArrival(lTotalBytes, sIncoming)
End Sub
```

```
'the sole tcpServer event
Private Sub tcpServer_ConnectionRequest(ByVal lRequestID As Long)
    RaiseEvent ServerConnectionRequest(lRequestID)
End Sub

'remaining events are for the control array
Private Sub link_DataArrival(lIndex As Integer, _
    ByVal lTotalBytes As Long)
    Dim sIncoming$
    link(lIndex).GetData sIncoming, vbString
    RaiseEvent DataArrival(lIndex, lTotalBytes, sIncoming)
End Sub

Private Sub link_Close(lIndex As Integer)
    RaiseEvent ConnectionClosed(lIndex)
End Sub

Private Sub link_Error(Index As Integer, ByVal Number As Integer, _
    Description As String, ByVal Scode As Long, _
    ByVal Source As String, ByVal HelpFile As String, _
    ByVal HelpContext As Long, CancelDisplay As Boolean)
    RaiseEvent SocketError(Index, Number, Description)
End Sub
```

The ServerSocket Class

Now that you have a foundation for socket communications through the frmLink form and the three controls that it contains, you are able to subclass the form (so to speak) and encapsulate the Winsock controls to make them play nice. After all, that is mainly what classes are for, right? Basically, any time a connection request comes into the tcpServer control, a new instance of the link control is loaded and connected to the outside line, thus freeing up the server for additional connection requests.

Basically, there are 255 sockets available within a single server. If you need more connections than that, you will have to set up additional servers with new port numbers to accommodate the load and then devise a way for players on different servers to communicate (or simply disallow it). For this, a control server is needed, which is beyond the scope of this chapter. What the ServerSocket class does provide, however, is a means to search through the socket array and look for unused sockets (clients that have disconnected). Take a look at Figure 16.9, which shows what happens when the first 255 sockets have been used. The ServerSocket class picks up socket #0, which was unused.

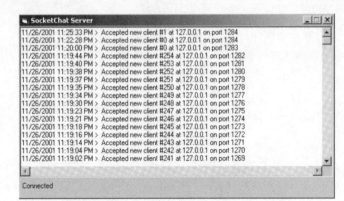

Figure 16.9

The SocketServer program, showing socket numbers from connecting clients

Since I was using just a single client to test this code, closing and then re-opening the connection again brought up socket #0. Only after I fired up a second instance of the SocketChat client did the server's socket count go up to #1 (because #0 was still being used). This mechanism of reuse should give the server quite a bit of use in an actual game.

```
'----------------------------------------------------------------------
' Visual Basic Game Programming With DirectX
' Chapter 16 : Multiplayer Programming With Windows Sockets
' ServerSocket Class Source Code File
'----------------------------------------------------------------------

Option Explicit
Option Base 0

'socket server events
Public Event DataArrival(ByVal lIndex As Long, _
    ByVal lTotalBytes As Long, ByVal sIncoming As String)
Public Event ServerConnectionRequest(ByVal lRequestID As Long)

'define the winsock control form
Dim WithEvents frm As frmLink

Dim sIncoming As String
Dim lCurrentLink As Long

'initialize the form
Private Sub Class_Initialize()
    Set frm = New frmLink
End Sub
```

```vb
    Private Sub Class_Terminate()
        Set frm = Nothing
    End Sub

    Public Function UserCount()
        Dim lCount&
        lCount = frm.link.count
        UserCount = lCount
    End Function

    Public Function OpenConnection(ByVal lRequestID As Long, _
        ByVal lPort As Long) As Long
        Dim count As Long
        Dim n As Long

        'look for an available socket
        count = frm.link.count
        If count >= 255 Then
            For n = 0 To 255
                If frm.link(n).State <> sckConnected Then
                    count = n
                    Exit For
                End If
            Next n

            'make sure it worked
            If n <> count Then
                OpenConnection = -1
                Exit Function
            End If
        Else
            Load frm.link(count)
        End If

        'set up the socket
        frm.link(count).Close
        frm.link(count).LocalPort = lPort
        frm.link(count).Accept lRequestID
        CurrentLink = count
        OpenConnection = count
    End Function
```

```
Public Sub CloseConnection(ByVal Index&)
    frm.link(Index).Close
End Sub

Public Property Get RemoteHostIP() As String
    RemoteHostIP = frm.link(CurrentLink).RemoteHostIP
End Property

Public Property Get RemotePort() As String
    RemotePort = frm.link(CurrentLink).RemotePort
End Property

Public Property Get LocalIP() As String
    LocalIP = frm.link(CurrentLink).LocalIP
End Property

Public Property Get LocalPort() As Long
    LocalPort = frm.tcpServer.LocalPort
End Property

Public Property Get State() As Long
    State = frm.link(CurrentLink).State
End Property

Public Sub Send(ByVal Index&, ByVal s$)
    If frm.link(Index).State = sckConnected Then
        frm.link(Index).SendData s$
        Delay 20
    End If
End Sub

Public Sub OpenServer(ByVal PORT As Long)
    frm.tcpServer.LocalPort = PORT
    frm.tcpServer.Listen
End Sub

Public Sub CloseServer()
    frm.tcpServer.Close
End Sub
```

```
Private Sub frm_DataArrival(ByVal Index&, ByVal bytesTotal As Long, _
    ByVal sData$)
    CurrentLink = Index
    RaiseEvent DataArrival(Index, bytesTotal, sData)
End Sub


Private Sub frm_ServerConnectionRequest(ByVal requestID As Long)
    RaiseEvent ServerConnectionRequest(requestID)
End Sub


Private Sub frm_SocketError(ByVal Index&, ByVal Number As Long, _
    ByVal Description As String)
    Debug.Print "SocketError: " & Number & " " & Description
End Sub


Public Property Get CurrentLink() As Long
    CurrentLink = lCurrentLink
End Property


Public Property Let CurrentLink(ByVal vNewValue As Long)
    lCurrentLink = vNewValue
End Property


Public Sub Delay(ByVal ms As Long)
    Dim lStart As Long
    lStart = GetTickCount
    Do Until GetTickCount > lStart + ms
        DoEvents
    Loop
End Sub
```

The ClientSocket Class

The client socket class also encapsulates frmLink to gain Winsock client functionality. The client socket class completely ignores the server stuff that is also available, so both classes can share the same form. Actually, the client only uses the tcpClient control, while the server uses both the tcpServer control and the link control array.

```
'---------------------------------------------------------------------------
' Visual Basic Game Programming With DirectX
' Chapter 16 : Multiplayer Programming With Windows Sockets
' clsClientSocket Source Code File
'---------------------------------------------------------------------------


Option Explicit
Option Base 0

'client socket events
Public Event DataArrival(ByVal lTotalBytes As Long, _
    ByVal sIncoming As String)

'define the winsock control form
Private WithEvents frm As frmLink

'initialize the form
Private Sub Class_Initialize()
    Set frm = New frmLink
    frm.tcpClient.RemoteHost = ""
End Sub

Private Sub Class_Terminate()
    Set frm = Nothing
End Sub

Public Property Let RemotePort(ByVal lPort&)
    frm.tcpClient.RemotePort = lPort
End Property

Public Property Get RemotePort() As Long
    RemotePort = frm.tcpClient.RemotePort
End Property


Public Property Get LocalIP() As String
    LocalIP = frm.tcpClient.LocalIP
End Property
```

```
Public Sub Send(ByVal s$)
    If frm.tcpClient.State = sckConnected Then
        frm.tcpClient.SendData s$
        Delay 20
    End If
End Sub

Public Sub CloseConnection()
    frm.tcpClient.Close
End Sub

Public Property Get RemoteHost() As String
    RemoteHost = frm.tcpClient.RemoteHost
End Property

Public Property Let RemoteHost(ByVal vNewValue As String)
    frm.tcpClient.RemoteHost = vNewValue
End Property

Public Sub Connect()
    frm.tcpClient.Connect
End Sub

Private Sub frm_ClientDataArrival(ByVal bytesTotal As Long, _
    ByVal sData As String)
    RaiseEvent DataArrival(bytesTotal, sData)
End Sub

Public Property Get State() As Long
    State = frm.tcpClient.State
End Property

Public Sub Delay(ByVal ms As Long)
    Dim lStart As Long
    lStart = GetTickCount
    Do Until GetTickCount > lStart + ms
        DoEvents
    Loop
End Sub
```

Building the Chat Server

The chat server uses the clsServerSocket class (which in turn requires the frmLink form) to establish a socket server for a chat program that is capable of accepting (in theory) hundreds of connections. What this means is basically that a couple hundred clients can connect to the server and send chat messages to each other. This chat server doesn't support any advanced features like sending messages to specific users, and does not even include a user list, like most chat programs (although that would be a great feature enhancement that you might tackle).

But why a chat program, and not something more interesting like a real game? Indeed, there is a game in Part Four, "Complete Game Projects," that shows how to use sockets. The reason behind a chat program is that it demonstrates how to send messages between client and server programs using TCP/IP. This is the "Hello, World!" of networking programs, so to speak. Once you have a messaging system that works, it is a simple matter to create a multiplayer game because messaging is the foundation of multiplayer gaming.

The SocketServer program is incredibly useful for building new game servers, since it has all the bases covered, and you can simply add new message types to the messaging system to incorporate sprite movement (such as player position and projectiles).

Creating the SocketServer Project

I hope you don't mind a little inconsistency, because this chapter is full of it! As you might recall, in previous chapters I have written code that set up the user interface of a form. That is only practical up to a certain point, and then it becomes messy. The chat program (both client and server) is easier to build using the form editor at design time. Fortunately, the SocketServer program has a simple user interface that includes just a TextBox (txtOutput), a Label (lblStatus), and a Timer (Timer1).

Feel free to size the form however you like, or refer to Figure 16.10 for an example of how I did it. The TextBox receives a log of commands and events that provides some feedback about what is going on with the server. The label simply shows the status of the socket connections, while the Timer control checks the status of the tcpServer at an interval of 250 milliseconds (which is four times per second).

The SocketServer program will need to include the following files in order to compile:

- ServerSocket.cls
- Declares.bas
- frmLink.frm

Figure 16.10

The main form of the SocketServer program in the form editor at design time

The ServerSocket.cls and frmLink.frm files were created earlier in the chapter, but the Declares.bas file is part of the game library, so you can copy it from the Chapter 13 directory where you created the VBGL project (or just copy it directly off the CD-ROM).

SocketServer Source Code

The source code for the SocketServer program includes primarily events generated by the serverLink object (instantiated from the ServerSocket class). Basically, this object communicates with the Winsock controls within frmLink and passes on events as they occur. For instance, when a client connection request comes in, it is passed to SocketServer as an event called serverLink_ServerConnectionRequest. All you need to do at that point is open the connection with the OpenConnection procedure (also built into the ServerSocket class).

From that point forward, events will come in through the serverLink as messages, or possibly as new connection requests from additional clients. Really, the event-driven nature of the process makes it very easy to understand how everything works. By abstracting the process of loading new controls into the link control array, the final game code is easier to write.

The ParseToken and ReplaceToken functions are simply used to break apart message strings to determine what kinds of messages are coming in through the DataArrival event.

```
'-----------------------------------------------------------------------
' Visual Basic Game Programming With DirectX
' Chapter 16 : Multiplayer Programming With Windows Sockets
' SocketServer Source Code File
'-----------------------------------------------------------------------


Option Explicit
Option Base 0
```

```
Dim WithEvents serverLink As clsServerSocket

Const PORT As Long = 10001
Const SEP As String = "ÿ" 'ASCII 255
Const PREFIX = "___" 'ASCII 254
Const PING_HDR = PREFIX & "111"
Const CHAT_HDR = PREFIX & "112"

Public sIncoming As String
Dim lPingCount As Long

Private Sub Form_Load()
    Set serverLink = New clsServerSocket
    serverLink.OpenServer PORT
    PrintOut "Server IP Address = " & serverLink.LocalIP
    PrintOut "Server Port = " & serverLink.LocalPort
    Timer1.Interval = 250
    Timer1.Enabled = True
End Sub

Private Sub serverLink_ServerConnectionRequest( _
    ByVal requestID As Long)
    Dim lCount As Long

    lCount = serverLink.OpenConnection(requestID, PORT)
    serverLink.Send lCount, CHAT_HDR & SEP & _
        "This is the server welcome message."
    PrintOut "Accepted new client at " & _
        serverLink.RemoteHostIP & " on port " & _
        serverLink.RemotePort
End Sub

Private Sub serverLink_DataArrival(ByVal link As Long, _
    ByVal bytesTotal As Long, ByVal receiveString As String)
    Dim msgHeader As String
    Dim msgBody As String
    Dim temp As String
    Dim Data As String
    Dim n As Long
    Dim Value As Long
    Dim tokens As Long
```

```
        msgHeader = ParseToken(receiveString, 1, SEP)
        msgBody = Mid$(receiveString, InStr(1, receiveString, SEP) + 1)

        Select Case msgHeader
            Case CHAT_HDR
                PrintOut "Broadcast: " & msgBody
                For n = 0 To 255
                    If serverLink.Connected(n) Then
                        serverLink.Send n, CHAT_HDR & SEP & msgBody
                    End If
                Next n

            Case PING_HDR
                lPingCount = lPingCount + 1
                Value = Val(msgBody)
                serverLink.Send link, PING_HDR & SEP & Value

            Case Else
                PrintOut "Unknown Message: " & receiveString
        End Select
End Sub

Public Sub PrintOut(ByVal msg$)
    txtOutput.Text = Now() & " >  " & msg$ & vbCrLf & _
        txtOutput.Text
End Sub

Public Sub PrintChar(ByVal char$)
    txtOutput.Text = txtOutput.Text & char$
End Sub

Private Sub Timer1_Timer()
    Static last&

    If serverLink.State <> last Then

        Select Case serverLink.State
            Case sckClosed:
                lblStatus = "Socket closed"
            Case sckOpen:
                lblStatus = "Socket open"
```

```vb
            Case sckListening:
                lblStatus = "Listening..."
            Case sckConnectionPending:
                lblStatus = "Connection pending"
            Case sckResolvingHost:
                lblStatus = "Resolving host..."
            Case sckHostResolved:
                lblStatus = "Host resolved"
            Case sckConnecting:
                lblStatus = "Connecting..."
            Case sckConnected:
                lblStatus = "Connected"
            Case sckClosing:
                lblStatus = "Socket closed"
            Case sckError:
                lblStatus = "Error"
        End Select
        last = serverLink.State
    End If
End Sub

Private Sub Form_Unload(Cancel As Integer)
    serverLink.CloseServer
    End
End Sub

Public Function ParseToken(ByVal sWork As String, _
    ByVal lTokenNum As Long, ByVal sDelimiter As String, _
    Optional ByVal sEncapChr As String) As String


    Dim bExitDo As Boolean
    Dim lDPos As Integer
    Dim lSPtr As Integer
    Dim lEPtr As Integer
    Dim lCurrentToken As Integer
    Dim lWorkStrLen As Integer
    Dim lEncapStatus As Integer
    Static lSPos As Integer
    Dim sTemp As String
    Static lDelimitLen As Integer
```

```
lWorkStrLen = Len(sWork)
If Len(sEncapChr) Then
    lEncapStatus = Len(sEncapChr)
End If

'grab the desired token
If lWorkStrLen = 0 Or (lSPos > lWorkStrLen And _
    lTokenNum = 0) Then
    lSPos = 0
    Exit Function
ElseIf lTokenNum > 0 Or lSPos = 0 Then
    lSPos = 1
    lDelimitLen = Len(sDelimiter)
End If

'loop once whether true or not
Do
    lDPos = InStr(lSPos, sWork, sDelimiter)
    If lEncapStatus Then
        lSPtr = InStr(lSPos, sWork, sEncapChr)
        lEPtr = InStr(lSPtr + 1, sWork, sEncapChr)
        If lDPos > lSPtr And lDPos < lEPtr Then
            lDPos = InStr(lEPtr, sWork, sDelimiter)
        End If
    End If

    If lDPos < lSPos Then
        lDPos = lWorkStrLen + lDelimitLen
    End If

    If lDPos Then
        'found the right token?
        If lTokenNum Then
            lCurrentToken = lCurrentToken + 1
            If lCurrentToken = lTokenNum Then
                sTemp = Mid(sWork, lSPos, lDPos - lSPos)
                bExitDo = True
            Else
                bExitDo = False
            End If
```

```
            Else
                sTemp = Mid(sWork, lSPos, lDPos - lSPos)
                bExitDo = True
            End If
            lSPos = lDPos + lDelimitLen
        Else
            lSPos = 0
            bExitDo = True
        End If
    Loop Until bExitDo

    If lEncapStatus Then
        'return desired token
        ParseToken = ReplaceToken(sTemp, sEncapChr, "")
    Else
        'return whole string
        ParseToken = sTemp
    End If

End Function

Private Function ReplaceToken(ByVal sWork As String, _
    ByVal sOld As String, ByVal sNew As String, _
    Optional bUpdated As Boolean) As String

    Dim lOldLen As Long
    Dim lNewLen As Long
    Dim lSPos As Long
    Dim n As Long

    lNewLen = Len(sNew)
    lOldLen = Len(sOld)

    lSPos = 1
    bUpdated = False

    'loop once whether true or not
    Do
        lSPos = InStr(lSPos, sWork, sOld, 0)
        If lSPos Then
            sWork = Left(sWork, lSPos - 1) & sNew & _
```

```
            Mid(sWork, lSPos + 10ldLen)
        lSPos = lSPos + lNewLen
        bUpdated = True
      End If
   Loop While lSPos

   ReplaceToken = sWork
End Function
```

Building the Chat Client

The SocketChat program is a bit more complicated than the SocketServer program because it has a bunch of ActiveX controls that need to be added to the form, so I'll go over the controls with you and explain how to set them all up.

Creating the SocketChat Project

Figure 16.11 shows the main form for the SocketChat program at design time. This should give you an idea how to set up the form.

Table 16.1 lists the ActiveX controls (with their respective properties) that you will need to set after adding the controls to the form.

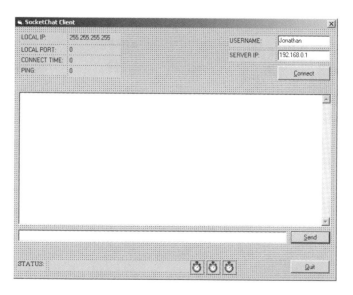

Figure 16.11

The main form of the SocketChat program in the form editor at design time

Table 16.1 SocketChat User Interface Control List

Control Name	Type	Caption/ Text	Position	Dimensions
Label1	Label	LOCAL IP:	12,12	90,17
lblLocalIP	Label	255.255.255.255	108,12	102,17
Label2	Label	LOCAL PORT:	12,36	90,17
lblLocalPort	Label	0	108,36	102,17
Label3	Label	CONNECT TIME:	12,60	90,17
lblConnectTime	Label	0	108,60	102,17
Label4	Label	PING:	12,84	90,17
lblPing	Label	0	108,84	102,17
Label6	Label	USERNAME:	424,12	90,17
txtNickname	TextBox	<username>	520,12	104,21
Label7	Label	SERVER IP:	424,36	90,17
txtConnectTo	TextBox	192.168.0.1	520,36	104,21
cmdConnect	CommandButton	&Connect	520,80	104,26
txtOutput	TextBox	""	8,128	617,255
txtInputLine	TextBox	""	8,388	532,23
cmdSend	CommandButton	&Send	548,388	78,23
Label5	Label	STATUS:	8,446	56,17
lblStatus	Label	""	68,448	463,17
cmdQuit	CommandButton	&Quit	548,448	78,23
clientPing	Timer	N/A	348,444	n/a
timerClient	Timer	N/A	380,444	n/a
timerConnect	Timer	N/S	412,444	n/a

Okay, that's all there is for the SocketChat main form. Note that you do not need to set the Interval property for any of the timers on the form, since it is set inside Form_Load. But you do need to set MultiLine = True for txtOutput so output messages will scroll properly.

The SocketChat program will need to include the following files in order to compile:

- ClientSocket.cls
- Declares.bas
- frmLink.frm

> **TIP**
>
> One final thing that you need to do is set a property of txtOutput to allow scrolling; set MultiLine = True in the Properties window for txtOutput.

The ClientSocket.cls and frmLink.frm files were created earlier in the chapter, but the Declares.bas file is part of the game library, so you can copy it from the Chapter 13 directory where you created the VBGL project (or just copy it directly off the CD-ROM).

SocketChat Source Code

The source code for SocketChat is similar to the code listing for SocketServer, and is made up mostly of events passed back by clientLink (which communicates directly with the Winsock controls). The best way to master the subject is to play with the code. I encourage you to add new types of messages to this program and the SocketServer program that was written earlier in the chapter.

Note that both the client and server programs must understand the types of messages being sent back and forth in order for a new type of message to work. One of the things you will likely notice right away is how easy it is to use the client and server classes that were developed in this chapter. The code is fairly simple, and yet it provides all the functionality you need to create compelling online multiplayer games.

```
'-------------------------------------------------------------------
' Visual Basic Game Programming With DirectX
' Chapter 16 : Multiplayer Programming With Windows Sockets
' SocketChat Source Code File
'-------------------------------------------------------------------

Option Explicit
Option Base 0

'define the ClientSocket class with events
Dim WithEvents clientLink As clsClientSocket
```

```
'define some socket messaging constants
Const PORT As Long = 10001
Const SEP As String = "ÿ" 'ASCII 255
Const PREFIX = "___" 'ASCII 254
Const PING_HDR = PREFIX & "111"
Const CHAT_HDR = PREFIX & "112"

'here are the program variables
Dim lBytesReceived As Long
Dim lBytesSent As Long
Dim lPingCount As Long
Dim lSecondsConnected As Long
Dim lPingStart As Long
Public sIncoming As String

Private Sub Form_Load()
    Set clientLink = New clsClientSocket
    clientLink.RemotePort = PORT
    lblLocalIP.Caption = clientLink.LocalIP
    txtConnectTo.Text = clientLink.LocalIP
    lBytesReceived = 0
    lBytesSent = 0
    Me.Show
    timerClient.Interval = 250
    clientPing.Interval = 1000
    timerConnect.Interval = 1000
    timerClient.Enabled = True
End Sub

Private Sub cmdSend_Click()
    clientPing.Enabled = False
    clientLink.Send CHAT_HDR & SEP & txtNickname.Text & ": " & _
        txtInputLine.Text
    txtInputLine.Text = ""
End Sub

Private Sub cmdQuit_Click()
    clientLink.CloseConnection
    End
End Sub
```

```
    Private Sub cmdConnect_Click()
        If cmdConnect.Caption = "&Connect" Then
            If Len(txtConnectTo.Text) > 0 Then
                clientLink.RemoteHost = txtConnectTo.Text
                clientLink.Connect
                cmdConnect.Caption = "&Close"
                clientPing.Enabled = True
                timerConnect.Enabled = True
            End If
        Else
            clientLink.CloseConnection
            clientPing.Enabled = False
            cmdConnect.Caption = "&Connect"
            lPingCount = 0
            lSecondsConnected = 0
            timerConnect.Enabled = False
        End If
    End Sub

    Private Sub clientLink_DataArrival(ByVal lTotalBytes As Long, _
        ByVal sIncoming As String)
        Dim lPingEnd As Long
        Dim lPingVal As Long
        Dim msgHeader As String
        Dim msgBody As String

        'parse the msg out of the string so data is left
        msgHeader = ParseToken(sIncoming, 1, SEP)
        msgBody = Mid$(sIncoming, InStr(1, sIncoming, SEP) + 1)

        'clear the socket buffer
        If TokenCount(msgBody, SEP) > 0 Then
            msgBody = ParseToken(msgBody, 1, SEP)
        End If

        Select Case msgHeader
            Case CHAT_HDR
                PrintOut msgBody
```

```
            Case PING_HDR
                lPingEnd = CLng(msgBody)
                lPingVal = GetTickCount() - lPingEnd + 1
                lblPing.Caption = lPingVal

        End Select

        'turn the ping back on now that responses have been received
        clientPing.Enabled = True

End Sub

Private Sub timerConnect_Timer()
    lSecondsConnected = lSecondsConnected + 1
    lblConnectTime = lSecondsConnected
End Sub

Private Sub clientPing_Timer()
    lPingStart = GetTickCount()
    clientLink.Send PING_HDR & SEP & lPingStart

End Sub

Private Sub timerClient_Timer()
    Static last As Long

    If clientLink.State <> last Then

        Select Case clientLink.State
            Case sckClosed:
                lblStatus = "Socket closed"
            Case sckOpen:
                lblStatus = "Socket open"
            Case sckListening:
                lblStatus = "Listening..."
            Case sckConnectionPending:
                lblStatus = "Connection pending"
            Case sckResolvingHost:
                lblStatus = "Resolving host..."
            Case sckHostResolved:
                lblStatus = "Host resolved"
```

```vb
            Case sckConnecting:
                lblStatus = "Connecting..."
            Case sckConnected:
                lblStatus = "Connected"
            Case sckClosing:
                lblStatus = "Closing..."
            Case sckError:
                lblStatus = "Error"
                cmdConnect_Click
                timerConnect.Enabled = False
        End Select
        last = clientLink.State
    End If
End Sub


Public Sub PrintOut(ByVal msg$)
    txtOutput.Text = msg$ & vbCrLf & txtOutput.Text
End Sub


Public Sub PrintChar(ByVal char$)
    txtOutput.Text = txtOutput.Text & char$
End Sub


Public Function TokenCount(ByVal sWork As String, _
    ByVal sDelimiter As String) As Long

    Dim n As Long
    Dim lCPos As Long
    Dim lSPos As Long
    Dim lCharLen As Long

    If Len(sWork) = 0 Then Exit Function

    lCharLen = Len(sDelimiter)
    lSPos = 1

    'process loop once whether true or not
    Do
        lCPos = InStr(lSPos, sWork, sDelimiter)
```

```
        If lCPos Then
            n = n + 1
            lSPos = lCharLen + lCPos
        End If
    Loop While lCPos

    If Right(sWork, lCharLen) <> sDelimiter Then
        TokenCount = n + 1
    Else
        TokenCount = n
    End If

End Function

Public Function ParseToken(ByVal sWork As String, _
    ByVal lTokenNum As Long, ByVal sDelimiter As String, _
    Optional ByVal sEncapChr As String) As String

    Dim bExitDo As Boolean
    Dim lDPos As Integer
    Dim lSPtr As Integer
    Dim lEPtr As Integer
    Dim lCurrentToken As Integer
    Dim lWorkStrLen As Integer
    Dim lEncapStatus As Integer
    Static lSPos As Integer
    Dim sTemp As String
    Static lDelimitLen As Integer

    lWorkStrLen = Len(sWork)
    If Len(sEncapChr) Then
        lEncapStatus = Len(sEncapChr)
    End If

    'grab the desired token
    If lWorkStrLen = 0 Or (lSPos > lWorkStrLen And _
        lTokenNum = 0) Then
        lSPos = 0
        Exit Function
```

```
    ElseIf lTokenNum > 0 Or lSPos = 0 Then
        lSPos = 1
        lDelimitLen = Len(sDelimiter)
End If


'loop once whether true or not
Do
    lDPos = InStr(lSPos, sWork, sDelimiter)
    If lEncapStatus Then
        lSPtr = InStr(lSPos, sWork, sEncapChr)
        lEPtr = InStr(lSPtr + 1, sWork, sEncapChr)
        If lDPos > lSPtr And lDPos < lEPtr Then
            lDPos = InStr(lEPtr, sWork, sDelimiter)
        End If
    End It

    If lDPos < lSPos Then
        lDPos = lWorkStrLen + lDelimitLen
    End If

    If lDPos Then
        'found the right token?
        If lTokenNum Then
            lCurrentToken = lCurrentToken + 1
            If lCurrentToken = lTokenNum Then
                sTemp = Mid(sWork, lSPos, lDPos - lSPos)
                bExitDo = True
            Else
                bExitDo = False
            End If
        Else
            sTemp = Mid(sWork, lSPos, lDPos - lSPos)
            bExitDo = True
        End If
        lSPos = lDPos + lDelimitLen
    Else
        lSPos = 0
        bExitDo = True
    End If
Loop Until bExitDo
```

```
        If lEncapStatus Then
            'return desired token
            ParseToken = ReplaceToken(sTemp, sEncapChr, "")
        Else
            'return whole string
            ParseToken = sTemp
        End If

End Function

Private Function ReplaceToken(ByVal sWork As String, _
    ByVal sOld As String, ByVal sNew As String, _
    Optional bUpdated As Boolean) As String

    Dim lOldLen As Long
    Dim lNewLen As Long
    Dim lSPos As Long
    Dim n As Long

    lNewLen = Len(sNew)
    lOldLen = Len(sOld)

    lSPos = 1
    bUpdated = False

    'loop once whether true or not
    Do
        lSPos = InStr(lSPos, sWork, sOld, 0)
        If lSPos Then
            sWork = Left(sWork, lSPos - 1) & sNew & _
                Mid(sWork, lSPos + lOldLen)
            lSPos = lSPos + lNewLen
            bUpdated = True
        End If
    Loop While lSPos

    ReplaceToken = sWork
End Function
```

SUMMARY

Well, that's the end of the socket chapter. I hope you learned a lot about socket programming and gained a solid understanding of the TCP/IP protocol and the Winsock control. There is no substitute for understanding how to program the Winsock API. Although you are using the Winsock control (in order to avoid multithreading issues), the code to program the control is the same as that found in the actual Winsock API. I personally prefer socket programming to DirectPlay, but I must admit that DirectPlay is growing on me.

To decide for yourself, turn the page and move on to the next chapter, where I will give you a crash course in DirectPlay and show you why it might be more enlightening than sockets. You might also want to skip the DirectPlay chapter for now and jump ahead to Chapter 21, "Stellar War: Multiplayer Space Combat Game," which uses DirectDraw and the Winsock code from this chapter to pit players against each other in space.

CHAPTER 17

NETWORK
PROGRAMMING
WITH
DIRECTPLAY

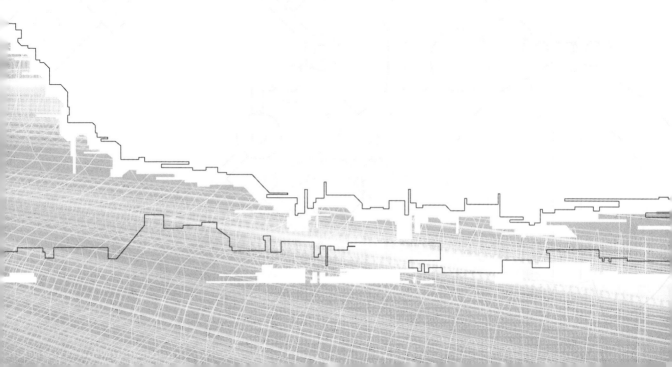

This chapter covers the new version of DirectPlay that was released with DirectX 8.0, with an introduction to the DirectPlay API and a description of the major features available. DirectPlay is an abstract form of socket programming, so much of the material will be familiar if you already read Chapter 16, "Multiplayer Programming with Windows Sockets." In fact, many of the main features of DirectPlay can be traced directly to similar subjects found in the lower-level Windows Sockets API library.

This chapter covers the following topics:

- Introduction to DirectPlay
- Learning about DirectPlay
- Programming DirectPlay

INTRODUCTION TO DIRECTPLAY

For starters, what is DirectPlay? Good question, Jedi Apprentice. Master Yoda might have said, "Like Winsock it is." Here's my version: "DirectPlay is just like Winsock, only different." I realize that there are millions of online gamers who still use a dial-up Internet service provider and a modem. DirectPlay supposedly takes away all the headache associated with dialing a modem and playing a game with a friend. What I wonder, however, is who in the world ever dials up a friend directly to play a game? Are any game developers still including two-player direct-connect modem code…*and why?*

I can't think of any situation where someone who has a 56k modem (or more likely, DSL or cable) would want to dial up their buddy to play a game, one on one. As far as I'm concerned, the modem and serial cable code built into DirectPlay are irrelevant. It's like when you have warp drive—why bother with impulse engines? (Sorry, bit of Star Trek in my past life.) The last big game I can recall that made serious use of serial ports and null modem cables was Blizzard's *StarCraft*, which supported a goofy four-player mode using PCs with dual serial ports and some very funky configurations. That seems like an awful lot of work for a feature that no one is going to use.

So, here's the deal. TCP/IP has taken over the world. Some protocol is likely to come along and eclipse TCP/IP some day. But until that day arrives—which is about as likely as electric cars outselling gasoline-powered cars—let's not waste time on initializing serial ports or dialing modems.

I'm going to completely ignore that material in this chapter and stick to TCP/IP client/server messaging. Doing so will make things like DirectPlay addresses much simpler, because hard-coding the IP header information won't be a problem.

LEARNING ABOUT DIRECTPLAY

The primary function of DirectPlay is to provide a messaging system that isolates your game code from the actual network hardware, software, and protocols. You might recognize many of the concepts presented in this chapter because DirectPlay is based on sockets (as are most Internet-enabled applications).

DirectPlay Protocol

The core of the DirectPlay networking capabilities is the DirectPlay protocol, which abstracts the actual messaging system (covered in Chapter 16, "Multiplayer Programming with Windows Sockets"). The ultimate goal of DirectPlay is to provide a simple means to send messages between linked programs (usually on separate PCs), allowing the programmer to focus on what must be communicated, rather than how it is done.

Message Delivery

Reliable and unreliable delivery is defined on a per-message basis. Reliable messages will be continually re-sent until they are received. Unreliable messages are "fire and forget." Sequential delivery involves sending messages from a queue in the order they were added. Congestion control is another thing that DirectPlay handles automatically. You might recall from the last chapter that Winsock will occasionally become "clogged" and combine packets. At least, this is what happens when you're working with string-based packets. The situation would be much less problematic with byte-based packets (such as those required by DirectPlay). Outgoing messages in DirectPlay are throttled on high-bandwidth connections if the destination cannot process the messages fast enough or if too many messages are being re-sent, to prevent the server from being overwhelmed with too much information from some clients and not enough information from others.

Client/Server Session Topology

Players connect to a central server, which handles all messaging among the players and requires individual players to communicate only with the server. The server handles all aspects of the game interaction, from chat messages to player position. The server handles the game universe, while clients only need to present the user interface.

A Note on Scalability

A client/server game is able to scale from two players to hundreds of players without very much additional effort. The initial investment in time to design and code the client/server core will usually allow the game a lot of flexibility and multiplayer support, if it was designed to handle several players. Usually a game is designed for a fixed number of players, as in the case of a sports game. However, some games are designed to support dozens, hundreds, or even thousands of players. The largest of these games is called *massively multiplayer*. The name alone is impressive enough without even considering the complexity of the subject. But don't confuse *architecture* with *gameplay* when considering the complexity of a game. Often the most enjoyable games are simple 2-D shooters.

Popular Multiplayer Games

The additional dimension that becomes available through online gameplay can increase a game's appeal by orders of magnitude. Such is the case with *Continuum*, a game that was developed by fans of the original *Subspace* game by Interplay. I was a big fan of space exploration and combat games back in the old days of *Star Control* and *StarFlight*. Galactic conquest games like *Master of Orion II* and *Imperium Galactica II* are fun (and I'm looking forward to the sequels!), but usually lose the intrigue of piloting a single ship through space, following whatever storyline or mini-quest happens to be going on in the game at any particular time. *Continuum* takes the space explorer-type game to a new level by allowing thousands of players to interact in the same universe. Visual appeal definitely takes a back seat next to gameplay in *Continuum*, but gameplay is usually all that is needed to keep a game from going the way of most RTS games—the discount bargain shelf.

Massively Multiplayer Online Games

Client/server is currently the best-known method of building massively-multiplayer games, which are further developed by linking multiple servers in a single massive online game universe.

Once a client/server game has shipped, there is the added problem of supporting the game on an ongoing basis, since the server is required for gameplay. Often, a game company alleviates this problem by making the server software available for fans so they can set up their own servers. This is generally only the case for limited-duration games. Massively-multiplayer games usually require a central collection of servers that is maintained by a single company rather than the fans, as in the case of *Ultima Online* and *EverQuest*.

Message Handling

Incoming packets (or messages) are handled by DirectPlay automatically, allowing the programmer to just grab pieces of information and use them on-the-fly, without having to worry too much about how the data is packed into the byte arrays. The important thing is that the information is delivered accurately, and is then easy to manipulate after it has been received. DirectPlay features two useful functions for grabbing data out of incoming packets: `GetStringFromBuffer` and `GetDataFromBuffer`. Basically, any time you need to send numeric data (such as the position of a sprite in your game), you can use `GetDataFromBuffer`, since it is more convenient to use `GetStringFromBuffer` for text messages. Likewise, you can use the `AddStringToBuffer` and `AddDataToBuffer` routines to assemble a packet prior to sending it.

PROGRAMMING DIRECTPLAY

Since the Chapter 16, "Multiplayer Programming with Windows Sockets," already featured a sample client/server chat program, I thought it would be too tedious to build yet another chat program for DirectPlay. However, there is no better way to demonstrate simple messaging—and no better way to teach the subject—than by building a chat program. Like I mentioned in the last chapter, writing a chat program is the online form of the infamous "Hello, World!" program.

DirectPlay is already an abstracted wrapper for the Windows Sockets API (Winsock), so there is no real need for YAWC. (That's short for "Yet Another Wrapper Class.") The DirectPlay message handler is similar to the socket classes I showed you in the last chapter. Sure, there are a whole bunch of events that you won't need, but it's nice to know that there are advanced features available if you want to take advantage of them (such as voice chat).

Figure 17.1 shows the DPChatServer with two clients connected to it, sending messages back and forth. The server allows you to send broadcast messages to the clients as well, without running a separate instance of the client.

The DPChatClient program (shown in Figure 17.2) connects to the server and is then able to send packets of data to and from the server, primarily with chat messages attached. There is an additional packet (other than the chat messages), involving the player count, that is updated when a player joins or leaves the server.

Here is a procedure I wrote for the chat program that assembles a packet of data with a chat message. Both the client and server use a variation of this routine for sending messages.

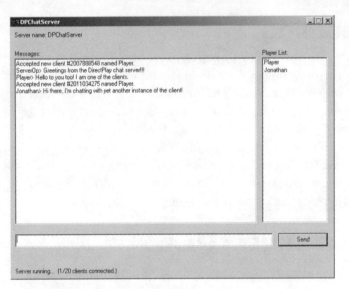

Figure 17.1

The DPChatServer program running with two clients connected

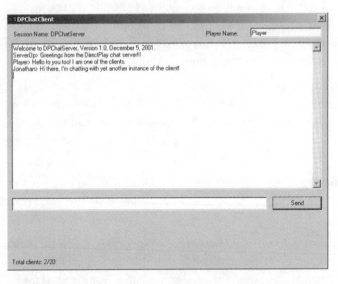

Figure 17.2

The DPChatClient program, showing messages coming in from the server

```
Private Sub SendMsg(ByVal sMsg As String)
    Dim oMsg() As Byte
    Dim lMsg As Long
    Dim lOffset As Long

    'set the message header
    lMsg = CHAT_MSG
```

```
    'create a new message packet
    lOffset = NewBuffer(oMsg)

    'add header to the packet
    AddDataToBuffer oMsg, lMsg, LenB(lMsg), lOffset

    'add chat message to packet
    AddStringToBuffer oMsg, sMsg, lOffset

    'fire off the packet!
    dpc.Send oMsg, 0, DPNSEND_NOLOOPBACK
End Sub
```

The DirectPlay Chat Server

The DirectPlay Chat test program includes a server program called DPChatServer and a client program called DPChatClient. To demonstrate DirectPlay programming, the two programs work together to exchange messages, with each client sending messages directly to the server, and the server broadcasting messages to all the clients. The packets are byte arrays, so the messaging system for DirectPlay is far more efficient than the String-based socket code that was presented in the last chapter (although sockets would run very fast with a byte array). Figure 17.3 shows the design-time form for DPChatServer.

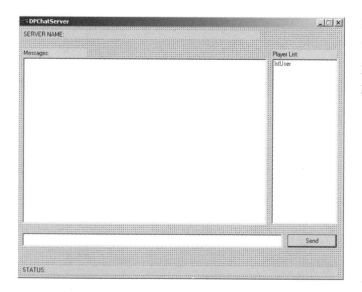

Figure 17.3

The DPChatServer form in the Visual Basic form editor window

The source code for DPChatServer is manageable, considering all that it accomplishes. Thankfully, the server code relies on DirectPlay for most of the hard work in establishing network connections and hosting the chat session.

```
'-------------------------------------------------------------------
' Visual Basic Game Programming With DirectX
' Chapter 17 : Network Programming With DirectPlay
' DPChatServer Source Code File
'-------------------------------------------------------------------


Option Explicit
Option Base 0

Implements DirectPlay8Event

'program constants
Const SERVERNAME As String = "DPChatServer"
Const MAXPLAYERS As Long = 20

'messaging constants
Const CHAT_MSG As Long = 1
Const PLYR_MSG As Long = 2

Private Type SERVER_INFO
    AppGuid As String
    ServiceName As String
    ServiceGuid As String
End Type

'DirectX objects
Dim dx As New DirectX8
Dim dps As DirectPlay8Server
Dim dpa As DirectPlay8Address

'program variables
Dim serverinfo As SERVER_INFO
Dim glNumPlayers As Long
Dim gfStarted As Boolean
Dim mfExit As Boolean
```

```vb
Private Sub Form_Load()
    Dim n As Long
    Dim dpn As DPN_SERVICE_PROVIDER_INFO

    Form1.Show
    lblStatus.Caption = "Initializing the server..."
    DoEvents

    serverinfo.AppGuid = "{5726CF1F-702B-4008-98BC-BF9C95F9E289}"

    'initialize the server object
    Set dps = dx.DirectPlayServerCreate
    Set dpa = dx.DirectPlayAddressCreate

    'start the DirectPlay message handler
    dps.RegisterMessageHandler Me

    'look for a TCP/IP service provider
    For n = 1 To dps.GetCountServiceProviders
        dpn = dps.GetServiceProvider(n)
        If InStr(1, dpn.Name, "TCP/IP") Then
            serverinfo.ServiceName = dpn.Name
            serverinfo.ServiceGuid = dpn.Guid
        End If
    Next

    'see if provider was found
    If InStr(1, serverinfo.ServiceName, "TCP/IP") = 0 Then
        MsgBox "TCP/IP service provider not found!"
        Shutdown
    End If

    lblServerName.Caption = "Server name: " & SERVERNAME
    lblStatus.Caption = "Server not running"

    InitServer

End Sub

Private Sub InitServer()
    Dim AppDesc As DPN_APPLICATION_DESC
    Dim lService As Long
```

```
        If gfStarted Then Exit Sub

        'Now set up the app description
        With AppDesc
            .SessionName = SERVERNAME
            .lMaxPlayers = MAXPLAYERS
            .guidApplication = serverinfo.AppGuid
            .lFlags = DPNSESSION_CLIENT_SERVER
        End With

        'set up service provider
        dpa.SetSP serverinfo.ServiceGuid

        'start the server
        dps.Host AppDesc, dpa

        gfStarted = True
        lblStatus.Caption = "Server running (" & CStr(glNumPlayers) & _
            " / " & MAXPLAYERS & " clients connected)"

End Sub

Private Sub Shutdown()
    'Shut down our message handler
    If Not dps Is Nothing Then dps.UnRegisterMessageHandler
    'Close down our session
    If Not dps Is Nothing Then dps.Close
    Set dps = Nothing
    Set dpa = Nothing
    Set dx = Nothing
    End
End Sub

Private Sub Form_Unload(Cancel As Integer)
    Shutdown
End Sub

Private Sub Form_KeyDown(KeyCode As Integer, Shift As Integer)
    If KeyCode = 27 Then Shutdown
End Sub
```

```
    Private Sub SendPlayerCount()
        Dim oBuf() As Byte
        Dim lMsg As Long
        Dim lOffset As Long

        'send player count to all clients
        lOffset = NewBuffer(oBuf)
        lMsg = PLYR_MSG
        AddDataToBuffer oBuf, lMsg, LenB(lMsg), lOffset
        AddDataToBuffer oBuf, glNumPlayers, LenB(glNumPlayers), lOffset
        AddDataToBuffer oBuf, MAXPLAYERS, SIZE_LONG, lOffset
        dps.SendTo DPNID_ALL_PLAYERS_GROUP, oBuf, 0, DPNSEND_NOLOOPBACK
    End Sub

    Private Sub cmdBroadcast_Click()
        PrintOut "ServerOp> " & txtChat.Text
        Broadcast "ServerOp> " & txtChat.Text
        txtChat.Text = ""
    End Sub

    Private Sub Broadcast(ByVal sMsg As String)
        Dim oMsg() As Byte
        Dim lMsg As Long
        Dim lOffset As Long

        'set the message header
        lMsg = CHAT_MSG

        'create a new message packet
        lOffset = NewBuffer(oMsg)

        'add header to the packet
        AddDataToBuffer oMsg, lMsg, LenB(lMsg), lOffset

        'add chat message to packet
        AddStringToBuffer oMsg, sMsg, lOffset

        'fire off the packet!
        dps.SendTo DPNID_ALL_PLAYERS_GROUP, oMsg, 0, DPNSEND_NOLOOPBACK
    End Sub
```

```vb
Private Sub SendTo(ByVal lPlayer As Long, ByVal sMsg As String)
    Dim oMsg() As Byte
    Dim lMsg As Long
    Dim lOffset As Long

    'set the message header
    lMsg = CHAT_MSG

    'create a new message packet
    lOffset = NewBuffer(oMsg)

    'add header to the packet
    AddDataToBuffer oMsg, lMsg, LenB(lMsg), lOffset

    'add chat message to packet
    AddStringToBuffer oMsg, sMsg, lOffset

    'fire off the packet!
    dps.SendTo lPlayer, oMsg, 0, DPNSEND_NOLOOPBACK
End Sub

Private Sub DirectPlay8Event_CreatePlayer(ByVal lPlayerID As Long, _
    fRejectMsg As Boolean)
    On Error Resume Next
    Dim dpPeer As DPN_PLAYER_INFO

    'try to retrieve new player info
    dpPeer = dps.GetClientInfo(lPlayerID)
    'if this is local player, just exit
    If Err Then Exit Sub

    glNumPlayers = glNumPlayers + 1
    lblStatus.Caption = "Server running: (" & CStr(glNumPlayers) & _
        " / " & MAXPLAYERS & " connections)"

    'add this player to the list
    lstUser.AddItem dpPeer.Name
    lstUser.ItemData(lstUser.ListCount - 1) = lPlayerID

    'display local message
    PrintOut "Accepted new client #" & lPlayerID & " named " & _
        dpPeer.Name & "."
```

```
    'send the server welcome message
    SendTo lPlayerID, "Welcome to DPChatServer, Version 1.0, " & _
        "December 5, 2001."

    'update all clients with player count
    SendPlayerCount
End Sub

Private Sub DirectPlay8Event_DestroyPlayer(ByVal lPlayerID As Long, _
    ByVal lReason As Long, fRejectMsg As Boolean)
    Dim lCount As Long
    For lCount = lstUser.ListCount - 1 To 0 Step -1
        'remove this player from the list
        If lstUser.ItemData(lCount) = lPlayerID Then
            lstUser.RemoveItem lCount
        End If
    Next
    glNumPlayers = glNumPlayers - 1
    lblStatus.Caption = "Server running...  (" & CStr(glNumPlayers) & _
        "/" & MAXPLAYERS & " clients connected.)"
    SendPlayerCount
End Sub

Private Sub DirectPlay8Event_Receive(dpnotify As DxVBLibA.DPNMSG_RECEIVE, _
    fRejectMsg As Boolean)
    Dim oNewMsg() As Byte
    Dim sTemp As String
    Dim lOffset As Long
    Dim lMsg As Long

    'incoming message received!
    With dpnotify
        GetDataFromBuffer .ReceivedData, lMsg, LenB(lMsg), lOffset
        Debug.Print "Received msg # " & lMsg

        Select Case lMsg
            Case CHAT_MSG
                'retrieve chat message
                sTemp = GetStringFromBuffer(.ReceivedData, lOffset)
                PrintOut sTemp
```

```
                'assemble new packet
                lOffset = NewBuffer(oNewMsg)
                AddDataToBuffer oNewMsg, lMsg, LenB(lMsg), lOffset
                AddStringToBuffer oNewMsg, sTemp, lOffset
                'send the chat message on to all clients
                dps.SendTo DPNID_ALL_PLAYERS_GROUP, oNewMsg, 0, _
                    DPNSEND_NOLOOPBACK
        End Select
    End With
End Sub


Private Sub PrintOut(ByVal sMsg As String)
    txtOutput.Text = txtOutput.Text & sMsg & vbCrLf
End Sub


Private Sub DirectPlay8Event_SendComplete(dpnotify As _
    DxVBLibA.DPNMSG_SEND_COMPLETE, fRejectMsg As Boolean)
End Sub


Private Sub DirectPlay8Event_TerminateSession(dpnotify As _
    DxVBLibA.DPNMSG_TERMINATE_SESSION, fRejectMsg As Boolean)
End Sub


Private Sub DirectPlay8Event_AddRemovePlayerGroup( _
    ByVal lMsgID As Long, ByVal lPlayerID As Long, _
    ByVal lGroupID As Long, fRejectMsg As Boolean)
End Sub


Private Sub DirectPlay8Event_AppDesc(fRejectMsg As Boolean)
End Sub


Private Sub DirectPlay8Event_AsyncOpComplete( _
    dpnotify As DxVBLibA.DPNMSG_ASYNC_OP_COMPLETE, _
    fRejectMsg As Boolean)
End Sub


Private Sub DirectPlay8Event_ConnectComplete( _
    dpnotify As DxVBLibA.DPNMSG_CONNECT_COMPLETE, _
    fRejectMsg As Boolean)
End Sub
```

```
Private Sub DirectPlay8Event_CreateGroup( _
    ByVal lGroupID As Long, ByVal lOwnerID As Long, _
    fRejectMsg As Boolean)
End Sub

Private Sub DirectPlay8Event_EnumHostsQuery( _
    dpnotify As DxVBLibA.DPNMSG_ENUM_HOSTS_QUERY, _
    fRejectMsg As Boolean)
End Sub

Private Sub DirectPlay8Event_EnumHostsResponse( _
    dpnotify As DxVBLibA.DPNMSG_ENUM_HOSTS_RESPONSE, _
    fRejectMsg As Boolean)
End Sub

Private Sub DirectPlay8Event_HostMigrate( _
    ByVal lNewHostID As Long, fRejectMsg As Boolean)
End Sub

Private Sub DirectPlay8Event_IndicateConnect( _
    dpnotify As DxVBLibA.DPNMSG_INDICATE_CONNECT, _
    fRejectMsg As Boolean)
End Sub

Private Sub DirectPlay8Event_IndicatedConnectAborted( _
    fRejectMsg As Boolean)
End Sub

Private Sub DirectPlay8Event_InfoNotify(ByVal lMsgID As Long, _
    ByVal lNotifyID As Long, fRejectMsg As Boolean)
End Sub

Private Sub DirectPlay8Event_DestroyGroup( _
    ByVal lGroupID As Long, ByVal lReason As Long, _
    fRejectMsg As Boolean)
End Sub
```

The DirectPlay Chat Client

The DPChatClient is far more complicated than the server, which is ironic because it is much more difficult to locate and connect to a server than it is for a server to just sit there and wait for a connection.

The DPChatClient Main Form

The primary task of the client program is to connect to the server. After that is accomplished, it is just a matter of sending and receiving packets of data back and forth with the server—basically, grunt work. Figure 17.4 shows the main form for the chat client program as it appears in the Visual Basic IDE.

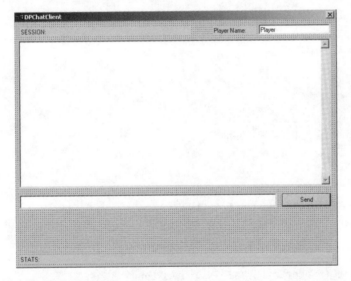

Figure 17.4

The main form for the DPChatClient program, as it appears in the Visual Basic IDE

The source code for DPChatClient is listed in the following pages. Simply type the code into the code window for Form1.

```
'-------------------------------------------------------------------------
' Visual Basic Game Programming With DirectX
' Chapter 17 : Network Programming With DirectPlay
' DPChatClient Source Code File
'-------------------------------------------------------------------------

Option Explicit
Option Base 0
```

```vb
Implements DirectPlay8Event

'program constants
Const MAXPLAYERS As Long = 20

'messaging constants
Const CHAT_MSG As Long = 1
Const PLYR_MSG As Long = 2

Private Type CLIENT_INFO
    AppGuid As String
    ServiceName As String
    ServiceGuid As String
End Type

'DirectX objects
Dim dx As New DirectX8
Dim dpc As DirectPlay8Client
Dim frm As DPlayConnect

Private mfCanUnload As Boolean

'program variables
Private clientinfo As CLIENT_INFO

Private Sub Form_KeyDown(KeyCode As Integer, Shift As Integer)
    If KeyCode = 27 Then Shutdown
End Sub

Private Sub Form_Load()
    Dim dpn As DPN_SERVICE_PROVIDER_INFO
    Dim n As Long

    'the guid should be the same on both client and server
    clientinfo.AppGuid = "{5726CF1F-702B-4008-98BC-BF9C95F9E289}"

    'initialize DirectPlay client object
    Set dpc = dx.DirectPlayClientCreate

    Set frm = New DPlayConnect
```

```vb
        'First lets get the dplay connection started
        If Not frm.StartWizard(dx, dpc, clientinfo.AppGuid, _
            MAXPLAYERS, Me) Then
            Shutdown
        End If

End Sub

Public Sub Shutdown()
        'Stop our message handler
        dpc.UnRegisterMessageHandler

        'Close down our session
        dpc.Close

        Set dpc = Nothing
        Set dx = Nothing

        'Get rid of our message pump
        frm.GoUnload

        End
End Sub

Private Sub Form_Unload(Cancel As Integer)
        Shutdown
End Sub

Private Sub cmdSend_Click()
        SendMsg txtUserName.Text & "> " & txtChat.Text
        txtChat.Text = ""
End Sub

Private Sub SendMsg(ByVal sMsg As String)
        Dim oMsg() As Byte
        Dim lMsg As Long
        Dim lOffset As Long

        'set the message header
        lMsg = CHAT_MSG
```

```
    'create a new message packet
    lOffset = NewBuffer(oMsg)

    'add header to the packet
    AddDataToBuffer oMsg, lMsg, LenB(lMsg), lOffset

    'add chat message to packet
    AddStringToBuffer oMsg, sMsg, lOffset

    'fire off the packet!
    dpc.Send oMsg, 0, DPNSEND_NOLOOPBACK
End Sub

Private Sub DirectPlay8Event_ConnectComplete( _
    dpnotify As DxVBLibA.DPNMSG_CONNECT_COMPLETE, _
    fRejectMsg As Boolean)
    Dim AppDesc As DPN_APPLICATION_DESC

    If dpnotify.hResultCode <> 0 Then
        MsgBox "Error establishing connection!"
        Shutdown
    Else
        AppDesc = dpc.GetApplicationDesc(0)
        lblSession = "Session Name: " & AppDesc.SessionName
        lblStats.Caption = "Total clients: " & _
            CStr(AppDesc.lCurrentPlayers) & "/" & _
            CStr(AppDesc.lMaxPlayers)
    End If
End Sub

Private Sub DirectPlay8Event_Receive( _
    dpnotify As DxVBLibA.DPNMSG_RECEIVE, _
    fRejectMsg As Boolean)
    Dim sPlayer As String
    Dim sTemp As String
    Dim lOffset As Long
    Dim lMsg As Long
    Dim lNum As Long
    Dim lMax As Long
```

```
            'incoming message received!
            With dpnotify
                'check the message header
                GetDataFromBuffer .ReceivedData, lMsg, LenB(lMsg), lOffset

                'determine the message type
                Select Case lMsg
                    'chat message
                    Case CHAT_MSG
                        sTemp = GetStringFromBuffer(.ReceivedData, lOffset)
                        PrintOut sTemp

                    'player count message
                    Case PLYR_MSG
                        GetDataFromBuffer .ReceivedData, lNum, _
                            LenB(lNum), lOffset
                        GetDataFromBuffer .ReceivedData, lMax, _
                            LenB(lMax), lOffset
                        lblStats.Caption = "Total clients: " & _
                            CStr(lNum) & "/" & CStr(lMax)
                End Select
            End With
    End Sub

    Private Sub PrintOut(ByVal sMsg As String)
        txtOutput.Text = txtOutput.Text & sMsg & vbCrLf
    End Sub

    Private Sub DirectPlay8Event_TerminateSession( _
        dpnotify As DxVBLibA.DPNMSG_TERMINATE_SESSION, _
        fRejectMsg As Boolean)
        If dpnotify.hResultCode = DPNERR_HOSTTERMINATEDSESSION Then
            MsgBox "The server has terminated the session."
        Else
            MsgBox "The session has been lost."
        End If
        Shutdown
    End Sub

    Private Sub DirectPlay8Event_SendComplete( _
        dpnotify As DxVBLibA.DPNMSG_SEND_COMPLETE, fRejectMsg As Boolean)
    End Sub
```

```
Private Sub DirectPlay8Event_AddRemovePlayerGroup( _
    ByVal lMsgID As Long, ByVal lPlayerID As Long, _
    ByVal lGroupID As Long, fRejectMsg As Boolean)
End Sub

Private Sub DirectPlay8Event_AppDesc(fRejectMsg As Boolean)
End Sub

Private Sub DirectPlay8Event_AsyncOpComplete( _
    dpnotify As DxVBLibA.DPNMSG_ASYNC_OP_COMPLETE, _
    fRejectMsg As Boolean)
End Sub

Private Sub DirectPlay8Event_CreateGroup(ByVal lGroupID As Long, _
    ByVal lOwnerID As Long, fRejectMsg As Boolean)
End Sub

Private Sub DirectPlay8Event_CreatePlayer( _
    ByVal lPlayerID As Long, fRejectMsg As Boolean)
End Sub

Private Sub DirectPlay8Event_DestroyGroup(ByVal lGroupID As Long, _
    ByVal lReason As Long, fRejectMsg As Boolean)
End Sub

Private Sub DirectPlay8Event_DestroyPlayer(ByVal lPlayerID As Long, _
    ByVal lReason As Long, fRejectMsg As Boolean)
End Sub

Private Sub DirectPlay8Event_EnumHostsQuery( _
    dpnotify As DxVBLibA.DPNMSG_ENUM_HOSTS_QUERY, _
    fRejectMsg As Boolean)
End Sub

Private Sub DirectPlay8Event_EnumHostsResponse( _
    dpnotify As DxVBLibA.DPNMSG_ENUM_HOSTS_RESPONSE, _
    fRejectMsg As Boolean)
End Sub

Private Sub DirectPlay8Event_HostMigrate(ByVal lNewHostID As Long, _
    fRejectMsg As Boolean)
End Sub
```

```
Private Sub DirectPlay8Event_IndicateConnect( _
    dpnotify As DxVBLibA.DPNMSG_INDICATE_CONNECT, _
    fRejectMsg As Boolean)
End Sub

 Private Sub DirectPlay8Event_IndicatedConnectAborted( _
    fRejectMsg As Boolean)
End Sub

 Private Sub DirectPlay8Event_InfoNotify(ByVal lMsgID As Long, _
    ByVal lNotifyID As Long, fRejectMsg As Boolean)
End Sub
```

The DPChatClient Connection Form

When the DPChatClient program starts running, the connection form appears, allowing you to type in an IP address for the server. The program then searches that address for any active sessions and displays them in the ListBox, as shown in Figure 17.5.

Figure 17.6 shows the DPlayConnect form at design-time. Note that there isn't much to this form, other than a couple buttons, a ListBox, and a timer.

Figure 17.5

The connection form allows you to select the session on the server before making the connection.

Figure 17.6

The DPlayConnect form searches for available sessions on the server.

Here is the source code for the DPlayConnect form's code window. Remember that all of the DirectPlay8Event routines must be present in the program, even though many are not even used.

```
'----------------------------------------------------------------------
' Visual Basic Game Programming With DirectX
' Chapter 17 : Network Programming With DirectPlay
' DPlayConnect Source Code File
'----------------------------------------------------------------------


Option Explicit
Option Base 0


Implements DirectPlay8Event


'Host expire threshold constant
Private Const HOST_EXPIRE_THRESHHOLD As Long = 2000


Private Type HostFound
    AppDesc As DPN_APPLICATION_DESC
    Address As String
    TimeLastFound As Long
End Type


Private Enum SearchingButton
    StartSearch
    StopSearch
End Enum


'Internal DirectX variables
Private moDPC As DirectPlay8Client
Private moDPA As DirectPlay8Address
Private moDX As DirectX8
Private moCallback As DirectPlay8Event
Private moDPN As DPN_SERVICE_PROVIDER_INFO


'App specific vars
Private msGuid As String
Private sUser As String
Private mlSearch As SearchingButton
Private sGameName As String
Private mlMax As Long
```

```
Private mlNumPlayers As Long
Private mfComplete As Boolean
Private mfHost As Boolean
Private mlEnumAsync As Long
Private mfGotEvent As Boolean
Private mfDoneWiz As Boolean

Private mfCanUnload As Boolean

'We need to keep track of the hosts we get
Private moHosts() As HostFound
Private mlHostCount As Long

'Declaration for our API
Private mfDoneEnum As Boolean
Private mfConnectComplete As Boolean

Public Function StartWizard(ByRef oDX As DirectX8, _
    ByRef oDPC As DirectPlay8Client, ByVal sGuid As String, _
    ByVal lMaxPlayers As Long, _
    ByRef oCallback As DirectPlay8Event) As Boolean

    Dim lCount As Long

    'Now we can start our connection
    mfCanUnload = False
    mlSearch = StartSearch
    mlHostCount = -1

    'First we need to keep track of our Peer Object, and app guid
    Set moDX = oDX
    Set moCallback = oCallback
    msGuid = sGuid
    mlMax = lMaxPlayers

    'start the DirectPlay message handler
    Set moDPC = oDPC
    moDPC.RegisterMessageHandler Me

    'look for a TCP/IP service provider
    For lCount = 1 To moDPC.GetCountServiceProviders
```

```
        moDPN = moDPC.GetServiceProvider(lCount)
        If InStr(1, moDPN.Name, "TCP/IP") Then Exit For
    Next

    'see if provider was found
    If InStr(1, moDPN.Name, "TCP/IP") = 0 Then
        MsgBox "TCP/IP service provider not found!"
        StartWizard = False
        Exit Function
    End If

    sUser = Form1.txtUserName.Text

    'Set up the address
    Set moDPA = moDX.DirectPlayAddressCreate

    moDPA.SetSP moDPN.Guid

    'Init the register handler here
    RegisterThisApp sGuid

    'Show this screen
    Me.Show

    Do While Not mfDoneWiz
        DoSleep 5
    Loop

    'Now we can return our success (or failure)
    StartWizard = mfComplete
End Function

Public Sub DoSleep(Optional ByVal lMilliSec As Long = 0)
    Sleep lMilliSec
    DoEvents
End Sub

Private Sub cmdJoin_Click()
    Dim HostAddr As DirectPlay8Address
    Dim dpApp As DPN_APPLICATION_DESC
```

```
'You must select a game before you try to join one
If lstGames.ListIndex < 0 Then
    MsgBox "You must first select a game from the list to join.", _
        vbOKOnly Or vbInformation, "Select game."
    Exit Sub
End If

'We no longer need to Enum since we're connecting now
If mlEnumAsync <> 0 Then cmdRefresh_Click

'Lets join the game
Dim pInfo As DPN_PLAYER_INFO
'Set up my peer info
pInfo.Name = sUser
pInfo.lInfoFlags = DPNINFO_NAME

moDPC.SetClientInfo pInfo, DPNOP_SYNC
mfDoneEnum = True

With moHosts(lstGames.ItemData(lstGames.ListIndex)).AppDesc
    dpApp.guidApplication = .guidApplication
    dpApp.guidInstance = .guidInstance
    mlNumPlayers = .lMaxPlayers
End With

mfGotEvent = False
mfConnectComplete = False
'Lets get our host address
Set HostAddr = moDX.DirectPlayAddressCreate
HostAddr.BuildFromURL moHosts(lstGames.ItemData( _
    lstGames.ListIndex)).Address

'Now we can join the selected session
moDPC.Connect dpApp, HostAddr, moDPA, 0, ByVal 0&, 0

Do While Not mfGotEvent
    DoSleep 5
Loop
If mfConnectComplete Then
    'We've joined our game
    mfComplete = True
```

```vb
            mfHost = False
            'Clean up our address
            Set moDPA = Nothing
            Unload Me
        End If
End Sub


Private Sub cmdRefresh_Click()
    Dim Desc As DPN_APPLICATION_DESC
    Dim dph As DirectPlay8Address

    If mlSearch = StartSearch Then
        'Time to enum our hosts
        mfDoneEnum = False

        Desc.guidApplication = msGuid

        Set dph = moDX.DirectPlayAddressCreate

        dph.SetSP moDPN.Guid

        mlEnumAsync = moDPC.EnumHosts( _
            Desc, dph, moDPA, INFINITE, 0, INFINITE, _
            DPNENUMHOSTS_OKTOQUERYFORADDRESSING, ByVal 0&, 0)

        cmdRefresh.Caption = "Stop Search"
        mlSearch = StopSearch

    ElseIf mlSearch = StopSearch Then
        mfDoneEnum = True

        If mlEnumAsync <> 0 Then _
            moDPC.CancelAsyncOperation mlEnumAsync, 0

        cmdRefresh.Caption = "Start Search"
        mlSearch = StartSearch
    End If
End Sub


Private Sub AddHostsToListBox(oHost As DPNMSG_ENUM_HOSTS_RESPONSE)
    Dim lFound As Long
```

```
If mfDoneEnum Then Exit Sub
If mlHostCount = -1 Then
    'clear the list and add this one to the list.
    lstGames.Clear
    ReDim moHosts(0)
    moHosts(0).AppDesc = oHost.ApplicationDescription
    moHosts(0).Address = oHost.AddressSenderUrl
    'Save the last time this host was found
    moHosts(0).TimeLastFound = GetTickCount
    With oHost.ApplicationDescription
        lstGames.AddItem .SessionName & " - " & _
        CStr(.lCurrentPlayers) & "/" & CStr(.lMaxPlayers) & _
        " - Latency:" & CStr(oHost.lRoundTripLatencyMS) & " ms"
    End With
    lstGames.ItemData(0) = 0
    mlHostCount = mlHostCount + 1
Else
    Dim lCount As Long
    Dim fFound As Boolean

    For lCount = 0 To mlHostCount
        If moHosts(lCount).AppDesc.guidInstance = _
            oHost.ApplicationDescription.guidInstance Then
            'Save the last time this host was found
            moHosts(lCount).TimeLastFound = GetTickCount
            fFound = True
            Exit For
        End If
    Next

    If Not fFound Then 'We need to add this to the list
        ReDim Preserve moHosts(mlHostCount + 1)
        moHosts(mlHostCount + 1).AppDesc = _
            oHost.ApplicationDescription
        moHosts(mlHostCount + 1).Address = _
            oHost.AddressSenderUrl
        With oHost.ApplicationDescription
            lstGames.AddItem .SessionName & " - " & _
            CStr(.lCurrentPlayers) & "/" & CStr(.lMaxPlayers) & _
            " - Latency:" & CStr(oHost.lRoundTripLatencyMS) & " ms"
        End With
```

```vb
                    'Save the last time this host was found
                    moHosts(mlHostCount + 1).TimeLastFound = GetTickCount
                    lstGames.ItemData(lstGames.ListCount - 1) = mlHostCount + 1
                    mlHostCount = mlHostCount + 1
                Else 'We did find it, update the list
                    For lFound = 0 To lstGames.ListCount - 1
                        With oHost.ApplicationDescription
                        If lstGames.ItemData(lFound) = lCount Then
                            lstGames.List(lFound) = .SessionName & " - " & _
                            CStr(.lCurrentPlayers) & "/" & _
                            CStr(.lMaxPlayers) & " - Latency:" & _
                            CStr(oHost.lRoundTripLatencyMS) & " ms"
                        End If
                        End With
                    Next
                End If
        End If
    End If
End Sub

Private Sub Form_QueryUnload(Cancel As Integer, UnloadMode As Integer)
    If Not mfCanUnload Then Cancel = 1
    Me.Hide
    mfDoneWiz = True
End Sub

Private Sub Form_Unload(Cancel As Integer)
    'Clean up our address
    Set moDPA = Nothing
End Sub

Private Sub lstGames_DblClick()
    cmdJoin_Click
End Sub

Public Property Get IsHost() As Boolean
    IsHost = mfHost
End Property

Public Property Get SessionName() As String
    SessionName = sGameName
End Property
```

```vb
Public Property Get UserName() As String
    UserName = sUser
End Property

Public Sub GoUnload()
    tmrExpire.Enabled = False
    mfCanUnload = True
    Unload Me
End Sub

Public Sub RegisterCallback(oCallback As DirectPlay8Event)
    Set moCallback = oCallback
End Sub

Public Property Get NumPlayers() As Long
    NumPlayers = mlNumPlayers
End Property

Private Sub RegisterThisApp(sGuid As String)
    Dim dplProg As DPL_PROGRAM_DESC
    'register the program
    With dplProg
        .ApplicationName = App.EXEName
        .Description = "VB DirectPlay SDK Sample"
        .ExecutableFilename = App.EXEName & ".exe"
        .ExecutablePath = App.Path
        .LauncherFilename = App.EXEName & ".exe"
        .LauncherPath = App.Path
        .guidApplication = sGuid
    End With
End Sub

Private Sub tmrExpire_Timer()
    'periodically expire the hosts
    Dim lCount As Long, lIndex As Long
    Dim lInner As Long

    'if there are no hosts, just exit
    On Error GoTo LeaveSub
```

```
    For lCount = 0 To UBound(moHosts)
        If (GetTickCount - moHosts(lCount).TimeLastFound) > _
            HOST_EXPIRE_THRESHHOLD Then
            'remove expired user from the list
            For lIndex = lstGames.ListCount - 1 To 0 Step -1
                If lstGames.ItemData(lIndex) = lCount Then
                    lstGames.RemoveItem lIndex
                End If
            Next
            moHosts(lCount).Address = vbNullString
            'remove all of the old info
            For lInner = lCount + 1 To UBound(moHosts)
                moHosts(lInner - 1).Address = moHosts(lInner).Address
                moHosts(lInner - 1).AppDesc = moHosts(lInner).AppDesc
                moHosts(lInner - 1).TimeLastFound = _
                    moHosts(lInner).TimeLastFound
            Next
            'decrement each of the remaining items in the listbox
            For lIndex = lstGames.ListCount - 1 To 0 Step -1
                If lstGames.ItemData(lIndex) > lCount Then
                    lstGames.ItemData(lIndex) = _
                        lstGames.ItemData(lIndex) - 1
                End If
            Next
            mlHostCount = mlHostCount - 1
            If UBound(moHosts) > 0 Then
                ReDim Preserve moHosts(UBound(moHosts) - 1)
            Else
                Erase moHosts
            End If
        End If
    Next
LeaveSub:
End Sub

Private Sub DirectPlay8Event_AddRemovePlayerGroup( _
    ByVal lMsgID As Long, ByVal lPlayerID As Long, _
    ByVal lGroupID As Long, fRejectMsg As Boolean)
    moCallback.AddRemovePlayerGroup lMsgID, lPlayerID, _
        lGroupID, fRejectMsg
End Sub
```

```vb
Private Sub DirectPlay8Event_AppDesc(fRejectMsg As Boolean)
    moCallback.AppDesc fRejectMsg
End Sub

Private Sub DirectPlay8Event_AsyncOpComplete( _
    dpnotify As DxVBLibA.DPNMSG_ASYNC_OP_COMPLETE, _
    fRejectMsg As Boolean)
    If dpnotify.AsyncOpHandle = mlEnumAsync Then _
        mlEnumAsync = 0
    moCallback.AsyncOpComplete dpnotify, fRejectMsg
End Sub

Private Sub DirectPlay8Event_ConnectComplete( _
    dpnotify As DxVBLibA.DPNMSG_CONNECT_COMPLETE, _
    fRejectMsg As Boolean)
    mfGotEvent = True
    If dpnotify.hResultCode = DPNERR_SESSIONFULL Then
        MsgBox "The server is full!"
    Else
        mfConnectComplete = True
        moCallback.ConnectComplete dpnotify, fRejectMsg
    End If
End Sub

Private Sub DirectPlay8Event_EnumHostsResponse( _
    dpnotify As DxVBLibA.DPNMSG_ENUM_HOSTS_RESPONSE, _
    fRejectMsg As Boolean)
    'add this to the list
    AddHostsToListBox dpnotify
    moCallback.EnumHostsResponse dpnotify, fRejectMsg
End Sub

Private Sub DirectPlay8Event_CreateGroup( _
    ByVal lGroupID As Long, ByVal lOwnerID As Long, _
    fRejectMsg As Boolean)
    moCallback.CreateGroup lGroupID, lOwnerID, fRejectMsg
End Sub

Private Sub DirectPlay8Event_CreatePlayer( _
    ByVal lPlayerID As Long, fRejectMsg As Boolean)
    moCallback.CreatePlayer lPlayerID, fRejectMsg
End Sub
```

```vb
Private Sub DirectPlay8Event_DestroyGroup( _
    ByVal lGroupID As Long, ByVal lReason As Long, _
    fRejectMsg As Boolean)
    moCallback.DestroyGroup lGroupID, lReason, fRejectMsg
End Sub


Private Sub DirectPlay8Event_DestroyPlayer( _
ByVal lPlayerID As Long, ByVal lReason As Long, _
fRejectMsg As Boolean)
    moCallback.DestroyPlayer lPlayerID, lReason, fRejectMsg
End Sub


Private Sub DirectPlay8Event_EnumHostsQuery( _
    dpnotify As DxVBLibA.DPNMSG_ENUM_HOSTS_QUERY, _
    fRejectMsg As Boolean)
    moCallback.EnumHostsQuery dpnotify, fRejectMsg
End Sub


Private Sub DirectPlay8Event_HostMigrate( _
    ByVal lNewHostID As Long, fRejectMsg As Boolean)
    moCallback.HostMigrate lNewHostID, fRejectMsg
End Sub


Private Sub DirectPlay8Event_IndicateConnect( _
    dpnotify As DxVBLibA.DPNMSG_INDICATE_CONNECT, _
    fRejectMsg As Boolean)
    moCallback.IndicateConnect dpnotify, fRejectMsg
End Sub


Private Sub DirectPlay8Event_IndicatedConnectAborted( _
    fRejectMsg As Boolean)
    moCallback.IndicatedConnectAborted fRejectMsg
End Sub


Private Sub DirectPlay8Event_InfoNotify( _
    ByVal lMsgID As Long, ByVal lNotifyID As Long, _
    fRejectMsg As Boolean)
    moCallback.InfoNotify lMsgID, lNotifyID, fRejectMsg
End Sub
```

```
Private Sub DirectPlay8Event_Receive( _
    dpnotify As DxVBLibA.DPNMSG_RECEIVE, _
    fRejectMsg As Boolean)
    moCallback.Receive dpnotify, fRejectMsg
End Sub

Private Sub DirectPlay8Event_SendComplete( _
    dpnotify As DxVBLibA.DPNMSG_SEND_COMPLETE, _
    fRejectMsg As Boolean)
    moCallback.SendComplete dpnotify, fRejectMsg
End Sub

Private Sub DirectPlay8Event_TerminateSession( _
    dpnotify As DxVBLibA.DPNMSG_TERMINATE_SESSION, _
    fRejectMsg As Boolean)
    moCallback.TerminateSession dpnotify, fRejectMsg
End Sub
```

SUMMARY

Well, that wraps up this quick jaunt into DirectPlay. After working through the socket-based code in the last chapter, this DirectPlay code seems much more refined and useable. Although understanding socket programming is important, there are clear advantages to using DirectPlay, not the least of which is performance. The load-balancing and bandwidth-throttling features alone are worth switching to DirectPlay, if you have been working with sockets for any period of time. DirectPlay is now a modern, streamlined, efficient, and powerful library for building multiplayer games.

CHAPTER 18

EFFECTIVE GAME DESIGN TECHNIQUES

Creating a computer game without at least a minimal design document or collection of notes is like building a plastic model kit of a car or airplane without the instructions. More than likely, a game that is created without the instructions will end up with missing pieces and loose ends. The tendency is always to jump right in and get some code working, and there is room for that step in the development of a new game! However, the initial coding session should be used to build enthusiasm for yourself and any others in the project, and should be nothing more than a proof of concept or an incomplete prototype.

This chapter goes over the software development process for game development, describing the main steps involved in taking a game from inspiration to completion. This is not about creating a hundred-page document with all the screens, menus, characters, settings, and storyline of the game. Rather, this chapter is geared for the programmer, with tips for following a design process that will keep a game in development until it is completed. Without a simple plan, most game programmers will become bored with a game that only weeks before had them up all night with earnest fervor.

Like most creative individuals, game programmers must have the discipline to stick to something before moving on, or they fall into the trap of half-completing a dozen or so games without much to show for the effort. The real difference between a hobbyist and a professional is simply that a professional game programmer will see the game through to completion no matter how long it takes.

This chapter covers the following topics:

- Game Design Basics
- Game Development Phases
- Post-Production
- Future-Proof Design

GAME DESIGN BASICS

I have mentioned several times already (because memory is based on repetition) that Visual Basic is a great language for writing games as long as you understand the limits. There is a world of possibilities with DirectX, but VB is just not suited for extremely demanding games because it is a high-level language.

Obviously, there are exceptions. Pick up the latest processor on the market, along with the fastest memory and video card, and you probably could port a first-person shooter like *Quake III* to Visual Basic. But that should not be your primary goal. The focus of this book is on general-purpose solutions to a variety of games. Why spend all your time on a first-person shooter when there is unlimited potential for writing an entirely new game?

Inspiration

Take a look at classic console games for inspiration and you will have no trouble coming up with an idea for a cool new game. Any time I am bug-eyed and brain-dead from a long coding session, I will take a walk outside and then return for a Dreamcast or Game Boy Advance gaming session (preferably with a friend). Consoles are great because they are usually fast paced and often based on arcade machines.

PC games, on the other hand, can be quite slow and even boring in comparison, because they have so much more depth. If you are in a hurry and just want to have a little fun, go with a console. Video games are full of creativity and interesting technology that PC gamers usually fail to notice.

Game Feasibility

The feasibility of a game is a difficult thing to judge, because so much is possible once you get started, and it is easy to underestimate your own capabilities (especially if you have a few people helping you). One thing that you must be careful about when designing a new game is scope. How big will the game be? You also don't want to bite off more than you can chew, to use the familiar euphemism.

Feasibility is the process of deciding how far you will go with the game, and at what point you will stop adding new features. But at the very least, feasibility is a study of whether the game can be done at all in the first place. Once you are certain that you have the capabilities to create a certain type of game, and you have narrowed the scope of the game to a manageable level, work can begin.

Feature Glut

As a general rule, you should get the game up and running before working on new features (also called "bells and whistles"). Never spend more than a day working on code without testing it! This is critical. Any time you change a major part of the game, you must completely recompile the game and run it to make sure you haven't broken any part of it in the process.

I can't tell you how many times I have thought up a new way to do something and gone through all the source code for a game, making changes here and there, with the result being that the game won't compile. Every change you make during the development of the game should be small and easy to undo if it doesn't work.

My personal preference is to keep the game running throughout the day. Every time I make even a minor change, I test the game to make sure it works before moving on to a new section of code. This is really where object-oriented coding pays off. By moving tried-and-tested code into a class, you are relatively safe in assuming the code works as expected, because you are not modifying it as often. The class files in the Visual Basic Game Library developed in this book are perfect examples.

Once the DirectDraw code was developed back in Chapter 10, "Diving into DirectDraw," there was no longer a need to rewrite the DirectDraw startup code for each new project. Rather, I simply instantiate a new object of the class and start using it. It really helps to eliminate bugs when you have put the startup and shutdown code inside a class, where the class handles these routines automatically. There is also another tremendous benefit to wrapping code inside a class—information overload.

There is a point where we humans simply can't handle any more information, and memory starts to fail. If you try to keep track of too many loose ends in a game you are bound to make a mistake! By putting common code in classes (or in a separate ActiveX DLL altogether) you reduce the amount of information that you must remember. It is such a relief when you need to do something quickly and you realize that all the code is ready to do your bidding at a moment's notice. The alternative (and old-school) method of copying sections of code and pasting them into your project is error prone and will introduce bugs into your game.

Back Up Your Work

Follow this simple advice or learn the hard way: Back up your work several times a day! If you don't, you are going to make a significant change to the game code that completely breaks it and you will not be able to figure out how to get the game back up and running. That is the point where you return to a backup and start again. Even if the backup is a few hours old, it is better than spending half a day figuring out the problem with the changes you made.

I have an informal method of backing up my work. I use an archive program to ZIP the entire project directory for a game—including all the graphics, sounds, and source code—into a file with the date and time stamped into the filename, like this: Game_071502_1030.zip.

The backup file might be huge, but what is disk space today? Now, you don't always need to back up the entire project directory if you haven't made any changes to the graphics or sound files for the game (which can be quite large). If you are working on source code for days at a time without making any changes to media files, you might just make a complete backup once a day, and then make smaller backups during the day for code changes. As a general rule, I don't use the incremental backup feature available with many compression programs, because I prefer to create an entirely new backup file each time.

If you get into the habit of backing up your files every hour or two, you will not be faced with the nightmare of losing a whole day's work if you mess up the source code or if something happens to your hard drive. For this reason, I recommend that you copy all backup files directly to CD (using packet-writing technology, which provides drag-drop capability from Windows Explorer) or ZIP disk. CD-RW drives are very affordable and are indispensable when it comes to saving your work. While most PCs have a CD-ROM drive capable of reading a CD-RW, few PCs have a ZIP drive (although ZIP disks are more reliable than CD-RWs).

In the end, how much is your time worth? Making regular backups is the smart thing to do.

Game Genres

The gaming press seems to differentiate between console and PC games, but the line that separates the two is diminishing as games are ported back and forth. I tend to group console and PC games together in shared genres, although some genres do not work well on both platforms. Following is a list of game genres, with a description of each and a list of sample games within that genre. It is important to consider the target genre for your game, because this affects your target audience. There are some gamers who are absolutely fanatical about first-person shooters, others who prefer real-time strategy, and so on. It is a good idea to at least identify the type of game you are working on, even if it is a unique game.

Fighting Games

2-D and 3-D fighting games are almost entirely bound to the console market due to the way these games are played. While a PC equipped with a game pad is a fine platform, fighting games really shine on console systems with multiple controllers.

One of my favorite Dreamcast fighting games is called *Power Stone 2*. This game is hilarious! Four players can participate on varied levels in hand-to-hand combat, with numerous obstacles and miscellaneous items strewn about on each level, and the action is fast paced.

Here is a list of my favorite fighting games:

- *Dead or Alive 3*
- *Mortal Kombat*
- *Power Stone 2*
- *Ready 2 Rumble*
- *Soul Calibur*
- *Street Fighter II*

- *Tekken*
- *Virtua Fighter 3*

Action/Arcade Games

Action/arcade games turned the fledgling video game industry into a worldwide phenomenon in the 1980s and 1990s, but started to drop off in popularity in arcades in the 2000s. The action/arcade genre encompasses a huge list of games; here are some of my favorites:

- *Akari Warriors*
- *Blasteroids*
- *Elevator Action*
- *Rolling Thunder*
- *Spy Hunter*
- *Star Control*
- *Super R-Type*
- *Teenage Mutant Ninja Turtles*

Adventure Games

The adventure game genre was once comprised of the largest collection of games in the computer game industry, with blockbuster hits like *King's Quest* and *Space Quest*. Adventure games have fallen out of style in recent years, but there is still an occasional new adventure game that inspires the genre to new heights. My definition of an adventure game might differ from someone else's, but most of the following games can be categorized as adventure games:

- *King's Quest IV*
- *Mean Streets*
- *Myst*
- *Space Quest V*
- *StarFlight III*

First-Person Shooters

The first-person shooter genre is the dominant factor in the gaming industry today, with so many new titles coming out every year that it is easy to overlook some extremely cool games while playing others. This list is by no means complete, but it includes the most common first-person shooters out today:

- *Doom III*
- *Half-Life*

- *HALO: Combat Evolved*
- *Jedi Knight*
- *Max Payne*
- *Return to Castle Wolfenstein*
- *Quake III Arena*
- *Unreal Tournament*
- *Wolfenstein 3-D*

Flight Simulators

Flight simulators (flight sims) are probably the most important types of games in the industry, although they are not always recognized as such. The technology required to render the world, when you think about it, is quite a challenge. The best of the best in flight sims usually push the envelope of realism. Here is my list of favorites, old and new:

- *Aces of the Pacific*
- *B-17 Flying Fortress*
- *Battlehawks 1942*
- *European Air War*
- *Falcon 4.0*
- *Iron Aces*
- *Jane's WWII Fighters*
- *Red Baron*

Galactic Conquest Games

Galactic conquest games have seen varied success at one time or another, with a popular title about once a year. One early success was a game called *Stellar Crusade*, which focused heavily on the economics of running a galactic empire. This might be debatable, but I believe that *Master of Orion* popularized the genre, while *Master of Orion II* perfected it. Even today, *MOO2* (as it is fondly referred to) still holds its own against modern wonders like *Imperium Galactica II*.

- *Imperium Galactica II*
- *Master of Orion 2*
- *Stellar Crusade*

Real-Time Strategy Games

Real-time strategy (RTS) games are second only to first-person shooters in popularity and success, with blockbuster titles selling in the millions. Westwood is generally given kudos for inventing the genre with *Dune II*, although the *Command & Conquer* series gave the genre a lot of mileage.

Warcraft and *Starcraft* (both by Blizzard) were huge in their time, and are still popular today. My personal favorite is *Age of Empires* and the follow-up games in the series. Here are the best RTS games on the market today:

- *Age of Empires II*
- *Dark Reign II*
- *Empire Earth*
- *Homeworld: Cataclysm*
- *MechCommander 2*
- *Real War*
- *Red Alert 2*
- *Starcraft*
- *Star Trek: Armada II*
- *Total Annihilation*

Role-Playing Games

What would the computer industry be without role-playing games? RPGs go back as far as most gamers can remember, with early games like *Ultima* and *Might & Magic* appearing on some of the earliest PCs. *Ultima Online* followed in the tradition of *Meridian 59* as a massively multiplayer online role-playing game (MMORPG), along with *EverQuest* and *Asheron's Call*. Here are some classic favorites:

- *Darkstone*
- *Diablo II*
- *Fallout 2*
- *Final Fantasy X*
- *Grandia II*
- *Might & Magic VII*
- *The Bard's Tale III*
- *Ultima VII*

Sports Simulation Games

Sports sims have long held a strong position in the computer game industry as a mainstay group of products covering all the major sports themes—baseball, football, soccer, basketball, and hockey. Here are some of my favorites:

- *Earl Weaver Baseball*
- *Madden 2001*
- *NBA 2K1*

- *NFL 2K1*
- *NHL 2K*
- *Wayne Gretzky and the NHLPA All-Stars*
- *World Series Baseball 2K1*

Third-Person Shooters

The third-person shooter genre was spawned by first-person shooters with an "over the shoulder" viewpoint. *Tomb Raider* is largely responsible for the popularity of this genre. Here are some favorite third-person shooters:

- *Delta Force*
- *Dino Crisis*
- *Operation: Flashpoint*
- *Rainbow Six*
- *Resident Evil: Code Veronica*
- *Tomb Raider*

Turn-Based Strategy Games

Turn-based strategy (TBS) games have a huge fan following because this genre allows for highly detailed games based on classic board games like *Axis & Allies*. Since TBS games do not run in real time, each player is allowed time to think about his next move, providing for some highly competitive and long-running games. Here is a list of the most popular games in the genre:

- *Alpha Centauri*
- *Axis & Allies*
- *Civilization III*
- *Panzer General III*
- *Shogun: Total War*
- *Steel Panthers III*
- *The Operational Art of War*

Space Simulation Games

Space sims are usually grand in scope and provide a compelling story to follow. Based loosely on movies like *Star Wars*, space sims usually feature a first-person perspective inside the cockpit of a spaceship. Gameplay is similar to that of a flight sim, but with science-fiction themes. Here are a couple of popular space sims:

- *Tachyon: The Fringe*
- *Wing Commander III*

Real-Life Games

Real-life sims are affectionately referred to as *God Games*, although the analogy is not perfect. How do you categorize a game like *Dungeon Keeper*? Peter Molyneux seems to routinely create his own genres. These games usually involve some sort of realistic theme, although it might be based on fictional characters or incidents. Here are some of the most popular real-life games:

- *Black & White*
- *Dungeon Keeper II*
- *Populous: The Beginning*
- *SimCity 3000*
- *The Sims*
- *Tropico*

Massively Multiplayer Online Games

I consider this a genre of its own, although the games herein might be categorized elsewhere. The most popular online games are called MMORPGs—massively multiplayer online role-playing games. This convoluted phrase describes an RPG that you can play online with hundreds or thousands of players—at least, in theory.

- *Anarchy Online*
- *Asheron's Call*
- *Conquest: Frontier Wars*
- *EverQuest*
- *Ultima Online*
- *WWII Online*

GAME DEVELOPMENT PHASES

While there are entire volumes dedicated to software development life cycles and software design, I am going to cover just the basics that you will need to design a game. You might want to go into finer detail with your game designs, or you might want to skip a few steps. It is all a matter of preference. But the important thing is that you at least attempt to document your ideas before you get started on a new game.

Initial Design

The initial design for a game is usually a hand-drawn figure showing what the game screen will look like, with the game's user interface or game elements shown in roughly the right places on the sketched screen. You can also use a program like Visio to create your initial design screens.

The initial design should also include a few pages that contain an overview of the components needed by the game, such as the DirectX components or any third-party software libraries. You should include a description of how the game will be played, what forms of user input will be supported, and how the graphics will be rendered (in 2-D or 3-D).

Game Engine

Once you have an initial design for the game down on paper, you can get started on the game engine. This will usually be the most complicated core component of the game, including the graphics renderer.

In the case of a 2-D sprite-based game, the game engine will be a simple game loop with a double buffer, a static or rendered background, and a few sprites moving around for good measure. If the game runs in real-time, you will want to develop the collision detection routine and start working on the physics for the game.

By the end of this phase of development—before you get started on a real prototype—you should try to anticipate (based on the initial design) some of the possible graphics and miscellaneous routines you will need later. Obviously, you will not know in advance all of the functionality the game will need, but you should at least code the core routines up front.

Alpha Prototype

After you have developed the engine that will power your game, the next natural step in development is to create a prototype of the game. This phase is really a natural result of testing the game engine, so the two phases are often seamless. But if you treat the prototype as a single, complete program, without the need for modification, then you will have recognized this phase of the game.

Once the prototype has been finished, I recommend that you compile and save it as an individual program or demo. At this point, you might want to send it to a few friends to get some feedback on general gameplay. This version of the game will not even remotely look as if it is complete. Bitmaps will be incomplete, and there might not even be any sound or music in the prototype.

However, one thing that the prototype must have is network capabilities from the start. If you are developing a multiplayer game, you must code the networking, along with the graphics and the game engine, early in development. It is a mistake to start adding multiplayer code to the game after it is half finished because most likely you will have written routines that are not suited for multiple players, and a lot of code will have to be re-written.

Game Development

The game development phase is clearly the longest phase of work done on a game, and consists of taking the prototype code base, along with feedback received from those who ran the demo, and building the game. Since this phase is the most important one, there are many different methods that you can follow. First, you will most likely be building on the prototype that you developed in the previous phase, because it usually does not make sense to start over from scratch unless there are some serious design flaws in the prototype.

You might want to stub out all of the functionality needed to complete the game, so that there is at least some sort of minimal response from the game when certain things happen or when a chain of events occurs. For instance, if you plan to support a high-score server on the Internet, you might code the high-score server with a simple response message, so that you can send a request to the server and then display the reply. This way, there is at least some sort of response from this part of the game, even if you do not intend to complete it until later.

Another positive note for stubbing out functionality is that you get to see the entire game as it will eventually appear. This allows you to go back to the initial design phase and make some changes before you are half-done with the game. Stubbing out nonessential functionality lets you see the entire game as an overview. You can then freeze the design and complete each piece of the game individually until the game is finished.

Quality Control

Individuals like you who are working on a game alone might be tempted to skip some of the phases of development, since the formality of it might seem humorous. But even if you are working on a game by yourself, it is a good idea to get into the habit of going through the motions of the formal game development life cycle as if you have a team of people working with you on the game. Some day, you might in fact find yourself working on a professional game with others, and the professionalism that you learned early on will pay off.

Quality control is the formal testing process that is required in order to correct bugs in a game. Since the lead developers of a game have been staring at the code and the game screens for months or years, a fresh set of eyes is needed to properly test a game. If you are working solo, you need to recruit one or more friends to help you test the game. I guarantee that they will be able to find problems that you have overlooked or missed completely. Since this is your pet project, you are very likely to develop habits when playing the game, while anyone else would find your machinations rather strange. Goofy keyboard shortcuts or strange user interface decisions might seem like the greatest thing since ketchup to you, but to someone else the game might not even be fun to play.

Consider quality control as an audit of your game. You need an objective person to point out flaws and gameplay issues that might not have been present in the prototype. It is a critical step when you think about it. After all the work you have put into a game, you certainly don't want a simple and easily correctable bug to tarnish the impression that you would like your game to have on others.

Beta Testing

Beta testing is a phase that follows the completion of the game's development phase, and should be recognized as significantly separate from the previous quality control phase. The beta version of a game absolutely should not be released if the game has known bugs. Any time you send out a game for beta testing when you know there are bugs, you are really still in the quality control phase and you should recognize it as such. Only when you have expunged every conceivable bug in the game should it be released to a wider audience for beta testing.

At this point in the game's life cycle, the game is complete and 100 percent functional, and you are only looking for a larger group of users to identify bugs that might have slipped past quality control. Before releasing a game to beta testers, make absolutely certain that all of the graphics, sound effects, and music are completely ready to go, as if the game is ready to be sent out to stores. If you do not feel confident that the game is ready to sit on a retail shelf, it is a sure sign that the game is not yet out of the quality control phase. When bugs are identified during the beta test phase, they should be collected on a regular time interval, and a new release should be sent out—regardless of whether your schedule is daily or weekly.

When users stop thinking of the game as a beta version and actually start to play for fun (with general trust in its stability), and when no new bugs have been identified for a length of time (such as a couple weeks or a month), then you can consider the game complete.

Post-Production

Post-production work on a game includes creating the install program that installs the game onto a computer system and writing the game manual. If you will be distributing the game via the Internet, you will definitely want to create a Web site for your game, with a bunch of screenshots and a list of the key features of the game.

Official Release

Once you have a complete package that is ready to go, burn the complete game installer with everything you need to play the game on a CD and give it to a few people who were not involved in the beta testing process. If you feel that the game is ready for prime time, you might send out copies of it to online and printed magazine editors for review.

Out the Door or Out the Window?

One thing is for certain; when you work on a game project for an employer who knows nothing about software development, you can count on having marketing run the show, which is not always good. Some of the best studios in the world are run by a small group of individuals who actually work on games, but who know very little about how to run a business or advertise a game to the general public. Far too often, those award-winning game designers and developers will turn over the reins of their small company to a full-time manager (or president), because the pressure of running the business becomes too much for the developers (who would rather write code than balance the accounts).

Managing the Game

The manager of a game studio might have learned the strategies to make a retail or wholesale company succeed. These strategies include concepts like just-in-time inventory, employee management, cost control, customer relationship management—all very good things to know when running a grocery store or sales department. The problem is, many managers fail to realize that software development is not a business, and programmers should not be treated like factory workers; rather, they should be treated like members of a research and development team.

Consider the infamous Bell Laboratories (or Bell Labs), an R&D center that has come up with hundreds of patents and innovations that have directly affected the computer industry (not the least of which was the transistor). While a couple of intelligent guys might have invented the microprocessor, the transistor was a revolutionary step that made the microprocessor possible. Now imagine if someone had treated Bell Labs like a factory, demanding results on a regular basis. Is that how human creativity works, with schedules and deadlines?

The case might be made that true genius is both creative and timely. Along that same train of thought, it might be said that genius is nothing but an extraordinary amount of hard work, with a dash of inspiration here and there.

There are some really terrific game publishers in the world, who give development teams the leeway to add every last bell and whistle to a game—those publishers should be applauded! But— you knew that was coming, didn't you?—far too often, publishers simply want results without regard for the quality of a game. When shareholders become more important than developers in a game company, it's time to find a new job.

A Note about Quality

What is the best way to work with game developers or management? The goal, after all, is to produce a successful game. Learn the meaning behind the buzzwords. If you are a developer, try to explain the technology behind your game throughout the development life cycle and provide options to managers. By offering several technical solutions to any given problem, and then allowing the decision makers to decide which path to follow, you will succeed in completing the game on time and within budget.

The accusations and jibes actually go both ways! Management is often faced with developers who are competing with other developers in the industry. The goal might be a sound one—high-end game engines are often so difficult to develop that many companies would rather license an existing engine than build their own. Quite often a game is nothing more than a technology demo for the engine, since licensing might provide even more income than actual game sales (especially if royalties are involved). When a game is nearing completion and a competitor's game comes out with some fancy new feature (like a software renderer with full anisotropic filtering—okay, that's impossible, but you get the point), the tendency is to cram a similar new feature into the game at the last minute for bragging rights. However, the new feature will have absolutely no bearing on the playability or fun-factor of the game, and might even reduce game stability.

This tendency is something that managers must deal with on a daily basis, in a struggle to keep developers from modifying the game's design (resulting in a game that is never finished). Rather than constantly modifying the design, developers should be promised work on a sequel or new game, using all the new things they have learned while working on the current game.

Empowering the Engine

Consider the game *Unreal*, by Epic Games (a company that was once called Epic Megagames, and has produced some very cool shareware games). The "Unreal Engine" was touted as a *Quake II* killer, with unbelievable graphics, all rendered in software. Of course, 3-D acceleration made *Unreal* even more impressive. The problem with *Unreal* was not the technology behind the mesmerizing graphics in the game, but rather the gameplay. Gamers were playing tournament-style games, a trend that was somewhat missed by the developers, publishers, and gaming media at the time. In contrast, *Quake II* had a large and engaging single-player game in addition to multiplayer support that spawned a cult following and put the game at the top of the charts.

Unreal was simply was developed from the start as a multiplayer game, since the game was in development for several years. Epic Games released *Unreal Tournament* about two years later, and it was simply awesome—a perfect example of putting additional efforts into a second game, rather than delaying the first. The only single-player component of *Unreal Tournament* is a game mode where you can play against computer-controlled bots, but *Unreal Tournament* is undeniably a multiplayer game throughout.

Quality Versus Trends

Blizzard was once a company that set the industry standard for creating extremely high quality games, such as *Warcraft II*, *Starcraft*, and *Diablo*. These games alone have outsold the entire lineup from some publishers, with multiple millions of copies sold worldwide. Why was Blizzard so successful with these early games? In a word: quality. From the installer to the end of the game, Blizzard exuded quality in every respect. Then something happened. The company announced a new game and then cancelled it. A new installment of *Warcraft* was announced and then forgotten for several years. *Diablo II* came out, with many scratching their heads, wondering why it took three years to develop a sequel that looked so much like the original.

Consider Future Trends

The problem is often not related to the quality of a game as much as the trends. When it takes several years to develop an extremely complicated game, design decisions must be made in advance. It requires a little guesswork on the part of the designer to try to determine where gaming trends are headed, and then take advantage of those trends in a game. A blockbuster game does not necessarily need to follow every new trend; on the contrary, the trends are set by the blockbuster games themselves. An otherwise fantastic game that was revolutionary and ambitious at one point might find itself outdated by the time it is released.

Take Out the Guesswork

Age of Empires was released for the holiday season in 1997, at the dawn of the real-time strategy revolution in the gaming industry. This game was in development for perhaps two years before release. That means work started on *Age of Empires* as early as 1995! Now, imagine the trends of the time and the average hardware on a PC, and it is obvious that the designer of the game had a good grasp of future trends in gaming.

Those RTS games that were developed with complete 3-D environments have still not seemed to catch on. In many ways, *Dark Reign II* is far superior to *Age of Empires II*, with gorgeous graphics and stunning 3-D particle effects. And yet, *Age of Empires II* has become more of a LAN party favorite, along with *Quake III Arena*, *Unreal Tournament*, and *Counter-Strike*. Perhaps RTS fans are not interested in complete 3-D environments. My personal suspicion is that the 3-D element is distracting to a gamer who would prefer to focus on his strategy instead of on navigating the 3-D terrain.

Innovation Versus Inspiration

As an aspiring game designer, what is the solution to the technology/trend problem? My advice is to play every game you can get your hands on (if you are not already an avid gamer). Play games that don't interest you to get a feel for a variety of games. Download and play every demo that comes out, regardless of the type of game. Demos are a great way for marketing to promote a game before it is finished, but they are also a great way for competitors to see what you have planned. As with most things in business or leisure, there is a tradeoff. While you play games, it is great to have some fun, but try to determine how the game works and what is under the hood, so to speak. If the game is based on a licensed engine rather than custom code, you might try to identify which engine powers the game.

Half-Life is probably one of the oldest games in the industry that is still being improved upon and packaged for sale on retail shelves. The single most significant reason behind the success of *Half-Life* (aside from the compelling story and gameplay) is the Half-Life SDK. This is a software development kit for the Half-Life engine that is available for free download. While hundreds of third-party modifications (MODs) have been created for *Half-Life*, by far the most popular is *Counter-Strike* (which was finally packaged for retail sale after over a year in beta).

The Infamous Game Patch

Regardless of the good intentions of developers, many games are rushed and sent out to stores before they are 100 percent complete. This is a result of a game that went over budget, a publisher who decided to drop the game but was convinced to complete it, or a publisher who was interested only in a first run of sales without regard to quality.

A common trap that publishers have fallen into is the belief that they can rush a game and then just release a downloadable patch for it. The reasoning is that customers are already used to downloading new versions and updates to software, so there is nothing wrong with getting a game out the door a week before Christmas in order to make it for the holiday season. The flaw behind this reasoning is that games are largely advertised by word of mouth, not by marketing schemes. Due to the huge number of newsgroups and discussion lists (such as YahooGroups.com) with millions of members sharing information, ideas, and stories, it is impossible for a killer new game to be released without a few hundred thousand gamers knowing about it.

But now you see the trap. The same gamers who swap war stories online and about their favorite games will rip apart a shoddy game that was released prematurely. Doing so is a sign of sure death for a game. Only rarely will a downloadable patch be acceptable for a game that is released before it is complete.

Expanding the Game

Most games that are successful are followed by an expansion pack of some sort, whether it is a map pack or complete conversion to a new theme. One of my favorite games of all time is *Homeworld*, which was created by Relic and published by Sierra. *Homeworld* is an extraordinary game of epic proportions, and is possibly the most engaging and realistic game I have ever played. Figure 18.1 shows a scene from *Homeworld*, featuring the Taiidan mothership.

When the sequel, *Homeworld: Cataclysm*, was released, I found that not only was there a new theme to the game (in fact, it takes place a number of years after the events in the original game), but the developers had actually added some significant new features to the game engine! Take a look at Figure 18.2 to see a capital ship about to engage the enemy.

The new technologies and ships in *Cataclysm* were enough to warrant buying the game, but *Cataclysm* is also a stand-alone expansion game that does not require the original to run. Figure 18.3 shows a research station that is a key factor in the plot of the game.

Expansion packs and enhanced sequels allow developers to complete a game on schedule, while still allowing them to exercise their creative and technical skill on an additional product based on the same game. This is a great idea from a marketing perspective, because the original game has already been completed, so the amount of work required to create an expansion game is significantly less and allows for some fine-tuning of the game.

Figure 18.1

The mothership is the focus of the game in Homeworld.

Figure 18.2

This heavy frigate is ready to dish out some damage.

Figure 18.3

The research station is an important part of the game's plot.

FUTURE-PROOF DESIGN

Developing a game with code reuse is one thing, but what about designing a game to make it future proof? That is quite a challenge given that computer technology improves at such a rapid pace. The ironic thing about computer games is that developers usually target high-end systems when building the game, without being able to fully estimate where mainstream computer hardware will be a year in the future. And yet, when a new high-end game is released, many gamers will go out and purchase upgrades for their computers in order to play the new game. You see the circular cause-and-effect that results.

Overall, designing a game for the highest end of the hardware spectrum is not a wise decision, because there are thousands of gamers in the world who do not have access to the latest hardware innovations—such as striped hard drives attached to a RAID (*Redundant Array of Independent Disks*) controller, or a 64MB DDR GeForce 3 video card (that's *double-data*

> **NOTE**
>
> These topics are not just relevant to Visual Basic programming, but to any language and to game development in general.

rate memory, by the way). While hardware improvements are increasing as rapidly as prices seem to be dropping, the average gaming rig is still light-years beyond the average consumer PC, and that should be taken into account when targeting system hardware.

Game Libraries

A solid understanding of game development usually precedes work on a game library for a particular platform, and this usually takes place during the initial design and prototype phases of game development. It is becoming more common now for publishers to contract with developers for multiple platforms. Whether the developers build an entirely new game library for each platform or develop a multi-platform game library is usually irrelevant to the publisher (who is only interested in a finished product).

Therefore, a development studio is likely to reap incredible rewards by developing a multi-platform game library that can be easily recompiled for any of the supported computer platforms. It is not unheard of to develop a library that supports PC, PlayStation 2, GameCube, and Xbox, all with the same code base.

Game Engines and SDKs

Game engines are rated in the media and online discussion groups as a complete solution to a developer's needs. Not true! Game engines are based on game libraries for one or more platforms, and the game engine is likely optimized to an incredible degree for a particular game.

Common engines today include the Half-Life SDK, the Unreal engine, and the Quake III engine (among others). These game engines can be used to create a completely new game, but that game is really just a total conversion for the existing engine. Some studios are up to the challenge of modifying the existing engine for their own needs, but far more often, developers will use the existing engine as-is and simply customize it for their own game project.

Examples of games based on an existing engine include *Star Trek Voyager: Elite Force, Counter-Strike,* and even *Quake IV* (which is based on the new Doom III engine).

PROMOTION!

You have now completed Part III, "Hardcore Game Programming." By finishing this section of the book, you have demonstrated mastery of advanced game programming subjects. You learned how to spawn artificial life forms that simulate intelligence; you learned to program multiplayer games with Windows Sockets and DirectPlay; and you now have a solid understanding of game design.

These are the final skills necessary to build not only a complete game, but also a challenging and entertaining one. You have learned all the theory that I have to teach you. From this point forward, you must demonstrate the patience and vision necessary to build complete games, which is what follows in the next four chapters.

You are hereby promoted to the rank of *Master Developer*, with all of the rights and privileges that come with the position. Use your new knowledge and skills wisely, and continue to push the envelope of Visual Basic gaming!

Here is a record of your progress so far:

1. **Newbie Gamer**
2. **Apprentice Hacker**
3. **Skilled Programmer**
4. **Veteran Coder**
5. **Master Developer**
6. Adept Game Designer

SUMMARY

This chapter covered the subject of game design and discussed the phases of the game development life cycle. You learned how to classify your games by genre, how to manage development and testing, how to release and market your game, how to improve quality while meeting deadlines, and some of the pitfalls of releasing an incomplete product.

You then learned how to follow trends, how to expand and enhance a game with expansion packs, and how game libraries and game engines work together.

This marks the end of Part III. Prepare for an adventure as you embark on an exciting tour through four complete games in Part IV, "Complete Game Projects."

PART IV

COMPLETE
GAME
PROJECTS

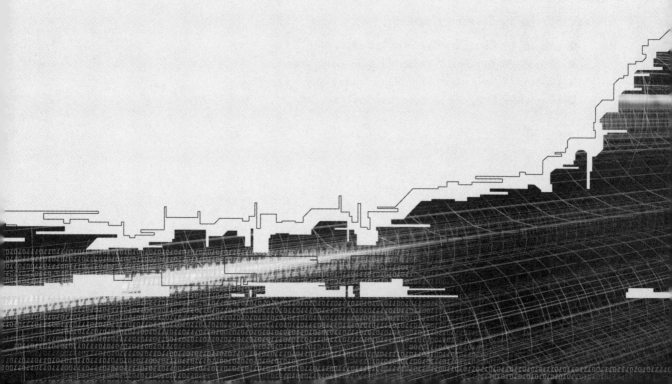

Welcome to Part IV of *Visual Basic Game Programming with DirectX*. Part IV includes four exciting chapters with actual game projects. The goal of each chapter in Part IV is to demonstrate the theory, design, and application of game programming topics that were covered in the earlier parts of the book, through the hands-on development of complete games.

Most of the material presented in Part IV was covered in earlier chapters, so there are few surprises here. The important point is that you will see the results of all the hard work that you have invested in learning the material up to this point. You will have an opportunity to put the game library through its paces by developing real-world games.

Each chapter in Part IV covers subjects of increasing difficulty, starting with the information presented in Part I, "Introducing Visual Basic and DirectX," moving on to the game library in Part II, "The Nuts and Bolts of Game Development," and up through the advanced topics in Part III, "Hardcore Game Programming." The DirectX classes will be used by all of the games in Part IV, although the first two games use the Windows API bitmap and sprite classes. Chapter 21 covers a complete multiplayer game, while in Chapter 22 you will develop a game based on Direct3D code.

Part IV includes the following chapters:

- Chapter 19: Block Attack: Classic Arcade Game
- Chapter 20: Warbirds 1944: Scrolling Shooter Game
- Chapter 21: Stellar War: Multiplayer Space Combat Game
- Chapter 22: Pong 3D: Modern Arcade Game

CHAPTER 19

BLOCK ATTACK! CLASSIC ARCADE GAME

W elcome to the first game chapter in the book! This chapter, like those that follow, is dedicated to building a complete game from scratch. The game is called Block Attack, and features a ball and paddle with a series of blocks on the screen that you must clear in order to move on to the next level. This is a type of classic arcade game that dates back to Atari's original game of *Pong* (as well as the follow-up game, *Breakout*).

This chapter covers the following topics:

- Playing Block Attack
- Building the Game Project
- Enhancing the Game

Playing Block Attack

Block Attack features a paddle at the bottom of the screen that is controlled by the player, and a ball that bounces off the walls and the paddle. Each level of the game is populated with blocks that must be cleared by hitting them with the ball. The goal of the game is to clear the blocks without letting the ball fall off the bottom of the screen!

Since Block Attack is the first sample game in the book, I purposely kept it simple. The game uses the Windows API bitmap and sprite classes rather than DirectDraw, although it does use DirectInput to handle the keyboard and DirectSound for playing sound effects.

Arcade Genre

The arcade game genre dates back to the late '70s, when pinball machine arcades started to feature video games in addition to pinball machines. These early games were simple in design and function, and rarely had a means to complete the game. Rather, the games usually wore on and on until the player lost or ran out of quarters. As I mentioned before, *Pong* was the game that started it all, and Block Attack is loosely based on that game (and even more so on Atari's later game, *Breakout*).

While this game is simple in design, it has a huge potential for greatness. I included only a few powerups, but there are countless fun things you can do with a game of this type once the foundation has been laid and the initial source code has been written. I designed the game so that it would be easy to add new blocks and powerups to the game.

Scoring and Powerups

Scoring in Block Attack is somewhat different from other games of this type (that is, block-bashing games). Rather than tallying the score for simply breaking blocks, the game drops point tokens each time a block is destroyed. The player must catch those tokens in order to gain points. It is a novel idea that I felt would add a little more intrigue to the game. As a player competing for points (seemingly with other players), you must judge which points are worth saving and which are worth sacrificing in the never-ending quest to keep the ball from falling off the bottom of the screen.

Would it be better to grab a few gold points or a single platinum point, or to go for a bonus life or growth powerup? These decisions must be made on-the-fly, which makes the game entertaining. Table 19.1 shows the blocks used in the game, along with the points associated with each block.

Get into the Action!

The next few pages will show a series of screenshots from the game, with a description of the situation shown in each figure.

The First Level

The first level of the game is a small section of blocks that is easy to clear, and is basically a good way for the player to become familiar with the game before some of the more difficult levels come along. Figure 19.1 shows the first level, as it appears when the game starts. Notice how the ball moves with the paddle until the player is ready to begin (by pressing the spacebar).

Table 19.1 Block Values for Scoring Points

Block	Value	Block	Value
Red	1	Cyan	5
Green	2	Silver	10
Blue	3	Gold	15
Violet	4	Platinum	20

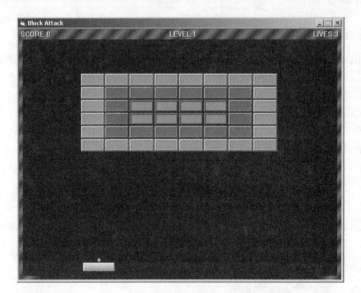

Figure 19.1

The first level of Block Attack is easy enough to give the player some practice before encountering more challenging levels.

Catching Points and Powerups

Figure 19.2 shows the second level in the game, with numerous points and a powerup falling toward the player's paddle. The only way to score in Block Attack is by grabbing the points that fall when a block has been destroyed. If you fail to catch any of the falling points, your score will never go up. Also note the "shrink" powerup above the paddle (it has an "S" on it). This is a powerup that you do not want to get, because it shrinks your paddle to half the normal size.

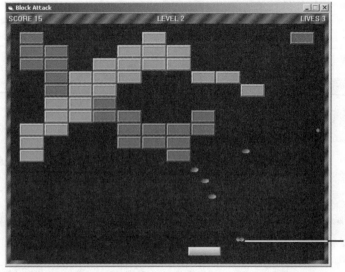

Figure 19.2

In order to score points in Block Attack, the player must catch falling points.

Shrink powerup

Indestructible Blocks

The third level of the game (shown in Figure 19.3) features indestructible tiles that cannot be destroyed by hitting them with the ball. The game takes this type of block into account when determining whether the level has been cleared, and simply bounces the ball off these blocks.

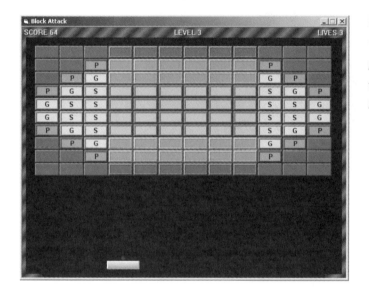

Figure 19.3

The third level features indestructible blocks that increase the challenge.

Mining for Precious Metals

In addition to the normal blocks in the game, there are bonus blocks that drop silver, gold, and platinum points that are worth considerably more than normal points. (See Table 19.1 for the list of blocks and their point values.) Figure 19.4 shows a level with veins of gold embedded in the blocks! Silver blocks are worth 10 points; gold blocks are worth 15 points; and platinum blocks are worth 20 points! The player must decide which points are worth catching as they fall, since a group of cyan points (each worth 5) might be more valuable than any single precious metal point. Note that powerups (shrink, grow, and bonus life) are worth no actual points.

Shrink and Growth Powerups

There are two powerups that change the size of the paddle. The shrink powerup causes the paddle to shrink to half its size, while the growth powerup causes the paddle to increase in size by 50 percent. Figure 19.5 shows the small paddle, with a growth powerup that the player needs to catch!

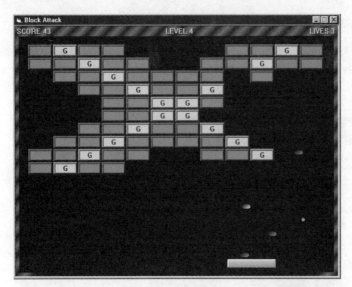

Figure 19.4

Precious metal blocks are worth considerably more than normal blocks, but only if you catch the points that fall.

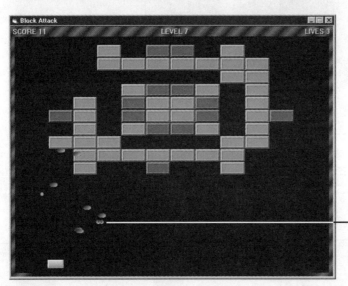

Figure 19.5

Catch the growth powerup to increase the size of the paddle.

—— Growth powerup

The Game Over Screen

The Game Over screen, shown in Figure 19.6, appears when you lose all your lives in the game or when you complete the last level. I know this is not a triumphant way to end the game after getting through all 10 stages of it, but it does get the point across.

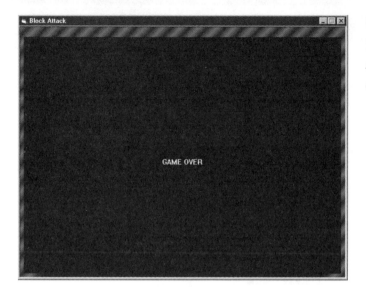

Figure 19.6

The Game Over screen simply gets the point across.

This might be a great way for you to enhance the game, by adding some sort of fanfare to the end if the player completes all the levels in the game. While 10 levels are sufficient to demonstrate the game, they are not nearly enough for a full-blown game. I found that the current set of powerups and fun features were far too lacking to add more levels to the game, because it becomes monotonous after a while. This game is definitely open for improvement! I can think of a dozen enhancements and powerups that would immediately improve the game. I encourage you to dive into the source code and have some fun with it!

Playing with the Level Editor

The levels in Block Attack were designed using a custom program called BlockEdit, which was adapted from a public domain level editor program specifically for this game (and is therefore not useful for other types of games). BlockEdit (shown in Figure 19.7) is really simple and gets the job done without any bells or whistles.

The BlockEdit level editor is included on the CD-ROM in the directory for this chapter, under \BlockEdit. The source code for the level editor is included as well.

BUILDING THE GAME PROJECT

Now that you have seen what the game looks like, it's time to create it from scratch. The following pages describe how to create the Block Attack project, how to add class files to the project, and how to configure the settings prior to actually typing in the source code.

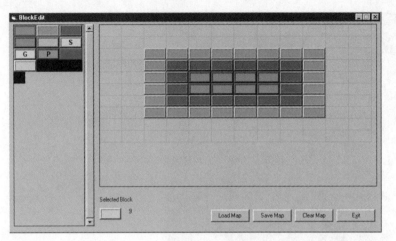

Figure 19.7

The BlockEdit program allows you to create custom levels for the Block Attack game.

Creating the Project

This game is like every other project in the book; it requires just a single form. Fire up Visual Basic and create a new project. As shown in Figure 19.8, select a Standard EXE program.

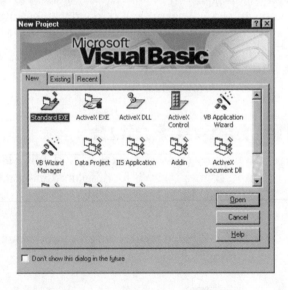

Figure 19.8

Selecting the project type for the game

Project Explorer

Block Attack uses numerous classes that were developed in earlier chapters and compiled into the game library in Chapter 13, "Building the DirectX Game Library." For this game, I have opted to include the class files directly inside the project in order to eliminate the need for the external VBGL.DLL file that results from compiling the game library. While it is usually not necessary to include all of the game library files in the later stages of game development, it is convenient to have the classes be part of the game project for debugging purposes.

You might want to use the compiled library for final release if you wish. It is certainly convenient to have all the classes instantly available just by creating a reference to the game library. Basically, do what is most convenient and most productive when it comes to using the game library.

Figure 19.9 shows the Project Explorer window for the Block Attack project, showing all the files required by the game. The easiest way to attach these files to the project is to simply drag them from Windows Explorer over the Project Explorer window in VB. But you can also add each file separately from the Project menu.

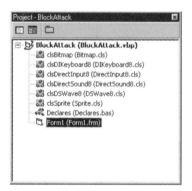

Figure 19.9

The Project Explorer shows the files needed to compile the game.

The Block Attack Project

The complete Block Attack project as it appears in VB is shown in Figure 19.10, with the code window for Form1 loaded. Notice how the editor window features a split screen.

References

Since the Block Attack game includes the needed class files directly and does not use the game library, you must reference the DirectX 8 for Visual Basic Type Library in the References dialog, as shown in Figure 19.11. This game does not use DirectDraw, so there is no need to reference DirectX 7.

Source Artwork

The source artwork for Block Attack includes several bitmap files that you will need in order to run the game. While you should feel free to draw the graphics from scratch, you will most likely want to copy the files off the CD-ROM into your project directory for Block Attack. Once there, you can make any changes you want to the bitmaps used in the game.

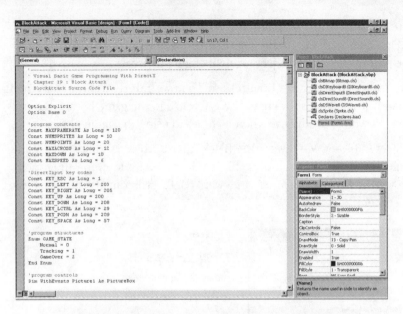

Figure 19.10

The Block Attack game project, open in the Visual Basic editor

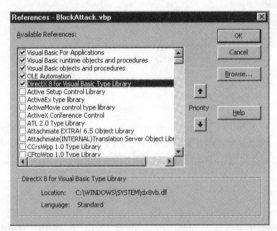

Figure 19.11

Referencing the DirectX 8 for Visual Basic Type Library is necessary to compile the game.

The Paddle

The paddle frames are stored in a file called paddle.bmp, which is shown in Figure 19.12. One easy enhancement that you can make to the game is to add new paddle sprites so that each level has a unique paddle image.

The Blocks

The blocks used in the game are very simple and are not even animated. The bitmaps for all of the blocks used in the game are stored in a file called blocks.bmp, shown in Figure 19.13.

Figure 19.12

The source image for the player's paddle

Figure 19.13

The blocks used in the game

The Ball

The ball used in the game (see Figure 19.14) features 16 frames of animation, which makes it seem to glow or pulsate as it moves about the screen.

Figure 19.14

The ball features 16 frames of animation.

The Points

Each time the ball hits a block, that block is destroyed (unless it is an indestructible block) and a point sprite the same color as the block will begin to float down the screen. When the player catches these sprites, his score is increased. Every time a point is dropped, there is a 10 percent chance that it will become a powerup instead of a point. Figure 19.15 shows the source image for the point sprites.

Figure 19.15

The points fall down the screen and must be caught by the player in order to score.

User Input

While Block Attack uses the enhanced Windows API game library routines that were developed earlier in the book for double buffering and sprite handling, the user input handler for the game was implemented with DirectInput and the input classes developed back in Chapter 12, "Getting a Handle on User Input." Block Attack does not use the mouse for input, primarily because it is a windowed program, and acquiring the mouse in a windowed game is complicated (for instance, when dealing with switching applications or pop-up windows).

Block Attack only uses the keyboard for input. I was going to include joystick support, but decided to stick with the keyboard for this first game to keep the source code listing as short as possible.

Here are the game library classes that are included in the game to handle input:

- clsDirectInput8
- clsDIKeyboard8

Sound Effects

The sound effects in Block Attack are very simple (with no positional effects), and there are only a few of them—block hit, paddle hit, and wall hit.

Here are the game library classes that are included in the game to handle audio:

- clsDirectSound8
- clsDSWave8

Block Attack Source Code

The source code for Block Attack is quite lengthy, so I will try to explain each part of the game along the way. For starters, you will want to have the code window for Form1 open, because that is where all of this code should be entered.

This first section of code includes the program variables, constants, structures, and objects needed by the game. I'm not going to explicitly explain every single detail of the game, because this is all repeat material from the theory chapters in the book up to this point. I will, however, explain everything that is relevant to the game and those routines that obviously require explanation.

```
'--------------------------------------------------------------
' Visual Basic Game Programming With DirectX
' Chapter 19 : Block Attack
' BlockAttack Source Code File
'--------------------------------------------------------------
```

```
Option Explicit
Option Base 0

'program constants
Const MAXFRAMERATE As Long = 120
Const NUMSPRITES As Long = 10
Const NUMPOINTS As Long = 20
Const MAXACROSS As Long = 12
Const MAXDOWN As Long = 10
Const MAXSPEED As Long = 6

'DirectInput key codes
Const KEY_ESC As Long = 1
Const KEY_LEFT As Long = 203
Const KEY_RIGHT As Long = 205
Const KEY_UP As Long = 200
Const KEY_DOWN As Long = 208
Const KEY_LCTRL As Long = 29
Const KEY_PGDN As Long = 209
Const KEY_SPACE As Long = 57

'program structures
Enum GAME_STATE
    Normal = 0
    Tracking = 1
    GameOver = 2
End Enum

'program controls
Dim WithEvents Picture1 As PictureBox

'DirectX objects
Dim WithEvents Keyboard As clsDIKeyboard8
Dim dinput As New clsDirectInput8
Dim dsound As New clsDirectSound8
Dim dswPaddleHit As New clsDSWave8
Dim dswBlockHit As New clsDSWave8
Dim dswWallHit As New clsDSWave8
```

```
'class objects
Dim Map(MAXACROSS, MAXDOWN) As Long
Dim csBlocks As New clsSprite
Dim cbBackBuffer As New clsBitmap
Dim cbBackgrnd As New clsBitmap
Dim csBall As New clsSprite
Dim csPaddle As New clsSprite
Dim csPoints(0 To NUMPOINTS) As New clsSprite

'program variables
Dim GameState As GAME_STATE
Dim bRunning As Boolean
Dim lFrameDelay As Long
Dim lScore As Long
Dim lLives As Long
Dim lLevel As Long
```

Okay, now for the first real procedure in the game, Form_Load. Since this is the first routine that
runs when the game starts, it makes sense to initialize the game and load all the graphics and
sounds from Form_Load, and then start the game loop running.

```
Private Sub Form_Load()
    Randomize GetTickCount
    GameState = Tracking
    lLives = 3
    lLevel = 1
    bRunning = True

    InitForm
    InitDirectInput
    InitDirectSound
    InitBackBuffer

    LoadPaddle
    LoadBall
    LoadPoints
    LoadBlocks
    LoadLevel App.Path & "\level" & lLevel & ".map"

    GameLoop
End Sub
```

```
Private Sub Form_Paint()
    Dim r As RECT_API
    GetClientRect Picture1.hWnd, r
    ValidateRect Picture1.hWnd, r
    cbBackgrnd.Draw 0, 0, Picture1.hdc
End Sub


Private Sub Form_QueryUnload(Cancel As Integer, UnloadMode As Integer)
    Shutdown
End Sub
```

Keyboard_KeyDown, might look like a standard Visual Basic event (like Form_Load), but it is actually a variable that was declared using the keyword WithEvents. The Keyboard object is declared as a clsDIKeyboard8, meaning it is a callback from a DirectX routine that was developed in an earlier chapter. I simply made it look like a built-in event because that keeps things nice and neat.

```
Private Sub Keyboard_KeyDown(ByVal lKey As Long)
    Static lLast As Long
    If GetTickCount > lLast + 80 Then
        lLast = GetTickCount
        Select Case lKey
            Case KEY_ESC
                Shutdown
            Case KEY_LEFT
                MovePaddle -2
            Case KEY_RIGHT
                MovePaddle 2
            Case KEY_SPACE
                If GameState = Tracking Then
                    GameState = Normal
                ElseIf GameState = GameOver Then
                    Shutdown
                End If
        End Select
    End If
End Sub
```

All of the initialization routines are included in the following pages of source code, and they are all called by Form_Load. They include InitForm, InitDirectSound, InitBackBuffer, and InitDirectInput.

```
Private Sub InitForm()
    'set up the main form
    Form1.Caption = "Block Attack"
    Form1.AutoRedraw = False
    Form1.BorderStyle = 1
    Form1.ClipControls = False
    Form1.KeyPreview = True
    Form1.ScaleMode = 3
    Form1.Width = 652 * Screen.TwipsPerPixelX
    Form1.Height = 510 * Screen.TwipsPerPixelY
    Form1.Show

    'create the PictureBox control for drawing
    Set Picture1 = Controls.Add("VB.PictureBox", "Picture1")
    Picture1.AutoRedraw = False
    Picture1.BorderStyle = 1
    Picture1.ClipControls = False
    Picture1.ScaleMode = 3
    Picture1.BackColor = RGB(0, 0, 0)
    Picture1.Left = 0
    Picture1.Top = 0
    Picture1.Width = Form1.ScaleWidth
    Picture1.Height = Form1.ScaleHeight
    Picture1.Visible = True
End Sub

Private Sub InitDirectSound()
    dsound.Startup Form1.hWnd
    dswPaddleHit.LoadSound dsound, App.Path & "\paddlehit.wav"
    dswPaddleHit.Interrupt = True
    dswBlockHit.LoadSound dsound, App.Path & "\blockhit.wav"
    dswBlockHit.Interrupt = True
    dswWallHit.LoadSound dsound, App.Path & "\wallhit.wav"
    dswWallHit.Interrupt = True
End Sub

Private Sub InitBackBuffer()
    'create the back buffer
    If Not cbBackBuffer.Create(Picture1.hdc, Picture1.ScaleWidth, _
        Picture1.ScaleHeight) Then
```

```
        MsgBox "Error creating back buffer"
        Shutdown
    End If

    'load the background
    If Not cbBackgrnd.Load(App.Path & "\background.bmp") Then
        MsgBox "Error loading background image"
        Shutdown
    End If
    cbBackgrnd.Draw 0, 0, cbBackBuffer.hdc

End Sub

Private Sub InitDirectInput()
    'initialize DirectInput
    dinput.Startup Form1.hWnd
    Set Keyboard = New clsDIKeyboard8
    Keyboard.Startup dinput, Form1.hWnd
End Sub
```

Are we having fun yet? Next in line are the load routines. Again, these are all called by Form_Load, and they were divided into these individual procedures for clarity. Some of the games in the following chapters follow this standard, while others simply include all of this code inside Form_Load. It really depends on the complexity and whether it seems cleaner to break apart all of this initialization. You might be tempted to move initialization code into a separate module file. That's not a bad idea, but I always prefer to have the main code for the game inside Form1. After all, the game library classes contain most of the code already.

```
Private Sub LoadBall()
    'load the ball
    If Not csBall.LoadFrames(App.Path & "\ball.bmp", _
        0, 0, 8, 8, 16) Then
        MsgBox "Error loading ball.bmp"
        Shutdown
    End If
    If Not csBall.GenerateAllMasks Then
        MsgBox "Error generating ball mask"
        Shutdown
    End If
    csBall.Transparent = True
    csBall.x = 320
```

```
        csBall.y = 300
        csBall.SaveUnder cbBackBuffer.hdc
        csBall.SpeedX = 1 + Random(2)
        csBall.SpeedY = 2 + Random(2)
        csBall.AnimCount = 0
        csBall.AnimRate = 3
End Sub

Private Sub LoadPaddle()
    'load the small paddle
    If Not csPaddle.LoadFrames(App.Path & "\paddle.bmp", _
        0, 0, 32, 16, 1) Then
        MsgBox "Error loading paddle.bmp"
        Shutdown
    End If

    'load the normal paddle
    If Not csPaddle.LoadFrames(App.Path & "\paddle.bmp", _
        0, 16, 64, 16, 1) Then
        MsgBox "Error loading paddle.bmp"
        Shutdown
    End If

    'load the big paddle
    If Not csPaddle.LoadFrames(App.Path & "\paddle.bmp", _
        0, 32, 96, 16, 1) Then
        MsgBox "Error loading paddle.bmp"
        Shutdown
    End If
    csPaddle.CurrentFrame = 2
    csPaddle.Transparent = False
    csPaddle.x = Picture1.ScaleWidth / 2 - csPaddle.Width / 2
    csPaddle.y = Picture1.ScaleHeight - csPaddle.Height * 2
    csPaddle.SaveUnder cbBackBuffer.hdc
    csPaddle.CurrentFrame = 1
End Sub

Private Sub LoadPoints()
    Dim n As Long
    For n = 0 To NUMPOINTS
        Set csPoints(n) = New clsSprite
```

```
            If Not csPoints(n).LoadFrames(App.Path & "\points.bmp", _
                0, 0, 16, 8, 8) Then
                MsgBox "Error loading points.bmp"
                Shutdown
            End If
            If Not csPoints(n).LoadFrames(App.Path & "\points.bmp", _
                0, 8, 16, 8, 3) Then
                MsgBox "Error loading points.bmp"
                Shutdown
            End If
            If Not csPoints(n).GenerateAllMasks Then
                MsgBox "Error generating point masks"
                Shutdown
            End If
            csPoints(n).Transparent = True
            csPoints(n).Active = False
            csPoints(n).SpeedY = 1
        Next n
End Sub

Private Sub LoadBlocks()
    'load the blocks
    If Not csBlocks.LoadFrames(App.Path & "\blocks.bmp", _
        0, 0, 48, 24, 9) Then
        MsgBox "Error loading blocks.bmp"
        Shutdown
    End If
    csBlocks.Transparent = False
    csBlocks.CurrentFrame = 0
End Sub
```

Here is the game loop. This is the most important procedure in the game because it is where all the action takes place. Seems small, doesn't it? The key word here is delegation. The Game_Update procedure does all the real work, although GameLoop does call Keyboard.Check_Keyboard to get an update on the status of the keyboard (which is required in order to receive DirectInput keyboard events without a callback function).

```
Private Sub GameLoop()
    Static lStartTime As Long
    Static lCounter As Long
```

```
        Static lNewTime As Long
        lStartTime = GetTickCount

        lFrameDelay = 1000 / MAXFRAMERATE
        Do While bRunning
            lCounter = GetTickCount() - lStartTime
            If lCounter > lNewTime Then
                Keyboard.Check_Keyboard
                Game_Update lCounter
                lNewTime = lCounter + lFrameDelay
            End If
            DoEvents
        Loop
    End Sub


    Private Sub Game_Update(ByVal MS As Long)
        Static bFirst As Boolean
        Static lCounter&
        Static lTimer&
        Static lStart&
        Dim n As Long

        'start counting milliseconds
        lStart = GetTickCount

        'erase sprites
        csPaddle.RestoreUnder cbBackBuffer.hdc
        csBall.RestoreUnder cbBackBuffer.hdc
        For n = 0 To NUMPOINTS
            If csPoints(n).Active Then
                csPoints(n).RestoreUnder cbBackBuffer.hdc
            End If
        Next n

        'erase text messages
        cbBackgrnd.Blt cbBackBuffer.hdc, 0, 0, _
            Picture1.ScaleWidth - 1, 20

        If GameState = GameOver Then
            cbBackgrnd.Draw 0, 0, cbBackBuffer.hdc
```

```
        cbBackBuffer.DrawText 280, 250, "GAME OVER", _
            RGB(255, 255, 255)
    Else
        'move everything
        UpdatePaddle
        UpdateBall
        UpdatePoints

        'save background
        csPaddle.SaveUnder cbBackBuffer.hdc
        csBall.SaveUnder cbBackBuffer.hdc
        For n = 0 To NUMPOINTS
            If csPoints(n).Active Then
                csPoints(n).SaveUnder cbBackBuffer.hdc
            End If
        Next n

        'draw sprites
        For n = 0 To NUMPOINTS
            If csPoints(n).Active Then
                csPoints(n).Draw cbBackBuffer.hdc
            End If
        Next n
        csPaddle.Draw cbBackBuffer.hdc
        csBall.NextFrame
        csBall.Draw cbBackBuffer.hdc

        'draw text messages
        cbBackBuffer.DrawText 5, 3, "SCORE " & lScore, _
            RGB(40, 40, 40)
        cbBackBuffer.DrawText 3, 1, "SCORE " & lScore, _
            RGB(230, 230, 230)
        cbBackBuffer.DrawText 302, 3, "LEVEL " & lLevel, _
            RGB(40, 40, 40)
        cbBackBuffer.DrawText 300, 1, "LEVEL " & lLevel, _
            RGB(230, 230, 230)
        cbBackBuffer.DrawText 586, 3, "LIVES " & lLives, _
            RGB(40, 40, 40)
        cbBackBuffer.DrawText 584, 1, "LIVES " & lLives, _
            RGB(230, 230, 230)
    End If
```

```
        'copy the back buffer to the screen
        cbBackBuffer.Draw 0, 0, Picture1.hdc

        'count the frames per second
        If MS > lTimer + 1000 Then
            lStart = GetTickCount - lStart
            Debug.Print "FPS = " & lCounter & ", MS = " & lStart
            lTimer = MS
            lCounter = 0
        Else
            lCounter = lCounter + 1
        End If
End Sub

Private Sub MovePaddle(ByVal lDir As Long)
    If lDir = 0 Then
        csPaddle.SpeedX = 0
    Else
        csPaddle.SpeedX = csPaddle.SpeedX + lDir
    End If

    If csPaddle.SpeedX < -MAXSPEED Then
        csPaddle.SpeedX = -MAXSPEED
    ElseIf csPaddle.SpeedX > MAXSPEED Then
        csPaddle.SpeedX = MAXSPEED
    End If
End Sub

Private Sub Shutdown()
    Dim n As Long

    bRunning = False
    Keyboard.Shutdown
    Form1.Hide

    'delete DirectInput objects
    Set Keyboard = Nothing
    Set dinput = Nothing

    'delete bitmaps and sprites
    Set csBlocks = Nothing
```

```
        Set cbBackBuffer = Nothing
        Set cbBackgrnd = Nothing
        Set csBall = Nothing
        Set csPaddle = Nothing
        For n = 0 To NUMPOINTS
            Set csPoints(n) = Nothing
        Next n

        'delete DirectSound objects
        Set dswPaddleHit = Nothing
        Set dswBlockHit = Nothing
        Set dswWallHit = Nothing
        Set dsound = Nothing

    End
End Sub
```

The various update procedures are called by Game_Update to move the paddle and ball, and to detect collisions with the blocks. Collision detection with the blocks involves locating the position of a block and testing whether the ball intersects with the block's rectangle. The blocks are not actually handled like regular sprites, or you would have simply called on the CheckCollision function that is built into clsSprite. To save memory and time, the blocks are simply stored as an array of Longs, and a single block sprite is used to draw the blocks.

```
Private Sub UpdatePaddle()
    Static lSlowdown As Long

    'move the paddle
    csPaddle.x = csPaddle.x + csPaddle.SpeedX
    If csPaddle.x < 8 Then
        csPaddle.x = 8
        csPaddle.SpeedX = 0
    ElseIf csPaddle.x > Picture1.ScaleWidth - csPaddle.Width - 8 Then
        csPaddle.x = Picture1.ScaleWidth - csPaddle.Width - 8
        csPaddle.SpeedX = 0
    End If

    'stop the paddle
    If GetTickCount > lSlowdown + 100 Then
        lSlowdown = GetTickCount
```

```
            If csPaddle.SpeedX > 0 Then
                csPaddle.SpeedX = csPaddle.SpeedX - 1
            ElseIf csPaddle.SpeedX < 0 Then
                csPaddle.SpeedX = csPaddle.SpeedX + 1
            End If
        End If
End Sub

Private Sub UpdateBall()
    Dim lCol As Long
    Dim lRow As Long
    Dim lBlockNum As Long
    Dim lNumBlocks As Long

    'see if ball is tracking the paddle
    If GameState = Tracking Then
        csBall.x = csPaddle.x + csPaddle.Width / 2 - csBall.Width / 2
        csBall.y = csPaddle.y - csBall.Height - 1
        csBall.DirY = -1
        csBall.DirX = 1
        csBall.SpeedX = 1 + Random(1)
        csBall.SpeedY = 2 + Random(1)
        Exit Sub
    End If


    'move the ball horizontally
    csBall.x = csBall.x + csBall.SpeedX * csBall.DirX
    If csBall.x < 7 Then
        'bounce off left wall
        csBall.x = 7
        csBall.DirX = 1
        dswWallHit.PlaySound
    ElseIf csBall.x > Picture1.ScaleWidth - csBall.Width - 7 Then
        'bounce off right wall
        csBall.x = Picture1.ScaleWidth - csBall.Width - 7
        csBall.DirX = -1
        dswWallHit.PlaySound
    End If


    'move the ball vertically
    csBall.y = csBall.y + csBall.SpeedY * csBall.DirY
```

```
If csBall.y < 19 Then
    'bounce off top wall
    csBall.y = 19
    csBall.DirY = 1
    dswWallHit.PlaySound
ElseIf csBall.y > Picture1.ScaleHeight - csPaddle.Height Then
    If csBall.x > 40 And csBall.x < 600 Then
        'player missed the ball
        GameState = Tracking
        csBall.SaveUnder cbBackBuffer.hdc
        lLives = lLives - 1
        If lLives < 1 Then GameState = GameOver
    Else
        'bounce off bottom corners
        csBall.y = Picture1.ScaleHeight - csPaddle.Height - 1
        csBall.DirY = -1
        dswWallHit.PlaySound
    End If
End If

'check for collision with paddle
If csBall.Collided(csPaddle) Then
    dswPaddleHit.PlaySound
    csBall.DirY = -1
    csBall.SpeedX = 1 + Random(2)
    csBall.SpeedY = 2 + Random(2)
    If csBall.x < csPaddle.x + csPaddle.Width / 2 Then
        csBall.DirX = -1
    Else
        csBall.DirX = 1
    End If
End If

'check for collision with blocks
For lCol = 0 To MAXACROSS - 1
    For lRow = 0 To MAXDOWN - 1
        lBlockNum = Map(lCol, lRow)
        If lBlockNum = 8 Then
            'hit solid block
```

```
                    If CheckCollision(csBall, lCol, lRow) Then
                        dswBlockHit.PlaySound
                    End If
                ElseIf lBlockNum <> -1 Then
                    'hit normal block
                    lNumBlocks = lNumBlocks + 1
                    If CheckCollision(csBall, lCol, lRow) Then
                        dswBlockHit.PlaySound
                        EraseBlock lCol, lRow
                        DropPoint lBlockNum, csBall.x, csBall.y
                        Map(lCol, lRow) = -1
                    End If
                End If
            Next lRow
        Next lCol

        If lNumBlocks = 0 Then
            'end of level
            lLevel = lLevel + 1
            If lLevel > 10 Then
                'end of game
                GameState = GameOver
            Else
                'load next level
                csPaddle.RestoreUnder cbBackBuffer.hdc
                csPaddle.CurrentFrame = 1
                csPaddle.SaveUnder cbBackBuffer.hdc
                LoadLevel App.Path & "\level" & lLevel & ".map"
                GameState = Tracking
            End If
        End If
    End If
End Sub

Private Function CheckCollision(ByRef ball As clsSprite, _
    ByVal lCol As Long, ByVal lRow As Long) As Boolean
    Dim r As RECT_API

    r.Left = 25 + lCol * 49
    r.Top = 35 + lRow * 25
    r.Right = r.Left + 48
    r.Bottom = r.Top + 24
```

```
        If ball.x > r.Left And ball.x < r.Right And _
            ball.y > r.Top And ball.y < r.Bottom Then
            CheckCollision = True

            'see if ball hit bottom of block
            If ball.y > r.Bottom - 5 Then
                ball.DirY = 1
                ball.SpeedX = 1 + Random(2)
                ball.SpeedY = 2 + Random(2)
                Exit Function
            End If

            'see if ball hit top of block
            If ball.y < r.Top + 5 Then
                ball.DirY = -1
                ball.SpeedX = 1 + Random(2)
                ball.SpeedY = 2 + Random(2)
                Exit Function
            End If

            'see if ball hit right side of block
            If ball.x > r.Left + 24 Then
                ball.DirX = ball.DirX * -1
                Exit Function
            End If

            'see if ball hit left side of block
            If ball.x < r.Left + 5 Then
                ball.DirX = ball.DirX * -1
                Exit Function
            End If
        End If

    CheckCollision = False
End Function
```

The UpdatePoints procedure requires a little more explanation because it is sort of critical to the game. (After all, if you can't keep track of score, the game isn't much fun). This routine will be important any time you want to make modifications to the game, such as adding new blocks or powerups.

UpdatePoints calls the AddScore procedure, which expects to receive the frame number of the point sprite. AddScore then determines how to increment the score (by taking into account the special silver, gold, and platinum tokens, for example). Any time you want to add new powerups to the game, you will simply add the token to the points.bmp file and then add a new index to the Select...Case statement to support the new powerup.

```
Private Sub UpdatePoints()
    Dim n As Long
    For n = 0 To NUMPOINTS
        'check
        If csPoints(n).Active Then
            csPoints(n).y = csPoints(n).y + csPoints(n).SpeedY
            If csPoints(n).y > Picture1.ScaleHeight Then
                csPoints(n).Active = False
            End If
            If csPoints(n).Collided(csPaddle) Then
                csPoints(n).Active = False
                'determine type of point
                Select Case csPoints(n).CurrentFrame
                    Case 0 To 7
                        AddScore csPoints(n).CurrentFrame
                    Case 8
                        'shrink
                        csPaddle.RestoreUnder cbBackBuffer.hdc
                        csPaddle.CurrentFrame = 0
                        csPaddle.SaveUnder cbBackBuffer.hdc
                    Case 9
                        'grow
                        csPaddle.RestoreUnder cbBackBuffer.hdc
                        csPaddle.CurrentFrame = 2
                        If csPaddle.x + csPaddle.Width + 8 > _
                            Picture1.ScaleWidth Then
                            csPaddle.x = Picture1.ScaleWidth - _
                                csPaddle.Width - 8
                        End If
                        csPaddle.SaveUnder cbBackBuffer.hdc
                    Case 10
                        'extra life
                        lLives = lLives + 1
                End Select
            End If
```

```
            End If
        Next n
    End Sub


    Private Sub AddScore(ByVal lBlockValue As Long)
        Select Case lBlockValue
            Case 1
                lScore = lScore + 1
            Case 2
                lScore = lScore + 2
            Case 3
                lScore = lScore + 3
            Case 4
                lScore = lScore + 4
            Case 5
                lScore = lScore + 5
            Case 6
                lScore = lScore + 10
            Case 7
                lScore = lScore + 15
            Case 8
                lScore = lScore + 20
        End Select
        If CLng(lScore Mod 100) = 0 Then
            DropPoint 10, csBall.x, csBall.y
        End If
    End Sub


    Private Sub DropPoint(ByVal lNum As Long, ByVal lLeft As Long, _
        ByVal lTop As Long)
        Dim n As Long

        For n = 0 To NUMPOINTS
            With csPoints(n)
                If Not .Active Then
                    If lNum < 5 And Random(10) = 0 Then
                        'random points become powerups
                        .CurrentFrame = 8 + Random(2)
                    Else
                        .CurrentFrame = lNum
                    End If
```

```
                    .x = lLeft
                    .y = lTop
                    .Active = True
                    .SaveUnder cbBackBuffer.hdc
                    Exit For
                End If
            End With
        Next n
End Sub


Public Function Random(ByVal num&) As Long
    Random = CLng(num * Rnd)
End Function


Private Sub DrawBlock(ByVal lCol As Long, ByVal lRow As Long)
    Dim lBlockNum As Long
    lBlockNum = Map(lCol, lRow)
    If lBlockNum > -1 And lBlockNum < 10 Then
        csBlocks.CurrentFrame = lBlockNum
        csBlocks.x = 25 + lCol * 49
        csBlocks.y = 35 + lRow * 25
        csBlocks.Draw cbBackBuffer.hdc
    End If
End Sub


Private Sub EraseBlock(ByVal lCol As Long, ByVal lRow As Long)
    Dim lLeft As Long
    Dim lTop As Long
    lLeft = 25 + lCol * 49
    lTop = 35 + lRow * 25
    cbBackgrnd.Blt cbBackBuffer.hdc, lLeft, lTop, _
        lLeft + 48, lTop + 24
End Sub


Private Sub LoadLevel(ByVal sFilename As String)
    Dim lFileNum As Long
    Dim lBlockNum As Long
    Dim lNumCols As Long
    Dim lNumRows As Long
    Dim lCol As Long
    Dim lRow As Long
```

```
    lFileNum = FreeFile
    Open sFilename For Input As #lFileNum

    'read the map data
    Input #1, lNumCols
    Input #1, lNumRows
    If lNumCols <> MAXACROSS Or lNumRows <> MAXDOWN Then
        MsgBox "Invalid level file: " & sFilename
        Close #lFileNum
        Exit Sub
    End If

    'load the level data
    For lCol = 0 To lNumCols - 1
        For lRow = 0 To lNumRows - 1
            Input #lFileNum, lBlockNum
            Map(lCol, lRow) = lBlockNum
            DrawBlock lCol, lRow
        Next lRow
    Next lCol

    'Close the file
    Close #lFileNum
End Sub
```

ENHANCING THE GAME

Here are some recommendations for improving the game:

- Convert the game to DirectDraw, using full-screen mode.
- Add more powerups, such as firepower, force fields, and multiple balls.
- Add new types of blocks, such as a castle block that requires multiple hits.
- Add fuzzy control to the ball, as explained in Chapter 15, "Artificial and Simulated Intelligence."
- Add animation to each of the blocks to make the game more interesting.
- Improve the accuracy of collision detection with better response for side hits.
- Add a musical score to each level by using clsDirectMusic8 and clsDISequence8.
- Add joystick support by using the clsDIJoystick8 class.

■ Keep track of high scores and ask players to enter their initials at the end of a game.

■ Add two-player support by adding a second paddle to the game.

■ Play a short jingle each time the player catches a powerup.

SUMMARY

Congratulations on completing your first Visual Basic game! Block Attack has shown how easy it is to develop a game once all the foundations have been laid. All of the chapters up to this point have covered the theory of game programming, while this chapter and those that follow demonstrate the design and function of actual game projects.

CHAPTER 20

WARBIRDS 1944: SCROLLING SHOOTER GAME

This chapter is focused entirely on building a vertical scrolling arcade game called Warbirds 1944, using techniques and code developed up to this point, with a focus on the Windows API version of the Visual Basic Game Library. DirectInput is used to provide keyboard and joystick support in the game, while DirectSound and DirectMusic are employed to handle sound effects and music.

This chapter covers the following topics:

- Playing Warbirds
- Building the Warbirds 1944 Project
- Enhancing the Game

PLAYING WARBIRDS

Warbirds 1944 was inspired by the classic Midway game *1942*, in which the player controls a P-38 Lightning fighter against waves of Japanese planes and ships somewhere in the Pacific. In contrast, Warbirds takes place over Europe against waves of German fighters and gun turrets. The game starts out difficult because early planes that you must fly do not handle well and have poor armaments and defensive strength. The game increases in difficulty in later missions, but you are equipped with better aircraft (such as the formidable P-51 Mustang and P-47 Thunderbolt).

Scrolling Shooter Genre

Warbirds 1944 is a top-view shoot-em-up game. This genre started with fixed-screen games like *Space Invaders* and *Galaxian*, and was enhanced with features like scrolling tile-based backgrounds in games like *R-Type*, *Spy Hunter*, and *Gradius*. The scrolling effect in typical shooters can be either vertical or horizontal. *R-Type* is a classic horizontal-scrolling arcade game that has been ported to nearly every video game system in existence (including Game Boy Advance). While horizontal-scrolling shooters do have advantages and can be just as much fun to play, vertical-scrolling shooters like Warbirds are generally easier to program.

Title Screen

The title screen for Warbirds displays some copyright information and shows the airplanes that the player will get to fly (see Figure 20.1). When the title screen appears, the background will

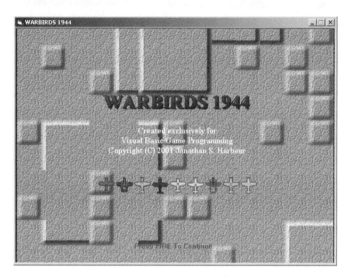

Figure 20.1

When the game starts, the title screen appears to the tune of Yankee Doodle Dandy.

scroll (providing a nice effect) while the opening musical score is played. The song I selected is a public domain MIDI version of Yankee Doodle Dandy, but feel free to replace it (along with all of the music tracks) with your own favorite sequence.

Mission Screen

The mission screen (shown in Figure 20.2) displays some information about the mission that is about to start. In Figure 20.2, you can see that Mission 1 is about to start, and that the airplane will be the P-40 Warhawk. Some attributes for this fighter are also included (top speed, attack, and defense), providing a glimpse into the performance of the plane.

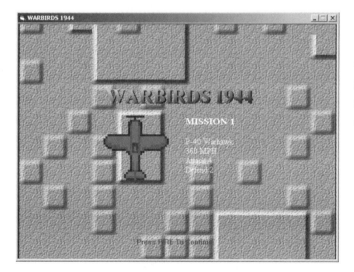

Figure 20.2

The mission screen shows the aircraft that you get to fly for the mission, along with the airplane's specs.

Take to the Skies!

The next few pages will show a series of screenshots from the game, with a description of the situation shown in each figure. Note in each image that debug text is listed in the top-left corner of the game window. Displaying vitals of the game can be a useful aid to debugging. At top-center is a countdown that shows how much time remains in the current mission. The red bar at the top-right shows the damage level of the player's aircraft.

Missile Volley

Figure 20.3 shows the first mission of the game, during which you must fly the poorly equipped P-40 Warhawk fighter. The goal of the game is not to make later missions easier, but to encourage the player to pass each level in order to acquire faster and more powerful airplanes.

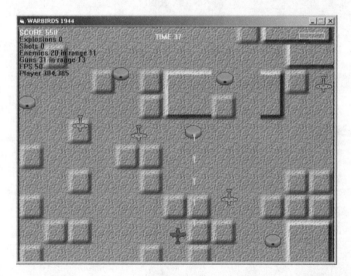

Figure 20.3

The P-40 Warhawk is a rather slow airplane, making the first mission extremely difficult.

Strafing the Enemy

Figure 20.4 shows the P-40 delivering a barrage of bullets into an enemy fighter and a turret, leaving nothing but debris and explosions in the wake. The turret and plane each got a few shots off before annihilation, but it looks like the P-40 will be able to move out of the way in time.

Caught in a Barrage

Figure 20.5 shows an enemy fighter (a German BF-109) launching a line of fire across the flight path of our trusty P-40. More than likely, the fate of this pilot is sealed, unless he can get off a shot at the last minute to stop the downpour of bullets.

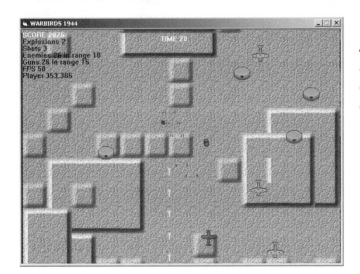

Figure 20.4

A volley of bullets fired by the P-40 decimates an enemy fighter and a turret.

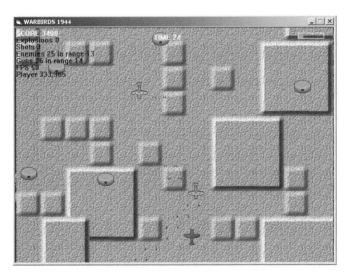

Figure 20.5

The P-40 is caught in a barrage of bullets fired by a strafing BF-109.

Lightning Strike

As Figure 20.6 shows, the P-38 Lightning is an awesome fighter plane, and beautifully styled at the same time. Mission 7 lets you fly this distinguished airplane against the German Luftwaffe. This screen is the title screen for the mission, showing that the P-38 has a balanced attack/defense value of 7, with a top speed of 410 MPH.

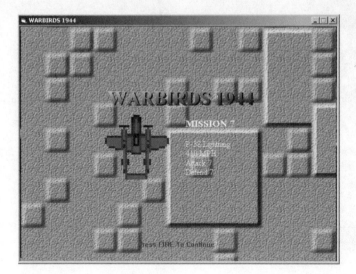

Figure 20.6

The P-38 Lightning is a beautifully styled airplane that you get to fly in Mission 7.

Superior Firepower

The fighter planes in later missions are far more capable than earlier models, with higher movement rates, faster rates of fire, and better armor for defense. The P-38 Lightning shown in Figure 20.7 is strafing two German BF-109 fighters while avoiding their return fire. Note the explosion sprites flaring up on the first enemy fighter.

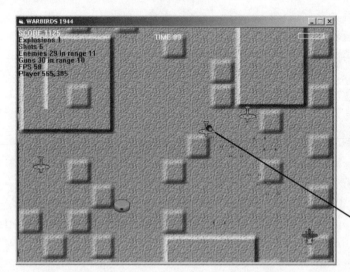

Figure 20.7

The P-38 Lightning chews up two enemy fighters. Note the explosions on the enemy plane and the sheer number of shots being fired.

Explosion sprite

Mutual Destruction

By the looks of things in Figure 20.8, it doesn't appear as if the P-39 Aircobra will survive the stream of rockets and bullets without some evasive maneuvers—and quick! On a positive note, the rocket turret will definitely be a smoking cinder soon.

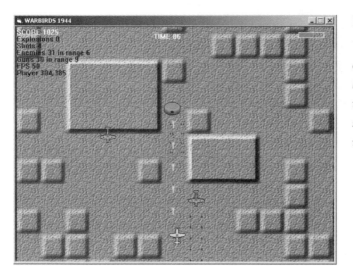

Figure 20.8

The P-39 Aircobra is caught between a volley of missiles fired by the turret and a stream of bullets from the BF-109.

Final Mission

The final mission of the game (Mission 9) puts you in the cockpit of the formidable P-47 Thunderbolt, which features an attack value of 9 and a defense value of 9. Just take a look at Figure 20.9 for an example of the P-47 in action. The modern A-10 Thunderbolt II was named after the good old P-47 because it too is capable of surviving a lot of punishment.

Figure 20.10 shows a zoomed-in version of the screen shown in Figure 20.9. This close-up view shows the explosion sprites trailing behind the P-47, as well as the detail of the BF-109 fighters. The turrets are not very attractive or functionally sound, but as far as programmer art goes, they're not bad.

Victory Screen

The victory screen is displayed when you complete the final mission of the game (Mission 9), as shown in Figure 20.11. Since you must restart each level when your plane is destroyed, it can take a while to get to the end of the game.

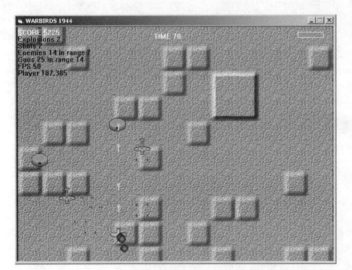

Figure 20.9

The P-47 Thunderbolt is a formidable fighter, capable of delivering as much punishment as it can take.

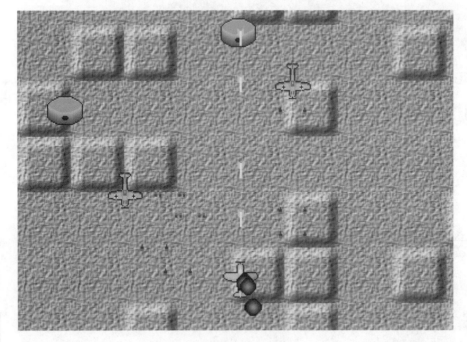

Figure 20.10

This close-up view of the battlefield in Warbirds 1944 shows the detail of the sprites in the game.

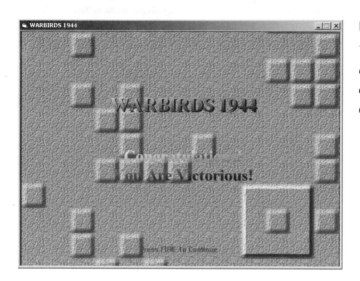

Figure 20.11

The victory screen appears after you complete the last stage of the game.

BUILDING THE WARBIRDS 1944 PROJECT

Now that you have seen what the game looks like, how would you like to create the game from scratch? Glad to hear it! The following pages describe how to create the Warbirds project, how to add game library files to the project, and how to configure the settings prior to actually typing in the source code.

Warbirds Project

This game is like every other game project in the book, requiring just a single (default) form and a new project. Fire up Visual Basic and create a new project. As indicated in Figure 20.12, select a Standard EXE project.

Figure 20.12

The New Project dialog box in Visual Basic

Project Explorer

Warbirds uses numerous classes that were developed in earlier chapters and compiled into the game library in Chapter 13, "Building the DirectX Game Library." I have opted to include the class files directly inside the project for this game in order to eliminate the need for the external VBGL.dll file that results from compiling the game library. While it is usually not necessary to include all of the game library files in the later stages of game development, it is convenient to have the classes be part of the game project for debugging purposes.

You might want to use the compiled library for the final release. It is certainly convenient to have all the classes instantly available just by creating a reference to the game library (which usually negates the need to also include the DirectX type libraries, since they are already referenced in the DLL). Basically, do what is most convenient and most productive when it comes to using the game library developed earlier.

Figure 20.13 shows the Project Explorer window for the Warbirds project, including all the files required by the game. The easiest way to attach these files to the project is to simply drag them from Windows Explorer over the Project Explorer window in VB. But you can also add each file separately from the Project menu.

Figure 20.13

The Project Explorer window in Visual Basic shows the files in the Warbirds project.

The complete Warbirds project is shown in Figure 20.14 as it appears in VB, with the code window for Form1 loaded. Notice how the editor window features a split screen. This is a really handy feature for keeping a section of code visible while scrolling around with the other window. You can split the code window from the Window menu.

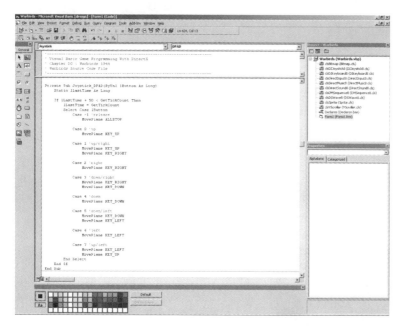

Figure 20.14

The Warbirds project loaded into Visual Basic

References

Since the Warbirds project includes the needed class files directly and does not use the game library, you must reference the DirectX 8 for Visual Basic Type Library in the References dialog box (as shown in Figure 20.15). Since this game does not use DirectDraw, there is no need to reference DirectX 7.

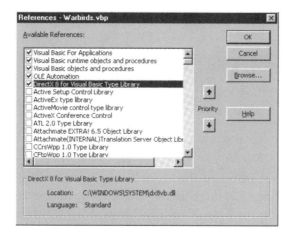

Figure 20.15

The References dialog box shows the DirectX 8 for Visual Basic Type Library.

Source Artwork

The source artwork for Warbirds includes several bitmap files that you will need in order to run the game. While you should feel free to draw the graphics from scratch, you will most likely want to just copy the files off the CD into your project directory for Warbirds. Once there, you can make any changes that you want to the bitmaps used in the game.

Projectiles

The projectiles (bullets and rockets) in the game are stored in a file called bullets.bmp, which is shown in Figure 20.16. One easy enhancement that you can make to the game is to add new bullet sprites so that each plane has a unique weapon sprite.

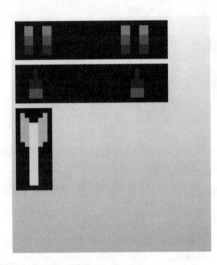

Figure 20.16

The bullets.bmp file holds the projectile graphics for the Warbirds game.

Enemy Fighters and Turrets

The enemy fighters and turrets used in the game are actually very simple and are not even animated. The bitmaps are stored in a file called enemies.bmp, as shown in Figure 20.17.

Explosions

The cool-looking explosions in the game (shown in Figure 20.18) are made up of three animated sprites, with each explosion sprite consisting of three frames (small, medium, and large), all stored in a file called explosions.bmp. By displaying these explosions with a slight randomness, a pretty good effect is created on the screen to demonstrate an explosion.

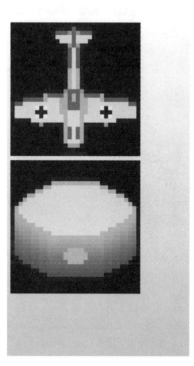

Figure 20.17

The enemies.bmp file holds the enemy fighter and turret sprites.

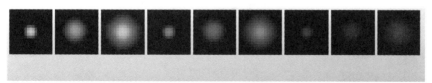

Figure 20.18

The explosions.bmp file holds three different animated explosion sprites.

Map Tiles

The map tiles for the game (shown in Figure 20.19) were the most difficult images for a mere programmer to draw. Creating your own map tiles by hand will quickly engender newfound adoration for skilled game artists. I was able to improve the scrolling map by drawing raised rectangles at random locations using tiles that are generated by a procedure called `CreateRandomLevel` (first introduced back in Chapter 9, "Let the Animation Begin").

Note that there are nine rows—one for each mission in the game. To really improve the visual appeal of the game, I would recommend that you create new tiles for each mission. The varied tiles I created are not sufficient and the missions all look nearly the same as a result.

Figure 20.19

The maptiles.bmp file holds the bitmaps used to construct the scrolling background.

Air Superiority

The planes.bmp file (shown in Figure 20.20) includes the bitmaps for each of the nine planes used in the game (with each plane featuring a left, right, and center image). The varied airplanes are definitely the coolest part of the game.

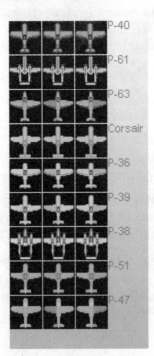

Figure 20.20

The planes.bmp file holds the animated sprite for each fighter plane controlled by the player.

Transparent Message Boxes

In case you were wondering about the mission screens that are drawn over the scrolling background at the start of each mission, take a look at Figure 20.21, which shows the bitmap for the title screen. Note that it is simply an image with a black background, which is loaded as a sprite and drawn transparently.

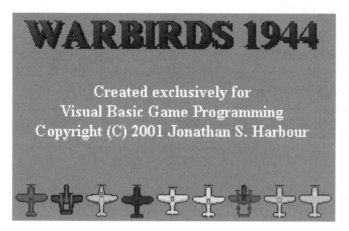

Figure 20.21

Bitmaps with black backgrounds (such as mission title screens) are drawn transparently in the game.

User Input

While Warbirds uses the enhanced Windows API game library routines that were developed earlier in the book for double buffering and sprite handling, the user input handler for the game was implemented with DirectInput and the input classes developed back in Chapter 12, "Getting a Handle on User Input." Warbirds does not use the mouse for input, primarily because it is a windowed program. Acquiring the mouse is complicated (for instance, when dealing with switching applications or pop-up windows).

Warbirds does support a joystick. The joystick handler actually uses the directional pad rather than the analog stick (since D-pad input is easier to handle).

The following DirectInput classes are used in this game:

- clsDirectInput8
- clsDIKeyboard8
- clsDIJoystick8

Sound Effects and Music

The music in Warbirds is comprised of MIDI files, one for each mission in the game. The songs are all public domain and feature United States military themes, past and present. Music playback is handled by DirectMusic.

The sound effects in Warbirds are very simple (with no positional effects), and there are only three of them—an explosion sound, a gun sound, and a rocket sound. I recorded all three sounds with the simple Sound Recorder that comes with Windows, using common household appliances. While the features in a program like Syntrillium's Cool Edit 2000 are impressive, there are times when the ultra-simple Sound Recorder can come in handy. Since there are no wave-editing features with the program, you have to be quick on the draw with the Record and Stop buttons.

Here are the game library classes that are included in the game to handle audio:

- clsDirectSound8
- clsDSWave8
- clsDirectMusic8
- clsDMSequence8

Warbirds Source Code

The source code for Warbirds 1944 is quite lengthy, so I will try to explain each part of the game along the way. For starters, you will want to have the code window for Form1 open, because that is where all of this code should be entered. This first section of code includes the program variables, constants, structures, and objects needed by the game.

```
'-------------------------------------------------------------------
' Visual Basic Game Programming With DirectX
' Chapter 20: Warbirds 1944
' Warbirds Source Code File
'-------------------------------------------------------------------
Option Explicit
Option Base 0

'Windows API functions
Private Declare Function GetTickCount Lib "kernel32" () As Long

'program constants
Const MAXFRAMERATE As Long = 120
Const MAXBULLETS As Long = 10
Const MAXENEMIES As Long = 30
```

```vb
Const MAXEXPLODES As Long = 10
Const MAXGUNS As Long = 30
Const MAXROCKETS As Long = 10

'DirectInput key codes
Const KEY_LEFT As Long = 203
Const KEY_RIGHT As Long = 205
Const KEY_UP As Long = 200
Const KEY_DOWN As Long = 208
Const KEY_LCTRL As Long = 29
Const KEY_ESC As Long = 1
Const KEY_PGDN As Long = 209
Const KEY_SPACE As Long = 57
Const ALLSTOP As Long = 999

'late-initialized constants
Dim CWHITE As Long
Dim CRED As Long
Dim CGREEN As Long
Dim CBLUE As Long
Dim CBLACK As Long

'program structures
Private Enum GAME_STATUS
    LOADING = 1
    SHOWTITLE = 2
    RUNNING = 3
    NEXTMISSION = 4
    ENDGAME = 5
End Enum

Private Type POSITION
    X As Long
    Y As Long
End Type

Private Type BOUNDARY
    Left As Long
    Top As Long
    Right As Long
    Bottom As Long
End Type
```

```vb
'program controls
Dim WithEvents Picture1 As PictureBox

'DirectX components
Dim dinput As clsDirectInput8
Dim WithEvents Keyboard As clsDIKeyboard8
Dim WithEvents Joystick As clsDIJoystick8
Dim dsound As clsDirectSound8
Dim dswFire As clsDSWave8
Dim dswBoom As clsDSWave8
Dim dswRocket As clsDSWave8
Dim dmusic As clsDirectMusic8
Dim dmsSong As clsDMSequence8

'game library objects
Dim csPlayerBullets(0 To MAXBULLETS) As clsSprite
Dim csEnemyBullets(0 To MAXBULLETS) As clsSprite
Dim csEnemyRockets(0 To MAXROCKETS) As clsSprite
Dim csEnemy(0 To MAXENEMIES) As clsSprite
Dim csGuns(0 To MAXGUNS) As clsSprite
Dim csExplosions(0 To MAXEXPLODES) As clsSprite
Dim WithEvents Scroller As clsVScroller
Dim cbBackBuf As New clsBitmap
Dim csPlane As New clsSprite
Dim csMission As clsSprite

'variables related to game status
Dim lMissionNumber As Long
Dim GameStatus As GAME_STATUS
Dim bGameOver As Boolean
Dim bMissionLoaded As Boolean
Dim lCurrentMission As Long

'variables related to player
Dim lPlayerHealth As Long
Dim lPlayerDamage As Long
Dim lPlayerSpeed As Long
Dim lPlayerAttack As Long
Dim lPlayerScore As Long
```

```
'variables related to projectiles
Dim lBulletCount As Long
Dim lBulletNum As Long
Dim lExplCount As Long
Dim lExplNum As Long
Dim lRocketCount As Long
Dim lRocketNum As Long
Dim lActiveGuns As Long
Dim lLastShot As Long
Dim lGunCount As Long

'misc program variables
Dim bRunning As Boolean
Dim lEnemyCount As Long
Dim lEnemiesInRange As Long
Dim lFrameRate As Long
```

The Form_Load procedure starts running when the game begins, and incorporates all of the initialization code needed to get the game up and running, including the code to load the bitmaps, sprites, sound effects, and music, as well as the code to initialize the DirectX components. This initialization code is lengthy, but fairly easy to understand. The large portions of code under each comment line include extra error-checking code to make sure the game objects are loaded properly. If anything fails to load, the game will error out.

Following Form_Load are two additional event procedures. Form_Paint is called any time the window is obstructed, and simply draws the back buffer to the screen in order to clean up things. This is not really needed in a game with a scrolling background, but it is good practice nonetheless. Form_QueryUnload is an event procedure that is called when you try to close the game window, and simply calls Shutdown to end the game.

```
Private Sub Form_Load()
    Dim n As Long
    Dim fn As String
    Dim ret As Boolean

    CWHITE = RGB(255, 255, 255)
    CRED = RGB(255, 0, 0)
    CGREEN = RGB(0, 255, 0)
    CBLUE = RGB(0, 0, 255)
    CBLACK = RGB(0, 0, 0)
```

```
Randomize GetTickCount
bRunning = True

'set up the main form
Form1.Caption = "WARBIRDS 1944"
Form1.AutoRedraw = False
Form1.BorderStyle = 1
Form1.ClipControls = False
Form1.KeyPreview = True
Form1.ScaleMode = 3
Form1.Width = 640 * Screen.TwipsPerPixelX
Form1.Height = 480 * Screen.TwipsPerPixelY
Form1.Show

'create the PictureBox control for drawing
Set Picture1 = Controls.Add("VB.PictureBox", "Picture1")
Picture1.AutoRedraw = False
Picture1.BorderStyle = 1
Picture1.ClipControls = False
Picture1.ScaleMode = 3
Picture1.BackColor = CBLACK
Picture1.Left = 0
Picture1.Top = 0
Picture1.Width = Form1.ScaleWidth
Picture1.Height = Form1.ScaleHeight
Picture1.Visible = True

'create DirectInput object
Set dinput = New clsDirectInput8
dinput.Startup Form1.hWnd

'create Keyboard object
Set Keyboard = New clsDIKeyboard8
Keyboard.Startup dinput, Form1.hWnd

'create Joystick object
Set Joystick = New clsDIJoystick8
If Not Joystick.Startup(dinput, Form1.hWnd) Then
    Debug.Print "Joystick not detected"
End If
```

```
'initialize DirectSound
Set dsound = New clsDirectSound8
dsound.Startup Form1.hWnd

'load fire sound
Set dswFire = New clsDSWave8
dswFire.LoadSound dsound, App.Path & "\fire.wav"
dswFire.Interrupt = True

'load boom sound
Set dswBoom = New clsDSWave8
dswBoom.LoadSound dsound, App.Path & "\boom.wav"
dswBoom.Interrupt = False

'load rocket sound
Set dswRocket = New clsDSWave8
dswRocket.LoadSound dsound, App.Path & "\rocket.wav"
dswRocket.Interrupt = True

'initialize DirectMusic
Set dmusic = New clsDirectMusic8
If Not dmusic.Startup(Form1.hWnd) Then
    MsgBox "Error initializing DirectMusic"
    Shutdown
End If

'load music sequence
Set dmsSong = New clsDMSequence8
dmusic.Volume = -1500
PlayMissionSong

'create the double buffer
ret = cbBackBuf.Create(Picture1.hdc, Picture1.ScaleWidth, _
    Picture1.ScaleHeight)
If ret = False Or cbBackBuf.hdc = 0 Then
    MsgBox "Error creating double buffer"
    Shutdown
End If

'create the scroller object
Set Scroller = New clsVScroller
```

```vbnet
'load some stuff temporarily needed
LoadNewMission


'load the enemy planes
For n = 0 To MAXENEMIES
    Set csEnemy(n) = New clsSprite
    csEnemy(n).Active = True
    csEnemy(n).Transparent = True
    ret = csEnemy(n).LoadFrames(App.Path & "\enemies.bmp", _
        1, 1, 32, 32, 1)
    If ret = False Or csEnemy(n).hdc = 0 Then
        MsgBox "Error loading enemy plane #" & n
        Shutdown
    End If

    csEnemy(n).GlobalX = Random(Scroller.MaxTileCols * _
        Scroller.TileWidth) - csEnemy(n).Width
    csEnemy(n).GlobalY = Random(Scroller.MaxTileRows * _
        Scroller.TileHeight) - csEnemy(n).Height
    csEnemy(n).SpeedX = Random(3) - 1
    csEnemy(n).SpeedY = 1
Next n
If n < MAXENEMIES Then
    MsgBox "Error loading enemy planes (count = " & n & ")"
    Shutdown
End If


'load the ground guns
For n = 0 To MAXGUNS
    Set csGuns(n) = New clsSprite
    csGuns(n).Transparent = True
    csGuns(n).Active = True
    ret = csGuns(n).LoadFrames(App.Path & "\enemies.bmp", _
        1, 34, 32, 32, 1)
    If ret = False Or csGuns(n).hdc = 0 Then
        MsgBox "Error loading enemies.bmp"
        Shutdown
    End If

    csGuns(n).GlobalX = Random(Scroller.MaxTileCols * _
        Scroller.TileWidth) - csGuns(n).Width
```

```
        csGuns(n).GlobalY = Random(Scroller.MaxTileRows * _
            Scroller.TileHeight) - csGuns(n).Height
        csGuns(n).SpeedX = 0
        csGuns(n).SpeedY = 0
    Next n
    If n < MAXGUNS Then
        MsgBox "Error loading enemy guns (count = " & n & ")"
        Shutdown
    End If


    'load the player bullets
    For lBulletNum = 0 To MAXBULLETS
        Set csPlayerBullets(lBulletNum) = New clsSprite
        csPlayerBullets(lBulletNum).Transparent = True
        ret = csPlayerBullets(lBulletNum).LoadFrames( _
            App.Path & "\bullets.bmp", 0, 0, 32, 8, 1)
        If ret = False Or _
            csPlayerBullets(lBulletNum).hdc = 0 Then
            MsgBox "Error loading bullets.bmp"
            Shutdown
        End If
    Next lBulletNum
    If lBulletNum < MAXBULLETS Then
        MsgBox "Error loading player bullets (count = " & _
            lBulletNum & ")"
        Shutdown
    End If


    'load the enemy bullets
    For lBulletNum = 0 To MAXBULLETS
        Set csEnemyBullets(lBulletNum) = New clsSprite
        csEnemyBullets(lBulletNum).Transparent = True
        ret = csEnemyBullets(lBulletNum).LoadFrames( _
            App.Path & "\bullets.bmp", 0, 9, 32, 8, 1)
        If ret = False Or _
            csEnemyBullets(lBulletNum).hdc = 0 Then
            MsgBox "Error loading bullets.bmp"
            Shutdown
        End If
    Next lBulletNum
```

```
If lBulletNum < MAXBULLETS Then
    MsgBox "Error loading enemy bullets (count = " & _
        lBulletNum & ")"
    Shutdown
End If


'load the enemy rockets
For lBulletNum = 0 To MAXROCKETS
    Set csEnemyRockets(lBulletNum) = New clsSprite
    csEnemyRockets(lBulletNum).Transparent = True
    ret = csEnemyRockets(lBulletNum).LoadFrames( _
        App.Path & "\bullets.bmp", 0, 18, 8, 16, 1)
    If ret = False Or _
        csEnemyRockets(lBulletNum).hdc = 0 Then
        MsgBox "Error loading bullets.bmp"
        Shutdown
    End If
Next lBulletNum
If lBulletNum < MAXROCKETS Then
    MsgBox "Error loading enemy rockets (count = " & _
        lBulletNum & ")"
    Shutdown
End If


'load the explosions
For n = 0 To MAXEXPLODES
    Set csExplosions(n) = New clsSprite
    csExplosions(n).Transparent = True
    csExplosions(n).Active = False
    ret = csExplosions(n).LoadFrames( _
        App.Path & "\explosions.bmp", 0, 0, 17, 16, 9)
    If ret = False Or csExplosions(n).hdc = 0 Then
        MsgBox "Error loading explosions.bmp"
        Shutdown
    End If
    ret = csExplosions(n).GenerateAllMasks
    If ret = False Or csExplosions(n).MaskDC = 0 Then
        MsgBox "Error generating explosion masks"
        Shutdown
    End If
Next n
```

```
        If n < MAXEXPLODES Then
            MsgBox "Error loading explosions (count = " & n & ")"
            Shutdown
        End If

        lMissionNumber = 0
        lCurrentMission = lMissionNumber
        lPlayerScore = 0
        GameStatus = SHOWTITLE

        GameLoop
End Sub

Private Sub Form_Paint()
    cbBackBuf.Draw 0, 0, Picture1.hdc
End Sub

Private Sub Form_QueryUnload(Cancel As Integer, _
    UnloadMode As Integer)
    Shutdown
End Sub
```

The DirectInput user input event procedures are next in the program listing for Warbirds. The
first event procedure, Keyboard_KeyDown, is triggered any time you press a key. Note that there is a
delay of 50 milliseconds in this procedure—an attempt to slow things down when a key is held
down. You might want to experiment with this value if keyboard input seems inefficient.

Following the keyboard handler are two event procedures for handling joystick input.
Joystick_ButtonDown is fired off any time a joystick button is pressed, while Joystick_DPAD is triggered when the directional pad is pressed.

```
Private Sub Keyboard_KeyDown(ByVal lKey As Long)
    Select Case lKey
        Case KEY_LEFT
            MovePlane KEY_LEFT
        Case KEY_RIGHT
            MovePlane KEY_RIGHT
        Case KEY_UP
            MovePlane KEY_UP
        Case KEY_DOWN
            MovePlane KEY_DOWN
```

```
            Case KEY_LCTRL
                'fire a shot
                If GameStatus = RUNNING Then PlayerFireShot
            Case KEY_ESC
                Shutdown
            Case KEY_PGDN
                GameStatus = NEXTMISSION
            Case KEY_SPACE
                Select Case GameStatus
                    Case SHOWTITLE
                        'display mission screen
                        bMissionLoaded = False
                        GameStatus = NEXTMISSION
                    Case NEXTMISSION
                        'start next mission
                        If lMissionNumber = 10 Then
                            Shutdown
                        Else
                            GameStatus = LOADING
                        End If
                    Case ENDGAME
                        'end game
                        Shutdown
                End Select
        End Select
End Sub


Private Sub Joystick_ButtonDown(ByVal lButton As Long)
    'fire a shot
    If GameStatus = RUNNING Then PlayerFireShot
End Sub


Private Sub Joystick_DPAD(ByVal lButton As Long)
    Static lLastTime As Long

    If lLastTime + 50 < GetTickCount Then
        lLastTime = GetTickCount
        Select Case lButton
            Case -1 'release
                MovePlane ALLSTOP
```

```
        Case 0 'up
            MovePlane KEY_UP

        Case 1 'up/right
            MovePlane KEY_UP
            MovePlane KEY_RIGHT

        Case 2 'right
            MovePlane KEY_RIGHT

        Case 3 'down/right
            MovePlane KEY_RIGHT
            MovePlane KEY_DOWN

        Case 4 'down
            MovePlane KEY_DOWN

        Case 5 'down/left
            MovePlane KEY_DOWN
            MovePlane KEY_LEFT

        Case 6 'left
            MovePlane KEY_LEFT

        Case 7 'up/left
            MovePlane KEY_LEFT
            MovePlane KEY_UP
        End Select
    End If
End Sub
```

The Scroller_Complete event procedure is called by the Vscroller class when a scrolling map reaches the end of the tile array. Since the scroller automatically wraps back up to the top of the list, it proved necessary to include an event notification when the bottom of a map is reached. In the case of Warbirds, that triggers the end of a mission.

```
Private Sub Scroller_Complete()
    'if game loop running, go to next mission
    If GameStatus = RUNNING Then
        GameStatus = NEXTMISSION
        bMissionLoaded = False
    End If
End Sub
```

The GameLoop procedure is launched by Form_Load to start the game loop running. GameLoop checks the GameStatus variable to determine how program flow should be handled, depending on which state the game is in. The really important code is found under Case RUNNING, where normal gameplay is handled.

```
Private Sub GameLoop()
    Static lStartTime As Long
    Static lCounter As Long
    Static lNewTime As Long
    Dim fn As String

    'store starting time
    lStartTime = GetTickCount

    'game loop
    Do While bRunning
        lCounter = GetTickCount() - lStartTime
        'if time for next frame...
        If lCounter > lNewTime Then
            'check the game status
            Select Case GameStatus
                Case SHOWTITLE
                    If Not bMissionLoaded Then
                        lMissionNumber = 0
                        lCurrentMission = lMissionNumber
                        LoadNewMission
                        bMissionLoaded = True
                    End If
                    Scroller.Scroll 1
                    Scroller.DrawTiles 13, 10, cbBackBuf.hdc
                    csMission.X = 160
                    csMission.Y = 120
                    csMission.Draw cbBackBuf.hdc
                    cbBackBuf.DrawText Picture1.ScaleWidth _
                        / 2 - 80, Picture1.ScaleHeight - 40, _
                        "Press SPACEBAR To Continue", CBLUE
                    DoEvents
```

```
        Case NEXTMISSION
            If Not bMissionLoaded Then
                lMissionNumber = lMissionNumber + 1
                lCurrentMission = lMissionNumber
                LoadNewMission
                ResetEnemies
                bMissionLoaded = True
                PlayMissionSong
            End If
            Scroller.Scroll 1
            Scroller.DrawTiles 13, 10, cbBackBuf.hdc
            csMission.X = 160
            csMission.Y = 120
            csMission.Draw cbBackBuf.hdc
            cbBackBuf.DrawText Picture1.ScaleWidth _
                / 2 - 80, Picture1.ScaleHeight - 40, _
                "Press SPACEBAR To Continue", CBLUE
            DoEvents

        Case LOADING
            Set csPlane = Nothing
            Set csPlane = New clsSprite
            csPlane.Transparent = True
            fn = App.Path & "\planes.bmp"
            If Not csPlane.LoadFrames(fn, 0, (lMissionNumber - 1) _
                * 32, 32, 32, 3) Then
                MsgBox "Error loading " & fn
                Shutdown
            End If

            'move fighter to starting position
            csPlane.CurrentFrame = 1
            csPlane.X = 320 - csPlane.Width / 2
            csPlane.Y = Picture1.ScaleHeight - _
                csPlane.Height * 2

            'LoadNewMission
            bMissionLoaded = False
            GameStatus = RUNNING
            DoEvents
```

```
                    Case RUNNING
                            Scroller.Scroll 1
                            Scroller.DrawTiles 13, 10, cbBackBuf.hdc
                            GameUpdate lCounter
                            lNewTime = lCounter + 1000 / MAXFRAMERATE
                            DoEvents

                    End Select

                    'blit double buffer to the screen
                    cbBackBuf.Draw 0, 0, Picture1.hdc

                    'check for user input
                    Keyboard.Check_Keyboard
                    Joystick.Check_Joystick
                End If
                DoEvents
        Loop
End Sub
```

The GameUpdate procedure is called from GameLoop for each frame. GameUpdate is responsible for moving and drawing all the objects in the game to the double buffer (which is blitted to the screen inside GameLoop).

```
Private Sub GameUpdate(ByVal MS As Long)
        Static lCounter As Long
        Static lTimer As Long
        Static lStart As Long
        Static lScroll As Long
        Dim lLeft As Long
        Dim lValue As Long
        Dim n As Long

        'begin screen update timing
        lStart = GetTickCount

        'process game objects
        MoveEnemies
        MoveGuns
        MoveBullets
        MoveRockets
```

```
MovePlayer
DrawExplosions

'display player damage level
lLeft = Picture1.ScaleWidth - 70
lValue = lPlayerHealth - lPlayerDamage
If lValue > 0 Then
    For n = 1 To lValue * 5
        cbBackBuf.DrawLine lLeft + n, 10, _
            lLeft + n, 20, CRED
    Next n
    cbBackBuf.DrawRect lLeft, 10, lLeft + 50, _
        20, CWHITE
End If

'display score and timer
cbBackBuf.DrawText 2, 2, "SCORE " & lPlayerScore, CWHITE
cbBackBuf.DrawText Picture1.ScaleWidth / 2 - 40, 10, _
    "TIME " & Scroller.MajorScroll, CWHITE

'display game info
cbBackBuf.DrawText 2, 15, "Explosions " & _
    lExplCount, CBLACK
cbBackBuf.DrawText 2, 28, "Shots " & lBulletCount, CBLACK
cbBackBuf.DrawText 2, 41, "Enemies " & lEnemyCount & _
    " in range " & lEnemiesInRange, CBLACK
cbBackBuf.DrawText 2, 54, "Guns " & lGunCount & _
    " in range " & lActiveGuns, CBLACK
cbBackBuf.DrawText 2, 67, "FPS " & lFrameRate, CBLACK
cbBackBuf.DrawText 2, 80, "Player " & csPlane.X & _
    "," & csPlane.Y, CBLACK

'end screen update timing
lStart = GetTickCount - lStart

'count the frames per second
If MS > lTimer + 1000 Then
    lTimer = MS
    lFrameRate = lCounter
    lCounter = 0
```

```
        Else
            lCounter = lCounter + 1
        End If
End Sub
```

The `PlayMissionSong` procedure loads and plays a MIDI file by reading a filename based on the current mission number.

```
Private Sub PlayMissionSong()
    Dim fn As String

    'stop currently playing music
    dmsSong.StopMusic

    'load MIDI file
    fn = App.Path & "\mission" & lMissionNumber & ".mid"
    If Not dmsSong.LoadMusic(dmusic, fn) Then
        MsgBox "Error loading MIDI file " & fn
        Shutdown
    End If

    'start song playing in a loop
    dmsSong.Looping = True
    dmsSong.PlayMusic
End Sub
```

The `ResetEnemies` procedure cleans up the enemy airplanes, turrets, bullets, and rockets at the start of each new mission. The enemies are placed randomly on the scrolling game map (using global positions).

```
Private Sub ResetEnemies()
    Dim n As Long

    'reset enemy planes
    For n = 0 To MAXENEMIES
        csEnemy(n).Active = True
        csEnemy(n).GlobalX = Random(Scroller.MaxTileCols * _
            Scroller.TileWidth) - csEnemy(n).Width
        csEnemy(n).GlobalY = Random(Scroller.MaxTileRows * _
            Scroller.TileHeight) - csEnemy(n).Height
    Next n
```

```
    'reset enemy bullets
    For n = 0 To MAXBULLETS
        With csEnemyBullets(n)
            .Active = False
            .X = 0
            .Y = 0
        End With
    Next n

    'reset enemy guns
    For n = 0 To MAXGUNS
        csGuns(n).Active = True
        csGuns(n).GlobalX = Random(Scroller.MaxTileCols * _
            Scroller.TileWidth) - csEnemy(n).Width
        csGuns(n).GlobalY = Random(Scroller.MaxTileRows * _
            Scroller.TileHeight) - csEnemy(n).Height
    Next n

    'reset enemy rockets
    For n = 0 To MAXROCKETS
        With csEnemyRockets(n)
            .Active = False
            .X = 0
            .Y = 0
        End With
    Next n
End Sub
```

The LoadNewMission procedure is called by GameLoop when the game status indicates it is time for the next mission. This procedure cleans up variables and objects for a new mission, generates and loads a new map, and initializes the player's airplane.

```
Private Sub LoadNewMission()
    Dim fn As String

    're-create the mission graphic
    Set csMission = Nothing
    Set csMission = New clsSprite

    'load the mission graphic
    csMission.Transparent = True
```

```
fn = App.Path & "\mission" & lMissionNumber & ".bmp"
If Not csMission.LoadFrames(fn, 0, 0, 320, 200, 1) Then
    MsgBox "Error loading " & fn
    Shutdown
End If


'load tiles for current map
fn = App.Path & "\maptiles.bmp"
If Not Scroller.LoadTiles(fn, 0, 0, 48, 48, 10) Then
    MsgBox "Error loading " & fn
    Shutdown
End If


'set left edge of map
Scroller.StartX = 2


'load the scrolling terrain
CreateRandomLevel App.Path & "\level.dat", 13, 50 + _
    lMissionNumber * 10
LoadLevel App.Path & "\level.dat"


'initialize plane stats
Select Case lMissionNumber
    Case 1 'P-40
        lPlayerHealth = 2
        lPlayerDamage = 0
        lPlayerAttack = 4
        lPlayerSpeed = 1

    Case 2 'P-61
        lPlayerHealth = 3
        lPlayerDamage = 0
        lPlayerAttack = 4
        lPlayerSpeed = 1

    Case 3 'P-63
        lPlayerHealth = 3
        lPlayerDamage = 0
        lPlayerAttack = 4
        lPlayerSpeed = 1
```

```
                lExplCount = lExplCount + 1
                'draw explosion sprite five times
                For n = 0 To 5
                    .X = .X + Random(3) - 1
                    .Y = .Y + Random(3) - 1
                    .Draw cbBackBuf.hdc
                    .CurrentFrame = Random(10)
                Next n
                'draw multiple times for effect
                .MoveRate = .MoveRate - 1
                If .MoveRate < 1 Then .Active = False
            End If
        End With
    Next lNum
End Sub
```

The MovePlane procedure is called by the keyboard and joystick handlers to update the airplane's speed based on the specific type of input that was generated.

Next, the MovePlayer procedure updates the player's aircraft position on the screen and draws the sprite for the airplane.

```
Private Sub MovePlane(ByVal lDir As Long)
    Select Case lDir
        Case KEY_LEFT
            csPlane.SpeedX = -lPlayerSpeed
        Case KEY_RIGHT
            csPlane.SpeedX = lPlayerSpeed
        Case KEY_UP
            csPlane.SpeedY = -lPlayerSpeed
        Case KEY_DOWN
            csPlane.SpeedY = lPlayerSpeed
        Case Else
            csPlane.SpeedX = 0
            csPlane.SpeedY = 0
    End Select
End Sub

Private Sub MovePlayer()
    With csPlane
        'set the current frame
        .CurrentFrame = .SpeedX - 1
```

```
            'update X position
            .X = .X + .SpeedX
            If .X < 1 Then
                .X = 1
            ElseIf .X > Picture1.ScaleWidth - .Width - 1 Then
                .X = Picture1.ScaleWidth - .Width - 1
            End If
            .SpeedX = 0

            'update Y position
            .Y = .Y + .SpeedY
            If .Y < 1 Then
                .Y = 1
            ElseIf .Y > Picture1.ScaleHeight - .Height - 1 Then
                .Y = Picture1.ScaleHeight - .Height - 1
            End If
            .SpeedY = 0

            'draw sprite
            .Draw cbBackBuf.hdc
        End With
    End Sub
```

The next three procedures (PlayerFireShot, EnemyFireShot, and GunFireRocket) each launch a projectile in a certain direction and from a certain starting position, with a set velocity. This information is later used to move and draw the projectiles on the screen.

```
Private Sub PlayerFireShot()
    'see if a sprite is available
    For lBulletNum = 0 To MAXBULLETS
        If Not csPlayerBullets(lBulletNum).Active Then
            Exit For
        End If
    Next lBulletNum

    'delay 1/10 second between shots
    If lLastShot + 100 < GetTickCount Then
        lLastShot = GetTickCount
        'limit number of shots
```

```
Private Sub MoveRockets()
    For lRocketNum = 0 To MAXROCKETS
        With csEnemyRockets(lRocketNum)
            'make sure rocket is alive
            If .Active Then
                'update rocket position
                .X = .X + .SpeedX
                If .X < 1 Or .X > Picture1.ScaleWidth Then
                    .Active = False
                End If
                .Y = .Y + .SpeedY
                If .Y < 1 Or .Y > Picture1.ScaleHeight Then
                    .Active = False
                End If

                'draw the rocket
                .Draw cbBackBuf.hdc

                'check for collision with player
                If .Collided(csPlane) Then
                    .Active = False
                    lPlayerDamage = lPlayerDamage + 1
                    StartExplosion csPlane
                    Debug.Print "Rocket " & lBulletNum & _
                        " hit PLAYER at " & .X & "," & .Y

                    'see if plane was destroyed (restart mission)
                    If lPlayerHealth - lPlayerDamage < 0 Then
                        bMissionLoaded = False
                        lMissionNumber = lCurrentMission - 1
                        GameStatus = NEXTMISSION
                        lPlayerDamage = 0
                    End If
                End If
            End If
        End With
    Next lRocketNum
End Sub
```

```
Private Sub MoveBullets()
    Dim n As Long

    lBulletCount = 0
    For lBulletNum = 0 To MAXBULLETS
        'move the player's shots
        With csPlayerBullets(lBulletNum)
            'make sure bullet is alive
            If .Active Then
                'update bullet position
                lBulletCount = lBulletCount + 1
                .X = .X + .SpeedX
                If .X < 1 Or .X > Picture1.ScaleWidth Then
                    .Active = False
                End If
                .Y = .Y + .SpeedY
                If .Y < 1 Or .Y > Picture1.ScaleHeight Then
                    .Active = False
                End If

                'draw the bullet sprite
                .Draw cbBackBuf.hdc

                'check for collision with enemy planes
                For n = 0 To MAXENEMIES
                    If csEnemy(n).Active Then
                        If .Collided(csEnemy(n)) Then
                            .Active = False
                            csEnemy(n).Active = False
                            StartExplosion csEnemy(n)
                            lPlayerScore = lPlayerScore + 50
                            Debug.Print "Bullet " & lBulletNum & _
                                " hit ENEMY at " & .X & "," & .Y
                            Exit For
                        End If
                    End If
                Next n

                'check for collision with enemy guns
                For n = 0 To MAXGUNS
```

```
                    If csGuns(n).Active And csGuns(n).X <> 0 And _
                        csGuns(n).Y <> 0 Then
                        If .Collided(csGuns(n)) Then
                            .Active = False
                            csGuns(n).Active = False
                            StartExplosion csGuns(n)
                            lPlayerScore = lPlayerScore + 75
                            Debug.Print "Bullet " & lBulletNum & _
                                " hit GUN at " & .X & "," & .Y
                            Exit For
                        End If
                    End If
                Next n
            End If
    End With


    'move enemy bullets
    With csEnemyBullets(lBulletNum)
        'make sure bullet is alive
        If .Active Then
            'update bullet position
            .X = .X + .SpeedX
            If .X < 1 Or .X > Picture1.ScaleWidth Then
                .Active = False
            End If
            .Y = .Y + .SpeedY
            If .Y < 1 Or .Y > Picture1.ScaleHeight Then
                .Active = False
            End If

            'draw enemy bullet sprite
            .Draw cbBackBuf.hdc

            'check for collision with player
            If .Collided(csPlane) Then
                .Active = False
                lPlayerDamage = lPlayerDamage + 1
                StartExplosion csPlane
                Debug.Print "Bullet " & lBulletNum & _
                    " hit PLAYER at " & .X & "," & .Y
```

```
                       'see if plane was destroyed (restart mission)
                       If lPlayerHealth - lPlayerDamage < 0 Then
                           bMissionLoaded = False
                           lMissionNumber = lCurrentMission - 1
                           GameStatus = NEXTMISSION
                           lPlayerDamage = 0
                       End If
                   End If
               End If
           End With
       Next lBulletNum
End Sub
```

The MoveEnemies and MoveGuns procedures update the position of each enemy fighter and rocket
turret in the game, if those items are currently active. The key to these routines is a check for the
global position of each. When an item's position places it in the area of the map that is currently
visible, then the appropriate sprite for that item is displayed in the correct location.

```
Private Sub MoveEnemies()
    Dim n As Long
    lEnemyCount = 0
    lEnemiesInRange = 0
    For n = 0 To MAXENEMIES
        With csEnemy(n)
            'make sure enemy plane is alive
            If .Active Then
                lEnemyCount = lEnemyCount + 1

                'update enemy plane position
                .GlobalX = .GlobalX + .SpeedX
                .GlobalY = .GlobalY + .SpeedY

                'rebound off screen edges
                If .GlobalX < 1 Then
                    .GlobalX = 1
                    .SpeedX = 1
                ElseIf .GlobalX > Picture1.ScaleWidth - 1 Then
                    .GlobalX = Picture1.ScaleWidth - 1
                    .SpeedX = -1
                End If
```

```
    Input #1FileNum, numcols, numrows
    Scroller.InitTileMap numcols, numrows
    For rows = 0 To numrows - 1
        'load map tile values
        For cols = 0 To numcols - 1
            Input #1FileNum, lTileValue
            Scroller.SetTile cols, rows, lTileValue
        Next cols
    Next rows

    Close #1FileNum
    LoadLevel = True
error1:
Fnd Function
```

The final code listing of the program is for the Shutdown procedure, which simply deletes all of the objects in the game, closes down the DirectX objects, and then ends the game.

```
Private Sub Shutdown()
    Dim n As Long

    'stop game loop
    bRunning = False

    'delete objects
    Set Scroller = Nothing
    Set cbBackBuf = Nothing
    Set csPlane = Nothing
    Set csMission = Nothing

    'delete bullets
    For n = 0 To MAXBULLETS
        Set csPlayerBullets(n) = Nothing
        Set csEnemyBullets(n) = Nothing
    Next n

    'delete rockets
    For n = 0 To MAXROCKETS
        Set csEnemyRockets(n) = Nothing
    Next n
```

```
    'delete enemy planes
    For n = 0 To MAXENEMIES
         Set csEnemy(n) = Nothing
    Next n

    'delete DirectInput objects
    Joystick.Shutdown
    Set Joystick = Nothing
    Keyboard.Shutdown
    Set Keyboard = Nothing
    Set dinput = Nothing

    'delete DirectSound objects
    Set dsound = Nothing
    Set dswFire = Nothing
    Set dswBoom = Nothing
    Set dswRocket = Nothing

    'delete DirectMusic objects
    dmsSong.StopMusic
    Set dmsSong = Nothing
    Set dmusic = Nothing

    'end program
    Form1.Hide
    End
End Sub
```

ENHANCING THE GAME

Here are some recommendations for improving the game:

- Add more enemy fighter planes and some bombers.
- Add moving vehicles, foot soldiers, anti-aircraft guns, and Panzer tanks.
- Add some scenery, such as shrubs, trees, rocks, roads, or water.
- Create a data file for each plane, rather than the hard-coded airplane values.
- Record additional sound effects to make each airplane sound unique.
- Add a shadow below each plane to improve the sense of depth in the game.
- Create some cloud sprites and draw random clouds floating across the screen.
- Keep track of high score and player names to improve playability and challenge.

- Make the enemies more intelligent by causing them to dodge incoming fire.
- Draw a crater at the position of any rocket turrets that are destroyed.
- Create an animation sequence of enemy planes crashing into the ground.
- Create a new version of the game with modern fighter airplanes.
- Convert the game to DirectDraw.

SUMMARY

Warbirds 1944 is a great example of what can be done with the standard game library that was developed in previous chapters, along with a little DirectX support for user input, sound, and music. Since this game is double buffered and features a scrolling background using just Windows API blitting routines, it requires a video card with 2-D hardware blitting functionality to run properly (which should not be a problem, since most video cards today include 2-D acceleration).

This game was an interesting exercise in arcade game design and featured some really good ideas that can be built upon for new games. One possible use for the vertical scroller is an old-school car driving game (like *Spy Hunter*), or any of the multitude of games that came out years ago with scrolling backgrounds.

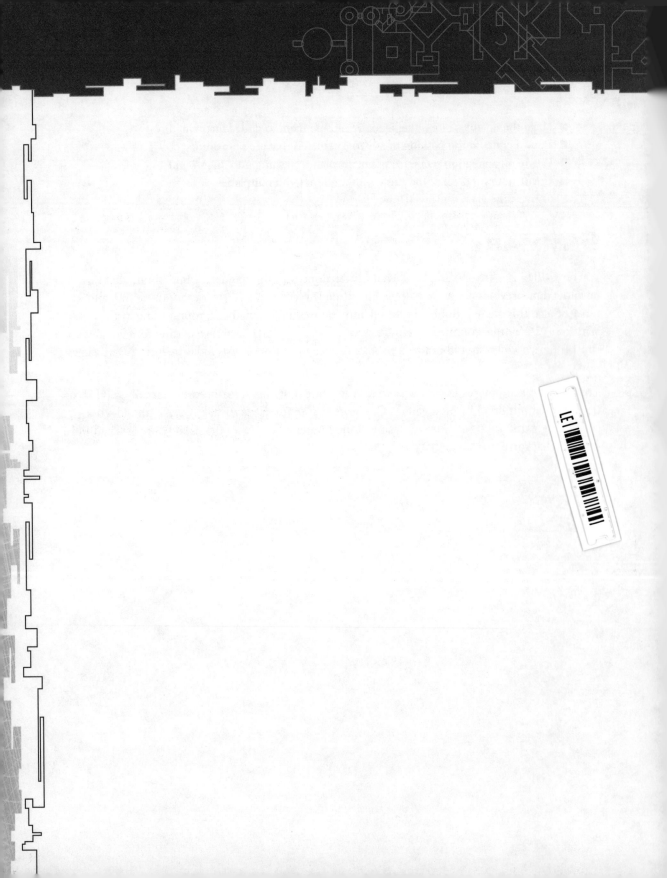

Figure 21.1

Stellar War, the multi-player game featured in this chapter

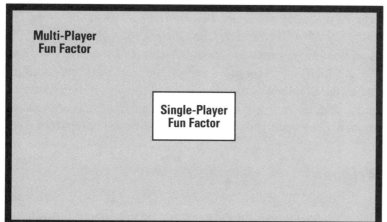

Figure 21.2

Single-player versus multiplayer fun factor

online game, before *Ultima Online*, *EverQuest*, or *Asheron's Call*. I know, *Diablo* is not a massively-multiplayer online game, and it is only a pseudo-RPG, but *Diablo* (and then *StarCraft*) were both huge in Blizzard's prime, around 1997–1999.

You just have to love a game that spirits away all of your free time! It's a funny paradox, similar to my feelings about *Counter-Strike*. Can't live with it, can't uninstall it. Thankfully, Microsoft released the Xbox, along with the game *HALO* (thank you, Bungie!), because I don't think I could have tolerated another round of DE_DUST.

Personally, I find the subject of programming multiplayer games even more fun than playing them. So, let's move along and talk about Stellar War.

Introducing the Game

Stellar War includes some fun gameplay mechanics reminiscent of sci-fi movies, such as plasma guns and black holes. The problem with modern cinema is that the scriptwriters and special effects people are too interested in wowing the audience. I wonder whether professional astronomers have a hard time sitting through a modern science fiction movie? Unfortunately, most moviemakers "dumb down" movies for the general population. I don't know about you, but I find that insulting, to say the least. To assume that I'm too dumb to enjoy a movie that is realistic; well, that just ticks me off.

Time travel movies are the worst, especially those episodes of Star Trek: *<insert your favorite series here>*, where they twist the physics of the universe to fit a cheesy plot. I have heard that rough draft Star Trek scripts actually have the phrase "*<insert technobabble>*" in the middle of dialog, and a technical advisor then fills in the technobabble using the latest scientific jargon. Hey, I like the show, so I have to overlook things like that.

But I have to give the producers of the latest series, *Star Trek: Enterprise*, a little more credit. There have been some very cool episodes, such as "Civilization," which was a spin-off of an original Star Trek episode called "Wink of an Eye." In "Civilization," the inhabitants of a planet are stuck in an accelerated space/time bubble in which several centuries pass on the planet for every hour in the rest of the universe (which makes me wonder why the inhabitants of the planet didn't just use their advanced technology and accelerated industry to take over the galaxy). Sci-fi stories like "Civilization," even on a medium like television, provide some great ideas for computer games.

Game Setting

Stellar War is based loosely on the classic PC game, *Star Control II*. (Okay, Accolade, when is number three coming out?) While my original design for the game was very ambitious, I had to scale it back significantly in order to complete the project. I wanted to have a vast area of space for players to explore, so they could discover resources such as planets and asteroids, alien races, and human starbases. The object was to pilot your own ship through the galaxy as a privateer, seeking out resources in order to make money, which could then be used to buy a better ship, better weapons, and so on. The game would have been open-ended, with player-created aliens (using the bot source code), and a galaxy editor for the server operator.

Alas, the game had to be scaled down or the source code for just this one game would have filled the entire book. Maybe some day I will complete a game like that. In the meantime, Stellar War is a small-scale space combat game with a dedicated server that keeps the game persistent.

Players can jump in and play at any time, with the game client or with a bot, and the server keeps things going.

The large-scale game would have allowed over 100 players to interact in the galaxy. But because Stellar War ended up being strictly a melee game, I have limited the number of players to eight. As it turns out, that is the practical limit for a Visual Basic server using String-based packets (more on server design later).

Game Strategy

The object of the game is to move your ship on the screen using the thrust key (up arrow) and rotation keys (left and right arrows). Since the game uses realistic gravitational propulsion (at least, realistic in a space setting), there is no stop key. To stop your ship, you need to twist the nose around and apply reverse thrust. When you blow stuff up, point markers are left behind. You have to fly your ship over the markers in order to grab them for points. This prevents players from racking up points just by shooting randomly. To score, you must grab point markers with your ship while avoiding destruction by projectiles.

Thankfully, the designer of the game—that would be me—purposely limited the firing rate of ships, so that only one or two live shots are traveling through space at a time. When you fire repeatedly, your shots are replaced by new projectiles coming out of your ship. This keeps the game server from being inundated with projectile packets, which would slow things down too much.

Gravitational Propulsion

The "killer feature" of Stellar War is the realistic simulation of gravity that is caused by two animated black holes. I decided that a black hole would be a cool feature for the game, but why stop there? Two black holes, each exerting pull on the players' ships, should provide for some very interesting gameplay. Just when you scream past the first black hole in a near miss, along comes the second one, dragging your ship down the gullet of near-infinite mass in fiery destruction.

Not only does the game feature black holes with gravity, but it also uses gravity to move the ships. When you press the up arrow key to apply thrust, there is a gravity well sitting in front of the ship that causes the ship to move toward it. Figure 21.3 shows an illustration of the gravity well's effect on ship motion.

The trick is keeping the gravity well in front of the ship, no matter what direction the ship is facing. This is accomplished by checking the direction of the ship and positioning the gravity well accordingly.

Can you think of any cool things that you could do with gravity other than black holes? It would be neat to implement a tractor beam weapon, in which one ship suddenly has a huge mass (like a

GRAVITY WELL
(Massive Object)

Figure 21.3

The gravity well is a massive object that exerts pull on the space ship.

GRAVITY WAVES
(Exert Pull On Ship)

SPACE SHIP
(Dead Weight)

black hole) and attracts the other ships to it. You could also apply this "tractor beam" to just a single opponent and drag their ship toward you.

The Theory of Gravity

In space, the object with the greater mass will pull the smaller object toward it. That is how the universe works, at any rate. The reason why our planet Earth is so far away from the sun (aside from being in the perfect spot, temperature-wise) is because it is in a stable orbit around the sun. At around 93 million miles, Earth is attracted to the sun's powerful gravitational pull, but that pull is balanced by the extreme distance, so that Earth rotates around the sun rather than just plunging into it. Orbit has been referred to as *freefall*, because that is essentially what is happening—one object is falling toward the other.

Jumping out of an airplane and parachuting to the ground is the same thing: Your body has a very small mass, and it is being pulled down toward the center of the earth. If you go far enough away from the surface of the earth, you will actually begin to orbit the earth rather than fall down into it. That is how satellites are placed above the earth to handle voice and data communications, global television and radio, global positioning, and even espionage. The Earth's moon is a gigantic object, about the size of the United States in diameter, so it has to be way, way, way out there (approximately 240,000 miles, actually) in order to keep from falling down and crashing into the Earth. Makes you wonder how many moons, asteroids, and space debris that were once in orbit actually crashed into the surface of our planet, doesn't it? Well, we do have the craters to show that it has happened in the past. Not only that, but how many planets were actually sucked into the sun as the solar system was forming several billion years ago?

The gist of this subject is that the heavier the objects in space, the farther away they need to be or else they will crash into each other. If two objects have exactly the same mass, they will orbit around each other perfectly. But if one object is heavier than the other, the smaller object will tend to orbit around the larger one. Did you know that there is actually a super massive black hole at the center of our Milky Way galaxy? That is what gives the galaxy a spiral shape, because all of the billions of stars in the galaxy are all orbiting around that central massive black hole, all the while exerting gravitational attraction with each other.

Which does bring up another subject—the effects of gravity. Have you ever wondered why so many things in the universe take on the shape of a sphere? When the solar system was forming, Earth was actually a cloud of hydrogen and other particles that began to coalesce by attraction over time. Gravity itself, which was discovered by Newton and put into theory by Einstein, actually warps space and time. The result is that things seem to "fall toward" massive objects, which take on the shape of a sphere because gravity exerts force in all three dimensions.

Calculating Gravitational Waves

Calculating gravity between two objects in space is not as difficult as it sounds, and you don't need a degree in mathematics or physics to simulate a simplistic model of gravity. Surprisingly, the most complicated formula used to calculate gravity looks sort of like the distance formula. If you recall basic trigonometry, to calculate the distance between two points, (X1,Y1) and (X2,Y2), use this formula:

$$d = \sqrt{(x_2-x_1)^2+(y_2-y_1)^2}$$

The formula for calculating the gravitational attraction between two points is a little more involved than just calculating distance. It actually involves velocity and acceleration of the two objects. If either object has zero mass, then there will be no attraction because without mass, that thing called *matter* does not exist. So, first things first—give your objects some mass. For the purpose of calculating gravity in the game, mass should be a value between 0.0 and 1.0 (which is housed in either a Single or Double variable), just to keep gameplay fun. Higher mass for the gravity well causes the ships to be dragged down into the black holes without prejudice.

First, start by calculating the distance (D) modifier:

$$D = \frac{1}{(X_2-X_1)^2+(Y_2-Y_1)^2}$$

After you have the distance modifier, you can calculate acceleration for both X and Y. The acceleration calculation for X (which is called AX) looks like the formula below. (Note that the second line of the formula is just a shorthand version of the first line.)

$$AX = -1 * Mass * D * (X_2-X_1)$$
$$AX = -MD(X_2-X_1)$$

Likewise, the acceleration calculation for Y (which is called AY) looks like the formula below. (Again, note that the second line of the formula is just a shorthand version of the first line.)

$$AY = -1 * Mass * D * (Y_2-Y_1)$$
$$AY = -MD(Y_2-Y_1)$$

Now you have the acceleration in terms of X and Y for a single object being "tugged" by another massive object in space. You can use a velocity value like I have done in the gravity code for Stellar War, or you can simply add (AX,AY) to a sprite's (X,Y) position, like this:

```
X = X + AX
Y = Y + AY
```

This formula works just fine, because when the object is moving left or up, the acceleration will be a negative number, while a right or down motion is reflected by positive acceleration values. You simply need a gravity well and a dead weight for each object in the game. To make things easier, you can just add these to the sprite class if you want.

Multiplayer Elements

Gravity is a lot of fun, but what really makes Stellar War interesting is the multiplayer component. Since there is no single-player component, the game actually requires access to a server in order to play. If you want to see how the game looks, you can simply run the server on your PC at the same time that you run the game. Figure 21.4 shows the game with five players—four bots and

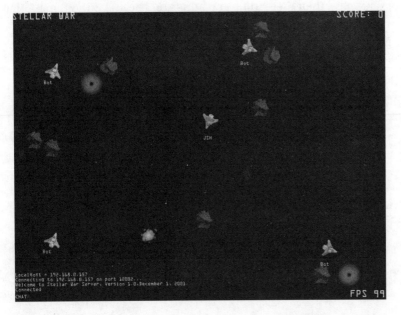

Figure 21.4

Stellar War allows multiple players to play against each other while avoiding black holes and asteroids.

my ship (with the initials "JSH"). I will explain the multiplayer components of the game in the next section.

STELLAR WAR GAME DESIGN

Stellar War is fairly efficient at handling game objects and passing packets of data between the server and the clients. Each player transmits ship and projectile positions every 50 milliseconds. This is not a theoretical "best" rate; it is just a value I came up with after extensive trial and error. You might find the packet communication speeds inefficient for a dial-up Internet connection, although 50 milliseconds provides an acceptable frame rate of 20, which shouldn't tax anyone's bandwidth.

The packets are very small, around 20 bytes on average, although Winsock does combine packets on-the-fly. For this reason, the DataArrival routines in both the client and server take care to break separate packets out of each string of incoming data. The server screen includes a field that tells you how many incoming packets are combined into a single string and must be split up (which slows things down). Figure 21.5 shows a diagram of the client/server architecture for Stellar War.

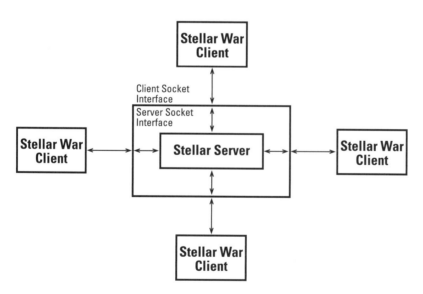

Figure 21.5

The socket layer relationship between the players and the game server

During testing, which involved tweaking the transmission time values, I ran into several instances where combined packets reached 300, 400, or even 500. The string-parsing functions were bogging down the system so badly that the game would hardly run at all. If you start tweaking the timing, be sure to keep an eye on the combined packet displays. A really nice feature might be to allow the server to dynamically change the timing to maximize efficiency.

Some tasks in Stellar War are handled by the server, while some tasks are handled by each client. The goal is to get server processes down to an acceptable level for each synchronization, so that lag does not occur. At a certain point, this is unavoidable because the server is a Visual Basic program as well. It is doubly limited since it is based on strings of data rather than bytes of data when sending and receiving packets.

A resourceful programmer might want to convert the string-based packets to a byte structure packet format, which would probably decrease lag by an order of magnitude. The server has to break up each packet using string-parsing functions, which is horribly slow. Again, it was a design decision intended to make the game easier to understand, rather than more efficient.

Server Design

The Stellar War server was designed as a learning tool, and is therefore not very efficient. All of the data flowing from the clients through the server is based on String data, with functions that parse the packets for the needed data. These packets start with a prefix character and a three-character header code, representing the type of packet. Table 21.1 shows the types of packets used in the game.

Table 21.1 Stellar War Packet Types

Name	Header	Description
PING_HDR	111	Ping (latency test) packet
CHAT_HDR	112	Chat message packet
SHIP_HDR	113	Player position packet
SHOT_HDR	114	Projectile position packet
ROCK_HDR	115	Asteroid position packet
HOLE_HDR	116	Black hole position packet
BOOM_HDR	117	Explosion position packet
SCOR_HDR	118	Player score packet
HITA_HDR	119	Hit asteroid packet
HITP_HDR	120	Hit player packet

Any time you want to add new functionality to the game, simply create a new packet header and program the server and client to recognize the new packet. It is then up to you to send whatever data you want with the new packet. But keep the data short, or the server will get bogged down. There's no problem with adding a dozen new types of packets if you are adding many cool new features to the game. Just remember that there is a finite amount of bandwidth available for every frame of the game (which runs at around 20 fps). Also, keep in mind that the server has to send out packets to every other player in the game. My advice is to pack as much data as possible into small packets, combining data where possible.

Client Design

The game client for Stellar War requires a server connection, or nothing will happen on the screen. This is because the server sends ship, asteroid, projectile, and other position information to each of the clients (which don't do very much on their own).

A Note about Security

The Stellar War server is really an open server that is prone to exploitation and overload. If you try to build a large-scale game server out of it (or even a small-scale system), and the game becomes popular, I guarantee that programmers will try to screw with your server by sending junk data, thus locking it up. Therefore, if you develop a game that does become popular, you might want to consider encrypting the packets of data. There are some simple and complex ways to encrypt packets of string data (and even byte data). You might want to look into encryption if you do write a popular game.

Source Artwork

Stellar War uses several 3-D rendered sprites for such objects as the player ships, black holes, and asteroids. The game also uses a bitmap font.

Player Ships

Figure 21.6 shows the animation sequence for the spaceships used in the game.

Figure 21.6

The ships in the game feature 16 frames of animation.

Figure 21.7 shows the same ship, animated at a slightly different angle, which provides a different look.

Figure 21.7

A second set of frames for the ship, animated at a slightly different angle

These spaceship frames of animation were rendered using a program called Imagine (shown in Figure 21.8). It is a simple 3-D modeler that was once popular on the Amiga.

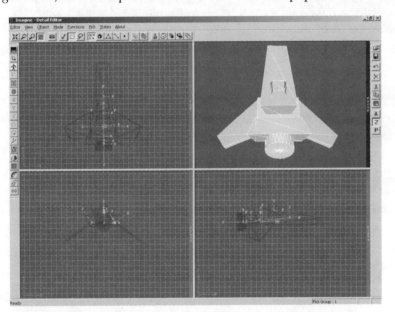

Figure 21.8

The 3-D modeling program, Imagine, with the spaceship model for Stellar War displayed

Black Holes

The black holes in the game (shown in Figure 21.9) are made up of blue-colored, 16-frame, animated sprites.

Asteroids

The asteroids (shown in Figure 21.10) are the most impressive sprites in the game; they were also rendered with Imagine. The asteroid sprite used in the game actually features 64 frames of animation. With so many frames, the rotating asteroids look extremely fluid, with realistic motion. Generally, the more frames in a 3-D model, the better the animation will look.

Figure 21.9

The black holes in the game are made up of 16-frame animated sprites.

Figure 21.10

The rendered 3-D asteroid sprite features 64 frames of animation.

Bitmapped Font

Figure 21.11 shows the bitmapped font used in the game. There are actually two sizes for the font. The primary font has characters that are 16×24 pixels each, while the smaller font has characters that are 8×12 pixels in size. This smaller font is more useful in the game, since the larger font is too big to display player names and the message lines at the bottom of the screen.

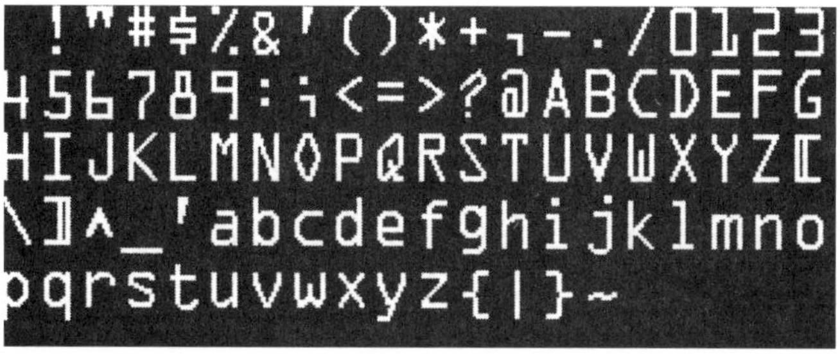

Figure 21.11

The bitmapped font is used to display text in the game.

User Input

Stellar War is a fairly simple game that features only keyboard input. The left and right arrow keys rotate the ship, the up arrow applies thrust to the ship, and the left CTRL key is used to fire the weapon. The reason the traditional spacebar is not used for the fire button is that the chat line at the bottom of the screen is always active. You can type in quick chat messages and send them without first pressing any chat key, which makes it easy to chat in the middle of playing the game.

The following DirectInput classes are used in this game:

- clsDirectInput8
- clsDIKeyboard8

BUILDING STELLAR WAR

The source code for Stellar War is quite lengthy, so I will try to explain each part of the game as I go. There are two programs: the Stellar Server program and the Stellar War client. In addition, I provided the source code for a bot that runs in the game. I will explain how to build the projects and enter the source code for all three programs in the following pages.

The Stellar War Client Program

The first part of the program that I want to cover is the Stellar War client. As I mentioned earlier, the game client requires a server connection in order to run. Otherwise, nothing happens in the game.

The Client Project

The Stellar War client is a full-screen DirectDraw program. You might recall covering DirectDraw back in Chapter 10, "Diving into DirectDraw." You can refer to that chapter if you don't under-

stand any aspects of how the source code for Stellar War handles the graphics. There is a background image (used to erase sprites), a double buffer (for smooth animation), and numerous sprites in the game.

So, how about if we get started on the project? Create a new Standard EXE project in Visual Basic. The default form, Form1, will house all the source

> **TIP**
>
> Remember, when building a full-screen DirectDraw game, you must set BorderStyle = 0 for the main form of the game.

code for the game (except the game library code). In order to make it a full-screen game, you need to set the BorderStyle property of the form to 0 - None. Otherwise, DirectDraw will not be able to override the default Visual Basic form handler, and the game will end up with a toolbar at the top and won't really run full-screen. It's not a pretty site! Figure 21.12 shows Stellar War loaded in the Visual Basic IDE.

Figure 21.12

The project for Stellar War in the Visual Basic IDE

The Project Explorer

Figure 21.13 shows the Project Explorer for Stellar War, listing the files needed to compile and run the game. You should be able to recognize all of the files in the project from previous chapters of the book. ClientSocket.cls and frmLink.frm were both covered in Chapter 16, "Multiplayer Programming with Windows Sockets." DirectDraw7.cls, DDSprite7.cls, and DDSurface7.cls were

Figure 21.13

The Project Explorer for Stellar War shows the files needed to compile the game.

all introduced in Chapter 10, "Diving into DirectDraw." DirectInput8.cls and DIKeyboard8.cls were created back in Chapter 12, "Getting a Handle on User Input." Finally, Declares.bas came from Chapter 13, "Building the DirectX Game Library."

References

The Project References dialog, which is shown in Figure 21.14, shows the components needed by the game. Aside from the usual Visual Basic components, note the reference to both DirectX 7 and DirectX 8. Both libraries are needed by Stellar War because DirectDraw is being used along with DirectInput8 (and other game library classes).

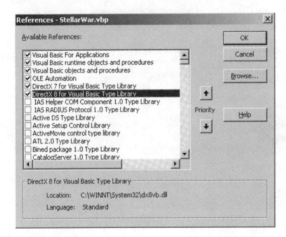

Figure 21.14

The Project References dialog shows the system components needed by the game.

There is no problem with linking to both libraries at the same time. However, you will occasionally encounter an error message when you try to use a common struct, such as RECT, which is defined by both versions of DirectX. If you get a weird error message based on a RECT, just prefix one of the library designations to it, like DxVBLib (for DirectX 7) or DxVBLibA (for DirectX 8), like this:

```
Dim rTemp as DxVBLib.RECT
```

Client Source Code

Okay, now on to the source code for Stellar War. I will discuss each section of code prior to listing it in the following pages. Just type the code into the code window for Form1 and save frequently!

The first section of code lists the constants, types, and variables for Stellar War.

```
'----------------------------------------------------------------------
' Visual Basic Game Programming With DirectX
' Chapter 21: Stellar War: Multiplayer Space Combat Game
' StellarWar Client Source Code File
'----------------------------------------------------------------------
Option Explicit
Option Base 0

'program constants
Const FULLSCREEN As Boolean = True
Const SCREENWIDTH As Long = 1024
Const SCREENHEIGHT As Long = 768
Const COLORDEPTH As Long = 32
Const MAXFRAMERATE As Long = 120
Const MAXSHOTS As Long = 3
Const MAXROCKS As Long = 10
Const MAXENEMIES As Long = 20
Const MAXBOOMS As Long = 20

'socket messaging constants
Const SEP As String = "ÿ" 'ASCII 255
Const PREFIX = "___" 'ASCII 254
Const PING_HDR = "111"
Const CHAT_HDR = "112"
Const SHIP_HDR = "113"
Const SHOT_HDR = "114"
Const ROCK_HDR = "115"
Const HOLE_HDR = "116"
Const BOOM_HDR = "117"
Const SCOR_HDR = "118"
Const HITA_HDR = "119"
Const HITP_HDR = "120"
Const DIED_HDR = "121"

'gravity constants
Const BLACKHOLEMASS As Double = 0.3
Const GRAVITYWELL As Double = 0.5
Const MASSADD As Double = 0.01
Const MAXMASS As Double = 0.1
Const MAXVELOCITY As Long = 1
Const MAXACCEL As Double = 0.05
```

```
'DirectInput key codes
Const KEY_LEFT As Long = 203
Const KEY_RIGHT As Long = 205
Const KEY_UP As Long = 200
Const KEY_DOWN As Long = 208
Const KEY_LCTRL As Long = 29
Const KEY_ESC As Long = 1
Const KEY_PGDN As Long = 209
Const KEY_SPACE As Long = 57
Const KEY_BSPACE As Long = 14
Const KEY_ENTER As Long = 28

'cut down on global variables
Private Type GAME_DATA
    Server As String
    Port As Long
    FrameRate As String
    PingStart As Long
    WindowHandle As Long
    ChatMessage As String
    Messages(0 To 7) As String
    Nicknames(MAXENEMIES) As String
    Nickname As String
    Score As Long
    Running As Boolean
End Type

'gravity struct
Private Type MASS_OBJECT
    mass As Double
    X As Double
    Y As Double
    ax As Double
    ay As Double
    vx As Double
    vy As Double
End Type

'program controls
Dim WithEvents Picture1 As PictureBox
```

```
Dim WithEvents clientPing As Timer
Dim WithEvents socketStatus As Timer

'socket class
Dim WithEvents clientLink As clsClientSocket

'DirectX objects
Dim ddraw As clsDirectDraw7
Dim dinput As clsDirectInput8
Dim WithEvents Keyboard As clsDIKeyboard8

'DirectDraw surfaces and sprites
Dim cddsBackground As clsDDSurface7
Dim cddsBackBuffer As clsDDSurface7
Dim cddsSprite As clsDDSurface7
Dim cdsPlayer As clsDDSprite7
Dim cddsShot As clsDDSurface7
Dim cdsShots(MAXSHOTS) As clsDDSprite7
Dim cddsBoom As clsDDSurface7
Dim cdsBooms(MAXBOOMS) As clsDDSprite7
Dim cddsAsteroid As clsDDSurface7
Dim cdsAsteroids(MAXROCKS) As clsDDSprite7
Dim cddsBlackHole As clsDDSurface7
Dim cdsBlackHoles(0 To 1) As clsDDSprite7
Dim cdsEnemy As clsDDSurface7
Dim cdsEnemies(MAXENEMIES) As clsDDSprite7
Dim cdsFont(2) As clsDDSprite7
Dim cdsCursor As clsDDSprite7

'program variables
Dim gameinfo As GAME_DATA
Dim shipMass1 As MASS_OBJECT
Dim shipMass2 As MASS_OBJECT
Dim blackHole1 As MASS_OBJECT
Dim blackHole2 As MASS_OBJECT
Dim rTemp As RECT
```

The LoadSettings procedure loads some program settings from the settings.ini file. The settings file includes the player name, server IP address, and the port on which the Stellar Server is running. Figure 21.15 shows the settings file loaded into Notepad.

Figure 21.15

The Stellar War client settings.txt file

```
Private Sub LoadSettings()
    Dim filenum As Long
    Dim sInput As String
    Dim sTemp As String

    On Error GoTo error1
    filenum = FreeFile
    Open App.Path & "\settings.txt" For Input As #filenum

    Do Until EOF(filenum)
        Line Input #filenum, sInput
        If Len(sInput) > 0 Then
            If Left$(sInput, 1) <> ";" Then
                If UCase$(Left$(sInput, 7)) = "PLAYER=" Then
                    sTemp = ParseToken(sInput, 2, "=")
                    If Len(sTemp) > 0 Then
                        gameinfo.Nickname = sTemp
                        If Len(gameinfo.Nickname) > 40 Then
                            gameinfo.Nickname = "Newb"
                        End If
                    Else
                        gameinfo.Nickname = "Newb"
                    End If
                ElseIf UCase$(Left$(sInput, 7)) = "SERVER=" Then
                    sTemp = ParseToken(sInput, 2, "=")
```

```
                    If Len(sTemp) > 0 Then
                        gameinfo.Server = sTemp
                    Else
                        gameinfo.Server = "localhost"
                    End If
                ElseIf UCase$(Left$(sInput, 5)) = "PORT=" Then
                    sTemp = ParseToken(sInput, 2, "=")
                    If IsNumeric(sTemp) Then
                        gameinfo.Port = CLng(sTemp)
                        If gameinfo.Port < 1024 Or _
                            gameinfo.Port > 60000 Then
                            gameinfo.Port = 10002
                        End If
                    Else
                        gameinfo.Port = 10002
                    End If
                End If
            End If
        End If
    Loop

    Close #filenum
    Exit Sub
error1:
    MsgBox "The settings.txt file is invalid!"
    Shutdown
End Sub
```

Form_Load is the startup procedure for the game; it handles initializing the entire game, including
DirectDraw and socket communications with the server.

```
Private Sub Form_Load()
    Dim lStartTime As Long
    Dim lCounter As Long
    Dim lNewTime As Long
    Dim lFrameRate As Long
    Dim lNum As Long
    Dim bRet As Boolean
    Dim n As Long
```

```
LoadSettings
InitForm
InitSocket

'initialize DirectInput
Set dinput = New clsDirectInput8
dinput.Startup Form1.hWnd
Set Keyboard = New clsDIKeyboard8
Keyboard.Startup dinput, Form1.hWnd

'create primary DirectDraw object
Set ddraw = New clsDirectDraw7
If Not ddraw.Startup(gameinfo.WindowHandle, SCREENWIDTH, _
    SCREENHEIGHT, COLORDEPTH, FULLSCREEN) Then
    MsgBox "Error creating DirectDraw primary display surface"
    Shutdown
End If

'create back buffer
Set cddsBackBuffer = New clsDDSurface7
If Not cddsBackBuffer.Create(ddraw.ddObj, _
    SCREENWIDTH, SCREENHEIGHT) Then
    MsgBox "Error creating back buffer surface"
    Shutdown
End If

'load the background image
Set cddsBackground = New clsDDSurface7
If Not cddsBackground.Load(ddraw, App.Path & _
    "\background.bmp") Then
    MsgBox "Error loading blueyellow.bmp"
    Shutdown
End If

'load the big font
Set cdsFont(0) = New clsDDSprite7
cdsFont(0).Create ddraw
If Not cdsFont(0).LoadFromFile(App.Path & "\ocrfont.bmp", _
    16, 24, 20, 95) Then
    MsgBox "Error loading ocrfont.bmp"
    Shutdown
End If
```

```
'load the small font
Set cdsFont(1) = New clsDDSprite7
cdsFont(1).Create ddraw
If Not cdsFont(1).LoadFromFile(App.Path & "\smallfont.bmp", _
    8, 12, 20, 95) Then
    MsgBox "Error loading smallfont.bmp"
    Shutdown
End If

'load the blinking cursor
Set cdsCursor = New clsDDSprite7
cdsCursor.Create ddraw
If Not cdsCursor.LoadFromFile(App.Path & "\cursor.bmp", _
    8, 12, 2, 2) Then
    MsgBox "Error loading cursor.bmp"
    Shutdown
End If
cdsCursor.AnimRate = 50

'load the sprite image
Set cddsSprite = New clsDDSurface7
If Not cddsSprite.Load(ddraw, App.Path & "\ship2_32.bmp") Then
    MsgBox "Error loading dxscale.bmp"
    Shutdown
End If

'initialize player sprite
Set cdsPlayer = New clsDDSprite7
With cdsPlayer
    .Create ddraw
    If Not .LoadFromSurface(cddsSprite, 32, 32, 8, 16) Then
        MsgBox "Error loading player ship"
        Shutdown
    End If
    .Active = True
    .AnimRate = 10
    .MoveRate = 10
    .X = (SCREENWIDTH + .Width) / 2
    .Y = (SCREENHEIGHT + .Height) / 2
End With
```

```
'initialize enemy sprites
For n = 0 To MAXENEMIES
    Set cdsEnemies(n) = New clsDDSprite7
    With cdsEnemies(n)
        .Create ddraw
        If Not .LoadFromSurface(cddsSprite, 32, 32, 8, 16) Then
            MsgBox "Error loading enemy ship"
            Shutdown
        End If
        .Active = True
        .AnimRate = 10
        .MoveRate = 10
        .X = 0
        .Y = 0
    End With
Next n


'load the projectile image
Set cddsShot = New clsDDSurface7
If Not cddsShot.Load(ddraw, App.Path & "\plasma.bmp") Then
    MsgBox "Error loading plasma.bmp"
    Shutdown
End If


'load the projectiles
For n = 0 To MAXSHOTS
    Set cdsShots(n) = New clsDDSprite7
    With cdsShots(n)
        .Create ddraw
        If Not .LoadFromSurface(cddsShot, 8, 8, 5, 5) Then
            MsgBox "Error copying projectile image"
            Shutdown
        End If
        .Active = False
        .MoveCount = 0
        .MoveRate = 0
    End With
Next n


'load the explosion frames
Set cddsBoom = New clsDDSurface7
```

```
If Not cddsBoom.Load(ddraw, App.Path & "\burst.bmp") Then
    MsgBox "Error loading burst.bmp"
    Shutdown
End If


'create the explosion sprites
For n = 0 To MAXBOOMS
    Set cdsBooms(n) = New clsDDSprite7
    With cdsBooms(n)
        .Create ddraw
        If Not .LoadFromSurface(cddsBoom, 64, 64, 8, 16) Then
            MsgBox "Error copying explosion surface"
            Shutdown
        End If
        .Active - False
    End With
Next n


'load the asteroid images
Set cddsAsteroid = New clsDDSurface7
If Not cddsAsteroid.Load(ddraw, App.Path & "\asteroid64.bmp") Then
    MsgBox "Error loading asteroid.bmp"
    Shutdown
End If


'create the asteroid sprites
For n = 0 To MAXROCKS
    Set cdsAsteroids(n) = New clsDDSprite7
    With cdsAsteroids(n)
        .Create ddraw
        If Not .LoadFromSurface(cddsAsteroid, 64, 64, 8, 64) Then
            MsgBox "Error grabbing asteroid surface"
            Shutdown
        End If
        .Active = False
        .AnimCount = 0
        .AnimRate = Random(5) + 5
    End With
Next n
```

```
'load the black hole images
Set cddsBlackHole = New clsDDSurface7
If Not cddsBlackHole.Load(ddraw, App.Path & "\redhole.bmp") Then
    MsgBox "Error loading redhole.bmp"
    Shutdown
End If

'create the blackhole sprites
For n = 0 To 1
    Set cdsBlackHoles(n) = New clsDDSprite7
    With cdsBlackHoles(n)
        .Create ddraw
        If Not .LoadFromSurface(cddsBlackHole, 64, 64, 8, 16) Then
            MsgBox "Error grabbing blackhole surface"
            Shutdown
        End If
        .Active = False
        .AnimRate = Random(5) + 5
    End With
Next n

ResetGravity

'draw the background image
cddsBackBuffer.BltFast 0, 0, cddsBackground.Surface, _
    cddsBackground.SurfaceRect

'gentlemen, start your engines!
clientPing.Enabled = True
gameinfo.Running = True
gameinfo.FrameRate = "FPS"
lFrameRate = 1000 / MAXFRAMERATE

'main game loop
Do While gameinfo.Running
    lCounter = GetTickCount() - lStartTime
    If lCounter > lNewTime Then
        Game_Update lCounter
        Keyboard.Check_Keyboard
        lNewTime = lCounter + lFrameRate
```

```
        End If
        DoEvents
    Loop
End Sub
```

The `Gravity` procedure calculates gravitational pull of one massive object upon another (as I discussed earlier in the chapter). Notice that the source code for this procedure resembles the formulas I presented for calculating gravity (although the source code is easier to follow). Also, the `ResetGravity` procedure initializes the gravity values for the ship and the black holes in the game.

```
Private Sub Gravity(ByRef obj1 As MASS_OBJECT, _
    ByRef obj2 As MASS_OBJECT)
    Dim distX As Double
    Dim distY As Double
    Dim dist As Double
    Dim distance As Double

    With obj1
        'move object based on velocity
        .X = .X + .vx
        .Y = .Y + .vy

        'calc distance
        distX = .X - obj2.X
        distY = .Y - obj2.Y

        'distance formula
        dist = distX * distX + distY * distY

        'avoid division by zero
        If dist <> 0 Then
            distance = 1 / dist
        Else
            distance = 0
        End If

        'calc acceleration based on distance
        .ax = -1 * obj2.mass * distX * distance
        .ay = -1 * obj2.mass * distY * distance
```

```
            'limit acceleration
            If .ax > MAXACCEL Then .ax = MAXACCEL
            If .ay > MAXACCEL Then .ay = MAXACCEL

            'calc velocity based on acceleration
            .vx = .vx + .ax
            .vy = .vy + .ay

            'limit velocity
            If .vx > MAXVELOCITY Then .vx = MAXVELOCITY
            If .vx < -MAXVELOCITY Then .vx = -MAXVELOCITY
            If .vy > MAXVELOCITY Then .vy = MAXVELOCITY
            If .vy < -MAXVELOCITY Then .vy = -MAXVELOCITY
        End With
End Sub

Private Sub ResetGravity()
        'initialize ship gravity well
        With shipMass1
            .mass = 0
            .ax = 0
            .ay = 0
            .X = cdsPlayer.X
            .Y = cdsPlayer.Y
            .vx = 0
            .vy = 0
        End With

        'initialize ship dead weight
        With shipMass2
            .mass = 0
            .ax = 0
            .ay = 0
            .X = shipMass1.X
            .Y = shipMass1.Y + 20
            .vx = 0
            .vy = 0
        End With
```

```
    'initialize black hole 1
    With blackHole1
        .mass = BLACKHOLEMASS
        .ax = 0
        .ay = 0
        .X = cdsBlackHoles(0).X + cdsBlackHoles(0).Width / 2
        .Y = cdsBlackHoles(0).Y + cdsBlackHoles(0).Height / 2
        .vx = 0
        .vy = 0
    End With

    'initialize black hole 2
    With blackHole2
        .mass = BLACKHOLEMASS
        .ax = 0
        .ay = 0
        .X = cdsBlackHoles(1).X + cdsBlackHoles(1).Width / 2
        .Y = cdsBlackHoles(1).Y + cdsBlackHoles(1).Height / 2
        .vx = 0
        .vy = 0
    End With
End Sub
```

The InitForm procedure is called by Form_Load to initialize the form and create the timer controls
needed by the socket routines.

```
Private Sub InitForm()
    'set up the main form
    Form1.Caption = "Stellar War"
    Form1.Width = SCREENWIDTH * Screen.TwipsPerPixelX
    Form1.Height = SCREENHEIGHT * Screen.TwipsPerPixelY
    Form1.AutoRedraw = False
    Form1.ClipControls = False
    Form1.KeyPreview = True
    Form1.ScaleMode = 3

    'create the PictureBox control for drawing
    Set Picture1 = Controls.Add("VB.PictureBox", "Picture1")
    Picture1.AutoRedraw = False
    Picture1.BorderStyle = 1
    Picture1.ClipControls = False
```

```
Picture1.ScaleMode = 3
Picture1.BackColor = RGB(0, 0, 0)
Picture1.Left = 0
Picture1.Top = 0
Picture1.Width = Form1.ScaleWidth
Picture1.Height = Form1.ScaleHeight
Picture1.Visible = Not FULLSCREEN

'add timers
Set clientPing = Controls.Add("VB.Timer", "clientPing")
clientPing.Enabled = False
clientPing.Interval = 5000

Set socketStatus = Controls.Add("VB.Timer", "socketStatus")
socketStatus.Enabled = False
socketStatus.Interval = 50

Form1.Show
If FULLSCREEN Then
    gameinfo.WindowHandle = Form1.hWnd
Else
    gameinfo.WindowHandle = Picture1.hWnd
End IfEnd Sub
```

The InitSocket procedure initializes the socket and attempts to connect to the Stellar Server using the server's IP address and port that were loaded from the settings.ini file. If the server connection fails, an error message is displayed.

```
Private Sub InitSocket()
    Set clientLink = New clsClientSocket
    clientLink.RemotePort = gameinfo.Port
    ScrollMessages "LocalHost = " & clientLink.LocalIP
    socketStatus.Enabled = True
    ConnectServer gameinfo.Server
End Sub
```

The Form_QueryUnload and Shutdown procedures are related to freeing up the memory used by game objects and shutting down the game.

```
Private Sub Form_QueryUnload(Cancel As Integer, _
    UnloadMode As Integer)
    Shutdown
End Sub

Private Sub Shutdown()
    Dim n As Long

    gameinfo.Running = False
    clientLink.CloseConnection
    clientPing.Enabled = False
    socketStatus.Enabled = False

    Keyboard.Shutdown
    Set Keyboard = Nothing
    Set dinput = Nothing
    ddraw.Shutdown
    Set ddraw = Nothing
    Set cddsBackground = Nothing
    Set cddsBackBuffer = Nothing
    Set cddsSprite = Nothing
    Set cdsPlayer = Nothing
    Set cddsShot = Nothing
    For n = 0 To MAXSHOTS
        Set cdsShots(n) = Nothing
    Next n
    Set cddsBoom = Nothing
    For n = 0 To MAXBOOMS
        Set cdsBooms(n) = Nothing
    Next n
    Set cddsAsteroid = Nothing
    For n = 0 To MAXROCKS
        Set cdsAsteroids(n) = Nothing
    Next n
    Set cddsBlackHole = Nothing
    For n = 0 To 1
        Set cdsBlackHoles(n) = Nothing
    Next n
    Set cdsEnemy = Nothing
    For n = 0 To MAXENEMIES
        Set cdsEnemies(n) = Nothing
```

```
        Next n
        For n = 0 To 2
            Set cdsFont(n) = Nothing
        Next n
        Set cdsCursor = Nothing

        Form1.Hide
        End
End Sub
```

The Random function has been present in nearly every program in the book, so it should come as no surprise that it makes itself useful in Stellar War as well. You can never have too many random variables in a game.

```
Public Function Random(ByVal lNum As Long) As Long
    Random = CLng(lNum * Rnd)
End Function
```

The Game_Update procedure is called by the game loop in Form_Load to update the game during every frame. This procedure calls EraseStuff, DrawBlackHoles, DrawAsteroids, DrawEnemies, DrawPlayer, DrawBullets, DrawBooms, and DrawMessages to process all of the graphics in the game. The procedure then blits the back buffer to the screen and calculates the frame rate. The support procedures are all listed below Game_Update, and are easy enough that they don't need any explanation.

```
Public Sub Game_Update(ByVal ms As Long)
    Static lTimer As Long
    Static lStart As Long
    Static lCounter As Long

    'start counting milliseconds
    lStart = GetTickCount

    EraseStuff
    DrawBlackHoles
    DrawAsteroids
    DrawEnemies
    DrawPlayer
    DrawBullets
    DrawBooms
    DrawMessages
```

```
    'copy back buffer to the screen
    ddraw.Draw cddsBackBuffer, cddsBackBuffer.SurfaceRect

    'count the frames per second
    If ms > lTimer + 1000 Then
        lStart = GetTickCount - lStart
        gameinfo.FrameRate = "FPS " & lCounter
        lTimer = ms
        lCounter = 0
    Else
        lCounter = lCounter + 1
    End If
End Sub

Private Sub EraseStuff()
    Dim n As Long

    'erase the top status line
    rTemp.Left = 0
    rTemp.Top = 0
    rTemp.Right = SCREENWIDTH - 1
    rTemp.Bottom = cdsFont(0).Height + 1
    cddsBackBuffer.BltFast 0, 0, _
        cddsBackground.Surface, rTemp

    'erase the frame rate message
    rTemp.Left = SCREENWIDTH - cdsFont(0).Width * _
        Len(gameinfo.FrameRate)
    rTemp.Top = SCREENHEIGHT - cdsFont(0).Height - 1
    rTemp.Right = SCREENWIDTH
    rTemp.Bottom = SCREENHEIGHT
    cddsBackBuffer.BltFast rTemp.Left, rTemp.Top, _
        cddsBackground.Surface, rTemp

    'erase the chat message
    rTemp.Left = 4
    rTemp.Top = 640
    rTemp.Right = 500
    rTemp.Bottom = 767
    cddsBackBuffer.BltFast 4, 640, _
        cddsBackground.Surface, rTemp
```

```
    'erase the player's ship and name
    rTemp.Left = cdsPlayer.X
    rTemp.Top = cdsPlayer.Y
    rTemp.Right = rTemp.Left + cdsPlayer.Width + 1
    rTemp.Bottom = rTemp.Top + cdsPlayer.Height + _
        cdsFont(1).Height
    cddsBackBuffer.BltFast rTemp.Left, rTemp.Top, _
        cddsBackground.Surface, rTemp

    'erase the asteroids
    For n = 0 To MAXROCKS
        EraseSprite cdsAsteroids(n)
    Next n

    'erase the explosions
    For n = 0 To MAXBOOMS
        If cdsBooms(n).Active Then
            EraseSprite cdsBooms(n)
        End If
    Next n

    'erase projectile sprites
    For n = 0 To MAXSHOTS
        If cdsShots(n).Active Then
            EraseSprite cdsShots(n)
        End If
    Next n
End Sub

Private Sub DrawBlackHoles()
    Dim n As Long

    'display the blackholes
    For n = 0 To 1
        With cdsBlackHoles(n)
            If .Active Then
                .NextFrame
                .Draw cddsBackBuffer
            End If
        End With
    Next n
End Sub
```

```
Private Sub DrawAsteroids()
    Dim n As Long

    'display the asteroids
    For n = 0 To MAXROCKS
        With cdsAsteroids(n)
            If .Active Then
                .NextFrame
                .Draw cddsBackBuffer
            End If
        End With
    Next n
End Sub

Private Sub DrawEnemies()
    Dim n As Long

    'display the enemy ships
    For n = 0 To MAXENEMIES
        With cdsEnemies(n)
            If .Active Then
                .Draw cddsBackBuffer
            End If
        End With

        'display enemy player name
        DrawText cdsEnemies(n).X + 1, cdsEnemies(n).Y + _
            cdsEnemies(n).Height, gameinfo.Nicknames(n)
    Next n
End Sub

Private Sub DrawBullets()
    Dim n As Long
    Dim lNum As Long

    'move and draw projectiles
    For n = 0 To MAXSHOTS
        With cdsShots(n)
            If .Active Then
                'update X position
                .MoveCount = .MoveCount + 1
```

```
        If .MoveCount > .MoveRate Then
            .MoveCount = 0
            .X = .X + .SpeedX * 2
            If .X < 1 Or .X > SCREENWIDTH - _
                .Width - 1 Then
                .Active = False
            End If

            'update Y position
            .Y = .Y + .SpeedY * 2
            If .Y < 1 Or .Y > SCREENHEIGHT - _
                .Height - 1 Then
                .Active = False
            End If
        End If

        'check for collision with asteroids
        For lNum = 0 To MAXROCKS
            If cdsAsteroids(lNum).Active Then
                If Collided(cdsShots(n), _
                    cdsAsteroids(lNum)) Then
                    .Active = False
                    'send "hit asteroid" message to server
                    clientLink.Send PREFIX & HITA_HDR & _
                        SEP & lNum
                    StartBoom cdsAsteroids(lNum).X, _
                        cdsAsteroids(lNum).Y
                    cdsAsteroids(lNum).Active = False
                    Exit For
                End If
            End If
        Next lNum

        'check for collision with other players
        For lNum = 0 To MAXENEMIES
            If cdsEnemies(lNum).Active Then
                If Collided(cdsShots(n), _
                    cdsEnemies(lNum)) Then
                    .Active = False
```

```
                                'send "hit player" message to server
                                clientLink.Send PREFIX & HITP_HDR & _
                                    SEP & lNum
                                StartBoom cdsEnemies(lNum).X, _
                                    cdsEnemies(lNum).Y
                                cdsEnemies(lNum).Active = False
                                Exit For
                        End If
                    End If
                Next lNum

                'animate and draw the sprite
                If .Active Then
                    .NextFrame
                    .Draw cddsBackBuffer
                End If
            End If
        End With
    Next n
End Sub

Private Sub DrawMessages()
    Dim n As Long
    Dim sTemp As String

    'display game title
    DrawText 1, 1, "STELLAR WAR", 0

    'display the score
    sTemp = "SCORE: " & CStr(gameinfo.Score)
    DrawText SCREENWIDTH - Len(sTemp) * _
        cdsFont(0).Width - 1, 1, sTemp, 0

    'display the frame rate
    DrawText SCREENWIDTH - cdsFont(0).Width * _
        Len(gameinfo.FrameRate), SCREENHEIGHT - _
        cdsFont(0).Height - 1, gameinfo.FrameRate, 0

    'display message lines
    For n = 0 To 7
```

```
        If Len(gameinfo.Messages(n)) > 0 Then
            DrawText 4, 640 + n * 13, gameinfo.Messages(n)
        End If
    Next n

    'display chat line and cursor
    DrawText 4, 750, "CHAT: " & gameinfo.ChatMessage
    With cdsCursor
        .X = 4 + Len("CHAT: " & gameinfo.ChatMessage) * _
            cdsFont(1).Width
        .Y = 750
        .NextFrame
        .Draw cddsBackBuffer
    End With

End Sub

Private Sub DrawPlayer()
    Dim n As Long

    'calculate gravitational forces
    Gravity shipMass2, shipMass1
    Gravity shipMass2, blackHole1
    Gravity shipMass2, blackHole2

    'important: nullify the gravity well!
    shipMass1.mass = 0

    'move and draw the player's ship
    With cdsPlayer
        'position sprite based on dead weight
        .X = shipMass2.X - 32
        .Y = shipMass2.Y - 32

        'check X bounds
        If .X < 1 Then
            .X = SCREENWIDTH - 65
            shipMass2.X = .X + 32
        ElseIf .X > SCREENWIDTH - 65 Then
            .X = 0
            shipMass2.X = .X + 32
        End If
```

```
        'check Y bounds
        If .Y < 1 Then
            .Y = SCREENHEIGHT - 80
            shipMass2.Y = .Y + 32
        ElseIf .Y > SCREENHEIGHT - 80 Then
            .Y = 0
            shipMass2.Y = .Y + 32
        End If

        'draw the sprite
        .Draw cddsBackBuffer
    End With

    'display player name
    DrawText cdsPlayer.X + 20, cdsPlayer.Y + _
        cdsPlayer.Height, gameinfo.Nickname
End Sub
```

There are two support procedures for drawing explosions on the screen: StartBoom and DrawBooms. The goofy names are simply easier to spell out than "explosion" throughout the source code. Basically, you pass an X and Y position, and StartBoom turns on the explosion and sets it to the position indicated. Game_Update then takes over and draws the explosion during the next frame.

```
Private Sub StartBoom(ByVal X As Long, ByVal Y As Long)
    Dim n As Long
    Dim lFound As Long
    'check for available sprites
    lFound = -1
    For n = 0 To MAXBOOMS
        If Not cdsBooms(n).Active Then
            lFound = n
            Exit For
        End If
    Next n
    'limit number of explosions
    If lFound > -1 Then
        'turn on the explosion
        cdsBooms(lFound).Active = True
        cdsBooms(lFound).X = X
        cdsBooms(lFound).Y = Y
    End If
End Sub
```

```
Private Sub DrawBooms()
    Dim n As Long
    Dim lNum As Long

    For lNum = 0 To MAXBOOMS
        With cdsBooms(lNum)
            'make sure burst sprite is alive
            If .Active Then
                'draw burst sprite
                .Draw cddsBackBuffer
                'increment frame
                If .CurrentFrame < 15 Then
                    .CurrentFrame = .CurrentFrame + 1
                Else
                    .Active = False
                    .CurrentFrame = 0
                End If
            End If
        End With
    Next lNum
End Sub
```

The next section of code lists several support routines that should be self-evident: ClearScreen, ScrollMessages, EraseSprite, DrawText, and DrawChar.

```
Private Sub ClearScreen()
    rTemp.Left = 0
    rTemp.Top = 0
    rTemp.Right = SCREENWIDTH - 1
    rTemp.Bottom = SCREENHEIGHT - 1
    cddsBackBuffer.BltFast rTemp.Left, rTemp.Top, _
        cddsBackground.Surface, rTemp
End Sub

Private Sub ScrollMessages(ByVal sText As String)
    Dim n As Long

    For n = 1 To 7
        gameinfo.Messages(n - 1) = gameinfo.Messages(n)
    Next n
    gameinfo.Messages(7) = sText
End Sub
```

```
Private Sub EraseSprite(ByRef sprite As clsDDSprite7)
    Dim rTemp As DxVBLib.RECT
    With sprite
        rTemp.Left = .X - 1
        rTemp.Top = .Y - 1
        rTemp.Right = rTemp.Left + .Width + 1
        rTemp.Bottom = rTemp.Top + .Height + 1
        cddsBackBuffer.BltFast .X, .Y, _
            cddsBackground.Surface, rTemp
    End With
End Sub


Private Sub DrawText(ByVal X As Long, ByVal Y As Long, _
    ByVal sText As String, Optional lFontNum As Long = 1)
    Dim n As Long
    For n = 1 To Len(sText)
        DrawChar X + (n - 1) * cdsFont(lFontNum).Width, _
            Y, Asc(Mid$(sText, n, 1)), lFontNum
    Next n
End Sub


Private Sub DrawChar(ByVal X As Long, ByVal Y As Long, _
    c As Byte, Optional lFontNum As Long = 1)
    cdsFont(lFontNum).X = X
    cdsFont(lFontNum).Y = Y
    cdsFont(lFontNum).CurrentFrame = c - 32
    cdsFont(lFontNum).Draw cddsBackBuffer
End Sub
```

The Network_Update procedure is called by the socketStatus timer to fire off a series of packets to update the server on the player's position and status.

```
Private Sub Network_Update()
    Static lLastScore As Long
    Dim n As Long

    If clientLink.State <> sckConnected Then Exit Sub

    'send ship position to server
    With cdsPlayer
        clientLink.Send PREFIX & SHIP_HDR & SEP & _
```

```
                .X & SEP & .Y & SEP & _
                .CurrentFrame & SEP & gameinfo.Nickname
        End With

        'send projectiles to server
        For n = 0 To MAXSHOTS
            With cdsShots(n)
                If .Active Then
                    clientLink.Send PREFIX & SHOT_HDR & _
                        SEP & .X & SEP & .Y
                End If
            End With
        Next n

        'send score to server
        If gameinfo.Score <> lLastScore Then
            lLastScore = lLastScore
            clientLink.Send PREFIX & SCOR_HDR & SEP & _
                gameinfo.Score
        End If

        'request black hole positions from server
        If cdsBlackHoles(0).Active = False Then
            'request blackhole positions
            clientLink.Send PREFIX & HOLE_HDR & SEP
        End If
End Sub
```

There are two procedures for handling keyboard input. First, the DirectInput keyboard handler, Keyboard_KeyDown, provides support for multiple key presses and is generally used to move the ship around the screen where the arrow keys and several simultaneous key presses are needed. Form_KeyPress is the standard Visual Basic form event for keyboard input, and is used to track regular key presses for typing messages into the chat line. To support chatting, an additional support routine is also included in this section: SendChatMessage.

```
Private Sub Keyboard_KeyDown(ByVal lKey As Long)
    Select Case lKey
        Case KEY_ESC
            Shutdown
        Case KEY_LEFT
            cdsPlayer.PrevFrame
```

```
            Case KEY_RIGHT
                cdsPlayer.NextFrame
            Case KEY_UP
                MoveShip
            Case KEY_LCTRL
                FireProjectile cdsPlayer.X, cdsPlayer.Y, _
                    cdsPlayer.CurrentFrame
            Case KEY_ENTER
                SendChatMessage gameinfo.ChatMessage
                gameinfo.ChatMessage = ""
        End Select
End Sub

Private Sub Form_KeyPress(KeyAscii As Integer)
    Select Case KeyAscii
        Case 8
            If Len(gameinfo.ChatMessage) > 0 Then
                gameinfo.ChatMessage = Mid$( _
                    gameinfo.ChatMessage, 1, _
                    Len(gameinfo.ChatMessage) - 1)
            End If
        Case 32 To 127
            If Len(gameinfo.ChatMessage) < 49 Then
                gameinfo.ChatMessage = _
                    gameinfo.ChatMessage & Chr$(KeyAscii)
            End If
    End Select
End Sub

Private Sub SendChatMessage(ByVal sMsg As String)
    If Len(sMsg) = 0 Then Exit Sub
    clientLink.Send PREFIX & CHAT_HDR & SEP & _
        gameinfo.Nickname & ": " & sMsg
End Sub
```

MoveShip and FireProjectile are somewhat similar in that both procedures must determine the
direction that the player's ship is facing. This involves a tedious Select statement that accounts for
all 16 rotation angles. MoveShip is called by Keyboard_KeyDown when the up arrow is pressed, and
handles thrust for the ship (using some of the gravity variables). FireProjectile searches for an
available projectile sprite and sets it up if available.

```
Private Sub MoveShip()
    Dim lStartX As Long
    Dim lStartY As Long

    With cdsPlayer
        .MoveCount = .MoveCount + 1
        If .MoveCount > .MoveRate Then
            .MoveCount = 0
        Else
            Exit Sub
        End If
    End With
    lStartX = shipMass2.X
    lStartY = shipMass2.Y
    shipMass1.mass = GRAVITYWELL
    shipMass2.mass = shipMass2.mass + MASSADD
    If shipMass2.mass > MAXMASS Then _
        shipMass2.mass = MAXMASS

    With shipMass1
        Select Case cdsPlayer.CurrentFrame
            Case 0
                .X = lStartX
                .Y = lStartY - 24
            Case 1
                .X = lStartX + 8
                .Y = lStartY - 24
            Case 2
                .X = lStartX + 14
                .Y = lStartY - 20
            Case 3
                .X = lStartX + 16
                .Y = lStartY - 12
            Case 4
                .X = lStartX + 16
                .Y = lStartY
            Case 5
                .X = lStartX + 16
                .Y = lStartY + 2
```

```
            Case 6
                .X = lStartX + 16
                .Y = lStartY + 12
            Case 7
                .X = lStartX + 6
                .Y = lStartY + 16
            Case 8
                .X = lStartX
                .Y = lStartY + 20
            Case 9
                .X = lStartX - 12
                .Y = lStartY + 16
            Case 10
                .X = lStartX - 20
                .Y = lStartY + 12
            Case 11
                .X = lStartX - 20
                .Y = lStartY + 4
            Case 12
                .X = lStartX - 24
                .Y = lStartY
            Case 13
                .X = lStartX - 22
                .Y = lStartY - 12
            Case 14
                .X = lStartX - 20
                .Y = lStartY - 20
            Case 15
                .X = lStartX - 12
                .Y = lStartY - 22
        End Select
    End With
End Sub

Private Sub FireProjectile(ByVal lStartX As Long, _
    ByVal lStartY As Long, ByVal lDir As Long)
    Static lLast As Long
    Dim lShot As Long
    Dim n As Long
```

```
'check timing on shots
If GetTickCount < lLast + 800 Then Exit Sub

'look for available projectile
lShot = -1
For n = 0 To MAXSHOTS
    If Not cdsShots(n).Active Then
        lShot = n
        Exit For
    End If
Next n
If lShot = -1 Then Exit Sub
lStartX = lStartX + 16
lStartY = lStartY + 16

'fire the shot
With cdsShots(lShot)
    .Active = True
    .AnimRate = 15
    .CurrentFrame = Random(5)

    'based on direction of player's ship
    Select Case lDir
        Case 0
            .X = lStartX + 12
            .Y = lStartY
            .SpeedX = 0
            .SpeedY = -2
        Case 1
            .X = lStartX + 20
            .Y = lStartY
            .SpeedX = 1
            .SpeedY = -2
        Case 2
            .X = lStartX + 24
            .Y = lStartY
            .SpeedX = 2
            .SpeedY = -2
```

```
Case 3
    .X = lStartX + 22
    .Y = lStartY + 6
    .SpeedX = 2
    .SpeedY = -1
Case 4
    .X = lStartX + 24
    .Y = lStartY + 12
    .SpeedX = 2
    .SpeedY = 0
Case 5
    .X = lStartX + 24
    .Y = lStartY + 20
    .SpeedX = 2
    .SpeedY = 1
Case 6
    .X = lStartX + 24
    .Y = lStartY + 24
    .SpeedX = 2
    .SpeedY = 2
Case 7
    .X = lStartX + 20
    .Y = lStartY + 24
    .SpeedX = 1
    .SpeedY = 2
Case 8
    .X = lStartX + 12
    .Y = lStartY + 24
    .SpeedX = 0
    .SpeedY = 2
Case 9
    .X = lStartX + 4
    .Y = lStartY + 24
    .SpeedX = -1
    .SpeedY = 2
Case 10
    .X = lStartX
    .Y = lStartY + 24
    .SpeedX = -2
    .SpeedY = 2
```

```
                    Case 11
                        .X = 1StartX
                        .Y = 1StartY + 20
                        .SpeedX = -2
                        .SpeedY = 1
                    Case 12
                        .X = 1StartX
                        .Y = 1StartY + 12
                        .SpeedX = -2
                        .SpeedY = 0
                    Case 13
                        .X = 1StartX
                        .Y = 1StartY + 4
                        .SpeedX = -2
                        .SpeedY = -1
                    Case 14
                        .X = 1StartX
                        .Y = 1StartY
                        .SpeedX = -2
                        .SpeedY = -2
                    Case 15
                        .X = 1StartX + 4
                        .Y = 1StartY
                        .SpeedX = -1
                        .SpeedY = -2
                End Select
            End With
            1Last = GetTickCount
End Sub
```

The two timers in the game are used to send information to the server at regular intervals. This
keeps the game loop free of the cluttered code that these socket events require. clientPing_Timer
sends a ping message to the server every five seconds. In addition, a call to ClearScreen cleans up
the display at regular intervals. I found this necessary because once in a while there is a missed
network packet that moves a game object out of sync. The graphics code erases everything when
needed, but occasionally a glitch is left on the screen. This call to ClearScreen makes sure the
glitch doesn't stay on the screen for very long. socketStatus_Timer sends a bunch of data to the
server and also checks the status of the socket for any errors (or a disconnection).

```
Private Sub clientPing_Timer()
    gameinfo.PingStart = GetTickCount()
```

```
    clientLink.Send PREFIX & PING_HDR & SEP & _
        gameinfo.PingStart
    ClearScreen
End Sub

Sub socketStatus_Timer()
    Static last As Long
    Dim sStatus As String

    'set player data to server
    Network_Update

    'check socket status
    If clientLink.State <> last Then
        Select Case clientLink.State
            Case sckClosed
                sStatus = "Socket closed"
            Case sckOpen
                sStatus = "Socket open"
            Case sckListening
                sStatus = "Listening..."
            Case sckConnectionPending
                sStatus = "Connection pending"
            Case sckResolvingHost
                sStatus = "Resolving host..."
            Case sckHostResolved
                sStatus = "Host resolved"
            Case sckConnecting
                sStatus = "Connecting..."
            Case sckConnected
                sStatus = "Connected"
            Case sckClosing
                sStatus = "Closing..."
            Case sckError
                sStatus = "Error"
        End Select
        last = clientLink.State
        ScrollMessages sStatus
    End If
End Sub
```

`ConnectServer` is a support routine called by `InitSocket` to establish a connection to the server. If the connection is successful, a message is added to the server message log, and gameplay will commence.

```
Private Sub ConnectServer(ByVal IP As String)
    If Len(IP) = 0 Then Exit Sub
    ScrollMessages "Connecting to " & IP & _
        " on port " & gameinfo.Port & "..."
    clientLink.RemoteHost = IP
    clientLink.Connect
End Sub
```

The socket data arrival routines are significant to the operation of the game. When an event comes into the client socket (clientLink), the class generates an event called `DataArrival`, which is found in the main program under the label of clientLink_DataArrival. This is the central socket message handler for the game, and it calls on numerous support procedures: `ProcessScore`, `ProcessBoom`, `ProcessShot`, `ProcessBlackHole`, `ProcessAsteroid`, `ProcessShip`, and `ScrollMessages` (for chat packets). These socket events are all processed with the string-parsing routines at the end of the source code listing.

```
Private Sub clientLink_DataArrival(ByVal lTotalBytes As Long, _
    ByVal sIncoming As String)

    Dim sWork As String
    Dim lPingEnd As Long
    Dim lPingVal As Long
    Dim msgHeader As String
    Dim msgBody As String
    Dim lTotal As Long

    'grab all packets out of this transmission
    Do While Len(sIncoming) > 3 And _
        TokenCount(sIncoming, PREFIX) > 0

        sWork = ParseToken(sIncoming, 2, PREFIX)
        sIncoming = Mid$(sIncoming, Len(PREFIX) + _
            Len(sWork) + 1)

        'parse the msg out of the string so data is left
        msgHeader = ParseToken(sWork, 1, SEP)
        msgBody = Mid$(sWork, InStr(1, sWork, SEP) + 1)
```

```
        Select Case msgHeader
            Case DIED_HDR
                DrawText SCREENWIDTH / 2 - 100, _
                    SCREENHEIGHT / 2, "YOU GOT KILLED!"
            Case SCOR_HDR
                ProcessScore msgBody
            Case BOOM_HDR
                ProcessBoom msgBody
            Case SHOT_HDR
                ProcessShot msgBody
            Case HOLE_HDR
                ProcessBlackHole msgBody
            Case ROCK_HDR
                ProcessAsteroid msgBody
            Case SHIP_HDR
                ProcessShip msgBody
            Case CHAT_HDR
                ScrollMessages msgBody
            Case PING_HDR
                lPingEnd = CLng(msgBody)
                lPingVal = GetTickCount() - lPingEnd + 1
                DrawText 1, 1, "PING " & lPingVal
        End Select
        lTotal = lTotal + 1
        DoEvents
    Loop
    If lTotal > 1 Then _
        Debug.Print "Combined packets: " & lTotal
End Sub

Private Sub ProcessScore(ByVal msgBody As String)
    Dim Score As Long
    On Error GoTo error1
    If TokenCount(msgBody, SEP) <> 1 Then Exit Sub
    'score packet is just a trigger to add one point
    gameinfo.Score = gameinfo.Score + 1
    Exit Sub
error1:
End Sub
```

```
Private Sub ProcessBoom(ByVal msgBody As String)
    Dim X As Long
    Dim Y As Long

    On Error GoTo error1
    If TokenCount(msgBody, SEP) <> 2 Then Exit Sub

    'store the data
    X = ParseToken(msgBody, 1, SEP)
    Y = ParseToken(msgBody, 2, SEP)

    'validate the data
    If Not IsNumeric(X) Then Exit Sub
    If Not IsNumeric(Y) Then Exit Sub

    'start the explosion
    StartBoom X, Y
    Exit Sub
error1:
End Sub

Private Sub ProcessShot(ByVal msgBody As String)
    Dim X As Long
    Dim Y As Long
    Dim n As Long

    On Error GoTo error1
    If TokenCount(msgBody, SEP) <> 2 Then Exit Sub

    'store the data
    X = ParseToken(msgBody, 1, SEP)
    Y = ParseToken(msgBody, 2, SEP)

    'validate the data
    If Not IsNumeric(X) Then Exit Sub
    If Not IsNumeric(Y) Then Exit Sub

    'update the shot array
    For n = 0 To MAXSHOTS
        With cdsShots(n)
```

```
                If Not .Active Then
                    .Active = True
                    .X = X
                    .Y = Y
                End If
            End With
        Next n
        Exit Sub
    error1:
    End Sub


    Private Sub ProcessAsteroid(ByVal msgBody As String)
        Dim X As Long
        Dim Y As Long
        Dim num As Long

        On Error GoTo error1
        If TokenCount(msgBody, SEP) <> 3 Then Exit Sub

        num = ParseToken(msgBody, 1, SEP)
        X = ParseToken(msgBody, 2, SEP)
        Y = ParseToken(msgBody, 3, SEP)

        'erase the asteroid
        EraseSprite cdsAsteroids(num)

        'validate the values
        If Not IsNumeric(num) Then Exit Sub
        If Not IsNumeric(X) Then Exit Sub
        If Not IsNumeric(Y) Then Exit Sub

        With cdsAsteroids(num)
            .Active = True
            .X = X
            .Y = Y
        End With
        Exit Sub
    error1:
    End Sub
```

```
Private Sub ProcessBlackHole(ByVal msgBody As String)
    Dim X As Long
    Dim Y As Long
    Dim num As Long
    Dim dest As Long

    On Error GoTo error1
    If TokenCount(msgBody, SEP) <> 3 Then Exit Sub

    num = ParseToken(msgBody, 1, SEP)
    X = ParseToken(msgBody, 2, SEP)
    Y = ParseToken(msgBody, 3, SEP)

    'validate the values
    If Not IsNumeric(num) Then Exit Sub
    If Not IsNumeric(X) Then Exit Sub
    If Not IsNumeric(Y) Then Exit Sub

    With cdsBlackHoles(num)
        .Active = True
        .X = X
        .Y = Y
    End With
    ResetGravity
    Exit Sub
error1:
End Sub

Private Sub ProcessShip(ByVal msgBody As String)
    Dim X As Long
    Dim Y As Long
    Dim dir As Long
    Dim num As Long
    Dim nick As String

    On Error GoTo error1
    If TokenCount(msgBody, SEP) <> 5 Then Exit Sub

    num = ParseToken(msgBody, 1, SEP)
    X = ParseToken(msgBody, 2, SEP)
    Y = ParseToken(msgBody, 3, SEP)
```

```
        dir = ParseToken(msgBody, 4, SEP)
        nick = ParseToken(msgBody, 5, SEP)

        'validate data
        If Not IsNumeric(num) Then Exit Sub
        If Not IsNumeric(X) Then Exit Sub
        If Not IsNumeric(Y) Then Exit Sub
        If Not IsNumeric(dir) Then Exit Sub
        If Len(nick) > 4 Then nick = Left$(nick, 4)

        With cdsEnemies(num)
            'erase enemy ship
            rTemp.Left = .X
            rTemp.Top = .Y
            rTemp.Right = .X + .Width + 1
            rTemp.Bottom = .Y + .Height + cdsFont(1).Height
            cddsBackBuffer.BltFast rTemp.Left, rTemp.Top, _
                cddsBackground.Surface, rTemp

            'update info
            .Active = True
            .X = X
            .Y = Y
            .CurrentFrame = dir
        End With
        gameinfo.Nicknames(num) = nick
        Exit Sub
error1:
End Sub

Public Function TokenCount(ByVal sWork As String, _
    ByVal sDelimiter As String) As Long

    Dim n As Long
    Dim lCPos As Long
    Dim lSPos As Long
    Dim lCharLen As Long

    On Error GoTo error1
    If Len(sWork) = 0 Then Exit Function
```

```
        lCharLen = Len(sDelimiter)
        lSPos = 1

        'process loop once whether true or not
        Do
            lCPos = InStr(lSPos, sWork, sDelimiter)
            If lCPos Then
                n = n + 1
                lSPos = lCharLen + lCPos
            End If
        Loop While lCPos

        If Right(sWork, lCharLen) <> sDelimiter Then
            TokenCount = n + 1
        Else
            TokenCount = n
        End If
        Exit Function
error1:
End Function

Public Function ParseToken(ByVal sWork As String, _
    ByVal lTokenNum As Long, ByVal sDelimiter As String, _
    Optional ByVal sEncapChr As String) As String

        Dim bExitDo As Boolean
        Dim lDPos As Integer
        Dim lSPtr As Integer
        Dim lEPtr As Integer
        Dim lCurrentToken As Integer
        Dim lWorkStrLen As Integer
        Dim lEncapStatus As Integer
        Static lSPos As Integer
        Dim sTemp As String
        Static lDelimitLen As Integer

        On Error GoTo error1

        lWorkStrLen = Len(sWork)
        If Len(sEncapChr) Then
            lEncapStatus = Len(sEncapChr)
        End If
```

```
'grab the desired token
If lWorkStrLen = 0 Or (lSPos > lWorkStrLen And _
    lTokenNum = 0) Then
    lSPos = 0
    Exit Function
ElseIf lTokenNum > 0 Or lSPos = 0 Then
    lSPos = 1
    lDelimitLen = Len(sDelimiter)
End If

'loop once whether true or not
Do
    lDPos = InStr(lSPos, sWork, sDelimiter)
    If lEncapStatus Then
        lSPtr = InStr(lSPos, sWork, sEncapChr)
        lEPtr = InStr(lSPtr + 1, sWork, sEncapChr)
        If lDPos > lSPtr And lDPos < lEPtr Then
            lDPos = InStr(lEPtr, sWork, sDelimiter)
        End If
    End If

    If lDPos < lSPos Then
        lDPos = lWorkStrLen + lDelimitLen
    End If

    If lDPos Then
        'found the right token?
        If lTokenNum Then
            lCurrentToken = lCurrentToken + 1
            If lCurrentToken = lTokenNum Then
                sTemp = Mid(sWork, lSPos, lDPos - lSPos)
                bExitDo = True
            Else
                bExitDo = False
            End If
        Else
            sTemp = Mid(sWork, lSPos, lDPos - lSPos)
            bExitDo = True
        End If
        lSPos = lDPos + lDelimitLen
    Else
```

```
                lSPos = 0
                bExitDo = True
            End If
        Loop Until bExitDo

        ParseToken = sTemp
        Exit Function
error1:
End Function
```

The `Collided` function checks to see whether the bounding boxes of two sprites overlap, resulting in a collision. The server handles most of the collision in the game, but there are some cases where collision detection is needed by the game client as well.

```
Private Function Collided(ByRef Sprite1 As clsDDSprite7, _
    ByRef Sprite2 As clsDDSprite7) As Boolean
    Dim r1 As RECT_API
    Dim r2 As RECT_API
    Dim r3 As RECT_API
    Dim lMod As Long

    'set up primary rect
    With Sprite1
        lMod = .Width / 5
        r1.Left = .X + lMod
        r1.Top = .Y + lMod
        r1.Right = r1.Left + .Width - lMod
        r1.Bottom = r1.Top + .Height - lMod
    End With

    'set up secondary rect
    With Sprite2
        lMod = .Width / 2
        r2.Left = .X + lMod
        r2.Top = .Y + lMod
        r2.Right = r2.Left + .Width - lMod
        r2.Bottom = r2.Top + .Height - lMod
    End With

    'check for collision
    Collided = IntersectRect(r3, r1, r2)
End Function
```

The Stellar Server Program

The Stellar Server program processes the packets of data for each player logged on to play the game. The server is a required part of this client/server game, and is called a *dedicated* server because it can reside on a powerful PC and it generally runs faster than a server that is hosted by one of the players. Figure 21.16 shows the Stellar Server program running. Notice the "radar window" showing the position of objects in the game.

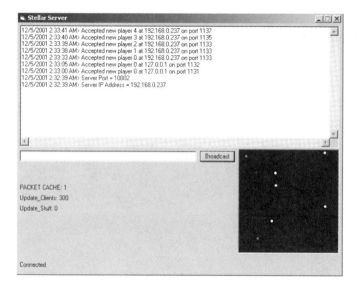

Figure 21.16

The Stellar Server shows game messages and a small window that displays player positions. It allows the server operator to send broadcast messages to the players.

The Project Explorer

The Project Explorer for Stellar Server (shown in Figure 21.17) shows the files needed to compile the game server. In addition to the default Form1, the project will need the following game library files: ServerSocket.cls, frmLink.lnk, and Declares.bas.

Figure 21.17

The Project Explorer for Stellar Server shows the files needed to compile the program.

The Stellar Server Project

The Stellar Server program also calls for a Standard EXE project with a single form. But in this case, the form will have a bunch of controls on it, and—*gasp!*—I'm going to have you add the controls to the form at design time. I know, it's contradictory to my faith, but some VB programs (like servers) are just easier to put together at design time. Take a peek at Figure 21.18 to see the Stellar Server project loaded into the Visual Basic IDE.

Figure 21.18

The Stellar Server project as it appears in the Visual Basic IDE

Building the User Interface

The source code for Stellar Server assumes that various controls are present on the form, as shown in Figure 21.19.

To build the user interface for Stellar Server, simply refer to Table 21.2 for a list of controls. Add the controls to Form1, with the appropriate caption or text, in the proper position, and with the designated dimensions. You can refer to Figure 21.19 for reference.

Project References

The References dialog box for Stellar Server, shown in Figure 21.20, does not need to include any DirectX type libraries because this is just a standard VB program that doesn't do much (other than process packets of data and display some status information).

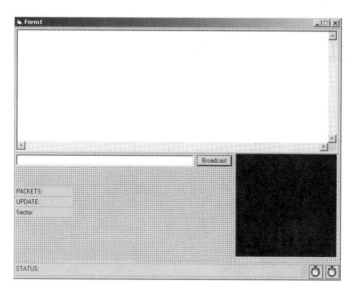

Figure 21.19

The user interface for Stellar Server at design time, showing the controls used in the program

Table 21.2 Stellar Server Control List

Control Name	Type	Caption/Text	Position	Dimensions
txtOutput	TextBox	""	4,4	630,230
txtBroadcast	TextBox	""	4,244	350,21
cmdBroadcast	CommandButton	Broadcast	360,244	70,21
picRadar	PictureBox	n/a	436,240	200,200
lblPackets	Label	PACKETS:	4,308	110,13
lblUpdate	Label	UPDATE:	4,328	110,13
lblSector	Label	SECTOR:	4,348	110,13
lblStatus	Label	STATUS:	4,456	560,17
Timer1	Timer	n/a	580,452	n/a
Timer2	Timer	n/a	612,452	n/a

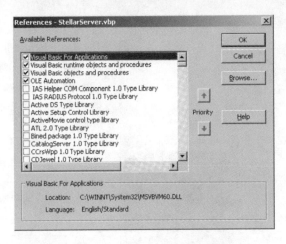

Figure 21.20

The Stellar Server References dialog box shows the standard components needed by the program.

Stellar Server Source Code

The source code listing for Stellar Server follows. I will explain each part of the program in the order in which it should be entered into the code window for Form1. The first section of code includes the constants, types, and variables for the program, as usual.

```
'-----------------------------------------------------------------------
' Visual Basic Game Programming With DirectX
' Chapter 21 : Stellar War: Multiplayer Space Combat Game
' Stellar Server Source Code File
'-----------------------------------------------------------------------

Option Explicit
Option Base 0

'program constants
Const SCREENWIDTH As Long = 1024
Const SCREENHEIGHT As Long = 768
Const MAXPLAYERS As Long = 8
Const MAXROCKS As Long = 2
Const MAXSHOTS As Long = 20
Const MAXBOOMS As Long = 20
Const ROCKREBIRTH As Long = 1000

'socket constants
Const CLIENTUPDATERATE As Long = 20
Const SEP As String = "ÿ" 'ASCII 255
Const PREFIX = "___" 'ASCII 254
Const PING_HDR = "111"
```

```
Const CHAT_HDR = "112"
Const SHIP_HDR = "113"
Const SHOT_HDR = "114"
Const ROCK_HDR = "115"
Const HOLE_HDR = "116"
Const BOOM_HDR = "117"
Const SCOR_HDR = "118"
Const HITA_HDR = "119"
Const HITP_HDR = "120"
Const DIED_HDR = "121"

'server data structure
Private Type SERVER_DATA
    Name As String
    Port As Long
    Players As Long
    HighScore As Long
    TopScorer As String
End Type

'basic bot data structure
Private Type PLAYER_DATA
    Active As Boolean
    X As Long
    Y As Long
    Dir As Long
    Nickname As String
    Scored As Boolean
End Type

'asteroid structure
Private Type ASTEROID_DATA
    Active As Boolean
    X As Long
    Y As Long
    SpeedX As Long
    SpeedY As Long
    MoveCount As Long
    MoveRate As Long
    AnimCount As Long
    AnimRate As Long
    CurrentFrame As Long
```

```
        Rebirth As Long
End Type

'generic all-purpose structure
Private Type MISC_DATA
        Active As Boolean
        Owner As Long
        X As Long
        Y As Long
End Type

'socket server class
Dim WithEvents serverLink As clsServerSocket

'program variables
Dim serverinfo As SERVER_DATA
Dim wormholes(2) As MISC_DATA
Dim shots(MAXSHOTS) As MISC_DATA
Dim booms(MAXBOOMS) As MISC_DATA
Dim asteroids(MAXROCKS) As ASTEROID_DATA
Dim Players(MAXPLAYERS) As PLAYER_DATA
```

The first procedure of the program, as usual, is Form_Load. This event is the first thing that
runs when the program starts, and it handles everything needed to initialize the server. The
LoadSettings procedure follows Form_Load and handles loading the server settings from the set-
tings.txt file, which is shown in Figure 21.21.

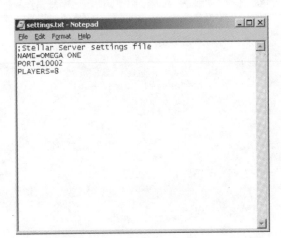

Figure 21.21

*The Stellar Server set-
tings file includes the
server name, port, and
maximum number of
players.*

```
Private Sub Form_Load()
    LoadSettings

    Form1.Caption = "Stellar Server"
    picRadar.ScaleWidth = SCREENWIDTH
    picRadar.ScaleHeight = SCREENHEIGHT

    Set serverLink = New clsServerSocket
    serverLink.OpenServer serverinfo.Port
    PrintOut "Server IP Address = " & serverLink.LocalIP
    PrintOut "Server Port = " & serverLink.LocalPort

    Randomize GetTickCount
    ResetPlayers
    ResetGame

    Timer1.Interval = CLIENTUPDATERATE
    Timer1.Enabled = True

    Timer2.Interval = CLIENTUPDATERATE / 2
    Timer2.Enabled = True
    Form1.Show
End Sub

Private Sub LoadSettings()
    Dim filenum As Long
    Dim sInput As String
    Dim sTemp As String

    On Error GoTo error1
    filenum = FreeFile
    Open App.Path & "\settings.txt" For Input As #filenum

    Do Until EOF(filenum)
        Line Input #filenum, sInput
        If Len(sInput) > 0 Then
            If Left$(sInput, 1) <> ";" Then
                If UCase$(Left$(sInput, 5)) = "NAME=" Then
                    sTemp = ParseToken(sInput, 2, "=")
```

```
                        If Len(sTemp) > 0 Then
                            serverinfo.Name = sTemp
                            If Len(serverinfo.Name) > 40 Then
                                serverinfo.Name = "OMEGA ONE"
                            End If
                        Else
                            serverinfo.Name = "OMEGA ONE"
                        End If
                    ElseIf UCase$(Left$(sInput, 5)) = "PORT=" Then
                        sTemp = ParseToken(sInput, 2, "=")
                        If IsNumeric(sTemp) Then
                            serverinfo.Port = CLng(sTemp)
                            If serverinfo.Port = 0 Or _
                                serverinfo.Port > 60000 Then
                                serverinfo.Port = 10002
                            End If
                        Else
                            serverinfo.Port = 10002
                        End If
                    ElseIf UCase$(Left$(sInput, 8)) = "PLAYERS=" Then
                        sTemp = ParseToken(sInput, 2, "=")
                        If IsNumeric(sTemp) Then
                            serverinfo.Players = CLng(sTemp)
                            If serverinfo.Players = 0 Or _
                                serverinfo.Players > 8 Then
                                serverinfo.Players = 8
                            End If
                        Else
                            serverinfo.Players = 8
                        End If
                    End If
                End If
            End If
    Loop

    Close #filenum
    Exit Sub
error1:
    MsgBox "The settings.txt file is invalid!"
    Shutdown
End Sub
```

The Broadcast and SendTo procedures are the main procedures for communicating with clients. While Broadcast sends a packet to every player in the game, SendTo just sends a packet to a specific player.

```
Private Sub Broadcast(ByVal msg As String)
    Dim n As Long
    Dim count As Long
    Dim total As Long

    'make sure message is not null
    If Len(msg) = 0 Then Exit Sub

    'get number of players
    total = serverLink.UserCount

    'broadcast message to all players
    For n = 0 To MAXPLAYERS - 1
        If serverLink.Connected(n) Then
            SendTo n, msg
            'sent to all players yet?
            count = count + 1
            If count > total Then Exit For
        End If
    Next n
End Sub

Private Sub SendTo(ByVal num As Long, ByVal msg As String)
    'send message to specific player
    serverLink.Send num, msg
    'critical: delay prevents packet clogging
    Delay 1
End Sub
```

Two procedures reset various settings on the server. ResetGame is called by Form_Load to initialize the object tracking structures. ResetPlayers is called by Form_Load and Client_Update to clear out the player list. Since players don't send a "goodbye" message when they leave (often due to a forced disconnection, rather than a farewell), the player list will quickly become outdated if it is not refreshed at every synchronization. Since each player sends ship position updates every frame, the server has a means to keep the list up-to-date.

```
Private Sub ResetGame()
    Dim n As Long
    Dim lAst As Long
    Dim lWorm As Long

    With wormholes(0)
        'place wormhole1 on left side
        .X = Random(SCREENWIDTH / 4) + 30
        .Y = Random(SCREENHEIGHT / 4)
    End With
    With wormholes(1)
        'place wormhole2 on right side
        .X = SCREENWIDTH - Random(SCREENWIDTH / 4 - 65)
        .Y = Random(SCREENHEIGHT - 65)
    End With

    'initialize asteroids
    For lAst = 0 To MAXROCKS
        With asteroids(lAst)
            .Active = True
            .X = Random(SCREENWIDTH - 64)
            .Y = Random(SCREENHEIGHT - 64)
            .SpeedX = Random(4) - 2
            .SpeedY = Random(4) - 2
            .MoveCount = 0
            .MoveRate = 1
        End With
    Next lAst
End Sub

Private Sub ResetPlayers()
    Dim n As Long

    For n = 0 To MAXPLAYERS
        With Players(n)
            .X = -1
            .Y = -1
        End With
    Next n
End Sub
```

The Update_Stuff procedure is called every 250 milliseconds (four times a second) to update all the objects in the game. This procedure moves the asteroids in the game, draws the objects in the mini radar, and checks for collisions between game objects. The support routine for Update_Stuff is called DrawCircle.

```
Private Sub Update_Stuff()
    Dim n As Long
    Dim lAst As Long
    Dim lPlay As Long
    Dim lTime As Long

    lTime = GetTickCount
    picRadar.Cls

    'move the asteroids
    For lAst = 0 To MAXROCKS
        With asteroids(lAst)
            If .Active Then
                'see if asteroid is ready to move
                .MoveCount = .MoveCount + 1
                If .MoveCount > .MoveRate Then
                    .MoveCount = 0
                    'update X
                    .X = .X + .SpeedX
                    If .X > SCREENWIDTH - 65 Then
                        .X = 1
                    ElseIf .X < 1 Then
                        .X = SCREENWIDTH - 65
                    End If
                    'update Y
                    .Y = .Y + .SpeedY
                    If .Y > SCREENHEIGHT - 65 Then
                        .Y = 1
                    ElseIf .Y < 1 Then
                        .Y = SCREENHEIGHT - 65
                    End If
                    'draw asteroid on radar
                    DrawCircle .X, .Y, 10, RGB(140, 140, 140)
                End If
```

```
                    Else
                        .Rebirth = .Rebirth + 1
                        If .Rebirth > ROCKREBIRTH Then
                            .Active = True
                        End If
                    End If
                End With
        Next lAst


        'draw wormholes on radar
        With wormholes(0)
            DrawCircle .X, .Y, 10, RGB(0, 0, 210)
        End With
        With wormholes(1)
            DrawCircle .X, .Y, 10, RGB(0, 0, 210)
        End With


        'draw players on radar
        For lPlay = 0 To MAXPLAYERS
            With Players(lPlay)
                If .X > -1 Then
                    DrawCircle .X, .Y, 10, RGB(255, 255, 255)
                End If
            End With
        Next lPlay


        'draw shots on radar
        For n = 0 To MAXSHOTS
            With shots(n)
                If .Active Then
                    If .X < 3 Or .X > SCREENWIDTH + 8 Or _
                        .Y < 3 Or .Y > SCREENHEIGHT + 8 Then
                        .Active = False
                    Else
                        DrawCircle .X, .Y, 10, RGB(255, 0, 0)
                    End If
                End If
            End With
        Next n
```

```
        lblSector.Caption = "Update_Stuff: " & GetTickCount - lTime
End Sub

Private Sub DrawCircle(ByVal X As Long, ByVal Y As Long, _
    ByVal Radius As Long, ByVal Color As Long)
    picRadar.FillColor = Color
    picRadar.FillStyle = 0
    picRadar.Circle (X, Y), Radius, Color
End Sub
```

The Update_Clients procedure is where all the socket messaging takes place, and is how the clients are updated with the positions of the objects in the game. Update_Clients calls numerous support routines, including SendPlayers, SendBullets, SendBooms, SendAsteroids, and SendScores. These routines all use Broadcast or SendTo to send packets of data to the players in the game.

```
Private Sub Update_Clients()
    Dim lSocket As Long
    Dim total As Long
    Dim count As Long
    Dim lTime As Long
    Dim n As Long

    lTime = GetTickCount
    total = serverLink.UserCount
    'process all sockets
    For lSocket = 0 To MAXPLAYERS - 1
        'make sure this socket is live
        If serverLink.Connected(lSocket) Then
            SendPlayers lSocket
            SendBullets lSocket
            SendBooms lSocket
            SendAsteroids lSocket
            'break if all players have been updated
            count = count + 1
            If count > total Then Exit For
        End If
    Next lSocket
    ResetPlayers
    ResetBooms
    lblUpdate.Caption = "Update_Clients: " & GetTickCount - lTime
End Sub
```

```
Private Sub SendAsteroids(ByVal lSocket As Long)
    Dim n As Long
    For n = 0 To MAXROCKS
        With asteroids(n)
            If .Active Then
                SendTo lSocket, PREFIX & ROCK_HDR & _
                    SEP & n & SEP & .X & SEP & .Y
            End If
        End With
    Next n
End Sub

Private Sub SendBooms(ByVal lSocket As Long)
    Dim n As Long
    For n = 0 To MAXBOOMS
        With booms(n)
            If .Active Then
                SendTo lSocket, PREFIX & BOOM_HDR & _
                    SEP & .X & SEP & .Y
            End If
        End With
    Next n
End Sub

Private Sub SendBullets(ByVal lSocket As Long)
    Dim n As Long
    For n = 0 To MAXSHOTS
        With shots(n)
            If .Active And .Owner <> n Then
                SendTo lSocket, PREFIX & SHOT_HDR & _
                    SEP & .X & SEP & .Y
            End If
        End With
    Next n
End Sub

Private Sub SendPlayers(ByVal lSocket As Long)
    Dim n As Long
    For n = 0 To MAXPLAYERS
```

```
            If n <> lSocket Then
                With Players(n)
                    If .Active Then
                        SendTo lSocket, PREFIX & SHIP_HDR & _
                            SEP & n & SEP & .X & SEP & .Y & _
                            SEP & .Dir & SEP & .Nickname
                    End If
                End With
            End If
        Next n
End Sub
```

There are two `ServerSocket` events in the Stellar Server program. The first, `ServerConnectionRequest`, handles any new players that attempt to join the game. The first thing that this event does is check to make sure there is an empty slot for the player, since there are a limited number of players allowed on the server. This number defaults to eight, but can be changed to any number up to eight in the settings.txt file.

As it was written, the practical limit for the server was eight players. The string-parsing packet code is just too slow to handle any more players without causing the game to have some serious lag. If you have access to the ASCI White supercomputer and happen to have a Visual Basic run-time library for the uber-machine, feel free to increase the player support. Actually, I jest: Stellar Server is not a multithreaded program, so not even ASCI White (which is powered by a few thousand desktop processors) would help it support more players.

The second `ServerSocket` event is called `DataArrival`. It handles all incoming message packets. Each of the four support routines handles a specific type of packet that comes in, including `KillPlayer`, `KillAsteroid`, `ProcessScore`, `ProcessShot`, `ProcessWormhole`, and `ProcessShip`. When a packet is received and passed to a support routine, the packet is ripped apart by the string parsers and the variables are retrieved out of the packet. As the support routines indicate, there are score, projectile, wormhole, and ship position packets received by the server. (Note that wormhole was called *black hole* in the game client.)

```
Private Sub serverLink_ServerConnectionRequest( _
    ByVal requestID As Long)
    Dim lCount As Long

    lCount = serverLink.OpenConnection(requestID, _
        serverinfo.Port)
```

```
        If lCount > -1 Then
            'send greeting
            SendTo lCount, PREFIX & CHAT_HDR & SEP & _
                "Welcome to Stellar War Server, Version 1.0," & _
                "December 1, 2001."

            'make sure there is room
            If serverLink.UserCount > serverinfo.Players Then
                'send "server full" message
                SendTo lCount, PREFIX & CHAT_HDR & SEP & _
                    "Server is full. Please try again later."
                serverLink.CloseConnection lCount
            Else
                PrintOut "Accepted new player " & lCount & " at " & _
                    serverLink.RemoteHostIP & " on port " & _
                    serverLink.RemotePort

            End If
        End If
End Sub

Private Sub serverLink_DataArrival(ByVal link As Long, _
    ByVal bytesTotal As Long, ByVal sIncoming As String)

    Dim msgHeader As String
    Dim msgBody As String
    Dim Value As Long
    Dim n As Long
    Dim sWork As String
    Dim lNumPackets As Long

    'grab all packets out of this transmission
    Do While Len(sIncoming) > 3 And _
        TokenCount(sIncoming, PREFIX) > 0

        'grab current packet data
        sWork = ParseToken(sIncoming, 2, PREFIX)
        sIncoming = Mid$(sIncoming, Len(PREFIX) + Len(sWork) + 1)

        'break out the header and body of the packet
        msgHeader = ParseToken(sWork, 1, SEP)
        msgBody = Mid$(sWork, InStr(1, sWork, SEP) + 1)
```

```
        Select Case msgHeader
            Case HITA_HDR
                KillAsteroid link, msgBody
            Case HITP_HDR
                KillPlayer link, msgBody
            Case SCOR_HDR
                ProcessScore link, msgBody
            Case SHOT_HDR
                ProcessShot link, msgBody
            Case HOLE_HDR
                ProcessWormhole link, msgBody
            Case SHIP_HDR
                ProcessShip link, msgBody
            Case CHAT_HDR
                PrintOut msgBody
                Broadcast PREFIX & CHAT_HDR & SEP & msgBody
            Case PING_HDR
                Value = CLng(msgBody)
                SendTo link, PREFIX & PING_HDR & SEP & Value
            Case Else
                PrintOut "Unknown Message: " & sIncoming
        End Select
        lNumPackets = lNumPackets + 1
    Loop
    lblPackets.Caption = "PACKET CACHE: " & lNumPackets
End Sub

Private Sub KillPlayer(ByVal link As Long, ByVal msgBody As String)
    Dim lPlayer As Long

    On Error GoTo error1
    If TokenCount(msgBody, SEP) <> 1 Then Exit Sub

    'store the data
    lPlayer = ParseToken(msgBody, 1, SEP)

    'validate the data
    If Not IsNumeric(lPlayer) Then Exit Sub

    'disable the player
    Players(lPlayer).Active = False
    SendTo lPlayer, PREFIX & DIED_HDR
```

```
        Exit Sub
error1:
End Sub

Private Sub KillAsteroid(ByVal link As Long, ByVal msgBody As String)
    Dim lAst As Long

    On Error GoTo error1
    If TokenCount(msgBody, SEP) <> 1 Then Exit Sub

    'store the data
    lAst = ParseToken(msgBody, 1, SEP)

    'validate the data
    If Not IsNumeric(lAst) Then Exit Sub

    'reset the asteroid
    With asteroids(lAst)
        .Active = False
        .X = Random(SCREENWIDTH - 64)
        .Y = Random(SCREENHEIGHT - 64)
        .SpeedX = Random(4) - 2
        .SpeedY = Random(4) - 2
        .MoveCount = 0
        .MoveRate = 1
        .Rebirth = 0
    End With
    Exit Sub
error1:
End Sub

Private Sub ProcessScore(ByVal link As Long, ByVal msgBody As String)
    Dim Score As Long

    On Error GoTo error1
    If TokenCount(msgBody, SEP) <> 1 Then Exit Sub

    'store the data
    Score = ParseToken(msgBody, 1, SEP)
```

```
        'validate the data
        If Not IsNumeric(Score) Then Exit Sub

        'update the high score
        If Score > serverinfo.HighScore Then
            serverinfo.HighScore = Score
            serverinfo.TopScorer = Players(link).Nickname
            PrintOut "New high score: " & serverinfo.TopScorer & _
                " = " & serverinfo.HighScore
        End If

    Exit Sub
error1:
End Sub

Private Sub ProcessShot(ByVal link As Long, ByVal msgBody As String)
    Dim X As Long
    Dim Y As Long

    On Error GoTo error1
    If TokenCount(msgBody, SEP) <> 2 Then Exit Sub

    'store the data
    X = ParseToken(msgBody, 1, SEP)
    Y = ParseToken(msgBody, 2, SEP)

    'validate the data
    If Not IsNumeric(X) Then Exit Sub
    If Not IsNumeric(Y) Then Exit Sub

    'update shot array
    With shots(link)
        .Active = True
        .Owner = link
        .X = X
        .Y = Y
    End With

    Exit Sub
error1:
End Sub
```

```vb
Private Sub ProcessWormhole(ByVal link As Long, ByVal msgBody As String)
    'send wormhole1 position
    With wormholes(0)
        SendTo link, PREFIX & HOLE_HDR & SEP & "0" & _
            SEP & .X & SEP & .Y
    End With
    'send wormhole2 position
    With wormholes(1)
        SendTo link, PREFIX & HOLE_HDR & SEP & "1" & _
            SEP & .X & SEP & .Y
    End With

End Sub

Private Sub ProcessShip(ByVal link As Long, ByVal msgBody As String)
    Dim X As Long
    Dim Y As Long
    Dim Dir As Long
    Dim Nick As String

    On Error GoTo error1
    If TokenCount(msgBody, SEP) <> 4 Then Exit Sub

    'store the data
    X = ParseToken(msgBody, 1, SEP)
    Y = ParseToken(msgBody, 2, SEP)
    Dir = ParseToken(msgBody, 3, SEP)
    Nick = ParseToken(msgBody, 4, SEP)

    'validate the data
    If Not IsNumeric(X) Then Exit Sub
    If Not IsNumeric(Y) Then Exit Sub
    If Not IsNumeric(Dir) Then Exit Sub

    'update player data
    With Players(link)
        .Active = True
        .X = X
        .Y = Y
        .Dir = Dir
```

```
            .Nickname = Nick
        End With

        Exit Sub
error1:
End Sub
```

There are two timers in the Stellar Server program. The first timer, Timer1, is fired every 20 milliseconds. This is the rate at which the server sends packets to the clients. I arrived at this rate through trial and error—you might want to tweak the rate depending on the performance of your PC. Timer1 calls Update_Clients to fire off all the packets of data needed to update each player on the position of everything in the game.

The second timer, Timer2, is fired twice as often as Timer1. So, if Timer1's interval is 20 milliseconds, then Timer2 will fire every 10 milliseconds. This ensures that the game objects are all updated at least once before the next synchronization with the clients.

```
Private Sub Timer1_Timer()
    Static lAst As Long

    'update all players
    Update_Clients

    'check status of server socket
    If serverLink.State <> lAst Then
        Select Case serverLink.State
            Case sckClosed:
                lblStatus = "Socket closed"
            Case sckOpen:
                lblStatus = "Socket open"
            Case sckListening:
                lblStatus = "Listening..."
            Case sckConnectionPending:
                lblStatus = "Connection pending"
            Case sckResolvingHost:
                lblStatus = "Resolving host..."
            Case sckHostResolved:
                lblStatus = "Host resolved"
            Case sckConnecting:
                lblStatus = "Connecting..."
```

```
              Case sckConnected:
                  lblStatus = "Connected"
              Case sckClosing:
                  lblStatus = "Socket closed"
                  PrintOut "Closed connection for player " & _
                      serverLink.CurrentLink & _
                      " at " & serverLink.RemoteHostIP & _
                        " on port " & serverLink.RemotePort
              Case sckError:
                  lblStatus = "Error"
          End Select
          lAst = serverLink.State
      End If
End Sub

Private Sub Timer2_Timer()
    'move all server-based game objects
    Update_Stuff
End Sub
```

The two string-parsing routines are listed next. `TokenCount` counts the number of tokens in a string, based on a delimiter character. `ParseToken` actually separates a packet into individual variables, again with the use of a delimiter. The delimiter character is called SEP; it is a constant that was listed at the top of the program. Note that if you change the delimiter character on the server, you must change it as well on the client, and vice versa.

The miscellaneous support routines used by the server are included in the last section of source code that follows, and include the following procedures: `ResetBooms`, `cmdBroadcast_Click`, `Random`, `SetPixel`, `Delay`, `Form_Unload`, `Shutdown`, `PrintOut`, and `PrintChar`. These routines are simple and should not need any explanation at this point.

> **NOTE**
>
> Copy the `TokenCount` and `ParseToken` functions from the **Stellar War** client program and paste the functions to the end of the source code listing for **Stellar Server**. No sense in typing them in all over again.

```
Private Sub ResetBooms()
    Dim n As Long
    For n = 0 To MAXBOOMS
        With booms(n)
            .Active = False
            .Owner = -1
```

```
            .X = -1
            .Y = -1
        End With
    Next n
End Sub

Private Sub cmdBroadcast_Click()
    Broadcast PREFIX & CHAT_HDR & SEP & _
        "ServerOp: " & txtBroadcast.Text
    txtBroadcast.Text = ""
End Sub

Public Function Random(ByVal lNum As Long) As Long
    Random = CLng(lNum * Rnd)
End Function

Public Sub Delay(ByVal ms As Long)
    Dim lStart As Long
    lStart = GetTickCount
    Do Until GetTickCount > lStart + ms
        DoEvents
    Loop
End Sub

Private Sub Form_Unload(Cancel As Integer)
    Shutdown
End Sub

Private Sub Shutdown()
    serverLink.CloseServer
    End
End Sub

Public Sub PrintOut(ByVal msg$)
    txtOutput.Text = Now() & "> " & msg$ & vbCrLf & _
        txtOutput.Text
End Sub

Public Sub PrintChar(ByVal char$)
    txtOutput.Text = txtOutput.Text & char$
End Sub
```

The Stellar Bot Program

The Stellar Bot program (shown in Figure 21.22) was developed in order to test the messaging system for Stellar War. It eventually evolved into a bot program, which is a miniature version of the game with rudimentary ship control. It is controlled by the computer on which you run the program.

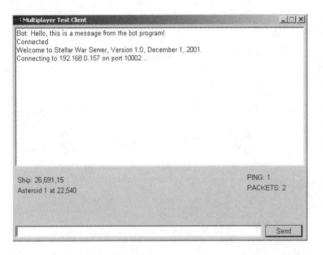

Figure 21.22

The Stellar Bot program shows incoming messages and moves a ship randomly, but it is primarily a skeleton program.

The Stellar Bot client is similar to the game client in that it uses the settings.txt file to find the server IP address and port in order to make the connection. The bot is not intelligent at all and it doesn't do much, but it is a skeleton program for building your own computer-controlled players for the game. I personally find it more enjoyable to just watch the bots cruise around the screen, rather than playing the game.

Bot programming is a great exercise in coding problem-solving routines into a program that runs without human intervention, and would be a great application for the classes developed in Chapter 15, "Artificial and Simulated Intelligence." I suspect that programming bots for Stellar War might eventually be the sole reason for running the game. Computer science teachers might use Stellar War as a means to teach client/server programming, or they might abstract all the communication and socket code into a separate module, and just have students write bot programs.

By providing simple events like ShotFired, EnemyInSight, and ShipPosition (for instance), younger programmers could write bots to compete with each other. Bot programmers could then watch the battles take place on separate terminals. This implementation differs from existing "robot war" games in which the server interprets bot programs on-the-fly, without any client/server aspect. I think there would be significant incentive to write intelligent bot programs if players could run their bots from anywhere on the Internet, as long as a server was running (presumably on the teacher's PC).

The Project Explorer

The Project Explorer for the Stellar Bot program is shown in Figure 21.23, and it lists the files needed to compile the bot program.

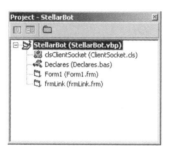

Figure 21.23

The Project Explorer for Stellar Bot shows the files needed to compile the program.

The Stellar Bot Project

The Stellar Bot program is a Standard EXE project with a single form. The form has a few controls that you will need to add at design time, so I will show you how to set up the controls. Take a peek at Figure 21.24 to see the Stellar Bot project loaded into the Visual Basic IDE.

Figure 21.24

The Stellar Bot project, as it appears in the Visual Basic IDE

Building the User Interface

The source code for Stellar Bot assumes that various controls are present on the form, as shown in Figure 21.25. The bot program really doesn't need a user interface at all. I included some status information for testing purposes, and then decided to leave it all alone for the final program. If you decide to improve the program (to make the bots more intelligent, for instance), then you might want to add your own labels to the form, or even a mini-radar display like the one on the server form. It would be very cool to see your own bot displayed on the game screen in a different color.

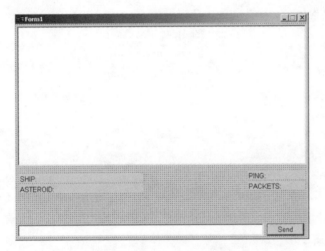

Figure 21.25

The user interface for Stellar Bot at design time

To build the user interface for Stellar Bot, simply refer to Table 21.3 for a list of controls. You will want to resize the form to match the positioning of the controls. By default, I set the form dimensions to 580 × 410. Add the controls to Form1 with the appropriate caption or text in the proper position, and with the designated dimensions. You can refer to Figure 21.25 for reference.

Project References

The References dialog box for Stellar Bot, shown in Figure 21.26, does not need to include any DirectX type libraries.

Stellar Bot Source Code

The Stellar Bot source code is similar to the Stellar War game client code, only shorter. Therefore, I'm not going to spend as much time explaining the code that follows. Everything in the Stellar Bot program should have already been explained earlier in the chapter. After all, this

Table 21.3 Stellar Bot Control List

Control Name	Type	Caption/Text	Position	Dimensions
txtOutput	TextBox	""	4,4	575,265
lblShip	Label	SHIP:	8,288	245,16
lblAsteroid	Label	ASTEROID:	8,308	245,16
lblPing	Label	PING:	464,284	110,16
lblPackets	Label	PACKETS:	464,304	110,16
txtChat	TextBox	""	4,384	490,23
cmdSend	CommandButton	Send	500,384	72,23

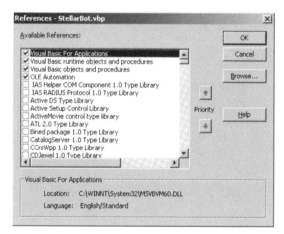

Figure 21.26

The Stellar Bot References dialog box

is a bot program that makes use of code that was already developed. Currently, the only thing that Stellar Bot does is move the ship in a random direction.

New support for firing weapons and tracking other players would be added by examining packets, using the routines in the game client. As mentioned earlier, I would recommend abstracting the bot programming model and storing all the "grunt code" elsewhere. Like the game library classes that abstract various components of DirectX, the bot class might intercept socket communications and just raise events to the bot program with the details, thus abstracting the programmer from the messy parts of the program. But until then, here is the "grunt code" for Stellar Bot.

```
'--------------------------------------------------------------------
' Visual Basic Game Programming With DirectX
' Chapter 21: Stellar War: Multiplayer Space Combat Game
' Stellar Bot Source Code File
'--------------------------------------------------------------------
Option Explicit
Option Base 0

'program constants
Const SCREENWIDTH As Long = 1024
Const SCREENHEIGHT As Long = 768
Const MAXSHOTS As Long = 10
Const MAXROCKS As Long = 10

'socket messaging constants
Const SEP As String = "ÿ" 'ASCII 255
Const PREFIX As String = "___"  'ASCII 254
Const PING_HDR = "111"
Const CHAT_HDR = "112"
Const SHIP_HDR = "113"
Const ROCK_HDR = "115"
Const DIED_HDR = "121"

Private Type GAME_OBJECT
    Server As String
    Port As Long
    Active As Boolean
    Nickname As String
    X As Long
    Y As Long
    SpeedX As Long
    SpeedY As Long
    Width As Long
    Height As Long
    Dir As Long
    MoveCount As Long
    MoveRate As Long
End Type

'program controls
Dim WithEvents clientPing As Timer
Dim WithEvents socketStatus As Timer
```

```
'DirectDraw surfaces and sprites
Dim player As GAME_OBJECT

'ClientSocket class with events
Dim WithEvents clientLink As clsClientSocket

'socket variables
Dim lPingCount As Long
Dim lPingStart As Long

'program variables
Dim bRunning As Boolean
Dim rTemp As RECT

Private Sub Form_Load()
    Static lStartTime As Long
    Static lCounter As Long
    Static lNewTime As Long
    Dim lNum As Long
    Dim bRet As Boolean

    Randomize
    LoadSettings
    InitForm
    InitSocket
    InitShip
    bRunning = True
    clientPing.Enabled = True
    lStartTime = GetTickCount

    'main game loop
    Do While bRunning
        lCounter = GetTickCount() - lStartTime
        If lCounter > lNewTime Then
            Game_Update lCounter
            Network_Update
            lNewTime = lCounter + 20
        End If
        DoEvents
    Loop
End Sub
```

```vb
Private Sub LoadSettings()
    Dim filenum As Long
    Dim sInput As String
    Dim sTemp As String

    On Error GoTo error1
    filenum = FreeFile
    Open App.Path & "\settings.txt" For Input As #filenum

    Do Until EOF(filenum)
        Line Input #filenum, sInput
        If Len(sInput) > 0 Then
            If Left$(sInput, 1) <> ";" Then
                If UCase$(Left$(sInput, 7)) = "PLAYER=" Then
                    sTemp = ParseToken(sInput, 2, "=")
                    If Len(sTemp) > 0 Then
                        player.Nickname = sTemp
                        If Len(player.Nickname) > 40 Then
                            player.Nickname = "Newb"
                        End If
                    Else
                        player.Nickname = "Newb"
                    End If
                ElseIf UCase$(Left$(sInput, 7)) = "SERVER=" Then
                    sTemp = ParseToken(sInput, 2, "=")
                    If Len(sTemp) > 0 Then
                        player.Server = sTemp
                    Else
                        player.Server = "localhost"
                    End If
                ElseIf UCase$(Left$(sInput, 5)) = "PORT=" Then
                    sTemp = ParseToken(sInput, 2, "=")
                    If IsNumeric(sTemp) Then
                        player.Port = CLng(sTemp)
                        If player.Port < 1024 Or _
                            player.Port > 60000 Then
                            player.Port = 10002
                        End If
                    Else
                        player.Port = 10002
                    End If
                End If
```

```
                End If
            End If
        End If
    Loop

    Close #filenum
    Exit Sub
error1:
    MsgBox "The settings.txt file is invalid!"
    Shutdown
End Sub

Private Sub InitShip()
    'initialize the ship
    With player
        .Active = True
        .X = Random(SCREENWIDTH - 33)
        .Y = Random(SCREENHEIGHT - 33)
        .Dir = Random(16)
        .MoveCount = 0
        .MoveRate = 0 'Random(1) + 1

        'set X,Y speed based on direction
        Select Case .Dir
            Case 0
                .SpeedX = 0
                .SpeedY = -2
            Case 1
                .SpeedX = 1
                .SpeedY = -2
            Case 2
                .SpeedX = 2
                .SpeedY = -2
            Case 3
                .SpeedX = 2
                .SpeedY = -1
            Case 4
                .SpeedX = 2
                .SpeedY = 0
            Case 5
                .SpeedX = 2
                .SpeedY = 1
```

```
            Case 6
                .SpeedX = 2
                .SpeedY = 2
            Case 7
                .SpeedX = 1
                .SpeedY = 2
            Case 8
                .SpeedX = 0
                .SpeedY = 2
            Case 9
                .SpeedX = -1
                .SpeedY = 2
            Case 10
                .SpeedX = -2
                .SpeedY = 2
            Case 11
                .SpeedX = -2
                .SpeedY = 1
            Case 12
                .SpeedX = -2
                .SpeedY = 0
            Case 13
                .SpeedX = -2
                .SpeedY = -1
            Case 14
                .SpeedX = -2
                .SpeedY = -2
            Case 15
                .SpeedX = -1
                .SpeedY = -2
        End Select
    End With

End Sub

Private Sub InitForm()
    'set up the main form
    Form1.Caption = "Multiplayer Test Client"
    Form1.Show
```

```
    'add timers
    Set clientPing = Controls.Add("VB.Timer", "clientPing")
    clientPing.Enabled = False
    clientPing.Interval = 5000

    Set socketStatus = Controls.Add("VB.Timer", "socketStatus")
    socketStatus.Enabled = False
    socketStatus.Interval = 250

End Sub

Private Sub InitSocket()
    Set clientLink = New clsClientSocket
    clientLink.RemotePort = player.Port
    socketStatus.Enabled = True
    ConnectServer player.Server
End Sub

Public Sub Game_Update(ByVal ms As Long)
    With player
        .MoveCount = .MoveCount + 1
        If .MoveCount > .MoveRate Then
            .MoveCount = 0

            .X = .X + .SpeedX
            If .X < 1 Then
                .X = SCREENWIDTH - 33
            ElseIf .X > SCREENWIDTH - 33 Then
                .X = 0
            End If

            .Y = .Y + .SpeedY
            If .Y < 1 Then
                .Y = SCREENHEIGHT - 33
            ElseIf .Y > SCREENHEIGHT - 33 Then
                .Y = 0
            End If
        End If
    End With
End Sub
```

```vb
Private Sub Network_Update()
    If clientLink.State <> sckConnected Then Exit Sub

    With player
        lblShip.Caption = "Ship: " & .X & "," & .Y & "," & .Dir
        clientLink.Send PREFIX & SHIP_HDR & SEP & _
            .X & SEP & .Y & SEP & _
            .Dir & SEP & .Nickname
    End With
End Sub

Private Sub socketStatus_Timer()
    Static last As Long
    Dim sStatus As String
    If clientLink.State <> last Then
        Select Case clientLink.State
            Case sckClosed
                sStatus = "Socket closed"
            Case sckOpen
                sStatus = "Socket open"
            Case sckListening
                sStatus = "Listening..."
            Case sckConnectionPending
                sStatus = "Connection pending"
            Case sckResolvingHost
                sStatus = "Resolving host..."
            Case sckHostResolved
                sStatus = "Host resolved"
            Case sckConnecting
                sStatus = "Connecting..."
            Case sckConnected
                sStatus = "Connected"
            Case sckClosing
                sStatus = "Closing..."
            Case sckError
                sStatus = "Error"
        End Select
        last = clientLink.State
        PrintOut sStatus
    End If
End Sub
```

```
Private Sub ConnectServer(ByVal IP As String)
    If Len(IP) = 0 Then Exit Sub
    PrintOut "Connecting to " & IP & " on port " & _
        player.Port & "..."
    clientLink.RemoteHost = IP
    clientLink.Connect
End Sub

Private Sub clientPing_Timer()
    lPingStart = GetTickCount()
    clientLink.Send PREFIX & PING_HDR & SEP & lPingStart
End Sub

Private Sub clientLink_DataArrival(ByVal lTotalBytes As Long, _
    ByVal sIncoming As String)

    Dim sWork As String
    Dim lPingEnd As Long
    Dim lPingVal As Long
    Dim msgHeader As String
    Dim msgBody As String
    Dim lTotal As Long
    Dim lTime As Long

    lTime = GetTickCount
    'grab all packets out of this transmission
    Do While Len(sIncoming) > 3 And _
        TokenCount(sIncoming, PREFIX) > 0

        sWork = ParseToken(sIncoming, 2, PREFIX)
        'sIncoming = ReplaceToken(sIncoming, sWork, "")
        sIncoming = Mid$(sIncoming, Len(PREFIX) + Len(sWork) + 1)

        'parse the msg out of the string so data is left
        msgHeader = ParseToken(sWork, 1, SEP)
        msgBody = Mid$(sWork, InStr(1, sWork, SEP) + 1)

        Select Case msgHeader
            Case DIED_HDR
                Shutdown
```

```vb
            Case ROCK_HDR
                ProcessAsteroid msgBody
            Case CHAT_HDR
                PrintOut msgBody
            Case PING_HDR
                lPingEnd = CLng(msgBody)
                lPingVal = GetTickCount() - lPingEnd + 1
                lblPing.Caption = "PING: " & lPingVal
        End Select
        lTotal = lTotal + 1
    Loop

    If lTotal > 1 Then lblPackets.Caption = "PACKETS: " & lTotal

    Debug.Print "DataArrival: " & GetTickCount - lTime
End Sub

Private Sub ProcessAsteroid(ByVal msgBody As String)
    Dim X As Long
    Dim Y As Long
    Dim num As Long
    Dim frame As Long

    If TokenCount(msgBody, SEP) <> 3 Then Exit Sub

    num = ParseToken(msgBody, 1, SEP)
    X = ParseToken(msgBody, 2, SEP)
    Y = ParseToken(msgBody, 3, SEP)

    'validate the values
    If Not IsNumeric(num) Then num = 0
    If Not IsNumeric(X) Then X = 0
    If Not IsNumeric(Y) Then Y = 0

    lblAsteroid.Caption = "Asteroid " & num & " at " & X & "," & Y

End Sub

Public Sub PrintOut(ByVal msg$)
    txtOutput.Text = msg$ & vbCrLf & txtOutput.Text
End Sub
```

```
Public Sub PrintChar(ByVal char$)
    txtOutput.Text = txtOutput.Text & char$
End Sub

Private Sub cmdSend_Click()
    clientLink.Send PREFIX & CHAT_HDR & SEP & player.Nickname & _
        ": " & txtChat.Text
    txtChat.Text = ""
End Sub

Private Sub Form_KeyDown(KeyCode As Integer, Shift As Integer)
    If KeyCode = 27 Then Shutdown
End Sub

Private Sub Form_QueryUnload(Cancel As Integer, _
    UnloadMode As Integer)
    Shutdown
End Sub

Private Sub Shutdown()
    bRunning = False
    clientLink.CloseConnection
    clientPing.Enabled = False
    socketStatus.Enabled = False
    End
End Sub

Public Function Random(ByVal lNum As Long) As Long
    Random = CLng(lNum * Rnd)
End Function
```

Now paste the TokenCount and ParseToken functions to the end of the source code listing, just like you did with the Stellar Server program. You can copy the functions from either the Stellar War Client or Stellar Server source code, because they are identical in all three programs.

ENHANCING THE GAME

There are so many neat things you can do with a space combat game, and a multiplayer one at that. I have only scratched the surface of what is possible with Stellar War. If you are a sci-fi fan, I encourage you to modify Stellar War and make it the game you think it should have been. Add all kinds of cool special effects, awesome new weapons, bonus points, and powerups, and turn it into the game you envision.

Stellar War is not actually a complete game; it is just a prototype—a basic space combat game. As you have seen, just the prototype for a multiplayer game can be quite lengthy. That is the primary reason why I chose not to include sound or joystick support. Those features are absolutely essential—I won't argue against it. The client, server, and bot programs for Stellar War are primarily meant to teach client/server game programming, and I believe that any more complexity would have tried your patience. I leave those additional features up to you.

I believe the networking code and the graphics code are easy enough to understand, so I'll leave the task up to you to make Stellar War into a truly great game. First and foremost, add support for playing sound effects using the clsDirectSound8 and clsDSWave8 classes, and add sound to game events like weapons firing and explosions. The game could also benefit from a title screen where players can chat before jumping into the game. It currently jumps right into the action and terminates completely when you hit ESC.

Here are some recommendations for improving the game:

- Add collision detection between ships and asteroids.
- Add joystick support using clsDIJoystick8.
- Add some new asteroids to give the game more variety.
- Add sound effects using clsDirectSound8 and clsDSWave8.
- Add a music soundtrack using clsDirectMusic8 and clsDMSequence8.
- Apply the gravity code to the asteroids so they are attracted to the black holes.
- Program commands into the chat parser so players can change game variables.
- Add collision detection so that the black holes are dangerous.
- Add some new starships and allow players to select a ship before joining the server.
- Write an automatic packet timing routine to optimize the packet send/receive rate.
- Convert the string-based packet format to an efficient byte-based structure.
- Create a standard bot programming interface with custom game events.
- Add a neural interface so players can control the ship with thought waves.

SUMMARY

Alas, that's the end of another great game. Stellar War is an ambitious multiplayer game that helps to demonstrate client/server programming techniques. Since the server is a separate program, you will need to run it before you are able to play the game. This chapter covered client/server game programming in excruciating detail, while developing a dedicated server and game client around the setting of a multiplayer space combat game. Stellar War aptly demonstrates the subject, and goes a step further to propose a bot programming language for competition and learning purposes.

CHAPTER 22

PONG 3D: MODERN ARCADE GAME

W elcome to the 3-D realm of gaming! The game that I will show you how to write in this chapter is called Pong 3D, and is a 3-D implementation of the classic Atari game called *Pong* (although this is a single-player game with just one paddle). Pong 3D includes some source code features that you might find useful in your own game projects, such as the ability to run in a window or full-screen without a hitch. These features will also enable you to run the game in any resolution supported by the host computer's video card. Even at 1600 × 1200, the game runs at a fairly decent frame rate. There is a feature (set within the source code) that runs the game in "extreme mode," in which the viewpoint follows the ball instead of the paddle!

This chapter covers the following topics:

- Playing Pong 3D
- Building the Pong 3D Game
- Enhancing the Game

PLAYING PONG 3D

Pong 3D features a player-controlled paddle positioned at the bottom of the screen (and actually sitting on top of a 3-D surface that acts as the floor in the game), and a ball that bounces off the walls and the paddle. The goal of the game is like that of many arcade games—to steal as many of your quarters as possible! Actually, Pong 3D was designed to simulate an arcade game, with simple flashing messages at the top (like "INSERT QUARTER"), and was influenced by pinball machines as well. As an arcade game, it has a certain appeal and novelty that makes the game more enjoyable. The sound effects also help to give it a certain arcade game feel that is hard to achieve in a PC game. The only thing missing is a two-player mode, where players take turns. I decided that it would be much easier to just keep track of a single player and high score, and let other players jump in when the current player loses three balls. Figure 22.1 shows Pong 3D running at 640 × 480, with debug mode enabled.

At the top of the game screen is the current score, the high score, and the number of balls remaining. This is all that is displayed in a normal build of the game. But if you enable the debug mode setting, you will see the debug messages, as shown at the bottom of Figure 22.1. The bottom-left of the screen shows the current position of the ball and paddle. The bottom-right shows the frame rate and draw rate in milliseconds.

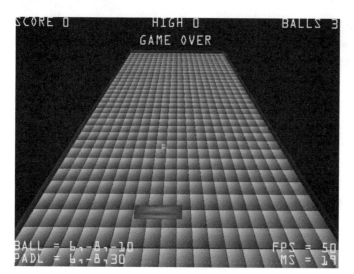

Figure 22.1

The Pong 3D game demonstrates how to write a complete 3-D game with Visual Basic and Direct3D 8.0.

Controlling the game is easy. The left and right arrow keys move the paddle, while the spacebar starts the game (or launches the ball after a miss). The up and down arrow keys adjust the game surface from a head-on perspective, all the way up to birds-eye view over the top. It is actually quite fun to play the game with the head-on viewpoint.

Demo Mode

When the game first starts, it will be in the default demo mode, in which the game plays on its own in typical arcade game style. During demo mode, sound effects and scoring are disabled. At the top of the screen (which is shown in Figure 22.2), a message is displayed, alternating between "INSERT QUARTER" and "GAME OVER." Basically, the paddle just tracks the ball's X position, and it does occasionally miss the ball. Figure 22.2 shows the frame rate at 1280 × 1024. The textures look nice at high resolutions, but the game is simple enough to run at any resolution.

Launch Mode

Launch mode is active either when the game starts and you press the spacebar to start a new game, or when you miss the ball. Figure 22.3 shows the game in launch mode, running at a resolution of 800 × 600. Note that the frame rate at this resolution is nearly 50 fps. The frame rate is limited by a constant called FRAMERATE, which was set to 60 in the program. Setting FRAMERATE to a higher value will result in faster gameplay, but the game becomes difficult to play at a certain point. During launch mode, the ball tracks along with the paddle until you press the spacebar.

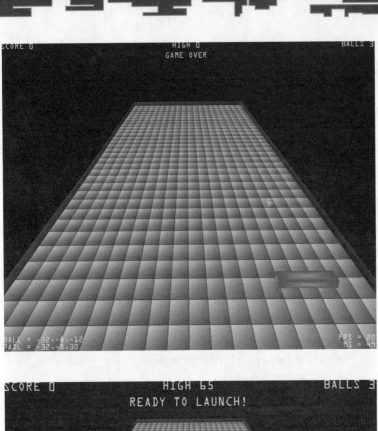

Figure 22.2

Pong 3D in demo mode.

Figure 22.3

During launch mode, the game waits for you to release the ball for the next round of play.

Normal Mode

Figure 22.4 shows the game running in normal mode (without debug messages) with the player controlling the paddle. As long as the ball isn't missed, the game will continue to run normally. There are no additional levels to the game, and the difficulty remains the same for as long as you continue to play.

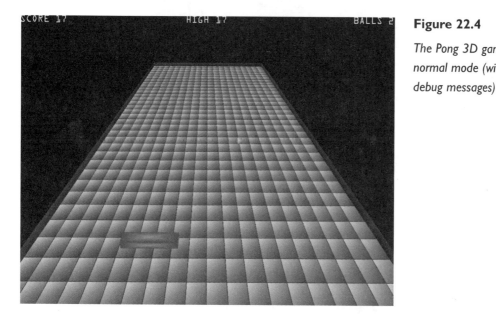

Figure 22.4

The Pong 3D game in normal mode (without debug messages)

When you run out of balls, the game is over, and you are returned to demo mode. For every hundred points you are awarded an extra ball, which comes in handy after a couple of misses.

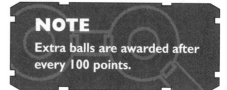

NOTE

Extra balls are awarded after every 100 points.

Extreme Mode

One interesting change you can make to the game is extreme mode (which is a source code setting, not to be confused with the three gameplay modes). Extreme mode is shown in Figure 22.5, running at a resolution of 1280 × 1024.

When you set the EXTREMEMODE constant to True (at the top of the game's source code), the game runs in a sort of first-person perspective, in which the camera follows the ball and looks back at the paddle. While in extreme mode, the paddle works in reverse, so it is not too confusing. (Otherwise, the left arrow would cause the paddle to seem to move right, and vice versa.)

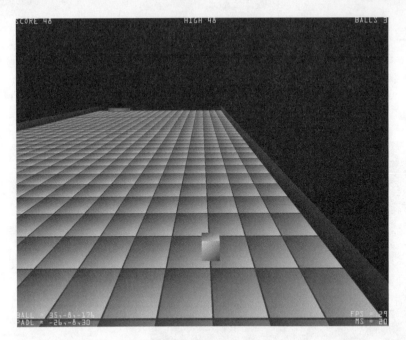

Figure 22.5

The Pong 3D game running in extreme mode, in which the camera follows the ball

Figure 22.6 shows a shot where the ball is close to the paddle. Note that with EXTREMEMODE set to True, the game will still function normally, including the demo. So you can simply sit back and watch extreme mode in action as the game plays by itself.

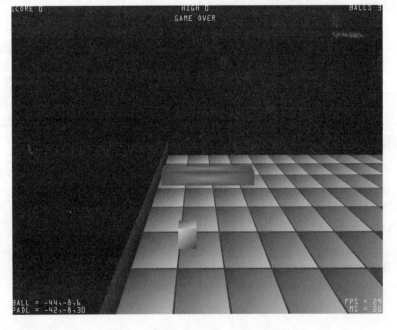

Figure 22.6

In extreme mode, it is sometimes difficult to judge the direction of the ball.

Tilting the Game Surface

Another cool feature of Pong 3D is the ability to tilt the surface of the game board up or down. This changes the perspective from a head-on view to a top-down view, with some interesting gameplay results. Figure 22.7 shows the game running in demo mode with the game surface tilted head-on. Notice how the bottom of the game board rises above the debug messages at the bottom of the screen. In my opinion, this type of gameplay is actually easier than the top-down view.

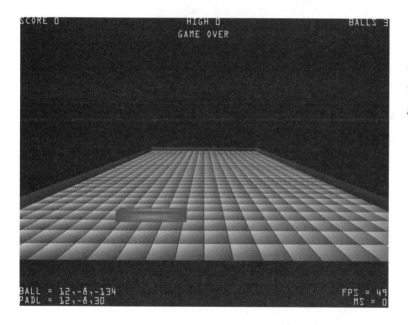

Figure 22.7

Tilting the game board to a head-on perspective adds variety to the game.

Likewise, Figure 22.8 shows the game tilted all the way up to a top-down view.

Performance

Figure 22.9 shows that performance is not really an issue because the game doesn't need a lot of graphics horsepower.

In all, this game renders a grand total of 20 textured polygons! Impressive, don't you think? I thought that was pretty funny, myself. After all, some games utilize 20 or so polygons just to represent a clock on the wall of an otherwise jampacked level. Hey, you have to start somewhere;

NOTE

It is fascinating how Direct3D scales objects in the game to the same size at every resolution without programmer intervention.

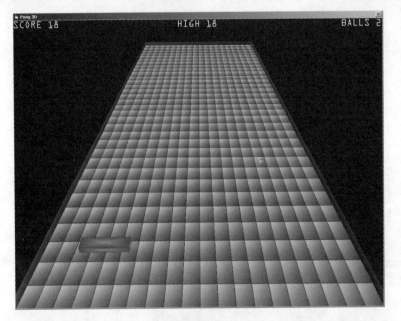

Figure 22.8

Tilting the game board to a top-down perspective gives it more of a 2-D appearance.

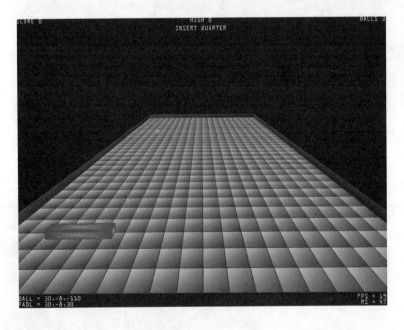

Figure 22.9

Even at 1600 × 1200, Pong 3D runs at a fair frame rate. Notice how small the bitmapped font looks.

that is what I always say when I'm getting into something new. If this is your first 3-D game, then I'm sure you will welcome the simplicity of it.

The important thing to remember when perusing the source code for Pong 3D (or while typing it in) is that you are writing a textured 3-D game. That is the key! From that point forward, the complexity and depth of a game is entirely up to you. If you play the game in extreme mode it's obvious that you could make all kinds of games with even this rudimentary 3-D engine, such as a cart-racing game. Just make the game surface much larger or link several surfaces together along with the walls to create a racetrack. Of course, anything more advanced would require a better 3-D object handler, because you can't generate the objects in a game that is much more involved than Pong 3D without difficulty. Loading X files or a custom file format would be a necessity.

Sound Effects

Pong 3D uses a lot of different sound effects to spruce up the game, and they are actually a significant part of the gameplay. There are several versions of each sound event, such as the ball hitting a wall or the paddle, and the player gaining an extra ball or missing the ball. There are even two different sounds for launching the ball at the start of the game.

The sound effects in Pong 3D feature positional 3-D audio effects that greatly enhance the game. For instance, when the ball hits the left or right wall, the rebound sounds are actually played as if coming from the left or right. In addition, when the ball hits the far edge of the game surface, the sound seems to be off in the distance. Several of the sounds pan left to right, and vice versa. This gives the game variety and makes it more fun to play.

BUILDING THE PONG 3D GAME

The Pong 3D project will be a Standard EXE project with a reference to the DirectX 8 for Visual Basic Type Library. Alternatively, you can link to the Visual Basic Game Library with all of the classes included in the pre-compiled vbgl.dll file. During development of a completely new game, I prefer to include the class files directly in the game project. How you prefer to write games is completely up to you. If you want the flexibility of having all the source code at your fingertips, then include the necessary files in your game projects. Figure 22.10 shows the Pong 3D project loaded into the Visual Basic IDE.

However, if you would prefer the simplicity of linking to the VBGL reference instead, then feel free to use that method. The resulting game will be the same with either method. The only thing to consider (which might be thought of as a downside to using the library), is that you must distribute the vbgl.dll file with the game. That is absolutely not a problem. Some large programs are best divided up into modules, and DLLs are a great way to go. In the case of the game library, I urge you to use whatever method works best for you.

Figure 22.10

Presenting the Pong 3D project in its entirety.

The Pong 3D game project needs all of the following files:

- D3DRectangle8.cls
- D3DSprite8.cls
- DIKeyboard8.cls
- Direct3D8.cls
- DirectInput8.cls
- DirectSound8.cls
- DSWave8.cls
- Declares.bas
- Form1.frm

Bitmapped Font Engine

Pong 3D uses a standard bitmap font, which is shown in Figure 22.11. I created this bitmap using the Text tool in Paint Shop Pro. This is actually the same font used for Stellar War back in Chapter 21, "Stellar War: Multiplayer Space Combat Game."

There are two important factors to consider when creating a bitmap font. First, you must use a consistent character size, which is easier if you use a monotype font. The font I chose for this game is called "OCR A Extended," which is a character recognition font used by programs that convert scanned text into an editable document. I just liked the way this font looked. If you

Figure 22.11

The bitmap font used in Pong 3D

would like to use a proportionally spaced font, you will need to carefully lay out each character in the image so that each one is the same size.

The second thing to consider is that you should turn off any anti-alias feature when creating a bitmap font, because anti-aliasing routines add fuzzy pixels (which are lighter in tone) to remove the jagged edges. The problem is that this looks terrible when blitted transparently over a background in a game. Most often, the jagged edges are not an issue because the font will look much smaller in the game, so anti-aliasing is not needed. The font I created is 16×24 pixels for each character.

Pong 3D Source Code Listing

Now for the source code listing. Everything in this game was pieced together from code that I wrote earlier in the book, so there is absolutely nothing new here. Most of the code involves setting up the scene. There is a tremendous amount of code required just to create the 3-D objects in the game because they are generated on-the-fly rather than loaded from disk. I did not want to get into the details of 3-D file formats and loading data from disk because that subject can get complicated in a hurry. Rather, this game just does it all in code. That's how most things have been done up to this point, so I figured this game might as well be consistent with earlier programs in the book.

```
'-----------------------------------------------------------------
' Visual Basic Game Programming With DirectX
' Chapter 22 : Pong 3D
' Pong3D Source Code File
'-----------------------------------------------------------------

Option Explicit
Option Base 0

'misc constants
Const DEBUGMODE As Boolean = False
Const EXTREMEMODE As Boolean = False
```

```
Const SCREENWIDTH As Long = 1024
Const SCREENHEIGHT As Long = 768
Const FULLSCREEN As Boolean = True
Const FRAMERATE As Long = 60
Const C_BLACK As Long = &H0
Const PI As Single = 3.141592654

'game board constants
Const FLOORWIDTH As Long = 50
Const FLOORDEPTH As Long = 200
Const FLOORTILES As Long = 32
Const FLOORY As Long = -10
Const WALLHEIGHT As Long = 3

'ball constants
Const BALLSPEED As Long = 3

'paddle constants
Const PADDLEWIDTH As Long = 8
Const PADDLEHEIGHT As Long = 1
Const PADDLEDEPTH As Long = 2

'game state values
Private Enum GAME_MODES
    DEMO = 1
    LAUNCH = 2
    RUNNING = 3
End Enum

'define a standard timer
Dim WithEvents timer1 As Timer

'define the DirectX objects
Dim d3d As New clsDirect3D8
Dim dinput As New clsDirectInput8
Dim WithEvents Keyboard As clsDIKeyboard8
Dim dsound As New clsDirectSound8
Dim dswStart(1) As clsDSWave8
Dim dswLaunch(0 To 2) As clsDSWave8
Dim dswMissed(0 To 1) As clsDSWave8
```

```
    Dim dswExtraLife(0 To 1) As clsDSWave8
    Dim dswDanger(0 To 1) As clsDSWave8
    Dim dswWall(0 To 2) As clsDSWave8

    'define the Direct3D game objects
    Dim paddle(0 To 5) As clsD3DRectangle8
    Dim ball(0 To 5) As clsD3DRectangle8
    Dim wall1 As clsD3DRectangle8
    Dim wall2 As clsD3DRectangle8
    Dim wall3 As clsD3DRectangle8
    Dim floor As clsD3DRectangle8
    Dim font1 As New clsD3DSprite8

    'define matrixes and vectors
    Dim matProj As D3DMATRIX
    Dim matView As D3DMATRIX
    Dim matWorld As D3DMATRIX
    Dim matTranslate As D3DMATRIX
    Dim vCameraSource As D3DVECTOR
    Dim vCameraTarget As D3DVECTOR
    Dim vBallPos As D3DVECTOR
    Dim vBallDir As D3DVECTOR
    Dim vBallSpd As D3DVECTOR
    Dim vPaddlePos As D3DVECTOR

    'program variables
    Dim gamestatus As GAME_MODES
    Dim sStatusMsg As String
    Dim bRunning As Boolean
    Dim lFrameRate As Long
    Dim sFrameRate As String
    Dim sDrawRate As String
    Dim lScore As Long
    Dim lHighScore As Long
    Dim lBallsLeft As Long

    Private Sub Form_Load()
        Static lStartTime As Long
        Static lCounter As Long
        Static lNewTime As Long
```

```
'set up the main form
Form1.Caption = "Pong 3D"
Form1.AutoRedraw = False
Form1.BorderStyle = 1
Form1.ClipControls = False
Form1.KeyPreview = True
Form1.ScaleMode = 3
If Not FULLSCREEN Then
    Form1.Width = Screen.TwipsPerPixelX * (SCREENWIDTH + 12)
    Form1.Height = Screen.TwipsPerPixelY * (SCREENHEIGHT + 30)
End If
Form1.Show

'initialize the timer
Set timer1 = Controls.Add("VB.TIMER", "timer1")
timer1.Interval = 500
timer1.Enabled = False

'initialize DirectSound
InitDirectSound

'initialize DirectInput
dinput.Startup Form1.hWnd
Set Keyboard = New clsDIKeyboard8
Keyboard.Startup dinput, Form1.hWnd

'initialize Direct3D
If Not d3d.Startup(Form1.hWnd, SCREENWIDTH, SCREENHEIGHT, _
    FULLSCREEN) Then
    MsgBox "Error initializing Direct3D"
    Shutdown
End If

'set up the 3D scene
If Not SetupScene() Then
    MsgBox "Error setting up the 3D scene"
    Shutdown
End If

'initialize the font
font1.Create d3d
font1.LoadFromFile App.Path & "\ocrfont.bmp", 16, 24, 20, 100
```

```
    'set some starting values
    Randomize GetTickCount
    bRunning = True
    lFrameRate = FRAMERATE
    lBallsLeft = 3
    gamestatus = DEMO
    timer1.Enabled = True

    'initialize ball direction and speed
    ResetBall

    'play opening sound
    dswStart(0).SetPosition 0, 0, -5
    dswStart(0).PlaySound

    'start main game loop
    Do While bRunning
        lCounter = GetTickCount() - lStartTime
        If lCounter > lNewTime Then
            RenderScene lCounter
            Keyboard.Check_Keyboard
            lNewTime = lCounter + 1000 / lFrameRate
        End If
        DoEvents
    Loop
End Sub

Private Sub Form_Unload(Cancel As Integer)
    Shutdown
End Sub

Private Sub InitDirectSound()
    dsound.Startup Form1.hWnd

    Set dswStart(0) = New clsDSWave8
    'remember to set positional mode before loading!
    SetPosition dswStart(0)
    dswStart(0).LoadSound dsound, App.Path & "\start1.wav"

    Set dswLaunch(0) = New clsDSWave8
    SetPosition dswLaunch(0)
    dswLaunch(0).LoadSound dsound, App.Path & "\launch1.wav"
```

```
        Set dswLaunch(1) = New clsDSWave8
        SetPosition dswLaunch(1)
        dswLaunch(1).LoadSound dsound, App.Path & "\launch2.wav"


        Set dswMissed(0) = New clsDSWave8
        SetPosition dswMissed(0)
        dswMissed(0).LoadSound dsound, App.Path & "\missed1.wav"


        Set dswMissed(1) = New clsDSWave8
        SetPosition dswMissed(1)
        dswMissed(1).LoadSound dsound, App.Path & "\missed2.wav"


        Set dswExtraLife(0) = New clsDSWave8
        SetPosition dswExtraLife(0)
        dswExtraLife(0).LoadSound dsound, App.Path & "\extralife1.wav"


        Set dswExtraLife(1) = New clsDSWave8
        SetPosition dswExtraLife(1)
        dswExtraLife(1).LoadSound dsound, App.Path & "\extralife2.wav"


        Set dswDanger(0) = New clsDSWave8
        SetPosition dswDanger(0)
        dswDanger(0).LoadSound dsound, App.Path & "\danger1.wav"


        Set dswDanger(1) = New clsDSWave8
        SetPosition dswDanger(1)
        dswDanger(1).LoadSound dsound, App.Path & "\danger2.wav"


        Set dswWall(0) = New clsDSWave8
        SetPosition dswWall(0)
        dswWall(0).LoadSound dsound, App.Path & "\wall1.wav"


        Set dswWall(1) = New clsDSWave8
        SetPosition dswWall(1)
        dswWall(1).LoadSound dsound, App.Path & "\wall2.wav"


        Set dswWall(2) = New clsDSWave8
        SetPosition dswWall(2)
        dswWall(2).LoadSound dsound, App.Path & "\wall3.wav"
End Sub
```

```
Private Sub SetPosition(ByRef sound As clsDSWave8)
    sound.Interrupt = True
    sound.Positional = True
    sound.SetPosition Random(8) - 4, -1, Random(8) - 5
End Sub
```

The SetupScene function requires a little explanation, because it is responsible for creating the
3-D game environment. First, the camera's source and target vectors are set, and the view matrix
is created, followed by the projection matrix. These are pretty standard things that must be done
at the beginning of a Direct3D program, and this was all explained back in Chapter 14, "DirectX
Graphics and Direct3D." At the end of this function are four calls to procedures that create the
floor, wall, ball, and paddle objects.

```
Private Function SetupScene() As Boolean
    vCameraSource.X = 0
    vCameraSource.z = 101
    If EXTREMEMODE Then
        vCameraSource.Y = 80
    Else
        vCameraSource.Y = 50
    End If

    vCameraTarget.X = 0
    vCameraTarget.Y = 0
    vCameraTarget.z = 0

    vPaddlePos.X = 0
    vPaddlePos.Y = -8
    vPaddlePos.z = 30

    'set up the camera view matrix
    D3DXMatrixLookAtLH matView, vCameraSource, vCameraTarget, _
        CreateVector(0, 1, 0)

    'use the camera view for the viewport
    d3d.Device.SetTransform D3DTS_VIEW, matView

    'set up the projection matrix (for perspective)
    D3DXMatrixPerspectiveFovLH matProj, PI / 4, 0.7, 1, 1000
```

```
      'tell device to use the projection matrix
      d3d.Device.SetTransform D3DTS_PROJECTION, matProj

      'create 3D objects
      CreateFloor
      CreateWalls
      CreateBall
      CreatePaddle

      SetupScene = True
End Function

Private Sub CreateFloor()
      Set floor = New clsD3DRectangle8
      floor.SetVertex 0, FLOORWIDTH, FLOORY, 50, -20, FLOORTILES
      floor.SetVertex 1, FLOORWIDTH, FLOORY, -FLOORDEPTH, -20, 0
      floor.SetVertex 2, -FLOORWIDTH, FLOORY, -FLOORDEPTH, 0, 0
      floor.SetVertex 3, FLOORWIDTH, FLOORY, 50, -20, FLOORTILES
      floor.SetVertex 4, -FLOORWIDTH, FLOORY, -FLOORDEPTH, 0, 0
      floor.SetVertex 5, -FLOORWIDTH, FLOORY, 50, 0, FLOORTILES
      floor.Create d3d
      floor.LoadTexture App.Path & "\floor2.bmp"
End Sub

Public Sub CreateWalls()
      'create the left wall
      Set wall1 = New clsD3DRectangle8
      wall1.SetTexturePos 0, 0, 1
      wall1.SetTexturePos 1, 0, 0
      wall1.SetTexturePos 2, 1, 0
      wall1.SetTexturePos 3, 0, 1
      wall1.SetTexturePos 4, 1, 0
      wall1.SetTexturePos 5, 1, 1

      wall1.SetPosition 0, FLOORWIDTH, FLOORY, 50
      wall1.SetPosition 1, FLOORWIDTH, FLOORY + WALLHEIGHT, 50
      wall1.SetPosition 2, FLOORWIDTH, FLOORY + WALLHEIGHT, _
          -FLOORDEPTH
      wall1.SetPosition 3, FLOORWIDTH, FLOORY, 50
      wall1.SetPosition 4, FLOORWIDTH, FLOORY + WALLHEIGHT, _
          -FLOORDEPTH
      wall1.SetPosition 5, FLOORWIDTH, FLOORY, -FLOORDEPTH
```

```
        wall1.Create d3d
        wall1.LoadTexture App.Path & "\wall.bmp"

        'create the back wall
        Set wall2 = New clsD3DRectangle8
        wall2.SetTexturePos 0, 0, 1
        wall2.SetTexturePos 1, 0, 0
        wall2.SetTexturePos 2, 1, 0
        wall2.SetTexturePos 3, 0, 1
        wall2.SetTexturePos 4, 1, 0
        wall2.SetTexturePos 5, 1, 1
        wall2.SetPosition 0, FLOORWIDTH, FLOORY, -FLOORDEPTH
        wall2.SetPosition 1, FLOORWIDTH, FLOORY + WALLHEIGHT, _
            -FLOORDEPTH
        wall2.SetPosition 2, -FLOORWIDTH, FLOORY + WALLHEIGHT, _
            -FLOORDEPTH
        wall2.SetPosition 3, FLOORWIDTH, FLOORY, -FLOORDEPTH
        wall2.SetPosition 4, -FLOORWIDTH, FLOORY + WALLHEIGHT, _
            -FLOORDEPTH
        wall2.SetPosition 5, -FLOORWIDTH, FLOORY, -FLOORDEPTH
        wall2.Create d3d
        wall2.LoadTexture App.Path & "\wall.bmp"

        'create the right wall
        Set wall3 = New clsD3DRectangle8
        wall3.SetTexturePos 0, 0, 1
        wall3.SetTexturePos 1, 0, 0
        wall3.SetTexturePos 2, 1, 0
        wall3.SetTexturePos 3, 0, 1
        wall3.SetTexturePos 4, 1, 0
        wall3.SetTexturePos 5, 1, 1
        wall3.SetPosition 0, -FLOORWIDTH, FLOORY, -FLOORDEPTH
        wall3.SetPosition 1, -FLOORWIDTH, FLOORY + WALLHEIGHT, _
            -FLOORDEPTH
        wall3.SetPosition 2, -FLOORWIDTH, FLOORY + WALLHEIGHT, 50
        wall3.SetPosition 3, -FLOORWIDTH, FLOORY, -FLOORDEPTH
        wall3.SetPosition 4, -FLOORWIDTH, FLOORY + WALLHEIGHT, 50
        wall3.SetPosition 5, -FLOORWIDTH, FLOORY, 50
        wall3.Create d3d
        wall3.LoadTexture App.Path & "\wall.bmp"
End Sub
```

```
Public Sub CreateBall()
    'create the six sides of the cube
    Set ball(0) = New clsD3DRectangle8
    ball(0).SetDefaultVertices
    ball(0).SetPosition 0, 1, -1, 1        'bottom left
    ball(0).SetPosition 1, 1, 1, 1         'top left
    ball(0).SetPosition 2, -1, 1, 1        'top right
    ball(0).SetPosition 3, 1, -1, 1        'bottom left
    ball(0).SetPosition 4, -1, 1, 1        'top right
    ball(0).SetPosition 5, -1, -1, 1       'bottom right
    ball(0).Create d3d
    ball(0).LoadTexture App.Path & "\cube2.bmp"

    Set ball(1) = New clsD3DRectangle8
    ball(1).SetDefaultVertices
    ball(1).SetPosition 0, -1, -1, 1
    ball(1).SetPosition 1, -1, 1, 1
    ball(1).SetPosition 2, -1, 1, -1
    ball(1).SetPosition 3, -1, -1, 1
    ball(1).SetPosition 4, -1, 1, -1
    ball(1).SetPosition 5, -1, -1, -1
    ball(1).Create d3d
    ball(1).LoadTexture App.Path & "\cube2.bmp"

    Set ball(2) = New clsD3DRectangle8
    ball(2).SetDefaultVertices
    ball(2).SetPosition 0, -1, -1, -1
    ball(2).SetPosition 1, -1, 1, -1
    ball(2).SetPosition 2, 1, 1, -1
    ball(2).SetPosition 3, -1, -1, -1
    ball(2).SetPosition 4, 1, 1, -1
    ball(2).SetPosition 5, 1, -1, -1
    ball(2).Create d3d
    ball(2).LoadTexture App.Path & "\cube2.bmp"

    Set ball(3) = New clsD3DRectangle8
    ball(3).SetDefaultVertices
    ball(3).SetPosition 0, 1, -1, -1
    ball(3).SetPosition 1, 1, 1, -1
    ball(3).SetPosition 2, 1, 1, 1
    ball(3).SetPosition 3, 1, -1, -1
```

```
        ball(3).SetPosition 4, 1, 1, 1
        ball(3).SetPosition 5, 1, -1, 1
        ball(3).Create d3d
        ball(3).LoadTexture App.Path & "\cube2.bmp"

        Set ball(4) = New clsD3DRectangle8
        ball(4).SetDefaultVertices
        ball(4).SetPosition 0, 1, 1, 1
        ball(4).SetPosition 1, 1, 1, -1
        ball(4).SetPosition 2, -1, 1, -1
        ball(4).SetPosition 3, 1, 1, 1
        ball(4).SetPosition 4, -1, 1, -1
        ball(4).SetPosition 5, -1, 1, 1
        ball(4).Create d3d
        ball(4).LoadTexture App.Path & "\cube2.bmp"

        Set ball(5) = New clsD3DRectangle8
        ball(5).SetDefaultVertices
        ball(5).SetPosition 0, -1, -1, 1
        ball(5).SetPosition 1, -1, -1, -1
        ball(5).SetPosition 2, 1, -1, -1
        ball(5).SetPosition 3, -1, -1, 1
        ball(5).SetPosition 4, 1, -1, -1
        ball(5).SetPosition 5, 1, -1, 1
        ball(5).Create d3d
        ball(5).LoadTexture App.Path & "\cube2.bmp"
End Sub

Public Sub CreatePaddle()
    'create the six sides of the cube
    Set paddle(0) = New clsD3DRectangle8
    paddle(0).SetDefaultVertices
    paddle(0).SetPosition 0, PADDLEWIDTH, -PADDLEHEIGHT, PADDLEDEPTH
    paddle(0).SetPosition 1, PADDLEWIDTH, PADDLEHEIGHT, PADDLEDEPTH
    paddle(0).SetPosition 2, -PADDLEWIDTH, PADDLEHEIGHT, PADDLEDEPTH
    paddle(0).SetPosition 3, PADDLEWIDTH, -PADDLEHEIGHT, PADDLEDEPTH
    paddle(0).SetPosition 4, -PADDLEWIDTH, PADDLEHEIGHT, PADDLEDEPTH
    paddle(0).SetPosition 5, -PADDLEWIDTH, -PADDLEHEIGHT, PADDLEDEPTH
    paddle(0).Create d3d
    paddle(0).LoadTexture App.Path & "\sunburstred.bmp"
```

```
Set paddle(1) = New clsD3DRectangle8
paddle(1).SetDefaultVertices
paddle(1).SetPosition 0, -PADDLEWIDTH, -PADDLEHEIGHT, PADDLEDEPTH
paddle(1).SetPosition 1, -PADDLEWIDTH, PADDLEHEIGHT, PADDLEDEPTH
paddle(1).SetPosition 2, -PADDLEWIDTH, PADDLEHEIGHT, -PADDLEDEPTH
paddle(1).SetPosition 3, -PADDLEWIDTH, -PADDLEHEIGHT, PADDLEDEPTH
paddle(1).SetPosition 4, -PADDLEWIDTH, PADDLEHEIGHT, -PADDLEDEPTH
paddle(1).SetPosition 5, -PADDLEWIDTH, -PADDLEHEIGHT, -PADDLEDEPTH
paddle(1).Create d3d
paddle(1).LoadTexture App.Path & "\sunburstred.bmp"

Set paddle(2) = New clsD3DRectangle8
paddle(2).SetDefaultVertices
paddle(2).SetPosition 0, -PADDLEWIDTH, -PADDLEHEIGHT, -PADDLEDEPTH
paddle(2).SetPosition 1, -PADDLEWIDTH, PADDLEHEIGHT, -PADDLEDEPTH
paddle(2).SetPosition 2, PADDLEWIDTH, PADDLEHEIGHT, -PADDLEDEPTH
paddle(2).SetPosition 3, -PADDLEWIDTH, -PADDLEHEIGHT, -PADDLEDEPTH
paddle(2).SetPosition 4, PADDLEWIDTH, PADDLEHEIGHT, -PADDLEDEPTH
paddle(2).SetPosition 5, PADDLEWIDTH, -PADDLEHEIGHT, -PADDLEDEPTH
paddle(2).Create d3d
paddle(2).LoadTexture App.Path & "\sunburstred.bmp"

Set paddle(3) = New clsD3DRectangle8
paddle(3).SetDefaultVertices
paddle(3).SetPosition 0, PADDLEWIDTH, -PADDLEHEIGHT, -PADDLEDEPTH
paddle(3).SetPosition 1, PADDLEWIDTH, PADDLEHEIGHT, -PADDLEDEPTH
paddle(3).SetPosition 2, PADDLEWIDTH, PADDLEHEIGHT, PADDLEDEPTH
paddle(3).SetPosition 3, PADDLEWIDTH, -PADDLEHEIGHT, -PADDLEDEPTH
paddle(3).SetPosition 4, PADDLEWIDTH, PADDLEHEIGHT, PADDLEDEPTH
paddle(3).SetPosition 5, PADDLEWIDTH, -PADDLEHEIGHT, PADDLEDEPTH
paddle(3).Create d3d
paddle(3).LoadTexture App.Path & "\sunburstred.bmp"

Set paddle(4) = New clsD3DRectangle8
paddle(4).SetDefaultVertices
paddle(4).SetPosition 0, PADDLEWIDTH, PADDLEHEIGHT, PADDLEDEPTH
paddle(4).SetPosition 1, PADDLEWIDTH, PADDLEHEIGHT, -PADDLEDEPTH
paddle(4).SetPosition 2, -PADDLEWIDTH, PADDLEHEIGHT, -PADDLEDEPTH
paddle(4).SetPosition 3, PADDLEWIDTH, PADDLEHEIGHT, PADDLEDEPTH
paddle(4).SetPosition 4, -PADDLEWIDTH, PADDLEHEIGHT, -PADDLEDEPTH
paddle(4).SetPosition 5, -PADDLEWIDTH, PADDLEHEIGHT, PADDLEDEPTH
```

```
        paddle(4).Create d3d
        paddle(4).LoadTexture App.Path & "\sunburstred.bmp"

        Set paddle(5) = New clsD3DRectangle8
        paddle(5).SetDefaultVertices
        paddle(5).SetPosition 0, -PADDLEWIDTH, -PADDLEHEIGHT, PADDLEDEPTH
        paddle(5).SetPosition 1, -PADDLEWIDTH, -PADDLEHEIGHT, -PADDLEDEPTH
        paddle(5).SetPosition 2, PADDLEWIDTH, -PADDLEHEIGHT, -PADDLEDEPTH
        paddle(5).SetPosition 3, -PADDLEWIDTH, -PADDLEHEIGHT, PADDLEDEPTH
        paddle(5).SetPosition 4, PADDLEWIDTH, -PADDLEHEIGHT, -PADDLEDEPTH
        paddle(5).SetPosition 5, PADDLEWIDTH, -PADDLEHEIGHT, PADDLEDEPTH
        paddle(5).Create d3d
        paddle(5).LoadTexture App.Path & "\sunburstred.bmp"
End Sub
```

Now that all the messy setup routines have been covered, the rest of the program listing is more interesting. First, the Keyboard_KeyDown procedure is actually an event passed back from the DirectInput keyboard handler. This event just sends the main program a key value for each key-press. There is no corresponding key release event. (For more information, refer to Chapter 12, "Getting a Handle on User Input.") This procedure handles key-presses differently, depending on which mode the game is in. During demo mode, the arrow keys are disabled so the player can't mess up the computer-controlled paddle. The other keys, such as the spacebar, ESC, and the up/down keys for changing the viewpoint, are available during demo mode.

```
Private Sub Keyboard_KeyDown(ByVal lKey As Long)
    Static lLastTime As Long

    If gamestatus = DEMO Then
        'move paddle in demo mode
        If lKey = 203 Then
            If vPaddlePos.X < FLOORWIDTH - PADDLEWIDTH Then
                vPaddlePos.X = vPaddlePos.X + 2
            End If
            Exit Sub
        ElseIf lKey = 205 Then
            If vPaddlePos.X > -(FLOORWIDTH - PADDLEWIDTH) Then
                vPaddlePos.X = vPaddlePos.X - 2
            End If
            Exit Sub
        End If
    End If
```

```
'handle regular user input
Select Case lKey
    Case 1 'escape
        Shutdown


    Case 57 'spacebar
        'pause one sec to display messages
        If GetTickCount > lLastTime + 1000 Then
            If gamestatus = DEMO Then
                gamestatus = LAUNCH
            ElseIf gamestatus = LAUNCH Then
                dswLaunch(Random(2)).PlaySound
                gamestatus = RUNNING
            End If
            lLastTime = GetTickCount
        End If


    Case 203 'left arrow
        If EXTREMEMODE Then
            If vPaddlePos.X > -(FLOORWIDTH - PADDLEWIDTH) Then
                vPaddlePos.X = vPaddlePos.X - 2
            End If
        Else
            If vPaddlePos.X < FLOORWIDTH - PADDLEWIDTH Then
                vPaddlePos.X = vPaddlePos.X + 2
            End If
        End If


    Case 205 'right arrow
        If EXTREMEMODE Then
            If vPaddlePos.X < FLOORWIDTH - PADDLEWIDTH Then
                vPaddlePos.X = vPaddlePos.X + 2
            End If
        Else
            If vPaddlePos.X > -(FLOORWIDTH - PADDLEWIDTH) Then
                vPaddlePos.X = vPaddlePos.X - 2
            End If
        End If
```

```
        Case 200 'up arrow
            If Not EXTREMEMODE Then
                If vCameraSource.Y < 65 Then
                    vCameraSource.Y = vCameraSource.Y + 5
                End If
                D3DXMatrixLookAtLH matView, vCameraSource, _
                    vCameraTarget, CreateVector(0, 1, 0)
                d3d.Device.SetTransform D3DTS_VIEW, matView
            End If

        Case 208 'down arrow
            If Not EXTREMEMODE Then
                If vCameraSource.Y > 10 Then
                    vCameraSource.Y = vCameraSource.Y - 5
                End If
                D3DXMatrixLookAtLH matView, vCameraSource, _
                    vCameraTarget, CreateVector(0, 1, 0)
                d3d.Device.SetTransform D3DTS_VIEW, matView
            End If
    End Select
End Sub
```

I decided to use a timer in this game because timers are extremely handy for repetitive functionality that clogs up the main logic routines. In this case, the timer is responsible for updating the status message at the top of the screen (just below the high score). It works great, so I recommend that you use timers any time you need to update status messages in a game. This is as close as you can get to multi-threading in VB.

```
Private Sub timer1_Timer()
    Static bSwitch As Boolean

    'change status message
    bSwitch = Not bSwitch
    If bSwitch Then
        Select Case gamestatus
            Case DEMO
                sStatusMsg = "INSERT QUARTER"
            Case LAUNCH
                sStatusMsg = "READY TO LAUNCH!"
            Case RUNNING
                sStatusMsg = ""
        End Select
```

```
        Else
            Select Case gamestatus
                Case DEMO
                    sStatusMsg = "GAME OVER"
                Case LAUNCH
                    sStatusMsg = "PRESS SPACEBAR"
                Case RUNNING
                    sStatusMsg = ""
            End Select
        End If
End Sub
```

The RenderScene procedure is called by the main loop in Form_Load to render each scene (or frame) of the game. This procedure calls UpdateBall, UpdatePaddle, and UpdateStats to move the ball and paddle, and to display text on the screen (respectively). Collision detection in the UpdateBall procedure simply involves a call to the IntersectRect function, which has been used extensively in the book. This is a great little helper function that would have been a pain to write from scratch if it were not available in the Windows API.

```
Public Sub RenderScene(ByVal MS As Long)
    Static lTimer As Long
    Static lStart As Long
    Static lCounter As Long
    Dim n As Long

    'start counting milliseconds
    lStart = GetTickCount

    d3d.Clear C_BLACK

    'start rendering
    d3d.BeginScene

    'draw the tiled floor and walls
    floor.Draw
    wall1.Draw
    wall2.Draw
    wall3.Draw

    'update the ball
    UpdateBall
    SetIdentity
```

```
        'update the paddle
        UpdatePaddle
        SetIdentity

        'display the game stats
        UpdateStats

        'stop rendering
        d3d.EndScene

        'draw the back buffer to the screen
        d3d.Present

        'count the frames per second
        If MS > lTimer | 1000 Then
            lStart = GetTickCount - lStart
            sFrameRate = "FPS = " & lCounter
            sDrawRate = "MS = " & lStart
            lTimer = MS
            lCounter = 0
        Else
            lCounter = lCounter + 1
        End If
End Sub

Private Sub UpdateBall()
    Dim r1 As RECT_API
    Dim r2 As RECT_API
    Dim r3 As RECT_API
    Dim n As Long

    If gamestatus = LAUNCH Then
        vBallPos.X = vPaddlePos.X
        vBallPos.z = vPaddlePos.z - 5
        vBallDir.z = -1
    Else
        'check for collision with left or right wall
        vBallPos.X = vBallPos.X + vBallSpd.X * vBallDir.X
        If vBallPos.X < -(FLOORWIDTH - 2) Then
```

```
            If gamestatus = RUNNING Then
                n = Random(3)
                dswWall(n).SetPosition 1, 0, 0
                dswWall(n).PlaySound
            End If
            vBallDir.X = 1
            AddScore 1
    ElseIf vBallPos.X > FLOORWIDTH - 2 Then
            If gamestatus = RUNNING Then
                n = Random(3)
                dswWall(n).SetPosition -1, 0, 0
                dswWall(Random(n)).PlaySound
            End If
            vBallDir.X = -1
            AddScore 1
    End If


    'check for collision with top or bottom wall
    vBallPos.z = vBallPos.z + vBallSpd.z * vBallDir.z
    If vBallPos.z < -FLOORDEPTH Then
            If gamestatus = RUNNING Then
                n = Random(3)
                dswWall(n).SetPosition 0, 0, 0
                dswWall(Random(n)).PlaySound
            End If
            vBallDir.z = 1
            AddScore 2
    ElseIf vBallPos.z > FLOORWIDTH - 2 Then
            MissedBall
    End If


    'check for collision with the paddle
    r1.Left = vBallPos.X - 1
    r1.Right = vBallPos.X + 1
    r1.Top = vBallPos.z - 1
    r1.Bottom = vBallPos.z + 1
    r2.Left = vPaddlePos.X - PADDLEWIDTH
    r2.Right = vPaddlePos.X + PADDLEWIDTH
    r2.Top = vPaddlePos.z - 2
    r2.Bottom = vPaddlePos.z + 2
    If IntersectRect(r3, r2, r1) Then
```

```
            If gamestatus = RUNNING Then
                dswWall(Random(2)).PlaySound
            End If
            vBallDir.z = -1
            vBallSpd.z = BALLSPEED + Random(3)
            If vBallPos.X < vPaddlePos.X Then
                vBallDir.X = -1
                vBallSpd.X = Random(1) + 1
            Else
                vBallDir.X = 1
                vBallSpd.X = Random(1) + 1
            End If
        End If
    End If

    'transform the ball within the scene
    D3DXMatrixTranslation matTranslate, vBallPos.X, _
        vBallPos.Y, vBallPos.z
    d3d.Device.SetTransform D3DTS_WORLD, matTranslate

    'draw the ball
    For n = 0 To 5
        ball(n).Draw
    Next n

    'in extreme mode, the camera follows the ball
    If EXTREMEMODE Then
        vCameraTarget.X = vBallPos.X
        vCameraTarget.z = vBallPos.z
        vCameraSource.X = vBallPos.X
        vCameraSource.Y = vBallPos.Y + 15
        vCameraSource.z = vBallPos.z - 30
        D3DXMatrixLookAtLH matView, vCameraSource, vCameraTarget, _
            CreateVector(0, 1, 0)
        d3d.Device.SetTransform D3DTS_VIEW, matView
    End If
End Sub

Private Sub UpdatePaddle()
    Dim matPaddle As D3DMATRIX
    Dim n As Long
```

```
        'in demo mode, move the paddle
        If gamestatus = DEMO Then
            If vBallPos.X < vPaddlePos.X Then
                'remember game board is -50 to +50
                Keyboard_KeyDown 205
            ElseIf vBallPos.X > vPaddlePos.X Then
                'seems reversed, but it is not
                Keyboard_KeyDown 203
            End If
        End If

        'transform the paddle within the scene
        D3DXMatrixTranslation matPaddle, vPaddlePos.X, _
            vPaddlePos.Y, vPaddlePos.z
        d3d.Device.SetTransform D3DTS_WORLD, matPaddle

        'draw the paddle
        For n = 0 To 5
            paddle(n).Draw
        Next n
    End Sub

    Private Sub UpdateStats()
        Static lLastTime As Long
        Static bSwitch As Boolean
        Dim temp As String

        'display the current score
        DrawText 1, 1, "SCORE " & lScore

        'display the high score
        temp = "HIGH " & lHighScore
        DrawText SCREENWIDTH / 2 - Len(temp) * font1.Width / 2, 1, temp

        'display the balls left
        temp = "BALLS " & lBallsLeft
        DrawText SCREENWIDTH - Len(temp) * font1.Width, 1, temp

        'display the status message
        DrawText SCREENWIDTH / 2 - Len(sStatusMsg) * font1.Width / 2, _
            35, sStatusMsg
```

```
        'display debug messages
        If DEBUGMODE Then
            DrawText SCREENWIDTH - Len(sFrameRate) * font1.Width, _
                SCREENHEIGHT - font1.Height * 2 - 1, sFrameRate
            DrawText SCREENWIDTH - Len(sDrawRate) * font1.Width, _
                SCREENHEIGHT - font1.Height - 1, sDrawRate

            DrawText 1, SCREENHEIGHT - font1.Height * 2 - 1, _
                "BALL = " & vBallPos.X & "," & vBallPos.Y & "," & _
                vBallPos.z
            DrawText 1, SCREENHEIGHT - font1.Height - 1, _
                "PADL = " & vPaddlePos.X & "," & vPaddlePos.Y & _
                    "," & vPaddlePos.z
        End If
End Sub

Private Sub AddScore(ByVal lValue As Long)
    Dim lMod As Long
    If gamestatus = RUNNING Then
        lScore = lScore + lValue
        If lScore > lHighScore Then
            lHighScore = lScore
        End If

        lMod = lScore Mod 100
        If lScore > 99 And (lMod = 0 Or lMod = 1) Then
            lBallsLeft = lBallsLeft + 1
            dswExtraLife(Random(2)).PlaySound
        End If
    End If
End Sub

Private Sub MissedBall()
    If gamestatus = RUNNING Then
        dswMissed(Random(2)).PlaySound
        gamestatus = LAUNCH
        lBallsLeft = lBallsLeft - 1
        If lBallsLeft = 1 Then
            dswDanger(Random(2)).PlaySound
```

```
            ElseIf lBallsLeft < 1 Then
                ResetBall
                lScore = 0
                gamestatus = DEMO
            End If
        End If
End Sub

Private Sub ResetBall()
    lBallsLeft = 3
    vBallPos.X = 0
    vBallPos.Y = -8
    vBallPos.z = 10
    vBallDir.X = Random(3) - 1
    vBallDir.z = -1
    vBallSpd.X = Random(1) + 1
    vBallSpd.z = BALLSPEED + Random(3)
End Sub

Public Sub SetIdentity()
    'set default position, scale, and rotation
    D3DXMatrixIdentity matWorld
    d3d.Device.SetTransform D3DTS_WORLD, matWorld
End Sub

Public Function CreateVector(X As Single, Y As Single, _
    z As Single) As D3DVECTOR
    CreateVector.X = X
    CreateVector.Y = Y
    CreateVector.z = z
End Function

Public Function Random(ByVal lMax As Long)
    Random = Int(Rnd * lMax)
End Function
```

The two bitmap font drawing routines are DrawText and DrawChar. Since the source bitmap image is already laid out in ASCII order, the only thing that DrawChar needs to do is subtract 32 from the ASCII value to draw the correct character. This is done by setting the CurrentFrame property of the sprite that holds the font characters. Simple!

```
Private Sub DrawText(ByVal X As Long, ByVal Y As Long, _
    ByVal sText As String)
    Dim n As Long
    For n = 1 To Len(sText)
        DrawChar X + (n - 1) * font1.Width, Y, Asc(Mid$(sText, n, 1))
    Next n
End Sub

Private Sub DrawChar(ByVal X As Long, ByVal Y As Long, c As Byte)
    font1.X = X
    font1.Y = Y
    font1.CurrentFrame = c - 32
    font1.Draw
End Sub
```

As usual, the trusty Shutdown procedure cleans up the mess, so to speak, before the game ends.

```
Private Sub Shutdown()
    Dim n As Long
    Set d3d = Nothing
    Set dinput = Nothing
    Keyboard.Shutdown
    Set Keyboard = Nothing
    Set floor = Nothing
    Set font1 = Nothing
    Set wall1 = Nothing
    Set wall2 = Nothing
    Set wall3 = Nothing
    For n = 0 To 5
        Set ball(n) = Nothing
        Set paddle(n) = Nothing
    Next n
    Set dsound = Nothing
    Set dswStart(0) = Nothing
    For n = 0 To 1
        Set dswLaunch(n) = Nothing
        Set dswMissed(n) = Nothing
        Set dswExtraLife(n) = Nothing
        Set dswDanger(n) = Nothing
    Next n
```

```
      For n = 0 To 2
            Set dswWall(n) = Nothing
      Next n
      End
End Sub
```

Enhancing the Game

Well, that is the end of the Pong 3D source code. Again, most of the code involves the 3-D scene, so the actual game logic is pretty short as far as games go. But that was the whole idea—to keep it simple because 3-D can be a tough subject to master, and studying simple code is definitely the best way to learn. Now, here are some recommendations for improving the game:

- Add some scenery to the background by displaying a bitmap before rendering.
- Add multiple levels with a different theme for each level.
- Add joystick and mouse support.
- Add a musical soundtrack to the game.
- Add dynamic lighting with colored light sources (advanced).
- Add z-buffer support for rendering (advanced).
- Load the 3-D objects from .X files rather than generating them.
- Change the ball object so it looks like a sphere instead of a cube.

Summary

Congratulations on completing your first complete 3-D game! I must admit, I had a lot of fun writing Pong 3D. I hope you had as much fun exploring the source code and seeing how the game works for yourself. Once you understand how to create 3-D objects and apply textures to them, it is fairly easy to build a game around those techniques (and quite fun at the same time!). Granted, this game could have been even better with more advanced techniques, such as the ability to load 3-D objects from disk rather than creating them at run-time. But simplicity rules the day.

PART V

APPENDIXES

Welcome to Part V of *Visual Basic Game Programming with DirectX*. Part V includes six appendixes that provide supplemental reference information which should be useful as you develop new games. The appendixes are also helpful when you need to look up a quick function or event for either DirectX or the game library.

The game library contains numerous classes and a considerable number of functions, procedures, and events. At times, it is difficult to search through source code to find the needed information. IntelliSense is a welcome and highly-useful feature of Visual Basic, but it does not always provide all the information you need. Therefore, I have provided a complete reference of the Visual Basic Game Library that was compiled in Part II, "The Nuts and Bolts of Game Development."

Part V includes a reference for the functions and events in DirectX 7.0 and DirectX 8.0 that were used in the book. While the DirectX reference is not complete, it is valuable because it describes those features used in the book and ignores the multitude of features that were not used for the source code in the book.

Also included in Part Five is a listing of DirectInput keyboard codes (which are not the same as traditional ASCII codes), a list of valuable game programming books, and some fascinating Web sites dedicated to Visual Basic game development.

Part V includes the following appendixes:

- Appendix A: Visual Basic Game Library Reference
- Appendix B: DirectX for Visual Basic Reference
- Appendix C: Windows API Reference
- Appendix D: DirectInput Keyboard Codes
- Appendix E: Recommended Reading
- Appendix F: Visual Basic Gaming Sites

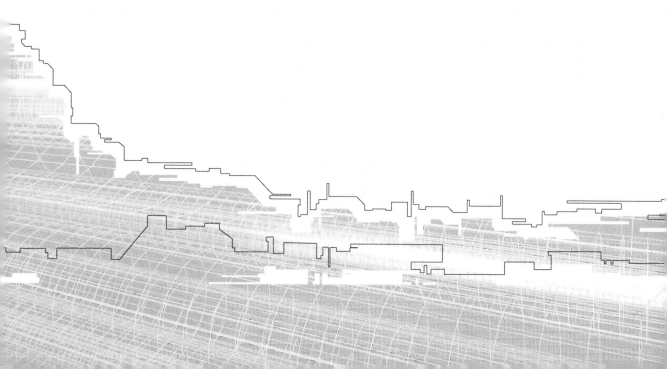

APPENDIX A

VISUAL BASIC
GAME LIBRARY
REFERENCE

This appendix lists the events, functions, and procedures for all of the classes developed in the book. Comprehensively, they form the Visual Basic Game Library (VBGL).

GRAPHICS LIBRARY

The graphics library is the most important aspect of writing a game, and the code developed in this book covered the Windows API, DirectDraw, and Direct3D.

Windows API

There are four classes that make up the core of the Windows API support: clsBitmap, clsSprite, clsDirtyRect, and clsVScroller.

clsBitmap

```
Property Get Width() As Long
Property Get Height() As Long
Property Get BitsPerPixel() As Long
Property Get Planes() As Long
Property Get TypeNum() As Long
Property Get WidthBytes() As Long
Property Get hdc() As Long
Property Get hWnd() As Long
Function Create(ByVal hdcDest As Long, _
    ByVal lWidth As Long, ByVal lHeight As Long) As Boolean
Function Load(ByVal Filename As String) As Boolean
Sub LoadBitmapIntoPicture(ByVal Filename As String, _
    ByVal pic As PictureBox)
Sub Draw(ByVal X As Long, ByVal Y As Long, _
    ByVal hdcDest As Long)
Sub Blt(ByVal hdcDest As Long, _
    ByVal Left As Long, ByVal Top As Long, _
    ByVal Right As Long, ByVal Bottom As Long)
```

```
Sub DrawText(ByVal Left As Long, ByVal Top As Long, _
    ByVal sText As String, ByVal lColor As Long)
    Dim hPen As Long
    Dim hOldPen As Long
Sub DrawEllipse(ByVal Left As Long, ByVal Top As Long, _
    ByVal Right As Long, ByVal Bottom As Long, ByVal Color As Long)
Sub DrawRect(ByVal Left As Long, ByVal Top As Long, _
    ByVal Right As Long, ByVal Bottom As Long, ByVal Color As Long)
Sub DrawPoint(ByVal X As Long, ByVal Y As Long, _
    ByVal Color As Long, Optional ByVal hdcDest As Long = 0)
Sub DrawLine(ByVal Left As Long, ByVal Top As Long, _
    ByVal Right As Long, ByVal Bottom As Long, _
    ByVal Color As Long, Optional ByVal Width As Long = 1)
```

clsSprite

```
Property Let X(ByVal lNewValue As Long)
Property Get X() As Long
Property Let Y(ByVal lNewValue As Long)
Property Get Y() As Long
Property Let GlobalX(ByVal lNewValue As Long)
Property Get GlobalX() As Long
Property Let GlobalY(ByVal lNewValue As Long)
Property Get GlobalY() As Long
Property Get SpeedX() As Long
Property Let SpeedX(ByVal lNewValue As Long)
Property Get SpeedY() As Long
Property Let SpeedY(ByVal lNewValue As Long)
Property Get DirX() As Long
Property Let DirX(ByVal lNewValue As Long)
Property Get DirY() As Long
Property Let DirY(ByVal lNewValue As Long)
Property Get Width() As Long
Property Get Height() As Long
Property Get Active() As Boolean
Property Let Active(ByVal bNewValue As Boolean)
PrivateProperty Get ColorDepth() As Long
Property Get CurrentFrame() As Long
Property Let CurrentFrame(ByVal lNewValue As Long)
```

```
Property Get hdc(Optional ByVal lFrame _
    As Long = -1) As Long
Property Get MaskDC(Optional ByVal lFrame _
    As Long = -1) As Long
Property Get Transparent() As Boolean
Property Let Transparent(ByVal bNewValue As Boolean)
Property Get HardwareTransparency() As Boolean
Property Let State(ByVal lNewValue As Long)
Property Get State() As Long
Property Let MoveRate(ByVal lNewValue As Long)
Property Get MoveRate() As Long
Property Let MoveCount(ByVal lNewValue As Long)
Property Get MoveCount() As Long
Property Let AnimRate(ByVal lNewValue As Long)
Property Get AnimRate() As Long
Property Let AnimCount(ByVal lNewValue As Long)
Property Get AnimCount() As Long
Sub NextFrame()
Sub PrevFrame()
Sub SaveUnder(ByVal hdcDest As Long)
Sub RestoreUnder(ByVal hdcDest As Long)
Function LoadFrames(ByVal sFilename As String, _
    ByVal lStartX As Long, ByVal lStartY As Long, _
    ByVal lWidth As Long, ByVal lHeight As Long, _
    ByVal lNumFrames As Long, _
    Optional bGenMasks As Boolean = True) As Boolean
Sub Draw(ByVal hdcDest As Long)
Function GenerateAllMasks() As Boolean
Function GenerateMask(ByVal lFrame As Long) As Boolean
Function Collided(ByRef OtherSprite As clsSprite) As Boolean
```

clsDirtyRect

```
Sub Init(ByRef pic As Variant)
Sub Reset()
Sub Resize(ByRef spr As clsSprite, _
    ByRef pic As Variant)
Sub Draw(ByRef hdcDest As Long, _
    cbSource As clsBitmap)
```

clsVScroller

```
Function GetTileDC(ByVal lTileNum As Long)
Property Get MajorScroll() As Long
Property Let MajorScroll(ByVal lNewValue As Long)
Property Get MinorScroll() As Long
Property Let MinorScroll(ByVal lNewValue As Long)
Property Get TileWidth() As Long
Property Get TileHeight() As Long
Property Get MaxTileCols()
Property Get MaxTileRows()
Property Get StartX() As Long
Property Let StartX(ByVal lNewValue As Long)
Sub SetTile(ByVal lCol As Long, _
    ByVal lRow As Long, _
Function GetTile(ByVal lCol As Long, _
    ByVal lRow As Long)
Sub InitTileMap(ByVal lCols As Long, _
    ByVal lRows As Long)
Function LoadTiles(ByVal sFilename As String, _
    ByVal lStartX As Long, ByVal lStartY As Long, _
    ByVal lWidth As Long, ByVal lHeight As Long, _
    ByVal lNumFrames As Long) As Boolean
Sub Scroll(ByVal lNumLines As Long)
Sub DrawTiles(ByVal lHorizTiles As Long, _
Sub DrawTile(ByVal lStartX As Long, _
    ByVal lCol As Long, ByVal lRow As Long, _
    ByVal hdcDest As Long)
```

DirectDraw 7.0

The game library includes three classes to support DirectDraw: clsDirectDraw7, clsDDSprite, and clsDDSurface7.

clsDirectDraw7

```
Function Startup(ByVal hWnd As Long, ByVal lWidth As Long, _
    ByVal lHeight As Long, ByVal lBPP As Long, _
    ByVal bFullscreen As Boolean) As Boolean
```

```
Sub Shutdown()
Sub Blt(ByRef ddsSource As DirectDrawSurface7, _
    ByRef srcRect As DxVBLib.RECT)
Sub Draw(ByRef cddsSource As clsDDSurface7, _
    ByRef srcRect As DxVBLib.RECT)
Property Get DXObj() As DirectX7
Property Get DDObj() As DirectDraw7
Property Get ScreenRect() As DxVBLib.RECT
```

clsDDSprite7

```
Property Let X(ByVal lNewValue As Long)
Property Get X() As Long
Property Let Y(ByVal lNewValue As Long)
Property Get Y() As Long
Property Let GlobalX(ByVal lNewValue As Long)
Property Get GlobalX() As Long
Property Let GlobalY(ByVal lNewValue As Long)
Property Get GlobalY() As Long
Property Get SpeedX() As Long
Property Let SpeedX(ByVal lNewValue As Long)
Property Get SpeedY() As Long
Property Let SpeedY(ByVal lNewValue As Long)
Property Get Width() As Long
Property Get Height() As Long
Property Get Active() As Boolean
Property Let Active(ByVal bNewValue As Boolean)
Property Get CurrentFrame() As Long
Property Let CurrentFrame(ByVal lNewValue As Long)
Property Get Transparent() As Boolean
Property Let Transparent(ByVal bNewValue As Boolean)
Property Let State(ByVal lNewValue As Long)
Property Get State() As Long
Property Let MoveRate(ByVal lNewValue As Long)
Property Get MoveRate() As Long
Property Let MoveCount(ByVal lNewValue As Long)
Property Get MoveCount() As Long
Property Let AnimRate(ByVal lNewValue As Long)
Property Get AnimRate() As Long
Property Let AnimCount(ByVal lNewValue As Long)
```

```
Property Get AnimCount() As Long
Property Let AnimDir(ByVal lNewValue As Long)
Property Get AnimDir() As Long
Property Get DirX() As Long
Property Let DirX(ByVal lNewValue As Long)
Property Get DirY() As Long
Property Let DirY(ByVal lNewValue As Long)
Property Get Surface() As DirectDrawSurface7
Property Get SurfaceRect() As DxVBLib.RECT
Sub Create(ByRef ddObj As clsDirectDraw7)
Sub NextFrame()
Sub PrevFrame()
Sub Draw(ByRef ddsDest As clsDDSurface7)
Function LoadFromFile(ByVal sFilename As String, _
    ByVal lSprWidth As Long, ByVal lSprHeight As Long, _
    ByVal lNumCols As Long, ByVal lNumFrames As Long) As Boolean
Function LoadFromSurface(ByRef ddsOther As clsDDSurface7, _
    ByVal lSprWidth As Long, ByVal lSprHeight As Long, _
    ByVal lNumCols As Long, ByVal lNumFrames As Long) As Boolean
```

clsDDSurface7

```
Property Get Surface() As DirectDrawSurface7
Property Get SurfaceRect() As DxVBLib.RECT
Property Get Width() As Long
Property Get Height() As Long
Function Create(ByRef objDD As DirectDraw7, _
    ByVal lWidth As Long, ByVal lHeight As Long, _
    Optional bPrimary As Boolean = False) As Boolean
Function Load(ByRef ddraw As clsDirectDraw7, _
    ByVal sFilename As String) As Boolean
Sub Blt(ByRef dstRect As DxVBLib.RECT, _
    ByRef ddsSource As DirectDrawSurface7, _
    ByRef srcRect As DxVBLib.RECT)
Sub BltTrans(ByRef dstRect As DxVBLib.RECT, _
    ByRef ddsSource As DirectDrawSurface7, _
    ByRef srcRect As DxVBLib.RECT)
Sub BltFast(ByVal X As Long, ByVal Y As Long, _
    ByRef ddsSource As DirectDrawSurface7, _
    ByRef srcRect As DxVBLib.RECT)
```

```
Sub BltColorFill(ByVal lColor As Long)
Sub DrawText(ByVal X As Long, ByVal Y As Long, _
    ByVal sText As String)              -
```

DirectX Graphics 8.0

The game library provides support for Direct3D with four classes: clsDirect3D8, clsD3DTriangle8, clsD3DRectangle8, and clsD3DSprite8.

clsDirect3D8

```
Function Startup(ByVal hWnd As Long, ByVal lWidth As Long, _
    ByVal lHeight As Long, _
    ByVal bFullscreen As Boolean) As Boolean
Property Get Device() As Direct3DDevice8
Property Get RefreshRate() As Long
Property Get DisplayMode() As Long
Property Get MaxPrimitiveCount() As Long
Property Get MaxActiveLights()
Property Get MaxTextureWidth()
Property Get MaxTextureHeight()
Sub Clear(ByVal lColor As Long)
Sub BeginScene()
Sub EndScene()
Sub Present()
```

clsD3DTriangle8

```
Sub Create(ByRef d3dObj As clsDirect3D8)
Function LoadTexture(ByVal sFilename As String) As Boolean
Sub Draw()
Sub SetVertex(ByVal lVert As Long, ByVal X As Single, _
    ByVal Y As Single, ByVal z As Single, _
    ByVal u As Single, ByVal v As Single)
Sub SetPosition(ByVal lVert As Long, ByVal X As Single, _
    ByVal Y As Single, ByVal z As Single)
Sub SetNormal(ByVal lVert As Long, ByVal X As Single, _
    ByVal Y As Single, ByVal z As Single)
```

```
Sub SetTexturePos(ByVal lVert As Long, ByVal u As Single, _
    ByVal v As Single)
Property Get VertexSize() As Long
```

clsD3DRectangle8

```
Sub Create(ByRef d3dObj As clsDirect3D8)
Function LoadTexture(ByVal sFilename As String, _
    Optional ByVal bAlpha As Boolean = False) As Boolean
Sub Draw()
Sub SetDefaultVertices()
Sub SetVertex(ByVal lVert As Long, ByVal X As Single, _
    ByVal Y As Single, ByVal z As Single, _
    ByVal u As Single, ByVal v As Single)
Sub SetPosition(ByVal lVert As Long, ByVal X As Single, _
    ByVal Y As Single, ByVal z As Single)
Sub SetNormal(ByVal lVert As Long, ByVal X As Single, _
    ByVal Y As Single, ByVal z As Single)
Sub SetTexturePos(ByVal lVert As Long, ByVal u As Single, _
    ByVal v As Single)
Property Get VertexSize() As Long
```

clsD3DSprite8

```
Sub Create(ByRef d3dObj As clsDirect3D8)
Sub LoadFromFile(ByVal sFilename As String, _
    ByVal lSprWidth As Long, ByVal lSprHeight As Long, _
    ByVal lNumCols As Long, ByVal lNumFrames As Long)
Sub LoadFromTexture(ByRef d3dtSprite As Direct3DTexture8, _
    ByVal lSprWidth As Long, ByVal lSprHeight As Long, _
    ByVal lNumCols As Long, ByVal lNumFrames As Long)
Sub Draw()
Property Get X() As Long
Property Let X(ByVal lNewValue As Long)
Property Get Y() As Long
Property Let Y(ByVal lNewValue As Long)
Property Get ScaleX() As Single
Property Let ScaleX(ByVal fNewValue As Single)
Property Get ScaleY() As Single
```

```
Property Let ScaleY(ByVal fNewValue As Single)
Property Get Width() As Long
Property Get Height() As Long
Property Get TotalFrames() As Long
Property Get CurrentFrame() As Long
Property Let CurrentFrame(ByVal lNewValue As Long)
Property Get SpeedX() As Long
Property Let SpeedX(ByVal lNewValue As Long)
Property Get SpeedY() As Long
Property Let SpeedY(ByVal lNewValue As Long)
Property Get DirX() As Long
Property Let DirX(ByVal lNewValue As Long)
Property Get DirY() As Long
Property Let DirY(ByVal lNewValue As Long)
```

Sound Library

Sound support in the game library is provided by DirectSound and DirectMusic with the following classes: clsDirectSound8, clsDSWave8, clsDirectMusic8, and clsDMSequence8.

clsDirectSound8

```
Property Get DSObj() As DirectSound8
Property Get DXObj() As DirectX8
Sub Startup(ByRef lWindowHandle As Long)
```

clsDSWave8

```
Property Get DSBObj() As DirectSoundSecondaryBuffer8
Property Set DSBObj(ByRef dssbNewValue As _
    DirectSoundSecondaryBuffer8)
Property Get Interrupt() As Boolean
Property Let Interrupt(ByVal bNewValue As Boolean)
Property Get Looping() As Boolean
Property Let Looping(ByVal bNewValue As Boolean)
Property Get Positional() As Boolean
Property Let Positional(ByVal bNewValue As Boolean)
Property Get Frequency() As Long
Property Get Channels() As Long
```

```
Property Get Samples() As Long
Property Get BitsPerSample() As Long
Property Get Size() As Long
Sub SetPosition(ByVal X As Long, _
    ByVal Y As Long, ByVal Z As Long)
Sub LoadSound(ByRef objDS As clsDirectSound8, _
    ByVal sFilename As String)
Sub PlaySound()
Sub StopSound()
```

clsDirectMusic8

```
Property Let Volume(ByVal lNewValue As Long)
Property Get ClockTime() As Long
Property Get MusicTime() As Long
Property Get LatencyTime() As Long
Property Get DXObj() As DirectX8
Property Get DMPerfObj() As DirectMusicPerformance8
Property Get DMPathObj() As DirectMusicAudioPath8
Function Startup(ByVal lWindowHandle As Long) As Boolean
```

clsDMSequence8

```
Property Get Length() As Long
Property Get Name() As String
Property Get Looping() As Boolean
Property Let Looping(ByVal bNewValue As Boolean)
Property Get Playing() As Boolean
Function LoadMusic(ByRef dm As clsDirectMusic8, _
    ByVal sFile As String) As Boolean
Sub PlayMusic()
Sub StopMusic()
```

USER INPUT LIBRARY

User input is provided by the game library through keyboard, mouse, and joystick handlers, which are implemented as the following four classes: clsDirectInput8, clsDIKeyboard8, clsDIMouse8, and clsDIJoystick8.

clsDirectInput8

```
Property Get DIObj() As DirectInput8
Property Get DXObj() As DirectX8
Sub Startup(ByRef lWindowHandle As Long)
```

clsDIKeyboard8

```
Event KeyDown(ByVal lKey As Long)
Sub Startup(ByRef di As clsDirectInput8, _
    ByVal hWindowHandle As Long)
Sub Check_Keyboard()
Sub Shutdown()
Property Get KeyName(ByVal lKey As Long) As String
```

clsDIMouse8

```
Event MouseMove(ByVal X As Long, ByVal Y As Long)
Event MouseDown(ByVal lButton As Long)
Event MouseUp(ByVal lButton As Long)
Property Get RelativeMotion() As Boolean
Property Let RelativeMotion(ByVal bNewValue As Boolean)
Sub Startup(ByRef di As clsDirectInput8, _
    ByVal hWindow As Long)
Sub Check_Mouse(ByVal lScreenWidth As Long, _
    ByVal lScreenHeight As Long)
Sub Shutdown()
```

clsDIJoystick8

```
Event AnalogMove(ByVal lNum As Long, _
    ByVal X As Long, ByVal Y As Long, ByVal Z As Long)
Event SliderMove(ByVal lSlider As Long, _
    ByVal lValue As Long)
Event ButtonDown(ByVal lButton As Long)
Event ButtonUp(ByVal lButton As Long)
Event DPAD(ByVal lButton As Long)
```

```
Function Startup(ByRef di As clsDirectInput8, _
    ByVal hWindow As Long) As Boolean
Sub Check_Joystick()
Sub Shutdown()
```

NETWORKING LIBRARY

Multiplayer networking support is included in the game library with the two socket classes: clsSocketServer and clsSocketClient. DirectPlay support is provided by straight code and is not implemented through classes.

Windows Sockets

The multiplayer networking classes that support socket connections are clsServerSocket and clsClientSocket.

clsServerSocket

```
Event DataArrival(ByVal lIndex As Long, _
    ByVal lTotalBytes As Long, ByVal sIncoming As String)
Event ServerConnectionRequest(ByVal lRequestID As Long)
Function UserCount()
Function OpenConnection(ByVal lRequestID As Long, _
    ByVal lPort As Long) As Long
Sub CloseConnection(ByVal Index&)
Property Get RemoteHostIP() As String
Property Get RemotePort() As String
Property Get LocalIP() As String
Property Get LocalPort() As Long
Property Get State() As Long
Function Connected(ByVal Index As Long) As Boolean
Sub Send(ByVal Index As Long, ByVal msg As String)
Sub OpenServer(ByVal Port As Long)
Sub CloseServer()
Property Get CurrentLink() As Long
Property Let CurrentLink(ByVal vNewValue As Long)
```

clsClientSocket

```
Event DataArrival(ByVal lTotalBytes As Long, _
    ByVal sIncoming As String)
Property Let RemotePort(ByVal lPort&)
Property Get RemotePort() As Long
Property Get LocalIP() As String
Sub Send(ByVal s$)
Sub CloseConnection()
Property Get RemoteHost() As String
Property Let RemoteHost(ByVal vNewValue As String)
Sub Connect()
Property Get State() As Long
```

APPENDIX B

DirectX for Visual Basic Reference

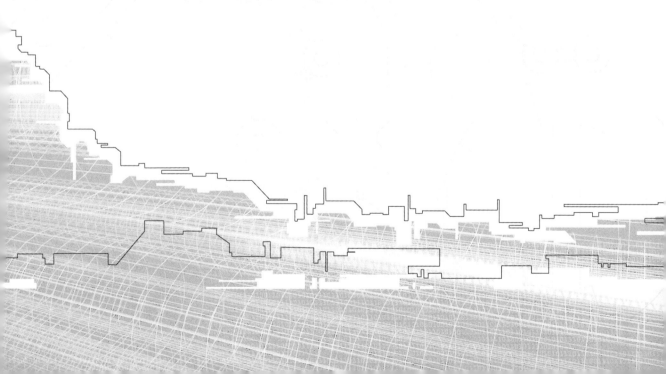

This is a reference of DirectX objects, structures, and functions that were used in the book. As such, this appendix is not a comprehensive DirectX reference. If it were a complete reference, it would have been bundled as a second volume, because the complete list of DirectX routines is huge. Basically, if any DirectX object, structure, or function was used in the book, it is listed in this appendix. You will not, however, find any constants or enumerations here, because Visual Basic programmers don't have to worry about lists, thanks to the IntelliSense drop-down menu that appears just when you need it for such things.

DIRECTX 7.0

The section on DirectX 7.0 includes the primary DirectX7 object and two objects related to programming DirectDraw: DirectDraw7 and DirectDrawSurface7.

DirectDraw7

The DirectDraw7 object is invoked through the following five routines.

CreateSurface Function

```
CreateSurface( _
    dd As DDSURFACEDESC2 _
) As DirectDrawSurface7
```

CreateSurface requires the following DDSURFACEDESC2 parameter:

```
Type DDSURFACEDESC2
    ddckCKDestBlt As DDCOLORKEY
    ddckCKDestOverlay As DDCOLORKEY
    ddckCKSrcBlt As DDCOLORKEY
    ddckCKSrcOverlay As DDCOLORKEY
    ddpfPixelFormat As DDPIXELFORMAT
    ddsCaps As DDSCAPS2
    lAlphaBitDepth As Long
    lBackBufferCount As Long
    lFlags As CONST_DDSURFACEDESCFLAGS
    lHeight As Long
```

```
        lLinearSize As Long
        lMipMapCount As Long
        lPitch As Long
        lRefreshRate As Long
        lTextureStage As Long
        lWidth As Long
        lZBufferBitDepth As Long
End Type
```

CreateSurfaceFromFile Function

```
CreateSurfaceFromFile( _
    file As String, _
    dd As DDSURFACEDESC2 _
) As DirectDrawSurface7
```

Refer to the definition of **DDSURFACEDESC2** in the definition of CreateSurface.

GetCaps

```
GetCaps(
    hwCaps As DDCAPS, _
    helCaps As DDCAPS _
)
Type DDCAPS
    ddsCaps As DDSCAPS2
    lAlignBoundaryDest As Long
    lAlignBoundarySrc As Long
    lAlignSizeDest As Long
    lAlignSizeSrc As Long
    lAlignStrideAlign As Long
    lAlphaBltConstBitDepths As Long
    lAlphaBltPixelBitDepths As Long
    lAlphaBltSurfaceBitDepths As Long
    lAlphaOverlayConstBitDepths As Long
    lAlphaOverlayPixelBitDepths As Long
    lAlphaOverlaySurfaceBitDepths As Long
    lCaps As CONST_DDCAPS1FLAGS
    lCaps2 As CONST_DDCAPS2FLAGS
    lCKeyCaps As CONST_DDCKEYCAPSFLAGS
```

```
        lCurrVideoPorts As Long
        lCurrVisibleOverlays As Long
        lFXCaps As CONST_DDFXCAPSFLAGS
        lMaxHwCodecStretch As Long
        lMaxLiveVideoStretch As Long
        lMaxOverlayStretch As Long
        lMaxVideoPorts As Long
        lMaxVisibleOverlays As Long
        lMinHwCodecStretch As Long
        lMinLiveVideoStretch As Long
        lMinOverlayStretch As Long
        lNLVBCaps As CONST_DDCAPS1FLAGS
        lNLVBCaps2 As CONST_DDCAPS2FLAGS
        lNLVBCKeyCaps As CONST_DDCKEYCAPSFLAGS
        lNLVBFXCaps As CONST_DDFXCAPSFLAGS
        lNLVBRops (0 To 7) As Long
        lNumFourCCCodes As Long
        lPalCaps As CONST_DDPCAPSFLAGS
        lReserved1 As Long
        lReserved2 As Long
        lReserved3 As Long
        lReservedCaps As Long
        lRops (0 To 7) As Long
        lSSBCaps As CONST_DDCAPS1FLAGS
        lSSBCKeyCaps As CONST_DDCKEYCAPSFLAGS
        lSSBFXCaps As CONST_DDFXCAPSFLAGS
        lSSBRops (0 To 7) As Long
        lSVBCaps As CONST_DDCAPS1FLAGS
        lSVBCaps2 As CONST_DDCAPS2FLAGS
        lSVBCKeyCaps As CONST_DDCKEYCAPSFLAGS
        lSVBFXCaps As CONST_DDFXCAPSFLAGS
        lSVBRops (0 To 7) As Long
        lSVCaps As CONST_DDSTEREOCAPSFLAGS
        lVidMemFree As Long
        lVidMemTotal As Long
        lVSBCaps As CONST_DDCAPS1FLAGS
        lVSBCKeyCaps As CONST_DDCKEYCAPSFLAGS
        lVSBFXCaps As CONST_DDFXCAPSFLAGS
        lVSRops (0 To 7) As Long
        lZBufferBitDepths As Long
    End Type
```

SetCooperativeLevel Procedure

```
SetCooperativeLevel( _
    hdl As Long, _
    flags As CONST_DDSCLFLAGS _
)
```

SetDisplayMode Procedure

```
SetDisplayMode( _
    w As Long, _
    h As Long, _
    bpp As Long, _
    ref As Long, _
    mode As CONST_DDSDMFLAGS _
)
```

DirectDrawSurface7

The DirectDrawSurface7 object is invoked through the following six routines.

Blt Function

```
Blt( _
    destRect As RECT, _
    ddS As DirectDrawSurface7, _
    srcRect As RECT, _
    flags As CONST_DDBLTFLAGS _
) As Long
```

BltColorFill Function

```
BltColorFill( _
    destRect As RECT, _
    fillvalue As Long _
) As Long
```

BltFast Function

```
BltFast( _
    dx As Long, _
    dy As Long, _
    ddS As DirectDrawSurface7, _
    srcRect As RECT, _
    trans As CONST_DDBLTFASTFLAGS _
) As Long
```

DrawText Procedure

```
DrawText( _
    x As Long, _
    y As Long, _
    text As String, _
    b As Boolean _
)
```

GetCaps Procedure

```
GetCaps( _
    caps As DDSCAPS2 _
)
```

GetSurfaceDesc Procedure

```
GetSurfaceDesc( _
    surface As DDSURFACEDESC2 _
)
```

Refer to the definition of DDSURFACEDESC2 in the definition of CreateSurface.

DirectX7

The DirectDrawSurface7 object is invoked through the following function.

DirectDrawCreate Function

```
DirectDrawCreate( _
    guid As String _
) As DirectDraw7
```

DIRECTX 8.0

DirectX 8.0 was used considerably more in the book than DirectX 7.0, which was simply a means to support DirectDraw. Since DirectX 8.0 includes a new, revamped graphics library, the only apparent reason why anyone would want to use DirectX 7.0 would be to support existing libraries that use DirectDraw. However, there are still many advantages to using DirectDraw, namely as support for older computers without 3-D video cards.

This section of the appendix includes the procedures and functions from the following DirectX 8.0 objects: D3DX8, DirectX8, Direct3D8, Direct3DDevice8, DirectInput8, DirectInputEnumDevices8, DirectMusicLoader8, DirectMusicPerformance8, DirectMusicSegment8, DirectPlay8Address, DirectPlay8Client, DirectPlay8Server, DirectPlay8Event, DirectSound3DBuffer8, DirectSound8, DirectSoundSecondaryBuffer8, and DirectX8.

D3DX8

The DirectDrawSurface7 object is invoked through the following nine routines.

CreateTextureFromFile Function

```
CreateTextureFromFile( _
    Device As Direct3DDevice8, _
    SrcFile As String _
) As Direct3DTexture8
```

CreateTextureFromFileEx Function

```
CreateTextureFromFileEx( _
    Device As Direct3DDevice8, _
    SrcFile As String, _
    Width As Long, _
    Height As Long, _
```

```
    MipLevels As Long, _
    Usage As Long, _
    Format As CONST_D3DFORMAT, _
    Pool As CONST_D3DPOOL, _
    Filter As Long, _
    MipFilter As Long, _
    ColorKey As Long, _
    SrcInfo As Any _
    Palette As Any _
) As Direct3DTexture8
```

D3DXMatrixIdentity Procedure

```
D3DXMatrixIdentity( _
    MOut As D3DMATRIX _
)
```

D3DXMatrixLookAtLH Procedure

```
D3DXMatrixLookAtLH( _
    MOut As D3DMATRIX, _
    VEye As D3DVECTOR, _
    VAt As D3DVECTOR, _
    VUp As D3DVECTOR _
)
Type D3DMATRIX
    m11 As Single
    m12 As Single
    m13 As Single
    m14 As Single
    m21 As Single
    m22 As Single
    m23 As Single
    m24 As Single
    m31 As Single
    m32 As Single
    m33 As Single
```

```
    m34 As Single
    m41 As Single
    m42 As Single
    m43 As Single
    m44 As Single
End Type
Type D3DVECTOR
    x As Single
    y As Single
    z As Single
End Type
```

D3DXMatrixPerspectiveFovLH Procedure

```
D3DXMatrixPerspectiveFovLH( _
    MOut As D3DMATRIX, _
    fovy As Single, _
    aspect As Single, _
    zn As Single, _
    zf As Single _
)
```

D3DXMatrixRotationX Procedure

```
D3DXMatrixRotationX( _
    MOut As D3DMATRIX, _
    angle As Single _
)
```

D3DXMatrixRotationY Procedure

```
D3DXMatrixRotationY( _
    MOut As D3DMATRIX, _
    angle As Single _
)
```

D3DXMatrixTranslation Procedure

```
D3DXMatrixTranslation( _
    MOut As D3DMATRIX, _
    x As Single, _
    y As Single, _
    z As Single _
)
```

D3DVertexBuffer8SetData Function

```
D3DVertexBuffer8SetData( _
    VBuffer As Direct3DVertexBuffer8, _
    Offset As Long, _
    Size As Long, _
    Flags As Long, _
    Data As Any _
) As Long
```

Direct3D8

The functionality of Direct3D8 is provided by the following two routines.

CreateDevice Function

```
CreateDevice( _
    Adapter As Long, _
    DeviceType As CONST_D3DDEVTYPE, _
    hFocusWindow As Long, _
    BehaviorFlags As Long, _
    PresentationParameters As D3DPRESENT_PARAMETERS _
) As Direct3DDevice8
Type D3DPRESENT_PARAMETERS
    AutoDepthStencilFormat As CONST_D3DFORMAT
    BackBufferCount As Long
    BackBufferFormat As CONST_D3DFORMAT
    BackBufferHeight As Long
    BackBufferWidth As Long
    EnableAutoDepthStencil As Long
    Flags As Long
```

```
    FullScreen_PresentationInterval As Long
    FullScreen_RefreshRateInHz As Long
    hDeviceWindow As Long
    MultiSampleType As CONST_D3DMULTISAMPLE_TYPE
    SwapEffect As CONST_D3DSWAPEFFECT
    Windowed As Long
End Type
```

GetAdapterDisplayMode Procedure

```
GetAdapterDisplayMode( _
    Adapter As Long, _
    Mode As D3DDISPLAYMODE _
)
Type D3DDISPLAYMODE
    Format As CONST_D3DFORMAT
    Height As Long
    RefreshRate As Long
    Width As Long
End Type
```

Direct3DDevice8

The functionality of Direct3DDevice8 is provided by the following twelve routines.

BeginScene Procedure

```
BeginScene()
```

Clear Procedure

```
Clear( _
    Count As Long, _
    ClearD3DRect As Any, _
    Flags As CONST_D3DCLEARFLAGS, _
    Color As Long, _
    Z As Single, _
    Stencil As Long _
)
```

CreateTexture Function

```
CreateTexture( _
    Width As Long, _
    Height As Long, _
    Levels As Long, _
    Usage As Long, _
    Format As CONST_D3DFORMAT, _
    Pool As CONST_D3DPOOL _
) As Direct3DTexture8
```

CreateVertexBuffer Function

```
CreateVertexBuffer( _
    LengthInBytes As Long, _
    Usage As Long, _
    FVF As Long, _
    Pool As CONST_D3DPOOL _
) As Direct3DVertexBuffer8
```

DrawPrimitive Procedure

```
DrawPrimitive( _
    PrimitiveType As CONST_D3DPRIMITIVETYPE, _
    StartVertex As Long, _
    PrimitiveCount As Long _
)
```

EndScene Procedure

```
EndScene()
```

Present Procedure

```
Present( _
    SourceRect As Any, _
    DestRect As Any, _
    DestWindowOverride As Long, _
    DirtyRegion As Any _
)
```

SetRenderState Procedure

```
SetRenderState( _
    State As CONST_D3DRENDERSTATETYPE, _
    Value As Long _
)
```

SetStreamSource Procedure

```
SetStreamSource( _
    StreamNumber As Long, _
    StreamData As Direct3DVertexBuffer8, _
    Stride As Long _
)
```

SetTexture Procedure

```
SetTexture( _
    Stage As Long, _
    Texture As Direct3DBaseTexture8 _
)
```

SetTransform Procedure

```
SetTransform( _
    TransformType As CONST_D3DTRANSFORMSTATETYPE, _
    Matrix As D3DMATRIX _
)
```

SetVertexShader Procedure

```
SetVertexShader( _
    VertexShaderHandle As Long _
)
```

DirectInput8

The functionality of DirectInput8 is provided by the following two routines.

CreateDevice Function

```
CreateDevice( _
    guid As String _
) As DirectInputDevice8
```

GetDIDevices Function

```
GetDIDevices( _
  deviceType As CONST_DI8DEVICETYPE, _
  flags As CONST_DIENUMDEVICESFLAGS _
) As DirectInputEnumDevices8
```

DirectInputDevice8

The functionality of DirectInputDevice8 is provided by the following eleven routines.

Acquire Procedure

```
Acquire()
```

GetCapabilities Procedure

```
GetCapabilities( _
    caps As DIDEVCAPS _
)
Type DIDEVCAPS
    lAxes As Long
    lButtons As Long
    lDevType As Long
    lDriverVersion As Long
    lFFMinTimeResolution As Long
    lFFSamplePeriod As Long
    lFirmwareRevision As Long
```

```
    lFlags As CONST_DIDEVCAPSFLAGS
    lHardwareRevision As Long
    lPOVs As Long
End Type
```

GetDeviceStateJoystick Procedure

```
GetDeviceStateJoystick( _
    state As DIJOYSTATE _
)
Type DIJOYSTATE
    Buttons(0 To 31) As Byte
    POV(0 To 3) As Long
    rx As Long
    ry As Long
    rz As Long
    slider(0 To 1) As Long
    x As Long
    y As Long
    z As Long
End Type
```

GetDeviceStateJoystick2 Procedure

```
GetDeviceStateJoystick2( _
    state As DIJOYSTATE2 _
)
Type DIJOYSTATE2
    arx As Long
    ary As Long
    arz As Long
    aslider (0 to 1) As Long
    ax As Long
    ay As Long
    az As Long
    Buttons(0 To 127) As Byte
    frx As Long
    fry As Long
    frz As Long
```

```
        fslider(0 To 1) As Long
        fx As Long
        fy As Long
        fz As Long
        POV(0 To 3) As Long
        rx As Long
        ry As Long
        rz As Long
        slider(0 To 1) As Long
        vrx As Long
        vry As Long
        vrz As Long
        vslider(0 To 1) As Long
        vx As Long
        vy As Long
        vz As Long
        x As Long
        y As Long
        z As Long
    End Type
```

GetDeviceStateKeyboard Procedure

```
GetDeviceStateKeyboard( _
    state As DIKEYBOARDSTATE _
)
Type DIKEYBOARDSTATE
    key(0 To 255) As Byte
End Type
```

GetDeviceStateMouse Procedure

```
GetDeviceStateMouse( _
    state As DIMOUSESTATE _
)
```

```
Type DIMOUSESTATE
    Buttons(0 To 3) As Byte
    lX As Long
    lY As Long
    lZ As Long
End Type
```

SetCommonDataFormat Procedure

```
SetCommonDataFormat( _
    format As CONST_DICOMMONDATAFORMATS _
)
```

SetCooperativeLevel Procedure

```
SetCooperativeLevel( _
    hwnd As Long, _
    flags As CONST_DISCLFLAGS _
)
```

SetEventNotification Procedure

```
SetEventNotification( _
    hEvent As Long _
)
```

SetProperty Procedure

```
SetProperty( _
    guid As String, _
    propertyInfo As Any _
)
```

Unacquire Procedure

```
Unacquire()
```

DirectInputEnumDevices8

The functionality of DirectInputEnumDevices8 is provided by the following function.

GetCount Function

```
GetCount() As Long
```

DirectMusicLoader8

The functionality of DirectMusicLoader8 is provided by the following function.

LoadSegment Function

```
LoadSegment( _
    filename As String _
) As DirectMusicSegment8
```

DirectMusicPerformance8

The functionality of DirectMusicPerformance8 is provided by the following four routines.

CreateStandardAudioPath Function

```
CreateStandardAudioPath( _
    lType As CONST_DMUSIC_STANDARD_AUDIO_PATH, _
    lPChannelCount As Long, _
    fActive As Boolean _
) As DirectMusicAudioPath8
```

InitAudio Procedure

```
InitAudio( _
    hwnd As Long, _
    lFlags As CONST_DMUS_AUDIO, _
    AudioParams As DMUS_AUDIOPARAMS, _
    Optional DirectSound As DirectSound8, _
    Optional lDefaultPathType As CONST_DMUSIC_STANDARD_AUDIO_PATH, _
    Optional lPChannelCount As Long _
)
```

PlaySegmentEx Function

```
PlaySegmentEx( _
    Source As Unknown, _
    lFlags As CONST_DMUS_SEGF_FLAGS, _
    StartTime As Long, _
    Optional From As Unknown, _
    Optional AudioPath As Unknown, _
) As DirectMusicSegmentState8
```

StopEx Procedure

```
StopEx( _
  ObjectToStop As Unknown,
  lStopTime As Long, _
  lFlags As Long _
)
```

DirectMusicSegment8

The functionality of DirectMusicSegment8 is provided by the following single procedure.

Download Procedure

```
Download( _
    downloadpath As Unknown _
)
```

DirectPlay8Address

The functionality of DirectPlay8Address is provided by the following two routines.

SetSP Procedure

```
SetSP( _
    guidSP As String _
)
```

BuildFromURL Procedure

```
BuildFromURL( _
    SourceURL As String _
)
```

DirectPlay8Client

The functionality of DirectPlay8Client is provided by the following eight routines.

Connect Function

```
Connect( _
    AppDesc As DPN_APPLICATION_DESC, _
    Address As DirectPlay8Address, _
    DeviceInfo As DirectPlay8Address, _
    lFlags As CONST_DPNOPERATIONS, _
    UserData As Any, _
    UserDataSize As Long _
) As Long
```

CancelAsyncOperation Procedure

```
CancelAsyncOperation( _
    lAsyncHandle As Long, _
    Optional lFlags As CONST_DPNCANCELFLAGS _
)
```

GetApplicationDesc Function

```
GetApplicationDesc( _
    Optional lFlags As Long _
) As DPN_APPLICATION_DESC
Type DPN_APPLICATION_DESC
    guidApplication As String
    guidInstance As String
    lCurrentPlayers As Long
```

```
        lFlags As Long
        lMaxPlayers As Long
        Password As String
        SessionName As String
End Type
```

GetCountServiceProviders Function

```
GetCountServiceProviders( _
    Optional lFlags As Long _
) As Long
```

GetServiceProvider Function

```
GetServiceProvider( _
    lIndex As Long _
) As DPN_SERVICE_PROVIDER_INFO
Type DPN_SERVICE_PROVIDER_INFO
    GUID As String
    lFlags As Long
    name As String
End Type
```

EnumHosts Function

```
EnumHosts( _
    ApplicationDesc As DPN_APPLICATION_DESC, _
    AddrHost As DirectPlay8Address, _
    DeviceInfo As DirectPlay8Address, _
    lRetryCount As Long, _
    lRetryInterval As Long, _
    lTimeOut As Long, _
    lFlags As   CONST_DPNOPERATIONS, _
    UserData As Any, _
    UserDataSize As Long _
) As Long
```

Send Function

```
Send( _
    buffer() As BYTE, _
    lTimeOut As Long, _
    Optional lFlags As CONST_DPNSENDFLAGS _
) As Long
```

UnRegisterMessageHandler Procedure

```
UnRegisterMessageHandler()
```

DirectPlay8Event

Since all of the routines for DirectPlay8Event must be present in a Visual Basic program that implements this interface, the complete list for DirectPlay8Event is included in the following seventeen events.

AddRemovePlayerGroup Event

```
AddRemovePlayerGroup( _
    lMsgID As Long, _
    lPlayerID As Long, _
    lGroupID As Long, _
    fRejectMsg As Boolean _
)
```

AppDesc Event

```
AppDesc( _
    fRejectMsg As Boolean _
)
```

AsyncOpComplete Event

```
AsyncOpComplete( _
    dpnotify As DPNMSG_ASYNC_OP_COMPLETE, _
    fRejectMsg As Boolean _
)
```

```
Type DPNMSG_ASYNC_OP_COMPLETE
    AsyncOpHandle As Long
    hResultCode As Long
End Type
```

ConnectComplete Event

```
ConnectComplete( _
    dpnotify As DPNMSG_CONNECT_COMPLETE,
    fRejectMsg As Boolean _
)
Type DPNMSG_CONNECT_COMPLETE
    AsyncOpHandle As Long
    hResultCode As Long
    ReplyData() as Byte
End Type
```

CreateGroup Event

```
CreateGroup ( _
    lGroupID As Long, _
    lOwnerID As Long, _
    fRejectMsg As Boolean _
)
```

CreatePlayer Event

```
CreatePlayer ( _
    lPlayerID As Long, _
    fRejectMsg As Boolean _
)
```

DestroyGroup Event

```
DestroyGroup( _
    lGroupID As Long, _
    lReason As Long, _
    fRejectMsg As Boolean _
)
```

DestroyPlayer Event

```
DestroyPlayer( _
    lPlayerID As Long, _
    lReason As Long, _
    fRejectMsg As Boolean _
)
```

EnumHostsQuery Event

```
EnumHostsQuery( _
    dpnotify As DPNMSG_ENUM_HOSTS_QUERY, _
    fRejectMsg As Boolean _
)
Type DPNMSG_ENUM_HOSTS_QUERY
    AddressDeviceUrl As String
    AddressSenderUrl As String
    lMaxResponseDataSize As Long
    ReceivedData() As Byte
    ResponseData() As Byte
End Type
```

EnumHostsResponse Event

```
EnumHostsResponse( _
    dpnotify As DPNMSG_ENUM_HOSTS_RESPONSE, _
    fRejectMsg As Boolean _
)
Type DPNMSG_ENUM_HOSTS_RESPONSE
    AddressDeviceUrl As String
    AddressSenderUrl As String
    ApplicationDescription As DPN_APPLICATION_DESC
    lRoundTripLatencyMS As Long
    ResponseData As Byte
End Type
```

HostMigrate Event

```
HostMigrate( _
    NewHostID As Long, _
    fRejectMsg As Boolean _
)
```

IndicateConnect Event

```
IndicateConnect( _
    dpnotify As DPNMSG_INDICATE_CONNECT, _
    fRejectMsg As Boolean _
)
Type DPNMSG_INDICATE_CONNECT
    AddressDeviceUrl As String
    AddressPlayerUrl As String
    UserData() As Byte
End Type
```

IndicateConnectAborted Event

```
IndicateConnectAborted( _
    fRejectMsg As Boolean _
)
```

InfoNotify Event

```
InfoNotify( _
    lMsgID As Long, _
    lNotifyID As Long, _
    fRejectMsg As Boolean _
)
```

Receive Event

```
Receive( _
    dpnotify As DPNMSG_RECEIVE,
    fRejectMsg As Boolean _
)
```

```
Type DPNMSG_RECEIVE
    idSender As Long
    iDataSize As Long
    ReceivedData() As Byte
End Type
```

SendComplete Event

```
SendComplete( _
    dpnotify As DPNMSG_SEND_COMPLETE, _
    fRejectMsg As Boolean _
)
Type DPNMSG_SEND_COMPLETE
    AsyncOpHandle As Long
    hResultCode As Long
    lSendTime As Long
End Type
```

TerminateSession Event

```
TerminateSession( _
    dpnotify As DPNMSG_TERMINATE_SESSION, _
    fRejectMsg As Boolean _
)
Type DPNMSG_TERMINATE_SESSION
    hResultCode As Long
    TerminateData() As Byte
End Type
```

DirectPlay8Server

The functionality of the DirectPlay8Server is provided by the following five routines.

GetCountServiceProviders Function

```
GetCountServiceProviders() As Long
```

GetServiceProvider Function

```
GetServiceProvider( _
    lIndex As Long _
) As DPN_SERVICE_PROVIDER_INFO
Type DPN_SERVICE_PROVIDER_INFO
    GUID As String
    lFlags As Long
    name As String
End Type
```

Host Procedure

```
Host( _
    AppDesc As DPN_APPLICATION_DESC, _
    Address As DirectPlay8Address _
)
Type DPN_APPLICATION_DESC
    guidApplication As String
    guidInstance As String
    lCurrentPlayers As Long
    lFlags As Long
    lMaxPlayers As Long
    Password As String
    SessionName As String
End Type
```

SendTo Function

```
SendTo( _
    idSend As Long, _
    buffer() As BYTE, _
    lPriority As Long, _
    lTimeOut As Long, _
    lFlags As CONST_DPNSENDFLAGS _
) As Long
```

UnRegisterMessageHandler Procedure

```
UnRegisterMessageHandler()
```

DirectSound3DBuffer8

The functionality of the DirectSound3DBuffer8 is provided by the following three routines.

SetConeAngles Procedure

```
SetConeAngles( _
    inCone As Long, _
    outCone As Long, _
    applyFlag As CONST_DS3DAPPLYFLAGS _
)
```

SetConeOutsideVolume Procedure

```
SetConeOutsideVolume( _
    coneOutsideVolume As Long, _
    applyFlag As CONST_DS3DAPPLYFLAGS _
)
```

SetPosition Procedure

```
SetPosition( _
    x As Single, _
    y As Single, _
    z As Single, _
    applyFlag As CONST_DS3DAPPLYFLAGS _
)
```

DirectSound8

The functionality of DirectSound8 is provided by the following five routines.

CreatePrimarySoundBuffer Function
```
CreatePrimarySoundBuffer( _
    bufferDesc As DSBUFFERDESC _
) As DirectSoundPrimaryBuffer8
```

CreateSoundBuffer Function
```
CreateSoundBuffer( _
    bufferDesc As DSBUFFERDESC _
) As DirectSoundSecondaryBuffer8
```

CreateSoundBufferFromFile Function
```
CreateSoundBufferFromFile( _
    filename As String, _
    bufferDesc As DSBUFFERDESC _
) As DirectSoundSecondaryBuffer8
Type DSBUFFERDESC
    fxFormat As WaveFormatEx
    guid3DAlgorithm As String
    lBufferBytes As Long
    lFlags As CONST_DSBCAPSFLAGS
End Type
```

GetCaps Procedure
```
GetCaps( _
    caps As DSCAPS _
)
Type DSCAPS
    lFlags As CONST_DSCAPSFLAGS
    lFreeHw3DAllBuffers As Long
    lFreeHw3DStaticBuffers As Long
    lFreeHw3DStreamingBuffers As Long
    lFreeHwMemBytes As Long
    lFreeHwMixingAllBuffers As Long
```

```
    lFreeHwMixingStaticBuffers As Long
    lFreeHwMixingStreamingBuffers As Long
    lMaxContigFreeHwMemBytes As Long
    lMaxHw3DAllBuffers As Long
    lMaxHw3DStaticBuffers As Long
    lMaxHw3DStreamingBuffers As Long
    lMaxHwMixingAllBuffers As Long
    lMaxHwMixingStaticBuffers As Long
    lMaxHwMixingStreamingBuffers As Long
    lMaxSecondarySampleRate As Long
    lMinSecondarySampleRate As Long
    lPlayCpuOverheadSwBuffers As Long
    lPrimaryBuffers As Long
    lReserved1 As Long
    lReserved2 As Long
    lTotalHwMemBytes As Long
    lUnlockTransferRateHwBuffers As Long
End Type
```

SetCooperativeLevel Procedure

```
SetCooperativeLevel( _
    hwnd As Long, _
    level As CONST_DSSCLFLAGS _
)
```

DirectSoundSecondaryBuffer8

The functionality of DirectSoundSecondaryBuffer8 is provided by the following five routines.

GetDirectSound3DBuffer Function

```
GetDirectSound3DBuffer() As DirectSound3DBuffer8
```

GetFormat Procedure

```
GetFormat( _
    format As WAVEFORMATEX _
)
```

```
Type WAVEFORMATEX
    lAvgBytesPerSec As Long
    lExtra As Long
    lSamplesPerSec As Long
    nBitsPerSample As Integer
    nBlockAlign As Integer
    nChannels As Integer
    nFormatTag As Integer
    nSize As Integer
End Type
```

Play Procedure

```
Play( _
    flags As CONST_DSBPLAYFLAGS _
)
```

SetCurrentPosition Procedure

```
SetCurrentPosition( _
    newPosition As Long _
)
```

Stop Procedure

```
Stop()
```

DirectX8

The functionality of DirectX8 (the root object) is provided by the following fifteen routines.

AddDataToBuffer Procedure

```
AddDataToBuffer( _
    Buffer() As Byte, _
    lData As Any, _
    lSize As Long, _
    lOffset As Long _
)
```

AddStringToBuffer Procedure

```
AddStringToBuffer( _
    Buffer() As Byte, _
    StringData As String, _
    lOffset As Long _
)
```

CreateEvent Function

```
CreateEvent( _
    event As DirectXEvent8 _
) As Long
```

DestroyEvent Procedure

```
DestroyEvent( _
    eventid As Long _
)
```

Direct3DCreate Function

```
Direct3DCreate() As Direct3D8
```

DirectInputCreate Function

```
DirectInputCreate() As DirectInput8
```

DirectMusicLoaderCreate Function

```
DirectMusicLoaderCreate() As DirectMusicLoader8
```

DirectMusicPerformanceCreate Function

```
DirectMusicPerformanceCreate() As DirectMusicPerformance8
```

DirectPlayAddressCreate Function

```
DirectPlayAddressCreate() As DirectPlay8Address
```

DirectPlayClientCreate Function

```
DirectPlayClientCreate() As DirectPlay8Client
```

DirectPlayServerCreate Function

```
DirectPlayServerCreate() As DirectPlay8Server
```

DirectSoundCreate Function

```
DirectSoundCreate( _
    guid As String _
) As DirectSound8
```

GetDataFromBuffer Procedure

```
GetDataFromBuffer( _
    Buffer() As Byte, _
    lData As Any, _
    lSize As Long, _
    lOffset As Long _
)
```

GetStringFromBuffer Function

```
GetStringFromBuffer( _
    Buffer() As Byte, _
    lOffset As Long _
) As String
```

NewBuffer Function

```
NewBuffer( _
    Buffer() As Byte _
) As Long
```

APPENDIX C

WINDOWS API REFERENCE

This appendix lists all of the Windows API structures and functions used by the source code in the book. When you consider that there are hundreds of functions in the Windows API, this short list is quite manageable.

WINDOWS API STRUCTURES

```
Public Type BITMAP_STRUCT
    bmType As Long
    bmWidth As Long
    bmHeight As Long
    bmWidthBytes As Long
    bmPlanes As Integer
    bmBitsPixel As Integer
    bmBits As Long
End Type

Public Type RECT_API
    Left As Long
    Top As Long
    Right As Long
    Bottom As Long
End Type

Public Type POINT
    X As Long
    Y As Long
End Type

Public Type RGBQUAD
    Blue As Byte
    Green As Byte
    Red As Byte
    alpha As Byte
End Type
```

```
Public Type OSVERSIONINFO
    dwOSVersionInfoSize As Long
    dwMajorVersion As Long
    dwMinorVersion As Long
    dwBuildNumber As Long
    dwPlatformId As Long
    szCSDVersion As String * 128
End Type
```

WINDOWS API FUNCTIONS AND PROCEDURES

```
Public Declare Function BitBlt _
    Lib "gdi32" ( _
    ByVal hDestDC As Long, _
    ByVal X As Long, _
    ByVal Y As Long, _
    ByVal nWidth As Long, _
    ByVal nHeight As Long, _
    ByVal hSrcDC As Long, _
    ByVal xSrc As Long, _
    ByVal ySrc As Long, _
    ByVal dwRop As Long _
) As Long


Public Declare Sub CopyMemory _
    Lib "kernel32" Alias "RtlMoveMemory" ( _
    lpvDest As Any, _
    lpvSource As Any, _
    ByVal cbCopy As Long _
)


Public Declare Function CreateCompatibleBitmap _
    Lib "gdi32" ( _
    ByVal hdc As Long, _
    ByVal nWidth As Long, _
    ByVal nHeight As Long _
) As Long
```

```
        Public Declare Function CreateCompatibleDC _
            Lib "gdi32" ( _
            ByVal hdc As Long _
        ) As Long

        Public Declare Function CreatePen _
            Lib "gdi32" ( _
            ByVal nPenStyle As Long, _
            ByVal nWidth As Long, _
            ByVal crColor As Long _
        ) As Long

        Public Declare Function DeleteDC _
            Lib "gdi32" ( _
            ByVal hdc As Long _
        ) As Long

        Public Declare Function DeleteObject _
            Lib "gdi32" ( _
            ByVal hObject As Long _
        ) As Long

        Public Declare Function Ellipse _
            Lib "gdi32" ( _
            ByVal hdc As Long, _
            ByVal X1 As Long, _
            ByVal Y1 As Long, _
            ByVal X2 As Long, _
            ByVal Y2 As Long _
        ) As Long

        Public Declare Function GetBitmapBits _
            Lib "gdi32" ( _
            ByVal hBitmap As Long, _
            ByVal dwCount As Long, _
            lpBits As Any _
        ) As Long

        Public Declare Function GetClientRect _
            Lib "user32" ( _
            ByVal hWnd As Long, _
            lpRect As RECT_API _
        ) As Long
```

```vb
Public Declare Function GetDC _
    Lib "user32" ( _
    ByVal hWnd As Long _
) As Long


Public Declare Function GetDesktopWindow _
    Lib "user32" ( _
) As Long


Public Declare Function GetDeviceCaps _
    Lib "gdi32" ( _
    ByVal hdc As Long, _
    ByVal nIndex As Long _
) As Long


Public Declare Function GetObjectA _
    Lib "gdi32" ( _
    ByVal hObject As Long, _
    ByVal nCount As Long, _
    lpObject As Any _
) As Long


Public Declare Function GetObjectW _
    Lib "gdi32" ( _
    ByVal hObject As Long, _
    ByVal nCount As Long, _
    lpObject As Any _
) As Long


Public Declare Function GetStockObject _
    Lib "gdi32" ( _
    ByVal nIndex As Long _
) As Long


Public Declare Function GetPixel _
    Lib "gdi32" ( _
    ByVal hdc As Long, _
    ByVal X As Long, _
    ByVal Y As Long _
) As Long
```

```
Public Declare Function GetTickCount _
    Lib "kernel32" ( _
) As Long


Public Declare Function GetVersionEx _
    Lib "kernel32" Alias "GetVersionExA" ( _
    lpVersionInformation As OSVERSIONINFO _
) As Long


Public Declare Function IntersectRect _
    Lib "user32" ( _
    lpDestRect As RECT_API, _
    lpSrc1Rect As RECT_API, _
    lpSrc2Rect As RECT_API _
) As Long


Public Declare Function LineTo _
    Lib "gdi32" ( _
    ByVal hdc As Long, _
    ByVal X As Long, _
    ByVal Y As Long _
) As Long


Public Declare Function LoadImage _
    Lib "user32" Alias "LoadImageA" ( _
    ByVal hInst As Long, _
    ByVal Filename As String, _
    ByVal un1 As Long, _
    ByVal Width As Long, _
    ByVal Height As Long, _
    ByVal opmode As Long _
) As Long


Public Declare Function MoveTo _
    Lib "gdi32" Alias "MoveToEx" ( _
    ByVal hdc As Long, _
    ByVal X As Long, _
    ByVal Y As Long, _
    lpPoint As POINT _
) As Long
```

```vbnet
Public Declare Function Polyline _
    Lib "gdi32" ( _
    ByVal hdc As Long, _
    lpPoint As POINT, _
    ByVal nCount As Long _
) As Long

Public Declare Function SelectObject _
    Lib "gdi32" ( _
    ByVal hdc As Long, _
    ByVal hObject As Long _
) As Long

Public Declare Function SetBkColor _
    Lib "gdi32" ( _
    ByVal hdc As Long, _
    ByVal crColor As Long _
) As Long

Public Declare Function SetBkMode _
    Lib "gdi32" ( _
    ByVal hdc As Long, _
    ByVal nBkMode As Long _
) As Long

Public Declare Function SetBitmapBits _
    Lib "gdi32" ( _
    ByVal hBitmap As Long, _
    ByVal dwCount As Long, _
    lpBits As Any _
) As Long

Public Declare Function SetPixel _
    Lib "gdi32" ( _
    ByVal hdc As Long, _
    ByVal X As Long, _
    ByVal Y As Long, _
    ByVal crColor As Long _
) As Long
```

```
Public Declare Function SetTextColor _
    Lib "gdi32" ( _
    ByVal hdc As Long, _
    ByVal crColor As Long _
) As Long

Public Declare Function TextOutA _
    Lib "gdi32" ( _
    ByVal hdc As Long, _
    ByVal X As Long, _
    ByVal Y As Long, _
    ByVal lpString As String, _
    ByVal nCount As Long _
) As Long

Public Declare Function TextOutW _
    Lib "gdi32" ( _
    ByVal hdc As Long, _
    ByVal X As Long, _
    ByVal Y As Long, _
    ByVal lpString As String, _
    ByVal nCount As Long _
) As Long

Public Declare Function ValidateRect _
    Lib "user32" ( _
    ByVal hWnd As Long, _
    lpRect As RECT_API _
) As Long
```

APPENDIX D

DIRECTINPUT KEYBOARD CODES

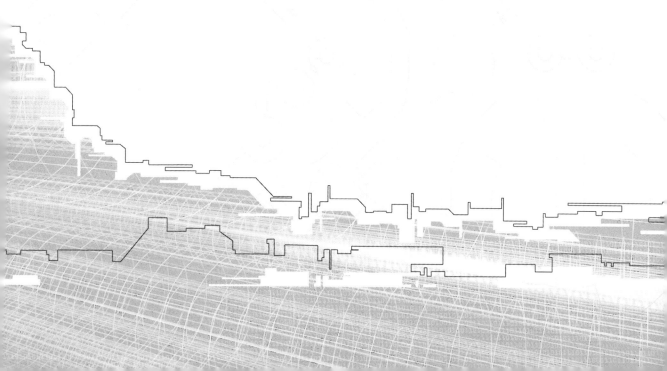

The following keyboard codes are specific to DirectInput and should not be confused with ASCII codes. These keyboard codes are mapped to the physical location of each key. They are therefore relevant only for programs that use DirectInput to process keyboard events.

Code	Key	Code	Key	Code	Key
1	ESC	21	Y	41	`
2	1	22	U	42	LSHIFT
3	2	23	I	43	\
4	3	24	O	44	Z
5	4	25	P	45	X
6	5	26	[	46	C
7	6	27	]	47	V
8	7	28	ENTER	48	B
9	8	29	LCTRL	49	N
10	9	30	A	50	M
11	0	31	S	51	,
12	-	32	D	52	.
13	=	33	F	53	/
14	BACKSPACE	34	G	54	RSHIFT
15	TAB	35	H	55	NUMPAD*
16	Q	36	J	56	LALT
17	W	37	K	57	SPACE
18	E	38	L	58	CAPSLOCK
19	R	39	;	59	F1
20	T	40	'	60	F2

Code	Key	Code	Key	Code	Key
61	F3	81	NUMPAD3	208	DOWN
62	F4	82	NUMPAD0	209	PAGE DN
63	F5	83	NUMPAD.	210	INSERT
64	F6	87	F11	211	DELETE
65	F7	88	F12	219	LWIN
66	F8	86	F13	220	RWIN
67	F9	84	F14	221	APPS
68	F10	85	F15	116	PAUSE
69	NUMLOCK	156	NUMPADENTER		
70	SCRLLOCK	157	RCONTROL		
71	NUMPAD7	91	NUMPAD,		
72	NUMPAD8	181	NUMPAD/		
73	NUMPAD9	183	SYSRQ		
74	NUMPAD-	184	RALT		
75	NUMPAD4	199	HOME		
76	NUMPAD5	200	UP		
77	NUMPAD6	201	PAGE UP		
78	NUMPAD+	203	LEFT		
79	NUMPAD1	205	RIGHT		
80	NUMPAD2	207	END		

APPENDIX E

RECOMMENDED READING

Following is a list of books that you might find useful in your quest to master the subject of game programming. This list includes books that I personally recommend. Some titles might be out of print; some might even cover subjects that are long outdated—but they are still useful as references.

Beginning Direct3D Game Programming by Wolfgang F. Engel, et al.
Premier Press, Inc. ISBN 0-7615-3191-2.

Black Art of 3D Game Programming: Writing Your Own High-Speed 3-D Polygon Video Games by André LaMothe.
Waite Group Press. ISBN 1-57169-004-2.

Black Art of Windows Game Programming by Eric R. Lyons.
Waite Group Press. ISBN 1-878739-95-6.

Game Design: The'Art & Business of Creating Games by Bob Bates.
Premier Press, Inc. ISBN 0-7615-3165-3.

Isometric Game Programming with DirectX 7.0 by Ernest Pazera.
Premier Press, Inc. ISBN 0-7615-3089-4.

Linux Game Programming by Mark Collins, et al.
Premier Press, Inc. ISBN 0-7615-3255-2.

Michael Abrash's Graphics Programming Black Book by Michael Abrash.
Coriolis Group Books. ISBN 1-57610-174-6.

More Tricks of the Game Programming Gurus by Greg Anderson, et al.
Sams Publishing. ISBN 0-672-30697-2.

Multiplayer Game Programming by Todd Barron.
Premier Press, Inc. ISBN 0-7615-3298-6.

OpenGL Game Programming by Dave Astle, et al.
Premier Press, Inc. ISBN 0-7615-3330-3.

Pocket PC Game Programming: Using The Windows CE Game API by Jonathan S. Harbour.
Premier Press, Inc. ISBN 0-7615-3057-6.

Programming Role-Playing Games with DirectX 8.0 by Jim Adams.
Premier Press, Inc. ISBN 0-7615-3521-7.

Special Effects Game Programming with DirectX 8.0 by Mason McCuskey.
Premier Press, Inc. ISBN 1-93184-109-8.

Swords & Circuitry: A Designer's Guide to Computer Role-Playing Games by Neal Hallford.
Premier Press, Inc. ISBN 0-7615-3299-4.

The Zen of Direct3D Game Programming by Peter Walsh.
Premier Press, Inc. ISBN 0-7615-3429-6.

Tricks of the 3D Game Programming Gurus: Advanced 3D Graphics and Rasterization by André LaMothe.
Sams Publishing. ISBN 0-672-31835-0.

Tricks of the Windows Game Programming Gurus by André LaMothe.
Sams Publishing. ISBN 0-672-31361-8.

Visual Basic Graphics Programming: Hands-On Applications and Advanced Color Development, 2nd Edition by Rod Stephens.
Wiley Computer Publishing. ISBN 0-471-35599-2.

Windows Game Programming for Dummies by André LaMothe.
Hungry Minds, Inc. ISBN 0-764-50337-5.

APPENDIX F

VISUAL BASIC GAMING SITES

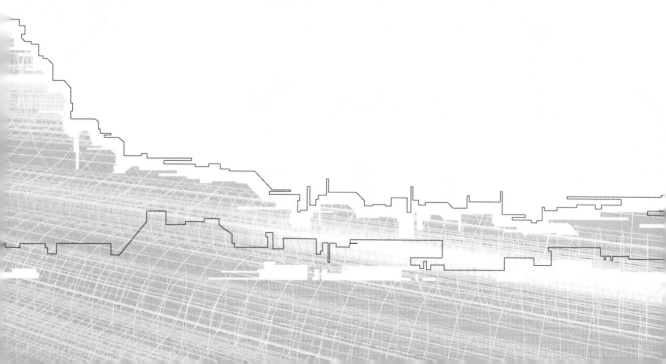

ollowing is a list of Web sites that are related to either Visual Basic or DirectX (or both). The focus of this list is primarily on Visual Basic development, so if you ever have a question or problem with a subject or piece of code, you should be able to find an answer at one of these sites or discussion lists. The book's primary support site is at http://www.jharbour.com/vb.

DISCUSSION GROUPS

The following Web sites provide links for joining a discussion group dedicated to Visual Basic, DirectX, or game programming in general.

> DirectX for Visual Basic Group
> http://www.yahoogroups.com/group/vbdirectx
>
> Visual Basic Game Programming Group (official book support list)
> http://www.yahoogroups.com/group/visual-basic-game-programming

VISUAL BASIC GAMES

The following Web sites are for specific games written with or for Visual Basic, or a derivation of the language. Several games include source code so you can see how they were written.

> 4000 A.D.
> http://4000ad.com
>
> Darkness Rising
> http://www.atypical-interactive.com
>
> Robot War 3D
> http://www.robotwar3d.com/advscripts/home.asp
>
> Senator Games
> http://www.senatorgames.com
>
> AckSoft's Space Shooter
> http://acksoft.hypermart.net

GAME RESOURCES

The following list of Web sites provides game development resources such as game graphics, sound effects, music libraries, and other media.

Free Character Animation Graphics
http://www.vbexplorer.com/charpack1.asp

Free Sound and Music Clips
http://www.vbexplorer.com/gamesound.asp

Edgar Ibarra's Pocket Ideas (3-D artwork)
http://www.pocketideas.com

DEVELOPMENT TOOLS

The following list of Web sites focuses on development tools, game libraries, compilers, and related resources, including sites specifically maintained by Microsoft.

Dark Basic: The Ultimate 3D Game Creator
http://www.darkbasic.co.uk

Microsoft DirectX Home
http://www.microsoft.com/directx

Microsoft Games
http://www.microsoft.com/games/home/default.asp

Microsoft Games for PC
http://www.microsoft.com/games/home/gameslist.asp?platform=Windows

Microsoft Games for Xbox
http://www.microsoft.com/games/home/gameslist.asp?platform=XBOX

Microsoft Visual Basic Home Page
http://msdn.microsoft.com/vbasic

Microsoft Visual Basic Online Product Documentation
http://msdn.microsoft.com/vbasic/technical/documentation.asp

Revolution 3D Engine
http://www.revolution3d.net

Visual Studio 6.0 Service Packs
http://support.microsoft.com/support/servicepacks/VS/6.0/Default.asp?SD=MSDN

PROGRAMMING SITES

The following list of Web sites is dedicated to the subject of game programming, with the majority of the sites focusing on Visual Basic.

Abstract VB
http://www.abstractvb.com

Anton's VB Gaming Site
http://www.angelfire.com/mi3/VBgaming/index.html

Carl & Gary's VB Home Page
http://www.cgvb.com

Dutch's VB Code Library
http://www.dutchthewiz.com/vb/Default.asp

GameDev.net
http://www.gamedev.net

Gary Beene's VB Information Center
http://www.vbinformation.com

AckyNet's Visual Basic Page
http://www.acky.net/vb

Larry Allen's VB Universe
http://www.desertware.com/vbuniverse/index.html

Lucky's VB Gaming Site
http://www.rookscape.com/vbgaming

Luhar's VB Page
http://www.geocities.com/SiliconValley/Park/3269

Planet Source Code
http://www.planet-source-code.com

Programmer's Heaven: VB Zone
http://www.programmersheaven.com/zone1

Simon Price's VB Game Site
http://www.vbgames.co.uk

The VB Compendium
http://www.cyber-matrix.com/vb.htm

VB-World
http://www.vb-world.net

VB Game Programming Web Ring
http://www.vbgamersring.com

VBA51
http://www.chez.com/scribe

VB CodeGuru
http://codeguru.earthweb.com/vb

VB Explorer
http://www.vbexplorer.com/games.asp

VB for Kids Tutorial
http://www.kidwaresoftware.com/vbkids.htm

VB Game Planet
http://vbgplanet.thenexus.bc.ca

VB RPG
http://www.vbrpg.net

VB Tips and Tricks
http://msdn.microsoft.com/vbasic/technical/tips.asp

VB Zone
http://www.homestead.com/vbgames6/game.html

Voodoo VB
http://voodoovb.thenexus.bc.ca

Zorro's VB Fun Page
http://www.geocities.com/SiliconValley/Heights/6429

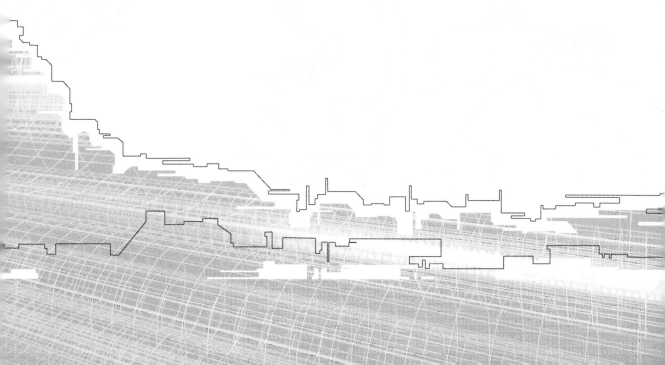

EPILOGUE

I would like to congratulate you for completing *Visual Basic Game Programming with DirectX*! I hope you have found this book as fascinating to read as it was for me to write. I must admit that I had no idea that the book would turn out as it did. The project seemed to take on a life of its own, demanding more and more of me with each new chapter. I found early on that I was not content to cover standard game development topics, but felt a need to dig into every feature of both the Windows API and DirectX. While the book could have covered DX7 or DX8, I felt a need to cover both. The resulting game library successfully combines all three major topics into a seamless whole.

I am pleased with the results. It is my sincere hope that you have found this book not only useful, but also essential. I have strived to leave no stone unturned in the quest to cover everything that you would possibly need to develop a game with Visual Basic. VB is my favorite language, and it is exciting to be able to do things with VB that previously required a language like Visual C++.

PROMOTION!

You have now learned not only everything that I can teach you about Visual Basic game programming, but also how to build complete games from start to finish. You have truly mastered the subject and demonstrated your willingness to succeed, no matter how difficult the challenge.

You are hereby promoted to the rank of *Adept Game Designer*, with all of the rights and privileges that come with the position. Use your new knowledge and skills wisely, and continue to push the envelope of Visual Basic gaming!

You have now completed all six ranks:

1. **Newbie Gamer**
2. **Apprentice Hacker**
3. **Skilled Programmer**
4. **Veteran Coder**
5. **Master Developer**
6. **Adept Game Designer**

Now that you have learned just about everything there is to learn about the subject of game programming with Visual Basic, where will you turn next for inspiration, ideas, and information?

There is but one thing to do—continue to learn and strive to build games that no one has ever before dreamed of creating. You must continue to push the limits of gaming and challenge others to do the same. When you have reached the final goal and learned everything there is to know about game development, then it will be up to you to try new things, invent new game genres, and fascinate the world with the artistic wizardry that we game developers alone can achieve.

Book Development History

This book had a difficult childhood, if I may use the analogy. Early in development, it was geared to beginners and actually had the title *Beginning Visual Basic Game Programming* for a few months. However, as I begin writing, I found that I wanted to cover so much more than was possible for a beginner book. The plan was to simply cover the Windows API for graphics and sound, with perhaps a sprinkling of DirectX here and there for good measure.

I was not happy with the results and found that such a book could be written in only a few hundred pages, unlike the tome of knowledge that this has become. Embracing DirectX was the key to raising the bar and pushing the possibilities of Visual Basic. The sample programs clearly demonstrate that this goal has been achieved, and the results need no explanation.

Premier Press, Inc.

It was also a bumpy ride as Prima Tech was transformed into Premier Press, Inc.! As soon as things settled and Premier Press, Inc. was announced, the book contract was promptly signed, a new schedule was drawn up, and work continued at a feverish pace.

I am absolutely thrilled that I was given the opportunity to write this book. It was a dream come true, because it's something that I have wanted to do for several years now—ever since Microsoft released DirectX 7.0 with Visual Basic support. I sincerely hope that you find this book to be a valuable resource as you develop increasingly more exciting games using Visual Basic.

How to Contact the Author

Although every effort was made to ensure that the source code presented in this book is accurate and free of errors, it is possible that errors might have escaped scrutiny and made it onto the printed page. I literally obsessed over every line of code right up to the last day of development, trying to find any bug that might pose a problem later. If you have any problems with the source code, sample projects, or general theory in this book, I welcome your feedback. Feel free to send an e-mail to jonathan@jharbour.com, and I will endeavor to help you work though any problems.

I also welcome constructive criticism and comments that you might have regarding the book in general or a specific aspect of the book. I usually respond to e-mail within a day or two. You might also want to visit my Web site at http://www.jharbour.com for updated information about the book.

Finally, whether you are an absolute beginner or a seasoned professional, I welcome you to join my discussion list at YahooGroups.com, where you will have an opportunity to share source code and game ideas and pose questions, along with other game developers. Membership is open to the public, so you are free to join. Just send an e-mail to the list server at Visual-Basic-Game-Programming-subscribe@yahoogroups.com, or visit the Web site at http://www.yahoogroups.com. I look forward to hearing from you!

Jonathan S. Harbour
Phoenix, Arizona
December, 2001

Index

B

GAME DEVELOPMENT.
IT'S SERIOUS BUSINESS.

"Game programming is without a doubt the most intellectually challenging field of Computer Science in the world. However, we would be fooling ourselves if we said that we are 'serious' people! Writing (and reading) a game programming book should be an exciting adventure for both the author and the reader."

—André LaMothe,
Series Editor

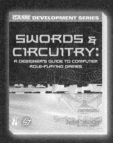

Gamedev.net

The most comprehensive game development resource

- The latest news in game development
- The most active forums and chatrooms anywhere, with insights and tips from experienced game developers
- Links to thousands of additional game development resources
- Thorough book and product reviews
- Over 1000 game development articles!
  Game design
  Graphics
  DirectX
  OpenGL
  AI
  Art
  Music
  Physics
  Source Code
  Sound
  Assembly
  And More!

Gamedev.net

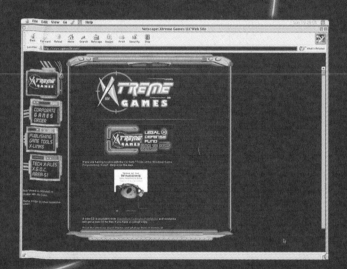

License Agreement/Notice of Limited Warranty